CW00802424

Comparative Competition Law and Economics

Comparative Competition Law and Economics

Roger Van den Bergh
Professor of Law and Economics, Rotterdam Institute of Law and Economics, Erasmus University Rotterdam, the Netherlands

with

Peter Camesasca
Partner Covington & Burling LLP, Assistant Professor, Rotterdam Institute of Law and Economics, the Netherlands

Andrea Giannaccari
Law and Economics Lab, LUISS Guido Carli, Rome, Italy

Cheltenham, UK • Northampton, MA, USA

© Roger Van den Bergh 2017

All rights reserved. No part of this publication may be reproduced, stored in a retrieval system or transmitted in any form or by any means, electronic, mechanical or photocopying, recording, or otherwise without the prior permission of the publisher.

Published by
Edward Elgar Publishing Limited
The Lypiatts
15 Lansdown Road
Cheltenham
Glos GL50 2JA
UK

Edward Elgar Publishing, Inc.
William Pratt House
9 Dewey Court
Northampton
Massachusetts 01060
USA

A catalogue record for this book
is available from the British Library

Library of Congress Control Number: 2017941893

ISBN   978 1 78643 830 0 (cased)
ISBN   978 1 78643 832 4 (paperback)
ISBN   978 1 78643 831 7 (eBook)

Typeset by Sparks – www.sparkspublishing.com
Printed and bound by CPI Group (UK) Ltd, Croydon, CR0 4YY

Contents in brief

Full contents

Boxes

Figures and tables

Figures

Tables

Abbreviations and acronyms

AAC	Average Avoidable Costs
ABA	American Bar Association
AEC	As Efficient Competitor Test
AML	Anti-Monopoly Law (China)
ATC	Average Total Costs
AVC	Average Variable Costs
BRIC	Brazil, Russia, India, China
CADE	Conselho Administratiovo de Defesa Econômica
CCI	Competition Commission of India
CJEU	Court of Justice of the European Union
DG COMP	Competition Directorate General
DoJ	Department of Justice
ECN	European Competition Network
EEC	European Economic Community
EU	European Union
FAS	Federal Antimonopoly Service of the Russian Federation
FRAND	Fair Reasonable and Non-Discriminatory Terms
FTC	Federal Trade Commission

HHI	Herfindahl–Hirschman Index
ICN	International Competition Network
IPR	Intellectual Property Right
LRAIC	Long-Run Average Incremental Costs
MOFCOM	Ministry of Commerce Anti-Monopoly Bureau (China)
NCA	National Competition Authority of the Member State
NDRC	National Development and Reform Commission (China)
OECD	Organisation for Economic Co-operation and Development
OEM	Original Equipment Manufacturer
OJ	Official Journal
R&D	Research and Development
SEP	Standard Essential Patent
SCP	Structure-Conduct-Performance
SIEC	Significantly Impede Effective Competition
SSNIP	Small but Significant and Non-Transitory Increase in Price
TFEU	Treaty on the Functioning of the European Union
UPP	Upward Pricing Pressure Analysis
US	United States of America

Preface

This book has grown out of the course on Competition Law and Economics that I am teaching in the EMLE programme (European Master in Law and Economics). It seeks to fill the gap of lacking textbooks on competition law that can be used in international courses at the masters level, which are open to both lawyers and economists. To make the topics discussed in this book equally enticing for students from different backgrounds, it adopts an interdisciplinary approach. In addition, thanks to the use of the comparative methodology, its suitability for educational purposes does not depend on differences in legal systems. I hope that this textbook will also be useful outside the EMLE programme, either as a main text for other masters courses taught to students of different disciplines (economics, management) or as supplementary reading in traditional competition law courses. Besides international students, the book also wants to reach an audience of antitrust law practitioners willing to reflect critically on the consistency of existing competition rules with economic insights and the challenges of competition law in a globalised economy.

This book builds upon an earlier book, co-authored by Peter Camesasca (*European Competition Law and Economics: A Comparative Perspective*, 1st ed., Intersentia, 2001; 2nd ed., Sweet & Maxwell, 2006). However, the book is different from the previous one in two respects. Whereas the former book contained only a limited number of comparisons with US antitrust law, this book offers a systematic comparison of EU and US competition rules and equally includes short discussions of the competition laws of the BRIC countries in separate boxes. Next, the book follows a rigorous interdisciplinary approach by a consistent use of concepts and methods from the economic analysis of law. The title 'Comparative Competition Law and Economics' clearly expresses both characteristics. I am very grateful to Peter Camesasca, who – in spite of his busy career as a practising antitrust lawyer – found the time to write the major part of the chapter on horizontal restrictions and also contributed to the chapters on market power and mergers. As principal author of this book, I also warmly welcome our new team member Andrea Giannaccari, who – as was the case with Peter – has been seriously infected with the Law and Economics approach in my competition law class. Andrea is the main author of the chapter on unilateral conduct of dominant firms and equally contributed to the chapters on market power and mergers. Further contributions to the book were made by Phil Warren, a colleague of Peter Camesasca at Covington, who took care of the part on US antitrust law in the chapter devoted to horizontal restrictions. I also thank my former and current (EMLE) students Yingyuan Ma, Maria Fernanda Caporale Madi and Sahib Singh Chadha, who authored boxes on the competition laws of China, Brazil and India.

A very special word of thanks goes to Roberto Pardolesi, who has always been eager to read and comment on draft chapters of the book. Roberto enjoyed the privilege of studying antitrust law at the University of Chicago at the time of the 'Chicago revolution', which has had a profound impact on the economic approach to competition problems. Thanks to his refreshing intellectual insights and never-ending enthusiasm, Roberto stimulated both colleagues and students to embark on the path of interdisciplinary studies in antitrust law. The current textbook is the fruit of three generations of European Competition Law and Economics scholars, for which Roberto has laid the foundations. All authors, each in their own way, owe him an immense gratitude. Thanks also go to Camilla Landi and all friends of Via Paternocchio 74 (a sinistra), who have made the life of the authors more enjoyable and provided the necessary support for making this book project a success.

Roger Van den Bergh
Montefiascone, February 2017

1

Introduction

Roger Van den Bergh

1.1 The increasing role of economic analysis in competition law

Economic analysis plays a prominent role in the formulation of substantive competition rules and their enforcement. In recent years, the legal competition regimes have exhibited significant changes. The importance of an economic approach to assess the anti-competitive effects and potentially outweighing efficiency benefits of particular agreements and types of conduct is now widely acknowledged. The way in which competition authorities and courts interpret competition rules has changed accordingly. These theoretical and practical changes have framed a modern antitrust, in which economic insights have acquired an increasingly relevant weight. The impact of economic analysis on competition law is clearly visible in the relevant legislation and the enforcement practice of the United States of America (US) and the European Union (EU). In current US antitrust law, almost all types of conduct have been submitted to a Rule of Reason analysis. The economic logic has similarly penetrated EU competition law and the competition laws of the Member States. In this regard, the efforts of the European Commission to adopt a so-called More Economic Approach are symptomatic (Schmidtchen, Albert, and Voigt 2007). Also in other jurisdictions, the effect of the increased use of economic analysis in deciding competition cases has been significant. Competition law and economics has influenced the legal regimes of other major economic players, such as China, India and Brazil. The increased importance of economic analysis thus goes hand in hand with the increasing globalisation of the economy.

Only if competition law consisted of unambiguously formulated *per se* rules could practitioners do without the tools of economic analysis. The concept of *per se* prohibitions has its origin in US antitrust law, which distinguishes between types of conduct that are *per se* unlawful and other types of conduct that may pass the test of reasonableness. A *per se* rule prohibits a certain act without regard to the particular effects of the act; it does not consider mitigating circumstances or offsetting benefits of anti-competitive practices. *Per se* prohibitions are justified for types of conduct that have manifestly anti-competitive implications and a very limited potential for pro-competitive benefits.[1] Conversely, a Rule of Reason requires an investigation of the effects of the challenged conduct, taking into account the particular facts of the case. According to the Rule of Reason, the courts must decide whether the questioned practice imposes an unreasonable restraint on competition. This implies that courts must take into account a variety of factors, including specific information about the relevant business, its condition before and after the restraint was imposed, and the restraint's history, nature and effect.[2]

Central questions of competition law are ultimately empirical issues. The questions whether cartel agreements raise prices above competitive levels (and, if yes, to what extent) or mergers cause price increases can be answered by quantitative evidence, thanks to the use of sophisticated econometric techniques (for an elaborate discussion of empirical methods, see Bishop and Walker 2010). The extent to which quantitative techniques are used to provide evidence in antitrust cases differs according to which side of the Atlantic Ocean one resides. US antitrust law has long moved beyond the stage of mere economic signalling. This is partly due to the more litigious nature of US antitrust law, which is very demanding in terms of supporting economic and factual evidence. Contrary to the enforcement procedure in Europe, expert testimony is more often required in the US since the adversarial process invites each party to expose the weakness of the other party's arguments and evidence. The US Supreme Court's *Daubert* rule has confirmed that it is 'virtually impossible to proceed with an antitrust case without an economist'.[3] In Europe, there is still less willingness to decide competition cases based on quantitative evidence. While the European Commission will use quantitative evidence whenever it is available and sufficiently sound, in many cases the assessment is still a qualitative analysis based on a mix of quantitative and qualitative evidence.

In spite of the growing importance of theoretical and empirical economics, the qualification of economic efficiency as the main goal of competition law is not necessarily the view of the politicians who wrote the laws. Considerations of distributive justice, such as fairness, different notions of consumer welfare, or the protection of small business, may create tensions with the efficiency goal. Also, within the legal community there may be objections to an

---

[1] See e.g. *Northern Pacific Railroad Co. v. United States*, 356 U.S. 1 (1958), at 5.
[2] *Board of Trade of Chicago v. United States*, 246 U.S. 231 (1918), at 238.
[3] *Daubert v. Merrill Dow Pharmaceuticals, Inc.*, 509 U.S. 579 (1993).

economic approach to competition law, if its attainment implies a different treatment of what (to most non-economists) appear to be identical cases. Besides concerns about the legitimacy of a competition law exclusively based on efficiency, the need for legal certainty remains an important obstacle to the reception of economic arguments in competition law. Courts may be hesitant to accept arguments based on probability statements, conceptions of frequency, and hypotheticals such as potential entry. Such considerations stem mainly from concerns of legal certainty (for further discussion of the lawyers' objections, see Van den Bergh 2016, 30–38).

However, a lack of precise economic analysis threatens to undermine competition law's foundations. This is an important insight to which the Court of Justice of the European Union (CJEU) has cleared the way in requesting a more positive economically inspired reasoning in *Walt Wilhelm*.[4] Within the existing framework of competition law, the general quality of reasoning may be improved substantially by referring to economic insights. On the one hand, economic theory supported by reliable quantitative measurement techniques necessitates a case-by-case approach, which may reduce the predictability of decisions and increase legal uncertainty in individual antitrust cases. On the other hand, these costs may be outweighed by reducing the inconsistencies which competition law still harbours. Ultimately, there may be a trade-off between legal certainty (administrative costs) and efficiency (deterrence) that can be solved only by developing optimally differentiated rules (Christiansen and Kerber 2006). Such rules should not be too complex, in order to save on administrative costs, but equally not too simple, in order to avoid error costs. The optimal degree of economic sophistication in applying competition law is a recurrent topic of this book. In the remainder of this Introduction, both the aim of the book and its structure and methodology are further elaborated.

1.2   The aim of this book

The aim of this book is to summarise the main insights of modern competition law and economics. It uses an interdisciplinary approach by integrating the lessons of competition economics and the existing legal framework as studied in competition law. Moreover, it adopts a comparative approach by contrasting the two major competition systems: the US antitrust laws and the EU competition rules. The book provides a well-documented economic analysis of the different practices and types of conduct governed by competition law. In addition, it critically scrutinises the ways in which competition

---

[4] Case 14/68 *Walt Wilhelm v. Bundeskartellamt* [1969] ECR 1, at 14.

authorities and courts make use of economic analysis in the enforcement practice. By using the comparative law and economics approach, the book is different from other textbooks on competition law. Textbooks on competition law seldom contain a systematic overview of the relevant economic theory (for excellent legal discussions of US antitrust law, see Hovenkamp 2016; Areeda and Hovenkamp 2011; Sullivan and Grimes 2006; on EU competition law, see Korah and Lianos 2017; Jones and Sufrin 2016; Whish and Bailey 2015). Conversely, in textbooks on industrial economics or introductions to competition economics, the analysis of competition law remains limited (for leading textbooks in industrial organisation, see Cabral 2017; Carlton and Perloff 2005; for an introduction of competition economics for lawyers see Niels, Jenkins and Kavanagh 2011). The available textbooks on competition law and economics limit themselves to a discussion of either US antitrust law (Hylton 2010; Hylton 2003) or EU competition law (O'Donoghue and Padilla 2013; Geradin, Layne-Farrar and Petit 2012; Bishop and Walker 2010; Motta 2004). Books with a comparative scope are either edited volumes or too extensive to be covered within a limited number of teaching hours (Elhauge and Geradin 2011; Drexl, Idot and Monéger 2009). More importantly, they do not follow the fully integrated approach adopted by this book. The structure of many books largely uses legal categories and does not provide a systematic analysis of the degree of integration between the legal and economic disciplines. Finally, this book aims at a worldwide audience by not only comparing the major legal competition regimes (US antitrust law and EU competition law) but also equally including short discussions of competition law of other important economic players, such as China and Brazil.

It would be premature to describe the current state of competition law as an unqualified victory for economic efficiency. First, differences between the two major antitrust systems remain. These differences are due largely to divergent views on the goals of competition law. Whereas in the US there seems to be unanimity that the goals to be reached can be defined in terms of allocative efficiency and consumer welfare, EU competition law attempts to achieve a broader set of goals. In particular, the emphasis put on the goal of market integration continues to cause inconsistencies with efficiency objectives (see Chapters 3 and 6). Second, in EU competition law the scope of economic analysis still must be expanded substantially, in order to eliminate fully the use of legalistic arguments and to avoid that decisions are taken that conflict with efficiency concerns. In addition, the quality of economic analysis must be further improved in order to avoid the use of outdated theories and to guarantee that poor economic arguments are identified. This book offers several examples of competition rules that remain at odds with mainstream economic insights, particularly in the areas of vertical restraints (Chapter 6), abuse of dominance (Chapter 7) and enforcement (Chapter 8).

The ambition of this book is to lay the foundations for an ever-closer co-operation between competition economists and competition lawyers. It is neither a substitute for textbooks on industrial organisation nor an overview of competition law. The central aim of this book is to stimulate an integrated approach, rather than assessing competition problems by either purely economic or strictly legal criteria. This reflects the key concern that both competition lawyers and competition economists should be ready to adapt their traditional analysis and methodology, in order to fully profit from an interdisciplinary approach. On the one hand, decisions in competition cases should not be based upon formalistic line drawing, using only technical legal categories. In order to develop a consistent and welfare enhancing competition policy, the economic effects of legal rules and decisions in competition cases should always be borne in mind. In order to avoid inconsistencies and adverse effects lawyers must be willing to adapt the existing substantive and procedural rules. On the other hand, economic theory should equally not be developed in a vacuum. An often-heard criticism among competition lawyers is that economic theories on competition are too abstract and too far away from the complexities of everyday practice. The need for industrial economists to inform themselves about the complexities of competition law is a similarly important undertaking to stimulate interdisciplinary research. It may prevent an industrial organisation theory from living a life of its own and enhance the development of economic models that are closer to reality. Theoretical models, which are informed by the institutional details of competition law, will be far more relevant for solving real-world problems in the field of competition law. In sum, openness to each other's approaches and willingness to adapt traditional concepts and methodologies are the corner-stones of a successful interdisciplinary approach to competition law.

1.3   Presentation of the book: structure and methodology

1.3.1   Structure

After this Introduction, Chapter 2 provides an overview of the evolution of economic thinking on competition law. In this way, different economic approaches are identified. Competition rules may be adapted as the underlying economic theory changes. An historical overview is well suited to reveal several schools of thought in the field of competition economics and point at both convergences and differences in economic approaches. Chapter 2 subsequently discusses: the concept of competition in classical economics, the models of perfect competition and monopoly developed in price theory, ordoliberalism, the Structure-Conduct-Performance paradigm, the views of the Chicago School, dynamic approaches to competition, the theory of contestable markets, transaction cost analysis, modern industrial organisation theory and behavioural antitrust law and economics. This chronological overview is particularly helpful to discuss whether and, if so, to what extent the outcomes of competition cases are affected by changes in economic theory. It also reveals that decisions in real-life cases may be based on value judgements that rarely surface if only the mainstream economic view is referred to.

Chapter 3 discusses the different goals that may underlie competition law. It starts with a clarification of different concepts of efficiency (static efficiency, dynamic efficiency) and the welfare goals (total welfare, consumer welfare) pursued by competition law. The chapter emphasises the negative welfare consequences of monopoly power, which traditionally justify the need for competition rules. At the same time, this chapter stresses that economic efficiency (total welfare) is not the only possible goal of competition policy. Rules of competition law may be inspired by other considerations, such as (particular notions of) consumer welfare, the protection of the competitive system and individual economic freedom, or concepts of equity. The two major goals of US antitrust law (total welfare and consumer welfare) are contrasted with the pluralist approach in the EU. Besides market integration (a goal which is absent in US antitrust), EU competition law is influenced by the objective of protecting the competitive order (ordoliberalism) and political goals (market integration) that do not coincide with a pure efficiency approach. Different goals may lead to different outcomes, as the comparisons of US antitrust law and EU competition law in later chapters of this book will illustrate.

Chapter 4 addresses the economic analysis of market power and shows how economic insights may be helpful in interpreting the legal concept of dominance. The largest part of this chapter is devoted to a critical analysis of the concept of the relevant market, which forms the basis of an indirect assessment of market power in competition law. The market share-market power paradigm is critically analysed. The inherent limitations of market share analysis are illuminated and comparisons are made with alternative approaches, which try to assess market power directly. Case examples are given to illustrate the limits of a legalistic approach and illuminate the possibilities and limitations of econometric tools. In addition, Chapter 4 contains an analysis of barriers to entry. In the absence of entry barriers, there is no possibility to exercise market power for a lasting period. A central question is whether, on top of entry requirements in public law, private firms may erect entry barriers by raising rivals' costs. Particular attention is devoted to intellectual property rights (patents, copyright) that create entry barriers and thus inhibit static efficiency but, at the same time, enhance dynamic efficiency by providing incentives to continuously innovate. Throughout the entire chapter, US antitrust law is compared with EU competition law.

Chapter 5 summarises the most important insights of economic theory relating to horizontal restrictions of competition. The focus is on the incentives of firms to collude, the requirements for successful collusion, the risk of cheating and the instruments to punish firms deviating from the collusive agreement. The chapter summarises the main insights from game theory and the economics of collusion regarding the potential for anti-competitive outcomes of horizontal agreements. Next to these anti-competitive effects, attention is devoted to the potential efficiency savings of horizontal restraints. Thereafter, the attention shifts to the legal analysis. Chapter 5 provides a comparative assessment of US antitrust law and EU competition law from an economic perspective. Hard-core cartels (price fixing, market sharing, bid rigging) are distinguished from other forms of competitor cooperation. Concerted practices (EU) and tacit agreements (US) are differentiated from tacit collusion in the economic sense. The distinction in EU competition law between 'restrictions by object' and 'restrictions by effect' is compared with the US Rule of Reason. It is also explained how the US and EU systems balance the anti-competitive and pro-competitive effects of horizontal restrictions. To that end, the four cumulative conditions for an exemption in EU competition law (Article 101(3) TFEU) are discussed. Chapter 5 has separate boxes with discussions of several US and EU cases and includes examples from other jurisdictions (Brazil, China, India) as well.

Chapter 6 addresses vertical restrictions of competition, which emanate from agreements between firms that are active at different stages of the supply chain. Also, this chapter starts with a summary of the major insights from economic theory. A distinction is made between price restraints and non-price restraints. Efficiency theories include, among others, the free-riding justification and transaction cost analysis, which focuses on problems of coordination between manufacturers and distributors. The anti-competitive effects arising from foreclosure and potential abuse of market power are contrasted with the efficiency explanation. Thereafter, Chapter 6 provides a comparative assessment of US antitrust law and EU competition law. It is shown why the Rule of Reason approach in the former system may be better reconciled with economic insights than the still-too-legalistic approach of the EU block exemptions. Also in this chapter, separate boxes discuss the competition laws of emerging economies and provide case discussions.

Chapter 7 analyses the prohibition of monopolisation (Section 2 US Sherman Act) and its European counterpart, the prohibition of abuse of a dominant position (Article 102 TFEU). Different types of monopolisation and potential abuses are analysed: refusals to deal, tying and bundling, predatory pricing, price discrimination, discounts, and rebates. Particular attention is devoted to the impact of divergent economic approaches on the contents of the legal prohibitions. Some of these approaches (in particular the Chicago School) had a clear impact on US case law but were not able to penetrate EU competition law. In this respect, the legacy of the Ordoliberal School is advanced as an explanation for the prohibition of certain practices (for example, tying) that would pose no problem from a purely efficiency-oriented competition policy perspective. Leading antitrust cases, such as *Wanadoo* and *Intel* (EU) and *Microsoft* (US and EU), are discussed in separate boxes. Recent examples from other jurisdictions are also provided, such as *Qualcomm* (China) and *Google* (Russia).

Chapter 8 discusses how the cartel prohibition and the rules on abuse of dominant position are enforced. Four dimensions of law enforcement are analysed: the choice of sanctions (fines on companies only or also fines on individuals and eventually imprisonment), the role of private and public enforcement mechanisms, the timing of the enforcement actions (*ex ante* control versus *ex post* monitoring), and the (de)centralisation of enforcement. Throughout the chapter, US antitrust law is compared with EU competition law. This discussion focuses on differences in the sanctioning system (criminal sanctions versus administrative fines) and the importance of public enforcement in the EU, which contrasts with a largely private enforcement system in the US. Chapter 8 also critically analyses the so-called modernisation of the EU enforcement system, which has changed the timing of the enforcement and the degree of centralisation. The system of self-assessment (Article 101(1) TFEU) and the increased decentralisation (application of EU competition law by authorities of the Member States) might be explained better by private interest theories, rather than efficiency objectives.

Chapter 9 contains an analysis of merger control. The chapter starts with an overview of the theoretical and empirical economic literature. It subsequently discusses the role of market share analysis, concentration ratios, competitive effects of mergers and potential efficiencies. It highlights the substantive issues raised by coordinated and non-coordinated effects and provides examples to illustrate these complex concepts and their application in recent antitrust practice. Several leading competition cases, including *Volvo Scania* (EU) and *General Electric/Honeywell* (EU/USA), are discussed in separate boxes. Besides a comparative analysis of merger control in the US and the EU, Chapter 9 also provides information about the control of concentrations in a number of developing economies (China, Brazil).

As indicated above, all chapters contain boxes, next to the main text. The use of boxes is instrumental to reach different objectives. First, competition law and economics is a vast and complex field of study. Summarising the main insights of competition economics and competition law from a comparative perspective is thus a challenging task. In order not to overburden the reader, it is useful to remove discussions of technical concepts and unsolved issues from the main text. Readers are then referred to boxes, where these concepts and additional problems are elaborated. Second, the reference legal regimes for the comparative approach are US antitrust law and EU competition law. The competition laws of other jurisdictions are largely inspired by these regimes. Nevertheless, both Member States' laws in the EU and the competition laws of major economic players (BRIC countries) may exhibit interesting differences that merit some discussion. Again, use is made of boxes to convey this information to the reader. Third, competition laws are phrased in deliberately general terms and get their precise meaning when competition authorities and courts interpret them. For this reason, leading cases must be analysed to find out whether their outcomes are consistent with economic principles. Detailed case discussions are not possible in the main text. Therefore, several leading antitrust cases taken from different legal systems are discussed in boxes. Examples include heavily debated cases, such as *Leegin* on vertical price fixing (see section 6.3.1), *Microsoft* on abuse of dominance (see Chapter 7, sections 7.2.3 and 7.3.2), and famous merger cases, such as *Volvo/Scania* and *General Electric/Honeywell* (see Chapter 9, boxes 9.3 and 9.5). Next to these US and/or EU cases, case studies from other jurisdictions are included in boxes.

1.3.2 Methodology

The methodology used in this book is comparative law and economics. This implies two major challenges: an integration of legal and economic approaches to problems of competition law and a comparative perspective contrasting different legal regimes. The integration of competition economics and competition law requires openness on both the lawyers' and the economists' side to each other's approaches. Legal regimes and economic frameworks are based on a different logic. Lawyers tend to emphasise the internal consistency of legal rules, that is to say, the need that rules are clear, predictable and do not contradict each other. Conversely, economists care about external consistency, which questions whether the legal regime conforms to the goal of economic efficiency. The challenge of this book is to integrate both approaches. In this way, it can be shown how economic insights may improve the formulation and enforcement of competition rules by profiting from theoretical and empirical economic studies. At the same time, the book highlights that particular economic insights have so far failed in permeating competition law. Remaining disharmonies between competition economics and competition law can be attributed to contrasting views on the goals to be achieved and differences relating to concepts and methods between competition economics and competition law.

The comparative law perspective is used to highlight the similarities and differences that still exist between different jurisdictions. In the field of competition, the legal systems most commonly discussed are US antitrust law and EU competition law. Both regimes contain a ban on cartel agreements, a prohibition of monopolisation (abuse of dominant position) and a system of merger control. The comparative legal approach in this book is functional: it is examined whether different rules achieve a similar goal, even though there may be formal differences in formulation and interpretation. This functional comparative approach allows assessment of the extent to which both US antitrust law and EU competition law achieve particular economic goals. Even though the emphasis is on the comparison of the US and EU approaches, the increasing globalisation justifies additional attention for the competition rules that apply in markets of important economic players and new emerging economies (BRIC countries). Therefore, the competition rules of countries such as China, India and Brazil are discussed in separate boxes. These rules are largely built upon the US and the EU frameworks and the competent authorities (public agencies and courts) increasingly rely on similar methods of enforcement. To the extent that they exhibit significant differences or provide important illustrations (case law), separate boxes will be devoted to the competition regimes of the latter countries.

The structure of this book reflects the methodology just described. After an overview of the evolution of the economic theory of competition (Chapter 2) and a discussion of the goals of competition law (Chapter 3), the book focuses on the main topics of antitrust. Chapter 2 adopts an institutional-historical perspective, since such an approach is indispensable to understanding how and to what extent different economic views have been able to penetrate competition law. The discussion of the goals of competition law in Chapter 3 is equally important to understanding the degree of integration between competition economics and competition law, as difficulties with the reception of economic insights may be caused by the degree to which competition law is hospitable to economic efficiency goals. Chapters 4 to 9 subsequently discuss the definition of market power, the legal regime of horizontal restrictions, the treatment of vertical restrictions, the prohibition of monopolisation (abuse of dominant position), enforcement issues and merger control. Following a comparative law and economics approach, as a first step these chapters systematically analyse the main economic insights (both economic theory and empirical studies) related to the anti-competitive effects and efficiency benefits of horizontal and vertical restraints, abuses of dominance (monopolisation), enforcement issues and merger control. As a second step, these chapters explore the way in which economic arguments are used in the legal practice of the two major antitrust regimes (US and the EU) and equally devote some attention to other jurisdictions (including EU Member States' competition laws, Brazil, China and India). This method allows an assessment of the extent to which economic analysis has been incorporated in the respective legal regimes and an indication of the areas where disharmonies between the economic and the legal approaches continue to exist. In this way, a balanced judgement on the integration of competition economics and competition law becomes possible.

The comparative law and economics approach adopted in this book explains the way in which the different chapters are structured. This structure uses economic categories rather than the legal categories of other textbooks. Whereas in the latter economic arguments are inserted if useful to interpret the meaning of legal terms or procedures, this book rigorously follows an interdisciplinary approach. Two examples seem useful to illustrate this difference. In traditional textbooks on EU competition law, the discussion of vertical restrictions follows the structure of Article 101 TFEU. In this book, the analysis of vertical restraints is organised according to the economic arguments relating to their anti-competitive effects and potential efficiency gains. Thereafter, the extent to which the legal regimes are hospitable to these economic arguments is examined. Similarly, in other textbooks the analysis of enforcement mechanisms is structured according to the different phases of the legal proceedings (commitments, formal decisions of the competition authorities, and appeal before the courts). In this textbook, the discussion of enforcement mechanisms follows the categories of the law and economics literature: the choice of sanctions to achieve deterrence, the efficiency of public and private enforcement, the economic effects of a shift from notifications to *ex post* legality and the economically optimal degree of centralisation.

In sum, this book provides an overview of the relevant economic insights on competition and shows how and to what extent these economic views have penetrated competition law worldwide. The book addresses the practical ways in which competition authorities and courts have implemented the economic logic in assessing real-life cases. The (sometimes difficult) reception of economic analysis is explained by taking account of the legal context and historical traditions permeating the different legal orders. The book is primarily written for courses on Competition Law and Economics taught at the postgraduate level. But it is also aimed at providing antitrust lawyers with crucial tools to successfully master the economic insights in their daily practice.

1.4 Bibliography

Areeda P, Hovenkamp H (2011), *Fundamentals of Antitrust Law* (Wolters Kluwer, 4th ed.)

Bishop S, Walker M (2010), *The Economics of EU Competition Law. Concepts, Application and Measurement* (Sweet & Maxwell, 3rd ed.)

Cabral L (2017), *Introduction to Industrial Organization* (MIT Press, 2nd ed.)

Carlton D, Perloff J (2005), *Modern Industrial Organization* (Pearson, 4th ed.)

Christiansen H, Kerber W (2006), 'Competition Policy with Optimally Differentiated Rules Instead of Per Se Rules vs Rule of Reason' 2 *Journal of Competition Law and Economics* 215

Drexl J, Idot L, Monéger J (eds.) (2009) *Economic Theory and Competition Law* (Edward Elgar)

Elhauge E, Geradin D (2011), *Global Competition Law and Economics* (Hart Publishing, 2nd ed.)

Geradin D, Layne-Farrar A, Petit N (2012), *EU Competition Law and Economics* (Oxford University Press)

Hovenkamp H (2016), *Federal Antitrust Policy. The Law of Competition and Its Practice* (West Academic Publishing, 5th ed.)

Hylton K (2010), 'Antitrust Law and Economics', in G De Geest (ed.), *Encyclopedia of Law and Economics* (Edward Elgar, 2nd ed.)

Hylton K (2003), *Antitrust Law. Economic Theory & Common Law Evolution* (Cambridge University Press)

Jones A, Sufrin B (2016), *EU Competition Law: Text, Cases and Materials* (Oxford University Press, 6th ed.)

Korah V, Lianos I (2017), *Competition Law. Text, Cases and Materials* (Hart, 4th ed.)

Motta M (2004), *Competition Policy. Theory and Practice* (Cambridge University Press)

Niels G, Jenkins H, Kavanagh J (2011), *Economics for Competition Lawyers* (Oxford University Press)

O'Donoghue R, Padilla J (2013), *The Law and Economics of Article 102 TFEU* (Hart, 2nd ed.)

Schmidtchen D, Albert M, Voigt S (eds.) (2007), *The More Economic Approach to European Competition Law* (Mohr Siebeck)

Sullivan L, Grimes W (2006), *The Law of Antitrust: An Integrated Handbook* (West Group, 2nd ed.)

Van den Bergh R (2016), 'The More Economic Approach in European Competition Law: Is More Too Much Or Not Enough?', in M Kovač and A Vandenberghe (eds.), *Economic Evidence in EU Competition Law* 13 (Intersentia)

Whish R, Bailey D (2015), *Competition Law* (Oxford University Press, 8th ed.)

2

Economic approaches to competition law

Roger Van den Bergh

2.1 Introduction

Competition economics and competition law are inextricably linked. Ever since competition law came into existence, the economic theory of competition has exercised its influence upon it. For a long period, the impact of economics on the antitrust laws of the United States of America (US) has been more pronounced than its impact on the competition rules of the European Union (EU). The US Sherman Act, dating from 1890, is now more than 125 years old.[1] During a period longer than a century, the economic theory of competition has naturally changed, and this has had an impact on competition law. This branch of the law has been characterised by a cyclical movement. The rules alter as and when the underlying economic theory changes, thus reflecting the fluctuating economic views of competition in the decision process.

In this chapter, a simple chronological structure is used to reveal various schools of thought[2] in the field of competition theory and competition law. A sketch of the evolution in economic thinking and the impact of changes in the dominant economic thinking of the time on competition law is the easiest way to explain how economic theory may have a concrete impact on legal issues. The presentation of different schools of thought is merely done for didactical reasons. It should not give the false impression that there is complete disagreement among economists, so that a systematic economic approach

---

[1] On the history of US antitrust law, see Peritz (2001). The Sherman Act is often referred to as the oldest competition law in the world. This is not entirely correct since the Canadian law is one year older; it is less known than the US Sherman Act, since it has not been as vigorously enforced.

[2] In the definition of Mackaay, a school of thought is 'a group of thinkers who adopt a common approach, including shared theoretical premises, on how and what to research in a particular field'. Mackaay states that such a school can be distinguished when a group of scholars project their own axioms and defend their views, which must have a certain complexity and logical coherence, against other views (Mackaay 2000, 402–403).

to competition law would only increase legal uncertainty and therefore be of little use. The qualification 'school' is a typical response to a paradigmatic change in a scholarly field, since new ideas are often threatening to established scholars. However, the views of different schools may be complementary, rather than contradictory, and their confrontation may allow policy makers a better assessment of specific forms of market conduct.

The origins of the economic concept of competition can be traced back in classical economics, where competition figured prominently as the 'invisible hand' guiding business decisions towards economic welfare. When mathematics began to penetrate economics at the end of the nineteenth century, this dynamic concept of competition as a 'process of rivalry' was replaced by the static notion of 'perfect competition'. The influence of competition theory on competition law increased dramatically once the Harvard School had articulated the basic perceptions of industrial organisation theory[3] in the well-known Structure-Conduct-Performance (SCP) paradigm and had claimed to be able to explain the relationships among these three variables (structuralist approach). This, together with the emergence of the new competitive ideal of 'workable competition' (Clark 1940), had a clear influence upon competition law. Many shifts in US antitrust law from the 1970s onwards can without doubt be attributed to the economic insights of the Chicago School. Chicago economists make a renewed use of concepts of price theory to explain firm behaviour and market structure. Contrary to the Harvard paradigm, which advanced structural remedies to improve market performance, the Chicago analysis led to a (much) less interventionist antitrust policy. In recent years, three additional theoretical approaches have won substantial support in industrial organisation theory: the model of contestable markets, transaction cost analysis and game theory (for an overview of Post-Chicago developments, see Cucinotta, Pardolesi and Van den Bergh 2002; Hovenkamp 1985). The latest entry in the continuing series of economic approaches to competition is behavioural economics. The behavioural antitrust literature attempts to integrate insights from psychology into economic analysis, in order to better explain the behaviour of firms.

---

[3] Industrial organisation (also termed 'industrial economics' in European countries) has developed into an influential branch of economic learning. This discipline is devoted to the application of explanations and predictions concerning economic results in real-life markets. The Harvard School applied the Structure-Conduct-Performance paradigm in order to determine whether the competition in various branches of industry is 'workable'. In European discussions, the 'Harvard label' is used because the approach was developed in the late 1930s and early 1940s at the University of Harvard. The denomination 'Harvard School' is less common in the US, though. American authors do not have a common way of referring to the pre-Chicago era. Usually, the case law is referred to as 'Warren Court' era, after the then-President of the Supreme Court.

So far, the evolution of economic thinking on competition seems a sole US endeavour. However, any historical overview would be seriously incomplete without a consideration of European views on competition policy. Even though the Ordoliberal School of thought did not contribute to neoclassical price theory, its proponents developed several competition principles that are relevant for a proper understanding of EU competition law as it has evolved up until today. In addition, the Harvard–Chicago debate in the US found its EU counterpart in the German discussion on competition policy from the 1960s until the 1980s. Meanwhile, the disciples of the Austrian School stressed the dynamic properties of competition. Today, the European economic literature has embraced the main insights of modern industrial organisation theory in its approach to competition law problems (Motta 2004).

For a long time economic views of efficiency had a negligible impact on European competition law. The rules of EU competition law and their application in practice were largely driven by the goal of achieving market integration. Putting emphasis on market integration and the concomitant promotion of parallel trade resulted in an interventionist competition law, which banned all forms of market division.[4] Moreover, rules of EU competition law were interpreted using technical legal distinctions and a focus on the economic effects of diverging interpretations was largely absent. Viewed from an economic perspective – and abstracting from the market integration goal – EU competition policy from the 1960s until the first half of the 1990s may be best understood as a manifestation of ordoliberalism, complemented by insights of the analytical model of the Harvard School. By contrast, the views of the Chicago School had no impact when the European Court of Justice (CJEU) interpreted the competition provisions of Articles 85 and 86 EEC Treaty (now Articles 101 and 102 TFEU). From the mid-1990s on, large parts of EU competition law have been revised and many ideas of modern industrial organisation theory have been integrated into the current legal framework. Further chapters of this book will investigate how far the old-fashioned formalistic legal approach has been replaced by what the European Commission calls a More Economic Approach.

The variety of economic views sketched above illustrates that there is no such thing as 'the' economic approach to competition law, which offers exact and authoritative answers to all kinds of competition law problems. This book

---

[4] It should be added that the prohibition of market partitioning has been somewhat relaxed in recent years but absolute territorial protection, without time limits, remains a severe infringement of the EU competition rules (see section 6.4.2 for further analysis). Also, price discrimination may still be prohibited as an abuse of a dominant position, in spite of resulting efficiency benefits achieved through increased output (see section 7.5 for further discussion).

will disappoint those who seek such guidance, for it contains nothing of the kind. Conversely, this chapter shows that there are different economic approaches to competition law. Even though most current industrial organisation research is grounded in the same formal economic theory, differences of opinion among economists on substantive points may not be excluded when it comes to policy issues. In this chapter, the overview of economic approaches to competition law will indicate both common opinions and the lines along which economists may disagree. The latter discord should by no means distract from the important added value to be derived from an economic analysis. It must be acknowledged that different opinions are often based upon differing underlying value judgements that rarely surface. The crucial point of diverging competition theories is that, from a non-ideological perspective, there can be no certainty about the 'right' competition theory and the 'right' competition rules. Competition policies should be sufficiently flexible to allow the creation and diffusion of innovative views.

The structure of this chapter is as follows. After this introduction, the second section describes the concept of competition as it figured in classical economics. The third section presents the main findings of price theory. It contrasts the model of perfect competition and the model of monopoly and discusses the ensuing welfare implications. In the fourth section, the ideas of the Freiburg School and later evolutions of the ordoliberal approach to competition policy are summarised. In the fifth section, the main arguments of the Harvard School are discussed. This School is also labelled the structuralist approach, since it produced numerous industry studies linking performance with structural characteristics of markets. In the sixth section, the Harvard–Chicago controversy is commented on in some detail, given its continuing relevance for understanding current competition policy issues. The basic tenets of the Chicago School are summarised and some first illustrations as to how these alternative views may influence antitrust law are given. The seventh section provides an overview of the most prominent dynamic approaches to competition: the work of Schumpeter, Austrian economics (Friedrich von Hayek, Ludwig von Mises) and the German concept of freedom of competition (*Konzept der Wettbewerbsfreiheit*, advanced by Erich Hoppmann). The eighth section discusses the theoretical concept of contestable markets and its relevance for competition policy. In the ninth section, it is shown how transaction cost analysis may supplement both the structuralist approach (Harvard School) and the relevant insights from price theory (Chicago School). The tenth section presents modern industrial organisation theory. The most recent literature builds upon the best insights from the Harvard–Chicago debate (without its extremes) and adds views from the theory of contestable markets, transaction cost economics and, more particularly, insights from game theory. In the eleventh section, this chapter introduces behavioural antitrust. This is the most recent evolution in the history of economic approaches to competition law. By abandoning the rationality assumption and creating scope for heuristics and cognitive biases, behavioural scholars claim to be better able to explain what is – in their view – systematic irrational behaviour of market participants. The twelfth section summarises the main findings and concludes.

2.2 Classical economics

The roots of the classical concept of competition go back at least to Adam Smith's famous book *The Wealth of Nations* (Smith 1776). Even before Smith's time competition was a familiar concept in economic writing.[5] Smith systematised earlier thinking on the subject and elevated competition to the level of a general organising principle of economic society. Although much of Adam Smith's analysis is now obsolete, his arguments concerning the efficiency of free competition are as valid as ever. Since the days of Adam Smith, economists have naturally updated their views of competition and have developed more refined competition models. Unfortunately, these formal models not infrequently sacrifice their explanatory power in favour of mathematical refinement. With overtly simple assumptions, important insights of the classical theory have been lost. A renewed acquaintance with the classical literature can, therefore, put us back on track to the origins of competition theory.

2.2.1 A dynamic view of competition

Classical economics presented competition as a dynamic concept, the essence of which is the effort of the individual seller to undersell, or the individual buyer to outbid, his rivals in the marketplace. Competition was seen as a power that forced prices to a level just covering costs (McNulty 1968, 647). Smith incorporated this concept into his *Wealth of Nations* and gave it a significance it never had before by presenting competition as a force that leads self-seeking individuals unconsciously to serve the general welfare. The reference to the invisible hand is the most frequently quoted passage of the book:

> [Each individual] generally, indeed, neither intends to promote the public interest,
> nor knows how much he is promoting it. (...) [He] intends only his own gain, and

---

[5] See McNulty (1967), with references to the seventeenth-century mercantilist Johann Joachim Becher, to writings by Turgot and Hume (1766) and to Sir James Steuart (1767), who provided the most complete pre-Smithian analysis of competition.

he is in this, as in many other cases, led by an invisible hand to promote an end which was no part of his intention.

Smith 1776, 127–128

Smith's invisible hand is the market prices, which emerge in reaction to competitive forces. These forces oblige producers to accept lower prices in order to attract demand; in this way competition increases economic welfare. If producers ignore the demands of consumers, they will be excluded from the market.

Smith's suspicion of cartels and monopolies is well summarised in another well-known passage of the *Wealth of Nations*:

> People of the same trade seldom meet together, even for merriment and diversion, but the conversation ends in a conspiracy against the public or in some contrivance to raise prices.

Smith 1776, 127–128

This quote illustrates that Smith was well aware of the problems caused by private restrictions of competition. The above quote is followed by a less well-known, but equally important, statement that the law cannot hinder people of the same trade from sometimes assembling together, but that nothing should be done to facilitate such assemblies or render them necessary (Smith, *ibid.*). Today, there is still great scepticism regarding the ability of competition law to effectively prevent collusive price fixing. Hence, Smith's warning that meetings of traders should not be favoured must be taken seriously. In the European context, the possibility of obtaining block exemptions (Article 103(3) TFEU) has incentivised associations of traders to organise meetings for developing a common view about how the European Commission may be convinced about the benefits of a cartel. Block exemptions may be counter-productive if the European Commission is captured by well-organised lobbies, which profit from their information advantage in convincing the competition authority about the benefits flowing from restraints of trade.[6]

---

[6] Many examples may be given, including the block exemptions for beer supply agreements (Regulation 1984/83, [1983] O.J. L 173/5), service and distribution agreements for cars (Regulation 1475/95 [1995] O.J. L 145/25) and cartels in the insurance industry (Regulation 3932/92 [1992] O.J. L 398/7; for a critical comment, see Faure and Van den Bergh (1995); later replaced by Regulation 267/2010 [2010] O.J. L 83/1. The two former exemptions no longer apply and the European Commission is currently also considering withdrawing the block exemption for the insurance industry.

The conception of competition as a dynamic ordering force dominated classical economics. When Adam Smith wrote of competition, he did not contrast competition and monopoly as market models but rather the level of prices resulting from the presence or absence of competition as a regulatory force (McNulty 1968, 643). In classical economics, competition was seen as a process of rivalry between competing firms possessing reasonable knowledge of the market opportunities. Freedom of trade was stressed as a necessary condition for competition to work. In addition, competition was seen as a process which achieves its results only in the long run. During the classical period, market theory was 'to open the door of opportunity wide and to trust the results' (Adams 1918, 27). Most importantly, competition was viewed as a price-determining force and not as a market structure, although it was acknowledged that competition was more effective with a larger number than with a smaller number of competitors. The idea of competition itself as a market structure is the distinguishing contribution of late nineteenth-century economics. In neoclassical economics, a more precise and elegant model of perfect competition was developed. This model, however, focuses exclusively on the effects of competition. It therefore, in spite of its elegance, loses sight of the dynamic processes leading to these results.

Nobel laureate George Stigler neatly summarised the Smithian conditions of competition as follows (Stigler 1957):

- The rivals must act independently, not collusively.
- The number of rivals, potential as well as present, must be sufficient to eliminate extraordinary gains.
- The economic units must possess tolerable knowledge of the market opportunities.
- There must be freedom (from social restraints) to act on this knowledge.
- Sufficient time must elapse for resources to flow in the directions and quantities desired by their owners.

2.2.2   Policy conclusions

What were the lessons of classical economics for competition law? In classical economics, competition signified both reciprocal rivalry and the absence of government restrictions, such as the exclusive privileges that characterised the mercantilist period. It is a widespread fallacy that classical economists blindly placed their trust in the *laissez faire* principle. Many classical economists were against government interference in the market. They were of the opinion that the competitive process would lead to efficient results. Some of them nevertheless advocated limited regulation of competition. Although competition was hailed as a process, they considered some sort of government interference to be necessary in order to ensure that markets could operate freely, so that competitors could enter and leave the market without hindrance. Adam Smith in particular was well aware of the need for a legal framework to guarantee freedom of competition by preventing collusion between firms and abuses by dominant firms, consisting of the erection of barriers to entry to combat the erosion of their market power.

The common law in relation to restraints of trade reflected the classical view of competition (Hovenkamp 1989). Certain modes of conduct limiting individual economic freedom were condemned as restraints on competition. The oldest common law cases often question the legality of non-competition clauses after the owner of a business had parted with ownership. Non-compete clauses obliging the seller of a store not to compete with the new owner for a limited period of time and within a restricted territorial area were usually held valid, whereas unlimited non-compete clauses were seen as unreasonably restrictive. This 'restraint of trade' doctrine was summarised in the case *Mitchel v. Reynolds*: covenants not to compete may be justified if they are reasonable and ancillary to a principal transaction and if they are limited in time and space.[7] The emphasis on economic freedom in classical economics may also explain why the older case law of the US Supreme Court relating to vertical restraints adopted a property rights approach to protect the economic freedom of retailers. This was reflected in the different treatment of contracts with agents or dealers. Limits on the formers' freedom were held legal but similar restrictions in contracts with dealers were seen as a violation of the antitrust laws, since the manufacturer had parted with ownership.[8] When the efficiency views of the Chicago School began to dominate the analysis of vertical restraints, the US Supreme Court labelled its former case law too legalistic and not based on the economic effects of the practices concerned. A renewed acquaintance with the classical view of competition reveals that the older view cannot simply be disqualified as legal formalism but that it also reflected a different kind of economics. In essence, the emphasis put on property rights reveals the concern for the protection of individual economic freedom cherished by the classical economists.

---

[7] 1 P.Wms.181, 24 Eng. Rep. 347 (K.B. 1711). Older cases involved contracts between a master and an apprentice stipulating that the apprentice is not allowed to start up in competition with the master within a year after completing his training. See for further discussion: Hylton (2003, 33–34).

[8] *United States v. Arnold, Schwinn & Co.*, 388 U.S. 365 (1967).

2.3 Price theory

2.3.1 A static view of competition

Adam Smith gave a positive reply on the desirability of a free market system, which has served as a policy guideline for more than two centuries now. However, the justification of his answer is not satisfactory according to the methodological standards of neoclassical micro-economics. With the mathematical economists (Cournot, Jevon, Edgeworth, Marshall), the concept of competition took a fundamentally different form. The emergence of price theory in the nineteenth century led to the development of a structural and static notion of competition: the model of perfect competition. In contrast with classical economics, which analysed competition as a dynamic process, price theory focuses on the properties of the market equilibrium.

A market equilibrium may be defined as a final state in which all possibilities for mutually beneficial exchanges between market parties have been exhausted. Price theory does not consider how this equilibrium is attained dynamically. Perfect competition is a static notion. If the conditions of the model are satisfied, no competitor can gain a lead on any of the others; this results in a slowing-down of the competitive process. In the German language, this phenomenon is concisely described as *Schlafmützenkonkurrenz* (nightcap competition, Lutz 1956). The equilibrium as a final state is a much simpler structure, but loses much of the richness of the classical model. Nevertheless, the structural concept of perfect competition is very useful to analyse the welfare properties of a market system. According to Smith, the invisible hand guided the economic actors through the incentives of the price system to an optimal resource allocation. To restate this proposition in a modern fashion, the behaviour of producers and consumers must be analysed more precisely and a yardstick must be introduced for measuring economic efficiency or social welfare. Neither aspect was convincingly developed in the original invisible hand theorem. The price to be paid for the progress in these questions is the unrealistic assumptions of the model of perfect competition.

2.3.2 The model of perfect competition

When economists speak of a perfectly competitive market, they have in mind a market that has the characteristics mentioned below. (For a technical description of the model of perfect competition, the interested reader may consult Hall and Lieberman 2007, 244; Carlton and Perloff 2005, 56) The conditions listed are commonly called assumptions; if they are not satisfied, so-called market failures occur.

- On the supply side of the market, there are a large number of producers acting as price-takers who decide independently, without collusion, on their actions. No single firm has a sufficiently large degree of market power to influence the market outcome or the actions of others.
- The demand side is similarly structured. The producers face a large number of buyers who are acting independently and have no power to control the market price through their behaviour.
- It is further assumed that entry and exit may occur instantaneously without prohibitively high costs for the new firms. Producers must be able to start up or shut down operations if they find it in their interest to do so. There is thus free and easy entry and exit.
- The products traded on the market are homogeneous. This means that consumers perceive no quality differences between the goods and decide based on prices alone from which producer they will buy.
- The transaction costs of a perfectly competitive market equal zero. The goods can be exchanged without costs and flow freely to their most valued use. Transaction costs are expenses that occur by the exchange of the produced good and cannot be considered as production costs.[9]
- The (final) assumption of perfect information covers a wide range of sub-assumptions, which will not be listed in full. Here, it suffices to reduce the assumptions to the following. The suppliers of the market know their production and cost function as well as the market price of the goods. Relying on this information, they are able to make decisions on the optimal output and on whether to enter or exit the market. The consumers know the utility they derive from the consumption of the goods and determine the purchased quantity by taking into account their utility, income and price of the goods.

In price theory, it is shown that the equilibrium of a perfectly competitive market is allocatively efficient. Perfect competition is a situation in which it is impossible to introduce a change to make at least one person better off without making another person worse off. This situation is also called Pareto-efficient. Pareto-optimality is achieved when it is no longer possible to enhance the welfare of one or more economic subjects by a change in the production or transaction conditions without diminishing the welfare of some other subject. The market equilibrium achieved under conditions of perfect competition is, therefore, optimal from a perspective of economic welfare. To describe the welfare consequences of perfect competition, the

---

[9] Originally, transaction costs were not considered in the description of competitive markets. After the seminal works by Nobel laureates Ronald Coase and Oliver Williamson, economists have realised that transaction costs may give rise to bilateral monopolies, even if the other conditions of perfect competition are satisfied (see section 2.9 for further discussion).

notions of consumer surplus and producer surplus must be introduced. On the one hand, consumers who are willing to pay higher sums for the product than the market price earn a consumer surplus. The consumer surplus can be defined as the difference between the market price and the consumer's willingness to pay. On the other hand, the producer surplus is the measure for the difference between the revenue and the production costs of firms. The producer surplus is the difference between the marginal cost of production and the selling price. The yardstick for measuring the efficiency of the market outcome is simply the sum of consumer and producer surplus. This joint surplus makes it possible to compare the social welfare consequences of the competitive equilibrium and a market in disequilibrium. Price theory shows that the equilibrium of a perfectly competitive market is allocatively efficient. Under perfect competition, the sum of producer surplus and consumer surplus is maximised. This implies that it is impossible to conceive a better use of the production factors or allocation of the goods produced.

2.3.3 The monopoly model

Monopoly is to be distinguished from perfect competition in two important respects. Instead of a large number of sellers there is only one firm supplying the entire market. In addition, it is assumed that new entrants do not challenge the monopoly position. The monopolist thus faces neither actual nor potential competition. In other aspects, the monopoly model does not differ from the assumptions made for the case of perfect competition: the goods sold are homogeneous, there is perfect information, transaction costs equal zero, and there is a large number of buyers. In contrast to a market characterised by perfect competition where firms act as price-takers, the monopolist can influence the equilibrium price and quantity by his production decisions. While the competitive market price is equal to marginal cost, the monopolist's price exceeds marginal cost. This leads to an inefficient allocation of resources because the consumers' wishes are not fully satisfied. Under perfect competition, with price equal to marginal cost, it is impossible to reallocate resources to achieve a higher output. By contrast, output is not maximised under monopoly. This difference lies at the heart of economists' pleas in favour of perfect competition and against monopoly[10] (for a

---

[10] Here, it is assumed that the monopolist is not able to discriminate between his customers according to their willingness to pay or, in other words, that the firm has no knowledge about their individual demand functions. This eliminates the possibility of price discrimination, where different prices are charged for different quantities and/or consumers. Price-discriminating behaviour is a possible extension of the model which will be covered in Chapter 7 (see section 7.5). Here, it may already be mentioned that the output under monopoly will equal the output under perfect competition if the monopolist can engage in first-degree price discrimination by charging every single consumer the maximum price (s)he is willing to pay. Generally speaking, price discrimination may

technical description of monopoly, the interested reader may consult Carlton and Perloff 2005, 88; Cabral 2000, 69).

The welfare consequences of monopoly can be summarised as follows:

- A part of the consumer surplus is redistributed to the monopolist as producer surplus or monopoly rent. This is the so-called 'price effect' of monopoly: consumers pay too much. This price effect in itself is not a loss of welfare, but it may be considered as a situation with a less preferable income distribution. In a political judgement, this transfer of income may be considered socially unacceptable.
- There is a deadweight loss, which lowers the welfare of the concerned economy. This is the so-called 'allocation effect' of monopoly: consumers purchase less of the product affected by monopoly pricing.

2.3.4 Competition law as an instrument to correct the undesirable effects of monopoly

The above analysis provides a strong theoretical basis for the design and implementation of a welfare-improving competition law. A great deal of the specialist literature on the economic effects of market power is dedicated to the magnitude of the deadweight loss triangle of an individual monopolist and the total deadweight loss caused by monopoly in the economy. The first attempt to measure the welfare costs of market power was made by Harberger. He estimated the deadweight loss due to market power for 73 American manufacturing industries. Harberger's empirical results for the period 1924–1928 showed that the welfare loss due to monopoly was a negligible part (0.1%) of US national income (Harberger 1954). Later studies investigated the losses for the American economy in the 'golden sixties' and estimated the deadweight loss at between 0.2% and 0.7% of national income (Worcester 1973). These low estimates can best be seen as a lower bound. In his study Harberger assumed a price elasticity of demand equal to 1; he estimated the normal rate of return on capital by the average rate of return on capital and used industry rather than firm data. By assuming higher price elasticities of demand and using a stock market measure of the normal rate of return and firm data, much higher estimates of welfare losses may be reached (for an overview of the literature Martin, see 1994, 31–36). Cowling and Mueller estimated the welfare losses due to market power for 734 American firms for the period 1963–1966; they suggested that monopoly power costs

---

improve upon efficiency and should, therefore, be carefully assessed in a fully fledged economic approach to competition law.

the American economy no less than 13% of national income per year. For the United Kingdom in the period 1968–1969, Cowling and Mueller calculated losses between 4% and 7% of national income (Cowling and Mueller 1978). For France in the period 1967–1970, Jenny and Weber estimated losses amounting to no less than 9% of national income in the worst scenario (Jenny and Weber 1983). In a classic survey written in 1990, after having corrected for a variety of errors and inconsistencies in Harberger's original methodology, Scherer and Ross suggested that 'the dead-weight welfare loss attributable to monopolistic resource misallocation in the United States lies somewhere between 0.5% and 2% of gross national product' (Scherer and Ross 1990, 667).

Economists believed for a long time that the deadweight loss was the only social cost of monopoly. However, allocative inefficiency is not the only cost of monopoly. Monopolist firms are also vulnerable to internal slack and, therefore, they may not take the necessary measures to keep the production cost at the lowest possible level. The resulting technical inefficiencies must be added to the welfare losses of monopoly. In addition, there may be so-called 'x-inefficiencies', which is the loss of management efficiency in markets where competition is limited. It should not be forgotten that one of the major benefits of a monopoly is a 'quiet life'. Once the competitive pressures have disappeared, a monopolist firm may become slower to reorganise production when that needs to be done because there are no competitors nipping at its heels. Earlier technical efficiencies will then be replaced by waste in the form of x-inefficiencies. With a lazy monopolist, innovative activity may also slow down.[11] Market power may thus also have harmful effects on factors other than price that are valued by consumers, such as product quality and variety. On top of these efficiency losses, other costs of monopoly result from the efforts of firms to become monopolists. Given the monopoly rents that firms may expect when they succeed in monopolising the market, would-be monopolists may spend substantial resources to obtain a monopoly position. This may take the form of lobbying governments to make the exercise of commercial activities dependent upon the possession of a licence. Efforts to obtain a monopoly position are labelled 'rent-seeking'.[12]

Gordon Tullock has convincingly argued that all the resources that are applied to achieving monopoly profits should likewise be included in the social

---

[11] The negative impact of monopoly on innovation is not generally accepted, though. See the discussion below in 2.7.1.

[12] A rent is the difference between the revenue to produce a good and the cost of production. Competition eliminates rents. By contrast, firms protected by regulation may retain rents. The process by which firms try to convince regulators to limit competition is thus called 'rent-seeking'.

costs. The analysis of the welfare losses caused by a monopoly cannot be complete if the sums expended on achieving the transfer from consumers to the monopolist are excluded (Tullock 1967). Firms may compete for market power not only by incurring expenditure to influence regulatory agencies but also by building excess capacity, excessive advertising, or sales efforts coaxed from dealers through vertical restrictions. To the extent that these practices contribute to the creation and/or preservation of monopoly power, they should be added to the social costs of monopoly. When these additional costs of monopoly are taken into account, the welfare losses may be quite substantial. In sum, the total costs of monopoly consist of allocative inefficiency, productive inefficiency, x-inefficiency, the risk of retarded innovation, and the rent-seeking expenditures. Given these costs combined with the distributional effects of monopoly (undesirable transfer of consumer surplus to the producer), the enactment and enforcement of competition laws may well be justified. The magnitude of the welfare losses under monopoly (in particular, allocative inefficiencies and rent-seeking) certainly seems to justify the costs of an antitrust law (Pindyck and Rubinfeld 1998, 334; id. 2017).

2.3.5 Typology of market forms

Perfect competition and monopoly are two extreme prototypes that differ from market structures that are found in real-life markets. Later developments in price theory have drawn attention to the effects of market imperfections, such as scale economies and product differentiation. Scale economies exist when the costs of production decrease with increasing output. Under such circumstances, the model of perfect competition is not appropriate for policy analysis. In the 1930s, more sophisticated forms of market analysis started to develop: the theory of monopolistic competition (Chamberlin 1933) and the analysis of imperfect competition (Robinson 1933). An important insight from the theory of monopolistic competition is that on markets with differentiated goods (where brands are important) also small and medium-sized firms may have limited market power, which enables them to increase their prices. Economists also started to study market forms that are distinguished in function of the number of firms on either the supply side or the buying side of the market. On the selling side, a common distinction is now made between a monopoly (a single seller), an oligopoly (a limited number of sellers) and a polypoly (many small sellers) confronting a large group of small buyers. On the buying side, sellers may face a monopsony (a single buyer) or an oligopsony (a limited number of buyers). If both market sides are concentrated, a bilateral monopoly or a bilateral oligopsony may exist. Table 2.1 shows that the market structure on the selling side may be further differentiated by taking account of the degree of product differentiation.

Table 2.1 Market forms

	One seller	Few sellers	Many sellers
Homogeneous products	Pure monopoly	Homogeneous oligopoly	Perfect competition
Differentiated products	Pure multi-product monopoly	Differentiated oligopoly	Monopolistic competition

The study of the welfare effects of each of these market forms has turned out to be very difficult. In recent years, game theory has offered new methodological tools that have been extremely useful to analyse the complex interaction between firms in an oligopolistic market. In this way, it has become possible to identify the factors that are needed to enable stable collusion (see for further discussion section 5.1 and section 9.2.2). If these factors are present, also prices in an oligopolistic market will be above the level of marginal cost and – even though not to the same extent as under monopoly – will enable firms to earn supra-competitive profits.

2.3.6 Policy conclusions

The attractiveness of the model of perfect competition as a blueprint for competition policy is limited, for several reasons. First, the static model loses sight of the importance of dynamic approaches that are closer to the everyday reality of competitive markets. Second, deviations from the model of perfect competition (information asymmetry, product differentiation) do not justify by themselves antitrust intervention. Finally, the model provides no policy answer if it is impossible to achieve a first-best optimum. These criticisms are further explained below.

First, the concept of perfect competition is totally devoid of behavioural content. In contrast with Adam Smith's view, competition is no longer the force that drives prices down to costs, but a description of a particular idealised situation. Perfect competition is a market situation that, although it is the result of the free entry of formerly competing firms, has evolved to the point where no further competition within the industry is possible. Competition is by definition also excluded under monopoly since the monopolist is identified as the entire industry. Neither the monopolist nor the perfectly competitive firm is able to compete in the Smithian sense. As Paul McNulty put it, the two concepts of competition are not only different but also fundamentally incompatible (McNulty 1968). Whereas classical economics provided insights that are very close to real-life business experience, the equilibrium achieved under perfect competition is far away from reality. Perfect competition is a state of affairs quite incompatible with the idea of all-encompassing competition. The idea of competition as a dynamic process, which is lost in price theory, has been elevated again to the status of a central policy concept in dynamic approaches of competition in the writings of Austrian economists (see section 2.7).

Apart from its unrealistic and abstract character, the concept of perfect competition reveals one of the great paradoxes of economic science: both perfect competition and monopoly are situations in which the possibility of competitive behaviour is ruled out by definition. Every act of competition in the classical sense of the word is valuable as evidence of welfare-enhancing conduct, while in neoclassical economic theory it would be proof of some degree of monopoly power. For Adam Smith, competition was a process (disequilibrium) through which a predicted result – the equation of price and costs – was achieved. With the mathematical economist Augustin Cournot, it became the realised result itself (McNulty 1967, 398). However, deviations from the equilibrium outcome may be the very essence of competitive processes. Therefore, those who favour a dynamic view on competition will refuse to base any policy recommendations on the model of perfect competition.

Second, the model of perfect competition may cause a serious bias in policy making. Even though the analysis of monopoly seems to demonstrate unambiguously that a monopoly is a bad thing, price theory does not allow easy conclusions as to the contents of competition policy in real life. A major problem in using the model of perfect competition is that it may lead policy makers to label every deviation from the perfectly competitive model caused by a less than perfectly elastic demand as a market imperfection. Here the risk of a so-called 'Nirvana approach' emerges (Demsetz 1973a). Policy makers should refrain from making comparisons between the real world and an imaginary ideal situation; they should rather compare the welfare outcomes of different institutions as they can be observed in reality (comparative institutional approach).

The danger of slipping from an idealised situation to real-world phenomena becomes clear when existing deviations from the model of perfect competition are used to justify antitrust intervention. Suppliers selling differentiated products face downward-sloping demand curves and, therefore, possess market power enabling them to increase prices above marginal cost. Uncertainty about the actions that competitors may undertake is a deviation from the assumption of perfect information, and another departure from the model of perfect competition. Non-conformity of real-world conditions with the assumptions of the perfectly competitive model is pervasive throughout the economy. However, these deviations are not imperfections in the antitrust policy sense. Taking advantage of uniqueness in pricing one's product is not anti-competitive, but it actually encourages the investments in product features and firm reputation that are valued by consumers. Product differentiation poses antitrust concerns only if it is used strategically to limit market entry (see 4.7.2). Likewise, the uncertainty about how competitors will behave stimulates competition, whereas competitive forces may slow down in the absence of information asymmetries.

Third, if a general competitive equilibrium is to be achieved, the conditions of perfect competition must be satisfied in all sectors of the economy. The impossibility of achieving a general competitive equilibrium, rather than a partial equilibrium in some sectors of the economy, gives rise to the problem of second-best. Apart from the hypothetical case in which all market imperfections either are absent or simultaneously corrected, the analysis set out above throws no light on the question of whether perfect competition is better than monopoly. Political pressure can hinder the removal of market imperfections, just as the presence of economies of scale can make their removal undesirable. Although the achievement of perfect competition in all sectors of the economy (the first-best solution) necessarily brings about an increase in welfare, this is by no means certain once one less-than-optimal situation is transformed by competition policy into another less-than-optimal situation. Given the imperfections in some markets, information about the most efficient market form in other markets (perfect competition, oligopoly, or even monopoly) is not easily available. To generate a second-best solution a lot of research has to be done and to be repeated if the situation in only one market changes. Frederic Scherer and David Ross conclude that: 'The theory of second best is a counsel of despair' (Scherer and Ross 1990, 37–38). According to these authors, aiming at a third-best solution is the best strategy for competition policy. An approach such as this involves choosing from the various forms of general policy those that, on average, result in the most desirable allocation of resources. Seen in this light, a policy that stimulates competition appears to be superior. Such a policy aims to achieve the amount of competition which is compatible with economies of scale and with the desired degree of product differentiation. Because there is no reliable information concerning the second-best solutions, an improvement in welfare may be achievable by eliminating monopoly power where it is present, rather than by encouraging fresh obstacles to monopoly in markets where these obstacles did not previously exist.

2.4 The Ordoliberal School

The term 'ordoliberalism' is closely connected with the policy views of the Freiburg School, which greatly affected the development of German economic policy in the period immediately after the Second World War. When the European Economic Community (EEC) was founded, the leading German representatives managed to introduce ordoliberal views in the competition policy of the EEC. It is a frequent misunderstanding that in the post-war period the allied occupation authorities imported US antitrust law in Europe and that the European competition rules were shaped after the prohibitions of the US Sherman Act – at that time the worldwide guiding example of antitrust law. Economic history tells us a different story (Giocoli 2009). The original Articles 85 and 86 of the Treaty establishing the EEC were not a by-product of US post-war debates on competition law but aimed at a goal that is extraneous to US antitrust law: the achievement of market integration by eliminating private trade barriers between the six original Member States. Ordoliberal scholars exerted an important influence on the process of European unification; it was through their impact that competition rules were enshrined in the original EEC Treaty. The goal of competition law specified in the original Treaty to establish a 'system of undistorted competition' (Article 3(f) EEC Treaty) has a clear ordoliberal wording. Up until today, the case law of the European Court of Justice is inspired by ordoliberal ideas. For this reason, any analysis of EU competition law that fails to take into account the influence of ordoliberalism would be seriously incomplete (see also Amato 1997).

In essence, ordoliberalism advances a competitive market as a preferred system of economic planning based on freedom and legally protected individual rights. At its origin, the ordoliberal view of society was distinguished by a search for a third way between capitalism (market economy) and socialism (command economy).[13] The third way between capitalism and socialism became known under the term 'social market economy', which is an open market with individual freedom and social justice (Gerber 1998, 236). Next to political freedom, economic freedom must be part of society's constitutional order. Consequently, the EEC Treaty itself has fixed the rules for the functioning of the economic system and awarded a key role to competition. The

---

[13] After the First World War, Europe experienced a renaissance of theoretical liberalism, which tried to avoid the disadvantages of the old liberal *laissez-faire* system, without moving to extreme state interventionism and centrally planned economic systems. In the German post-Second World War discussion, both socialists and liberals agreed on the need for anti-monopoly measures (*Dekartellierungsgesetze*) in order to discontinue the cartel-stimulating policy of the Hitler regime (war-related *Zwangskartelle*). Contrary to the socialists, the liberals took the position that individual freedom is a primary social goal, which can be guaranteed only if private property and economic freedom are protected by legal rules.

primary goal of competition law is to protect competition as a system within which there is freedom of action on both the supply and demand side of the market. The ordoliberal views on the desirable contents of specific competition rules (prohibition of cartels, control of monopoly power and mergers) have evolved over time and do not constitute a monolithic school of thought. For a proper understanding of ordoliberalism, it is helpful to distinguish between the original ideas of the Freiburg School (developed already in the 1930s and 1940s), the impact of ordoliberalism on the formulation of the competition provisions of the EEC Treaty (1950s) and later evolutions of ordoliberal thinking (Behrens 2014).

The founding fathers of the Freiburg School were the economist Walter Eucken and the lawyer Franz Böhm. The Freiburg School endorsed a clear instrumentalist view of the legal system by viewing legal rules, such as a cartel prohibition, as tools to attain economic goals. As stated by Böhm (1928, 1933), the language of economics must be translated into the language of law to create the conditions for an effectively functioning competitive market. The property rights of individuals, which are guaranteed by the private law system, are limited by rules that determine the borderline between (lawful) competitive and (unlawful) anti-competitive market conduct. According to Böhm, competition rules protect the economic freedom of individuals, which is an indispensable condition for attaining effective competition.

The distinguishing difference between classical liberalism and ordoliberalism is the emphasis put on the need to transfer responsibility for achieving competition from *laissez-faire* to a strong state. Apart from individual freedom and legally protected individual rights, ordoliberalism is characterised by its systemic approach to competition: the concept of 'ordo' as 'order' in the sense of systemic arrangement, not to be confused with order in the sense of command (Behrens 2015). The originality of ordoliberalism does not lie in the development of an alternative economic theory of competition (that would replace neoclassical economic views based on price theory), but rather in the formulation of a number of competition principles that must be embedded in an economic constitution and implemented by an independent competition authority.

In Eucken's view, the goal to be achieved was *vollständiger Wettbewerb* (complete competition). This notion is close to the notion of perfect competition. As explained above, numerous unrealistic criteria must be satisfied to achieve perfect competition. However, in Eucken's view, it should suffice to ensure that firms active in the market must behave as price-takers. In this vein, Eucken also emphasised the importance of free access to the market; this excludes scope for coercion by incumbent firms. In a market of *vollständiger Wettbewerb*, no firm has the power to forcibly influence the conduct of other firms (Eucken 1965; see for further discussion Möschel 1989). Hence, for the first generation of ordoliberals, the ideal market form was a polypoly. Two policy recommendations resulted from this view. First, the state should create the legal framework to make complete competition (*vollständiger Wettbewerb*) possible and must, where this ideal cannot be attained, enact regulations to simulate the outcome of complete competition. According to the original ordoliberal views, a strict and general prohibition of horizontal cartels and a preventive merger control should prevent the creation of monopolies in markets where the conditions of complete competition are still satisfied. In other markets, state intervention requiring dissolution of cartels, divestitures, and control of remaining monopolies should realise or simulate the outcomes under complete competition. Second, firms possessing economic power should be forced to behave as if complete competition existed, in particular with respect to their pricing decisions. The latter standard, which became known as *Als-Ob Wettbewerb* (as-if competition) was formulated by another ordoliberal thinker, Leonhard Miksch (see for further discussion Giocoli 2009, 774). The concept of as-if competition implies that the competition authority may require a dominant firm to act as if it was subject to competition: in price-theoretical jargon to act as a price-taker (firm subject to perfect competition) rather than as a price-maker (monopolist).

The writings of the Freiburg School, which used complete competition as a benchmark for the design of competition rules, have led commentators to conclude that ordoliberalism inevitably leads to a highly regulated economy (Gerber 1998, 232). This is a misunderstanding. Following the view of Böhm competition rules must be regarded as rules of the game and should not be conceived as prescriptive state intervention. The role of the legislature is to define the basic rules governing economic activities in an economic constitution and then step back. Economic processes should remain free but need a framework to achieve their beneficial results. As formulated by Eucken: 'Staatliche Planung der Formen – ja; Staatliche Planung und Lenkung des Wirtschaftsprozesses – nein'.[14] Consequently, competition law too should consist of general, broad rules and not be interventionist. Importantly, the enforcement of the competition rules should be entrusted to an independent, quasi-judicial competition authority, which is free from pressure by the executive power and interest groups. The competition authority should apply legal norms according to objective standards and there should be little room for discretionary behaviour. The current German enforcement system still

---

[14] 'State planning of structures – yes; State planning and direction of economic processes – no' (author's translation), see Eucken (1949, 93).

reflects these ordoliberal principles. The German Act Prohibiting Restraints of Competition (*Gesetz gegen Wettbewerbsbeschränkungen*) is enforced by the relatively autonomous German Competition Authority (*Bundeskartellamt*). The German enforcement system thus differs from its European counterpart. The European Commission is not free from (direct or indirect) political influences and may take decisions that are not in harmony with principles of competition policy but are influenced by other policies, such as social or environmental considerations (see 3.5.5).

In the 1950s, the original view that monopolies are harmful *per se* because they are incompatible with the standard of complete competition was given up by the second generation of ordoliberals. Also the concept of as-if competition had lost momentum (Behrens 2015). However, the fundamental ideological principles of ordoliberalism remained intact and they have been reflected in the wording of the original EEC Treaty. The goal of EU competition as specified in Article 3(f) is to establish a 'system of undistorted competition' (Article 3(f) EEC Treaty, later Article 3 (1(g) EC Treaty). This goal reflects the systemic approach to competition that is characteristic of the Ordoliberal School. Ordoliberalist thinking also underlies the formulation of Article 101(3) TFEU, which stipulates that competition may not be eliminated for a substantial part of the relevant market as one of the four cumulative conditions to grant an exemption from the cartel prohibition. In addition, the case law of the CJEU on abuses of a dominant position (Article 102 TFEU) has a clear ordoliberal touch. For example, the notion that dominant firms have a 'special responsibility' not to limit competition reflects ordoliberal thinking that is extraneous to US antitrust law, where such a notion is completely unknown in the case law on Section 2 of the Sherman Act (for further discussion, see Chapter 7).

2.5 The Harvard School

2.5.1 The structural conception of industrial organisation

In what follows the term 'Harvard School' will be employed to indicate the extensive literature on competition policy that constituted the dominant approach until the 1970s. Researchers working in the Harvard tradition tried to find causal relationships to predict possible results in real-life markets (characterised by a limited number of large firms next to a fringe of small competitors). In the Harvard approach to competition policy the performance of specific industries was seen as dependent on the conduct of firms, which in turn is dependent on the market structure of the industry under investigation. This has become widely known as the Structure-Conduct-Performance

(SCP) paradigm, which emphasises the direction of causality from structure to conduct to performance. Since the first industrial economists accorded an influential or even determinant role to market structure, their view is characterised as the structuralist conception of industrial organisation. On the normative level, Harvard scholars discarded perfect competition as the ideal to be aimed at. The concept of 'workable competition' was suggested instead as a blueprint for competition policy. In order to determine whether a specific industry satisfies the criteria of workable competition, structural components, modes of conduct and performance criteria must be taken into account.

The Structure-Conduct-Performance (SCP) paradigm

The Structure-Conduct-Performance paradigm was developed by Edward Mason at Harvard University in the late 1930s and early 1940s (Mason 1939, 1949). Some authors suggest that Edward Chamberlin, who, simultaneously with Joan Robinson, developed the model of monopolistic competition, laid the theoretical basis for the work on structure, conduct and performance (Hay and Morris 1991). In the works of Chamberlin and Robinson the theoretical relationship between industry structures, on the one hand, and prices and profits, on the other hand, was examined, and it was precisely this type of relationship that Harvard scholars started to test empirically in the 1950s. The original empirical applications of the Harvard approach were made by Mason's colleagues and students, the most famous of whom was Joe Bain.

The SCP paradigm implies that market performance (the success of an industry in producing benefits for consumers) is dependent on the conduct of sellers and buyers (as regards, for example, prices, advertising, research and development). Conduct, in turn, is determined by the structure of the relevant market (number of buyers and sellers, barriers to entry of new firms and degree of product differentiation). The structure of an industry depends on basic conditions on both the supply side (such as raw materials, technology and unionisation of the labour force) and the demand side (such as price elasticity, rate of growth and purchase method). Government policy, through antitrust laws, regulation and taxes, may affect the basic conditions, the structure of an industry, the conduct of the economic players and the ultimate performance of an industry.[15] In the initial years of classical industrial organisation, the reciprocal relationship between market structure and performance was the principal topic of investigation. Chamberlin proceeded upon the reasonable assumption that firms are maximising profit and showed

[15] In their classic textbook Scherer and Ross (1990) introduced Public Policy as a fifth block, next to Basic Conditions, Market Structure, Market Conduct and Market Performance.

that under monopolistic competition long-run equilibrium would be achieved where price is equal to average cost. In this vein, Bain stated that the conduct component did not add much information, since information about market structure is sufficient for predictions about performance (Bain 1968). Later publications by scholars working in the Harvard tradition also included conduct criteria as explanatory variables, insofar as the relevant information was available. By the addition of conduct, a much richer model arises and predictions can be made with more precision and confidence.

The relationship among basic conditions, structure, conduct, performance and government policy is complex. The Bain paradigm analysed industries in terms of a causative chain from structure to conduct to performance. However, there are also feedback effects from conduct to market structure and basic conditions and from market structure to basic conditions. For example, sellers' pricing policies (conduct) may either encourage entry or drive firms out of the market, thereby affecting the number of competitors (market structure). Also advertising (conduct) may be used to make the demand for products offered less elastic (basic conditions). Together with the criticisms by the Chicago School relating to the weaknesses of the empirical work conducted by Harvard scholars, these feedback effects diminish the predictive power of the SCP paradigm. Modern industrial organisation theory emphasises the effects of conduct (strategic interaction) on industry structure (see section 2.10).

There are hundreds of studies that attempt to relate market structure to market performance. In these studies three major measures of market performance are used: (i) the rate of return, which is based upon profits earned per dollar of investment; (ii) the price-cost margin, which should be based upon the difference between price and marginal cost, although in practice some form of average cost is used instead; and (iii) Tobin's q, which is the ratio of the market value of a firm to its value based upon the replacement cost of its assets (Tobin 1969). To examine how performance varies with structure, additional measures of market structure are needed. Industry concentration is typically measured as a function of the market shares of some or all of the firms in a market. In the early empirical research concentration was measured by using the eight-firm concentration ratio (CR8), which is the sum of the market shares of the eight largest firms, or the four-firm concentration ratio (CR4), which focuses attention on the top four firms in measuring concentration. Today, market concentration is measured by using a function of all the individual firms' market shares. The Herfindahl–Hirschman Index (HHI) is the sum of the squares of the market share of every firm in the relevant market. Compared to the CR4 and CR8, the HHI is a superior method to measure the degree of market concentration (see section 9.2.2).

Already in 1951 Bain had investigated 42 industries and separated them into two groups, depending upon whether the CR8 was higher than 70%. He found evidence that the rate of return was higher for the more concentrated industries (11.8%) than for the less concentrated industries (7.5 %). In 1956 Bain published his seminal book *Barriers to New Competition*, in which he argued that profit rates are higher in industries with high concentration and high barriers to entry. Bain's sample included 20 manufacturing industries with relatively high concentration levels. The CR4 was used as a measure of market concentration. Even though Bain recognised the theoretical superiority of the price-marginal cost margin, he used the accounting rate of return on stockholders' equity as a measure of profitability because of informational reasons. Bain's 1956 study also included a detailed (but subjective)[16] analysis of entry conditions, based on publicly available material and information from a survey. The relationship between concentration and profitability appeared to be consistent with his earlier work, especially when entry barriers were substantial. In addition, Bain discovered that large firms in industries with very high barriers to entry (e.g. automobiles, cigarettes, liquors) generally earned higher rates of return (23.9% in the automobile industry and 18.6% in the liquor industry) than large firms in industries with lower entry barriers (e.g. 10.1% in the flour industry and 5.1% in the meat packaging industry). In the Bain sample, higher barriers to entry were associated with greater profitability for large firms. Bain concluded that concentration allows collusion (explicitly or tacitly) and that collusion generates excess profit if entry into the industry is difficult. These effects were observed mainly for large firms (Bain 1956). Other authors replicated Bain's work for later periods. The results were generally consistent with Bain's findings (see e.g. Mann 1966). An early econometric study by Collins and Preston equally confirmed the relationship between profitability, used as a measure of market power, and various structural characteristics of industries.[17]

---

[16] In contrast to Bain's subjective judgements, later empirical work uses objective standards to measure entry barriers: minimum efficient scale as a fraction of industry output (to assess scale economies) and the advertising sales ratio (to assess product differentiation).

[17] Collins and Preston (1969). This study did not explicitly control for differences in entry conditions across industries. Later empirical work showed the importance of product differentiation in determining price-cost margins (Strickland and Weiss 1976). See also: Domowitz, Hubbard and Petersen (1986).

The concept of workable competition

The concept of workable competition came about as a result of the publication, in 1940, of John Clark's classic article 'Toward a Concept of Workable Competition'. This publication brought about a radical change in thinking concerning competition policy. In the 1930s Robinson and Chamberlin had developed models of imperfect competition (oligopoly, monopolistic competition), but their viewpoints contained no radically altered perspective as far as policy recommendations were concerned. Economic analysis of competition problems was reoriented towards real-life market situations, but the model of perfect competition was still applied as a policy guideline. Market imperfections had to be corrected whenever and wherever possible in order to achieve, or at least approximate, perfect competition.

Clark had an aversion to mathematic static equilibrium models and he followed Mason's approach of case studies. Initially, Clark also tried to maintain perfect competition as a norm. In his later work, which was influenced by Schumpeter, Clark emphasised the dynamics of competition once he had realised that perfect competition did not exist, could not exist and had probably never existed (Clark 1961). Accordingly, the theoretical model of perfect competition does not provide a reliable standard by which to evaluate real market conditions. Furthermore, Clark stressed that, in the long run, market imperfections are not bound to be injurious *per se*. Not all market imperfections should be eliminated by competition policy, for market imperfections can neutralise each other. This became known as the antidote theory. For example, informational uncertainty may be desirable to prevent collusion in markets with few suppliers. Persistent market imperfections are therefore no obstacle to workable competition. Competition policy should not seek to achieve the ideal of perfect competition, but should, instead, formulate criteria for judging to what extent an industry is workably competitive.

The views of Mason and Clark initiated a great number of case studies, starting from the SCP paradigm, in order to assess the existence of workable competition in different sectors of the economy. Sosnick (1958) published an admirable overview of the almost unmanageable bulk of US literature on this subject. Taking their cue from Sosnick's scheme, Scherer and Ross (1990) established criteria for judging whether an industry is workably competitive. The relevant criteria can be grouped into three categories, as summarised in Box 2.1.

Box 2.1: The Structure-Conduct-Performance paradigm: criteria

Structural criteria

- The number of firms must be at least as great as economies of scale permit.
- There must be no artificial restraints on entry or mobility.
- The products on offer must have moderate and price-sensitive differences in quality.

Conduct criteria

- Competitors must be subject to a degree of uncertainty as to the extent to which price initiatives will be followed.
- Firms must pursue their objectives independently, without reciprocal agreements.
- No unfair trade practices or exclusion measures must be used.
- Inefficient suppliers and customers must not be constantly protected.
- Advertising must be informative and not misleading.
- There must be no harmful, persistent price discrimination.

Performance criteria

- Firms' production and distribution processes must be efficient and must not waste resources.
- Production levels and product quality (differentiation, product life, safety and reliability) must accord with customers' wishes.
- Profits must reach just the right level to ensure investment, efficiency and innovation.
- Price levels must encourage rational choice, steer markets towards equilibrium and prevent the reinforcement of cyclical instability.
- Opportunities to introduce superior technical products and processes must be exploited.
- Advertising expenditure must not be excessive.
- Success must go to the sellers who respond best to consumers' wishes.

Box 2.1 shows, among other things, that there are a number of criteria whose fulfilment is very difficult to measure. More important still is the fact that it is not clear how the presence of workable competition is to be established if some, but not all, of the criteria are satisfied. If the performance criteria are satisfied but the structural ones are not, the main criterion in Harvard writings seems to be the acceptability of performance. Such difficulties will increase if some, but not all, performance dimensions are fulfilled. When the workability test is applied, the resulting second-best problems can thus be particularly serious. In addition, it must be stressed that the performance criteria may not be completely consistent with each other. Good performance is multi-dimensional. It embodies productive efficiency, allocative efficiency and dynamic efficiency (innovation). If workable competition is to be used as the normative criterion, what decision must be taken when a proposed merger may allow firms to earn supra-normal profits (allocative inefficiency) but at the same time produces substantial cost savings (increased productive efficiency)? How does one solve Clark's well-known dilemma according to which economic progress requires acceptance of restrictions on competition (for example, patents)? In the absence of unbiased empirical evidence, these conflicts cannot be resolved without invoking basic value judgements.

2.5.2 Policy conclusions

The Harvard School's vision, which emphasises the relationship between market power, business conduct and market results, considerably extends the scope of liability based on competition law. In its simplest version the SCP paradigm condemns positions of strength and barriers to entry if they are not related to economies of scale. In the US, the Harvard analysis became the cornerstone of competition policy in the 1960s and remained so until the neoclassical and neo-institutional approaches began to win the upper hand in the mid-1970s.

Harvard axioms

The principal tenets of the Harvard School of industrial organisation can be summarised as follows:

- The perfect competition and monopoly models must be supplemented with the more realistic and useful models of imperfect competition (monopolistic competition and oligopoly).
- Investigation should be concentrated not on individual economic agents but on whole branches of industry or on a group of firms within a given industry.
- The objective at which antitrust law should aim is not perfect competition but workable competition.
- The appraisal of the competitiveness of a given activity cannot be the result of logical-theoretical deductive reasoning; it must be a factual judgement. Empirical investigation is essential in order to be able to evaluate the competitiveness of particular branches of industry. Such a factual judgement is based on structural determinism: the structure of the market

influences the conduct of firms and the conduct of firms in turn influences performance (SCP paradigm).

From the late 1960s onwards, partly as a response to the emerging opposite views of the Chicago School, the preoccupation with market structure evolved into a wider concern incorporating exclusionary conduct. The focus shifted towards business behaviour creating market power where it otherwise would not exist or business behaviour enabling existing market power to sustain supra-competitive prices over a long period. According to the Harvard view, the most onerous of these exclusionary practices is business conduct erecting barriers to entry. Joe Bain used a wide notion of barriers to entry and included in the list: scale economies, absolute cost advantages of existing firms and product differentiation supported by intensive advertising (Bain 1951). Later empirical research, conducted by Harvard scholars, showed substantial differences in profit rates between firms with and without differentiated products and concluded that much of this profit rate differential is accounted for by the entry barriers created by advertising expenditure and the resulting achievement of market power (Comanor and Wilson 1967). In contemporary writings, the old Harvard view on entry barriers is criticised and a more balanced analysis has gained acceptance (see section 4.7).

Objectives of competition policy

At the policy level, the Harvard approach includes both economic and non-economic objectives. In their influential book *Antitrust Policy, An Economic and Legal Analysis*, Carl Kaysen and Donald Turner distinguished four objectives of competition policy: first, to achieve favourable economic results; second, to create and maintain competitive processes; third, to prescribe norms of fair conduct; and fourth, to restrict the growth of large firms.[18] Their most important views concerning a proper competition policy can be summarised as follows. Efficiency and progress (implying increased sales, the development of new techniques, and the production of new and better products) are considered the most important economic results which can be substantially influenced by competition policy. Thereafter, stability of employment and a fair distribution of income are stated to be the desired results for the whole economy. For Kaysen and Turner, the second aim which competition policy can achieve is essential. The need to create competitive processes receives special emphasis, namely by promoting competition as an aim in itself instead of as a means to achieve desired economic results. Competition is justified from the point of view of limiting the power of firms. It is therefore linked

---

[18] Kaysen and Turner (1959). Compare also Sullivan (1991), giving a complete and orthodox description of the Harvard views.

with the fourth objective of competition policy. The discussion by Kaysen and Turner concerning fair competition is also founded on the importance of competition. Because competition replaces personal control by large firms or by state bureaucracies with impersonal control by the market, it is presented as a means of guaranteeing fairness. According to Kaysen and Turner, it is fairer if restraints on conduct are imposed by the market rather than through a dominant position or state regulation. Competitive processes can provide one yardstick for measuring the fairness of business conduct, but it is certainly not the only one. The concept of fairness can thus have various meanings. It can signify similar treatment of firms in similar circumstances. The term can likewise be considered as being synonymous with 'fair play', which can be interpreted, in the market context, as refraining from the use of market power and thus seeking to achieve reasonable profits rather than maximum profits. According to these views of the concept of fairness, it seems permissible to protect smaller firms at the expense of society as a whole. In the latter case, guaranteeing fairness coincides with the fourth objective of competition policy by spreading economic power through restrictions on large firms. Competition policy can reduce the size of firms both directly (for example, by dismantling dominant positions) and indirectly by restrictions on conduct (for example, through rules prohibiting abuse of a dominant position). It should be noted that Kaysen and Turner admitted that the four possible objectives of competition policy are partly inconsistent with each other. In relation to economies of scale, for example, the aims of seeking fairness and redistributing power as between large and small firms were placed on a lower hierarchical level of policy.

Impact on competition law: United States

The Harvard view had a substantial impact on US antitrust policy in the 1950s and 1960s. The broad generalisation that price-cost margins and profits vary with the number of rivals and the size of barriers to entry entered US antitrust policy and exerted a noticeable influence upon it, especially in the field of merger control. The original Harvard view, characterised by the book of Kaysen and Turner, was that market power is *per se* harmful and therefore should be illegal. The focus of analysis was on market structure rather than on business conduct as the source of adverse economic performance. The Harvard School also emphasised structural solutions. A clear example of an extreme interventionist view is Donald Turner's proposal of structural remedies in oligopolistic markets if it is legally impossible to ban tacit collusion (Turner 1962). If it is believed that large firms use their market power to earn supra-normal profits, mergers also must be closely scrutinised. Bain suggested divestitures in highly concentrated markets. In his view, if the eight largest firms account for two thirds of production, powerful firms must be broken up so as to produce an oligopoly with only a moderate degree of concentration (Bain 1968, 648).

In the US Department of Justice's (DoJ) 1968 Merger Guidelines, it was stated that an analysis of market structure is fully adequate for showing that the effect of a merger, as spelled out in Section 7 of the Clayton Act, 'may be substantially to lessen competition or tend to create a monopoly'. The DoJ announced that its merger policy would focus on market structure 'because the conduct of the individual firms in a market tends to be controlled by the structure of that market'.[19] An enforcement policy emphasising a limited number of structural factors would not only produce adequate economic predictions for the showing of anti-competitive effects but would also facilitate both enforcement decision making and business planning. Only in exceptional circumstances would structural factors alone be inconclusive (for example, in the case of conglomerate mergers). With respect to horizontal mergers, the 1968 Merger Guidelines used the CR4 ratio as a market concentration measure: when the shares of the four largest firms amounted to approximately 75% or more, the market was regarded as highly concentrated. The DoJ stated its intention to challenge mergers when the market shares of both the acquiring firms and the acquired firms exceeded a certain threshold. For example, in highly concentrated markets, mergers between firms both accounting for approximately 4% of the market would be challenged; in less highly concentrated markets a 5% market share for both the acquiring and the acquired firms was used as the relevant threshold. The Merger Guidelines were revised several times (in 1982, 1984, 1992, 1997 and 2010) to take account of developments in economic thinking concerning the competitive effects of mergers. From the 1997 Merger Guidelines onwards, there has been no longer an explicit reference to the SCP paradigm; mergers are also no longer challenged if the merging firms have extremely low market shares. Moreover, the more recent US Merger Guidelines explicitly allow for an efficiency defence, which clearly reflects the influence of the Chicago School. The latest Guidelines (2010) show a remarkable reception of the newest economic learning on market definition and employ advanced economic techniques for assessing anti-competitive effects and efficiency savings (see section 9.3.2 for further discussion).

---

[19] U.S. Department of Justice, Antitrust Division, press release, Merger Guidelines, May 30, 1968, *reprinted in* Trade Reg. Rep. 4, at 13, 101 (1978).

Impact on competition law: European Union

From what is said above, it should be clear that the Harvard School was sympathetic to far-reaching government intervention and extended the scope of liability based on competition law. In addition, the concept of workable competition, which, albeit undefined, is used as a blueprint for competition policy, conferred large discretionary powers on the competition authorities. These views also had a clear impact on European competition policy until the 1990s and relics of the SCP paradigm and the old Harvard views remain present today.

Up until the end of the previous century, the competition law of the EU could adequately be described as a piecemeal policy aiming at workable competition in the common (internal) market. It dramatically reflected the difficult choices that have to be made when the first-best solutions are not available. Notwithstanding the fact that it is unlikely that the authors of the Treaty of Rome (EEC Treaty) were aware of the concept of workable competition,[20] many of the distinguishing features of European competition policy seem to fit nicely into this analytical framework. It is noteworthy that the Court of Justice of the European Union (CJEU), in its leading *Metro* judgment, referred to the concept of workable competition as being the type of competition that was necessary to achieve the economic objectives of the EEC Treaty.[21] This judgment was concerned with the lawfulness of selective distribution agreements. Once technical and luxury products are sold, for resale, only to recognised distributors, one can no longer discern a market which accords with the model of perfect competition. However, it is still possible to speak of workable competition if the product differentiation, which is thus created, is moderate (see also the criteria in Box 2.1). In *Metro*, the CJEU emphasised that price competition is not the only form of competition for wholesalers and retailers. It considered that it was in the consumers' interests for prices to be set at a certain level in order to be able to support a network of specialised dealers, alongside a parallel system of dealers who themselves provide services and undertake other actions to keep distribution

---

[20] It was mainly a political necessity, rather than a particular economic theory, which made an active competition policy necessary in the eyes of the authors of the EEC Treaty. The elimination of market fragmentation caused by restrictions on competition was necessary in order to achieve the central objective of integrating national markets. European competition policy was an instrument for opening up new sales territories in order to stimulate economic progress, sustained by the efforts of independent firms from all the Member States. This aim of market integration is essential for an understanding of the principal characteristics of EU competition law.

[21] Case 26/76 *Metro SB-Großmärkte GmbH & Co. KG v. Commission* [1977] ECR 1875, para. 20. In another case, however, the CJEU used the expression 'normal competition', which is not based on any economic theory at all. See Case 85/76 *Hoffmann-La Roche v. Commission (Vitamins)* [1979] ECR 461. One must thus be cautious when subjecting judgments of the CJEU to an economic analysis.

costs down. This choice was made available to certain sectors in which high-quality, technically advanced and durable goods are produced and distributed. In its effect, the *Metro* judgment has given the green light to selective distribution systems. In Chapter 6 of this book the current EU law on vertical restraints in distribution contracts will be described and critically examined. It will then become clear that up until today – in spite of the launch of the so-called More Economic Approach in the late 1990s – many relics of the old Harvard ideas on workable competition remain intact.

In the late 1960s and 1970s, the US Harvard/Chicago debate on the appropriateness of competition policy and the desirability of certain legal prohibitions found its German counterpart in the debate between Erhard Kantzenbach and Erich Hoppmann. The former favoured a structuralist approach, based on the belief that a concentrated market structure produces bad economic performance, whereas the latter rejected structuralism and focused on types of firm conduct that would hinder the economic freedom of competitors. The Harvard approach became very popular in Germany when Kantzenbach published his well-known book on the workability of competition in 1967. In this work, Kantzenbach plainly rejected the use of the perfect competition model as a policy guideline and defended the position that workable competition can be achieved in a broadly oligopolistic market structure with a low degree of product differentiation and informational uncertainty. The structuralist conception of competition policy was challenged by Hoppmann, who advanced the alternative concept of freedom of competition (*Konzept der Wettbewerbsfreiheit*) as a blueprint for competition policy. The concept of freedom of competition advanced by Hoppmann was inspired by both ordoliberal thinking and insights from dynamic theories of competition (see section 2.7.3 for further discussion).

2.6   The Chicago School

Chicago lawyer-economists caused a revolution in thinking about antitrust issues. The basic ideas of the Chicago approach to competition law originated with the economist Aaron Director, who, in the 1950s, taught the antitrust course at Chicago University together with the lawyer Edward Levi.[22] Numerous authors such as Robert Bork (1954),[23] Ward Bowman (1957), John McGee (1958) and Lester Telser (1960) elaborated further upon Director's core ideas. The Chicago School's starting point can be found in neoclassical price theory. The confrontation between the legal dogmatic

---

[22]   Director formulated his ideas mainly orally. See Posner (1979).
[23]   Bork's famous monograph *The Antitrust Paradox* gives the most complete and orthodox overview of the doctrine of the Chicago School.

approach to antitrust law and the micro-economic mode of analysis gave rise to a new theory of competition based on efficiency.

2.6.1 The new learning of the Chicago School

The re-emergence of price theory

The notion that the Chicago approach to competition policy is merely the result of the rejection of government intervention in the economy is a mis-understanding of frequent occurrence. On the contrary, Director reached his conclusions by viewing competition problems through the lenses of price theory (Posner 1979). Harvard economists devoted themselves to studying specific industries and examining competition problems based on observable phenomena through empirical research instead of having recourse to a general economic theory. By contrast, Director sought an explanation for practices observed in real markets, which tallied with economic theory's profit-maximisation principle.

The Chicago views are derived from the central tenets of neoclassical price theory. From this perspective, the Chicago School has developed a powerful, if controversial, theory of competition. As stated above, price theory proceeds upon the assumption that firms, which behave in a rational economic manner, will seek to maximise their profits; firms that do not behave in this way will not survive over time. Director adds to this the assumption that, failing proof to the contrary, conduct based on the maximisation of profits can be considered as competitive conduct and that, in principle, markets are capable of correcting eventual imperfections by themselves. Most markets are believed to be competitive, even if they contain relatively few firms; if price competition is reduced, other non-price forms of competition will fill the gap. The Chicago School also believes that monopolies will not last for ever. High profits earned by dominant firms will attract new entries that will erode the positions of dominance. Based on these axioms it becomes possible to explain the market conduct of firms and to formulate two guidelines for antitrust policy. The first guideline states that conduct aimed at maximising profits must, in principle, be regarded as lawful. The second guideline states that the question whether a given conduct is or is not competitive should not be answered based on a structural analysis; what should be examined instead is whether the conduct is economically efficient (Posner 1976). Antitrust law should present no hindrance to efficient forms of conduct, as the legal rules should be aimed solely at promoting efficiency.

The most remarkable differences between the Harvard School and the Chicago School can be summarised as follows:

- The Harvard School is criticised for lack of theory.[24] Chicago economists seek explanations for practices observed in real markets, which conform to the foundations of economic theory. In this vein, practices that were previously thought to be anti-competitive (such as vertical restrictions) are economically rationalised.
- The Structure-Conduct-Performance paradigm is rejected. The positive correlation between structure and performance is not seen as a loss of welfare caused by market power but simply as the consequence of higher efficiency. The allocative efficiencies associated with economies of scale and scope are thought to be of paramount importance.
- In contrast to the multitude of goals accepted by the Harvard School, productive efficiency and allocative efficiency are advanced as the only objectives to be taken into account in interpreting and applying antitrust law. When markets generate inefficient outcomes (which is considered unlikely), government intervention (which is considered prone to failure) is appropriate only if it improves economic efficiency.

These differences are further explained below by focusing on a number of examples: vertical restraints, merger control and entry barriers (for more elaborate discussions, see Chapters 6 and 9).

Vertical restraints

The Chicago School provided industrial organisation with something that the Harvard School did not have: a theory to explain anti-competitive practices (collusion, vertical restraints) and mergers. A well-known example is the efficiency explanation of minimum resale price maintenance, which traditionally had been seen as a way of keeping prices high to the benefit of traders and to the detriment of consumers. In 1960, Lester Telser published an article on vertical restraints, which has since become a classic. In this essay, the free-riding problem plays a central role in explaining minimum resale price maintenance. It is important to understand well a producer's motives for imposing minimum retail prices. If the dealers' margins increase, retail prices

---

[24] One of the harshest critics is Posner, who argues that Harvard's version of industrial organisation theory consists of 'casual observation of business behavior, colorful characterizations (such as the term "barriers to entry"), eclectic forays into sociology and psychology, descriptive statistics, and verification by plausibility which took the place of the careful definitions and parsimonious logical structure of economic theory. The result was that industrial organization regularly advanced propositions that contradicted economic theory', see Posner (1979, 931).

will also rise and a drop in the number of products sold will ensue. A fall in the producer's profits should therefore be expected. However, there are also circumstances in which resale price maintenance improves the producer's position because the advantages arising from efficiency exceed the short-term, disadvantageous consequences flowing from the reduction in demand resulting from the (dealers') higher profit margins. An increase in services and in publicity as a result of fixing minimum retail prices can enhance the value of the product to a more extensive group of consumers and may thus generate increased demand. Therefore, it should be potentially advantageous for a rational producer marketing differentiated products to use resale price maintenance with a view to encouraging his retailers to offer special services. Sales promoting publicity in the form of advertisements, displays of goods and demonstrations add to the retail price. A competing retailer who does not invest in the same publicity can profit from the advertising of others and will thus be able to sell at a lower price. Without higher prices, however, fewer services will be provided because consumers could buy from low-price dealers while still receiving the services from full-service dealers. Resale price maintenance imposed by the producer prevents this sort of free-riding and encourages retailers to offer an optimum level of presales services (for further discussion of this argument, see 6.2.2).

The free-riding argument is not only used in the analysis of resale price main-tenance but has been extended to other intra-brand restraints, such as the reservation of exclusive sales territories (exclusive distribution) and exclusive sales channels (selective distribution, franchising). Protection against free-riding may also explain inter-brand restraints such as exclusive purchasing. Exclusive distribution agreements address free-riding of one dealer on the efforts of another, whereas exclusive purchasing agreements address free-riding of one manufacturer on the efforts of another. Exclusive purchasing agreements can be understood as a means of protecting the manufacturer's property rights in cases in which he possesses informational advantages and is therefore better placed to regulate the sale of his own products (Marvel 1982).

Merger control

It is in the field of merger control that the approaches of the Chicago School and the Harvard School diverge most strongly. The nub of this difference lies in the explanations for the positive relationship, established in many empirical investigations, between concentration and price-cost margins or profits. Policy makers who lean towards the Harvard School refer to studies that are alleged to prove that concentrations lead to the acquisition of market power that facilitates collusion, which, in turn, makes it possible to set prices above the competitive level. It is claimed that leading firms in highly concentrated industries knowingly develop parallel conduct aimed at achieving supra-normal profits. Writers of the Chicago School have initiated an intense debate about the linkage between structure and performance and its implications for competition policy. They argue that large firms are more efficient than smaller ones and will therefore grow more rapidly at a given price level, thus strengthening the tendency towards a higher degree of concentration without thereby causing problems of abuse of market power. If the efficient firms are given room to grow, consumers will profit in the end because scarce resources are then set free to satisfy consumers' wishes in other sectors of the economy.

Nobel prize winner George Stigler emphasised the difficulties in maintaining collusion, rendering it profitable only at the highest levels of concentration (Stigler 1964). The trend of the Chicago School's thinking is that the positive relationship between structure and performance is not necessarily indicative of a loss of welfare caused by market power, but is simply the consequence of higher efficiency. Harold Demsetz argued that large firms more efficiently produce some products, while in other industries large market shares are not necessary for achieving efficiency (Demsetz 1973b). Industries in which large firms have cost advantages will become more concentrated than industries where scale economies are less important. Large firms will have higher profit rates than small firms because their costs are lower, not because they are able to hold the price above the level needed to cover the costs of smaller, less efficient firms. Market concentration and high industry average rates of return both result from efficiency savings realised by large firms. According to prominent Harvard scholars (Demsetz 1973a, 1973b, 1974; and Brozen 1970, 1971), the empirical studies of the Harvard School did not justify the conclusion that the profitability of firms in concentrated sectors is significantly higher than that of firms in sectors where there is no concentration. Rather, the correlation coefficients were very low; there was no linear relationship between concentration and profitability; the samples were too limited and the studies were carried out over too short a period. In concentrated branches of industry, profitability is higher in the short term, while in the long term profits fall again. This is simply the result of the operation of the market. The Chicago School's assertion is that branches of industry become concentrated because larger firms are more efficient than smaller firms are. The market selects the best-adapted form of organisation for each branch of industry; the degree of concentration thus reflects the most efficient form of organisation. To test this thesis empirically, Harvard studies of SCP relationships across large groups of industries were found to be inadequate.

Following Harold Demsetz, the appropriate empirical test for examining whether collusion or efficiency causes the link between sector performance and concentration consists of comparing the rates of return of large and small firms in specific concentrated industries. If concentration represents collusion, both small and large firms will profit. By contrast, if concentration is the consequence of greater efficiency of large firms, only the rates of return of the latter will be high (Demsetz 1973a).

Entry barriers

In the vision of Harvard scholars, barriers to entry are an alternative explanation for continuing concentration and above-normal profits. Following Stigler's attacks on the Harvard School's intellectual foundations, some of the force of this argument has been lost (Stigler 1968, 67 and 94). In the Chicago view, there are no significant barriers to entry except those created by government (licensing laws). Stigler defined a barrier to entry as:

> a cost of producing (at some or every rate of output) that must be borne by a firm which seeks to enter the industry but is not borne by firms already in the industry.[25]

Barriers to entry are present only if the costs for firms entering the market turn out to be higher than the costs for the existing firms. If, for example, it costs $10,000,000 to build the smallest possible efficient factory having an economic life of ten years, then the annual costs for a new entrant will be $1,000,000. The existing firms will be confronted with the same annual cost; at least if it is assumed that they also intend to replace their factories. Accordingly, there is no cost disadvantage for the new entrant. In Stigler's approach, the importance of barriers to entry is reduced. If his approach is followed, classic barriers to entry such as, for example, significant capital requirements will present no serious hindrance to market entry. If monopoly profits are achieved and the capital markets are functioning efficiently, it is presumably possible to raise the necessary capital in order to start up in competition. In this approach, advertising potential and product differentiation will likewise not constitute barriers to entry. Whereas the Harvard School qualified a great many things as barriers to entry, the Chicago School stressed that one must distinguish between forms of efficiency, such as product differentiation, and artificial entry barriers (Bork 1978, 311–312). The question for antitrust law is then limited to finding out whether there are any artificial

---

[25] Stigler (1968, 67). Compare with Bain, who defines entry barriers as 'the advantages of established sellers in an industry over potential entrants, these advantages being reflected in the extent to which established sellers can persistently raise their prices above a competitive level without attracting new firms to enter the industry' (Bain 1956, 3).

impediments apart from government regulations (licensing requirements), which restrict entry into the market (see section 4.7 for further discussion).

2.6.2 Policy conclusions

Chicago's guide on antitrust

Where the Harvard School assigned a multitude of goals to competition law, providing the basis for an interventionist policy, Chicago scholars acknowledge only one goal of antitrust law: the pursuit of economic efficiency. The purpose of antitrust law is to eliminate inefficiencies resulting from collusive price increases and output restrictions. Disciples of the Chicago School strongly warn against a competition policy that ignores considerations of efficiency. Vertical restraints, for example, may cope with free-riding and provide incentives for dealers to optimally invest in sales efforts. In addition, mergers may achieve cognisable efficiencies such as economies of scale, better integration of production facilities, specialisation, lower transportation costs and reduction of administrative expenses. If antitrust law does not consider these efficiencies, welfare losses will occur.

Already in the early 1970s, members of the Chicago School were sharply contesting an antitrust policy that was based on a prejudice against the market results associated with high levels of concentration. The orthodox Chicago approach heavily criticises a policy that protects individual (small) competitors at the expense of competition (and of large competitors). A firm becomes large because it is efficiently organised: 'big is beautiful'.[26] A policy that attacks the big firms for fear of growing concentration can be disastrous for economic welfare. Richard Posner stressed that persistent market concentration is not at all synonymous with market power. It is the result of either large-scale economies or the ability of some firms to attain economic profits persistently thanks to cost reductions and product improvements. The relevant inquiry is not how concentration can cause collusion but rather how economic rents can persist over a period without being eroded by new entry (Posner 1979, 945).

Chicagoans, moreover, stress that the fear that the market will be dominated by efficient firms abusing their market power is often exaggerated. Should a dominant firm try to exploit consumers by increasing its price far above the level of its cost, smaller firms will extend their market shares beneath the price umbrella of the dominant firm. In the improbable event that mergers

---

[26] A suitable answer to Schumacher's 'small is beautiful' theory; see Schumacher (1993).

drive all the other firms out of the market, new firms from other geographical markets will enter the monopolised market. Potential competition then becomes actual competition. Newcomers will seize the opportunity to reap monopoly profits. They will enter the market and undermine the high prices when these overshoot the level that is necessary to exclude less efficient firms. Concentration can persist only if economies of scale preclude the existence of a multiplicity of firms or if monopoly profits are a just reward for having achieved a higher degree of efficiency, by means of price reductions or product improvements that competing firms and new entrants were unable to achieve. Also, the view that monopolistic firms may leverage their monopoly power in related markets and achieve two monopoly profits is rejected. In the next chapters of this book, the Chicago views will be further elaborated and contrasted with modern industrial organisation theories.

Impact on US antitrust law

The Chicago School acquired a strong influence on US antitrust law from the mid-1970s onwards and reached the apogee of its influence in the 1980s. Many competition theorists and jurisdictions accepted Chicago's competition ideas. Several examples can be given to illustrate the altered judgment on forms of market conduct which, until the Chicago School emerged, seemed to cause competition problems but which, through the renewed application of price theory, no longer give rise to problems (Hovenkamp 1985). Later chapters of this book will show how the Chicago learning influenced the assessment of vertical restraints, predatory pricing and mergers. Even though it would be inappropriate to qualify the 1997 Merger Guidelines as a Chicago document, a comparison with the earlier 1968 Merger Guidelines shows that the old Harvard approach was adapted by taking into account some of Chicago's findings. A more complete overview of the assessment of mergers will be provided in Chapter 9 of this book. Here a few examples must suffice to illustrate the Chicago School's impact. Throughout the 1997 Merger Guidelines the analysis is focused on whether consumers or producers 'likely would' take certain actions, that is, whether the action is in the player's economic interest. This reflects the Chicago concern to explain, rather than to merely describe – as Harvard economists do – behaviour in (concentrated) markets, in order to be able to avoid inappropriate regulatory interventions. Chicagoans stress that the possibility of market entry may prevent the post-merger firm from earning above-normal profits. Following this view, the 1997 Merger Guidelines state that mergers in markets where entry is easy raise no antitrust concerns. Finally, the Guidelines explicitly say that the primary benefit of mergers to the economy is their efficiency enhancing potential that can increase the competitiveness of firms and result in lower prices for consumers: 'as a consequence, in the majority of cases, the Guidelines will allow firms to achieve available efficiencies through mergers'. Efficiency gains of mergers will be assessed and may serve as a defence for the benefit of the merging firms (US Merger Guidelines 1997, at 3–4).

Impact on EU competition law

In Europe, the substantive rules of competition law and practice of the European Commission remained largely unchanged during the antitrust revolution in the US. The Chicago views hardly affected EU competition law that, in the 1970s and 1980s, was still based on insights of the Ordoliberal School and the SCP paradigm. This, together with the emphasis on the market integration goal, explains remaining differences between US antitrust law and EU competition law. A few examples may suffice at this point to show that Brussels (and Luxembourg) is still far away from Chicago. Minimum vertical price fixing, which may be justified on several efficiency grounds, is outlawed by Regulation 310/2010 on vertical agreements (see section 6.4.2). In contrast with the US Supreme Court's case law that, in accordance with the Chicago view, considered predatory pricing as an irrational strategy, the EU Court of Justice has adopted a strict attitude towards price wars as a result of which dominant firms selling below average variable costs will be heavily fined for infringement of Article 102 TFEU (see section 7.4.3).

2.7 Competition as a dynamic process

The Harvard approach has been characterised as the structural conception of competition policy. The particular attention which disciples of the Harvard School devote to market structure stands in sharp contrast to the central concern of competition theories which analyse competition not as a structure but as a process. The opinions of prominent economists such as Joseph Schumpeter, writers of the Austrian School, including Nobel laureate Friedrich von Hayek, Ludwig von Mises and Israel Kirzner, and disciples of the concept of free competition, such as Erich Hoppmann and Dieter Schmidtchen, are diametrically opposed to the structuralist theories of competition which have been discussed above. The importance of this largely German-based literature in the field of competition theory should not be underestimated, even though it is less well known than the Harvard–Chicago controversy.

2.7.1   Schumpeter and dynamic innovation

The first important author in the series of competition theoreticians who advocate a dynamic vision of competition is Joseph Schumpeter. In Schumpeter's work competition is regarded as a dynamic process of 'creative destruction'. Pioneer firms introduce new products and new production methods, thereby opening up new markets. The dynamism of these firms initially gives them a temporary monopoly position in the market, but at the same time stimulates others to imitate them. These successive innovations and imitations promote economic progress (Schumpeter 1950). Seen from the perspective of competition as a dynamic process, deviations from the perfect competition model, such as product differentiation and lack of market transparency, are prerequisites for the 'workability' of that process.

The ensuing rejection of an ideal market structure as a fixed point of reference by which competition should be judged has worked its way through to competition policy. Whereas in price theory monopoly is unambiguously considered to be something bad, this is no longer the case in a dynamic view. Indeed, monopolies are seen as a decisive factor in promoting competition. Schumpeter argued that a monopoly might be necessary in order to finance research and development (R&D) costs. Under perfect competition firms will not dare to undertake expensive research because of the associated costs and risks. Large expenditures on R&D without any results to show for it can be enough to eliminate a firm from a competitive market. Large firms can more readily indulge in research and development because for them it is cheaper and less risky (Schumpeter 1950).

Apart from cost reductions, dynamic issues may indicate a preference for more concentrated market structures, even though in static terms this is allocatively inefficient. By contrast, a more fragmented market structure may be allocatively efficient but at the same time inhospitable to innovation. The question of how to take technological progress into account has become one of the most heavily discussed topics in the industrial organisation literature. Ever since the time Schumpeter presented the issue of a possible link between market structure and the rate of innovation, as well as firm size and innovation, implying that it would be advisable to allow for higher market shares in innovation markets, this has been a prolonged field of controversy.[27] Nobel laureate Kenneth Arrow showed that, theoretically, a monopolist has less incentive to invest in innovation than a new entrant or a firm in a

---

[27]   Passionately argued by Galbraith (1952) and dismissed with similar vigour by MacLaurin (1953). Empirical research highlights the importance of big and small for innovative activity; see Mansfield (1983), Gilbert and Sunshine (1995).

competitive industry.[28] Empirical evidence, however, still fails to demonstrate any definitive relationship between firm size, market concentration and the pace of innovation.[29] General conclusions to be drawn from a structural innovation markets analysis are thus reduced to long-shot value for the purpose of antitrust (Rapp 1995). Instead, the individual circumstances of the industry under scrutiny weigh heavily on the final outcome (Roberts and Salop 1995/1996).

2.7.2 Austrian economics

The dynamic vision of competition has been advanced in its most extreme form by the disciples of the Austrian School. Neither von Mises nor von Hayek were particularly interested in market equilibrium, which in any case can never be achieved. In the writings of the Austrian School, emphasis is placed on the time factor, which is absent in price theoretical models. Unlike Schumpeter, the Austrians do not accept the tendency towards market equilibrium as being axiomatic. According to von Hayek (1968), this tendency is an empirical matter; and for von Mises (1996) it is the result of entrepreneurial activity. Building on this notion, Kirzner (1978) has emphasised that it is the entrepreneur who establishes and consolidates the market. For the Austrian School, competition is a process of continuous interaction between the entrepreneur and the environment. It is the entrepreneur, as coordinator of the market, who makes the market.

The starting point in the analysis of von Hayek is that – contrary to the assumptions of the model of perfect competition – suppliers have only imperfect, subjective knowledge of buyers' preferences. It is the task of the competitive process itself to find out the best products and production methods. The price system provides market participants with important signals that enable them to adapt to events and circumstances of which they are unaware. This basic insight, which initiated a Copernican revolution in economics, has far-reaching consequences for competition policy. Von Hayek defended the position that numerous interventions by competition law, such as determining the optimum size for firms, or the degree of workable competition, and the requirement that costs must be justified, are vacuous and erroneous. Costs, prices and market results cannot be determined by market simulations but are revealed by the competitive process itself. To remain in business, firms must constantly obtain information about market conditions and how they change. Individuals hold important economic information

---

[28] See Arrow (1962). His findings have in the meantime been refined; see Reinganum (1989).
[29] Scherer (1992) provides for a survey of numerous studies. Empirical work arguing a positive correlation between product market competition and productivity growth includes Nickell (1996).

in an extremely non-aggregated way. No single economist, administrator or judge can answer the relevant questions of competition law better than the competitive process itself. Von Hayek rejects both a prohibition against cartels and the control of abuses by firms in a dominant position because of their negative effects on the dynamic competitive process (von Hayek 1967). Kirzner likewise considers even the extreme case of an entrepreneur getting permanent control over the whole supply of a particular raw material as being the result of the imaginativeness of a pioneer firm (Kirzner 1978, 168). According to the Austrian view, interference by competition law must be avoided because of its potentially negative effects on the competitive incentive system.

By concentrating on competitive processes, Austrian writers place great emphasis on potential competition. Traditional competitive concepts relate to actual competition. According to dynamic views, competition can also exist in a latent or potential form. Although Schumpeter already endorsed the concept of potential competition, above all the economists of the Austrian School have elaborated this concept (Armentano 1996; Reekie 1979). This School's approach implies that the exploitation of monopolistic positions is rendered impossible by the existence of potential competition (new firms, or pre-existing large firms in competing countries), at least in the long run. The attention that Schumpeter and the Austrians devoted to potential competition has recently taken formal shape in the theory of contestable markets (see next section).

2.7.3 The German concept of freedom of competition (*Konzept der Wettbewerbsfreiheit*)

Erich Hoppmann was a prominent author among the German theoreticians who reject the Structure-Conduct-Performance paradigm. Hoppmann (1968, 1966) advances the concept of freedom of competition as an alternative approach for assessing restrictions on competition. Hoppmann's ideas are based upon both ordoliberal thinking and dynamic views on competition. Instead of focusing on structural solutions, Hoppmann puts emphasis on individual freedom of action, which reflects the ordoliberal foundations of his approach. Since the pursuit of individual freedom also leads to the positive economic effects of competition, Hoppmann advances freedom of competition as the central aim of competition policy.

Authors, such as Kantzenbach (1966), who suggested optimal market structures were sharply criticised by Hoppmann. In Hoppmann's writings, competition is seen as a dynamic market process and not as a static equilibrium. As already mentioned above, Clark, in his later writings, criticised the concept of perfect competition on account of its static nature. Consequently, economic progress is accepted as an important indicator of good market performance. However, the need to accept restrictions on competition (like patents limiting the number of suppliers and thus negatively affecting market structure) in order to improve competition in terms of market performance is thus seen as a dilemma. Hoppmann rejects this finding as, in his view, no conclusions regarding market performance can be drawn from market structure criteria. In Hoppmann's view, competition is a process of spontaneous coordination and evolution. Freedom of competition is also regarded as the guarantor of economic advantages (*ökonomische Vorteilhaftigkeit*), which manifests itself in two ways: spontaneous coordination of business plans and evolution (Hoppmann 1968). The rejection of market performance tests also makes clear that the idea of competition as a learning process is taken seriously.

The conceptual approach of freedom of competition also has elaborated the notion of restrictions of competition. In Hoppmann's view, only forms of conduct that significantly restrict freedom of competition by fostering unreasonable market power should be prohibited by competition law. According to Hoppmann, freedom of competition embraces two components: on the one hand, the freedom to emulate the performance of competitors and to introduce innovations (*Wettbewerb im Parallelprozess*) and, on the other hand, the freedom to choose one's trading partners (*Wettbewerb im Austauschprozess*). Legal prohibitions should, according to Hoppmann, be formulated as *per se* rules in order to minimise legal uncertainty for firms. Hoppmann's advocacy of *per se* rules was criticised by other German authors, because it is difficult to give a description of practices which are, by their very nature, restrictive of competition (for an overview of this discussion, see Clapham 1981). Other proponents of the concept of freedom of competition have argued that the requirements of justice and legal certainty do not require *per se* rules, but can also be satisfied by the formulation of abstract rules that do apply in a general way and are sufficiently stable (Schmidtchen 1988). Taking account of the requirement in current EU competition law to define a relevant market on which the prohibited restrictions of competition materialise, a striking feature of the German conceptual approach of freedom of competition is that the market system is seen as unique and indivisible (Hoppmann 1977, 9). All products and services compete with each other and competition cannot be divided in different market segments. Consequently, in Hoppmann's view, the concept of a relevant market is meaningless (for further discussion, see Chapter 4).

2.8 The theory of contestable markets

2.8.1 Contestability as a theoretical yardstick

Among the more recent economic approaches towards competition law, contestability theory is closely related to the general thrust and ideas of the Chicago School. The most complete, but also very technical, description of the theory is given by William Baumol, John Panzar and Robert Willig (1982). An important distinction between the structuralist theories of competition and the theory of contestable markets has already been indicated in the previous section devoted to dynamic theories of competition: it is the emphasis which the theory of contestable markets puts on potential competition. Under the theory of contestable markets, market performance is judged without any regard at all to market structure. If contestability is taken as a yardstick, the fact that the market structure is concentrated says nothing, by itself, about the degree of efficiency. Even with a high degree of concentration, allocative efficiency is not excluded because potential entrants exercise a controlling discipline over monopolists and oligopolists. In contestable markets, abnormally high profits are not achieved and inefficiencies are likewise not possible in the long run. Perfect contestability produces an outcome similar to the optimality achieved under perfect competition. Hence, perfect contestability can be seen as a new ideal of welfare economics. In the extreme case of a perfectly contestable market, the performance of the incumbent firms is the same as the performance of firms operating in a perfectly competitive market.

A perfectly contestable market is characterised by free entry and the absence of exit costs (free exit). Free entry does not imply that entry costs absolutely nothing, or that it is easy, but rather that the entrant has no relative cost disadvantages compared with participants who are already active in the market. Potential entrants find it appropriate to judge the profitability of market entry on the basis of the entry costs of the firms which are already present in the market. Free exit implies that a firm can leave the market without hindrance and, in so doing, also recoup any entry costs incurred. Contestable market theory makes an important distinction between fixed costs and sunk costs: fixed costs do not vary with output but are recoverable if the firm leaves the market; sunk costs are costs that cannot be recouped if the firm leaves the market. Free exit implies that sunk costs equal zero.

Firms which operate in a perfectly contestable market are exposed to hit-and-run competition (Baumol 1982). If the market price increases beyond marginal cost, a potential entrant can effectively enter, make significant profits by setting his price somewhat below the market price, and leave the market again before the market price changes. The threat of a hit-and-run strategy makes above-normal profits impossible, even in a monopolistic market.[30] The only equilibrium which can be maintained is that at which prices are equal to average costs. It must be stressed that vulnerability to hit-and-run competition implies that entrants can establish their operations and undercut incumbents before the latter respond to the entry with price cuts.

At the policy level the theory of contestable markets leads to conclusions minimising the need for competition law. First, the degree of concentration yields no decisive conclusion as to the degree of efficiency. Unlike the theory of perfect competition, which is applicable only to markets with a large number of sellers, the doctrine of contestable markets equally applies to oligopolistic markets. A market may even be contestable with a single seller and can operate just as competitively as a market with perfect competition. Monopolies and oligopolies are not objectionable *per se* from a welfare economics point of view. A high degree of concentration can even be a healthy sign. Second, in contestable markets the existing monopolies and oligopolies can prevent market entry only by asking competitive prices. Any prices which exceed that level will attract hit-and-run entrants.

Many authors are sceptical of the claims of the contestability theory and its resulting policy recommendations (Utton 2003, 132–135; Martin 1994, 223–224). In their view, the theory is not robust. Small departures from its assumptions cause major alterations to the predictions. As long as the entrants are able to realise their investments without suffering a loss before the producers already present in the market can react, the market can be regarded as contestable and intervention by the antitrust authorities will be superfluous. In a more realistic scenario, however, where the incumbent can respond before the entrant is sufficiently established to start production and supply the market, some sunk costs would deter all entry (Utton 2003, 129). If small departures from perfect contestability produce dramatically different results, it may not make sense to analyse markets according to the degree to which they are contestable (or 'workably' contestable).

2.8.2 Policy conclusions

Compared with other economic approaches, which require long periods before they get an impact on policy decisions, contestability theory gained almost immediately influence on US antitrust policy. The argument that the

---

[30] If two or more firms operate in the market, price will be equal to marginal costs. If the market is a natural monopoly, price will only be sufficient to cover average costs; compare Utton (2003, 128).

airline industry was perfectly contestable was part of the justification for its deregulation in the US (Brodley 1981). In a deregulated market, so it was argued, airline companies can simply fly planes into airports to compete with existing companies already serving the routes from that airport. Potential entrants have cheap access to the market, since capital assets – i.e. planes – are perfectly mobile and can likewise be withdrawn from the market at practically no cost. Therefore, natural monopoly[31] routes were considered to be contestable. Mergers between large carriers (rising market share from around 50% to practically 75%) were not considered anti-competitive because airline markets were considered readily contestable. The airline example illustrates the danger of slipping from theory to a real-world scenario. Entry conditions in the airline market are indeed far from easy. The airport is a major sunk facility and guaranteeing equal access to competing airlines has proved to be difficult. Environmental concerns make it troublesome to increase the availability of runways; likewise, political considerations lead to the protection of national airlines and cause discrimination in the allocation of slots. Given the non-robust nature of the theory, in practice there is no reason to expect outcomes which resemble the theoretical results (Bailey 1981).

In spite of the above criticisms, the contestability theory has some merits. First, the Contestability School assumes that firms adjust their strategy to what market structures could become, rather than determining a strategy on the basis of what market structures actually are. In this view, firms follow a sort of pre-emptive or entry-deterring strategy. Hence, the issue to be tackled by competition law is not concentration, as is the case in the structuralist view, but lack of contestability. In perfectly contestable markets, competition problems are excluded. Such problems are caused precisely by obstacles which hinder free entry to, and withdrawal from, the market and thus make the market incontestable. All business practices which erect such barriers must therefore be resisted with the aid of competition law. From this perspective, both the existence of vertical restrictions in concentrated markets and the creation of excess capacity can justifiably be subjected to antitrust surveillance. Also, contestable market theory illustrates the fundamental importance of sunk costs in the analysis of barriers to entry. Incumbent firms may possess strategic (first-mover) advantages in the presence of sunk costs: advertising expenditures, which are not recoverable in case of exit, provide an example.

Second, the theory of contestable markets emphasises that not only firms but also, and above all, governments can adopt measures that are detrimental

---

[31] A natural monopoly is an industry in which economies of scale are so large (average cost declines as output increases) that the efficient level of production for one firm satisfies the entire market demand.

to market contestability. Government action restricting freedom of entry to (and withdrawal from) the market goes against a competition policy which attaches great significance to contestability. It follows from the theory of contestable markets that states ought not to enact any regulations hindering competitive entry to the market, but should, instead, create precisely those conditions promoting contestability. Unfortunately, the reality is often different. It is remarkable that the attainment of efficient results in relatively contestable markets is, on numerous occasions, hindered by regulatory activity which protects the existing firms. On the basis of the theory of contestable markets there must be serious doubt as to the desirability of state interventions such as licensing laws which make market entry difficult for newcomers. Rules regarding the establishment of firms, which cannot be justified as appropriate measures to cure informational asymmetries,[32] regularly turn out to have as their principal economic consequence the provision of interest groups with economic rents, while, in so doing, transforming relatively contestable markets into protected monopolies.[33]

Third, the theory of contestable markets likewise focuses policy makers' attention on the necessity of competition *for* a given market and stresses the limitations of a policy which concentrates exclusively on competition within that market. Even if a market has room for only one firm (a natural monopoly), competition can play an important role in deciding which firm is entitled to enter the market, how long that firm may remain in the market and what prices it will ask. These insights also have proved to be useful for assessing the possibilities of liberalising traditional network industries, such as gas and electricity.[34] For example, avoiding the high costs of duplication arising as a result of the establishment of new networks, competition may be served equally well by granting newcomers access to existing networks (Dunne 2015; Newbery 1999).

---

[32] On information remedies in cases of market failure, see Ogus (1994).

[33] In spite of deregulation efforts, examples remain numerous. It suffices to mention restrictions regarding travelling salespersons and the regulations concerning the exploitation of taxi services. These rules cause inefficiencies instead of reducing them. Several competition laws have created possibilities of repealing provisions which hinder market contestability. According to Article 21 of the Italian Competition Act, the Italian Competition Authority (Autorità Garante della Concorrenza e del Mercato) can judge what steps are necessary in order to eliminate distortions of competition caused by laws, regulations and general administrative decisions and can make appropriate recommendations for reform. In Belgium there are no such express provisions, but similar problems can nevertheless be indicated in a report by the Competition Council (Raad voor de Mededinging).

[34] See for a discussion of the regulation of utilities the articles in Van den Bergh and Pacces (eds.) (2012).

2.9   The transaction cost approach

2.9.1   Minimising transaction costs

In his classical contribution *The Nature of the Firm,* Nobel Prize winner Ronald Coase (1937) laid one of the foundations for the new institutional economics[35] by offering an explanation for the choice between the market and the firm as alternative decision-making mechanisms for completing transactions. Although there are no traditional cost differences in the form of production costs and transportation costs between these two institutions, there can still be cost differences which may be described as transaction costs. Transaction costs are search and information costs, negotiation costs, and the costs of implementing and enforcing the resulting agreements.

Transaction costs have become the central concept for explaining the borderline between the market and the firm. Economic actors regularly engage in transactions through which they change or transfer property rights. Each transaction must be coordinated; this takes place within a so-called governance structure that fixes the rights and duties of the parties involved. Governance structures can take the form of contracts (market solution) or a particular form of organisation (the firm or a strategic alliance). In the transaction cost literature both governance structures are also called institutional arrangements or briefly institutions. The extent of the transaction costs in the alternative institutions (the market or the firm) may explain the choice in favour of market contracts as an instrument of coordination, or in favour of the firm with its distinctive, hierarchical, organisational structure. In managerial terms, this choice may be referred to as the make-or-buy decision. When transactions between contract parties are too expensive and an organisation could coordinate them at a lower cost than if they were market transactions, then firms emerge as organisational structures. As a result, such transactions will not be carried out in ordinary markets, but will be internalised within the firm. The reason is that making (a product) is cheaper than buying (this product). According to the transaction cost approach, the reason for the establishment of firms lies precisely in the existence of transaction costs.

The transaction cost approach has meanwhile developed into an important pillar of the new institutional economics. In Williamson's work[36] emphasis is placed on the need to take into account considerations concerning transaction costs in the analysis of competition problems. The transaction cost ap-

---

[35] On the new institutional economics, consult Ménard and Shirley (2005); Furubotn and Richter (1991).
[36] On transaction cost economics, see Williamson's review article (1989). See also Williamson (1975) and Williamson (1985). For an early application to antitrust, see Williamson (1979).

proach superimposes transaction cost considerations upon micro-economic price theory, thus being more of a complement to, instead of a substitute for, price theory. The starting point in Williamson's analysis is not the subject matter of the sale-purchase transaction of goods or services, but the transaction itself. The transaction is an exchange between two or more individuals whereby they change or transfer property rights, that is, rights to dispose of scarce resources, which may be limited not only by other individuals' ownership rights but also by rules of legal liability and the provisions of competition law.[37] Transactions differ perceptibly so far as costs are concerned and these differences in transaction costs influence the choice of the right organisational form or governance structure. Markets and firms are regarded as alternative instruments for implementing transactions (Williamson 1986, 199–202). The transaction costs across markets and within firms are affected by human and market factors. The transaction costs of writing contracts vary with the characteristics of the human decision makers (bounded rationality, danger of opportunism) and the objective properties of the market (degree of uncertainty, frequency of the transactions, grade of asset specificity).

Whether a set of transactions is carried out via the market (by entering into agreements) or through a single firm depends on the relative efficiency of these two institutions. A hierarchical form of organisation may be superior to a market-based solution. The relative efficiency of the two forms is determined, on the one hand, by the costs of entering into, and carrying out, agreements in a market (market factors or transactional factors) and, on the other hand, by the characteristics of the individuals who are affected by the transaction (human factors). Transactions differ from each other in a number of respects: the uncertainty to which the transactions are exposed, the frequency with which market participants repeat the transactions (once, occasionally or regularly) and the extent to which transactions must be supported by transaction-specific investments (asset specificity). By asset specificity Williamson means the extent to which suppliers and customers must make relation-specific investments in order to be able to carry out the transactions. The value of these investments exceeds the value of the best alternative use and thus creates a quasi-rent. Asset specificity refers either to physical or to human elements in the transaction. Examples include the location of plants close to the site of the principal customer (for example, manufacturing of spare parts close to the production site of the final product) or the building-up of human capital to exercise a specific occupation. Asset specificity follows from the fact that there is no second-hand market for the investments in question, as these investments are idiosyncratic to particular transactions (for

---

[37] 'Property rights' in economics carries a much broader meaning than the legal concept of property; compare Cooter and Ulen (2011, 55).

example, particular skills in an employer-employee contract). Transaction-specific investments bind the supplier and the customer closely together. If the supplier cannot readily exploit his specific investments elsewhere, and the purchaser, because of his specific investments, cannot readily place his order elsewhere, the supplier and the purchaser are bound to each other for a substantial period of time. In cases of 'small numbers exchange', where market participants are very much dependent upon each other, serious lock-in effects will emerge. Circumstances not contracted upon *ex ante* allow one party possessing *ex post* bargaining power to decide over the division of the quasi-rents, to the counterparty's disadvantage. This is the hold-up problem arising from contractual incompleteness. The more specific the asset, the greater the need for continuity, and the more likely it will be that internal governance replaces market governance.

Besides the transactional factors, Williamson emphasises a number of human factors which influence the level of transaction costs. Accordingly, bounded rationality and opportunism distinguish the individuals who implement a transaction. Bounded rationality refers to the limited capacity of the human mind to formulate and solve (highly) complex problems (Simon 1957, 198). Opportunistic conduct alludes to the lack of honesty in transactions; economic actors may deliberately provide wrong information, abuse existing information asymmetries or bluntly cheat the counterparty. The pursuit of self-interest in combination with a high degree of asset specificity can be disastrous for the success of the transaction.

The combination of a number of transactional and human factors can impede the conclusion of an exchange. In particular, the combination of uncertainty and bounded rationality and the linking of small numbers exchange in case of high asset specificity with opportunistic conduct increase transaction costs significantly. In the case of small numbers exchange the opportunistic tendency to pursue self-interest will generate serious risks for the trading partners. Within a firm the transactional factors and the human factors which hinder exchanges between firms manifest themselves in different ways. Because hierarchical forms of organisation reduce transaction costs, a firm can be a better governance structure than the market. As shown in Table 2.2, efficient governance structures depend on the frequency of the transactions and the degree of asset specificity. In-between markets and hierarchies, there are several intermediate or hybrid governance structures that aim at adequately reducing transaction costs (Ménard 2004).

The market is the appropriate structure for standardised transactions (on which uncertainty has no bearing) or for transactions which require no

Table 2.2 Governance structures

Frequency	Degree of asset specificity		
	Not specific	Moderately specific	Specific
Occasionally	Market	Coordination; arbitrage	Coordination; arbitrage
Regularly	Market	Bilateral coordination	Vertical integration

specific investments, irrespective of their frequency. By contrast, if non-standard transactions are frequent and characterised by asset specificity, a transaction-specific structure will be the most appropriate form. In this way, Williamson distinguishes between bilateral structures and hierarchy. Bilateral structures lend themselves to transactions which are repeated regularly and for which moderate specific investments are needed. Franchising is an example of such transactions. In cases of frequent transactions a high degree of asset specificity will necessitate a hierarchical form of organisation (vertical integration). Lastly, hybrid forms are appropriate if transactions require that moderate specific investments occur on an occasional basis (trilateral coordination).

2.9.2 Policy conclusions

The transaction cost approach affects older competition theory and competition law. Conclusions derived from models of perfect competition or monopoly, without taking account of transaction costs, are often premature and misleading (Williamson 1986, 202–237). Most importantly, Coase's point of view provides an explanation for changes in market structure. His insights are therefore of great importance for competition policy and law. Price theory analyses stating how allocative efficiency can be realised lose their validity when high transaction costs have to be incurred in order to achieve an efficient outcome. These transaction costs must be taken into account explicitly before any welfare judgement can be pronounced. The Harvard approach, which draws conclusions as to market conduct and market results from data on market structure, must be critically examined anew in the light of transaction cost economics. If the choice between the market and the firm is made as a function of savings in transaction costs, the structure of the market (that is, the degree of concentration) is influenced by differences in transaction costs. These differences thus determine market structure and likewise, indirectly, market conduct.

Also, competition law must create a legal framework within which the market participants are free to choose the most advantageous institutional arrangements. If legal rules make it more difficult to choose institutions saving transaction costs (for example, by prohibiting or restricting vertical integration), welfare losses are inevitable. First, concentrations can be appropriate instruments for realising the necessary transaction cost savings within firms. A welfare-maximising competition law must take account of these efficiency aspects. In the context of merger control, it is necessary to consider what transaction cost savings will be prevented by a merger prohibition and whether these (possibly substantial) costs are compensated by the anticipated advantages of more intensive competition. This necessitates a trade-off between transaction cost savings and the elimination of restraints on competition (potential price increases). Second, one of the most important contributions of the transaction cost approach is the fundamental change which it has brought about in the thinking regarding vertical restraints as a competition problem. Vertical restraints – not just territorial restrictions but also restrictions on the circle of purchasers and vertical price fixing – reduce transaction costs. And finally, the transaction cost approach also makes clear that the problem of oligopoly cannot be equated with the problem of monopoly. The transaction costs, which go hand in hand with negotiating and implementing an extensive cartel agreement, may jeopardise the achievement of a profit-maximising outcome. A firm in a dominant position does not need to take these problems into account in its internal organisation. An economically rational competition law must therefore address first of all the industries in which dominant firms operate before dealing with oligopolies. It is apparent from these examples that transaction cost analysis is an important complement to the Chicago view. The need to save on transaction costs may provide an additional explanation (and, possibly, justification) for mergers and practices that, in the old Harvard view, were seen as exclusionary conduct.

2.10   Modern industrial organisation

In spite of the differences between them, many of the theories discussed above can in many respects be considered to have become part of current mainstream industrial organisation theory. In contrast with a widespread belief in Europe, Chicago economics is not necessarily seen by US researchers as biased, ideological or inappropriate. Many of the Chicago views have been adopted in modern industrial organisation and the Chicago learning has established itself as central to the entire discipline. Obviously, the initial excesses of the Chicago approach have been mitigated, as is also the case with the immoderations of the Harvard approach. The debate over the size of the firm and its profitability and the related issues of concentration, market power and efficiency continues. Thanks to the Harvard–Chicago controversy a balanced view towards these issues has found its way into modern industrial organisation and a consensus has been reached on large number of issues, even though opinions may continue to differ on the assessment of the competitive impact of certain practices in real-life cases. The consensus among economists does not, however, extend to the Austrian approach, which remains outside the mainstream of industrial organisation.

This section on modern industrial organisation may strike the reader as relatively short, compared with the other sections of this chapter. The reason is that the modern economic views on antitrust problems are integrated in the next chapters of this book devoted to specific fields of competition law, including measurement of market power, horizontal collusion, vertical restraints, abuses of dominance (monopolisation) and mergers. The historical overview in this chapter has as its only purpose to illustrate the variety of economic approaches and to make clear the underlying value judgements of choosing a particular economic approach. Knowledge of the history of economic thought on competition allows a proper understanding of the current debate on the remaining hot issues of competition law. Since this debate is extensively presented in the next chapters, the goal of this section is limited to a broad characterisation of modern industrial organisation, in particular with respect to the seminal Harvard–Chicago debate. Also, the major tools of modern industrial organisation based on game theory are briefly introduced.

How do the modern views of industrial organisation theory relate to the structuralist Harvard view and the efficiency approach of the Chicago School? First, the linearity of the structuralist view has come into question. Structure, conduct and performance may indeed be interdependent. Whereas the Harvard paradigm analysed industries in terms of a causative chain from structure to conduct to performance, the new approach emphasises that conduct (strategic interaction) affects industry structure and performance. This modern insight has, for example, shed a new light on the Harvard–Chicago debate with respect to the existence of entry barriers. Whereas the dominant Chicago view accepted only entry barriers resulting from government regulation and qualified other barriers as the consequence of the higher efficiency of incumbent firms, the modern view accepts that entry barriers may be created not only by state regulation but also by strategic behaviour of market participants. Second, in the structuralist view, collusion increases profits so that firms can be expected to collude and collusion is deemed most likely in concentrated markets. The Chicago criticisms to this view stressed that collusion is difficult for firms to enforce and thus unlikely; consequently, collusion would occur mostly in industries with government regulation or protection. The modern view asserts that collusion is possible when competitors are repeat players and most likely in industries with repeated encounters and easy monitoring, as well as in regulated and protected industries. Third, as to the relationship between the number of competitors and market performance, it is no longer argued that having more competitors automatically implies more competition and it is accepted that competition can be effective with a smaller number of competitors. Fourth, as to the sources of market power, the modern view is that market power not only arises from horizontal restraints (as was argued by the Chicago School) but that it can be extended through vertical arrangements and strategic behaviour.[38] Fifth, the debate has stilled concerning the interpretation of the relationship between concentration and profits. Most economists have accepted Demsetz's compromise that market concentration can reflect both elements of efficiency and market power. It is now well understood that high profits for large firms may be explained not only by greater market power but also by greater efficiency of the large firms. Large, efficient firms may succeed in colluding and set prices at a level that yields high rates of return for them but not for less efficient, more moderately sized firms (Demsetz 1974, 178–179). Policy makers should take both efficiency savings (scale economies or other advantages of large firms) and market power (high profit rates) into account.

Modern industrial organisation stresses the need for an analysis of strategic interaction to understand industry structure and concentration. Game theory offers formal tools helping to understand these strategic interactions.[39] Strategic behaviour arises when two or more individuals interact and the behaviour of each individual turns on what this individual expects other individuals to do. Game theory offers important insights with respect to the need for competition rules, as it makes clear under what conditions (assumptions) strategic behaviour may cause welfare losses. Competition rules may subsequently limit the scope for strategic interaction by outlawing certain types of conduct revealed by game theory as detrimental. Game theory may thus help in shaping competition rules that give parties an incentive to act in ways that enhance economic welfare. Game theoretical insights are particularly relevant for assessing the degree of competition in oligopolistic markets. Since oligopolistic interdependencies are made more difficult by the mutual expectations of the oligopolists with respect to the reactions of their competitors, the game theoretical toolbox is very appropriate to analyse such

---

[38] This summary is based on the overview of the differences between the structural view, the Chicago School and new industrial organisation theory in Baron (2013).

[39] Games are a scientific metaphor for human interactions, where the outcomes depend on the interactive strategies of two or more human players. It is a mathematical theory of bargaining and an interdisciplinary approach to human behaviour. The first work is: von Neumann and Morgenstern (1944). For an overview of the state of the art, see: Fudenberg and Tirole (1991) and Rasmusen (2006).

markets. Aside from the analysis of strategic behaviour on oligopolistic markets, game theory has also been able to show – contrary to the thesis of the Chicago School – that firms enjoying market power may be able to erect private barriers to entry, by raising the costs of their rivals (Salop and Scheffman 1987). Game theoretical theories are becoming increasingly important in competition policy discussions and have also been given particular emphasis in assessing competition in high technology and network industries (Cass 2013; Carrier 2009; Rubinfeld 1998; Ordover and Willig 1999).

Compared with traditional price theory, game theory allows a more precise and differentiated analysis of different market forms. The equilibrium concept in game theory does not relate to the structure of a market (as in the theory of perfect competition) but to the conduct of firms. An equilibrium is a combination of strategies that the players of a game are likely to adopt. The aim in game theory is to identify each player's best strategy, that is to say the strategy that will maximise the player's pay-off, taking the other player's strategy into account. The most important instrument to analyse strategic interaction is the concept of a Nash equilibrium. Such an equilibrium is reached when no player has the possibility to profit from a unilateral change of conduct, given the conduct of the other player. In the context of competition, it is the combination of output levels chosen by firms so that no firm can increase its profit by changing its level of output given the outputs chosen by its rivals (Nash–Cournot equilibrium).[40] Game theory has been able to provide a theoretical explanation for the instability of cartels, which is caused by the incentive for individual cartel members to deviate from the collusive price. This insight may be derived from the so-called 'prisoner's dilemma', in which the strategy combination that is in the joint interests of both players is not played. Oligopolists would prefer an outcome in which both charge a high price to that in which they both charge a low price. However, the incentive to charge a low price, while the rival firm charges a high price, results in both firms charging a low price (for further discussion, see 4.2.2).

The tools of game theory are highly technical and many of them have been developed only in recent years. Given that this body of literature is largely close to pure theory and not yet meaningfully verified by empirical research, some commentators warn against drawing generalised conclusions to be implemented by competition law (Kobayashi 1997; Peltzman 1991). On the sceptical side, it is argued that the results of the game theoretical research are insufficiently complete to provide firm conclusions or to allow an assessment

---

[40] A Nash equilibrium is the central solution concept in game theory. It is named after John Nash, who, together with Harsanyi and Selten, was awarded the Nobel Prize in 1994 (Nash 1950, 36). If the decision variable is price, the equilibrium will be called a 'Nash–Bertrand equilibrium', after another French economist.

of what will happen in particular cases (Fisher 1989). On the optimistic side, it is argued that game theory allows the analysis of a much broader range of business competitive strategies than before (Shapiro 1989). Within the limited format of this book it is not possible to introduce lawyers to the complexities of game theory; those interested in such an introduction are invited to read other publications.[41] In Chapters 5 and 7 of this book the lessons of game theory with respect to two hot issues in competition law (horizontal collusion and predatory pricing, respectively) will be summarised. Within the confines of this book, this is to be seen as a modest attempt to illustrate how game theory may be helpful in solving complex problems of competition law.

Modern industrial organisation also offers advances on the empirical side. Several sector-specific models that simulate the effects of mergers and detect collusive behaviour have been developed. As it will be explained in Chapter 9, in the context of merger control simulation models may allow a prediction of likely price increases and, eventually, an estimate of likely cost efficiencies of a proposed merger. These predictions may allow a better assessment of the market power of the post-merger firm. At the same time, it may make the (usually questionable) market definition exercise redundant. In spite of its large potential, economic models do not yet exist for every sector of industry. Moreover, the studies often rely on historical data; they do not allow firm conclusions for today's markets. Efforts to find robust results that can be applied to every industry have been made in the pioneering contributions by Panzar and Rosse (1987) and Porter (1983), but above all by Sutton (1998). The latter approach appears to indicate an upper and lower bound to concentration: predictions are possible as to within which boundaries a sector will move without providing precise evidence on market outcomes. The new empirical literature shows how shaky the traditional Harvard approach was when it claimed it could make exact predictions.

2.11 Behavioural antitrust

2.11.1 Abandoning the rationality assumption

The entry of behavioural economics and the ongoing discussion on its policy implications represent the most recent stage in the evolution of economic approaches to competition law. Since the pioneering work of Marshall, Edgeworth and Hicks at the end of the nineteenth century, neoclassical

---

[41] An excellent introduction for lawyers is Baird, Gertner and Picker (1994). This book applies game theory to a large number of classic legal problems, ranging from contract law and tort law to labour law, environmental regulations and antitrust law. On a more advanced level, see Philips (1995).

economics assumes that firms and consumers are well-informed, rational agents who maximise profit or utility within given constraints. This paradigm is still the backbone of modern economics; in the field of competition policy it explains a rich variety of practices and types of market conduct that may harm economic welfare. However, critics argue that consumers and firms are not always well informed and may systematically behave in an irrational way. In such circumstances neoclassical principles would not be able to reliably explain market phenomena and lead to incorrect predictions and biased policy conclusions. The last section of this chapter introduces the basic tenets of the behavioural antitrust literature, which abandons the rationality assumption.

Nobel Prize winner Herbert Simon wrote the first major contribution to behavioural economics by developing the notion of 'bounded rationality' (Simon 1957). Rationality is not necessarily perfect; it may be limited in the sense that individuals attempt to overcome the impossibility of collecting and digesting all available information through the extensive use of heuristics (rules of thumb) and other short-cuts. Next to bounded rationality, further deviations from rationality are caused by bounded willpower and bounded self-interest. Bounded willpower refers to actions whereby an individual systematically behaves against his or her preferences due to an over-valuation or under-valuation of present or future welfare benefits and costs. Bounded self-interest refers to the fact that people also care about the well-being of others. The psychologists Daniel Kahneman (another Nobel Prize laureate) and Amos Tversky further elaborated behavioural economics by developing Simon's ideas. Their 'prospect theory' is largely based upon experiments conceived to identify deviations from rational behaviour. Kahneman and Tversky classified the heuristics and associated biases into three categories: anchoring, availability and representativeness. Anchoring occurs when people make estimates by starting from an initial value ('anchor') and then make insufficient adjustments before reaching a final answer. The availability heuristic is often used to assess the frequency or the probability of events. Events that are easier to recall appear more common; people can also better imagine dramatic events and, therefore, such events appear more likely. Representativeness is used to assess the likelihood that an event belongs to a certain class. Relying on representativeness, decision makers may confuse random events with causal patterns and give too much weight to anecdotal evidence (Kahneman and Tversky 1982, 38–47). The behavioural economics literature has rapidly developed in the past 20 years (for an early overview, see Camerer 1995). To support their arguments, behavioural economists have conducted several laboratory and field experiments, which suggest that individual choices systematically deviate from those predicted by neoclassical economics.

If behavioural economics provides a better explanation of human behaviour, the normative question whether more regulatory intervention in markets is needed still remains unanswered. Any type of regulation restricts choices and causes costs that may not be counterbalanced by corresponding benefits. Two main proponents of Behavioural Law and Economics, Richard Thaler and Cass Sunstein, attempt preserving freedom of choice by proposing 'soft paternalism' (or 'libertarian paternalism'). Consequently, legal rules are presented as instruments that steer consumers' behaviours to better outcomes by means of 'nudges'.[42] Individuals may be 'nudged' toward taking a decision that is in their best interest, but they should remain free to opt out of the default rule set by the regulator. This proposal invites several critical comments. First, it is likely that most individuals will stick to the default rule (opt-out rates tend to be very low) and, as a result, 'soft' paternalism risks having effects similar to hard-core paternalism. Second, nudges are not costless and should thus be subject to a cost-benefit analysis; without such assessment, there remains a risk of adverse effects. Third, a more general objection is that regulation is needed only if irrationalities cannot be cured by learning processes and market-oriented remedies. Finally, it remains unclear why regulators and judges would not themselves be subject to exactly the same behavioural biases that they attempt to cure.

2.11.2 The relevance of behavioural economics for competition law

Behavioural economics aims at incorporating irrationality into the antitrust analysis and, in this way, it attempts at more accurately reflecting decisions by economic agents. Opinions on the relevance of behavioural economics for competition law differ. A first group of antitrust commentators sees it as a potentially severe criticism of the predominant Chicago School approach to antitrust and the Post-Chicago game theoretic models. In their view, behavioural antitrust may open the door for a modified application of traditional antitrust concepts, if not their outright rejection (Reeves and Stucke 2011; Bennett *et al.* 2010). Other commentators remain sceptical of the behavioural approach to antitrust; they deny any clear policy implications following from a behavioural approach and certainly reject a more interventionist competition policy (Van den Bergh 2013; Wright and Stone 2012). This section summarises this general discussion; the relevance of the behavioural approach to the analysis of particular antitrust problems (such as

---

[42] Nudges steer people's choices in directions that will improve their welfare. Thaler and Sunstein welcome governance by nudges if it is in the interests of boundedly rational consumers and does not prevent rational consumers from taking different decisions. This approach is called asymmetric paternalism (since it does not affect rational consumers) or libertarian paternalism (since freedom of choice is kept intact). See Thaler and Sunstein (1998).

vertical restraints, predatory pricing and mergers) will be addressed in later chapters. The behavioural biases that seem most relevant for antitrust law are presented in Box 2.2.

Box 2.2: Behavioural biases and their relevance for competition law

The main message of behavioural economics as regards competition law is that market participants (manufacturers, distributors and consumers) possess limited cognitive resources. To function in a complex environment, they use mental and emotional heuristics and rely on situational cues when they make judgements under uncertainty. These heuristics and cue-dependent choices systematically and predictably deviate from strictly rational decisions. There are a large number of behavioural biases; some of the ones that seem most relevant for competition law are listed below. Following Bennett *et al.* (2010) the behavioural biases are classified in two groups: errors in preference formation and errors in decision making.

Errors in preference formation

Endowment effect

Once individuals become owner of a good (or service), they require greater compensation to divest themselves of the good than what they would be willing to spend to acquire a similar good. This bias can be linked to the well-known gap between the Willingness to Pay and the Willingness to Accept. An individual will pay a fixed amount of money to acquire an object, but will require a greater amount of money to part with the same object. The relevance of the endowment effect for competition law may be illustrated by the difficulties to design a leniency programme (for a comparison of US antitrust law and EU competition law, see section 8.2.2). Cartels will be more stable if all participants are biased by the endowment effect. Differences in the conditions for granting immunity may have an impact on the extent of the endowment effect. If de-biasing cannot be achieved, it may be necessary to increase the level of sanctions or change the conditions for immunity to counteract the endowment effect.

Status quo bias

Individuals assess outcomes vis-à-vis their current position and thus are tempted to prefer the *status quo*. For example, loss-averse manufacturers who make use of resale price maintenance may engage in costly preventive efforts to preserve the *status quo* and prevent the painful potential loss of price competition. Buyers may remain passive and stick with the *status quo* even though changing their purchasing behaviour would bring additional benefits. This behavioural bias may be relevant for assessing the anticompetitive effects of tying and bundling (see section 7.3).

Framing bias

When individuals are confronted with an identical set of options surrounded by different environments they will make different choices. Consumers are influenced by the way in which price is framed. They have greater difficulties in calculating the full price in cases of add-on pricing, when the price of additional services must be added to a base price (for example, prices of airline tickets that start from a base price to which costs of luggage, better seating, insurance and other expenses must be added). The framing bias may be strategically exploited by firms wishing to increase sales at higher prices.

Hyperbolic discounting

This bias refers to an inconsistent set of time preferences in which an individual places exceptionally high weight on present benefits but would reverse that preference in retrospect. By contrast, a rational individual would use a consistent discount rate for avoiding that current benefits are valued disproportionally higher than future costs. Hyperbolic discounting may distort decisions of managers considering a merger, whereby the expectation of short-run profits interferes with a less positive long-term assessment of the post-merger efficiencies.

Loss aversion bias

Individuals find the pain associated with the negative prospect of a potential loss far stronger than the pleasure of the prospect of a comparable gain. Individuals are less likely to pursue a course of action with defined costs and undefined benefits, even when the risk is cost-justified. Loss aversion may explain why manufacturers make use of minimum vertical price fixing, also when there are no associated efficiency benefits. The perceived risk of income losses due to price reductions may be felt more strongly than the potential benefits of increased purchases thanks to better presale services.

Errors in decision making

Anchoring

In reaching a decision individuals make insufficient adjustments from a starting anchor point. For example, consumers reason by starting from an anchor point and then make insufficient corrections. Profiting from this irrational behaviour, sellers may boost demand by comparing an artificially high recommended price and an actual low retail price.

Overconfidence bias

Over-optimism makes individuals believe that good things are more likely to happen than bad things. Consumers may overestimate how much they will use of a good or underestimate how much it will cost them. Individuals may be overconfident in their ability to perform difficult tasks (such as managing a company) and systematically underestimate the difficulties of seemingly easy tasks. The overconfidence bias may explain excessive merger activity. Managers may make too optimistic assessments of potential synergies between merging firms and underestimate disturbances that may result from the merger.

Availability heuristic

The probability of an event is assessed by searching for relevant examples in the recent past. A consumer's utility is thus affected by using past actions as a reference point (relative utility). In the field of competition law, the likelihood that cartels are detected and punished may be affected by increased enforcement activity of antitrust authorities and the imposition of high fines in a number of high-profile cases. This availability heuristic may counteract the overconfidence bias in markets where potential cartelists underestimate the cost of engaging in price conspiracies. If it is unclear which of both biases (overconfidence or availability) is most important, behavioural theory will not be able to reliably predict market outcomes.

Hindsight bias

People judge the *ex ante* probability of an event on the basis of their information about the actual outcome. There is a tendency to increase the likelihood of an event's occurrence after learning that it actually did occur. Judges may also be vulnerable to this bias: they may fail to recognise that anticompetitive behaviour may have been rational at its conception even though it failed when it was implemented.

Confirmation bias

Decision frames influence choices by making individuals prefer the alternative that is more directly compatible with a problem. For example, manufacturers who wish that their dealers will provide adequate pre-sales services will resort more easily to resale price maintenance than to other devices (such as territorial exclusivity, recommended prices and refusals to deal). The reason is that resale price maintenance tackles the problem of price cutting directly, while the other arrangements only indirectly serve that purpose. Also, antitrust enforcers may be subject to a confirmation bias if they try to find evidence that confirms their prior beliefs about competition law infringements.

The antitrust literature critically discusses both the positive and normative component of the behavioural approach. On the positive side, the question arises whether conduct of companies operating in a market can be better explained by assuming that decision makers systematically behave in an irrational way. Behavioural biases are usually documented at the level of individual people. In the antitrust context, decisions are taken by firms and it largely remains unclear how individual biases translate at the collective level. In particular, it must be investigated at which level of decision making within firms behavioural biases occur and persist. Generally, firms may have better possibilities to overcome cognitive biases and may thus act in a more rational way than consumers. Hierarchical structures within firms may supersede forms of irrationality.[43] Firms have greater incentives to rationally profit maximise under competitive pressures. Market participants typically are repeat players who learn from mistakes and consequently adapt their behaviour. Firms may also hire experts to profit from specialised knowledge. Nevertheless, both the management literature and behavioural economics emphasise the cognitive limitations of managers and the effect of organisational structures on firm behaviour (Bhattacharya and Van den Bergh 2014). Also, decision makers within firms may resort to shortcuts and entrepreneurs may be overconfident and take irrational risks. The task of behavioural economics is to identify in which markets and under which circumstances particular types of behavioural biases occur. It should also be investigated which competitors are vulnerable to those biases: incumbents, entrants, or both. A further question is why the biases cannot be overcome

---

[43] The firm as a means to reduce transaction costs was discussed above (see 2.9.1). Linking the theory of the firm and the behavioural approach may prove very fruitful in improving our understanding of biases at the firm's level. From this perspective, the most important research question ahead is to what extent decisions within firms may overcome biased views of individuals concerning market behaviour.

by competitive pressures and the learning processes resulting thereof. If irrational firms are driven out of the market by their rational competitors, antitrust intervention is redundant.

Up until today, large parts of US antitrust law are firmly grounded in the rationality assumption.[44] This is certainly true for the Chicago School's theories favouring a Rule of Reason approach to resale price maintenance and the immunisation of economically irrational conduct in cases of alleged predatory pricing. Also, the Post-Chicago game theoretic models do not throw away the rationality assumption but merely clarify the conditions underlying the efficient market outcomes postulated by the Chicago disciples. Does behavioural antitrust advance compelling arguments to change this state of things? If it does, would a change of direction, eventually towards a more interventionist policy, be desirable? Those who are tempted to answer these questions positively should realise the difficulties underlying a normative use of behavioural economics in competition law. Such a use requires that the theoretical foundations of behavioural antitrust allow identifying the relevant cognitive biases, such as overconfidence or loss aversion, that may cause consumer harm. Ideally, these biases must be documented empirically and behaviouralists should propose a rule that allows decision makers to overcome the biased decisions of firms without succumbing themselves to cognitive biases, such as hindsight bias or confirmation bias. Up until today there is no general behavioural theory that can replace the Chicago and post-Chicago theorems. A particular problem is that not all firms may be subject to the same cognitive biases, for example in predation cases only the incumbent but not the entrant may act irrationally. Also, if firms' decisions are affected by more than one bias, it is not clear how the combination of different biases in the decision process works out.

2.12 Conclusions

This chapter has revealed different schools of thought in the field of competition policy. Even though most current industrial organisation research is grounded in the same formal economic theory, differences of opinion among economists may exist when it comes to policy issues. A simple chronological overview has been extremely helpful in discovering both common grounds and lines along which economists may disagree. In classical economics, competition was defined as a price-determining force (Adam Smith's 'invisible

---

[44] European competition law has not been strongly affected by Chicago economics and still reflects ordoliberal views. It has been argued that this difference may make it easier to accommodate behavioural insights (see Bhattacharya 2016).

hand'), which guides business decisions towards economic welfare, and not as a market structure. In neoclassical price theory, the formal models of perfect competition and monopoly were developed. These models focus on the properties of the market equilibrium and describe competition as a market structure. They show that perfect competition is Pareto-efficient, whereas monopoly causes a welfare loss. These models, in spite of their elegance, focus exclusively on the effects of competition and lose sight of the dynamic processes leading to these results. Most real markets cannot be characterised by either perfect competition or monopoly. This insight has led to the development of more sophisticated economic approaches. This evolution was not without cost, since consensus among economists disappeared.

Looking at the evolution of economic thinking on competition policy in the US during the past century, it becomes clear that the discussion mainly centred around two different approaches: the structural view of the Harvard School and the efficiency theory of the Chicago School. The structural approach argues that market performance is dependent on the conduct of firms, which in turn is dependent on the market structure of the industry under investigation. This vision of things has become known as the Structure-Conduct-Performance paradigm. The Harvard writers argued that high concentration in markets enables the exercise of market power (collusion) and the achievement of high profits to the detriment of consumers. This view led to a very interventionist antitrust policy, including *per se* rules on anticompetitive behaviour (such as resale price maintenance) and divestitures in highly concentrated markets. From the 1940s onwards, perfect competition as a blueprint for competition policy was replaced by the concept of 'workable competition'. The latter notion accepts that different market imperfections may neutralise each other and that restrictions of (certain forms of) competition may be necessary to further (other forms of) competition. Consequently, there can be different ideas about the ideal market structure (and ultimate performance) for different sectors of the industry and large discretionary powers are given to antitrust authorities.

The views of the Harvard School were severely criticised by scholars belonging to the Chicago School. In the writings of the latter School, the empirical studies showing a mono-causal and mono-dimensional relation between market concentration and profits were challenged by a different approach comparing profits of large and small firms in specific concentrated industries. If concentration is the consequence of greater efficiency, only the profits of large firms will be high. The SCP paradigm was rejected by the Chicagoans and the loose concept of 'workable competition' had to give way to the view that productive and allocative efficiency are the only acceptable goals for competition policy. To explain business practices in real-life markets, use was again made of price theory. The vision of things of the Chicagoans led to dramatically different policy conclusions. Vertical restraints of competition (in particular resale price maintenance) were rationalised as mechanisms to cure free-riding and considered legal. High profits were not seen as the consequence of collusion but as the result of higher efficiency (economies of scale and scope). Persistent market concentration was seen as the result of minimum efficient firm size and a merger policy not taking account of efficiency savings was rejected. In the US, the Chicago revolution led to a number of changes in the antitrust policy during the 1970s and 1980s, which decisively softened the previously more interventionist antitrust laws.

Today, in the US, Chicago economics has established itself as central to the entire discipline and the term Chicago School does not necessarily have a negative connotation. The Harvard paradigm (SCP) and the Chicago paradigm (price theory) are not incompatible as organising principles and may therefore be used as complementary rather than as mutually exclusive. Conversely, in European policy discussions, the term 'Chicago' has still a negative connotation and shooting at Chicago remains a popular sport. In this way, the baby is often thrown away with the bathwater and useful insights may get lost. Up until the end of the twentieth century, much of EU competition policy remained affected by the structural view. However, to fully understand the underlying principles of EU competition law and the precise meaning of the cartel prohibition and the ban on abuses of a dominant firm, it is important to realise that the wording of Articles 101–102 TFEU was influenced by ordoliberal ideas. The latter approach favoured a strong competition policy to protect individual economic freedom. Moreover, EU competition rules have been used as instruments to achieve market integration, and this also explains a number of persisting differences with US antitrust law.

As to the schools of thought, it must be added that dynamic approaches to competition policy continue to challenge the policy prescriptions of mainstream economic theories. The Austrian School questions the feasibility of a competition policy due to the lack of knowledge on the part of competition authorities. According to the Austrian scholars, information is hidden in the market in a vastly decentralised way and it is discovered only by innovative firms. Public authorities and judges lack the capability to collect this information and, consequently, their interventions in markets are often counterproductive. In the view of Hayek, only competitive processes themselves can reveal the necessary information on costs, prices and market results. The German concept of freedom of competition rejects a structuralist approach and favours rules of conduct that protect competition in both horizontal and vertical relations.

In modern industrial organisation theory, the immoderations of both the structuralist view (Harvard School) and the Chicago School have been mitigated. Current EU competition law and US antitrust law profit from this modern learning. Modern industrial organisation teaches that concentration can have different causes: market power, lower costs or strategic opportunities. Three important extensions of the Chicago approach have gained importance in the more recent literature: the theory of contestable markets, the transaction cost approach and insights from game theory. Contestable markets theory has provided the important insight that potential competition may be an effective deterrent to anti-competitive behaviour if there is free market entry and free market exit. The structuralist view must also be reassessed on the basis of transaction cost theory. Vertical mergers (and vertical restraints in long-term contracts) may achieve important transaction cost savings that should be traded off against potential restrictions of competition. Finally, with respect to the discussion on the possibility of collusion in oligopolistic markets and barriers to entry, insights from game theory have appeared to be very enlightening. Harvard scholars described markets as fragile and prone to failure, whereas the Chicago scholars argued that markets can largely correct themselves. Modern industrial organisation accepts that most markets are resilient but imperfections may be caused by strategic behaviour limiting efficiency. The Harvard School identified many barriers to entry (also erected by private firms), whereas the Chicago School qualified private entry barriers as the result of the higher efficiency of incumbent firms. The modern insights on sunk costs (contestable markets theory) and strategic behaviour (game theory) have revitalised the debate on entry barriers and made clear that they can be more persistent than Chicagoans thought.

The most recent development in the evolution of economic theories on competition is behavioural antitrust: the application of insights from behavioural economics to competition law. Behavioural economics is an area of economics that uses insights from psychology to more accurately describe decision making by individuals. Contrary to neoclassical price theory, consumers are not presented as rational, well-informed individuals who maximise their personal utility. Attention is drawn towards the difficulties that consumers may face in absorbing and processing information (anchoring effects, availability biases and representativeness biases). Also, the way in which information is presented (framing biases), the difficulties in anticipating the future (optimism bias) and loss aversion may have an impact on consumer behaviour and, consequently, the functioning of markets. Expanding behavioural economics into the realm of competition law meets criticisms from antitrust commentators. Indeed, there are several reasons to believe that firms are less vulnerable to behavioural biases: firms may profit from economies of scale in information gathering, they may hire information experts and may be disciplined by the presence of rational firms that drive bad decision makers out of the market. The behavioural literature on firm behaviour is still in its infancy and empirical evidence is limited. The future will show whether behavioural antitrust will turn out to be useful for the analysis of competitor behaviour and the design of legal rules addressing anti-competitive conduct.

2.13 Bibliography

Adams H (1918), *Description of Industry: An Introduction to Economics* (Holt and Company)

Amato G (1997), *Antitrust and the Bounds of Power* (Hart Publishing)

Armentano D (1996), *Antitrust and Monopoly: Anatomy of a Policy Failure* (Wiley, 2nd ed.)

Arrow K (1962), 'Economic Welfare and the Allocation of Resources for Invention', in R Nelson (ed.), *The Rate and Direction of Inventive Activity* 609 (Princeton University Press)

Bailey E (1981), 'Contestability and the Design of Regulatory and Antitrust Policy' 71 *American Economic Review. Papers and Proceedings* 178

Bain J (1968), *Industrial Organization* (Wiley, 2nd ed.)

Bain J (1956), *Barriers to New Competition. Their Character and Consequences in Manufacturing Industries* (Harvard University Press)

Bain J (1951), 'Relation of Profit Rate to Industry Concentration: American Manufacturing 1936–1940' 65 *Quarterly Journal of Economics* 293

Baird D, Gertner R and Picker R (1994), *Game Theory and the Law* (Harvard University Press)

Baron D (2013), *Business and Its Environment* (Pearson, 7th ed.)

Baumol W (1982), 'Contestable Markets: An Uprising in the Theory of Industry Structure' 72 *American Economic Review* 1

Baumol W, Panzar J and Willig R (1982), *Contestable Markets and the Theory of Industry Structure* (Harcourt Brace Jovanovich)

Behrens P (2015), 'The Ordoliberal Concept of "Abuse" of a Dominant Position and its Impact on Article 102 TFEU', Proceedings of the 10th ASCOLA Conference Tokyo 2015 <https://ssrn.com/abstract=2658045>

Behrens P (2014), 'The "Consumer Choice" Paradigm in German Ordoliberalism and Its Impact Upon EU Competition Law', Europa-Kolleg Hamburg, Discussion Paper no. 1/14 <https://ssrn.com/abstract=2568304>

Bennett M, Fingleton J, Fletcher A, Hurley L, Ruck D (2010), 'What Does Behavioral Economics Mean for Competition Policy?' 6 *Competition Policy International* 111

Bhattacharya S (2016), *Competition Law and the Bounded Rationality of Firms* (Erasmus University Rotterdam)

Bhattacharya S, Van den Bergh R (2014), 'The Contribution of Management Studies to Understanding Firm Behaviour and Competition Law' 37 *World Competition* 517

Böhm F (1928), 'Das Problem der privaten Macht' 3 *Die Justiz* 324

Böhm F (1933), *Wettbewerb und Monopolkampf. Eine Untersuchung zur Frage des wirtschaftlichen Kampfrechts und zur Frage der rechtlichen Strukturen der geltenden Wirtschaftsordnung* (Carl Heymanns Verlag)

Bork R (1978), *The Antitrust Paradox: A Policy at War with Itself* (Basic Books)

Bork R (1954), 'Vertical Integration and the Sherman Act: The Legal History of an Economic Misconception' 22 *University of Chicago Law Review* 157

Bowman W (1957), 'Tying Arrangements and the Leverage Problem' 67 *Yale Law Journal* 19

Brodley J (1981), 'Antitrust Policy under Deregulation: Airline Mergers and the Theory of Contestable Markets' 61 *Boston University Law Review* 823

Brozen Y (1971), 'The Persistence of "High Rates of Return" in High-Stable Concentration Industries' 14 *Journal of Law and Economics* 501

Brozen Y (1970), 'The Antitrust Taskforce Deconcentration Recommendation' 13 *Journal of Law and Economics* 279

Cabral L (2000), *Introduction to Industrial Organization* (MIT Press)

Camerer C (1995), 'Individual Decision Making', in J Kagel and A Roth (eds.), *The Handbook of Experimental Economics* 587 (Princeton University Press)

Carlton D, Perloff J (2005), *Modern Industrial Organization* (Pearson, 4th ed.)

Carrier M (2009), *Innovation for the 21st Century: Harnessing the Power of Intellectual Property and Antitrust Law* (Oxford University Press)

Cass R (2013), 'Antitrust for High-Tech and Low: Regulation, Innovation, and Risk' 9 *Journal of Law, Economics and Policy* 169

Chamberlin E (1933), *The Theory of Monopolistic Competition* (Cambridge University Press)

Clapham R (1981), 'Das wettbewerbspolitische Konzept der Wettbewerbsfreiheit', in H Cox, U Jens, and K Markert (eds.), *Handbuch des Wettbewerbsrechts*, 129 (Vahlen)

Clark J (1961), *Competition as a Dynamic Process* (Brookings Institution)

Clark J (1940), 'Toward a Concept of Workable Competition' 30 *American Economic Review* 241

Coase R (1937), 'The Nature of the Firm' 4 *Economica* 386

Collins N, Preston L (1969), 'Price-Cost Margins and Industry Structure' 51 *Review of Economics and Statistics* 271

Comanor W, Wilson T (1967), 'Advertising, Market Structure and Performance' 49 *Review of Economics and Statistics* 423

Cooter R, Ulen T (2011), *Law and Economics* (Pearson, 6th ed.)

Cowling K, Mueller D (1978), 'The Social Costs of Monopoly' 88 *Economic Journal* 727

Cucinotta A, Pardolesi R, Van den Bergh R (eds.) (2002), *Post-Chicago Developments in Antitrust Law* (Edward Elgar)

Demsetz H (1974), 'Two Systems of Belief about Monopoly', in H Goldschmid, H Mann and J Weston (eds.), *Industrial Concentration: The New Learning* 164 (Little, Brown & Company)

Demsetz H (1973a), 'Industry Structure, Market Rivalry and Public Policy' 16 *Journal of Law and Economics* 1

Demsetz H (1973b), *The Market Concentration Doctrine* (American Enterprise Institute)

Domowitz I, Hubbard G, Petersen B (1986), 'Business Cycles and the Relationship between Concentration and Price-Cost Margins' 17 *RAND Journal of Economics* 1

Dunne N (2015), *Competition Law and Economic Regulation: Making and Managing Markets* (Cambridge University Press)

Eucken W (1965), *Die Grundlagen der Nationalökonomie* (Springer, 8th ed.)

Eucken W (1949), 'Die Wettbewerbsordnung und ihre Verwirklichung', 2 *Ordo-Yearbook* 1

Faure M, Van den Bergh R (1995), 'Restrictions of Competition on Insurance Markets and the Applicability of EC Competition Law' 48 *Kyklos* 65

Fisher F (1989), 'Games Economists Play: A Noncooperative View' 20 *RAND Journal of Economics* 113

Fudenberg D, Tirole J (1991), *Game Theory* (MIT Press)

Furubotn E, Richter R (1991), 'The New Institutional Economics: An Assessment', in E Fu-
    rubotn and R Richter (eds.), *The New Institutional Economics. A Collection of Articles from the
    Journal of Institutional and Theoretical Economics* 1 (Mohr Siebeck)
Galbraith J (1952), *American Capitalism. The Concept of Countervailing Power* (Houghton Mifflin)
Gerber D (1998), *Law and Competition in Twentieth Century Europe* (Clarendon Press)
Gilbert R, Sunshine S (1995), 'Incorporating Dynamic Efficiency Concerns in Merger Analysis:
    The Use of Innovation Markets' 63 *Antitrust Law Journal* 567
Giocoli N (2009), 'Competition versus Property Rights: American Antitrust Law, the Freiburg
    School, and the Early Years of European Competition Policy' 5 *Journal of Competition Law and
    Economics* 747
Hall R, Lieberman M (2007), *Economics: Principles & Applications* (South-Western, 6th ed.)
Harberger A (1954), 'Monopoly and Resource Allocation' 44 *American Economic Review* 77
Hay D, Morris D (1991), *Industrial Economics and Organization: Theory and Evidence* (Oxford
    University Press, 2nd ed.)
Hoppmann E (1977), *Marktmacht und Wettbewerb* (Mohr Siebeck)
Hoppmann E (1968), 'Zum Problem einer wirtschaftspolitisch praktikablen Definition des Wett-
    bewerbs', in H Schneider (ed.), *Grundlagen der Wettbewerbspolitik* 27 (Schriften des Vereins für
    Socialpolitik, N. F. Bd. 48)
Hoppmann E (1966), 'Das Konzept der optimalen Wettbewerbsintensität. Rivalität und Freiheit
    des Wettbewerbs: Zum Problem eines wettbewerbspolitisch adäquaten Ansatzes der Wettbe-
    werbstheorie' 179 *Jahrbuch Für Nationalökonomie und Statistik* 286
Hovenkamp H (1989), 'The Sherman Act and the Classical Theory of Competition' 74 *Iowa Law
    Review* 1019
Hovenkamp H (1985), 'Antitrust Policy after Chicago' 84 *Michigan Law Review* 213
Hylton K (2003), *Antitrust Law: Economic Theory and Common Law Evolution* (Cambridge
    University Press)
Jenny F, Weber A (1983), 'Aggregate Welfare Losses due to Monopoly Power in the French
    Economy: Some Tentative Estimates' 32 *Journal of Industrial Economics* 113
Kahneman D, Tversky A (1982), 'Subjective Probability: A Judgment of Representativeness' in
    D Kahneman *et al.* (eds.), *Judgment under Uncertainty: Heuristics and Biases* 32 (Cambridge
    University Press)
Kantzenbach E (1966), *Die Funktionsfähigkeit des Wettbewerbs* (Vandenhoeck & Ruprecht)
Kaysen C, Turner D (1959), *Antitrust Policy, An Economic and Legal Analysis* (Harvard University
    Press)
Kirzner J (1978), *Wettbewerb und Unternehmertum* (Mohr Siebeck)
Kobayashi B (1997), 'Game Theory and Antitrust: A Post-Mortem' 5 George Mason Law Review
    411
Lutz F (1956), 'Bemerkungen zum Monopolproblem' 8 *Ordo* 32
Mackaay E (2000), 'History of Law and Economics', in B Bouckaert and G De Geest (eds.),
    Encyclopedia of Law and Economics I (Edward Elgar)
MacLaurin W (1953), 'The Sequence from Invention to Innovation' 67 *Quarterly Journal of
    Economics* 107
Mann H (1966), 'Seller Concentration, Barriers to Entry and Rates of Return in Thirty Indus-
    tries, 1950–1960' 48 *Review of Economics and Statistics* 296
Mansfield E (1983), 'Technological Change and Market Structure: An Empirical Study' 73
    American Economic Review 205
Martin S (1994), *Industrial Economics: Economic Analysis and Public Policy* (Prentice Hall)
Marvel H (1982), 'Exclusive Dealing' 25 *Journal of Law and Economics* 6

Mason E (1949), 'The Current State of the Monopoly Problem in the United States' 62 *Harvard Law Review* 1265

Mason E (1939), 'Price and Production Policies of Large Scale Enterprises' 29 *American Economic Review* 61

McGee J (1958), 'Predatory Price Cutting. The Standard Oil (N.J.) Case' 1 *Journal of Law and Economics* 137

McNulty P (1968), 'Economic Theory and the Meaning of Competition' 82 *Quarterly Journal of Economics* 639

McNulty P (1967), 'A Note on the History of Perfect Competition' 75 *Journal of Political Economy* 395

Ménard C (2004), 'The Economics of Hybrid Organizations', 160 *Journal of Theoretical and Institutional Economics* 345

Ménard C, Shirley M (2005), *Handbook of New Institutional Economics* (Springer)

Möschel W (1989), 'Competition Policy from an Ordo Point of View', in A Peacock and H Willgerodt (eds.), *German Neo-Liberals and the Social Market Economy* 142 (Palgrave Macmillan)

Motta M (2004), *Competition Policy. Theory and Practice* (Cambridge University Press)

Nash J (1950), 'Equilibrium Points in N-Person Games' 36 *Proceedings of the National Academy of Sciences of the United States of America* 48

Newbery D (1999), *Privatization, Restructuring, and Regulation of Network Utilities* (MIT Press)

Nickell S (1996), 'Competition and Corporate Performance' 104 *Journal of Political Economy* 724

Ogus A (1994), *Regulation: Legal Form and Economic Theory* (Clarendon Press)

Ordover J, Willig R (1999), 'Access and Bundling in High Technology Markets' in J Eisenach and T Lenard (eds.), *Competition, Innovation and the Microsoft Monopoly: Antitrust in the Digital Marketplace* 103 (Springer)

Panzar J, Rosse J (1987), 'Testing for Monopoly Equilibrium' 35 *Journal of Industrial Economics* 443

Peltzman S (1991), 'The Handbook of Industrial Organisation: A Review Article' 99 *Journal of Political Economy* 201

Peritz R (2001), *Competition Policy in America, 1888–1992: History, Rhetoric, Law* (Oxford University Press, 2nd ed.)

Philips L (1995), *Competition Policy: A Game-Theoretic Perspective* (Cambridge University Press)

Pindyck R, Rubinfeld D (2017), *Microeconomics* (Pearson, 9th ed.) (to be published)

Pindyck R, Rubinfeld D (1998), *Microeconomics* (Macmillan, 4th ed.)

Porter R (1983), 'A Study of Cartel Stability: The Joint Executive Committee 1880–1886' 14 *Bell Journal of Economics* 301

Posner R (1979), 'The Chicago School of Antitrust Analysis' 127 *University of Pennsylvania Law Review* 925

Posner R (1976), *Antitrust Law, an Economic Perspective* (University of Chicago Press)

Rapp R (1995), 'The Misapplication of the Innovation Market Approach to Merger Analysis' 64 *Antitrust Law Journal* 19

Rasmusen E (2006), *Games and Information. An Introduction to Game Theory* (Wiley, 4th ed.)

Reekie D (1979), *Industry, Prices and Market* (Wiley)

Reeves A, Stucke M (2011), 'Behavioral, Behavioral Antitrust' 86 *Indiana Law Journal* 1527

Reinganum J (1989), 'The Timing of Innovation: Research, Development and Diffusion', in R Schmalensee and R Willig (eds.), *The Handbook of Industrial Organization* I, 849 (North Holland)

Roberts G, Salop S (1995/1996), 'Dynamic Analysis of Efficiency Benefits' 19 *World Competition* 5

Robinson J (1933), *The Economics of Imperfect Competition* (Macmillan)

Rubinfeld D (1998), 'Antitrust Enforcement in Dynamic Network Industries' 43 *Antitrust Bulletin* 859

Salop S, Scheffman D (1987), 'Cost-Raising Strategies' 36 *Journal of Industrial Economics* 19

Scherer F (1992), 'Schumpeter and Plausible Capitalism' 30 *Journal of Economic Literature* 1416

Scherer F, Ross D (1990), *Industrial Market Structure and Economic Performance* (Houghton Mifflin Company, 3rd ed.)

Schmidtchen D (1988), 'Fehlurteile über das Konzept der Wettbewerbsfreiheit' 39 *ORDO Jahrbuch für die Ordnung von Wirtschaft und Gesellschaft* 111

Schumacher E (1993), *Small is Beautiful: A Study of Economics as if People Mattered* (Vintage, 2nd ed.)

Schumpeter J (1950), *Capitalism, Socialism and Democracy* (Harper & Brothers, 3rd ed.)

Shapiro C (1989), 'The Theory of Business Strategy' 20 *RAND Journal of Economics* 125

Simon H (1957), *Models of Man, Social and Rational: Mathematical Essays on Rational Human Behavior in a Social Setting* (Wiley)

Smith A (1776), *An Enquiry into the Nature and Causes of the Wealth of Nations* (Methuen & Co.)

Sosnick S (1958), 'A Critique of Concepts of Workable Competition' 72 *Quarterly Journal of Economics* 380

Stigler G (1968), *The Organisation of Industry* (Richard Irwin)

Stigler G (1964), 'A Theory of Oligopoly' 72 *Journal of Political Economy* 44

Stigler G (1957), 'Perfect Competition, Historically Contemplated' 65 *Journal of Political Economy* 2

Strickland A, Weiss L (1976), 'Advertising, Concentration, and Price-Cost Margins' 84 *Journal of Political Economy* 1109

Sullivan E (1991), *The Political Economy of the Sherman Act, The First One Hundred Years* (Oxford University Press)

Sutton J (1998), *Technology and Market Structure* (MIT Press, 2nd ed.)

Sutton J (1991), *Sunk Costs and Market Structure* (MIT Press)

Telser L (1960), 'Why Should Manufacturers Want Fair Trade?' 3 *Journal of Law and Economics* 86

Thaler R, Sunstein C (2008), *Nudge: Improving Decisions about Health, Wealth, and Happiness* (Yale University Press)

Tobin J (1969), 'A General Equilibrium Approach to Monetary Theory' 1 *Journal of Money, Credit and Banking* 15

Tor A, Rinner W (2011), 'Behavioral Antitrust: A New Approach to the Rule of Reason after *Leegin*' 11 *University of Illinois Law Review* 805

Tullock G (1967), 'The Welfare Costs of Tariffs, Monopolies and Theft' 5 *Western Economic Journal* 224

Turner D (1962), 'The Definition of Agreement Under the Sherman Act: Conscious Parallelism and Refusals to Deal', 75 *Harvard Law Review* 655

Utton M (2003), *Market Dominance and Antitrust Policy* (Edward Elgar, 2nd ed.)

Van den Bergh R (2013), 'Behavioural Antitrust; Not Ready for the Main Stage' 9 *Journal of Competition Law & Economics* 203

Van den Bergh R, Pacces A (eds.) (2012), *Regulation and Economics, Encyclopedia of Law and Economics IX* (Edward Elgar, 2nd ed.)

Von Hayek F (1968), *Wettbewerb als Entdeckungsverfahren* (Mohr Siebeck)

Von Hayek F (1967), 'Grundsätze einer liberalen Gesellschaftsordnung' 18 *ORDO* 11

Von Mises L (1996), *Human Action: A Treatise on Economics* (NY Foundation for Economic Education) von Neumann J, Morgenstern O (1944), *The Theory of Games and Economic Behaviour* (Princeton University Press)

Williamson E (1989), 'Transaction Cost Economics', in R Schmalensee and R Willig (eds.), *Handbook of Industrial Organisation I*, 135 (North Holland)

Williamson O (1986), *Economic Organisation, Firms, Markets and Policy Control* (New York University Press)

Williamson O (1985), *The Economic Institutions of Capitalism: Firms, Markets, Relational Contracting* (Free Press)

Williamson O (1979), 'Assessing Vertical Market Restrictions: Antitrust Ramifications of the Transaction Cost Approach', 127 *University of Pennsylvania Law Review* 953

Williamson O (1975), *Markets and Hierarchies: Analysis and Antitrust Implications: A Study in the Economics of Internal Organisation* (Free Press)

Worcester D (1973), 'New Estimates of the Welfare Loss to Monopoly in the United States 1956–1969' 40 *Southern Economic Journal* 234

Wright J, Stone J (2012), 'Misbehavioral Economics, The Case Against Behavioral Antitrust' 33 *Cardozo Law Review* 1517

3

The goals of competition law

Roger Van den Bergh

3.1   Introduction

There is no better opening for this chapter than the following quote from the seminal book *The Antitrust Paradox* by Robert Bork: 'Antitrust policy cannot be made rational until we are able to give a firm answer to one question: What is the point of the law – what are its goals? Everything else follows from the answer we give.' (Bork 1978, 50). This citation stresses the instrumental use of antitrust law: competition is not a goal in itself but a means to achieve other (economic) objectives. Today, there is no agreement on a single, unifying antitrust goal. A survey done by the International Competition Network (ICN), which comprises more than 100 member countries, revealed a wide variety of economic and political goals.[1] A lively debate on the goals of competition law has not only emerged in the antitrust enforcement practice; this discussion has been accompanied by a parallel debate on the goals of competition law in academia. Several thought-provoking articles on this subject have been published in the US from the incipiency of the Sherman Act onwards (see the collection of articles in Sullivan 1991), and in the EU from the 1960s until recently (see the articles published in Ehlermann and Laudati 1998; Zimmer 2012). Most antitrust commentators advance economic objectives as the goals competition policy should aim at. In their analysis, they mention different concepts of efficiency (productive efficiency, allocative efficiency and dynamic efficiency), total welfare and consumer welfare. Other antitrust scholars stress the protection of the competitive process and individual economic freedom, rather than (total or consumer) economic welfare as the main (economic) goal of antitrust. Finally, some commentators argue

---

[1] The 2007 ICN Report mentions: ensuring an effective competitive process, promoting consumer welfare, enhancing efficiency, ensuring economic freedom, ensuring a level playing field for small and mid-sized enterprises, promoting fairness and equality, promoting consumer choice, achieving market integration, facilitating privatisation and market liberalisation, and promoting competitiveness in international markets. See International Competition Network (2007), 'Report on the Objectives of Unilateral Conduct Laws, Assessment Of Dominance/Substantial Market Power, And State-Created Monopolies', Annex A http://www.internationalcompetitionnetwork.org/uploads/library/doc353.pdf.

that competition law should also aim at non-economic objectives and create scope for considering other goals of public interest.

The major reference systems for the comparative law and economics analysis in this book are US antitrust law and EU competition law. On top of the efficiency and consumer welfare objectives embraced by US antitrust law, EU competition rules are permeated by the goal of creating an internal (common) market. Besides bringing economic advantages resulting from increased trade, market integration is a European key objective that should enhance political unification. Such an approach, which may cause difficult trade-offs between market integration and efficiency, is absent in US antitrust law. Together with a greater emphasis on a unifying economic goal (total economic welfare or consumer welfare), this is the most distinct difference between US antitrust law and EU competition law. The history of both competition laws further shows a varying emphasis on industrial policy arguments (creating chances for national champions in worldwide markets), the wish to protect small and medium-sized firms (fairness, equal opportunities), as well as social, cultural and ethical considerations (Gerber 2008). Even though in today's enforcement practice the emphasis lies on the economic goals, the debate on the need to consider other goals of public interest has not stilled.

At the time of writing, competition laws have been adopted by more than 120 countries. Antitrust goals that prevail in one jurisdiction are not necessarily equally important in other jurisdictions (see the quotes in Box 3.1). The emphasis that the major antitrust systems (US and EU) put on economic objectives may not be shared by the policy makers in developing economies (BRICS countries). The competition laws of China, Russia and South Africa include many non-economic factors, which may give a new boost to a discussion of competition goals at the global level. Striking political objectives formulated in legislative texts include fairness considerations (China; see also South Africa: protection of small and medium-sized companies, 'great spread of ownership') and industrial policy objectives (China: 'healthy development of the socialist market economy'; South Africa: promoting competitiveness on worldwide markets). In the enforcement practice of these countries, the pluralist approach to competition goals is further exacerbated by undefined national security considerations (merger control in China and Russia; see Farmer 2013) and other goals of public interest. Companies that are active in world markets may deplore the lack of a unifying goal and the resulting legal uncertainty. The existence of different goals has initiated a debate on the desirability of harmonisation of competition laws. Whereas industry tends to favour more uniformity in order to create a 'level playing field' for businesses worldwide, a more cautious approach to harmonisation has been advocated in the academic literature (Van den Bergh 1996).

This chapter focuses on the micro-economic objectives of competition law (welfare maximisation) and does not discuss its potential macro-economic consequences. From the 1990s onwards, the adoption of competition laws by low-income countries has been motivated also by the wish to increase foreign direct investment and thus contribute to economic growth. So far, the literature on the relation between the enactment of competition laws and economic growth is less developed than the analysis of (particular) competition rules on total welfare or consumer welfare. Some authors warn against too much optimism concerning the effect of the enactment of a competition law on productivity growth. Ma argues that a defective institutional framework inhibits significant effects in poor, less developed, countries. Moreover, she finds that the positive contribution to economic growth in developed countries and middle-income developing countries depends on the efficiency of law enforcement (Ma 2011; see also Hylton and Deng 2007, who stress the importance of the age and scope of the competition laws). Other authors criticise the above studies (for the choice of subjective indicators of quality) and find a significant effect on growth by using also objective indicators. Gutman and Voigt find that overall investment gets a boost from the introduction of competition legislation (even though there is no statistically significant effect on total factor productivity or foreign direct investment) and conclude that competition laws significantly increase growth rates. In addition, corruption appears to decline after the introduction of competition laws in low-income countries (Gutmann and Voigt 2014; see also Petersen 2013).

Box 3.1: The goals of competition law

The quotes in this box show that the goals of competition law evolve over time. For example, the wish to protect small and medium-sized businesses has lost momentum in US antitrust law, which now almost exclusively focuses on welfare maximisation goals. Looking at competition law worldwide, there remains a broad spectrum of potential goals for competition policy. Some antitrust laws focus on a single economic goal (examples include Norway and the current practice of the US enforcement agencies), whereas competition laws in other jurisdictions pursue a broad variety of economic and non-economic objectives (examples include the EU, China, and South Africa).

US antitrust law

Senator Sherman defended his bill partly on the following ground:

> If we will not endure a king as a political power we should not endure a king over the production, transportation, and sale of any of the necessities of life. If we would not submit to an emperor we should not submit to an autocrat of trade, with power to prevent competition and fix the price of any commodity.
>
> Quoted by Martin 1994, 49

> Of course, some of the results of large integrated or chain operations are beneficial to consumers (...) But we cannot fail to recognize Congress' desire to promote competition through the protection of viable, small, locally owned business. Congress appreciated that occasional higher costs and prices might result from the maintenance of fragmented industries and markets. It resolved these competing considerations in favour of decentralization.
>
> *Brown Shoe Co. v. United States*, 370 US 294 (1962)

> United States' primary commitment in enforcement of its antitrust laws is to serve the goal of the welfare of consumers.
>
> Former FTC chairman R. Pitofsky, Speech held at New York, 15 October 1999

> The opportunity to charge monopoly profits, at least for a short period, is what attracts 'business acumen' in the first place: it induces risk taking that produces innovation and economic growth.
>
> US Supreme Court, *Verizon Communications Inc. v. Trinko, LLP*, 540 US 398 (2004)

EU competition law

> Effective competition preserves the freedom and right of initiative of the individual economic operators and it fosters the spirit of enterprise.
>
> European Commission, *Fifteenth Annual Report on Competition Policy*, 1986

> The objective of Article 81 is to protect competition on the market as a means of enhancing consumer welfare and of ensuring an efficient allocation of resources. Competition and market integration serve these ends since the creation and preservation of an open single market promotes an efficient allocation of resources throughout the Community for the benefit of the consumer.
>
> European Commission, Guidelines on the application of Article 81(3) of the Treaty, O.J. 27.4.2004, C 101, 98, at nr. 13

Our aim is simple: to protect competition in the market as a means of enhancing consumer welfare and ensuring an efficient allocation of resources. An effects-based approach, grounded in solid economics, ensures that citizens enjoy the benefits of a competitive, dynamic market economy.

Neelie Kroes, Competition Commissioner, Speech held in London, 15 September 2005

China

According to Article 1 of the Chinese competition law, the law is enacted:

for the purpose of preventing and restraining monopolistic conducts, protecting fair competition in the market, enhancing economic efficiency, safeguarding the interests of consumers and social public interest and promoting the healthy development of the socialist market economy.

Article 1 Anti-Monopoly Law of August 30, 2007 <http://www.china.org.cn/government/laws/2009-02/10/content_17254169.htm>

India

The Competition Act 2002 provides that:

keeping in view of the economic development of the country, the Act establishes a Commission to prevent practices having adverse effect on competition, to promote and sustain competition in markets, to protect the interests of consumers and to ensure freedom of trade carried on by other participants in markets, in India, and for matters connected therewith or incidental thereto.

South Africa

The South African Competition Act mentions a broad variety of economic and non-economic objectives: efficiency, competitive prices and choices for consumers, promotion of employment and social and economic welfare, expanding opportunities for South African firms to participate in world markets, equal opportunities for small and medium-sized enterprises and a great spread of ownership. See: § 2 Competition Act of 1998 <http://www.saflii.org/za/legis/num_act/ca1998149.pdf>.

Norway

At the opposite side of the above examples of a pluralist approach, the most dramatic single-goal approach can be found in the Norwegian Competition Act:

The purpose of the Act is to further competition and thereby contribute to the efficient utilization of society's resources. When applying this Act, special consideration shall be given to the interests of consumers.

Section 1 Competition Act 2005 <http://www.konkurransetilsynet.no/en/legislation/The-Competition-Act>

The structure of this chapter is as follows. After this introduction, section 3.2 discusses how the different concepts of economic efficiency relate to each other and why competition law cannot escape from difficult trade-offs if different efficiency goals are pursued simultaneously. Section 3.3 elaborates the consumer welfare standard; it suggests two ways of clarifying the goals of consumer protection. Section 3.4 contrasts the welfare economics approaches to competition law with the view rooted in the Ordoliberal School that competition law protects the competitive process as such and fosters an economic order (in the sense of system, not command) that guarantees economic freedom. Section 3.5 investigates how the current rules of US antitrust law relate to the efficiency concepts and the consumer welfare standard. A similar analysis of EU competition law is presented in section 3.6, which discusses at some length the typical policy conflicts of the pluralist tradition of EU competition policy. Section 3.7 introduces insights from the political economy of antitrust. The Public Choice literature helps in understanding the contents of antitrust laws and their enforcement that can be observed in real-life practice. These positive insights are surveyed in section 3.7. Section 3.8 concludes.

3.2   Conflicting concepts of efficiency and the ensuing welfare trade-offs

In Chapter 2, the economic models of perfect competition and monopoly were contrasted with each other (see section 2.2). Whereas allocative efficiency is reached in a perfectly competitive market, monopoly causes welfare losses: prices are persistently held above marginal cost and output is reduced. This chapter introduces a number of complications that limit the attractiveness of allocative efficiency as the universal yardstick for competition law. To start with, it is unclear whether it is either the allocation effect or the price effect of monopoly that should be seen as the major justification for competition law. Policy makers often tend to stress the low prices that competition brings to consumers. In this way, distributional concerns are emphasised; it is not the allocation effect (deadweight loss) but the price effect that becomes the main concern for competition law. However, economists do not offer an easy answer to the question of how the 'best' distribution of resources should look. In policy discussions, the economic welfare notion is often replaced by a consumer welfare notion, which incorporates distributional concerns. The consumer welfare criterion is further examined in the third section of this chapter. In this section, another complication of using efficiency as the yardstick for competition law is discussed. There are no less than three different concepts of efficiency that may be relevant for the design of competition rules: allocative efficiency, productive efficiency and dynamic efficiency (Brodley 1987). These concepts have different meanings. Hence, competition policy cannot simply aim at efficiency without acknowledging potential conflicts and necessary trade-offs between different forms of efficiency.

First, allocative efficiency may conflict with productive efficiency. Productive or technical efficiency implies that output is maximised by using the most effective combination of inputs. The goal of productive efficiency implies that firms which are more efficient should not be prevented from taking business away from less efficient ones. Obviously, the achievement of productive efficiency is not a Pareto improvement since the less efficient firms are made worse off. Merger control illustrates how productive and allocative efficiency may conflict. A merger may enable the merging firms to achieve important scale economies and thus improve productive efficiency. At the same time, the merger may enable previously independent firms to collude and raise price above competitive levels. The gains in terms of productive efficiency may thus be outbalanced by losses in terms of allocative efficiency. This situation gives rise to the well-known welfare trade-off in merger control that was formulated by Nobel laureate Oliver Williamson (see section 9.2.2 for further discussion).

Second, allocative efficiency may conflict with dynamic efficiency. It is important to note that allocative efficiency, as defined in price theory, is a static concept. The set of products, production technologies, production factors and preferences is assumed as given and constant. Static efficiency must be contrasted with dynamic efficiency, which is achieved through the invention, development and diffusion of new products and production processes that better satisfy consumer preferences and increase social welfare. Whereas productive efficiency and allocative efficiency are precisely defined in price theory, dynamic efficiency is a vague concept that loosely indicates the optimal rate of technological progress. Dynamic efficiency does not mean much more than that it is preferable that innovations are generated and spread throughout the market (Kerber 2012). As was the case with the achievement of productive efficiency gains, there will be losers also in the dynamic competitive struggle since less innovative firms will be confronted with a decreasing market share. Again, Pareto improvements are not possible.

When the different efficiency goals are not consistent with each other, Pareto efficiency cannot be reached. To enable policy decisions, welfare economics offers the alternative normative criterion of Kaldor–Hicks efficiency. A Kaldor–Hicks improvement allows changes in which there are both winners and losers, but requires that the gainers gain more than the losers lose. This condition being satisfied, the winners could compensate the losers and still have a surplus left for them. The relevant measure is potential compensation and not actual compensation, since the latter would again satisfy the Pareto criterion (Kaldor 1939; Hicks 1941). A Kaldor–Hicks improvement is also referred to as a potential Pareto improvement: compensation is possible but is not effectively required.

By using the Kaldor–Hicks criterion, the conflicts between, on the one hand, allocative efficiency and productive or dynamic efficiency, on the other, may be solved. Restrictions of competition that lead to allocative inefficiency may at the same time generate benefits in terms of productive efficiency. The best-known example is a merger that increases consumer prices but allows the post-merger firm to reduce production costs. Obviously, this does not constitute a Pareto improvement since there are both winners and losers. However, the resulting policy conflict can be solved by a welfare trade-off. The merger can be cleared if the cost savings are sufficiently large to outbalance the losses in terms of allocative efficiency, so that total welfare increases.

As is the case with productive efficiency, an improvement in terms of dynamic efficiency does not satisfy the Pareto criterion, since this will harm less innovative firms, which will lose customers to their technically superior competitors. Again, such improvements may nevertheless satisfy the Kaldor–Hicks criterion since benefits to both pioneering firms and consumers may outweigh losses to non-innovative firms. If competition law adopts both goals of static and dynamic efficiency, this will have important consequences for the assessments that competition authorities must undertake. For example, in the case of a merger, the focus should be not only on the short-term effects on consumer prices but also on the long-term effects on innovation. The post-merger firm may finance costly research and development (R&D) projects thanks to monopoly profits; cost inefficiencies may thus be outbalanced by dynamic efficiencies. In the EU context, a similar trade-off may arise in the assessment of parallel imports that may reduce price disparities among EU Member States. The pharmaceutical industry has been arguing strongly that the impossibility of charging higher prices in less regulated markets also reduces the possibility of financing the costly research needed to develop new drugs (for further discussion, see Box 3.2). If the analysis of dynamic efficiencies remains largely outside the competitive assessment, compared to the emphasis put on short-term static effects, policy failures cannot be excluded. There is an inherent risk that the decision practice of the competition authorities does not appropriately consider the long-term effects of business behaviour and mergers on innovation (for a criticism of the European Commission's 'more economic approach' from a dynamic perspective, see Kirchner 2007).

The major objection to the Kaldor–Hicks efficiency concept is that it neglects distributional effects. The total welfare model of antitrust rejects the view that competition authorities should require firms to pass on efficiency benefits to consumers, as this is unnecessary because total welfare is already increased by the very act of achieving efficiencies within the firm (Hovenkamp 1994, at para. 2.3c; for a summary of the critique, see Lande 1989, 639–639 and Fox 1987). The central value judgement underlying Kaldor–Hicks efficiency is that an exchange of money has a neutral impact on aggregate well-being, which may not be the case when the incomes of gainers and losers differ. The achievement of total welfare is not compatible with the Pareto criterion since it allows a balancing of positive and negative wealth effects between different individuals. Clearly, total welfare is also different from consumer welfare. In price-theoretical terms, the total welfare standard implies that in a particular market the sum of producer and consumer surplus is maximised (total surplus). It is not required that consumer surplus itself is larger, since eventual losses of consumers can be compensated for by larger increases of producer surplus. In terms of total welfare, it is irrelevant that producers rather than consumers capture the surplus produced by achieving efficiencies, as the monopoly overcharge paid by purchasers to stockholders is treated as a transfer from one member of society to another and so is ignored in the balance.

It may be added that applying the different efficiency criteria of welfare economics in real-life cases will give rise to serious problems of proof. When the benefits concern productive efficiency, it must be shown that cost savings are realised and that these efficiencies are sufficiently large to outweigh the losses caused by price increases. In the case of dynamic efficiency, it must be shown that new and improved products create sufficient value for consumers. Whereas in the former case, it could still be possible to measure the amount of the productive efficiencies, it seems very difficult to assign values to dynamic efficiencies. In both cases, also the calculation of the losses in terms of allocative inefficiency (size of the deadweight loss) may be problematic.

3.3 Consumer welfare

In policy statements of competition authorities, the objective of furthering consumer welfare is usually quoted alongside the goal to improve allocative efficiency. In the Guidelines on the application of Article 81(3) EC, the European Commission states that: 'The objective of Article 81 EC is to protect competition on the market as a means of enhancing consumer welfare and of ensuring an efficient allocation of resources' (Guidelines, at para 13). In recent years, consumer welfare has become the most articulated goal of antitrust law in the US. It should be no surprise that consumer welfare has achieved the status of the most publicised goal of competition laws across the globe. The consumer welfare proposition combines popular appeal with a flavour of economic erudition and thus has great rhetorical power. In spite of its popularity in the public policy debate, consumer welfare lacks a clear basis in industrial organisation theory (Orbach 2011). The question arises as to how consumer welfare relates to the economic concepts of efficiency discussed in section 3.2. Since the notion of consumer welfare may be understood in different ways, it needs to be defined explicitly before this question can be answered. In an attempt to overcome the current vagueness and potential confusion surrounding the notion of consumer welfare, two potential interpretations are presented below: (i) consumer welfare as the result of maximising (or at least saving) consumer surplus; (ii) consumer welfare resulting from improving consumer choices as the ultimate expression of consumer sovereignty.

3.3.1 Maximisation of consumer surplus

In a first interpretation of the consumer welfare notion, competition law should maximise consumer surplus or at least guarantee that consumer surplus is not reduced. By examining the size of consumer surplus rather than total surplus, consumer welfare may be reformulated in price theoretical terms. Consumer surplus is defined as the difference between the amount a buyer is willing to pay for a good and the amount (s)he actually pays for it. Consumer surplus is maximised under perfect competition. If consumer welfare is to be understood as the protection of consumer surplus, the consumer welfare goal of competition can be theoretically grounded in neoclassical price theory. Besides its theoretical appeal, consumer welfare understood as safeguarding consumer surplus has great practical advantages. Assessing the external effects on consumers requires much less information than assessing the overall welfare effect. For competition authorities, it is much easier to apply this standard than alternative welfare standards (in particular total surplus) because the inquiry can be limited to an estimate of future market prices. Merger simulation models, which allow a comparison of prices before and after the merger, nicely fit this interpretation (Carlton 2007; Farell and Katz 2006; Motta 2004, 20–22; Neven and Röller 2000; Besanko and Spulber 1993). Generally, this definition implies that a pre-eminent objective of competition law should be to prevent increases in consumer prices due to the exercise of market power by dominant firms (Fisher, Johnson and Lande 1989).

Following this first interpretation, the difference between a consumer welfare standard and a total welfare standard can be explained easily. Under the conditions of perfect competition, both allocative efficiency and consumer welfare are optimally served. Producer surplus and consumer surplus are simultaneously maximised. In reality, policy decisions that make producers better off without making any consumer worse off will be rare. Examples include mergers increasing the profits of the merging firms and at the same time leading to lower prices for consumers (Fisher, Lande and Vandaele 1983) or mergers allowing cost savings without any negative impact on consumer prices. If a dynamic perspective augments a static approach, increasing producer surplus may also be in the interest of consumers. When profits are the necessary return on previous innovation or provide the funding for future innovation, consumers may be harmed if antitrust intervention focuses on low consumer prices only. To guarantee innovation (dynamic efficiency), the size of producer surplus should matter inasmuch as it generates future increases of consumer surplus.

However, if the interests of producers and consumers do not (at least, partly) coincide, applying the consumer welfare criterion may entail a ban on anticompetitive agreements or mergers. The goal of safeguarding consumer surplus requires that consumers are made better off, or at least not made worse off. The total welfare standard implies that in a particular market the sum of producer and consumer surplus is maximised. Within the analytical framework of the Williamsonian trade-off the total welfare standard asks whether an increase in producer surplus, which may be the result of an increase of productive efficiency created by the merger (for example, economies of scale), is larger than the deadweight loss (allocative inefficiencies), which is the consequence of an increase in market power. From a total welfare perspective, it is not necessary to consider the distributional effects of the merger. A part of the former consumer surplus is transferred to the post-merger firm (and, therefore, becomes producer surplus) but this does not affect total welfare as the sum of consumer surplus and producer surplus increases. Unlike the total welfare approach, the consumer welfare model views redistribution in the form of wealth transfers from consumers to producers as harmful rather than neutral (Lande 1982). Hence, it is not possible to accept gains that ac-crue to producers only, even if these gains are sufficiently large to compensate potentially the losses to consumers.

It is important to note that the rejection of the total welfare criterion has no basis in welfare economics and can be justified on equity grounds only. Adopting the consumer welfare criterion in competition law may lead to welfare losses, as the following two examples illustrate. The rejection of a Williamsonian trade-off in merger control is a prime example. Improvements in terms of allocation may be opposed if they increase producer surplus only. The requirement that efficiency savings are passed on to consumers – partly or entirely, immediately or within a set time frame – is not reconcilable with the total welfare criterion. Another telling example is price discrimination, which increases output but enables the dominant firm to capture a larger part of the consumer surplus. Even though more consumers may get access to products or services, some of them will have to pay prices that are (sub-stantially) higher than those charged to other buyers. For this reason, price discrimination may be regarded negatively under a consumer welfare stand-ard (for further discussion, see section 7.5). The scope for conflicts between efficiency goals and consumer welfare seem to be smaller if dynamic efficien-cies are realised, since also consumers will benefit from product innovation. However, savings in terms of dynamic efficiency may be regarded negatively if they do not lead to immediate price decreases benefiting consumers. These negative policy judgements will be overcome if the size of the total surplus (Kaldor–Hicks efficiency) rather than consumer surplus is used as a bench-mark for policy decisions. The important insight is that allocative efficiency (assessed in terms of total welfare, i.e. total surplus in the markets under anti-trust scrutiny) and consumer welfare (defined as maximisation of consumer surplus) are conflicting concepts and that policy makers cannot escape from trade-offs if these goals are to be pursued simultaneously.

In essence, the discussion about the appropriateness of a consumer welfare standard is a debate about the use of competition law as an instrument of redistribution. The main objection against a consumer welfare standard, advanced by those who favour a total welfare approach, is that this standard discriminates between individuals in different interest groups. It cannot eas-ily be justified why consumers should be treated more favourably than other individuals (shareholders, workers) should. The Kaldor–Hicks criterion pre-cisely avoids this type of discrimination. Moreover, individuals have different capacities and do not only participate in markets as consumers; they can be also shareholders or workers (employees) of firms that are subject to anti-trust sanctions. If a merger is allowed, individuals may ultimately profit since the benefits that accrue to them in their capacity as shareholder or worker outweigh the costs they bear as consumers. To overcome discrimination among individuals, the Chicago School has voiced most clearly the promotion of total economic welfare as the sole aim of antitrust law (Bork 1978, 90–91). It is indeed not obvious why competition law should pursue goals of distributive justice. A related and widespread answer to distributional concerns voiced in the Law and Economics literature is that tax law is a better instrument to achieve goals of redistribution than other legal rules. Taxes can be imposed on a regular basis and can also be targeted at the wealthier groups of the population. By contrast, the distributive effects of private law occur only incidentally and randomly (Kaplow and Shavell 1994). In a political decision process, though, equity concerns may dominate efficiency concerns. The emphasis put on consumer welfare by antitrust authorities at both sides of the Atlantic is a signal of the likely greater importance of the protection of consumers' interests relative to the total economic welfare of society.

3.3.2 Enhancing consumer choice

Neoclassical welfare economics discusses consumer welfare in terms of price. As explained in the second chapter of this book, there are two main objections to monopoly: allocative inefficiency and wealth transfers. It is unclear whether total welfare (allocative efficiency) or distributional concerns (ban of wealth transfers) should be the relevant standard to measure consumer welfare, but in both cases the measurement is commonly expressed in the amount of consumer prices. However, consumers' choice is not only dependent on price; buyers decide on the basis of several variables: price, quality, safety, variety and innovation. In a static neoclassical analysis, price is used as a proxy for quality (Kaplow and Shapiro 2007). An alternative view links the notion of consumer welfare with the concept of consumer sovereignty and takes explicit account of non-price criteria that shape consumers' choices.

Consumer sovereignty implies that economic actors act primarily in response to the aggregate signals of consumer demand and in line with the preferences of individual businesses or government decisions (Averitt and Lande 1997, 715). Consumer choice is defined as the state of affairs where the consumer has the power to define his or her own wants and the ability to satisfy these wants at competitive prices (Lande 2001). Robert Lande, who may be regarded as the main proponent of a consumer choice approach in US antitrust law, has argued that consumers not only seek competitively priced goods but also consider quality, variety and safety in their purchase decision (Lande 1999). If the goal of antitrust is redefined as enhancing individual consumers' well-being, several other factors affecting the satisfaction of consumers' happiness and their wants must be added to the competitive assessment: material living standard, health, environmental quality, education, work satisfaction, political voice, social connections and (economic or physical) security.

In spite of its likely popular appeal, there are several problems with the consumer choice standard. First, consumer welfare becomes a very broad, not well-defined goal that incorporates different economic, social and moral values. Such a broad notion will be difficult to apply in antitrust practice; it lacks predictability and creates legal uncertainty. Second, measuring consumer welfare will become impracticable, if not impossible. One advantage of the consumer surplus notion is that it lends itself easily to quantification, for example when a merger is controlled for its potential negative unilateral effects (Carlton 2007).[2] Comparing prices before and after the merger may be only a proxy for other criteria that affect consumers' satisfaction, but it is more amenable to everyday antitrust enforcement. Third, the consumer choice criterion may generate perverse effects by ultimately protecting competitors rather than consumers. The emphasis put on variety may be abused to justify the survival of small companies, which add to the variety of the product offer. Clearly, the number of competitors should not be seen as an indicator of the consumers' degree of happiness. A competition policy focusing on the structure of the market may inhibit creative adaptations that lower the number of competitors but increase quality competition and overall competitiveness. In sum, the consumer choice criterion does not overcome the general criticisms of the consumer welfare approach limiting its practical usefulness: lack of clarity, predictability and objectivity.

Before turning to a discussion of ordoliberalism, a final remark on the economic welfare approaches discussed above seems appropriate. From a perspective of constitutional economics, it is not evident why total welfare or consumer welfare should be the only normative goals of competition law. Nobel prize winner James Buchanan has argued that the decisive normative criterion in policy discussions is voluntary individual consent (Buchanan and Tullock 1962). Based upon this criterion, Kerber argues that the preferences of the citizens should be the relevant normative criterion for appropriate decisions about the objectives of competition policy. Buchanan's normative criterion is close to the Pareto criterion, but clearly distinct from Kaldor–Hicks efficiency. It is unlikely that citizens would agree to a total welfare standard, since this will entail losses in the short run and it is unlikely that all individuals would win in the long run (which would be possible only if they

---

[2] The anti-competitive effects of mergers manifest themselves in two ways: through facilitating collusion in the post-merger market and by allowing unilateral price increases of the merged firm. For a discussion, see section 9.2.1.

are both winners and losers in different situations). In addition, a consumer welfare standard is unlikely to be accepted from a constitutional economics perspective, since citizens of a society are not only consumers but also owners of production factors (capital and labour) and will have different interests in the latter capacity. Citizens may also have different preferences about the types of business behaviour that should be accepted as 'normal' competitive behaviour and which conduct is 'morally acceptable'. Kerber concludes that a (very) broad set of goals may be acceptable from a constitutional economics perspective and that mainstream industrial organisation theory does not sufficiently take account of concerns different from total and consumer welfare (Kerber 2009).

3.4 Ordoliberalism: competition as a system (order) protecting economic freedom

Several authors do not agree with the instrumental view sketched above. These commentators attribute an intrinsic normative value to the competition process as such. Hence, competition is favoured irrespective of the consequences that the competitive process may have for (economic or consumer) welfare. In this alternative view, competition is not praised because of the expected beneficial economic outcomes but because of the intrinsic virtues of the competitive process itself. Competition may be seen as a natural right that all other individuals should respect. Robert Nozick famously claimed that the just distribution of resources in society depends on the competitive process that puts limits on anyone's right to pursue his self-interest (Nozick 1974, 120). Nobel prize winner Friedrich von Hayek stressed that we can assess the actions of individuals only by inquiring whether they conform to prescribed rules of conduct and not by assessing their outcomes (von Hayek 1967, 90). According to Hayek's ideas, competition authorities cannot judge consequences in terms of efficiency since they lack information to accurately balance economic costs and benefits. This information is hidden in the market in a decentralised way and can be discovered only through the competitive process itself. The latter brings about a 'spontaneous order' that should not be jeopardised by ill-conceived decisions of competition authorities.

The view that competition law should protect competition as a system finds its most prominent place in ordoliberal thinking. Originally, ordoliberals adopted the welfare ideal of 'complete competition' (which is similar to the neoclassical concept of perfect competition) and thus accepted an outcome-driven perspective (see section 2.4). This view was typical of the old Freiburg School but has been given up by modern ordoliberal thinkers (Behrens 2015). In more recent literature emphasis is put on freedom of action rather than the achievement of allocative efficiency. In ordoliberal thinking competition is described as a beneficial process because it is the embodiment of liberty. According to the German concept of *Wettbewerbsfreiheit* (freedom of competition), restrictions of competition may occur both in relations with competitors and in relations with firms that are active as suppliers or buyers. As defined by Hoppmann, economic freedom manifests itself in two ways: the freedom to choose a business partner and the freedom to decide which competitive (price or non-price) strategy to use (Hoppmann 1968). Ordoliberal authors launched the concept of *Leistungswettbewerb*, i.e. competition on the merits, to distinguish legal from illegal types of conduct. The normative criterion of 'performance on the merits' should allow drawing the border line between beneficial competitive conduct and harmful restrictions of economic freedom. In the ordoliberal view, firms may gain a competitive advantage if they perform better than their competitors do. However, certain forms of conduct must be prohibited if this advantage materialises because of market power that is not based on performance.

3.5 The goals of US antitrust law

The current policy debate in the US centres around the question whether to apply a total or consumer welfare standard (Carlton 2007). Historically, however, US antitrust policy recognised multiple goals. In the mid-1960s, the historian Richard Hofstadter wrote an article with the suggestive title 'What happened to the antitrust movement?'. In this article, Hofstadter argues that, besides economic goals, antitrust law also embodied social and moral goals. The competitive process was believed to be a kind of disciplinary machinery for the development of character and the competitiveness of people was seen as the fundamental stimulus to national morale, which needs protection (Hofstadter 1965). As the quote from Senator Sherman in Box 3.1 illustrates, in the early days of antitrust economic power was judged equally dangerous as political power. This view created scope for considerations of fairness, economic freedom, equal opportunities, and protection of small and medium-sized firms. The policy discussion in the 1950s and 1960s was neatly reflected in Kaysen and Turner's well-known book on the goals of antitrust law (see section 2.5.2). Even though the European Ordoliberal School was not explicitly referred to, Kaysen and Turner equally mentioned the protection of the competitive process as a goal of the US antitrust law. This goal had to be balanced against other values, including efficiency goals. There was also a 'populist' view of antitrust stressing political and cultural values (Hofstadter 1965). Taking these approaches together, it may be concluded that the first 70 years of US antitrust law enforcement showed a very diversified and fragmented set of policy goals.

From the late 1970s onwards, this picture changed dramatically because of the impact of the Chicago School. After a period of strong antitrust intervention (mid-1940s until 1970s), antitrust enforcement in the US substantially contracted, with the use of neoclassical economic theories focusing on allocative efficiency. The new mantra 'Competition law should protect competition, not competitors' discredited the objective to protect small businesses. Also, moral and social goals disappeared from the policy discussion. As a consequence of the Chicago Revolution, US antitrust law became at the same time more technical and less interventionist. The degree of technicality further increased in the Post-Chicago era, mainly under the influence of game theoretical analyses (see section 2.10). The increasing technicality has broadened the gap between antitrust enforcement and public concerns about fairness, equal opportunities and equity that might still subsist in parts of the American population. In spite of the increasing degree of economic sophistication, the debate between the proponents of allocative efficiency and the advocates of consumer protection, who stress distributional concerns, has never stilled. The famous Chicago scholar Robert Bork argued that allocative efficiency is the only value and goal that underlies the oldest US antitrust statute (Bork 1966). Robert Lande objected to this view by proposing that distributional concerns, rather than efficiency, were the original and primary concern of US antitrust (Lande 1982). Recently voices are heard that favour a 'blended goal approach which incorporates non-economic values to maximize overall well-being' (Stucke 2012). Other commentators have put forward the goal of reducing inequality as an objective of antitrust law (Baker and Salop 2015). However, it may be doubted that antitrust law is an appropriate and effective instrument to achieve redistributive goals (see the discussion above at section 3.3.1).

The case law of the US Supreme Court reflects an evolution similar to the changes in US enforcement practice. In the *Standard Oil* case (1911), the Supreme Court reviewed the legislative history of the Sherman Act and noted the non-economic concerns of Congress about the concentration of wealth and power in the hands of a few monopolies.[3] During the interventionist period of antitrust, the Supreme Court stressed the importance of protecting small, locally owned business even at the cost of ensuing inefficiencies. Back in 1945, a Court of Appeal stated that it is 'possible, because of its indirect social or moral effect, to prefer a system of small producers, each dependent for his success upon his own skill and character, to one in which the great mass of those engaged must accept the direction of a few.'[4] Later on, in the 1960s, this approach was supported by the US Supreme Court,

---

[3] *Standard Oil Co. v. United States,* 221 U.S. 18–19 (1911).
[4] *United States v. Aluminium Co. of Am.,* 148 F.2d 416, 427 (2d Cir. 1945).

which added explicitly that inefficiencies that may result from the protection of small and medium-sized firms should be accepted. Highly illustrative for the 'small is beautiful' approach is the quote from the *Brown Shoe* case, cited in Box 3.1.[5] In 1972, the US Supreme Court called the federal antitrust laws 'the Magna Carta of free enterprise' and thus qualified competition rules as an instrument to preserve economic freedom.[6] This statement should not be understood as an explicit embrace of European-like ordoliberal ideas but it shows that, for a long time, the US Supreme Court's case law was hospitable to a variety of antitrust goals.

When the Chicago School gained ascendancy, the US Supreme Court gradually embraced its learning. Chicagoans favour a unifying, single economic goal: total welfare. Consequently, the antitrust laws should be enforced with the help of micro-economic tools and not be based on formalistic legal rules. The changes in the US Supreme Court's case law on vertical restraints and monopolisation reflect the impact of the Chicago learning. In the early days of US antitrust, vertical restraints were judged in formalistic legal terms.[7] In the *Sylvania* case (1977), the US Supreme Court departed from this tradition and decided that evidence of economic effects and not formalistic line drawing should be decisive for judging the legality of non-price vertical restraints.[8] Three decades later, in *Leegin* the US Supreme Court opted in favour of a coherent approach for all vertical restraints by rejecting a *per se* prohibition of resale price maintenance.[9] Therefore, all vertical restraints are to be judged by assessing their conformity with economic welfare goals. Arguments based on legal conceptions of competitive distortions and administrative requirements of the legal system had to give way to a pure economic approach. In addition, the case law on monopolisation reflects the increased impact of the Chicago learning. In predatory pricing cases, the Supreme Court decided that such practices are unlikely in the absence of a reasonable prospect of recoupment.[10] This reasoning embraces the Chicago analysis, which is based on the assumption of rationally behaving companies and accepts allocative efficiency as the policy goal to aim at.[11] The ultimate approval of an economic approach, which completes the Chicago revolution in the US

---

[5] See also: *United States v. Von's Grocery Co.*, 384 U.S. 270, at 275 (1966): 'the basic purpose (…) was to prevent economic concentration in the American economy by keeping a large number of small competitors in business.'

[6] *United States v. Topco Assocs., Inc.*, 405 U.S. 596, 610 (1972).

[7] *Schwinn* case. See the discussion in section 6.4.3.

[8] *Continental TV Inc. v GTE Sylvania*, 433 U.S. 36 (1977). See the discussion of this case in Chapter 5, section 5.4.2.

[9] *Leegin Creative Leather Products, Inc. v. PSKS, Inc.*, 551 U.S. 877 (2007).

[10] Cases *Matsushita* and *Brooke*; see for a discussion of these cases Chapter 7, section 7.4.2.

[11] For a critique from a Behavioural Law and Economics perspective, see Chapter 7, section 7.4.1, with further references.

Supreme Court, can be read in the Court's statement in its *Trinko* judgment that monopoly profits are an important element of the free-market system. As illustrated by the quote in Box 3.1, the Supreme Court is ready to accept that monopoly profits may be justified if they create scope for innovation and economic growth. In sum, the US Supreme Court has evolved from a multiple goals perspective to a pure economic welfare approach, focusing on all types of economic efficiency (static efficiency, dynamic efficiency and their potential trade-off).

Today, consumer welfare ranks high on the list of goals presented by US antitrust authorities (see the quotes in Box 3.1). This may be due to its current pleasant popular ring, whereas in the past other goals, such as the protection of small companies, had a larger public appeal. Interestingly, it took until 1975 before the US Supreme Court mentioned consumer welfare in an antitrust case.[12] The term appeared also in the seminal book *The Antitrust Paradox* by Robert Bork. However, Bork gave it an unduly broad meaning by equating the term with total welfare (Orbach 2011). Today, the US antitrust authorities seem to favour the consumer welfare standard as the most appropriate benchmark for developing their policies. Rather than total surplus, consumer surplus seems to be the decisive normative criterion. Besides the flavour of economic erudition enjoyed by the consumer welfare concept, above all practical reasons may explain this preference. As explained in section 3.3, the consumer welfare standard is different from the notion of consumer surplus in micro-economic textbooks and it is, therefore, not without ambiguity. Nevertheless, the focus on the impact of agreements, unilateral conduct and mergers on consumer prices has a double advantage: it is based on economic insights about market power and it can be applied relatively easily in real-world cases. Indeed, calculating changes in consumer surplus (for example, by comparing prices before and after a contemplated merger) is far more feasible than quantifying total surplus. In this way, the US antitrust agencies opt for an economic approach that is both attractive and realistic. Nevertheless, two objectives may be raised against a consumer surplus standard. First, the certainty provided by empirical analyses (such as merger simulation models) may be illusory. The empirical studies may be based on questionable assumptions and subjective choices that are obscured by the seemingly persuasive power of the data set (Bishop 2013). Second, the decisions to start an investigation may be driven by the availability of data, rather than the seriousness of potential distortions in a particular industry. Data sets on the sale of consumer goods are broadly available but potential distortions in differentiated goods markets (where entry is relatively easy) seem to require less concern

---

[12] *United States v. Citizens & S. Nat'l Bank*, 422 U.S. 86, 131 (1975).

than anti-competitive effects in homogeneous goods markets, for which it is more difficult to obtain the data needed for calculating the effects on consumer prices. From this perspective, investing scarce resources on antitrust investigations in retailing markets might be problematic.

3.6   The goals of EU competition law

Whereas the current discussion in the US centres around the choice of either a total welfare or a consumer welfare standard, there is no unifying economic goal in EU competition law. Those who look for a uniting principle may find it rather in the political aim to achieve an internal market (Article 3(3) TFEU). Competition law is not a goal in itself but is linked inextricably to the objectives of the European Union. After the Treaty of Lisbon, the instrumental use of competition law and its subordinate role to the goal of market integration has become clearer than ever before. The old text of the Treaty recognised the vital importance of competition by mentioning in its Principles the establishment of 'a system ensuring that competition in the internal market is not distorted' (Article 3(1)(g) EC Treaty). Both the European Commission and the European Courts relied upon this article to increase the effectiveness of the competition law provisions (for example, by enacting additional rules on merger control or requiring effective enforcement of competition law by every individual).[13] Progressively, the role of competition law evolved from an instrument to an objective of the Community. This upgraded role was reflected in the ill-fated Constitutional Treaty, which listed competition not only as a guiding principle but also as one of the objectives of the EU. Competition was portrayed as the fifth freedom, next to the four existing freedoms (free movement of goods, services, persons and capital). France objected to this evolution and wanted to downgrade the role of competition to that of a means to accomplish the broader tasks of the Union (Lianos 2013). The new Article 3(3) TFEU states:

> The Union shall establish an internal market. It shall work for the sustainable development of Europe based on balanced economic growth and price stability, a highly competitive social market economy, aiming at full employment and social progress, and a high level of protection and improvement of the quality of the environment. It shall promote scientific and technological advance.

It is remarkable that neither the protection of competition nor the safeguarding of consumers' interests is mentioned in the current text of the TFEU.[14]

---

[13] Case 453/99, *Courage Ltd v Bernard Crehan* [2001] ECR I-6297, at para. 20.
[14] Protocol No. 27 provides that the internal market as set out in Article 3 TFEU includes a system ensuring that competition is not distorted. This Protocol may neutralise the repeal of the former Article 3(1)g, which

Today EU competition law is best understood as a means to accomplish the broader tasks of the Union: the internal market and the social market economy. Consequently, the discussion on the goals of competition law cannot be narrowed down to a US-like debate on the choice between consumer welfare and total welfare. In addition, competition policy cannot be decided independently but must take account of various other economic and non-economic (social, cultural) policies. The pluralist tradition of EU competition law is illustrated by the quotes in Box 3.1. The consequences of this 'many values' tradition of EU competition law are discussed below.

3.6.1 EU competition law viewed from the perspective of welfare economics

Careful reading of the Treaty's formulations immediately makes clear that total welfare (Kaldor–Hicks efficiency) cannot be used as the benchmarking standard for the purpose of EU competition law. The formulation of Article 101(3) TFEU excludes that maximising the sum of consumer and producer surplus is seen as the goal of EU competition law. Article 101(3) TFEU provides for agreements being exempt from the ban on cartels if four conditions are met (see section 5.3.3 for further discussion). The explicit requirement that consumers must receive a fair share of the resulting benefits excludes that gains incurred by producers are seen as a potential (Kaldor–Hicks) compensation justifying consumer losses. The Merger Regulation contains a similar wording and, therefore, equally disallows a trade-off between productive efficiency and allocative efficiency. Under a total welfare standard, cost savings brought about by a merger could offset price increases, but such an approach is at odds with the requirement that efficiencies should be taken into account only if they are 'to consumers' advantage and (do) not form an obstacle to competition' (Article 2(1)(b) Merger Regulation). It may be added that the notion of Pareto efficiency did not receive support in the early case law of the Court of Justice of the European Union (CJEU). In its landmark *Metro/Saba* judgment, the CJEU stated that perfect competition (where Pareto efficiency is realised) is not the goal of European competition law. Instead, the Court advanced the criterion of 'workable competition', which allows that some market imperfections are kept in place (see the discussion in section 2.5.2).

---

in any case loses the salience it had before. It is remarkable that the Protocol does not link competitive markets with the 'social market economy'. The meaning of the latter concept remains obscure; it might be understood as a market economy with social corrections to undo undesirable redistributive consequences of economic liberalism.

Later chapters of this book will discuss the most important policy documents (Guidelines) of the European Commission concerning the requirements for exemption of the cartel prohibition and merger control. Here, it may suffice to mention that these documents confirm that Kaldor–Hicks efficiency is not the benchmarking yardstick in European competition law (see sections 5.3.2 and 9.3.2 for further discussion). This obviously raises the question whether there is another welfare standard that underlies the current substantive rules. Is the goal of European competition law the promotion of consumer welfare? Here, a balanced answer seems necessary. In its Guidelines on the application of Article 81(3) EC, the European Commission does not require that any individual consumer receives a share of each single efficiency gain. This would amount to a Pareto criterion, which is extremely difficult to implement in practice. Instead, the Commission suggests the following pragmatic solution:

> The concept of 'fair share' implies that the pass-on of benefits must at least compensate consumers for any actual or likely negative impact caused to them by the restriction of competition (…) The net effect must at least be neutral from the point of view of those consumers directly or likely affected by the agreement. If such consumers are worse off following the agreement, the second condition of Article 81(3) EC is not fulfilled.

Guidelines, at para. 85

The requirement that a fair share of the benefits must be passed on to consumers limits the scope of efficiencies claims. In the Commission's view, the second condition for exemption incorporates a sliding scale: 'The greater the restriction of competition found under Article 81(1) EC the greater must be the efficiencies and the pass-on to consumers' (Guidelines, at para. 90). Clearly, the scope for an efficiency defence in everyday antitrust practice will depend on the requirements of proof relating to the achievement of static or dynamic efficiencies (see for further discussion: section 5.3.3 on the requirements for exemption of the cartel prohibition, and section 9.4.4 on merger control).

3.6.2 The impact of ordoliberalism on EU competition law

For a proper understanding of EU competition law, one should always keep in mind the impact of the Ordoliberal School on the original wording of the Treaty provisions and their subsequent interpretation by the European Court of Justice (ECJ).[15] The wording that competition law aims at the

---

[15] It has been argued by Akman (2012) that the impact of ordoliberalism on EU competition law has been overstated. However, her reading of ordoliberalism has been criticised as incomplete, since it relies largely on

establishment of 'a system ensuring that competition in the internal market is not distorted' (Article 3(1)(g) EC Treaty) clearly reflects the goal of protecting the competitive order as such. Also, the last condition to grant an exemption can be best understood from this perspective. This requirement holds that the agreement should not allow the possibility of eliminating competition in respect of a substantial part of the products in question (Article 101(3) *in fine* TFEU). This wording again reveals the ordoliberal view that competition is to be protected as a system (order) which fosters economic freedom. References to the protection of individual competitors also permeate the enforcement practice. The Article 81(3) EC Notice states that:

> a general principle underlying Article 81(1) EC, which is expressed in the case law of the Community Courts, is that each economic operator must determine independently the policy which he intends to adopt on the market.

Guidelines, at para. 14

The emphasis on freedom of action explains why the Commission often objects to contracts limiting the freedom of parties to take independent decisions (e.g. vertical restraints in distribution agreements).

The ordoliberal influence is clearly visible in the case law of the CJEU. In several judgments, the Court stated that the goal of competition law is not only or not mainly the protection of individual competitors or consumers but the protection of the competitive market structure, in other words the protection of competition as an institution.[16] An instrumental view, which sees competition rules as a tool to reach economic objectives, is not adhered to. Hence, neither total welfare nor consumer welfare is an autonomous goal of EU competition law. Consequently, consumers are protected only indirectly through the prohibition of competitive distortions. Gerber argues that all other potential goals of competition law can be achieved only as far as they relate to the central objective of combatting distortions of the competitive system and are developed in the service of that objective (Gerber 2008). The influence of the Ordoliberal School can be seen most clearly in the case law on abuse of a dominant position. Article 102 TFEU protects the market as an institution (*Institutionsschutz*) and only indirectly the interests of competitors and consumers. In a market where there is a dominant player, the structure of the market is negatively affected and competition as an institution is endangered. Because of the threat that it poses to competition as such,

---

the older writings of the Freiburg School and does not take account of later developments (see Behrens 2015).
[16] See, for example, Joined Cases C-501/06 P, C-513/06 P, C-515/06 P and C-519/06 P, *GlaxoSmithKline Services Unlimited v. Commission* [2009] ECR I-9291, para. 63.

a dominant firm may not engage in certain types of conduct that would cause no problem if practised by firms without market power. According to the ECJ, the European dominant firm is endowed with a 'special responsibility' vis-à-vis its customers: *Quod licet bovi non licet Iovi*. The competitive system has already been harmed by the simple presence of a dominant firm and should not be further weakened. For example, a refusal to supply can be prohibited as an abuse of a dominant position, irrespective of the fact that such conduct is perfectly lawful when practised by its non-dominant competitors. As a result of the ordoliberal influence, the European approach to dominant firms has been less hospitable to an analysis of economic effects as compared with US antitrust law. The assessment of exclusionary conduct under Article 102 TFEU has been the last field where the European Commission suggested a policy change by adopting a so-called more economic approach. The major obstacle to modernise this part of EU competition law is the long-standing case law of the ECJ, which has been heavily influenced by ordoliberal thinking (see for further discussion Chapter 7 of this book).

3.6.3   The market integration goal

EU competition law must be understood in the context of the need to break down the national boundaries between the Member States of the European Union. Since the ECJ's *Grundig*[17] case, the link between creating an internal (common) market and competition policy has been clearly established. The goal of market integration can be defined as the elimination of economic frontiers between two or more economies. Neither Member States nor private enterprises may engage in practices that are in conflict with or undermine the unification of the European market. The former should not maintain or issue regulations that hinder the free movement of goods, services, persons or capital. The latter should not agree to restrictive business practices that could equally form effective barriers against competition originating in other Member States. From an internal market perspective, efforts aimed at removing national regulatory barriers to the full deployment of the four freedoms should not be jeopardised by business conduct aimed at partitioning national markets. For example, national regulation on the composition of goods hindering free inter-state trade[18] should not be replaced by agreements between producers limiting their commercial activities to particular Member States.

---

[17] Joined Cases 56/64 and 58/64 *Consten Sarl and Grundig-Verkaufs GmbH v. Commission* [1966] ECR 299. See the discussion in Box 6.3.

[18] A classic example is the German purity law reserving the denomination 'beer' to beer brewed from specific approved ingredients; see: Case 178/84 *Commission v. Germany* [1987] ECR 1227 ('Reinheitsgebot'). In spite of German (unconvincing) attempts to justify this restriction on health grounds, the purity law was considered an infringement of the free movement of goods principle.

The removal of public barriers may not be made ineffective by the creation of private barriers. Competition policy should ensure that such substitution cannot arise. Therefore, the CJEU decided in *Grundig* that market partitioning by private firms which agree on territorial clauses is to be qualified as a very serious infringement of EU competition law.

The view that competition law is an instrument to inhibit private initiatives (either agreements or unilateral practices) against the process of market integration has left EU competition law with a heavy legacy. To reduce price differences across EU Member States, European competition law promotes intra-brand competition and stimulates parallel trade.[19] Two examples may illustrate the potential conflicts between the objective of market integration, on the one hand, and the efficiency goals and the goal of consumer welfare, on the other. The first example is the persistent (almost *per se*) ban on absolute territorial protection. In spite of possible efficiency benefits in the organisation of distribution, the practice is outlawed as an obvious instrument to segregate markets along national borders. The efficiency savings that are regularly attributed at intra-brand restrictions, such as coping with free-riding and providing incentives for dealers to increase sales efforts, are sacrificed on the altar of the internal market. The discussion in Chapter 6 on vertical restrictions will show that the Commission is currently willing to be more tolerant with regard to territorial restraints if they are objectively necessary in order for a distributor to penetrate a new market. However, the harmony with economic insights is still far from complete (see section 6.4.2).

The second example is the persisting uneasy attitude towards price discrimination across different Member States. Parallel imports limit the scope for price differences; the ensuing price uniformity (average prices) has ambiguous effects on welfare. Even though these effects highly depend on market characteristics, a general conclusion is that price uniformity imposed by parallel imports reduces total welfare when demand dispersion across markets is large (Malueg and Schwartz 1994; see also Varian 1985). The impact of parallel trade on consumer welfare is equally ambiguous. Since some consumers gain and others lose from uniform prices, the overall consumer surplus may either increase or decrease. If, in response to price uniformity, firms withdraw from high-elasticity markets, more consumers, particularly the poorest, may face a reduction in product choice. The overall effect of uniform prices may thus be detrimental in terms of both efficiency (total welfare) and equity

---

[19] A common distinction in competition law is the one between intra-brand competition and inter-brand competition. The latter indicates competition between sellers of different brands, whereas the former relates to competition between sellers of the same brand. If there is scope for intra-brand competition, parallel traders will import cheaper goods into markets where prices for the same brand are higher.

(Rey 2003). However, different prices in different geographical areas seem to fly in the face of the market integration goal. Hence, price convergence within the EU Member States may be pursued at the expense of losses in terms of economic welfare.

Unfortunately, the case law of the European Courts has not done much to resolve the normative conundrum that results from pairing the market integration goal and rules of competition law. The pharmaceutical products saga (see Box 3.2) shows that the General Court (at that time: Court of First Instance) was willing to downscale the importance of the market integration goal, but that the CJEU ultimately reverted to the old axioms. It may be concluded that the pharmaceutical cases have brought a number of nuances, rather than a real change, in the attitude towards parallel imports. Clearly, the market integration goal is still prominently present in the case law of the European Courts. Moreover, there are no indications that a more hospitable assessment of restrictions on parallel trade will be introduced outside the pharmaceutical sector. As long as the *Grundig* prohibition is not overruled, tensions between market integration and economic welfare goals (both allocative and dynamic efficiency) will persist and the impact of consumer welfare of the restrictive case law will remain ambiguous.

Box 3.2: The pharmaceutical saga

Prices of prescription drugs vary across EU Member States. This is due to differences in the organisation of the health systems: in some Member States prices are fixed by the State, which acts as the sole buyer of medicines. In other Member States, health care markets have been deregulated and consequently prices are lower than in neighbouring countries. These price differences create scope for parallel imports. Pharmaceutical companies have used a dual pricing policy to restrict the scope for such parallel trade. The dual pricing policy implies that the sales prices to wholesalers depend on the ultimate country of resale. The sales conditions of medicines specify that wholesalers who resell the medicines within the same Member State receive a discount. However, if the wholesalers buy medicines also with the purpose of reselling them for export to other EU Member States they lose this discount. The purpose of the dual pricing policy is to prevent parallel trade of prescription drugs from a low-price country to a high-price country. According to the dominant view of the European Commission, parallel trade brings savings that accrue to consumers or national health care services, by exerting a downward competitive pressure on the price of the medicines in high-price countries. Given the emphasis on the market integration goal of EU competition law, the dual pricing system has been qualified as an infringement of Article 101 TFEU by object (see section 5.3.2 for an explanation of this concept). Pharmaceutical companies have objected to this qualification, arguing that high profit margins in some Member States are needed to finance costly research in the development of new medicines. Accordingly, there seems to be a conflict between allocative efficiency (high consumer prices) and dynamic efficiency (innovation). Over the years, there have been some shifts in the way in which EU competition law is dealing with this trade-off.

A first sign that market integration was losing importance could be found in the *Adalat* case. The General Court (formerly: Court of First Instance) censured an attempt of the European Commission to achieve price convergence by supporting parallel trade in the pharmaceutical industry. To this end, the Commission had extended the applicability of Article 101 TFEU (which requires the proof of an agreement) to a case where no concurrence of wills between economic operators could be shown. By annulling the Commission's decision, the Court made clear that Article 101 TFEU cannot be used to eliminate in a generic way the obstacles to interstate trade.[20] Even clearer signs that the benefits of parallel trade cannot be taken for granted could be found in the two *Glaxo* cases. The first case concerned a dual pricing system, which required wholesalers to charge higher prices for medicines sold outside Spain that were not subject to a Spanish price cap.[21] The second case arose as the consequence of a refusal to sell medicines to wholesalers in Greece, where a price cap equally applied, when these wholesalers wanted to resell the medicines into higher-priced Member States.[22] In the first *Glaxo* case, the General Court stated that 'parallel trade must be given a certain protection' but that Article 101(1) TFEU applies only in so far as the agreement may be presumed to deprive final consumers of the benefit of reduced prices.[23] Moreover, the possibility of an exemption must be examined with particular attention in a market, such as the pharmaceutical sector, where competition is distorted by national price regulations. The Court concluded that the European Commission failed to consider whether efficiency advantages outbalanced the disadvantages to competition of a dual pricing system.[24] Glaxo had maintained that parallel trade prevented it from realising the profits necessary for financing its R&D. In the pharmaceutical industry, innovation is the crucial parameter of inter-brand competition and gains in dynamic efficiency may offset losses resulting from higher prices due to restrictions of intra-brand competition (losses in allocative efficiency). The General Court stressed that such claims must be carefully examined and that an outright rejection of a dual pricing system cannot be accepted.

---

[20] Case T-41/96 *Bayer AG v. Commission* [2000] ECR II-3383, confirmed by Court of Justice in joined cases C-2/01P and C-3/01P *Commission v. Bayer* [2004] ECR I-23.
[21] Case T-168/01, *GlaxoSmithKline v. Commission* (2006) ECR-II.
[22] Cases C-468/06, C-478/06, *Sot. Lelos v.Glaxo Smith AEVE* (2008) ECR-I.
[23] Case T-168/01 *GlaxoSmithKline v. Commission* (2006) ECR-II, at paras 12 and 147.
[24] *Ibid.*, at paras 262 and 276.

The CJEU seemed to be more reluctant than the General Court to depart from the earlier case law. The Court expressed its continuing concern about restraints on parallel trade[25] and concluded, in line with its 30 years old *United Brands* (Chiquita) judgment (see section 7.5.3 for a discussion), that wholesalers cannot refuse to meet 'ordinary orders', taking account of the size of those orders and the previous business relations. Hence, a legal formalistic argument superseded economic concerns relating to the adverse impact of restraints on parallel trade. The CJEU again confirmed its old-fashioned approach when it overturned the judgment of the General Court in the first Glaxo case. The Court decided that a dual pricing system limiting parallel trade is a restriction of competition by object, which infringes Article 101(3) TFEU without the need for showing competitive harm. Such restrictions can be justified only if the four cumulative conditions for an exemption are met. Again, legal formalistic line drawing superseded an analysis focusing on efficiency effects.

Within the limited scope of this book, the pharmaceutical case cannot be discussed at length (for an extensive discussion, see Desogus 2011). Here it may suffice to say that both the parallel trade argument and the dynamic efficiencies justification need some qualifications. The magnitude of savings resulting from parallel trade is uncertain and depends on several factors, such as the absence of regulatory entry barriers, the number of parallel traders and the price strategies used by competitors. A case-by-case analysis is also needed to assess the size of the dynamic efficiency gains. If a trade-off is to be made in a real-life competition case, the outcome will flow from the division of the burden of proof. If efficiency gains must be proven in light of a standard of proof based on the preponderance of evidence, it is likely that the gains from parallel trade (lower prices) will weigh more heavily in the final balance.

As a final remark, it may be added that the appropriateness of market integration as a goal of competition law can be doubted. In the EU context, the objective of market integration may be fully legitimate but it is not clear why it should not be pursued by other legal instruments. It is highly questionable whether competition law is an appropriate tool to further market integration. This goal is largely impeded by factors, such as fiscal disparities and different regulatory interventions by the Member States, which are external to concerns of competition policy. Illustrative examples are the car industry, where price differences are caused by differences in tax levels, and the pharmaceutical industry (see the discussion in Box 3.2), where price differences are the consequence of differences in the health policies of the Member States (such as the existence of price caps and the presence of single buyers). Prohibiting companies active in the EU to adapt their sales policies to heterogeneous

---

[25] Cases C-468/06, C-478/06, *Sot. Lelos v. Glaxo Smith AEVE* (2008) ECR-I, at paras 65–66.

local conditions is nothing else but combatting effects without reaching the causes of the existing disparities. Using rules of competition law to bring about price convergence by means of the arbitrage flowing from parallel trade comes down to imposing the costs of non-Europe on companies, whereas the primary responsibility of persisting price differences lies with the governments of the Member States.

3.7 The political economy of competition law

So far, the economic analysis in this chapter has been a normative approach that has aimed at clarifying the goals of competition law mainly in terms of allocative efficiency and consumer welfare. In this section, brief attention is paid to positive economic theories (in particular Public Choice) that try to explain why rules of competition law are enacted and how they are enforced. Government decisions, including the enactment of (competition) laws, can be seen as the outcome of actions by different groups of people, who all are willing to increase their ability in reaching their utility-maximising goals. The Public Choice literature discusses political institutions in the same manner as the economists discuss the market. Political decisions are explained as the result of utility-maximising behaviour by politicians, legislators and bureaucrats. Also, antitrust authorities are not seen as omniscient and benevolent agents seeking the public good but as a collection of agents pursuing their own objectives. Compared with the voluminous normative literature, the political economy of antitrust is less developed. Nevertheless, competition law lends itself to a positive analysis, which explains the existing legal rules rather than prescribing their content. Such a positive analysis focuses on behaviour of actors that deviates from the goal of aggregate welfare but rather fosters particular interests. Decisions of politicians may be explained by their wish to be re-elected and the behaviour of bureaucrats may be better understood by focusing on the goals of budget maximisation, increased power and prestige. On top of this, interest group theories may shed light on the relative strengths and weaknesses of particular industries in the enactment of competition rules and decisions in real-life cases that foster their private interests (see the collection of articles in McChesney and Shughart 1995).

Nobel prize winner George Stigler argued that the passing of the Sherman Act can be best explained on private interest grounds. His research demonstrated that the Sherman Act was supported by small enterprises, whereas large firms (monopolies and would-be monopolies) were opposed to the passing of the Act (Stigler 1985). The wish to protect particular interest groups also explains the 1936 Robinson–Patman Act. This US antitrust statute was inspired by the wish to protect small, locally owned retailers from competition by large national retail stores. The Robinson–Patman Act bans forms of price discrimination without requiring adequate proof of competitive injury and prohibits large retail stores from requiring non-cost-justified price rebates from a manufacturer. There is a large literature that criticises this Act as a set of rules protecting inefficient individual competitors (see for example: Elman 1969, Mezines 1973, Neal 1976). The Robinson–Patman Act seems an aberration of US antitrust policy, which can be explained only on private interest grounds. A blanket provision of price discrimination fits into a reduced emphasis on competitiveness that may materialise in a period of economic crisis, during which there is more concern about guaranteeing an occupation for independent small retailers.

The wish to protect small businesses has also permeated EU competition law in various fields. The goal of protecting small businesses has been endorsed in the case law. The CJEU referred to the independence of small and medium-sized firms in *United Brands*[26] to counter the alleged ability of large firms to extract unfair prices and conditions from smaller enterprises. The protection of small firms is often justified by referring to a particular concept of fairness: the preservation of equal opportunities. This concept finds its roots in philosophical thought and has no direct link with allocative efficiency. In spite of its shaky foundations, the view that the powers of large firms should be curtailed for reasons of economic democracy is not alien to EU competition policy. Apart from efficiency goals, current competition policy embodies rules that aim to decentralise power, protect freedom of decision of independent firms and maintain equal opportunities of competition for small businesses. Current competition laws, both at the level of the EU and the Member States, continue to be influenced by the 'small is beautiful' ideology (Schumacher 1974) and fairness considerations. Cartel agreements between small and medium-sized enterprises, which can often compete effectively with larger enterprises only by means of this sort of cooperation, are shielded from the ban on cartels.[27] Additionally, in some EU Member States, laws on 'unfair' competition contain rules that are not consistent with an efficiency-oriented competition policy.[28]

As explained in section 3.5, the protection of small business has been discredited in the US and replaced by a total (consumer) welfare approach.

---

[26] Case 27/76 *United Brands v. Commission* [1978] ECR 207.
[27] Provided they do not contain hard-core restrictions, such as price agreements and horizontal market partitioning (*De Minimis Notice* of the European Commission, see section 5.3).
[28] An example is the prohibition of sales at loss prices, which applies irrespective of the existence of a dominant market position (France, Belgium, Germany). From an efficiency perspective, this rule is over-inclusive since it also outlaws competitive pricing.

There is also a political economy explanation of why this has happened. Over the years, the number of citizens agreeing that small companies need to be protected from large companies may decline and the popular appeal of the consumer protection goal may increase at the expense of the 'small is beautiful' ideology. Compared with US citizens, European voters may have less confidence in big companies and this may explain why the protection of small businesses still has a larger popular ring. Focusing antitrust decisions on the effects for consumers might compensate the latter for advantages that producers might obtain through rent-seeking (as effective lobbyers) or regulatory capture (profiting from information asymmetries between firms and competition authorities).

Next to the concerns for protecting weak market participants discussed above, parts of competition law may be explained by considerations of social policy. The inclusion of social policy considerations may make competition law incoherent. Below two examples of such inconsistencies are given: the enforcement of competition rules in times of economic crisis and the legal status of collective labour agreements. The protection of workers and the attainment of social goals may become prominent policy objections in times of economic crisis. In 1933, the National Industrial Recovery Act suspended the prohibitions of US antitrust law for 18 months. A European example of a 'crisis' exemption can be found in the former version of the German competition law, providing an exemption for *Strukturkrisenkartelle*. Even though there seems to be agreement among economists that relaxing competition law in times of economic crisis is counterproductive and may retard economic growth, economic crisis conditions continue to have an impact on the enforcement practice. For example, the recent economic crisis has fed demands for speeding up the approval of contemplated mergers, in order to provide job security to workers as soon as possible. The second example of a potential conflict between competition policy and social policy is the legality of collective labour agreements under competition law. Both US antitrust law and EU competition law have excluded the application of the ban on cartels in this field, even though in different ways. The CJEU has exempted collective labour agreements from the scope of Article 101(1) TFEU.[29] This decision was justified by fears that protection of workers would be jeopardised if negotiations between employers and employees regarding wages and labour conditions were to be qualified as a cartel agreement.

---

[29] Case C-67/96 *Albany International v. Stichting Bedrijfspensioenfonds Textielindustrie* [1999] ECR I-5751; joined cases C-115/97, C-116/97 and C-117/97 *Brentjens' Handelsonderneming BV v. Stichting Bedrijfspensioenfonds voor de Handel in Bouwmaterialen* [1999] ECR I-6025; Case C-219/97 *Maatschappij Drijvende Bokken BV v. Stichting Pensioenfonds voor de Vervoer- en Havenbedrijven* [1999] ECR I-6121. For critical comments, see Van den Bergh and Camesasca (2000).

Another potential conflict area is cultural policy. As regards the potential undesirable consequences of price competition on cultural policy, the 'evergreen' in competition law discussions is the desirability of fixed book prices. In the political discussion, resale price maintenance for books is often justified by cultural objectives: increasing the availability and accessibility of books in order to promote reading. These objectives generally create tension with particular goals of competition policy, such as the promotion of innovative distribution systems for books. It is to be expected that the discussion on the efficiency of vertical price fixing for books will not still soon. The reason is that the theoretical arguments point in opposing directions. On the one hand, the free-riding rationale (see sections 2.6.1 and 6.2.2) may be advanced to substantiate the survival of specialised bookstores. In this way, the traditional policy argument that cross-subsidisation is needed to finance the publication and distribution of less popular books gets theoretical support. On the other hand, it may be argued that small bookstores use vertical price fixing as a surrogate for a horizontal price conspiracy, which keeps prices high also for consumers who do not desire special services. When theories diverge, only empirical studies may provide final answers. Unfortunately, there is no hard empirical evidence that a fixed pricing system for book is superior to free pricing (see for an overview of the empirical evidence in the United Kingdom and Scandinavian countries: Ringstad 2004). Given this inconclusiveness, government proposals to (re)introduce price fixing for books may be best explained as private interest legislation.

Another persisting conflict area is the tension between competition policy and industrial policy. The latter proposes an intervention in the free workings of the market, as opposed to competition policy's trust in the beneficial welfare outcomes of the competitive process. Industrial policy may work against competition policy if the wish to protect national champions is used as an argument to clear horizontal cartels or anti-competitive mergers. Conversely, competition policy may work against industrial policy in R&D-intensive industries. Prohibiting certain types of behaviour of dominant firms (such as price discrimination) is counterproductive if large (and potentially dominant) firms are likely to invest more in R&D than small competitive firms. Both policies may thus reflect fundamentally different views of policy makers on the impact of government intervention in competitive markets. The potential for policy conflicts is consequently quite large. Nevertheless, competition policy and industrial policy may be seen as complementary if competition among firms is perceived as a major force behind industrial performance. As is the case with the other conflicts discussed above, a Public Choice approach may help in understanding the reasons why changes to competition law are introduced that create tensions with the economic welfare objectives discussed in the second and third sections of this chapter.

Insights from Public Choice may not only explain substantive rules that deviate from the (total or consumer) welfare objectives but also different enforcement levels of the existing prohibitions. In real-life markets, the scope and degree of the antitrust enforcement practice is determined by the relative strength of various interest groups, the degree of independence enjoyed by competition authorities and the career objectives of civil servants. Competition authorities are properly seen as a collection of agents that can take decisions deviating from the welfare objectives of competition law. Rather than focusing on efficiency goals, enforcement priorities may be put on dubious high-profile cases that may advance the career objectives of bureaucrats (bureaucratic capture). Economists generally agree that the detection and punishment of horizontal price fixing should be the first priority for competition authorities, but bureaucratic capture may cause a shift of attention towards cases that have a more appealing popular ring (big companies are bad). The degree to which bureaucratic capture can arise is dependent on the degree of independence of competition authorities, the degree of accountability that bureaucrats are subject to and the transparency of the decision-making processes. Clearly, the availability of judicial review and the bureaucrats' expectations about the likely outcome of appeal decisions may affect the type and degree of antitrust enforcement (see, for example, the discussion of the *GE/Honeywell* merger case in Box 9.5). A private interest perspective may also better explain changes in enforcement systems than a theory based on the assumption that enforcement maximises economic efficiency. In this respect, the shift from an *ex ante* notification regime to a legal exception regime (with *ex post* control) in EU competition law will be critically analysed in section 8.4.

3.8   Conclusions

In spite of the lack of consensus on the goals to be achieved, an extensive body of US antitrust law and EU competition law has developed. Obviously, different goals may be inconsistent with each other and necessitate difficult trade-offs. The goal of a competition policy that is primarily intended to increase economic welfare can be defined in terms of total welfare and consumer welfare. The total welfare view asserts that the chief objective of antitrust law is increasing allocative efficiency by allocating resources through the price system to those users who value these resources most. Allocative efficiency may conflict with other efficiency goals: productive efficiency (maximisation of output at a given input) and dynamic efficiency (invention, development, and diffusion of new products and production processes). To enable policy decisions when different efficiency goals are not consistent with each other, welfare economics offers the criterion of Kaldor–Hicks efficiency. This approach allows changes that increase total welfare, irrespective of the distribution of the gains that results from these modifications.

The consumer welfare standard may be interpreted in two different ways: (i) maximisation or protection of consumer surplus, and/or (ii) guaranteeing consumer choice and consumer sovereignty. The first interpretation requires that also consumers profit from productive and dynamic efficiencies. In this way the neglect of distributional effects by applying the Kaldor–Hicks criterion is overcome. The second interpretation gives a broader meaning to the concept of consumer welfare by focusing on choice (which is based on price, variety, quality, as well as innovation) and not only on price as it is done when the neoclassical concept of consumer surplus is used. Conflicts between efficiency (total welfare) and consumer welfare (defined in terms of consumer surplus) cannot be excluded. This will be the case when distributional considerations prevail, so that improvements in terms of total welfare will be opposed because consumers are not made better off. The origins of producer surplus are inevitably mixed: sometimes market power, sometimes reward for efficiency or innovation. Distributional considerations prevent consumer losses (increased prices) being accepted since they lead to higher gains for producers (increased profits), even though consumers may also profit in their capacities as owners of capital (shareholders) or workers (employees).

In the US, there has been an intense debate over the goals of antitrust law during the more than 120-year history of the Sherman Act. In the early days of antitrust, much of the policy discussion reflected a preoccupation with the wish of protecting small businesses. From the 1960s onwards, the Chicago School has heavily criticised a policy of protecting competitors rather than competition. Scholars working in the Chicago School tradition have rejected the propriety of any other goal for antitrust law than economic efficiency. For Chicagoans, antitrust law should promote total welfare (maximisation of producer surplus and consumer surplus in the sectors of the economy that are under antitrust investigation). The Chicago School had a profound impact on US antitrust law in the 1970s and 1980s. However, recent policy statements of the US enforcement agencies stress consumer welfare, rather than total welfare, as the main goal of antitrust law. If making consumers better off is seen as the major goal, the efficiency analysis will need to be supplemented by an investigation of distributional effects; and trade-offs between efficiency benefits and negative distributional consequences for consumers cannot be avoided. Hence, the discussion on the goals of US antitrust law boils down to a choice between a total welfare standard and a consumer welfare standard.

The picture is different in the EU, where a broader variety of goals continues to have an impact on competition law. Reading together its policy documents, it seems that the European Commission has found a pragmatic way to avoid interpretations of consumer welfare that are impracticable (Pareto efficiency) for policy making. It is remarkable that policy statements of the 1970s, which urged for price decreases to the benefit of consumers, have been replaced by the less demanding criterion that consumers should not be made worse off. However, other passages of the more recent policy documents still describe consumer benefits in terms of lower prices. It would bring important benefits in terms of clarity and consistency if the Commission would clearly define its consumer welfare standard and openly endorse it, rather than obscuring policy choices by paying lip service to efficiency arguments.

A traditional objective of EU competition law is the achievement of market integration. The goal of market integration has put a heavy legacy on European competition law. Up until today, it has kept prohibitions in place (such as the ban on absolute territorial protection and the strict attitude towards price discrimination) which may cause substantial inefficiencies in the organisation of production or distribution. EU competition law is further distinct from US antitrust law in its continuing embrace of small and medium-sized firms as a positive competitive force and the related emphasis on fairness (equity) rather than efficiency. In particular, the ordoliberal view, according to which any limitation of economic freedom should be held as a virtual restriction of competition, has had an impact on the formulation of prohibitions in EU competition law. This has led to different and conflicting perspectives on the goals of competition law: total welfare contrasted with consumer welfare, market integration, protection of small businesses and protection of individual economic freedom. On top of the different views on competition policy, EU political leaders and bureaucrats stress the need of interaction between competition policy objectives and other goals, such as industrial policy, social policy, and cultural policy.

Insights from Public Choice may help in understanding why real-life competition policy deviates from the outcomes aimed at by normative approaches, which propose total welfare and consumer welfare as goals of competition law. The last section of this chapter discussed several examples to illustrate how competition rules may favour private interests rather than allocative efficiency. Tension exists between economic welfare goals and arguments of social policy (protection of small independent traders and workers), cultural policy (think of fixed book prices as an example) and industrial policy (protection of national champions). The outcome of the political decision process may be explained as the result of lobbying by powerful interest groups. The problems created by the 'multiple goals' tradition of EU competition law and the ensuing normative conundrum of conflicting policy goals are a recurrent topic of this book.

3.9   Bibliography

Akman P (2012), *The Concept of Abuse in EU Competition Law: Law and Economic Approaches* (Hart Publishing)

Averitt N, Lande R (1997), 'Consumer Sovereignty: A Unified Theory of Antitrust and Consumer Protection Law' 65 *Antitrust Law Journal* 713

Baker J, Salop S (2015), 'Antitrust, Competition Policy, and Inequality' 104 *Georgetown Law Journal* 1

Behrens P (2015), 'The Ordoliberal Concept of "Abuse" of a Dominant Position and its Impact on Article 102 TFEU' (Proceedings of the 10th ASCOLA Conference Tokyo 2015) <https://ssrn.com/abstract=2658045>

Besanko D, Spulber D (1993), 'Contested Mergers and Equilibrium Antitrust Policy' 9 *Journal of Law, Economics, & Organization* 1

Bishop S (2013), 'Snake-Oil with Mathematics is Still Snake-Oil: Why Recent Trends in the Application of So-Called "Sophisticated" Economics is Hindering Good Competition Policy Enforcement' 9 *European Competition Journal* 67

Bork R (1978), *The Antitrust Paradox: A Policy at War with Itself* (Basic Books)

Bork R (1966), 'Legislative Intent and the Policy of the Sherman Act' 9 *Journal of Law and Economics* 7

Brodley J (1987), 'The Economic Goals of Antitrust: Efficiency, Consumer Welfare and Technological Progress' 62 *New York University Law Review* 1020

Buchanan J, Tullock G (1962), *The Calculus Of Consent* (University of Michigan Press)

Carlton D (2007), 'Does Antitrust Need to be Modernized?' 21 Journal of Economic Perspectives 155

Desogus C (2011), *Competition and Innovation in the EU Regulation of Pharmaceuticals: The Case of Parallel Trade* (Intersentia)

Ehlermann C, Laudati L (1998), *European Competition Annual 1997: Objectives of Competition Policy* (Hart)

Elman P (1969), 'The Robinson-Patman Act and Antitrust Policy: A Time for Reappraisal' 1 *Journal of Reprints for Antitrust Law and Economics* 561

Farmer S (2013), 'Recent Developments in Regulation and Competition Policy in China: Trends in Private Civil Litigation', in M Faure and X Zhang (eds.), *The Chinese Anti-Monopoly Law* 15 (Edward Elgar)

Farrell J, Katz M (2006), 'The Economics of Welfare Standards in Antitrust', 2 *Competition Policy International* 3

Fisher A, Johnson F, Lande R (1989), 'Price Effects of Horizontal Mergers' 77 *California Law Review* 777

Fisher A, Lande R, Vandaele W (1983), 'Could a Merger Lead to both Monopoly and Lower Price?' 71 *California Law Review* 1697

Fox E (1987), 'The Battle for the Soul of Antitrust' 75 *California Law Review* 917

Gerber D (2008), 'The Future of Article 82: Dissecting the Conflict', in C Ehlermann and M Marquis (eds.), *European Competition Law Annual 2007: A Reformed Approach to Article 82 EC* (Hart Publishing)

Gutmann J, Voigt S (2014), 'Lending a Hand to the Invisible Hand? Assessing the Effects of Newly Enacted Competition Laws' <https://ssrn.com/abstract=2392780>

Hicks J (1941), 'The rehabilitation of consumers' surplus', 8 *Review of Economic Studies* 108

Hofstadter R (1965), 'What Happened to the Antitrust Movement?', in R Hofstadter (ed.), *The Paranoid Style in American Politics and Other Essays* 188 (Alfred A. Knopf), reprinted in E Sullivan (ed.) (1991), *The Political Economy of the Sherman Act: The First One Hundred Years* 20 (Oxford University Press)

Hoppmann E (1968), 'Zum Problem einer wirtschaftspolitisch praktikablen Definition des Wettbewerbs', in H Schneider (ed.), *Grundlagen der Wettbewerbspolitik* 27 (Schriften des Vereins für Socialpolitik, N. F. Bd. 48)

Hovenkamp H (1994), *Federal Antitrust Policy. The Law of Competition and Its Practice* (West Publishing Company)

Hylton K, Deng F (2007), 'Antitrust Around the World: An Empirical Analysis of the Scope of Competition Laws and their Effects' 74 *Antitrust Law Journal* 271

ICN (2007), 'Report on the Objectives of Unilateral Conduct Laws, Assessment Of Dominance/Substantial Market Power, and State-Created Monopolies' <http://www.internationalcompetitionnetwork.org/uploads/library/doc353.pdf>

Kaldor N (1939), 'Welfare Propositions in Economics' 49 *Economic Journal* 549

Kaplow L, Shapiro C (2007), 'Antitrust', in M Polinsky and S Shavell (eds.), *Handbook of Law and Economics* II 1073 (North Holland)

Kaplow L, Shavell S (1994), 'Why the Legal System is Less Efficient than the Income Tax in Redistributing Income', 23 *Journal of Legal Studies* 667

Kerber W (2012), 'Competition, Innovation and Maintaining Diversity Through Competition Law', in J Drexl, W Kerber and R Podszun (eds), *Competition Policy and the Economic Approach* (Edward Elgar)

Kerber W (2009), 'Should Competition Law Promote Efficiency? Some Reflections of an Economist on the Normative Foundations of Competition Law', in J Drexl, L Idot and J Monéger (eds.), *Economic Theory and Competition Law* 93 (Edward Elgar)

Kirchner C (2007), 'Goals of Antitrust Revisited', in D Schmidtchen, M Albert and Voigt S (eds.), *The More Economic Approach To European Competition Law* 7 (Mohr Siebeck)

Lande R (2001), 'Consumer Choice as the Ultimate Goal of Antitrust' 62 *University of Pittsburgh Law Review* 503

Lande R (1999), 'Proving the Obvious: The Antitrust Laws Were Passed to Protect Consumers (Not Just to Increase Efficiency)' 50 *Hastings Law Journal* 959

Lande R (1989), 'Chicago's False Foundation: Wealth Transfers (not just Efficiency) Should Guide Antitrust' 58 *Antitrust Law Journal* 631

Lande R (1982), 'Wealth Transfers as the Original and Primary Concern of Antitrust: The Efficiency Interpretation Challenged' 34 *Hastings Law Journal* 65

Lianos I (2013), 'Some Reflections on the Question of the Goals of EU Competition Law', in I Lianos and D Geradin (eds.), *Handbook On European Competition Law: Substantive Aspects* 1 (Edward Elgar)

Ma T-C (2011), 'The Effect of Competition Law Enforcement on Economic Growth' 7 *Journal of Competition Law & Economics* 334

Malueg D, Schwartz M (1994), 'Parallel Imports, Demand Dispersion and International Price Discrimination' 37 *Journal of International Economics* 167

Martin S (1994), *Industrial Economics. Economic Analysis and Public Policy* (Macmillan Publishing, 2nd ed.)

McChesney F, Shughart W (eds.) (1995), *The Causes and Consequences of Antitrust. The Public-Choice Perspective* (University of Chicago Press)

Mezines B (1973), *The Robinson-Patman Act: A Current Appraisal* (Federal Trade Commission)

Motta M (2004), *Competition Policy. Theory and Practice* (Cambridge University Press)

Neal P (1976), 'Let's Reform It' 45 *ABA Antitrust Law Journal* 52

Neven D, Röller L (2000), 'Consumer Surplus vs, Welfare Standard in a Political Economy Model of Merger Control', CEPR Discussion Papers No. 2620

Nozick R (1974), *Anarchy, State and Utopia* (Basic Books)

Orbach B (2011), 'The Antitrust Consumer Welfare Paradox' 7 *Journal of Competition Law & Economics* 133

Petersen N (2013), 'Antitrust Law and the Promotion of Democracy and Economic Growth' 9 *Journal of Competition Law & Economics* 593

Rey P (2003), *The Impact of Parallel Imports on Prescription Medicines*, Mimeo

Ringstad V (2004), 'On the Cultural Blessings of Fixed Book Prices' 10 *International Journal of Cultural Policy* 351

Schumacher E (1974), *Small Is Beautiful: A Study of Economics as if People Mattered* (Blond & Briggs)

Stigler G (1985), 'The Origin of the Sherman Act' 14 *Journal of Legal Studies* 1

Stucke M (2012), 'Reconsidering Antitrust's Goals' 53 *Boston College Law Review* 551

Sullivan E (ed.) (1991), *The Political Economy of the Sherman Act, The First One Hundred Years* (Oxford University Press)

Van den Bergh R (1996), 'Economic Criteria for Applying the Subsidiarity Principle in the European Community: The Case of Competition Policy' 16 *International Review of Law and Economics* 363

Van den Bergh R, Camesasca P (2000), 'Irreconcilable Principles? The Court of Justice Exempts Collective Labour Agreements from the Wrath of Antitrust' 25 *European Law Review* 492

Varian H (1985), 'Price Discrimination and Social Welfare' 75 *American Economic Review* 870

Von Hayek F (1967), *Studies in Philosophy, Politics and Economics* (Routledge)

Zimmer D (ed.) (2012), *The Goals of Competition Law* (Edward Elgar)

4

Market power, market definition and entry barriers

Roger Van den Bergh, Peter Camesasca and Andrea Giannaccari

4.1 Introduction

The crucial concern of competition policy is the possible inefficiencies of market power. Before addressing the ways in which market power is acquired and exploited, the preliminary question of how market power may be identified must be addressed. The establishment of market power is the central issue of this chapter. Definitions of market power, which may be found in the economic literature on industrial organisation, are influenced by the characteristics of the model of perfect competition. For example, in their classic textbook, Denis Carlton and Jeoffrey Perloff define market power as 'the ability of a firm to set price profitably above competitive levels (marginal costs)' (Carlton and Perloff 2005, 642). Many industrial economics books equally refer to discretion over price (the extent to which firms can hold price above marginal cost, measured by the Lerner index) as the relevant test for market power (Hildebrand 2006; Motta 2004, 102; see also Martin 1994, 14). The economic literature further emphasises that market power causes concerns from a competition policy viewpoint only if prices can be kept above the competitive level (through output restrictions) for a sustained period of time, because of the existence of entry barriers. If firms cannot easily enter and exit a market, incumbent firms enjoying market power may deploy forms of anti-competitive behaviour enabling them to earn supra-normal economic profits by hindering the growth of other firms and impeding the entry of newcomers.

The economic definition, which focuses on an individual firm's pricing discretion in the absence of entry barriers, differs from the traditional definition of a dominant firm found in European competition law. The relevant case law of the Court of Justice of the European Union (CJEU) defines market power in terms of independent behaviour in markets as 'a position of economic strength enjoyed by an undertaking which enables it to prevent effective competition being maintained on the relevant market by giving it the power to behave to an appreciable extent independently of its competitors, customers, and, ultimately, consumers'.[1] Whereas the economic definition emphasises the ability of a firm to keep prices above competitive levels for the near future, the traditional legal definition focuses on the degree of independence of firms and is not restricted to a focus on price. From a mainstream industrial organisation perspective, the emphasis on the degree of independence is rather odd, since even a monopolist cannot behave independently without taking account of potential entrants' responses. In addition, price is commonly considered as a useful proxy for other types of consumer harm (Kaplow and Shapiro 2007). Conversely, according to the definition of market power in the case law, concerns about limitations of the market participants' economic freedom[2] and protection of consumers' choices (product quality, innovation, product variety) should explicitly be taken into consideration. In more recent policy documents, the European Commission proposes to link the traditional economic and legal approaches by defining an undertaking as dominant if it is capable of profitably increasing prices above the competitive level for a significant period of time without facing sufficiently effective competitive constraints.[3]

The most striking difference between economic and legal definitions of market power is the emphasis on market definition issues in the legal writings. Application of the relevant competition rules requires competition lawyers to define the boundaries of the relevant market where market power is exercised. In many competition law cases, the outcome falls neatly from the resolution of the market definition issue. The market shares held by competitors in the relevant market are seen as an indication of their relative market power. In narrowly defined markets, mergers may be blocked and exclusionary practices of dominant firms may be prohibited which, if a wider market definition had been adopted, could have been cleared. Ill-defined relevant markets will have the consequence that the prohibitions of competition law

---

[1] Case 27/76 *United Brands v. Commission* [1978] ECR 207; see also case 85/76 *Hoffmann-La Roche v. Commission (Vitamins)* [1979] ECR 461.

[2] This approach can be related to the discussion on the goals of competition law: allocative efficiency and/or protection of individual economic freedom. See section 3.5 for an elaboration.

[3] Communication from the Commission — Guidance on the Commission's enforcement priorities in applying Article 82 of the EC Treaty to abusive exclusionary conduct by dominant undertakings (2009/C 45/02), at paras 9–22; see also Horizontal Guidelines, at 39; 'Market power is the ability to profitably maintain prices above competitive levels for a period of time or to profitably maintain output in terms of product quantities, product quality and variety or innovation below competitive levels for a period of time' (*Guidelines on the applicability of Article 101 of the Treaty on the Functioning of the European Union to horizontal co-operation agreements*, O.J. 14.1.2011, C 11/10).

are either over-inclusive or under-inclusive (type I and type II errors).[4] The quality of the study of industrial organisation is not similarly dependent on market definition decisions. The common approach of defining markets and assessing market shares does not play a central role in the economics of market power. The irrelevance of the market definition/market share paradigm explains why the economists' profession has, for a long time, not offered much practical help to the competition lawyers' community in establishing reliable economic criteria allowing a delineation of relevant markets for legal purposes. Since the 1990s, together with a greater openness towards economic arguments on the lawyers' side, economic input in competition law cases has become increasingly important.

The next issue on which lawyers' view differs from the economic approach is the analysis of entry barriers. The traditional legal definition does not explicitly mention entry barriers as a constitutive element of dominance. Consequently, high market shares are generally seen as the major indicator of antitrust problems. Rather than serving as an argument to deny the existence of market power when they are absent, the presence of entry barriers may be advanced as constitutive elements of dominance in cases where market shares are low. Most notably, product differentiation and advertising are commonly quoted in the case law as elements that confer a dominant position on firms possessing only moderate market shares. Again, the legal and economic approaches differ. Economic theory makes clear that market power can be exercised for a significant period only if barriers to market entry exist. The theory of contestable markets (see section 2.8), which is the most dramatic exponent of this view, even questions the desirability of antitrust intervention in cases of monopoly. Generally, if markets are easily accessible and if new entrants can leave without impediments, the threat of new entry will withhold incumbent firms from raising prices above competitive levels. Economists agree that government regulation making market entrance dependent on the possession of a licence is an important entry barrier. Opinions differ, however, on the extent to which private firms themselves may create entry barriers through exclusionary behaviour by raising rivals' costs. In addition, the question of whether product differentiation and advertising may be used to deter market entry is a subject of great controversy.

---

[4] Unfortunately, the terms 'type I error' and 'type II error' as well as the expressions 'false positives' and 'false negatives' are not used in a consistent way in the legal and economic literature. In this book, a type I error (false positive) denotes an erroneous prohibition of a conduct which would have increased welfare. Conversely, a type II error (false negative) refers to a conduct generating negative welfare effects which is wrongly allowed. This is the classification most common in the antitrust literature. For a different classification, see: Polinsky and Shavell (1989).

This chapter is structured as follows. After this introduction, sections 4.2 to 4.5 discuss methods of market definition for antitrust purposes (hence, for establishing market shares) and relate them to the economic concept of market power. Section 4.2 elaborates the economic definition of market power. It introduces a number of economic concepts that are crucial for determining the degree of market power: the Lerner index, the market elasticity of demand and the firm's elasticity of demand. Section 4.3 discusses the traditional legal definition of a relevant market, which focuses on the (dis) similar characteristics of different products and the (lack of) homogeneity of competitive conditions in different regions. Products are seen as belonging to the same relevant market if they have similar characteristics, uses and price: in other words, when they are 'reasonably interchangeable' or potential substitutes (in cases of non-homogeneous goods). Regions are seen as being part of the same geographical market if the conditions of competition in those areas are sufficiently homogeneous. Attention is paid to the extensive criticisms of these old-fashioned definitions: the risk of subjective decisions, regulatory capture, arbitrariness and the over-emphasis on cross-price elasticity (for measuring the degree of substitutability) as the relevant econometric measure. Besides the pitfalls of the traditional legal approach, section 4.3 also stresses the potential confusion among economists with regard to market definition issues.

Section 4.4 introduces the SSNIP methodology, which claims to give a reflection of economic learning on the market share–market power paradigm. SSNIP is the abbreviation of 'Small but Significant and Non-transitory Increase in Price'; the SSNIP test asks which products and geographical locations a hypothetical monopolist would need to control in order to impose such a price increase. Particular attention is devoted to the European Commission's Notice on market definition:[5] it is investigated in how far the guidance offered in this Notice coincides with economic theory. Section 4.5 introduces modern econometric techniques to measure market power empirically. Attention is successively paid to the estimation of demand elasticity, price correlation tests, critical loss analysis and shipment tests for defining relevant geographical markets. In addition, the relevance of qualitative evidence, in particular surveys, for market delineation purposes is discussed. Section 4.6 takes up the suggestion to abandon market definition (because of its many pitfalls) and to define market power directly. In the context of merger control, this may be done with quantitative techniques, such as simulation models and diversion ratios. Even though in this way some of the criticisms relating to the market share–market power paradigm

---

[5] Commission Notice on the definition of the relevant market for the purposes of Community competition law [1997] O.J. C 372/1.

may be overcome, direct assessments of market power that bypass the stage of market definition pose their own problems. Throughout sections 4.2 to 4.6, comparisons of EU competition law with US antitrust law are made to allow an overall assessment of the (dis)harmony between the state of the art in economics and the current rules of competition law. In addition, case discussions can be found in separate boxes: they provide real-life examples that aptly illustrate the problems faced by competition authorities and judges in defining relevant antitrust markets.

In section 4.7, the emphasis shifts to the analysis of entry barriers. As indicated above, market power may be exercised in the long run only if firms face difficulties in entering markets and incumbents are thus protected from competition by newcomers. Empirical research grounded in the Structure-Conduct-Performance paradigm indicated a great number of entry barriers, including economies of scale, product differentiation and advertising. It will be investigated how modern industrial organisation has reshaped thinking on these issues and how current competition law assesses alleged barriers to entry. Intellectual property rights (in particular patents and copyright) are a particular form of entry barriers. On the one hand, they confer monopoly power on their owners enabling them to limit entry and earn monopoly profits. On the other hand, the gains achieved may be defended from a dynamic perspective if they contribute to a higher degree of innovation. The trade-off between static inefficiency (high prices) and dynamic efficiency (innovation) surfaces also in real-life cases (see Box 4.4 devoted to intellectual property rights). Section 4.8 concludes.

4.2   Economic definition of market power

The standard theoretical economic approach assesses the degree of market power as an increase in the Lerner index (Lerner 1934). A firm in a perfectly competitive market faces a perfectly elastic (horizontal) demand curve and is said to possess no market power, since it can only act as a price-taker. By contrast, a monopolist sets its price at the point on the demand curve where marginal cost equals marginal revenue. The Lerner index formalises this concept of market power as the setting of price in excess of marginal cost by measuring the proportional deviation of price at the firm's profit-maximising output from the firm's marginal cost at that output. Its simplest formulation is:

$$L = \frac{(P - MC)}{P}$$

The Lerner index thus measures the difference between price and marginal cost; the greater the deviation between these standards of measurement, the greater the market power of the firm and the ensuing allocative inefficiency. By re-arranging the above formula, the mark-up factor can be defined as $1/(1 - L)$. The higher the elasticity of demand for the firm's product at the firm's profit-maximising price, the closer that price will be to the competitive price, and the less, therefore, the monopoly overcharge will be. If the elasticity of demand is infinite at the firm's profit-maximising price, the Lerner index equals zero. An infinite elasticity in demand means that the slightest increase in price will cause the quantity demanded to fall to zero. Conversely, as long as the firm is in the inelastic region of its demand curve (where the elasticity of demand is less than one), prices may be profitably raised (for a more elaborate analysis, see Motta 2004, 116; Tirole 1988, 66).

Due to information problems (size of marginal cost), the practical relevance of the marginal cost concept is very limited. Therefore, antitrust economics has focused mainly on the elasticity of demand to determine market power (Landes and Posner 1981, 941). It is important to distinguish between the elasticity of demand for a product[6] and the elasticity of demand faced by a firm. The former concept refers to the impact of the change in price on the market's demand; the latter concept includes any changes in demand for the firm's product after a price rise, as a result of any induced changes in the price of competing products. Since the Lerner index is a measure for the firm's market power, the relevant elasticity is the firm's elasticity of demand, for it is the response of the firm's output to a change in price that determines the degree to which it has market power (Landes and Posner 1981, 940–941). It may be shown that the proportionate price-cost margin charged by a profit-maximising firm is equal to the reciprocal of the absolute value of the price elasticity of demand faced by that firm. This elasticity itself has two components: first, the direct own-price elasticity of demand for the product(s) produced by the firm, and, second, the indirect sum of the cross-price elasticities with respect to competing products because of changes in the prices set by other firms.[7]

The market power of a firm (or group of firms) is limited by the degree of both demand substitution and supply substitution. The residual demand

---

[6] In general, the elasticity of demand for a product describes what happens when the price of that product changes, holding constant the prices of all other products.

[7] Own-price product demand elasticity is negative, and measures the extent to which a firm can raise the price of its product without experiencing a decline in total revenue. The cross-elasticities measure the extent to which changes in the prices of related products affect the sales of the product in question, and will be positive if products are substitutes. The induced changes in price of competing products will be positive if firms coordinate their behaviour and negative if they compete aggressively.

elasticity captures both competitive constraints. Unfortunately, its direct measurement by advanced econometric techniques requires extensive, reliable data and is therefore (very) difficult (Perekhozhuk et al. 2016; Kerber and Schwalbe 2006, 184 and 196–199). As mentioned above, in daily antitrust practice the most common way to define market power is by calculating market shares on a relevant market. To gear the use of market shares to the economic concept of market power, the so-called SSNIP test has been developed. It will be examined in section 4.4 of this chapter whether market shares are a reliable indicator for the degree of market power of the firm(s) under investigation, if use is made of the SSNIP methodology.

4.3 Definition of the relevant market

The economic definition implies that the degree of market power may be measured directly if the relevant figures about price and marginal cost are known. If the figures needed for direct measurement are not available, market power can be assessed only in an indirect way. The common approach in both US antitrust law and EU competition law requires market definition and an assessment of market power by relying on the size of market shares held by particular firms. Market definition is a necessary preliminary step before the analysis of competitive effects. High market shares are generally seen as an indicator of antitrust worries whereas low market shares provide firms with a 'safe harbour', a place free of antitrust scrutiny.

Market shares of 50–70% in US antitrust law and 40–60% in EU competition law are generally considered sufficient evidence of the ability to monopolise (US Sherman Act) or the possession of a dominant position (Article 102 TFEU). Exclusionary practices may be prohibited if the firm tries to monopolise the relevant market or abuses its dominant position according to the legal definitions of monopolisation (Section 2 Sherman Act) or abuse of dominance (Article 102 TFEU). If information about market shares is available, concentration indices (such as the CR4 and the HHI)[8] can be calculated also. Mergers may be blocked if the post-merger firm increases the degree of concentration above the legal threshold for merger control. Hence, in day-to-day antitrust practice, definition of relevant markets and calculation of market shares are common and give rise to a market definition/market share paradigm. However, one should always firmly keep in mind that market shares derived from relevant markets are not more than a proxy for market power. If market power can be measured directly by using

---

[8] The CR 4 is computed by summing up the market shares of the four largest firms in the relevant market, whereas the Herfindahl–Hirschman index (HHI) is the sum of the squares of the market shares held by all firms. For further discussion and comments, see Chapter 9, section 9.2.2.

reliable econometric techniques, the exercise of market definition may become superfluous.

Within the framework of the so-called More Economic Approach, the increasing reliance on market shares has been presented as an economically oriented approach, to contrast it with the legalistic tradition of EU competition law. However, it is misleading to present rules based on market shares as an (or even 'the') economic approach to all kinds of competition law problems. Rather, the concept of a relevant market should be qualified as the last legalistic bulwark of a competition law that only gradually, and often reluctantly, evolves towards economic analysis. There are several reasons why it may be misleading to present market share analysis as 'the' economic approach to problems of competition law. To start with, dynamic economic approaches to competition law reject market definition as a tool of decision-making. The Schumpeterian view, which perceives competition as a process of fierce rivalry, discovery and spontaneous coordination, implies that the market cannot be easily divided into various segments. At this point, also the German theory of freedom of competition may be recalled (see section 2.6). In the latter conceptual approach, both the market and the process of competition are seen as unique and indivisible. Every single euro the consumer spends on buying a certain product cannot be spent on other purchases. Consequently, all firms compete with each other to get the largest possible share of the consumer's purchases. For example: if the price of apples increases, consumers may switch to other fruits (pears, bananas, peaches) but also decide to consume less fruit and spend their money on other food products (chocolate, ice cream) or different necessities (washing powder, make-up, electric appliances). According to the theory of *Wettbewerbsfreiheit*, the exercise of market definition is meaningless, since all products compete with all remaining products. The above criticisms on the market delineation exercise are a reminder that the relevant market is a concept that builds upon the Structure-Conduct-Performance paradigm, which relates market performance to market structure. However, market definition is superfluous in an approach – such as the German concept of freedom of competition – that makes only a distinction between permitted and prohibited practices (Schmidtchen 1988, 130–132; Hoppmann 1977).

The dynamic views on competition are not the only part of the antitrust literature that rejects market share analysis altogether. Within the structuralist framework, which relates high consumer prices to increased concentration, efforts to formally define a relevant market are criticised as time-consuming, unduly costly and unnecessary when the size of future price increases may be predicted by using reliable econometric techniques. After all, as Richard

Posner wrote already in 1976: '[i]t is only because we lack confidence in our ability to measure elasticities, or perhaps because we do not think of adopting so explicitly an economic approach that we have to define markets instead (…)'[9] The use of an indirect approach often focuses attention on market definition, not on the fundamental question of market power. This may lead to biased decisions, in which the market is defined in such a way that an infringement of the competition rules becomes unquestionable. The most recent developments in the antitrust scene have suggested to abandon market definition altogether in favour of a direct assessment of the competitive effects resulting from particular types of conduct (Kaplow 2010). This section discusses the traditional legal (indirect) approach to market power and elaborates on the risks that a misguided use of market share analysis poses for antitrust law. Misunderstandings of an antitrust market may be caused not only by formalistic legal approaches but also by inadequate definitions of a 'market' in the economic discipline. The desirability of abandoning the market share/market power paradigm will be discussed in section 4.6. It will then become clear that also a direct assessment of market power that bypasses the delineation of a relevant antitrust market poses problems of its own.

4.3.1 Market definition: case law

In competition law cases, three consecutive steps are common. First, a relevant market is defined. This market definition process is aiming at choosing between different candidate markets the (relevant) market which most accurately depicts the extent of market power. Second, the competitive surroundings on the relevant market are analysed, paying particular attention to the number of suppliers. This allows it to be established how market shares are distributed among competitors and for the market share of the firm(s) under antitrust scrutiny to be measured. Third, competition analysts infer from the market share the degree of market power and assess it against the applicable legal standard.

The traditional definitions of the relevant product and geographical markets can be traced back in a number of leading cases on both sides of the Atlantic. In the *Du Pont* (Cellophane) case, the US Supreme Court enunciated the standard for product market definition by holding that two products are in

---

[9] Quote from Posner (1976, 125). More recently, similar views have been expressed by other commentators: 'From the perspective of economic theory, antitrust law's preoccupation with market definition has always seemed somewhat peculiar. Arguments for and against a merger that turn upon distinctions between broad and narrow market definition are, to an economic pursuit, an inadequate substitute for, and a diversion from direct assessment (…)' (Ordover and Wall 1989, 20–21).

the same market if they are 'reasonably interchangeable'.[10] Unfortunately, the percentage of interchangeability required has never been set (nor would this seem possible), while the presence of substitutes is not necessarily an indication of the absence of market power (as was held in *Du Pont*, see the discussion below in section 4.4.2). Following the concept of reasonable interchangeability, the CJEU has defined the relevant product market as comprising all those products and/or services that are regarded as interchangeable or substitutable by the consumer because of the products' characteristics, their prices and their intended use.[11] The definition of the relevant geographical market has been focused on the homogeneity of competitive conditions. It is the area in which the conditions of competition are sufficiently homogeneous and which can be distinguished from neighbouring areas because the conditions of competition are appreciably different in those areas.

Over the years, market definition issues have been given an ever-increasing importance. For example, the US Merger Guidelines have been using concentration ratios (HHI index) to classify mergers in different categories that reflect their relative impact on the functioning of competition in the relevant antitrust market (see section 9.3.2). Under the EU competition rules low market shares may guarantee antitrust immunity to firms (see, for example, the 'safe harbours' in the Guidelines on horizontal cooperation, the Regulation on vertical restraints and the Merger Regulation).[12] Obviously, the quality of the decisions based on market shares is crucially dependent on the value of the market definition exercise. There is a risk that the market definition may be biased towards finding an infringement of the competition rules. But even if markets are appropriately defined, one should be careful not to underestimate or overestimate the conclusions that can be drawn from market share analysis.

Both US antitrust law and EU competition law offer a number of cases that allow a good understanding of the inherent risks and limitations of the market definition exercise. In *Brown Shoe*, the US Supreme Court distinguished three distinct markets for shoes: men's shoes, women's shoes and children's shoes.[13] This conclusion followed from an examination of the characteristics of those three product groups, following the traditional legal definition of a relevant market as a group of products that are substitutable. Today, antitrust analysts will no longer distinguish three different sub-markets for shoes. The

---

[10] See *United States v. E.I. DuPont de Nemours & Co. (Cellophane)*, 351 US 377 (1956, 394–395).

[11] *United Brands* case; *Vitamins* case, both cited *supra*, note 1.

[12] For discussion of these legislative documents, see sections 5.3, 6.4.2 and 9.4, respectively. All other 'modern' block exemptions also contain market share based 'safe harbours'.

[13] *Brown Shoe Co v United States*, 370 U.S. 294 (1962).

analysis of the Supreme Court focused only on demand substitution and erroneously omitted the possibility of supply substitution. In deciding whether to increase the price of men's shoes, manufacturers are not only limited by potential responses of buyers but also by the possibility of manufacturers adapting their production machines and switching from manufacturing women's and children's shoes to men's shoes. If such supply substitution is easy, all three types of shoes belong to the same relevant market.

The leading case in Europe of ill-defined markets is *United Brands*, also known as the 'banana fallacy'. In this well-known case, the CJEU defined a relevant market for bananas, based upon the specific characteristics of this type of fruit, making it particularly suitable for specific consumer groups, including the very old and very young consumers. The banana case is further discussed in Box 4.1. From this discussion, one may learn that there likely is a wider market for fresh fruit and that distinguishing between consumer groups for purposes of market definition makes economic sense only if price discrimination is feasible. This classic European case offers a nice illustration of the difficulties competition law enforcers will encounter if they heavily rely on (differences in) product characteristics for defining relevant markets.

Box 4.1: The banana case

Among the oldest EU competition law cases, *United Brands* (Chiquita)[14] still manages to be referred to as a 'classic'. Concerning the relevant product market, the CJEU stated that this was formed by bananas (as distinguished from the wider market of fresh fruit in general). The Court reached this conclusion in alluding to the banana's special product attributes (such as appearance, taste, softness, seedlessness and easy handling), which enable it to satisfy the constant needs of an important section of the population consisting of 'the very young, the old, and the sick'.[15] Furthermore, bananas are characterised by an uninterrupted level of production, leading to limited effects on price competition from other fresh fruit (such as grapes and peaches) at the banana's seasonal peak periods. These considerations, so the CJEU inferred, outweighed others such as the fall in price of, and the demand for, bananas at times when more fruits are available, as the latter showed merely a limited interchangeability.[16]

---

[14] Case 27/76 *United Brands v. Commission* [1978] ECR 207. The issue before the CJEU was whether United Brands' pricing and distribution policy for bananas was in breach of Article 102 TFEU.

[15] *Ibid.*, at para. 34.

[16] Indeed, '[f]or the banana to be regarded as forming a market which is sufficiently differentiated from other fruit markets it must be possible for it to be singled out by such special factors distinguishing it from other fruits that it is only to a limited extent interchangeable with them and is only exposed to their competition in a way that is hardly perceptible'; see Case 27/76 *United Brands v. Commission* [1978] ECR 207, para. 22.

By ruling out the existence of significant cross-price elasticities between bananas and other summer fruits, this case depicts well the risks attached to delineating markets based solely on product characteristics. There is no convincing economic reason for a market defined so narrowly as to exclude melons, strawberries, plums and the like. Besides, *United Brands* highlights the limited applicability of the cross-elasticity concept as a stand-alone device for defining relevant antitrust markets. The issue is not whether certain groups of customers have strong preferences for the product in question, but whether, for a 5% or 10% increase above the competitive price, generally significant inter-product substitution would take place. The fact that particular groups of consumers (in the CJEU's vision of things: the 'toothless', being the very young, the old and the sick) will perceive differences in product characteristics when comparing bananas, peaches, pears and other types of fresh fruit does not allow for the conclusion that price increases for bananas will be profitable. Identifying a distinct sub-group of consumers is possible only in those cases where it may be established that producers can effectively distinguish between such sub-groups (*in casu* between those consumers able to chew and the toothless), thus barring arbitrage. If this would seem an impossible task, then United Brands' alleged position of dominance could not be abused. In its Notice on market definition, the European Commission has meanwhile acknowledged that the scope for narrow markets is dependent on the feasibility of price discrimination: '[a] distinct group of customers for the relevant product may constitute a narrower, distinct market when such a group could be subject to price discrimination. This will usually be the case when two conditions are met: first, it is possible to identify clearly which group an individual customer belongs to at the moment of selling the relevant products to him, and, second, trade among customers or arbitrage by third parties should not be feasible' (Market Definition Notice, at 43). This has been an important innovative aspect, as the European Commission in more recent cases seems less inclined to conclude upon separate narrow sub-markets.[17]

4.3.2 Problems on the lawyers' side: pitfalls of the traditional legal approach

Criticisms of the market definition/market share paradigm in everyday antitrust practice have been extensive (Kaplow 2010; Camesasca and Van den Bergh 2002; Werden 2002). Quite regularly, the use of an indirect approach in assessing market power leads to focusing the attention on market definition, not on the fundamental question of the potentially anti-competitive

---

[17] In the *Veba/Degussa* merger, for example, the Commission declined to separate isophoron diamines from the overall market of diamines (hardeners for epoxy resin systems used in varnishes, steel and concrete coatings), although they make up 30% of the value of the total market and it had been established that up to 20% of the applied isophoron diamines are limited in their substitutability (Case IV/M.942 *Veba/Degussa* [1998] O.J. L 201/102, para. 33).

(exclusionary) effects of market power. Whatever market shares may mean, their interpretation depends on how the market is defined. In a market too narrowly defined, a high share does not carry much information. In a market defined overly broadly, a low share does not allow any conclusion either. The concept of a relevant market, in the end, is but a deliberate attempt, for the sake of workability, to oversimplify the very complex interactions between a number of diversely situated buyers and sellers, each of whom has in reality different costs, needs and substitutes. Market definition only provides a foundation on which it is possible to evaluate likely competitive effects. It is definitely not an end in itself.

If market definition becomes the goal of the assessment by the competition authority, rather than an instrument to understand better the antitrust problems at hand, decisions in real-world cases may be biased. This risk is particularly severe when the old-fashioned legal definition focusing on product characteristics is used. The policy problems which may then arise are numerous: lack of transparency leading to large discretionary powers of competition authorities, danger of regulatory capture[18] and lack of objectivity. There is indeed no clear benchmark against which the degree of substitution must be measured and, consequently, it is not clear how much substitution is necessary to speak of a relevant market. In the literature, serious concerns have been expressed with respect to the risk of subjective decisions. It has been noted that the European Commission did not always establish dominance independently, but tended to determine that an abuse had occurred and then defined the market in such a way that dominance became unquestionable. These concerns are substantiated by examples of market definitions including non-substitutable goods (such as the market for 'vitamins')[19] or findings of dominance in cases of quite modest firms. An example of the latter is the *Hugin* case,[20] in which the relevant product market was identified by the CJEU as spare parts for cash registers manufactured by Hugin required by independent undertakings. Hugin had argued that the relevant market was to be cash registers as a whole, where the company had a market share of only 13%.[21] Although touching on the fascinating issue of aftermarkets, the

---

[18] Political theory explains that decisions tend to benefit regulated industries since the regulator is dependent on information provided by the regulated firms in those industries. The concept of regulatory capture, which is grounded in information deficiencies, should not be confused with the problem of corruption.

[19] In *Hoffmann-La Roche*, the complaint was directed against fidelity rebates based on aggregate purchases of the whole range of vitamins produced by the company. The CJEU relied on the company's share of particular vitamins to prohibit a strategy that applied to the whole range. Clearly, the relevant market cannot include all vitamins because they are not substitutable by either consumers or producers. Consequently, the Court's decision thus ultimately rests on fudging the market concept. See Utton (2003, 79).

[20] Case 22/78 *Hugin v. Commission* [1979] ECR 1869.

[21] *Hugin*, at paras 3–4.

CJEU did not pose the relevant questions to decide under what circumstances aftermarkets may constitute a separate antitrust market.[22] Obviously, the boundaries of the market should not be contracted in such a way that it becomes possible to identify the accused firm as a dominant producer within it. If not done objectively, distinguishing between products inside and outside the boundaries of a relevant market may wrongly depict the market's competitiveness in some instances and be arbitrary in others (Fisher 2001, 562).

The relevance of market shares and concentration indices is not only dependent upon the objectivity of the definition of the market in question. It also depends on the characteristics of the markets under scrutiny and the type of anti-competitive effects encountered. Market shares may give reliable indications as to whether markets for homogeneous goods are conducive to collusion, but will be less reliable indicators of antitrust worries when anti-competitive effects in differentiated product markets arise.[23] Market shares will be difficult to calculate and, even if those difficulties can be overcome, they will only give an imperfect indication of the intensity of competition in differentiated product markets (see already Chamberlin 1950, 86–87; compare Schmalensee 1982, 1800). The market definition exercise is inherently complex and difficult in such settings. There is no obvious chain of substitutes; competition authorities and judges may disagree as to whether to include particular substitutes. Even if a ranking of substitutes can be made, it will be still unclear where the boundaries of the relevant product market must be drawn. As will be clarified below, this problem is not mitigated but rather exacerbated when figures on cross-price elasticities are used in applying the traditional legal definition. The ultimate result may be multiple competing market definitions (Rubinfeld 2000, 177). The next problem in differentiated goods markets is that low market shares may overestimate the competitive constraints between products. In particular, cases where there is also a (relatively) low market share may confer price discretion to a firm, enabling it to charge supra-competitive prices. A prime example is merger control, where concerns arise not only when coordination of prices between a smaller number of competitors becomes likely but also when the post-

---

[22] Later enforcement decisions have brought more clarity on this issue. In its 1997 Guidelines on Market Definition, the European Commission concedes that a narrow definition of markets for secondary products (spare parts are explicitly mentioned) should result only when compatibility with the primary product is important, together with the existence of high prices and a long lifetime of the primary product. See for further discussion: Camesasca and Van den Bergh (2002).

[23] Products can be differentiated in a number of ways, including characteristics relating to the product itself (such as brands, physical characteristics or utility for the end user), or relating to how and to whom the product is sold (such as channels of distribution and targeted customers). See, for an overview, Keyte (1995, 701–703).

merger firm is able to unilaterally increase its prices (without engaging in co-ordinating behaviour). Also, when mergers do not lead to high market shares, competitive constraints may be substantially weakened. This may necessitate antitrust intervention to avoid lasting supra-normal profits (see section 9.2 for a discussion).

The adequacy of market definition is particularly questionable in high-technology markets, which exhibit constantly changing products that have parallel uses and overlapping functionalities (Newman 2015). To the above problems, the difficulties of assessing competition on two-sided markets must be added. A prominent example of such markets is social media, where information is provided at no cost to users of search engines and the operation of the latter is subsidised by financial contributions of advertisers. Market definition may become very complex and difficult to handle in this case. At any rate, market definition should not take place in a vacuum (in-dependent from the potential abusive behaviour) and a direct assessment of the competition effects of particular practices may be preferable to relying on imperfect indicators of market power (Salop 2000, 191–192).

In the US, the criticisms on the market share/market power paradigm have started to exert a clear impact on antitrust authorities and judges. Whereas EU competition law still largely cherishes the traditional market definition exercise, its US counterpart increasingly recognises that direct measurement of market power by making use of econometric techniques (figures about price elasticity and diversion ratios) may be a superior way of determining market power in the antitrust context. In US merger control less emphasis is now put on traditional methods of market definition in determining the market players' positions and, ultimately, market power. Simulation models, diversion ratios and price-concentration analyses are commonly applied techniques for directly assessing market power, in particular the anti-competitive unilateral effects of proposed mergers. These and other techniques will be further discussed in Chapter 9 on merger control (see section 9.3.2). Besides merger control, the message that direct estimates of market power may be preferred as alternative to traditional market definition exercises has also reached the US judiciary. In *Eastman Kodak* it was found that 'price elasticities are better measures of market power'[24] as compared with a pure market share approach. In an earlier case, a US court argued 'if market power is

---

[24] *United States v. Eastman Kodak Co.*, 853 F. Supp. 1454 (W.D.N.Y. 1994), aff'd, 63 F.3d 95 (2d Cir. 1995), at 1472. After having established Kodak's market shares in the US to be 67% of unit sales and 75% of dollar sales, the Court followed the econometric analysis conducted (based on the analysis of scanner data of film purchases), which revealed film purchasers to be price sensitive, in concluding that Kodak does not possess market power.

the ability to raise prices and maintain such prices above competitive levels, then a high degree of price sensitivity in a market exemplifies a lack of market power.'[25] Such a clear opening towards direct estimates of market power cannot (yet) be observed in European competition law, where market definition seems to remain the last legalistic bulwark of competition law.

4.3.3 Problems on the economists' side: possible misconceptions about the relevant antitrust market

Not only lawyers but also economists may be criticised for having adopted market definitions that are not suitable for competition law purposes. The exercise of defining a relevant market has as its ultimate goal to identify the most important competitive constraints that exist between products and regions. In everyday antitrust practice, the definition of the relevant market must capture the products and regions where the firms under antitrust scrutiny compete with other firms for obtaining buyers' preferences. The relevant market is the market where this battle takes place. Concepts of markets that do not capture the limitations on profitable lasting price increases are misleading. Here, three such misleading concepts will be presented: industries, economic markets and strategic markets (see also Geroski 1998).

Industries

As was explained in Chapter 2 of this book, Harvard scholars tended to base their investigations upon assessing competition effects in industries taken as a whole. In 1951, Joe Bain defined an industry as a group of products featuring high cross-price elasticities with each other, but low cross-price elasticities with other products (Bain 1951). The notion of a relevant market has its roots in the US Supreme Court's precedent law, which in turn was based on economic theory common at the time of the first major antitrust proceedings (Simons and Williams 1993, 799; Pitofsky 1990). In 1956, the US Supreme Court referred to Bain in its *Cellophane* ruling,[26] stressing the importance of assessing whether buyers could switch to substitute products and indicating cross-price elasticities as the standard of measurement to be determined econometrically. Two decades later, the CJEU, in its notorious *Chiquita* judgment (see Box 4.1), similarly applied the concept of cross-price elasticities. The Court defined the relevant product market as comprising 'the totality of products which, with respect to their characteristics, are

---

[25] *State of New York by Abrams v. Anheuser-Busch, Inc.*, 811 F. Supp. 848 (E.D.N.Y. 1993), at 873.
[26] *United States v. E.I. DuPont de Nemours & Co. (Cellophane)*, 351 US 377 (1956); para. 400.

particularly suitable for satisfying constant needs, and are only to a limited extent interchangeable with other products in terms of price, usage, and consumer preference.'[27]

Industry classifications as forwarded by Harvard scholars may at best be applied for statistical aims. However, they do not carry practical information for antitrust cases. The definition of an industry may not be confused with the relevant market in competition law, since the cross-price elasticities brought up by Bain may be inappropriate to decide pending antitrust cases. What can be learned from cross-price elasticities will be explained in the discussion of empirical techniques of market definition below (see section 4.5). Here, it should suffice to say that cross-price elasticities allow a ranking of substitutes but that, based on these figures alone, it remains unclear where the borderline between the different substitutes must be drawn, in order to delineate the relevant antitrust market. Only the (critical) residual demand elasticity at the firm's level allows for a direct delineation of the relevant market for antitrust purposes. In sum, one should be very cautious in drawing conclusions as to market definition based on cross-price elasticity figures.

Economic markets

The Bainian notion of an industry (and the related measurement of cross-price elasticities) is not the only potential cause of confusion surrounding the notion of a relevant market. The relevant market for antitrust purposes should equally not be confused with an economic market (or a strategic market). Economic markets (as defined in economics textbooks) are markets for goods (and/or geographical areas) where supply and demand lead to equilibrium. Put concisely, economic markets are areas where the law of one price holds (Marshall 1961, 325). In an economic market, if firm A increases its price, this may cause buyers to switch to firm B. Because of this 'arbitrage', B's output will increase and price differences will become smaller. This possibility of arbitrage tempers but does not necessarily eliminate the exercise of market power. It is not excluded that A is able to profitably increases its prices if not too many sales are lost to firm B (because B's output is relatively small and supply elasticity is low). In the example given, the relevant antitrust market is smaller than the economic market. Conversely, the relevant antitrust market may also be larger than the economic market. Two distant geographical areas, where homogeneous goods (produced competitively under constant marginal costs) are sold, may form two separate economic markets (since price levels are similar in each market considered individually) but constitute

---

[27] Case 27/76 *United Brands v. Commission* [1978] ECR 207, at paras 12 and 31.

a single antitrust market. Even if there is no similarity of price levels across both markets, an increase of prices in territory A may incite a producer in territory B to enter territory A if the transportation costs are lower than the price increase. This risk of entry may refrain producer A from imposing a price increase. In the latter case, the relevant antitrust market will comprise two territories with different price levels and thus consist of two separate economic markets (Scheffman and Spiller 1987, 127).

In sum, studies by econometricians showing positive price correlations between two or more products should be treated with care. Similarity of price movements over time allows the identification of an economic market, but does not automatically justify the conclusion that this economic market is also the relevant antitrust market. This insight will be further elaborated upon in Chapter 9 on merger control, where this type of econometric evidence is often used (see section 9.2.4).

Strategic markets

Another source of confusion among economists is the concept of a strategic market, which can be found in marketing literature (Kotler and Armstrong 2013). Strategic markets comprise consumer groups and geographical territories at which marketing activities are targeted. It is quite possible that the marketing techniques used in different geographical areas are largely similar. This similarity does not, however, indicate a single relevant antitrust market. For example, the sales methods, distribution techniques and promotion schemes (in particular advertising) of clothes may be the same in distant parts of the European Union, but these parts will form separate antitrust markets if lasting profitable price increases are possible in each of them. Therefore, the strategic market will be much wider than the relevant antitrust market.[28]

The distinction between a strategic market and the relevant antitrust market shows that competition authorities should be cautious in interpreting economic evidence. Marketing specialists may not be the right experts to be consulted in antitrust cases. Marketing studies are often quite informative but they are designed for understanding consumer buying patterns and do not ask the crucial question of how buying behaviour changes in response to changes in price. Hence, the information provided by such studies must be

---

[28] The European Commission decided that retailing markets are national in scope since price setting, advertising and assortment composition are fixed at the national level and not locally (Case IV/M.1221 *Rewe-Meinl*. 03.02.1999, C (1999) 228final, at paras 19–20). This decision may be criticised: it is likely that the Commission has defined a strategic market rather than an antitrust market.

interpreted with care: it is not directly relevant for the issue of market definition and is useful only in as far as that information complements econometric evidence about demand elasticities.[29]

4.4 The SSNIP test

The SSNIP test, also known as the hypothetical monopolist test, has gained popularity from the 1990s onwards and is often presented as a More Economic Approach for establishing market power. The SSNIP test seeks to recognise the smallest group of products and geographical areas for which a hypothetical monopolist could impose a profitable price increase, ranging between 5% and 10%, lasting for the foreseeable future (at least one year).[30] This examination reflects the economic definition of market power, which stresses power over price. The SSNIP test is thus different from the traditional legal approach, which seeks to define relevant markets upon the basis of a comparison of the characteristics of goods and geographical areas. In spite of its economic flavour, the SSNIP test is not without its own problems: its application in competition law practice is not straightforward and the test poses several methodological issues (see also Nevo 2014). The discussion in this section proceeds as follows. In a first step, the rise of the SSNIP test (in both US antitrust law and EU competition law) and its relation to economic concepts will be highlighted. Thereafter, the analysis focuses on the Guidelines of the European Commission on market definition (hereinafter referred to as the Market Definition Notice) and the use it makes of the economic insights flowing from the SSNIP test. Finally, the problems of applying the SSNIP test in high-technology markets are discussed.

4.4.1 The rise of the SSNIP test in US antitrust law and EU competition law

The SSNIP test was adopted by the US antitrust agencies in the 1982 Merger Guidelines.[31] This method of defining the product and geographical dimension of the market starts with a narrowly defined product (or geographical area) of one of the merging firms and judges the profitability of at least a 'Small but Significant and Non-transitory Increase in Price' (SSNIP,

[29] See Rubinfeld (2000, 167). The author provides the following clarifying example: if 80% of the average adult's cereal consumption is of adult cereals and 70% of the average child's consumption is of kid cereals, both products may still be in the same relevant antitrust market if a 10% increase in price of adult cereals would be unprofitable because consumers of all ages switch to kid cereals.
[30] These figures are based on a normative judgement, according to which price increases exceeding these limits are deemed unacceptable from a competition policy perspective.
[31] US Department of Justice, Antitrust Division, Merger Guidelines, August 9, 1982, Fed. Reg. 47, 1982, 28,493, *reprinted* in: Trade Reg. Rep. 4, Chicago, CCH, 1978, para. 13,102; at Section 1.

normally 5% lasting for the foreseeable future) by a hypothetical monopolist of the product in question. Products are included at each stage of the next best substitute, until a group of products is formed so that, at least, a SSNIP for a product of one of the merging firms would be maximally profitable for the hypothetical monopolist of that group. The relevant product market is the smallest set of products for which a hypothetical monopolist would find it profitable to increase prices by 5%. The analysis continues until markets are delineated around each of the products of each of the merging firms. The two sets of product markets are then compared to determine whether the two merging firms are participants in any of the same product markets. An identical procedure is used to define the geographical market. The 1997 Merger Guidelines thus defined the relevant market as:

> a product or group of products and a geographical area in which it is produced or sold so that a hypothetical profit-maximising firm, not subject to price regulation, that was the only present and future producer or seller of those products in that area would likely impose at least a 'small but significant and non-transitory' increase in price, assuming the terms of sale of all other products are held constant.

> 1997 Merger Guidelines, at 1.11

This approach has been confirmed in the most recent 2010 US Merger Guidelines (at 4.1.1).

The reduction in demand for a hypothetical monopolist's products in response to a projected price increase has three components: demand-side substitution, supply-side substitution of existing products outside the relevant market, and supply-side substitution of new products (potential competition). According to Section 4.1.3. of the 2010 Merger Guidelines, the US antitrust agencies take into account 'any reasonably available and reliable evidence', including, but not limited to: (i) evidence that customers have shifted purchases between products in the past in response to relative changes in price or other competitive variables; (ii) information collected from buyers concerning how they would respond to price changes; (iii) evidence that sellers base business decisions on the prospect of buyer substitution between products in response to relative changes in price; (iv) evidence on industry's participants behaviour in tracking and responding to price changes by rivals; (v) objective information about product characteristics and the timing and costs of switching products; (vi) the percentage of sales lost (as a consequence of a price rise) that is recaptured by other products in the candidate market; (vii) evidence from other industry participants; (viii) legal or regulatory requirements; and (ix) the influence of downstream competition faced by customers in their output markets. Apart from the inherent arbitrariness of choosing the appropriate level for a SSNIP (the range is usually between 5% and 10% and the time period at least one year), the procedure as contained in the Merger Guidelines provides for a tightly focused technique on how to define the market, thereby providing consistency among cases. The Guidelines also present a comprehensive approach to the question of an integrated product and geographical market definition.

The SSNIP's European presence was upstaged in the Commission's *Nestlé/Perrier* decision,[32] subsequently formalised in *Saint-Gobain/Wacker-Chemie/NOM*[33] and eventually adopted as the common standard for defining relevant antitrust markets in the EU Commission's 1997 Notice. Notable already at this point is the Notice's general reference to the SSNIP test, not only in cases of controlling concentrative activity, as in the US, but also related to findings of dominance. Applying, however, the SSNIP test in instances already characterised by existing market power may lead to unwanted results, as will be further elaborated upon below (see the discussion of the Cellophane fallacy).

Since the SSNIP test has been adopted by both the EU and US competition authorities, the question naturally arises how this approach relates to the economic insights on market definition. Among economists, there is a consensus that the critical concept underlying the definition of an antitrust market is the residual demand facing a given group of producers.[34] Residual demand methodology raises a particular firm's costs without raising the costs of its competitors, and this induces the firm to exercise market power over price if it can, and this, in turn, enables the measurement of market power (Baker and Bresnahan 1992). Products with a high residual demand elasticity would lose a large proportion of their sales in response to a small increase in price. If the residual demand elasticity is sufficiently high that the price increase is unprofitable, then the market must be expanded to include the next best substitute. Hence, the residual demand elasticity measures the extent to which a firm would be able to raise a price by reducing output, after taking into account the demand responses of buyers and the supply responses of rivals (Baker and Bresnahan 1988). It thus combines demand-side and supply-side substitution. The US 1982 Merger Guidelines applied a similar estimation technique to define markets (for a discussion, see Simons and Williams 1993, 823–828).

[32] Case IV/M.190 *Nestlé/Perrier* [1992] O.J. L 356/1.
[33] Case IV/M.774 *Saint-Gobain/Wacker-Chemie/NOM* [1997] O.J. L 247/1, para. 220.
[34] Introduced by Landes and Posner (1981) and elaborated in Scheffmann and Spiller (1987, 130–131). Although attractive in many ways, the residual demand analysis does have its own difficulties, summarised in Kaserman and Zeisel (1996, 677–678).

Unfortunately, the 1992/1997 Merger Guidelines deviated from their pre-decessors in qualifying Section 1.0 so that now the terms of sale of all other products are to be held constant when applying the SSNIP. In so doing, it is assumed that all potential substitutes have infinitely elastic supply at current prices, and this principally removes the assessment of competitors' reactions from the market delineation stage (1997 Merger Guidelines, sections 1.0 and 1.3). This supposition suggests that the econometric estimation underlying market definition is to proceed solely through the estimation of own-price elasticities of demand and cross-price elasticities of demand. Properly con-sidered, both concepts of elasticity are of course important for incorpora-tion into the antitrust process of market definition (Shughart, Tollison and Reed 1996, 85–86; Werden 1998). However, this approach turns out to be deficient if it is traced back to the original goal of market delineation, to wit the identification of market power. To estimate the size of market power, both demand substitution and supply substitution need to be considered. Accordingly, the inclusion of supply-side considerations at some point of the competitive assessment is essential. In the 2010 US Merger Guidelines, the responsive actions of suppliers are considered in the sections dealing with the identification of market participants, the measurement of market shares, the analysis of competitive effects and entry. Similar to the current version of the US Merger Guidelines, the European Commission has opted for a market definition that focuses primarily on demand substitution factors (Market Definition Notice, at 39, footnote 5).

4.4.2 The European Commission's Notice

Economic insights injected into a legal straitjacket

The European Commission's Notice is a somewhat peculiar document in that one is left with the impression of new theories and techniques being injected into an orthodox legal straitjacket.[35] At the outset, the Commission repeats the traditional legal definition of the relevant market, related to functional interchangeability (Market Definition Notice, at 7–8). According to the CJEU in *Hoffmann-La Roche*, this amounts to determining which products are sufficiently similar in function, price, and attributes to be regarded by consumers as reasonable substitutes for each other, concluding that:

> [t]he concept of the relevant product market in fact implies that there can
> be effective competition between the products which form part of it and this
> presupposes that there is a sufficient degree of interchangeability between all the

---

[35] This cannot really surprise, however, as the Notice dates back to 1997 and came at a pivotal moment where the European Commission was commencing a real push away from old-fashioned legalistic thinking.

products forming part of the same market insofar as a specific use of such products is concerned.[36]

Subsequently, the European Commission states that companies are restrained in their competitive scope of action by three factors, namely demand-side substitution, supply-side substitution and potential competition (Market Definition Notice, at 13). Of these, demand-side substitution focusing on consumer preferences is considered the most relevant and important. Overall, the explicit adoption of the hypothetical monopolist test should imply that the European Commission intends to put more weight on an economic approach to market definition. However, the passage on the realms of economical foundations was not entirely completed, as the old-style definition based on product characteristics remains a prominent feature in the textual build-up of the Notice.

The criterion of functionable interchangeability does not carry as its central aim the ultimate task of identifying market power, as the products' attributes contain relevance only inasmuch as they influence the extent of competition in-between commodities and locations. A comparison of product characteristics does not allow one to judge whether products belong to the same relevant market. Products with different characteristics may constitute the same relevant market (for example, beer and wine, trains and buses, or small and large trucks).[37] Conversely, products having the same characteristics may constitute different relevant markets (for example, branded products and non-branded products that are physically identical). The same criticism applies to products in the same price range[38] or products with a similar intended use. Consequently, a market definition based upon irrelevant product characteristics, similarity of price levels or intended uses may lead to distorted conclusions on the firms' market power.[39] What antitrust authorities should be figuring out instead is whether the companies under investigation can significantly and lastingly raise their prices because buyers do not enjoy

---

[36] Case 85/76 *Hoffmann-La Roche v. Commission* [1979] ECR 461, para. 24.

[37] In *Mercedes-Benz/Kässbohrer*, the European Commission distinguished different markets according to the loading capacity of trucks: between 5 and 6 tons and above 16 tons (Case IV/M.477 *Mercedes-Benz/Kässbohrer* [1995] O.J. L 211/1.

[38] In *Orkla/Volvo*, the European Commission argued that the price of beer is only one quarter of the price of a similar quantity of wine and distinguished two separate markets accordingly (Case IV/M.582 *Orkla/Volvo* [1996] O.J. L 66/17). This decision may be criticised, since the relevant question is whether a sufficient number of consumers would switch to beer in case of a 5–10% increase of the price of wine, so that the price increase would be unprofitable.

[39] Compare Desai (1997, 476) and Van den Bergh (1996, 82–83). Paragraph 36 of the Market Definition Notice does contain a nuance to the importance of product characteristics in that 'product characteristics and intended use are insufficient to show whether two products are demand substitutes.' If one accepts this statement at face value, the question remains why the traditional definition was not scrapped completely.

substitutes to turn to. Further, if it is thought that a price increase of 5–10% as compared with the competitive price is unacceptable, then the regulators have to determine which products and geographical areas the hypothetical monopolist has to control in order to be able to sustain such a price increase profitably, as it is precisely those products and areas that its buyers would transfer to in response to the increase in price. Only in this way do judgements on the potential exercise of market power become possible.

Further inconsistencies

Where new insights find themselves bottled in old definitions, there is clearly a risk of overall inconsistency. Unfortunately, this is also the case with the Notice, which suffers from ill-conceived attempts at dealing with supply-side substitution, the neglect of potential competition at the stage of market definition, and consecutive (instead of simultaneous) delineation of the relevant product and geographical market areas. The most serious inconsistency of the Notice is the application of the SSNIP test to Article 102 TFEU cases. When prices are already set at the monopoly level, a SSNIP test does not convey any information on the profitability of price increases from a competitive level (Cellophane fallacy).

Supply substitution

The aim of the hypothetical monopolist test is to assess the profitability of a price increase. Apart from taking into account demand-side substitution, this also requires considering supply-side substitution (competing firms' reactions inside the relevant market) and potential competition (competing firms' reactions outside the relevant market). Supply-side substitution is recognised as potentially equivalent to demand-side substitution (Market Definition Notice, at 20). The European Commission envisions this to be the case when suppliers are able to switch production to the relevant product and market it without incurring significant additional costs or risks. Such a situation would typically occur when companies market a wide range of qualities and grades of one product. Supply-side substitution is consequently accepted when its 'effectiveness' and 'immediacy' are similar to demand-side substitution, whereto it must be timely and occur without significant additional costs or risks in response to small and permanent changes in relative prices. It has been noted that identifying these costs or risks and quantifying how much is 'significant' will be a contentious issue (Baker and Wu 1998). There is thus a risk that the analysis remains incomplete and does not allow conclusions on market power. Therefore, it becomes very important to ensure that supply-side considerations are fully considered at a later stage of the assessment before conclusions on market power are reached.

On top of this, neither a clear line is drawn nor an explicit allusion is made to applying the SSNIP test to supply-side substitution also. The Commission's own example relating to the paper market does not bring enlightenment; rather, it provides for additional confusion. From a demand point of view, it is stated that different qualities of paper cannot be used for any given function, as the example of an art book printed on low-quality paper is to illustrate. On the supply-side, the Commission would not define a separate market for each quality of paper and its respective use, as paper manufacturers are able to compete for orders of the various qualities, given the absence of particular distribution hurdles and sufficient lead-time to allow for modification of production plants (Market Definition Notice, at 22). Therefore, the question of whether producers of low-quality paper (such as for newspapers) could profitably and permanently raise their prices with 5–10% is not even posed – although this may very well be the case. Producers of high-quality paper (such as for art books) may have good reasons not to switch production to manufacturing low-quality paper (such as for newspapers). Potential reasons may include: the higher profitability of the up-scale market segment, its faster rate of growth, or the existence of long-term contracts for delivering high-quality paper. Hence, the different types of paper can each constitute a separate relevant product market.

Potential competition

The European Commission clarifies that the analysis of potential competition and the assessment of barriers to entry, if required, will be carried out only after the relevant market has been defined (Market Definition Notice, at 24). At the stage of market definition, the Commission intends not to consider strategic decisions surpassing the short term (elucidated as 'a period that does not entail a significant adjustment of existing tangible and intangible assets' – Market Definition Notice, paragraph 23 *juncto* 20). Concluding *ab initio* upon a relevant market without taking into account the reactions of competitors operating outside this market, however, will prevent the taking into account of such companies' incentives to switch into the initial market after this has become profitable because of the price rise. When deciding upon increasing prices, firms have to take notice of their market surroundings. If their customers anticipate a medium-term response by related producers, a temporary fall in quantity demanded will ensue. As this loss in sales might also influence the profitability of the envisioned price increase, it needs to be included in some way during the market definition stage. If, instead, one follows the Commission's approach of assessing such potential competition only on a market where market power is already ascertained, it is implicitly acknowledged that its starting point was not correctly defined. Again, heightened transparency would have been opportune, as now one needs to distinguish between market definition-stage supply-side substitution and subsequent stage potential competition according to the ductile criterion of 'significant adjustments'.

Consecutive definition of product and geographical relevant markets

The techniques for defining the geographical relevant market are distinct from their product market counterparts. The conventional definition relating to the homogeneity of competitive conditions remains the determinative factor for delineating the geographical market (Market Definition Notice, at 8), with no reference being made to consumers' behaviour in switching locations as a reaction to a price increase. Additionally, the evidential material relied on to define relevant product and geographical markets differs (compare Market Definition Notice, at 36–43 and 44–52). As a result, the Market Definition Notice preserves the European practice of defining both areas consecutively instead of simultaneously, as is the case under paragraph 4 of the 2010 US Merger Guidelines. This heightens the risk of a market being defined too narrowly, as total demand substitution towards both other products and other locations will normally exceed that in either dimension separately (Willig 1991, 281–184). A price increase that is just about profitable under the sequential procedure may no longer be profitable under the simultaneous procedure. As long as consumers who switch to other products are not exactly the same as those consumers who switch towards other locations, the total substitution effect will always be larger than under a sequential definition of the product and geographical market area. In extreme cases, in which none of the consumers who would have substituted towards other products belonged to the group of consumers who would have substituted towards other locations, for example, the elasticity of demand would be halved.

Cellophane fallacy

The last critical remark on the Notice's theoretical framework concerns the application of the SSNIP test to abuse cases (Article 102 TFEU). In such disputes, the use of prevailing prices to define markets will cause considerable problems because of what has become known as the 'Cellophane fallacy'.[40]

---

[40] See Stocking and Mueller (1955) and many subsequent articles. An overview is presented in Hovenkamp (1994, 98–102).

In *Du Pont*, the US Supreme Court argued that cellophane is only one of a number of products making up the market of flexible packing materials, as a high level of cross-price elasticity of demand was determined between cellophane and other wrapping materials. Cellophane could thus not constitute a separate market as, obviously, consumers would switch to substitute products when confronted with monopoly prices for cellophane. The key issue remaining untouched, however, is whether consumers treat the products as close substitutes under competitive prices. In the *Cellophane* case, Du Pont, being the sole producer of cellophane, had already set prices at levels where alternative products provided an effective competitive constraint on the pricing of its product, implying, in fact, that the high cross-price elasticities indicated that Du Pont was exercising monopoly power.

In abuse of dominance cases (Article 102 TFEU), it may be difficult for a competition authority to apply the SSNIP test (as a deviation of 5–10% from competitive market prices) since information about what would be a competitive price is not easily available. The picture is different in merger cases. In not yet highly concentrated markets, pre-merger prices may be an appropriate point of reference for the SSNIP test. By contrast, if market concentration is high and collusion is already a problem, this approach to market definition will be biased in favour of permitting mergers. In Article 102 TFEU investigations, the information problem relating to the application of the SSNIP methodology is pervasive. Although the European Commission is aware of the issue (Market Definition Notice, at 19), nowhere is there a solution offered.

4.4.3 High-technology markets

The SSNIP test poses particular problems when market power must be defined in high-technology markets. Market definition regarding online search and social networking provides a good illustration of these difficulties. As far as the users' market is concerned, a price-related test seems futile when the price is not the decisive variable of consumers' choices. Therefore, it has been suggested to rephrase the SSNIP test in qualitative terms by asking whether consumers would switch to another company's service if the market leader suffered a small but significant non-transitory decrease in the quality of its online service (Gebicka and Heinemann 2014). As far as the advertisers' market is concerned, price constitutes a decisive parameter and an unchanged version of the SSNIP test (asking whether advertisers would switch to a different platform, such as television or newspapers) can be used. However, the problem remains as to how both sides of the market can be integrated in a full competition assessment. A potential solution to this problem is to analyse how platforms monetise their innovations, which leads to a definition of the relevant market as 'the monetization of user's data to advertisers' (Thépot 2013). All these proposals illustrate the risk that market definition may take place in a vacuum, whereas the crucial question remains the competitive effects of a given conduct. Consequently, in high-technology markets, market definition should certainly not be pursued as a goal in itself.

4.5   Empirical methods

The SSNIP test is not a test in itself but a conceptual framework, within which several qualitative and quantitative tests can be employed to address the market delineation question. Consequently, the real added value of the SSNIP methodology needs to be determined by assessing whether and how its hypothetical monopolist settings may actually be put into antitrust practice. This raises the question of the availability of empirical evidence and econometric techniques for estimating market power. The European Commission's Market Definition Notice is fairly confirmatory in this respect, by registering both qualitative and quantitative evidence to be used for determining the profitability of a hypothetical price increase. However, the Notice does not make it sufficiently clear how the different empirical techniques relate to the SSNIP test and what conclusions can be drawn from the available data. More information about the relevance of empirical methods to define relevant markets can be found in the Commission's decisions, particularly in merger cases. Hereinafter, different empirical methods for delineating relevant markets are critically analysed. First, qualitative studies are discussed: event studies and surveys (interviews of competitors and consumers). Second, the attention shifts to quantitative tests for market definition and the related econometric techniques: demand elasticities (own-price elasticity and cross-price elasticity) and price correlations. Critical loss analysis is presented as a tool to implement the SSNIP test. Third, shipment tests used for geographical market definition are discussed.

4.5.1   Qualitative studies

Event studies

In the context of product market definition, probative evidence may be deduced from substitution to competing products in the past. This circumstantial evidence of substitution in the recent past may take different forms. First, sudden events or shocks may indicate likely substitution effects. Second, changes in relative prices in the past may have led to reactions in quantities demanded. Third, launches of new products may have resulted in lost sales to established products.[41]

Surveys

Competition authorities often rely on survey evidence to define the boundaries of the relevant market. Such evidence may be classified into two broad categories: market investigations and customer surveys. The former involve enquiries usually addressed to competitors, in order to better understand the nature of the products in question and the supply and demand sides of the industry under investigation. Obviously, competition authorities will need to assess competitors' views on the definition of the relevant market with utmost care, since the answers provided may be biased towards the establishment of an antitrust infringement.

Customer surveys may provide direct and valuable evidence about consumers' behaviour. However, the appropriate design of customer surveys poses a number of challenges and difficulties that cannot always easily be overcome in the context of antitrust proceedings. The power of surveys is their ability to predict the behaviour of a large group of the population from responses received from a smaller sample of interviewed persons belonging to that group. To generate reliable predictions, the sample should be sufficiently large (not tens or hundreds but thousands of interviewed persons) and the interviewees should be selected randomly. The error margin should not exceed a tolerable percentage (for example, 3% if 1000 people have been interviewed) and also the non-response rate should be low.[42] In the political arena, surveys have been used quite successfully to predict the result of general elections. However, drawing an analogy between a political poll and the definition of a relevant antitrust market is far from obvious. Whereas respondents may relatively well understand the consequences on their well-being of voting for a particular political party, few interviewees will be familiar with competition law. On top of this, several additional factors will limit the reliability of customer surveys. The actual buying behaviour of consumers may be different from the hypothetical scenario of future purchasing patterns. At the time of buying consumers may dispose of more alternatives or, alternatively, may be subject to (budget) constraints that did not exist, or were not taken into consideration, when they answered questions about their likely future buying behaviour.

---

[41] Market Definition Notice, at 38. On the probative evidence of demand substitutability, see Desai (1997, 474–475); on interpreting competitors' and customers' views, see Baker and Wu (1998, 279–280).
[42] OECD (2013), 'The Role and Measurement of Quality in Competition Analysis' DAF/COMP(2013)17. See also Hurley (2011).

Given the intrinsic risk of biased conclusions, the design of the customer surveys is crucial. The wording of the questionnaire can have a dramatic effect
on how respondents react and the ensuing conclusions relating to the boundaries of the relevant antitrust market. Assume the following question: 'Would
you switch to vodka if the price of whisky increased by 5–10%?' The wording
of this question is inappropriate because it does not allow distinguishing between marginal and infra-marginal consumers. The former consumers have
weak preferences for a given product and may decide to switch to substitutes
in case of a SSNIP. The latter consumers are less price-sensitive; asking them
whether they would switch to a competing product may provide misleading
information about the relative importance of alternatives from the perspective of market definition. It is the group of marginal consumers which limits
the pricing discretion of the hypothetical monopolist. These marginal consumers may be identified and their preferences for competing products may
be discovered by making use of the following questions: 'Would you switch
to other products in the event of a 5–10% increase in the price of product x?
If yes, to which products (in order of your preference) would you switch?'[43]
In this way, the risk that the views of infra-marginal consumers are over-
represented is avoided. However, considering only the responses of marginal
consumers may reduce the sample size substantially, which may in turn limit
the reliability of the survey.

The requirements underlying reliable questionnaires are such that their use
for market definition purposes will necessarily remain limited. For practical
reasons, the sample size will often be small. With the exception of retailing
markets (groceries) it may be difficult to identify and survey a sufficiently
large group of customers.[44] Next, the formulation of the questions remains
a daunting task if the consumers who would switch in the event of a SSNIP
must be separated from those who would not and a list of competing alternatives must be put together. Finally, also the need to correct for behavioural
biases must be stressed. Framing effects and 'leading questions' may distort
the answers given by the respondents. The self-selection bias, which gives too
much weight to strong views of a minority of consumers, must also be corrected for. For all these reasons, surveys cannot provide conclusive evidence
on market definition. At best, surveys provide qualitative information that

---

[43] Open-ended questions provide more (reliable) information than closed questions but increase the costs
of the survey. Similar considerations apply to the choice between postal surveys (or via the internet) and
telephone surveys.
[44] The Commission concluded that it would not be possible to implement a representative consumer survey
in the *Olympic/Aegean Airlines* merger case. The market was defined mainly on information gathered during
the market investigation. Sea transport (ferry services) was not regarded as constituting the same relevant
market as the airline services' target of time-sensitive passengers. The proposed merger was blocked. See: Case
COMP/M.5830 *Olympic/Aegean Airlines*, 26.01.2011.

may be used in combination with other indicators that are helpful in delineating antitrust markets.

4.5.2 Quantitative tests

With regard to quantitative tests, the European Commission's Notice lists three econometric techniques, namely price elasticities of demand, cross-price elasticities of demand and price movements over a period of time (Market Definition Notice, at 39). The Notice does not elaborate on the concept of critical demand elasticity and the technique of critical loss analysis, which puts this concept into practice. Conversely, the 2010 US Merger Guidelines explicitly discuss the 'breakeven' approach of critical loss analysis (section 4.1.3).

Cross-price elasticities

To determine cross-price elasticities, it is asked whether certain products (for example, pears, melons, strawberries) are in the same market as the product under investigation (for example, bananas). Will a price increase for the latter product result in (significant) demand substitution towards one or more of the former products? This enquiry focuses on the significance of individual substitutes rather than on the collective competitive significance of all substitutes. Cross-price elasticities do not address the market definition question directly, since they do not indicate how much substitution is enough to constrain the profitability of a SSNIP. Nevertheless, cross-price elasticities may provide useful information in antitrust proceedings. They may confirm that there is demand-side substitution between products inside and outside the proposed market. This can be a powerful defence in cases where the investigating competition authority proposes a narrow market definition (for example, corn flakes), which neglects substantial demand-side substitution (other breakfast products).[45]

Figures on cross-price elasticities also allow a ranking of substitutes to be made. However, information about the critical (residual) demand elasticity, which is the threshold elasticity above which a price increase by the hypothetical monopolist is no longer profitable, is needed to define the boundaries

---

[45] Shughart, Tollison and Reed (1996, 85–92). See also: *State of New York v. Kraft General Foods, Inc.*, 926 F. Supp. 321, 356 (S.D.N.Y. 1995). The latter case shows that demand elasticities can have a considerable impact on assessing the sensibility of further subdivisions of the antitrust market. The State of New York proposed a relevant market containing only adult cereals. The defence convincingly argued the market should comprise all ready-to-eat cereals, based in part on evidence of relatively high cross-price elasticities between adult and children cereals.

of the relevant market. For example, the cross-price elasticities of products B, C and D with respect to product A may amount to 2, 1.8 and 1.4 respectively. These figures allow a ranking of substitutes but do not allow one to decide whether A constitutes a market in itself, or the market also includes product B and eventually also products C and D. To define the market, information is needed about the critical demand elasticity. If the latter elasticity amounts to 5, a 10% price increase for A will not be profitable, since this will result in a 52% loss of sales: 20% to product B, 18% to product C and 14% to product D. By contrast, if the hypothetical monopolist producing product A also controls the market for product B, the price increase will pay off since only 32% of sales will be diverted to products C and D. Consequently, in this example the relevant product market comprises products A and B. Figures about cross-price elasticities must thus be complemented with figures on critical demand elasticities to define the relevant antitrust market.

In sum, cross-price elasticities and price correlations carry a great intuitive appeal but suffer from serious shortcomings, which may distort the definition of the relevant market. Cross-price elasticities are a useful device for determining an appropriate chain of substitutes and showing why a proposed market definition cannot be valid. Hence, the proper role of cross-price elasticities in antitrust cases will vary depending on the nature of the product market being studied and on the issues raised in a particular case. Econometric techniques may be used for two separate purposes: either negatively, to reject a market definition suggested by a party or the competition authority, or positively, to define the boundaries of the relevant market. The data needed to perform the second task is more comprehensive than the information requirements for the first job. Even though the data available may be insufficient to define the boundaries of the relevant market, it may be enough to reject the definition suggested by a party in the antitrust case. For example, if the price elasticity of a particular product shows a high negative value and the cross-price elasticities with other products are high, it is unlikely that this product will constitute in itself a relevant product market.

Importantly, only figures of own-price elasticities based on a residual demand function estimation can address the market definition question directly. A low own-price elasticity indicates the existence of a separate relevant product market.[46] The choice of the residual demand model to investigate the relationship between prices charged and quantities sold is a technical question

---

[46] An example may further illustrate this. An own price-elasticity of −0.5% implies that a price increase of 10% will lead to a loss of sales not higher than 5%. If 100 products are sold at a price of 80, the total income is 8000. In case of a 10% price increase, demand will drop by 5%, but the remaining products will be sold at the higher price of 88. This leads to an increased gain of 4.5%: $95 \times 88 = 8360$.

that cannot be discussed within the confines of this book.[47] The crucial challenge for the econometric delineation of the relevant market is to compare the actual elasticity with the threshold elasticity (critical elasticity) above which a price increase is no longer profitable.

Similarity of price levels and price-correlation analysis

The choice of the empirical techniques used in antitrust proceedings often depends on the data that is available (compare generally Baker and Rubinfeld 1999). Ideally, which technique is to be preferred rests upon the question asked: econometric evidence must be related to the antitrust issue at hand. In practice, there is a risk that particular quantitative techniques will be used more often because the data needed to perform the analysis is more easily available. Hence, the choice of the methodology may be biased. For example, it may be the case that data on price movements is available, while data on demand elasticities is lacking. Here, one should keep in mind that, as evidential sources, price parallelism tests and price-correlation analyses do not enjoy the same analytical rigour as econometric estimates of demand elasticity and are not fully trustworthy techniques to define antitrust markets.

Similarity of price levels

In several high-profile decisions, the European Commission relied on differences in absolute price levels to delineate product markets.[48] Unfortunately, similarity of price levels is not necessarily a reliable criterion to define relevant antitrust markets since price differences do not need to imply that products cannot be considered substitutes. Inferring that products with substantially different prices are not close substitutes overlooks the relevant question for competition law analysis. The relevant inquiry is whether an increase in the price of the candidate market's product will induce enough consumers to switch, so that the price increase would be unprofitable. Defining relevant markets based on observed differences in absolute prices may be misleading if price differentials reflect actual or perceived quality differences. To capture the consumers' price-quality trade-off, the inquiry should focus on the degree to which the pricing of the high-quality or the branded product is constrained by the existence of lower quality or

---

[47] A widely adopted model among antitrust practitioners is the Almost Ideal Demand System (AIDS). See: Ulrick (2014); Deaton and Muelbauer (1980).

[48] For example: Case IV/M.53 *Aerospatiale/Alenia/de Havilland* [1991] O.J. L 334/42 (price differences between different types of aircraft); Case IV/M.190 *Nestlé/Perrier* [1992] O.J. L 356/1 (price gap between retail prices of source water and other soft drinks); Case IV/M.2609 *HP/Compaq* [2002] O.J. C 39/23 (division of market for computer servers according to price ranges).

unbranded (private label) products (Bishop and Walker 2002, 108–110). For example, branded and unbranded products may be in the same market despite obvious price differences if the cross-price elasticities between the products are high (see the discussion of the *Kimberly-Clark* case in Box 4.2).

Box 4.2: The *Kimberly-Clark* case: an EU–US comparison

In its 1996 decision declaring Kimberly-Clark's acquisition of Scott compatible under certain conditions,[49] the European Commission made extensive use of toilet tissue market studies submitted by both the parties and major competitors which addressed the impact of the operation on competition in the United Kingdom. Albeit featured only when discussing the parties' positions on markets already defined, the studies focused on whether prices of branded products are constrained by prices of private label products, drawing direct inference from price quantity data.[50] The price elasticities of demand estimated for the whole market, comprising both branded and private-label segments, showed overall market demand for toilet tissue to be inelastic (i.e. demand elasticity lower than 1). Hence, the relevant market was certainly not wider than all toilet tissues, since a 5% price increase would be followed by a less than 5% drop in sales. Concerning the cross-price elasticity estimates, the studies submitted by the parties led to quite different results and the Commission reached the conclusion that there existed 'a certain price competition' between the private-label and branded segments. Yet, accounting for the high market shares of the parties and the strong brand loyalty, the inelastic total demand for toilet tissues was seen as creating scope for the parties to abuse their position on the British market for toilet tissues after the merger.

Even though hampered by the decision's deletion of data for reasons of business secrecy, some deductions may still be made when comparing the European case with the parallel consent settlement issued in the US in Kimberly-Clark.[51] The likely price effects of the proposed merger on the toilet tissue market were econometrically estimated using Nielsen supermarket scanner data from five major US cities for five years. Contrary to the Department of Justice's preliminary imputations (based on the parties' substantial market share) showing a substantial increase in concentration in a market already considered highly concentrated (1997 Merger Guidelines Section 1.51), the figures presented by the defence allowed the clearing of the merger.

---

[49] Case IV/M.623 *Kimberly-Clark/Scott Paper* [1996] O.J. L 183/1. The two companies are among the largest world producers of hygienic paper products.

[50] *Ibid.*, at paras 172–177.

[51] *United States and State of Texas v. Kimberly-Clark Corp. and Scott Paper Co.*, Civil No. 3:95 CV 3055-P (D.C. Texas). See the case discussion in Hausman and Leonard (1997, 335–336), also including a detailed description of the price-concentration analysis applied.

First, evidence showed two separated market segments (see the tables in Hausman and Leonard 1997, 344–346): the premium (designated branded in the European counterpart) market and the economy (private-label in the European counterpart) market. Kimberly-Clark produced the premium brand Kleenex, while Scott produced a premium brand, Cottonelle, and an economy brand, ScotTissue. The premium segment was dominated by Charmin, a competing Procter & Gamble brand, with a 30.9% share of the whole tissue market. The share of the second and third brands, Northern and Angel Soft, were 12.4% and 8.8% respectively; Kleenex held a share of 7.5%, and Cottonelle 6.7%. The economy brands were dominated by ScotTissue with a 16.7% share of the total market, followed by other brands (together 9.4%) and Private Label with 7.6%. Hausman and Leonard's estimated demand system found that the own-price elasticity for Kleenex, Cottonelle and ScotTissue were −3.4, −4.5, and −2.9 respectively, implying sales reduction of 34%, 45% and 29% in response to a 10% increase in their price. The estimated cross-price elasticities were very low; the largest Kleenex cross-elasticity was with Charmin at 0.69, indicating Charmin to be the closest substitute for Kleenex (and implying that sales of Kleenex would go up by 6.9% in response to a 10% increase in the price of Charmin). The next largest cross-price elasticities were all estimated to be with other premium brands.

Second, the relevant products' cross-price elasticities were all different from each other and asymmetric. Using the estimated elasticities of demand, the parties predicted the price effects from the merger of Kimberly-Clark's and Scott's toilet tissue activities to constitute a price increase of 2.4% for Kleenex, 1.4% for Cottonelle and 1.2% for Scot Tissue (the parties' respective products), assuming no cost efficiencies. As these are very low figures, the merger was consequently approved. The toilet tissue case illustrates the decreasing significance to be attached to pre-merger computations of market shares in heterogeneous product markets (see for further discussion sections 9.3.2 and 9.4.4).

Price correlations

The European Commission mentions price movements over a period of time as one of the possible empirical methods to define relevant markets (Market Definition Notice, at 39). The statistical technique used to measure the degree of interdependence between prices of two different products or regions is called 'price-correlation analysis'. The underlying idea is that if two products A and B are in the same relevant product market, then the price of each will constrain the other. A reduction in the price of product A will put pressure on the producer of product B to reduce its price too, because of the demand and supply substitution that would otherwise arise. Hence, prices of products in the same relevant product market should move together over time (Bishop and Walker 2002, 382). Similarly, if two regions lie within a single relevant market, demand and/or supply substitution between those regions will cause their prices to move similarly.

Price correlation studies are widely used as a tool for market delineation in many EU competition law investigations, particularly in merger cases. This is due to the simple intuition behind the technique and the relatively modest data requirements. However, price correlation tests suffer from a number of inherent shortcomings that may undermine their reliability. First, the risk of spurious correlations (when similarity of price movements is caused by non-competition factors) must be overcome. Second, it is unclear how high the price correlation coefficient needs to be for reaching the conclusion that different products or regions are within the same relevant market. Since price correlation tests are mostly used in the context of merger control, these complications are further discussed in Chapter 9 (see section 9.2.4 and Box 9.1).

Critical loss analysis

Economists generally prefer residual demand analysis to define relevant markets. The informational requirements for the latter type of analysis are more bothersome, however. Only if figures about the (critical) residual demand elasticity faced by a (group of) firm(s) are available will it be possible to judge whether a price increase in the range of the SSNIP test will be profitable. The elasticity above which a price increase becomes unprofitable is called 'critical elasticity of demand'. If the prevailing elasticity of demand in the candidate market is lower than the critical value, the hypothetical monopolist will not refrain from increasing prices above the current level.

A technique which enjoys increasing popularity in the US is critical (sales) loss analysis. The Merger Guidelines define the critical loss as the number of lost unit sales that would leave profits unchanged (break-even analysis). The predicted loss (actual loss) is the number of sales that the hypothetical monopolist is predicted to lose as a consequence of the price increase. If the actual loss is less than the critical loss, the price increase will be profitable. Conversely, if the predicted loss is greater than the critical loss, a broader definition of the market is called for. To calculate the critical loss, the effects of a price increase must be balanced. On the one hand, a price increase raises the profit margin on all units sold; on the other hand, it also reduces the overall quantity demanded. The critical loss values depend on the initial price cost margins and the size of the price increase (see Box 4.3). Price-cost margins can be calculated from accounting data on the industry under investigation. Higher pre-merger margins indicate a smaller predicted loss as well as a smaller critical loss. Information about actual elasticities and actual losses can be obtained in several ways: through econometric estimations (regression analysis, figures on diversion ratios, shock analyses)[52] or qualitative evidence (surveys and third-party sources) that buyers shifted their purchases between alternative products or locations in response to a price increase. The US 2010 Merger Guidelines consider all evidence of customer substitution in assessing the size of the actual loss.

Box 4.3: Critical loss analysis in antitrust practice: cruise mergers

The following table illustrates how critical loss values change for various price increases and initial price-cost margins:

Initial margin	Price increase			
	5%	10%	15%	20%
0.1	0.33	0.5	0.6	0.67
0.2	0.2	0.33	0.43	0.5
0.3	0.14	0.25	0.33	0.4
0.4	0.11	0.20	0.27	0.33
0.5	0.09	0.17	0.23	0.29
0.6	0.08	0.14	0.20	0.25
0.7	0.07	0.13	0.18	0.22
0.8	0.06	0.11	0.16	0.2
0.9	0.05	0.10	0.14	0.18

For example, if the pre-merger margin is 60%, the critical sales loss following a 5% price increase should be about 8%. Intuitively, the larger the margin, the greater the profit lost from a given reduction in quantity, so the smaller the reduction in quantity (i.e. critical loss) required for a given price increase to be unprofitable. If the price-cost margin is quite high (e.g. 80–100%), a loss in sales of only about 5% would be sufficient to deter the hypothetical monopolist from increasing price by 5%. If the margin is quite low (e.g. less than 20%), a loss in sales of more than 20% would be necessary to dissuade the monopolist from increasing the price by 5% (Werden 1992, 116).

---

[52] In a regression analysis, the demand for a good (dependent variable) is defined as a function of several independent variables (such as the price of the good, the price of substitute products and complements) and the demand function is econometrically estimated. Such an analysis requires high-quality data for a sufficiently long period and can be carried out only by experts in econometrics. A diversion ratio indicates the effects of a price increase on the demand of a given product (for example, a diversion ratio of 0.60 for product 1 with respect to product 2 indicates that the seller of product 1 will lose 60% of its sales to the seller of product 2). A shock analysis investigates the effects of a sudden and unexpected event on the demand for a product.

The investigations undertaken by three different competition authorities (European Commission, Federal Trade Commission, UK Competition Commission) into mergers in the cruise industry illustrate the importance attached to critical loss analysis in differentiated product markets (see for a more detailed discussion Nevo 2013). The merger of P&O Princess with either Carnival Corporation or Royal Caribbean cruises would have created an operator with a market share above 60% in the UK market. The British Competition Commission, which analysed the latter operation, presented the critical loss methodology, stating that the fall in passenger numbers would be around 9.5–11.5% if prices were raised by 5%, and to be around 17–21% for a hypothesised 10% price increase. The concept of critical loss was, however, merely used to launch the discussion on the boundaries of the relevant market. The market definition was ultimately simply left open since the Competition Commission was not able to come to a single view.

In contrast with the UK approach, the European Commission did not attempt to quantify the impact of a hypothetical price increase. The Commission noted the possibility of unilateral effects within a narrow sub-set of cruises and examined these as a part of the competitive assessment. The Commission argued that a mix of demand and supply substitution justified a broad prohibition. In this way, the Commission recognised that market definition is not an end in itself but just an intermediate stage in the evaluation that must be augmented by consideration of the specific impact of the merger, given the nature of the competition in the differentiated cruise market.

The American Federal Trade Commission investigated both transactions for their impact on the US market. In the discussion on market definition, the FTC used reviews of prices revealing that the cruise industry's critical loss was extremely low, corresponding to a very high overall industry elasticity of demand. It was found that in order for a hypothetical monopolist to increase price profitably, its margins would have to be below 50%, much lower than short-run cruise ship margins. Even though these figures made clear that an across-the-board price increase would be unprofitable and defining the relevant market as a broader vacation market would have been appropriate, the FTC identified cruises as a separate relevant market.

In sum, all three competition authorities differed in their approaches towards market definition in general and to the use of econometric analysis in particular. None of the authorities decided on a narrow market definition, such as luxury oceanic cruises. In addition, the importance given to supply-side responses at the stage of the competitive assessment shows that a market definition solely inspired by demand-side factors would have been deficient.

The Elzinga–Hogarty test for defining the relevant geographical market

Next to the quantitative techniques mentioned above, which have been developed mainly for the purpose of product market definition,[53] a specific test has been proposed to delineate a relevant geographical market. The method is known as the Elzinga–Hogarty test, named after the professors who developed it. Even though neither the European Commission's Notice nor the 2010 US Merger Guidelines mention this test, the Elzinga–Hogarty approach for defining geographical markets has been used in a number of antitrust cases and is, therefore, briefly discussed below.

The Elzinga–Hogarty test specifies two criteria that are based on shipments data: LIFO (little in from outside) and LOFI (little out from inside). A low LIFO indicates that the demand is primarily served by local production (few imports), whereas a low LOFI indicates that the majority of the local production is used to serve the local market (few exports). If trade patterns observed in a region fail either the LIFO or LOFI conditions, this testifies that the region is subjected to external competition. The candidate geographical market is expanded until the inflow and export rate (calculated over the total number of sales) is sufficiently low, for example 10% (see Elzinga and Hogarty 1973).

This test has provoked several criticisms. First, the choice of the threshold (for example 0.9 as the critical value for both LIFO and LOFI) is arbitrary and not always appropriate for each individual case (Bishop and Walker 2002, 408). Second, conclusions on the geographical size of the entire market are taken by referring to the purchasing behaviour of a minority of consumers. If the silent majority of consumers faces high transportation costs and if the demand for the products concerned is rather inelastic, suppliers may enjoy strong market power. If a broader market definition is chosen on the basis of the low number of purchases outside the geographical area, the result of the Elzinga–Hogarty test will be unreliable. Third, on a more general level, the criteria proposed by Elzinga and Hogarty are inappropriate since they are independent of the supply elasticity of the exporting region. As a consequence, an economic market is defined instead of a relevant antitrust market (Scheffman and Spiller 1987, 129).

4.6 Direct measurement of market power

In a number of thought-provoking articles, Louis Kaplow severely criticises the current market definition process in antitrust law (Kaplow 2011; Kaplow

---

[53] Price correlations have been used also to define the boundaries of geographical markets.

2010). Given its many pitfalls, Kaplow concludes that market definition should simply be abandoned. His arguments consist of four prongs. First, market shares are relevant to infer market power in homogeneous goods markets only. Once markets are redefined to include imperfect substitutes, one needs a new mechanism for translating market shares into market power. The only correct way to do so requires invalidating the formerly established market definition. Second, making market power inferences from market shares presupposes some sort of benchmark for interpreting market shares. Discussions of market shares often operate on the implicit assumption that each share level is associated with some benchmark amount of market power. However, a given market share does not imply a unique level of market power. A market share approach would need a standard reference market, which could be either an average market or an abstract hypothetical market. Up until now, there have been no attempts in antitrust law to construct such a reference market. Third, the market definition exercise may yield conflicting market definitions. The decision maker may then select the definition which is least prone to error and provides a market power inference that is as close as possible to the actual level. In this way, the decision process presumes that the best estimate of market power is already available. This is ironic since the whole point of market definition is adequately assessing market power. Alternatively, the decision maker may choose the market definition that provides the best legal answers, in which case the process is circular and superfluous. Fourth, antitrust practice shows a strong focus on cross-price elasticity, rather than on the market elasticity of demand which is directly relevant to proper market power inferences (Kaplow 2010).

In its Market Definition Notice, the EU Commission has tied the traditional method of market definition to the economic concept of the SSNIP. The explicit adoption of the hypothetical monopolist test seems to imply that the Commission intends to put more weight on economic analysis in the market delineation exercise. However, Kaplow's criticisms remain intact: the SSNIP applies to heterogeneous goods markets; there is no indication of a standard reference market and too much emphasis is put on cross-price elasticities. The key point is that market power is not defined directly. The SSNIP continues the tradition of an indirect approach to market power by identifying the products and geographical regions that may exert competitive pressure on the company under investigation. By contrast, the development of empirical techniques in the US has initiated an evolution that puts less emphasis on the role that traditional methods of market definition play in determining the market players' positions and, ultimately, market power. Particularly in the field of merger control, econometric evidence may be available that allows a direct assessment of market power (see section 9.2.4). As already noted by

Stigler and Sherwin, the SSNIP test coupled with a judgement concerning the level and changes in concentration is not in any way easier than asking directly whether the merger under investigation will result in an increased price (Stigler and Sherwin, 1985). Where sufficient data is available, a simulation model may allow quantifying the unilateral price effects from mergers. Through simulation analysis the market power may be deduced or the change in market power through a merger may be calculated.[54] Such a merger simulation method needs not to rely on market definition. Also, diversion ratios (i.e. information about the lost sales that are captured by the post-merger firm in case of a price increase) may be able to assess market power directly, thus equally bypassing the need of market definition. Another advantage of the direct identification of market power is that also other factors, which are relevant for the overall competitive assessment, can be incorporated in the analysis. A merger simulation analysis captures not only the future price increases but also potential efficiencies generated by a proposed merger. This analysis may thus allow answering the question whether the cost savings resulting from a merger will be sufficiently passed on to consumers, which allows the competition authority to judge whether the anti-competitive effects will be compensated by efficiency gains.

Given their potential to alleviate the coercive character of market definition, the econometric techniques allowing direct inferences on market power are prone to controversy. The market definition exercise enjoys a respectable status in legal writings because of its logical simplicity and the legal certainty that safe harbour provisions[55] offer to companies. However, it follows from the economic insights that a dominant role for market shares in the decision-making process no longer appears warranted in all cases. Hence, also, the 'certainty' linking low market shares to the absence of market power disappears. Safe harbours for firms holding low market shares in vertical relations and low concentration safe harbours in merger control may thus become less of a haven (Hausman and Leonard 1997). Moreover, price increases shown by merger simulation analyses by no means should imply that differentiated goods mergers are to be rated negative *per se*, as the efficiency gains made possible through such mergers can outdo the anti-competitive effects attached, leading to lower prices for consumers.[56] In addition, (the threat of)

---

[54] Examples of simulation analyses include the telecommunications industry (Hausman and Leonard 1997) and the trucks market (Ivaldi and Verboven 2000).

[55] These are rules that exclude the application of the prohibitions of competition law to the benefit of undertakings possessing only a low market share on the relevant market. Examples include the 25% market share for R&D agreements (see the discussion in section 5.3.2) and the 30% market shares for suppliers and distributors in cases of vertical agreements (see the discussion in section 6.4.2).

[56] This still holds even under most dire conditions; see Werden (1996).

new entry may be able to counterbalance the increase in market power (compare Gilbert 1989).

The above discussion forcefully raises the question whether competition law could do without the market definition exercise. At this point, a cautious answer is necessary. Although the market share/market power paradigm is subject to many criticisms, the traditional approach accommodates a more wide-ranging view of available evidence. Also, it does not require the calculation of parameters (such as diversion ratios) that are difficult to measure. Coming back to Kaplow's criticisms, one may conclude that his remarks are theoretically valid but that also the practical implementation of econometric techniques exhibits a number of drawbacks, due to difficulties of measurement and manageability requirements. Hence, it seems too soon to abandon traditional ways of market definition entirely. Given the imperfections of the relevant market definition methods discussed in this chapter, competition authorities and judges may prefer a combined use of alternative techniques. If divergent approaches point in the same direction, a particular market definition will be better able to withstand close scrutiny.

4.7   Barriers to entry

The analysis of barriers to entry is another fundamental component of the assessment of market power. A firm may exercise market power for a significant period of time only if barriers to new entry exist. When one decides whether a firm is abusing market power or a merger will cause welfare losses, analysis of entry conditions is thus of major importance. This is acknowledged by the European Commission in its Horizontal Merger Guidelines, where it is stated: 'When entering a market is sufficiently easy, a merger is unlikely to pose any significant anti-competitive risk.'[57] Entry barriers may result from a wide variety of factors and may be present at the supplier's or buyer's level, or both. In later chapters of this book, it will be discussed in greater detail how competition authorities analyse entry barriers as part of their competitive assessment (see in particular Chapter 7 on market dominance and Chapter 9 on merger control). Here, the focus will be on the economic insights that enable one to distinguish anti-competitive entry barriers from entry impediments that should not pose antitrust worries.

In the past, economists conducted an intense debate on the contribution to entry barriers of determinants such as economies of scale, product differentiation and capital requirements. Together with absolute cost advantages, Bain

---

[57] Guidelines on the assessment of horizontal mergers under the Council Regulation on the control of concentrations between undertakings [2004] O.J. C 31/5, para. 68.

mentioned those factors in his seminal book as entry barriers (Bain 1956). Bain laid the foundations for what became known as the Harvard School of industrial organisation: followers of this approach qualify a great many things as barriers to entry. Conversely, the Chicago School, represented in the writings of Stigler, Bork and Posner, argue that most factors qualified by Harvard scholars as barriers to entry are, in fact, natural barriers and that antitrust law should be concerned only with artificial barriers to entry. Recent work in industrial organisation has clarified to a great extent the approach that should be taken in the analysis of entry conditions in general, and product differentiation and advertising in particular. A description of the Harvard–Chicago controversy (see section 2.6), however, remains useful to understand the issues at hand. An important contribution to the current understanding of entry barriers has been made by the recent theory of contestable markets (see section 2.10). The latter approach has revealed the fundamental importance of sunk costs. In assessing the feasibility of market entry, exit conditions are equally as important as entry conditions. Entry is particularly likely if suppliers in other markets already possess production facilities that could be used to enter the market, thus reducing the sunk costs of entry. Conversely, firms may abstain from entering if barriers to exit, prohibiting them from recouping entry costs, exist. Hence, barriers to exit are crucial in assessing market power. Finally, game theory has shown that incumbent firms may engage in strategic behaviour to alter the perceptions of rivals concerning the cost conditions in the industry, in order to deter entry (Salop and Scheffman 1987). For example, strategic behaviour may raise rivals' costs by foreclosing important inputs to production (for example, through exclusive dealing agreements), or incumbent firms may build a reputation for aggressive responses to entry (predatory pricing). Such strategies may successfully deter entry or at least minimise its competitive impact (see section 7.4.1 for a discussion).

The scope of this book does not allow for a complete overview of the economic theories on entry barriers (see for further analysis: OECD 2006; Schmalensee 2004; Harbord and Hoehn 1994). Here, common views and points of disagreement are only briefly sketched. There is agreement among economists that government regulation creates entry barriers.[58] Opinions differ with respect to non-regulatory entry barriers: some economists take a critical view of private market participants' possibilities to erect entry barriers. A useful distinction can be made between absolute advantages and strategic advantages that derive from the asymmetry of timing between incumbent firms and entrants (so-called first-mover advantages of incumbents). The latter category includes scale economies and product differentiation (supported

---

[58] See also Guidelines on the assessment of horizontal mergers under the Council Regulation on the control of concentrations between undertakings [2004] O.J. C 31/5, para. 71(a).

by advertising) as the most prominent examples. In addition, recent litera-ture also discusses vertical foreclosure and predatory pricing as entry barriers caused by strategic behaviour of incumbent firms (Cubero 2010). Contrary to entry impediments that afford only temporary protection for a limited period of time, barriers to entry allow incumbent firms to make long-run super-normal profits without being more efficient than potential rivals. Only barriers to entry benefiting incumbent firms that are not more efficient than newcomers should raise antitrust concerns.

4.7.1   Absolute advantages

Absolute cost advantages for incumbents arise if some factor of production is denied to the potential entrant and, but for this omitted factor, the latter firm would be as efficient as incumbent firms (Gilbert 1989). Absolute advantages are easy to identify by looking at government regulation. Monopoly rights granted to a single trader or a group of professionals constitute entry barriers for potential competitors who are not allowed to sell similar goods or perform similar services. Monopoly rights that were granted to public utilities to supply customers with gas, electricity and water are clear examples of legal barriers to entry. The same conclusion holds with respect to licensing systems in the sector of the liberal professions and entry regulation in retailing. In each of these sectors of industry, deregulation measures have been taken to promote competition. It would be premature, however, to conclude that the deregulation wave has created the conditions to guarantee efficient outcomes.[59]

Intellectual property rights (IPRs: patents, copyright) also belong to the category of absolute cost advantages. However, IPRs require a different eval-uation because of their potential to generate dynamic efficiencies. The eco-nomic rationale of patent protection is to promote competition in innovation by making sure that firms are able to reap the profits from their investments in research and development (R&D). Similarly, copyright protection grants monopoly rights to authors to protect them from free-riding and guarantee an optimal level of literary and artistic production. From an economic per-spective, the granting and protection of property rights, including IPRs, is the legal instrument for providing the necessary incentives to encourage so-cially beneficial investments and to achieve long-run returns higher than the marginal costs. The ability to exploit the investments made allows the owner to acquire the resulting rents, through his right to exclude others. If the legal systems did not protect IPRs, the *ex ante* incentives to make the necessary

---

[59] See, for example, on the liberal professions: Van den Bergh (1999); Van den Bergh and Montagnie (2006) and on telecommunications: Renda (2012).

investments to innovate would not be provided. The proprietary protection takes the form of a legal monopoly that allows the IPR holder to extract a profit greater than the marginal cost, which represents the highest incentive to invest. Moreover, it has been pointed out that this right to exclude others should receive a high level of protection because the investments needed to develop the assets protected by IPRs tend to be more risky and burdensome than those concerning traditional properties.

Intellectual property exhibits marked traits of similarity with public goods, particularly their non-rivalrous and non-exclusive features. Economic theory has shown that there are small incentives to create a public good since the marginal cost to which the price should be equal in a competitive market tends to be zero. On top of this, consumers are used to adapt a marked free-riding on this type of goods. Therefore, lacking a strong protection of IPRs, able to award monopoly profits in the long run, potential innovators may decide not to make investments at all or to perform this activity at a suboptimal level (Leveque and Ménière 2006; Scotchmer 2004, 65).

In the context of competition law, the wide protection scope of IPRs is usually contested by claims of individual competitors to force dominant firms to license their IPRs for a 'fair' price and in a non-discriminatory way. In different technological fields – such as information and communication technologies, biotechnology or the pharmaceutical sector – requests for compulsory licences have been made regularly. The question of under which conditions a refusal to license IPRs may be considered an infringement of competition law is the focus of Chapter 7 on unilateral behaviour (see section 7.2). Here, only two general remarks are made. First, it should be clear that the mere possession of an IPR does not allow to conclude that the firm is dominant. Overzealous competition authorities may underestimate the competitive pressures in markets characterised by widespread innovation and a large scope of IPRs (see, for example, the discussion of the *Ericsson* case in Box 4.4). The intervention of competition authorities in industries that have shown rapid innovation with substantial price decreases seems against the consumer welfare objective of competition law. Second, a cautious approach towards compulsory licensing is needed. Several studies have clarified the reasons why a compulsory licence on patents or other IPRs can be justified. Phenomena such as the patent race and the strategic use of patents have shown that, especially in economic contexts characterised by cumulative innovation, the refusal to grant licences can severely damage the innovation process. Patent holders should not be able to block innovation by refusing to grant licences on products, processes or technology platforms, thus compromising the ability of competitors to enter or compete (Hovenkamp, Janis, Lemley and Leslie 2010).

Ultimately, the effects of compulsory licensing IPRs in terms of consumer welfare are ambiguous. On the one hand, the granting of a compulsory licence generates beneficial effects in the short term. Input sharing with competitors is likely to increase competition in the market and to consequently reduce the deadweight loss associated with the dominant firms' market power. Whenever the compulsory licence allows competitors to develop their own products, consumer welfare can be increased even in the long run. On the other hand, the imposition of a compulsory licence is likely to reduce the incentives to innovate in the long term. In the latter case, the negative impact on consumer welfare can be particularly large and potentially equal to the reduction of the total surplus resulting from reduced innovation in the affected markets (Hovenkamp 2012; Ritter 2005). In sum, although compulsory licensing can enhance the benefits linked to the emergence of a competitive playground (reduction of the deadweight loss and an increase in the short run consumer welfare), there are notable objections that suggest a limited use of this legal obligation. From this perspective, competition authorities should be advised to take a cautious attitude towards claims for compulsory licensing of IPRs in high-technology industries characterised by rapid innovation and decreasing consumer prices (see the discussion of the Indian *Ericsson* case in Box 4.4).

Box 4.4: India: the *Ericsson* case
Sahib Singh Chadha

In March 2013 Telefonaktiebolaget LM Ericsson's (Ericsson) sought an injunction against Micromax Informatics Pvt. Ltd. (Micromax) for infringement of its Standard Essential Patents (SEPs) before the Delhi High Court. The Court ordered Micromax to pay an interim royalty until the pendency of the suit.[60] During the pendency of the suit, Micromax filed a complaint before the Competition Commission of India (CCI), alleging that Ericsson was abusing its dominant position by, *inter alia*, imposing an excessive royalty rate, an inappropriate royalty base and the refusal to disclose licensing terms with other licensees. It also had reneged on its obligation to license its SEPs on Fair Reasonable and Non-Discriminatory Terms (FRAND). In January 2014, the CCI examined the conduct of Ericsson and found that there was a *prima facie* case of abuse of dominance and asked the Director General to institute an investigation

---

[60] Delhi High Court, Order dated March 19 2013 in CS(OS) 442/2013.

into the practices of Ericsson.[61] This order was challenged by Ericsson by filing a writ petition before the Delhi High Court, arguing, *inter alia*, that any issue relating to royalty claims falls within the scope of the Patents Act and accordingly claimed that the impugned orders passed by the CCI were without jurisdiction. The Delhi High Court, in a detailed judgment,[62] found that there is no irreconcilable repugnancy or conflict between the Competition Act and the Patents Act. Therefore, the CCI has the jurisdiction to entertain complaints for abuse of dominance in respect of patent rights. Ericsson has preferred an appeal against this judgment before a division bench of the Delhi High Court, disputing CCI's jurisdiction to investigate into and adjudicate upon issues pertaining to patent licensing. At the time of writing, this appeal is still pending final determination, while the investigation before the Director General/CCI is simultaneously still in progress.

The order passed by the CCI shows the trend to interfere, without any consistent method and without addressing the teachings of economics predominant today. The CCI held Ericsson to be dominant in the market for licensing of SEPs in GSM-compliant mobile communication devices using 2G, 3G and 4G technologies in India. According to the CCI, Ericsson is the sole owner of SEPs and therefore enjoys immense and unassailable market power over its present and prospective licensees in the relevant market. This view invites some criticisms. The mere fact that an undertaking owns SEPs does not necessarily mean that it holds a dominant position; the question of market power can only be assessed on a case-by-case basis.[63] SEP holders, like Ericsson, are not in a position to operate independently of competitive forces or to affect their competitors and consumers in India. Implementers exert sufficient countervailing power on these patent holders. They have strong incentives to moderate royalty rates so as to ensure a widespread and fast adoption of the standard. Furthermore, SEP holders are constrained by the fact that many members of standards development organisations are also likely licensees/customers of products reading on the standard. Therefore a SEP owner who has attempted to charge non-FRAND rates in the past risks having its technologies excluded from future standards.[64]

Besides the dubious definition of dominance, competition law is not the appropriate instrument to assess the legality of price decisions made by a dominant firm (see, for further discussion, Chapter 7). In order to determine whether or not the licensing terms, including the royalty rates, offered by Ericsson are unfair or excessive, the CCI would first need to determine what a reasonable royalty rate should be. This assessment

[61] CCI Order dated November 12, 2013, in Case no. 50 of 2013.
[62] Delhi High Court, Judgment dated March 30, 2016.
[63] EC 2011C 11/01, *Guidelines on the applicability of Article 101 of the Treaty on the Functioning of the European Union to horizontal co-operation agreements*. See also, in the US: *Chrimar Systems vs. Cisco* United States District Court for the Northern District of California (October 29, 2014).
[64] Standard setting is a repeated game; see Epstein, Kieff and Spulber (2012).

cannot be undertaken under the provisions of the Competition Act: not only would the CCI be deviating from its own established practice of not determining prices,[65] it would also be exercising powers beyond its jurisdiction. With regard to discriminatory pricing, the CCI concluded (*prima facie*) that the royalty rates being charged by Ericsson had no linkage to the patented product, contrary to what is expected from a patent owner holding licences on FRAND terms. The CCI found that the pricing offered by Ericsson is discriminatory as it will result in different licence fees for different phones. By this holding, the CCI appears to be diverging from the industry-wide practice that is to use the end-user device as a royalty base.[66] Courts and authorities have also acknowledged that setting prices on an end-user level is in consonance with FRAND principles.[67] Basing royalties on the value of the patented technology to the end-product helps to ensure that they reflect the value which patented standardised technology brings to consumers through the interaction with complementary technologies. Setting prices in a manner that reflects the different values that different users attribute to a good enables more consumers to buy the end product.

The dispute between Ericsson and several Indian handset manufacturers is of immense importance to the continuing SEP jurisprudence, which is evolving all around the world (see, in particular, the comparative study of US antitrust law and EU competition in section 7.2). The case gives legal backing to licence seekers in cases where the patent is essential and the negotiations come to a halt. As a result patent holders find it risky to avoid FRAND compliance and grant licences in complete accordance with FRAND. The Ericsson case aims to provide clarification on the interface between patent law and competition law and tries to acknowledge the ambit of antitrust intervention which may, at times, curtail the exercise of the exclusivity rights held by a patent holder.

4.7.2 Strategic advantages

Scale economies

In Bain's view, scale economies were considered as an important source of barriers to entry. Bain argued that minimum efficient scale may impede entry;

---

[65] See: *Prints India v. Springer India Private Limited &Ors*, Case no. 16 of 2010, *Manjit Singh Sachdeva v. Director General, DGCA*, Case no. 68 of 2012.

[66] Keith Mallinson, *Mallinson on Intel & Wilmer Hale Smartphone Royalty Stack*, IP Finance, September 19, 2014, Eric Stasik, *Royalty Rates and Licensing Strategies for Essential Patents on LTE (4G) Telecommunication Standards*, les Nouvelles, at 114 (September 2010).

[67] *Guidelines on the application of Article 101 of the Treaty on the Functioning of the European Union to Technology Transfer Agreements*, 2014/C 89/03 at p. 184. Also see: *CSIRO v. Cisco* (Federal Circuit, December 5, 2015) http://www.cafc.uscourts.gov/sites/default/files/opinions-orders/15-1066.Opinion.12-1-2015.1.PDF. In India too in the case of *Telefonaktiebolaget LM Ericsson v. Micromax Informatics Ltd.* passed interim orders requiring the defendants to deposit the royalty calculated as a percentage of the net selling price of the mobile phones.

coming in at less than the minimum efficient scale would not be feasible if it involved average costs substantially higher than those of established firms. In Bain's view, economies of multi-plant operation and economies of scale in distribution equally limit entry. In the former case, an entrant may have to enter several geographical markets at once; in the latter case an entrant may have to come in on a vertically integrated basis. The modern view is that scale economies can constitute a barrier to entry if they are combined with sunk costs. The more costs are sunk, the more potential entrants have to weigh the risks of entering. Incumbents will be able to deter potential entrants if sunk costs are high: for the former it is costly to leave the market and for the latter the sum of fixed and sunk costs acts as a deterrent.

Recent evolution in high-technology markets has fuelled discussion about a new type of entry barrier. To effectively compete, firms need access to data. The more data a search engine has, the more refined and accurate will be the search results. 'Big data' are the new scale economies; together with network effects they may give rise to the creation of a dominant position if newcomers cannot offset their scale disadvantages. The ability to process large volumes of heterogeneous data displays an increasingly central role, not only in the digital ecosystem but also in traditional economic sectors. The implications of this phenomenon are not limited to the privacy of individuals as they heavily affect the functioning of markets and consumer welfare. Big Data fosters innovation, but it also poses antitrust concerns, mainly stemming from its extensive commercial use (OECD 2016).

In some economic sectors, the Big Data phenomenon is closely linked to market power. The ability to capture and analyse large amounts of information may give companies the possibility to acquire significant market power. In these circumstances, the main concerns for the competitive viability of the market surface. The use of Big Data by dominant firms may pose the risk that they exploit their market power to hinder the entry of new competitors in the market, harming also consumers (Rubinfeld and Gal 2017).

In markets characterised by dominant firms, the simple use of Big Data does not *per se* amount to an unlawful conduct under the different antitrust regimes. It is only under specific circumstances that the use of Big Data might allow dominant firms to drive competitors out of the market or limit their ability to enter and compete. Furthermore, Big Data may be also relevant in the competitive assessment of cartels. Competitors may have an interest in sharing information to the detriment of other operators. Lastly, it is increasingly common that mergers involve digital world actors, for which Big Data is a central aspect of their business, as symbolised by the *Google/DoubleClick*[68] and *WhatsApp/Facebook* mergers.[69]

Product differentiation: the Harvard–Chicago debate

In the perfect competition model firms sell homogeneous products. They have no incentives to use non-price strategies (such as physical differentiation and services provided with the product) to increase sales, since they can sell as much as they want without such extra effort. In real-world markets, firms use product differentiation to make their product(s) special to more and more consumers, so that sales increase. The view that product differentiation (and advertising) must be qualified as first-mover advantages and strategic entry barriers is not universally accepted. There are, broadly speaking, two conflicting approaches.

Some commentators have argued that product differentiation alters the public's perception of the product. According to Bain, product differentiation 'refers to the extent to which buyers differentiate, distinguish, or have specific preferences among the competing outputs of the various sellers' (Bain 1968, 223). A lot of product differentiation is perceived rather than real. Real differences include those in product reliability and performance as well as the quality of connected services (delivery time, pre-sales and post-sales services). Perceived product differentiation refers to the subjective appreciation of a product. Examples include colour, packaging, design and prestige brand names. Hence, firms that were the first to introduce changes in the product enjoy a first-mover advantage. Rival firms then have the choice of offering similar products or implementing their own strategies to make their products special to consumers. With an inferior image new entrants may be condemned more or less permanently to charge lower prices than the incumbent(s) and may have to spend more on promotion to change the consumers' brand loyalty or inertia. If the presence of the incumbent raises the marketing entry costs of the second firm, then the first firm has a permanent advantage (a long-run barrier to entry) and can maintain high prices.

Bork stressed the fact that many barriers to entry are inherent in the nature of different industries and thus natural. Anybody understands that it is more difficult to enter the computer industry than to open a candy store. Hence, it is necessary to distinguish carefully between forms of efficiency and artificial entry barriers. The key question for antitrust policy is to find out whether there are any artificial entry barriers (Bork 1993, 311). Regarding product

---

[68] Case COMP/M.4731, *Google/DoubleClick*, 11 March 2008.
[69] Case COMP/M.7217, *Facebook/ WhatsApp*, 03 October 2014.

differentiation, Bork disagreed with the Bainian approach which assessed this as a barrier to entry. Following the Chicago view, sellers differentiate their products to increase their appeal to consumers and such differentiation is profitable only if consumers value it. Hence, successful product differentiation must be classified as a form of efficiency. Even though an incumbent firm's product differentiation policy may create an entry barrier when consumers prefer established products to new rival products, entrants remain free to design their products as they wish. It all comes down to consumers' preferences.

Advertising: the Harvard–Chicago debate

In the tradition of Bain, Harvard scholars see advertising as persuasion: by changing the consumers' preferences, firms may increase their market power. If advertising campaigns are successful, consumers will perceive the advertised brand(s) as the best and most reliable. Since advertising is a means of building up consumer loyalty, it may make entry by new firms into the market difficult. The Chicago view on advertising originated with George Stigler; it regards advertising as information. Stigler showed that if consumers lack information about the prices charged by different sellers of a product, then the sellers would be able to charge higher prices than if the consumers had been perfectly informed (Stigler 1961). Advertising reduces search costs of consumers and is pro-competitive. The scope of this section does not allow an elaboration on the question of whether and to what extent advertising is informative. But even if advertisements are seen as merely persuasive, the informative value of advertising does not automatically fall to zero. Nelson argued that high expenditure on advertising is in fact a signal of high quality of the product: the advertiser's confidence in the product is such that he is willing to spend money on it.[70] Under some circumstances the amount of persuasive advertising may indeed be a signal of quality. High-quality firms selling experience goods will earn high confidence premiums; as a consequence they have a greater incentive to advertise than low-quality firms do. Obviously, this argument only holds if high-quality and low-quality firms have the same variable costs. If low-quality firms (fly-by-night firms) can easily enter the market, sell worthless products that are almost costless to produce and leave the market before consumers are able to retaliate, the amount of the premiums for opportunistic behaviour may be higher than the amount of the confidence premiums. The fly-by-night firms make larger profits on their initial sales (opportunism premiums) since they have

---

[70] See the seminal article by Nelson (1974). Building on Nelson's work, Bagwell and Ramey argue that even where advertising is ostensibly uninformative, it may achieve coordination economies if it directs consumers towards the firms that offer the best deals: Bagwell and Ramey (1994).

no intention of being around for very long; for them earning confidence premiums is not an objective. Low-quality firms may mimic the actions of high-quality firms by raising advertising to high levels. A related problem is false advertising. In markets in which opportunism premiums exceed confidence premiums, false advertising should be combatted by appropriate legal rules. From an efficiency point of view, in cases where there is a danger of opportunistic behaviour, confidence is to be protected if information costs are reduced and a confidence premium is paid. Both conditions are satisfied here: advertising reduces the search costs of consumers and the costs of advertising are passed on to consumers via higher resale prices. Hence, a prohibition of false advertising is warranted to cope with the danger of opportunistic behaviour. Even though there is thus a clear economic rationale for a prohibition of 'false' advertising, in practice the law prohibits 'misleading' advertising. This is a broader category of deception, which also includes true, but misleading, advertising. A major problem is how to apply a broad prohibition of misleading advertising without reducing efficient information flows by banning true advertising in consumer goods markets.

Modern industrial organisation

The modern industrial organisation literature has further contributed to our understanding of product differentiation and advertising as entry barriers. It now appears that a cautious approach is warranted. Product differentiation and advertising can, under certain conditions, reduce consumer welfare. Advertising may be used either to increase the objective knowledge of products or to create consumers' preferences for a particular brand, thereby making the demand for those products less elastic and market entry by newcomers more difficult. However, to qualify as an entry barrier and not just as an entry impediment, the effects of advertising must last sufficiently long to enable incumbent firms to earn supra-normal profits persistently. On the latter point, the relevant empirical evidence is mixed: some researchers found that the effects of advertising lasted for several years, whereas others found that advertising effects are gone within a year (compare Ayanian 1983; Boyd and Seldon 1990).

Modern industrial organisation stresses the importance of sunk costs in assessing whether advertising may function as a barrier to entry. Sunk costs are central to the calculations of potential entrants: advertising costs to build consumer loyalty are normally sunk costs, unless a firm that exits the market could either sell its brand name or use it somewhere else without a loss. The higher are the advertising and promotion expenditures that cannot be recovered on exiting a particular market, the more entry will be deterred.[71] The literature in industrial organisation on product differentiation also includes the view that it may be used as an instrument to obstruct market entry. To deter entrants looking for unfilled product design or brand image niches established sellers might seek to crowd product space with enough brands (brand proliferation), so that no room for profitable new entry remains (Schmalensee 1978). Consumer switching costs are a closely related topic. Goods or services which are perfect substitutes prior to the first purchase may become differentiated for a consumer who has already purchased because of *ex post* switching costs. Examples include bank accounts and airlines with frequent flyer programmes. Consumers who have already purchased from incumbent firms are locked in to a greater or lesser extent and, hence, are less available to entrants than uncommitted consumers (Klemperer 1987a, Klemperer 1987b). Recently, the behavioural economics literature has provided further arguments that warn against anti-competitive lock-in effects. Traders may exploit behavioural biases on the side of consumers (such as the endowment effect and the *status quo*/confirmation bias) to bind them to powerful suppliers (Cooper and Kovacic 2012; Bloomfield 2006). In sum, a competitive assessment of advertising and product differentiation requires a careful weighing of the following: the duration of advertising effects, the magnitude of sunk costs and the use of marketing techniques in a strategic way (brand proliferation, switching costs).

4.8 Conclusions

Competition law is an instrument to avoid that companies enjoying market power impose lasting price increases surpassing the competitive level. The first task of competition authorities thus consists of identifying market power. The economic definition of market power, which focuses on the difference between market price and marginal cost and the existence of entry barriers, differs from the legal concept of dominance. The latter focuses on the degree of independence of a powerful firm, which limits the individual economic freedom of competitors and consumers. The most striking difference between the assessment of market power in competition law and industrial organisation theory is the requirement to define a so-called relevant market and the market definition's primary position in competition analysis. Figures about firms' residual demand elasticities are immediately relevant for defining their degree of market power. Conversely, calculating market shares on a previously determined relevant market is only an indirect approach for assessing market power. Moreover, the market definition exercise is fraught

---

[71] Sutton classifies advertising as endogenous sunk costs, as opposed to exogenous sunk costs such as investments in production capacity (Sutton 1991).

with many difficulties: lack of transparency, danger of regulatory capture and lack of objectivity.

The main function of market definition is to identify in a systematic way the competitive constraints faced by the firms involved in an antitrust proceeding. These constraints include products and regions which are such close substitutes in the eyes of customers that they restrain the behaviour of their suppliers. According to the traditional legal definition, a relevant product market comprises all those products which are regarded as interchangeable or substitutable by the consumers by reason of the product's characteristics, their prices and their intended use. The relevant geographical market is defined by assessing whether the conditions of competition in a given region are sufficiently homogeneous. The SSNIP test defines the relevant market as a product or group of products and a geographical area in which it is sold so that a hypothetical profit-maximising firm, that was the only present and future seller of those products in that area would impose a profitable Small but Significant and Non-transitory Increase in Price above prevailing or likely future levels. In contrast with the traditional legal definition, the SSNIP test gears the delineation of the market to the crucial question of market power. It takes into account three forces that might simultaneously discipline market power: demand substitution, supply substitution and potential competition. The SSNIP test also defines the product market and the geographical market simultaneously instead of sequentially.

The concept of the relevant antitrust market is sometimes confused with other notions of markets. Industry classifications do not provide a sound basis for assessing the competitive impact of agreements, exclusionary practices or mergers. Economic markets are markets for goods or geographical areas where supply and demand lead to equilibrium prices. Strategic markets are groups of consumers and geographical areas at which marketing activities are targeted. By contrast, the relevant antitrust markets are markets where profitable price increases are possible. Consequently, industry classifications, economic markets and strategic markets provide no sound foundation on which it is possible to evaluate likely competitive effects, since they do not allow identification of the group of products and geographical areas worth monopolising.

The Notice of the European Commission on market definition is not fully consistent with insights from the economic analysis of market power. The Notice is a somewhat peculiar document since modern economic views are injected into an orthodox legal straitjacket. This causes several inconsistencies: the focus on product characteristics leads to inappropriate decisions if they do not influence the extent of competition in-between commodities and locations; there is no clear indication whether the SSNIP test should apply to supply substitution; there is no emphasis on the need to define product markets and geographical markets simultaneously; and there is no solution for the specific problem of applying a SSNIP test in dominance cases (to avoid the *Cellophane* fallacy, the test should start from competitive prices that cannot easily be established). Apart from these inconsistencies, the Notice may also be criticised for not offering sufficient guidance concerning the use of quantitative techniques for defining a relevant market.

In the past decades, the necessary data for quantitative analysis has become available on a wider scale and direct econometric measurements of the relevant elasticities to define market power have thus come within the reach of day-to-day competition law practice. The SSNIP test is not a test in itself but provides an economic framework in which quantitative techniques for measuring market power may be used. Cross-price elasticities of demand allow a ranking of substitutes and may equally provide sufficient proof of substitution to reject a proposed (narrow) market definition. However, it is not possible to define the relevant market on the basis of figures on cross-price elasticities without information about the critical demand elasticity at the firm's level. The most direct approach to market definition focuses on the own-price elasticity of demand for the product(s) in the potential relevant market. Comparing the critical demand elasticity (that is, the threshold above which a price increase becomes unprofitable) with the actual demand elasticity brings the SSNIP test from the world of theoretical economics into daily antitrust practice. A technique to directly define a relevant market is critical loss analysis. In this approach, the critical loss is calculated taking into account the initial profit margin and then compared with the actual loss. If the latter exceeds the former, a broader definition of the market is called for until the borderline is reached, where the critical value is no longer exceeded.

Market share analysis does not always capture the relevant concerns of competition law enforcement. In the literature, the market share/market power paradigm has been severely criticised. It has even been suggested to abandon the exercise of market definition entirely. Market shares are less reliable indicators of antitrust worries when, as a consequence of mergers, unilateral effects in differentiated product markets arise. In such cases, merger simulation models may allow for a direct assessment of market power and avoid burdensome market definition debates. However, also the use of econometric techniques may be biased. The availability of data, rather than the seriousness of particular competitive distortions, may determine the actions taken by competition authorities. Moreover, econometric techniques also involve some degree of subjectivity in choosing the relevant benchmarks for deriving conclusions on the competitive functioning of markets. Hence, both a disproportionate focus on data that is easily available and the risk of subjectivity in choosing the parameters to be measured must be avoided. Ultimately, a combined use of different techniques, which all point in the direction of a unique market definition, may be the most powerful way of defining market power.

This chapter concluded with an analysis of entry barriers. After having recalled the Harvard–Chicago debate on this topic, the most important insights from modern industrial organisation theory were summarised. Sunk costs and strategic behaviour are crucial factors in assessing the existence of entry barriers. In addition, a distinction can be made between absolute cost advantages (licensing laws, intellectual property rights) and strategic or first-mover advantages (economies of scale combined with sunk costs, lasting effects of advertising and brand proliferation through product differentiation). Competition authorities should carefully distinguish between both categories of entry barriers, on the one hand, and obstacles to entry that are caused by higher efficiency, on the other. Most recently, the availability and use of Big Data has proven to pose new antitrust policy concerns.

4.9   Bibliography

Ayanian R (1983), 'The Advertising Capital Controversy' 56 *Journal of Business* 349

Bagwell K, Ramey G (1994), 'Coordination Economies, Advertising and Search Behaviour in Retail Markets' 84 *American Economic Review* 498

Bain J (1968), *Industrial Organisation* (Wiley, 2nd ed.)

Bain J (1956), *Barriers to New Competition* (Harvard University Press)

Bain J (1951), 'Relation of Profit Rate to Industry Concentration: American Manufacturing' 65 *Quarterly Journal of Economics* 293

Baker J, Bresnahan T (1992), 'Empirical Methods of Identifying and Measuring Market Power' 61 *Antitrust Law Journal* 3

Baker J, Bresnahan T (1988), 'Estimating the Residual Demand Curve Facing a Single Firm' 6 *International Journal of Industrial Organization* 283

Baker J, Rubinfeld D (1999), 'Empirical Methods Used in Antitrust Litigation: Review and a Critique' 1 *American Law and Economics Review* 386

Baker S, Wu L (1998), 'Applying the Market Definition Guidelines of the European Commission' 19 *European Competition Law Review* 273

Bishop S, Walker M (2002), *Economics of EC Competition Law: Concepts, Application and Measurement* (Sweet & Maxwell, 2nd ed.)

Bloomfield R (2006), 'Behavioral Finance' (Johnson School Research Paper No. 38-06) <https://ssrn.com/abstract=941491>

Bork R (1993), *The Antitrust Paradox: A Policy at War with Itself* (Free Press, 2nd ed.)

Boyd R, Seldon B (1990), 'The Fleeting Effect of Advertising' 24 *Economics Letters* 375

Camesasca P, Van den Bergh R (2002), 'Achilles Uncovered: Revisiting the European Commission's 1997 Market Definition Notice' 47 *Antitrust Bulletin* 143

Carlton D, Perloff J (2005), *Modern Industrial Organization* (Pearson, 4th ed.)

Chamberlin E (1950), 'Product Heterogeneity and Public Policy' 40 *American Economic Review* 85

Cooper J, Kovacic W (2012), 'Behavioral Economics and Its Meaning for Antitrust Agency Decision Making' 8 *Journal of Law, Economics and Policy* 779

Cubero A (2010), *Barriers to Competition: The Evolution of the Debate* (Routledge)

Deaton A, Muelbauer J (1980), 'An Almost Ideal Demand System' 70 *American Economic Review* 312

Desai K (1997), 'The European Commission's Draft Notice on Market Definition: A Brief Guide to the Economics' 18 *European Competition Law Review* 473

Elzinga K, Hogarty T (1973), 'The Problem of Geographical Market Delineation in Antimerger Suits' 18 *Antitrust Bulletin* 45

Epstein R, Kieff F and Spulber D (2012), 'The FTC, IP, and SSOs: Government Hold-Up Replacing Private Coordination', 8 *Journal of Competition Law and Economics* 15

Fisher F (2001), 'Antitrust and Innovative Industries' 68 *Antitrust Law Journal* 559

Gebicka A, Heinemann A (2014), 'Social Media and Competition Law' 37 *World Competition* 149

Geroski P (1998), 'Thinking Creatively about Markets' 16 *International Journal of Industrial Organization* 77

Gilbert R (1989), 'Mobility Barriers and the Value of Incumbency', in R Schmalensee and R Willig (eds.), *The Handbook of Industrial Organization* I, 475 (North Holland)

Harbord D, Hoehn T (1994), 'Barriers to Entry and Exit in European Competition Policy' 14 *International Review of Law and Economics* 411

Hausman J, Leonard G (1997), 'Economic Analysis of Differentiated Products Mergers Using Real World Data' 5 *George Mason Law Review* 321

Hildebrand D (2006), 'Using Conjoint Analysis for Market Definition: Application of Modern Market Research Tools to Implement the Hypothetical Monopolist Test' 29 *World Competition* 315

Hoppmann E (1977), *Marktmacht und Wettbewerb* (Mohr)

Hovenkamp H (2012), 'Antitrust and the Movement of Technology' 19 *George Mason Law Review* 1119

Hovenkamp H (1994), *Federal Antitrust Policy. The Law of Competition and Its Practice* (West Publishing Company)

Hovenkamp H, Janis M, Lemley M, Leslie C (2010), 'IP and Antitrust: An Analysis of Antitrust Principles Applied to Intellectual Property Law' (Aspen Publishers, 2nd ed.)

Hurley S (2011), 'The Use of Surveys in Merger and Competition Analysis' 7 *Journal of Competition Law and Economics* 45

Ivaldi M, Verboven F (2000), 'Quantifying the Effects from Horizontal Mergers in European Competition Policy' 23 *International Journal of Industrial Organization* 669

Kaplow L (2011), 'Market Share Thresholds: On The Conflation of Empirical Assessments and Legal Policy Judgements' 7 *Journal of Competition Law and Economics* 243

Kaplow L (2010), 'Why (Ever) Define Markets?' 124 *Harvard Law Review* 437

Kaplow L, Shapiro C (2007), 'Antitrust', in M Polinsky and S Shavell (eds.), *Handbook of Law and Economics* II 1073 (North Holland)

Kaserman D, Zeisel H (1996), 'Market Definition: Implementing the Department of Justice Merger Guidelines' 41 *Antitrust Bulletin* 665

Kerber W, Schwalbe U (2006), 'Ökonomische Grundlagen des Wettbewerbsrechts', in G Hirsch, F Montag, and F Säcker (eds.), *Münchener Kommentar zum Europäischen und Deutschen Wettbewerbsrecht*, Bd I, 207 (C.H. Beck Verlag)

Keyte J (1995), 'Market Definition and Differentiated Products: The Need for a Workable Standard' 63 *Antitrust Law Journal* 697

Klemperer P (1987a), 'Markets with Consumer Switching Costs' 102 *Quarterly Journal of Economics* 375

Klemperer P (1987b), 'The Competitiveness of Markets with Switching Costs' 18 *RAND Journal of Economics* 138

Kotler P, Armstrong G (2013), *Principles of Marketing* (Prentice Hall, 15th ed.)

Landes W, Posner R (1981), 'Market Power in Antitrust Cases' 94 *Harvard Law Review* 937

Lerner A (1934), 'The Concept of Monopoly and the Measurement of Monopoly Power' 1 *Review of Economic Studies* 157

Leveque F, Ménière Y (2006), *Patents and Innovation: Friends or Foes?* <https://ssrn.com/abstract=958830>

Marshall A (1961), *Principles of Economics* (Macmillan, 9th ed.)

Martin S (1994), *Industrial Economics: Economic Analysis and Public Policy* (Prentice Hall)

Motta M (2004), *Competition Policy. Theory and Practice* (Cambridge University Press)

Nelson P (1974), 'Advertising as Information' 81 *Journal of Political Economy* 729

Nevo H (2014), *Definition of the Relevant Market: (Lack of) Harmony between Industrial Economics and Competition Law* (Intersentia)

Nevo H (2013), 'Market Definition Under Attack: How Relevant is the Relevant Market?', in M Faure and X Zhang (eds.), *The Chinese Anti-Monopoly Law* 301 (Edward Elgar)

Newman J (2015), 'Antitrust in Zero-Price Markets: Applications' 94 *Washington University Law Review* 49

OECD (2016), 'Big Data: Bringing Competition Policy to the Digital Era' DAF/Comp(2016)

OECD (2013), 'The Role and Measurement of Quality in Competition Analysis' DAF/COMP(2013)17

OECD (2006), 'Barriers to Entry' DAF/COMP(2005)42

Ordover J, Wall D (1989), 'Understanding Econometrics Methods of Market Definition' 3 *Antitrust* 20

Perekhozhuk O, Glauben T, Grings M, Teuber R (2016), 'Approaches And Methods For The Econometric Analysis Of Market Power: A Survey And Empirical Comparison' 31 *Journal of Economic Surveys* 303

Pitofsky R (1990), 'New Definitions of Relevant Market and the Assault on Antitrust' 90 *Columbia Law Review* 1805

Polinsky A, Shavell S (1989), 'Legal Error, Litigation and the Incentive to Obey the Law' 5 *Journal of Law, Economics and Organization* 99

Posner R (1976), *Antitrust Law. An Economic Perspective* (University of Chicago Press)

Renda A (2012), 'Telecommunications Regulation', in R Van den Bergh and A Pacces (eds.), *Regulation and Economics* 341 (Edward Elgar)

Ritter C (2005), 'Refusal to Deal and Essential Facilities: Does Intellectual Property Require Special Deference Compared to Tangible Property?' 28 *World Competition* 281

Rubinfeld D (2000), 'Market Definition with Differentiated Products: The Post/Nabisco Cereal Merger' 68 *Antitrust Law Journal* 163

Rubinfeld D, Gal M (2017), 'Access Barriers to Big Data' <https://ssrn.com/abstract=2830586>

Salop S (2000), 'The First Principles Approach to Antitrust, Kodak, and Antitrust at the Millenium' 68 *Antitrust Law Journal* 187

Salop S, Scheffman D (1987), 'Cost-Raising Strategies' 36 *Journal of Industrial Economics* 19

Scheffman D, Spiller P (1987), 'Geographical Market Definition under the U.S. Department of Justice Merger Guidelines' 30 *Journal of Law and Economics* 123

Schmalensee R (2004), 'Sunk Costs and Antitrust Barriers to Entry' (MIT Sloan Working Paper No. 4457-04) <https://ssrn.com/abstract=486944>

Schmalensee R (1982), 'Another Look at Market Power' 95 *Harvard Law Review* 1780

Schmalensee R (1978), 'Entry Deterrence in the Ready-to-Eat Breakfast Cereal Industry' 9 *Bell Journal of Economics* 305

Schmidtchen D (1988), 'Fehlurteile über das Konzept der Wettbewerbsfreiheit' 39 *ORDO Jahrbuch für die Ordnung von Wirtschaft und Gesellschaft* 111

Scotchmer S (2004), *Innovation and Incentives* (MIT Press)

Shughart W, Tollison R, Reed E (1996), 'Breakfast at the Federal Trade Commission', in F McChesney (ed.), *Economic Inputs, Legal Outputs: The Role of Economists in Modern Antitrust* 85 (Wiley)

Simons J, Williams M (1993), 'The Renaissance of Market Definition' 39 *Antitrust Bulletin* 799

Stigler G (1961), 'The Economics of Information' 69 *Journal of Political Economy* 213

Stigler G, Sherwin R (1985), 'The Extent of the Market' 28 *Journal of Law and Economics* 555

Stocking G, Mueller W (1955), 'The Cellophane Case and the New Competition' 45 *American Economic Review* 29

Sutton J (1991), *Sunk Costs and Market Structure* (MIT Press)

Thépot F (2013), 'Market Power in Online Search and Social Networking: a Matter of Two-Sided Markets' 36 *World Competition* 195

Tirole J (1988), *The Theory of Industrial Organization* (MIT Press)

Ulrick S (2014), 'A Primer on AIDS-Based Models in Antitrust Analysis' 10 *European Competition Journal* 123

Utton M (2003), *Market Dominance and Antitrust Policy* (Edward Elgar, 2nd ed.)

Van den Bergh R (1999), 'Self-regulation of the Medical and Legal Professions: Remaining Barriers to Competition and EC Law', in B Bortolotti and G Fiorentini (eds.), *Organized Interests and Self-Regulation* 89 (Oxford University Press)

Van den Bergh R (1996), 'Modern Industrial Organisation versus Old-fashioned European Competition Law' 17 *European Competition Law Review* 75

Van den Bergh R, Montangie Y (2006), 'Are Latin Notaries Different?' 2 *Journal of Competition Law and Economics* 189

Werden G (2002), 'Assigning Market Shares' 70 *Antitrust Law Journal* 67

Werden G (1998), 'Demand Elasticities in Antitrust Analysis' 66 *Antitrust Law Journal* 363

Werden G (1996) 'A Robust Test for Consumer Welfare Enhancing Mergers among Sellers of Differentiated Products' 44 *Journal of Industrial Economics* 409

Werden G (1992), 'Four Suggestions on Market Delineation' 37 *Antitrust Bulletin* 107

Willig R (1991), 'Merger Analysis, Industrial Theory, and Merger Guidelines' 1991 *Brookings Papers on Economic Activity. Microeconomics* 281

5

Horizontal restrictions

Peter Camesasca, Phil Warren and Roger Van den Bergh

5.1   Introduction

Competing firms that decide to join forces can do so in different, more or less structured or permanent, ways. They can exchange information, cooperate in certain fields, such as research and development (R&D), set up a joint venture, merge with or acquire a competitor. These forms of competitor cooperation can be seen on a sliding scale of intensity. Horizontal cooperation between companies preserves some sort of competition. In contrast, mergers end competition completely between the parties involved. Mergers, which occur either through forming a new company owning the assets of the founders or by acquiring all or part of the stock or assets of another company, are also designed to be permanent, whereas competitor collaboration is typically of a more limited duration. The former's potential for excluding future competition necessitates a modified antitrust approach.[1] Mergers are covered by a separate set of rules,[2] which will be discussed in Chapter 9 of this book. Instead of opting for a full merger, firms may also bring together capital, production assets, technology and knowledge to create a joint venture, which will produce a new product or take over activities (for example, research and marketing) from the founding companies. Legally, joint ventures are also treated separately; their treatment depends on the degree of integration achieved (see the discussion in section 5.3.4).

This chapter deals with forms of cooperation between actual and potential competitors, which imply horizontal restrictions of competition. Vertical restrictions are dealt with in the next chapter of this book. Each form

---

[1] Competition authorities recognise these differences; compare the Guidelines on the application of Article 81(3) [now Art. 101 (3) TFEU] of the Treaty [2004] O.J. C 101/97 (hereinafter EU General Guidelines), at 12–13; and US Antitrust Guidelines for Collaborations Among Competitors, April 2000 (hereinafter US Horizontal Guidelines), at 1.3.

[2] Notwithstanding the residuary applicability of Article 101 TFEU in the wake of the ECJ's *Philip Morris* judgment (Joined cases 142/84 and 156/84 *British American Tobacco Company Ltd. and R.J. Reynolds Industries, Inc. v. Commission* [1987] ECR 4487).

of horizontal restriction has potential pro- and anti-competitive effects. Agreements on price increases or output reductions (traditional cartels) as well as market sharing (territorial or customer restrictions) are clear examples of harmful horizontal restrictions. Besides collusion, anti-competitive horizontal restrictions may also take different forms: agreements may aim at harming rivals not party to the collusion (for example, boycotts) or changing the conditions under which competition in the market is to take place (for example, restrictions on advertising), which may lead to foreclosure of potential rivals. In contrast to these anti-competitive effects (collusion and market foreclosure), horizontal cooperation among competitors may also generate benefits. Cooperation often covers areas such as R&D, common schemes of production, purchasing, marketing or expanding into foreign markets. Companies need to respond to the increasing dynamism of the globalising marketplace and its growing complexity. To this end, cooperation can offer a means of sharing risks, saving costs, pooling know-how and stepping up innovative activity. Contrary to agreements on prices and output or foreclosure to change the competitive market surroundings, the latter form of cooperation is benign. The efficiencies achieved notwithstanding, horizontal cooperation of the benevolent kind may also lead to anti-competitive concerns, as the firms involved can simultaneously agree to fix prices or output, share markets or generally try to obtain or increase collective market power. The resulting trade-off between benefits and drawbacks to cooperation has been explicitly recognised by antitrust authorities, both in the US and in the EU.[3]

European competition law seeks to restrain anti-competitive coordination of companies' behaviour. In a first step, Article 101(1) TFEU bans cartel agreements, decisions of associations of undertakings and concerted practices that harm competition. This ban covers not only hard-core cartels, which are explicit agreements between competitors having as their object the restriction of competition, but also agreements whose effects are anti-competitive and concerted practices where the collusive agreement is merely implicit (soft cartels). Agreements between competitors, decisions of associations of undertakings and concerted practices that harm competition are null and void (Article 101(2) TFEU). In a second step, Article 101(3) TFEU addresses the potential benefits of horizontal cooperation. It is an exception rule, which grants an exemption from the prohibition contained in Article 101(1) TFEU when the benefits of the agreement in terms of efficiencies and consumer welfare are deemed to prevail without causing disproportionate restrictions or eliminating competition for a substantial part of the products

---

[3] Compare the EU General Guidelines, at 2–4; and the US Horizontal Guidelines, at the Preamble.

in question.[4] Article 101(3) TFEU provides a defence for undertakings against a finding of an infringement of Article 101(1) TFEU. Agreements, decisions of associations of undertakings and concerted practices caught by Article 101(1) TFEU that satisfy the conditions of Article 101(3) TFEU are valid and enforceable, no prior decision to that effect being required.

The first competition law in the United States, the Sherman Act, which was enacted in 1890, gave the government authority to seek criminal penalties for agreements in 'restraint of trade'.[5] The Sherman Act is exceedingly vague, as it does not specify what conduct it outlaws. Read literally, it would pro-hibit not only anti-competitive conduct but all manner of pro-competitive or competitively neutral agreements that simply restrict conduct. However, soon after the Sherman Act's adoption, the US Supreme Court narrowed its scope by ruling that it proscribes only restraints that *unreasonably* restrict competition.[6] Hence, the Sherman Act has been given content and meaning through more than 125 years of judicial interpretation. Horizontal restric-tions are analysed under the Rule of Reason, which allows a balancing of both anti-competitive and pro-competitive effects.

This chapter is structured as follows. After this introduction, section 5.2 summarises the most important insights of economic theory relating to hori-zontal restrictions of competition. The welfare losses that may be caused by market power have already been described in Chapter 2 of this book (see sec-tion 2.3.3). Here, the focus is on the welfare losses caused by different forms of horizontal (explicit or implicit) restrictions of competition. Thereafter, the incentives of firms to form cartels and the difficulties of monitoring these anti-competitive agreements are analysed. Game theory is particularly help-ful in revealing under which circumstances oligopolistic markets may reach a collusive outcome. Economic theory can assist in detecting whether col-lusion is more likely to occur and cartels are likely to succeed or fail. Factors that may make collusion either harder or easier will be highlighted. A major factor inhibiting successful cartelisation is the risk of cheating. Therefore, after the analysis of the incentives for cartelisation, the monitoring problem will be addressed. It will be explained how cartels may detect and punish de-viations from the collusive outcome. Section 5.2 concludes with an analysis of the potential benign effects of horizontal cooperation. The different ef-ficiencies (such as economies of scale and scope) which may be generated by horizontal restrictions are described and balanced against their potential anti-competitive effects. Section 5.3 assesses whether Article 101 TFEU

---

[4] For a detailed legal analysis, see Jones and Sufrin (2014, 192).
[5] 15 U.S.C. §§ 1–7.
[6] *Standard Oil Co. v. United States*, 221 US 1, 52 (1911).

provides an adequate legal platform for an economically balanced consideration of both the anti-competitive effects and the efficiencies of horizontal cooperation.[7] It subsequently focuses on the benchmark for cartelisation, the need for proof of explicit or implicit coordination and the assessment of efficiencies. References to the relevant case law are included to illustrate the importance of economic criteria that determine the (lack of) success of cartels. Section 5.4 discusses US antitrust law.[8] The Rule of Reason approach is compared with the distinction in EU competition law between restrictions by object and restrictions by effect. As in the other chapters of this book, the comparison with US antitrust law allows a clearer understanding of the most debated issues of the relevant competition laws. The similarities and remaining differences between EU competition law and US antitrust law are analysed from an economic perspective. Problems of enforcement, such as the level of fines, leniency programmes and the role of public versus private enforcement will be discussed in Chapter 8 of this book. Section 5.5 summarises the main findings of the comparative law and economics approach regarding horizontal restrictions of competition.

5.2 Lessons from economics

5.2.1 Forms of collusion and welfare effects

Economic theory is helpful in explaining why competitors have incentives to cooperate and why cartels are formed. On oligopolistic markets firms may increase their profits by cooperating. Anti-competitive collusion can take three forms (Werden 2004). First, firms may agree to fix prices, restrict output, freeze market shares or divide markets. Such agreements allow cartel members to maximise their profit directly. In practice, horizontal fixing of minimum prices also requires agreements on limiting production capacities and a concomitant discipline among cartel members not to exceed the production limits agreed upon. Most far-reaching is the founding of a common sales office (also called a syndicate), which represents the cartel in its relations with clients and divides the orders as well as the resulting profits among the cartel members. The second category of collusion consists of agreements to take action to harm rivals who are not party to the collusion. Firms can reduce their rivals' revenues through boycotts or raise rivals' costs by forcing the latter to increase prices (allowing the cartel members to sell under the rivals' price umbrella). Third, firms can collude to change the rules of competition in a manner that lessens other forms of competition than price competition. The

---

[7] Competition authorities, too, stress the need to base the analysis on economic criteria; compare the EU General Guidelines, at 6–7 and the US Horizontal Guidelines, at 1.2.

[8] For an in-depth overview of the relevant US antitrust rules, see Hovenkamp (1994), Kovacic (1993).

latter category includes agreements to limit advertising or raising consumers' search costs in another way (for example, restricting opening hours of shops). In the literature, the second and the third forms of collusion are commonly grouped under the heading of 'market foreclosure'.

Collusion of the first type directly raises price and causes a wealth transfer from consumers to the cartel as well as a deadweight loss (allocative inefficiency). From society's perspective the costs of forming and enforcing the cartel (rent-seeking) are also welfare-reducing (see section 2.3.4). In addition, the prospect of profits that are easy to make may reduce incentives to keep production costs low (productive inefficiency) or lower innovation incentives (dynamic inefficiencies). Since cartels of the second category lead to supra-competitive pricing, they may cause all the above types of detrimental effects. In addition, collusion to disadvantage rivals causes wasteful defensive measures by the victims and wasteful expenditure of resources by the cartel members to accomplish the cartel's objectives. The welfare effects of cartel agreements of the third type are even more numerous and complex. Consumer prices will be higher – because of the restrictions on advertising (or other sales methods) – so that losses in terms of allocative efficiency and rent-seeking will again ensue. In addition, the latter cartels will cause increased consumer search costs and lower the quality and variety of products offered in the market.

5.2.2 The economics of collusion

The problem of oligopolistic markets

As soon as the number of suppliers is limited and the products sold are not homogeneous, perfect competition no longer exists. Deviations give rise to different types of markets, of which monopoly is only one alternative. When products are differentiated, a distinction can be made between a pure multi-product monopoly (in which case there is only one seller), a differentiated oligopoly (in which case there are a few sellers) and monopolistic competition (in which case a large number of sellers offer differentiated products). The latter market form does not give rise to significant competitive concerns. Although it allows for price discrimination, this is not to be equated with the monopoly problem. The gains from product diversity can be large and may easily outweigh the inefficiencies resulting from small monopoly power (Pindyck and Rubinfeld 2005, 439–440). When products are homogeneous, there are once again three types of market: a pure monopoly, a homogeneous oligopoly and perfect competition. In this section, the focus will be on oligopolistic markets.

Economic theory teaches that the formation of cartels is easier if the firms involved are few and the industry concerned is concentrated. It must be added that antitrust practice shows that the opposite may also be true, as some of the most notorious cartels consisted of numerous participants.[9] In spite of their propensity to profitable and sustainable collusion, it would be premature to characterise all oligopolistic markets as prone to causing substantial welfare losses. The most important element distinguishing oligopolistic markets from monopoly and/or perfect competition is that profits of an oligopolistic firm are strongly dependent on the actions chosen by its competitors. A monopolist firm can maximise its profits by producing exactly the output where marginal revenue equals marginal cost. A firm in a perfectly competitive market must take price as given since it is too small to have an impact on the market price; hence price equals marginal cost. In oligopolistic markets, firms face a choice between cooperating (entering into cartel agreements) and competing (staying out of the cartel or cheating). In choosing one of these alternatives, an oligopolist firm will have to consider the plausible reactions of its competitors.

Insights from game theory

In game theory, economic models have been developed that describe the behavioural choices of firms in an oligopolistic market, which have to take the reactions by their competitors into account. Game theory supplements and refines the traditional insights of micro-economics with respect to welfare losses caused by oligopolies, by stressing that both cooperative and non-cooperative outcomes can be achieved. The game-theoretical literature on oligopolies is very extensive and cannot be covered within the limited scope of this book.[10] Economists have developed different models of oligopolistic industries, each carrying its own assumptions. The conclusions from this theoretical literature are highly dependent upon the underlying assumptions made. For the purposes of this book, it suffices to highlight the mainstream economic insights into the typical competitive problems encountered in oligopolistic markets. Game theory is helpful for revealing under which conditions price levels in oligopolistic markets may be above the competitive price.

Game theory distinguishes between cooperative and non-cooperative games. Under the former, the parties can make binding agreements. In the latter, this is not possible and strategic interaction may lead to an outcome which is suboptimal in comparison with what would be feasible if agreements were made.

---

[9] For example, see Cases IV/33.126 & IV/33.322 *Cement* [1994] O.J. L 343/1 and Case IV/33.833 *Cartonboard* [1994] O.J. L 243/1.

[10] For more detailed but also technical analyses, see Burkett (2006, 180); Vives (2001); Phlips (1995).

The best-known game providing the most relevant insights is the classic one-shot prisoner's dilemma. Two criminals, who together committed a crime, are caught and put in separate cells. Not having enough direct evidence, the police need a confession from one of them in order to convict both of them for the crime and impose a high sentence. The criminals are questioned separately and each prisoner is told that if (s)he testifies against the other, (s)he will receive a lighter sentence. Neither prisoner can speak with the other before making the decision whether to talk or remain silent. The best solution for both prisoners is that neither of them testifies. Having insufficient evidence, the public prosecutor will not be able to ask for a high sentence. However, if one prisoner talks, it is better for the other to testify as well in order to escape from a more severe punishment. If the other remains silent, testifying is also the best choice since it once again guarantees a lighter punishment. In the jargon of game theory, testifying is the dominant strategy.[11] As a result, both prisoners will be severely punished. The optimal outcome from the prisoners' perspective would have been a lighter sentence because of lack of evidence. However, this result will not be obtained because the two criminals cannot make a prior binding agreement not to testify.

The prisoner's dilemma in oligopolistic markets

The above analysis can be extended to the study of oligopolies. Given the existing interdependencies as a result of which a firm's actions depend on a rival's decisions, oligopolistic markets are characterised by strategic behaviour. Firms will face a choice between cooperative and non-cooperative strategies (colluding or cheating). On the one hand, they will recognise the possibility of earning higher profits through coordinating their activities. Price agreements or joint decisions to restrict output will achieve this goal. On the other hand, though, the collective incentive to collude will be opposed by strong private incentives of each individual firm to cheat on its fellow cartel members. If other firms respect the price agreement, the cheating firm will achieve additional profits. The numerical example below shows the different pay-offs for two firms which both face a choice between collusion (obeying the cartel agreement) and cheating (price undercutting or output expansion to attract additional customers). The numbers in each row denote the profits resulting from the outcome of the two firms' decisions. The first number shows the profits which Firm A makes and the second the profits which Firm B obtains. Considering the various outcomes, both firms would prefer an outcome in which both charged a high price (top left quadrant) to that in which they both charged a low price (bottom right quadrant). However, the duopoly

---

[11] A strategy that is a best choice for a player in a game for every possible choice by the other player is called a dominant strategy. See for further clarification: Baird, Gertner and Picker (1998, 306).

is characterised by a prisoner's dilemma (Figure 5.1) so that the outcome (Nash equilibrium)[12] will be that both firms cheat.

		Firm B	
		Collude	Cheat
Firm A	Collude	20, 20	15, 22
	Cheat	22, 15	17, 17

Figure 5.1 Prisoner's dilemma

If both firms coordinate their behaviour and collude, they will charge higher prices (or restrict output) and obtain joint profits amounting to 40, with each firm individually earning 20. If one firm cheats on the other by price undercutting (or expanding production) while the other firm adheres to the cartel agreement, the cheating firm will earn 22 while the other firm's profit declines to 15. Clearly, both firms are better off collectively if they collude. The joint collusive profits equal 40 and exceed the joint profits of 34 in case of price undercutting (or output expansion) by both firms. It is equally clear, however, that each firm has an incentive to forsake collusion and improve its own position through cheating. On the one hand, the latter option will increase profits by 2 (22 − 20) if the second duopolist does not cheat as well. On the other hand, if the rival cheats, adhering to the cartel agreement reduces profits by 3 (17 − 20). Given the extra profit in the case of cheating and the fear of losing money if the rival cheats, each duopolist will decide to cheat. In game-theoretical terms, the non-cooperative strategy will be dominant. To the duopolists the final outcome of the game (joint profits of 34) is worse than the cooperative outcome (joint profits of 40). To avoid this non-cooperative outcome the duopolists must be able to detect and punish cheating.

The fact that firms do meet in practice makes a collusive outcome more likely. In a one-shot game, a price increase is unlikely to convey enough information about the firm's intent to coordinate. In real-world oligopolistic markets, rivals do not play one-shot games. The Folk theorem in economics states that joint profit maximisation without communication among firms is possible if firms can observe each other's actions and interact with one another sufficiently frequently (Marshall and Marx 2012, 9). Non-cooperative games that are subject to repeated interaction (suggesting an infinite repetition of the

---

[12] An equilibrium is reached when no firm has a further incentive to change its behaviour taking account of the likely responses by other firms. The concept is named after Nobel laureate John Nash.

prisoner's dilemma) may lead to a collusive outcome, even in the absence of explicit agreements. In industries where only a few firms compete over a long period under stable demand and cost conditions, cooperation (tacit collusion) prevails even though no contractual arrangements are entered into.[13] In repeated games, it is possible that rivals can indicate their intention to collude by patterns of price movements and responses. The game theoretical insights relating to tacit collusion have been confirmed in experimental economics. Experiments suggest that tacit collusion is likely if there are (very) few rivals, many buyers, visible pricing, homogeneous products and firms compete over many time periods. Under these circumstances, each firm may be able to predict whether its rivals will reciprocate an announcement of a price increase (Haan *et al.* 2009, 13). Even limited communications (private expressions of intention) may reduce strategic uncertainty and facilitate coordination (Fonseca and Normann 2012). The theoretical and empirical insights on the possibility of a collusive equilibrium in oligopolistic markets may inform the legal debate on the interpretation of concerted practices (EU competition law) or tacit agreements (US antitrust law). If antitrust laws require hard evidence of explicit agreements (for example, written documents) to prove a violation of the cartel prohibition, they may fall short of adequately controlling serious anti-competitive concerns (for further discussion, see sections 5.3.1 and 5.4.1).

5.2.3 Requirements for successful collusion

In the remainder of this section, two issues are addressed in more detail: the incentive to collude and the problem of cheating. The potential of cartels to profitably increase prices depends on the market characteristics, the size of the attainable gains and the possibility to overcome organisational problems. A major factor inhibiting successful cartelisation is the risk of cheating. Below, it is discussed how deviations from the collusive outcome can be detected and punished.

The incentive to collude: conditions for successful cartelisation

Oligopolistic markets do not necessarily lead to collusive outcomes. Some cartels will succeed, while others will fail. In this section, three requisites for cartel success are discussed: the potential for monopoly power, given the characteristics of the market, expected high gains, and the need to overcome the organisational problems of cartels (see also Pindyck and Rubinfeld 2005, 463).

---

[13] For a technical discussion of Cournot competition and the relation with the basic prisoner's dilemma, the reader may refer to Pindyck and Rubinfeld (2005, 474).

Market characteristics

A number of market characteristics complicate collusion and thus decrease the potential for monopoly power: they may be apportioned among demand, supply, and other factors.[14] Complicating factors on the demand side include: (i) elastic demand; (ii) the existence of large and sophisticated buyers; (iii) differentiated products; (iv) volatile demand; and (v) demand booms. The more inelastic is the demand curve facing a cartel, the higher the price the cartel can set and the higher its profits. Examples of markets where cartels can be profit-maximising thus include cigarettes and services provided by utilities. Buyer power might counteract the cartel's power to increase prices: large buyers may succeed in obtaining secret discounts, causing the cartel to unravel (see the discussion of bilateral monopoly in Blair and Harrison 2010, 123–145). Heterogeneous products make traditional price fixing unlikely; most cartels involve homogeneous products, such as cement, glass, salt and cartonboard.[15] Cartels are also facilitated if the market is mature, rather than dynamic. If the technology used is well known and widespread, no major innovations are to be expected and demand is relatively stable or declining, negative effects are more likely than in more dynamic markets.

On the supply side, factors complicating collusion include: (i) low seller concentration; (ii) the existence of a competitive fringe with an elastic supply; (iii) ease of entry; and (iv) cost asymmetries. Entry by non-member firms or close substitutes produced in other industries prevents cartels from increasing prices. By contrast, collusion will be facilitated if the number of suppliers is limited and entry barriers exist. In general it is thought that cartels are to be found in concentrated industries, where competitors are few. Economists will hesitate to give a clear number indicating precisely what 'few' in this context means. A theoretical model developed by Nobel prize winner Reinhard Selten[16] shows that if there are fewer than five competitors, they will all find it profitable to collude explicitly; if there are more than five competitors, however, it becomes more attractive to be an outsider to the cartel. The subtitle of Selten's article neatly summarises the main insight: 'four are few and six are many'. However, as is the case with all economic models, the outcome is dependent on the assumptions made and antitrust practice also shows

---

[14] For an overview of the relevant literature, both theoretical and empirical, see Dick and Knight (1998, 17) and Carlton and Perloff (2005). Some of the relevant factors have been listed by the European Commission (EU General Guidelines, at 30). For additional discussion in the context of mergers, see section 9.2.2.

[15] For real-life examples, see Cases IV/33.126 & IV/33.322 *Cement* [1994] O.J. L 343/1; Case IV/33.833 *Cartonboard* [1994] O.J. L 243/1; Case IV/29.869 *Italian Cast Glass* [1980] O.J. L 383/19.

[16] Selten (1973). The argument is reinforced in Phlips (1995, 56–66). It should be noted that in Selten's model there are no statements made on the impact the number of competitors has on the enforcement of a cartel agreement, as there is no room for cheating in the chosen non-cooperative Nash equilibria with perfect information.

examples of high number cartels. It must also be added that in Selten's model there is no room for cheating or untruthful cost reporting (see for further discussion: Phlips 1995, 24).

Finally, other factors complicating collusion include the absence of prior collusion and one-shot competition. It should be noted, though, that some of these complicating factors will often be present without posing a serious risk to successful collusion. There is indeed no need for collusion to be perfect in order to work; firms only need to figure out convincingly that they are better off when coordinating instead of competing by independent pricing. Firms may also be able to adopt facilitating practices that help to offset or mitigate complicating factors. In general, empirical research warrants caution when making predictions, as studies vary widely by methodologies and samples (Page 2010; Dick 1996; Asch and Seneca 1976).

Expected high gains

If the potential gains from monopoly power achieved through cooperation are large, firms will have more incentives to form cartels and develop devices to make them effective instruments for raising prices persistently above competitive levels. If competition authorities strictly enforce the cartel prohibition, the expected penalties effectively reduce the expected value of collusion and fewer cartels will be formed.[17] During periods when the American Department of Justice was relatively lax in enforcing the antitrust laws, price-fixing conspiracies were more prevalent (Posner 1970). In Europe, in the period between both world wars, governments took a positive attitude towards cartels in an attempt to support national industry from foreign competition. Since the creation of the common market by the EEC Treaty, government-aided collusion has become a clear infringement of the Member States' duty not to take action inhibiting the achievement of the internal market goals.[18]

Cartels will not succeed if their members can and want to cheat on the agreement because the expected gains from cheating exceed the profits generated

---

[17] This does not imply that enforcement will be socially optimal. See section 8.2.2 for more on this issue.

[18] An example can be found in Case 311/85 *Vereniging van Vlaamse Reisbureaus v. Sociale Dienst* [1987] ECR 3801. The Belgian government endorsed a price-fixing agreement by travel agents and made it compulsory for outsiders by enacting a royal decree, which explicitly prohibited the granting of discounts. Article 101 TFEU does not apply if anti-competitive conduct is required by national legislation or if the latter creates a legal framework that precludes all scope for competitive activity (Case C-280/08 P, *Deutsche Telekom* [2010] ECR I-9555, at 80–81). It must be added that in such cases national legislators infringe their duty of loyalty towards the fundamental rules of the internal market, with the consequence that national competition authorities and judges must disapply those national rules; see Case C-198/01 *Consorzio Industrie Fiammiferi v. Autorità Garante della Concorrenza e del Mercato* [1993] ECR I-8055.

by the price-fixing agreement. In this respect, the moment at which deviation is detected and punished is crucial: the longer a firm can cheat without being detected, the more profitable price-cutting becomes. If cartel members can undermine the price-fixing agreement by granting secret discounts and are able to continue this practice for a sufficiently long period, cheating can be more profitable than respecting a price-fixing agreement. In order to succeed, a cartel must detect deviations from the collusive outcome and effectively and severely punish the firms that cheat. Devices that can be used to enforce cartels successfully will be further discussed below.

Low organisational costs

The transaction cost approach has made it clear that competition law should first address distortions of competition caused by dominant firms, since agreements among oligopolists may face great difficulties in minimising the costs of negotiating and enforcing agreements (see section 2.9.2). The greater the number of firms, the higher the transaction costs will be. Firms will also face more difficulties in agreeing on prices when each firm's product has different qualities or properties. This strengthens the argument advanced above that successful cartelisation is more likely in homogeneous goods markets.

Even before transaction cost theory had developed, the view was held that cartels did not raise significant concerns for competition policy (Stigler 1964). A cartel is inherently more fragile than a monopoly situation, since the interest of the cartel as a whole diverges substantially from the interests of its individual members.[19] With explicit coordination between firms (and thus the possibility of communication and negotiation) being prohibited, cooperative strategies can only be designed with considerable difficulty, as a result of which their implementation will remain unstable. The view that cartels will not be formed because of high transaction costs is too optimistic, however. The collective exercise of market power does not always require elaborate explicit coordination. If firms interact with each other on a prolonged basis, then the pursuit of individual interests – without any explicit communication or negotiation between firms – may be consistent with the collective exercise of market power. The formal theory of repeated games describes how firms might resist taking advantage of their competitors in the short term, because they would otherwise risk endangering a profitable long-term arrangement (Friedman 1971). Deviation from an established equilibrium situation will require a profitable trade-off between the resulting short-term gains and the long-term consequences. The outcome of this trade-off will depend on the

---

[19] The formal treatment may be retrieved from Phlips (1995, 49–66).

market circumstances as well as on whether the competitors can credibly announce that short-term deviations will be severely punished. If repeated interactions thus provide adequate surroundings for enforcing outcomes with substantial market power, then soft cartels may become a concern of competition policy as serious as hard core cartels – their intrinsic volatility notwithstanding. In short, from a welfare point of view, prohibiting explicit coordination does not solve all problems. Coordination may also result in a form of tacit agreement. In oligopolistic markets, there may be a situation of 'joint dominance' under which prices are kept high out of fear of retaliation.

Enforcement of cartels: reaching agreements to restrict competition, cheating and punishing deviations

Successful collusion requires that (i) competitors reach an understanding on prices, output, or another factor of competition; (ii) they can detect deviations from the common understanding; and (iii) they can credibly punish deviations from the collusive outcome. These requirements draw attention again to the cartel members' need of communicating with each other. Cartels collapse if their members are trapped in a prisoner's dilemma. It was shown above that duopolists who cannot influence each other's decision will choose not to cooperate and thus achieve a result which is worse than the one in case of collusion (see 5.2.2). A non-cooperative outcome (in technical terms: a non-cooperative Nash equilibrium) can be avoided if firms are able to control each other's behaviour. In other words, if firms can reach an agreement (explicitly or implicitly), cartels will be profit-maximising strategies if cheating can be detected and prevented.

The meeting of the minds

The successful formation of a cartel requires a 'meeting of the minds'. However, the repeated interaction of firms in an oligopolistic market leads by no means voluntarily to a coordinated outcome. Rather, multiple equilibria frequently exist, with the firms' profits differing accordingly. It is thus essential for firms to indicate to their potential fellow conspirators which strategy to pick. Below two strategies for reaching an understanding on the parameters of competition are discussed: cheap talk and basing point pricing.

Providing rivals with advance notice of intended prices may allow time to gauge the other firms' willingness to respond as well as to adjust prices if necessary. One way of doing so is so-called 'cheap talk', such as pre-announcing a price (Farrell 1987). A prominent example is the *Wood Pulp* cartel case,[20] which is built on evidence of parallel quarterly announcements of prospective price rises (see the discussion in Box 5.1). A variant is posed by referring to 'focal points', such as preserving existing price differentials or existing market shares.[21] Another strategy for making accomplices meet in unison is 'basing point pricing' (Haddock 1982). This scheme implies that sellers who produce at geographically dispersed locations set their prices according to a common price for delivered goods (thereby negating transportation as variable costs), typically designating a major production hub as its basing point. The price thus becomes independent of the actual distance between the seller and the buyer. A multiple basing point system ensures that at any given geographical location the delivered price to be quoted by all the competitors will be equal to the lowest combination of a base price plus freight (to that location) calculated from all basing points existing in the system. As a result, a single delivered price will be charged at every location.

Detecting deviations from the collusive outcome

Successful collusion is by no means self-enforcing. The profit opportunities created by collusion will attract entry into the market that the established members of the collusion must prevent. Otherwise, they have to persuade the new entrants to abide by the established code of conduct. As a consequence, members of a successful cartel often have to spend substantial resources to monitor their fellow accomplices' actions and restore discipline should cheating be detected. The ease of cheating varies considerably with the type of market involved. Cartels are most successful (cheating is most difficult) when markets are characterised by large-scale, infrequent sales and determined through secret bids with publicly announced results (compare Hovenkamp 1994, 145–146). Monitoring will be more difficult when information deficiencies exist or if the number of buyers is high. Conversely, monitoring costs may be alleviated when firms interact repeatedly.

Devices for detecting violations from the collusive outcome include information sharing, meeting competition clauses and repeated interaction. Imperfect or incomplete information available to the firms can impede coordination if they hold divergent views about demand conditions. Detecting the ensuing cheating may be facilitated if information is shared (Malueg and Tsutsui 1997; Kühn and Vives 1995). Information sharing presents antitrust

---

[20] Joined cases C-89/85, C-104/85, C-114/85, C-116/85, C-117/85 and C-125-129/85 A. Åhlström *Osakeyhtio and others v. Commission (Wood Pulp II)* [1993] ECR I-1307. A discussion from a game theoretical perspective is provided by Phlips (1995, 131–136).

[21] The theory of focal points was first devised by Schelling (1960) and later formalised by Sugden (1995).

with a dilemma. On the one hand, pooling information provides benefits to consumers (by facilitating comparison of alternative offers) as long as firms behave competitively. On the other hand, shared information makes anti-competitive agreements easier to construct (Clarke 1983). A second impediment to an unruffled collusive cohabitation arises when firms sell to many buyers, making it difficult to detect all instances of price undercutting. By adopting a 'meeting competition' clause, however, their buyers are guaranteed that, should they find another firm offering a lower price, the selling firm will match it or release the buyer from the contract. Also, monitoring may be alleviated when firms interact repeatedly, as firms will find it easier to observe the other cartel members' behaviour, given more frequent interaction.

Punishing deviations from the collusive outcome

The detection of deviations from collusion must be reinforced by some credible threat of punishment to serve as a meaningful deterrent. If secret price cuts or output reductions are traceable, the introduction of punishment causes a further series of problems. Given that competition law prohibits anti-competitive collusion, punishment must make cheating unprofitable without causing the cartel or collusion to be detected. Even if this is possible, the disciplinary measure will be effective only if the expected costs to the cheating member exceed the additional profits to be made. Ideally, cheating should be detected immediately and punished without exception, rendering it unprofitable. Among the more credible intimidations is threatening the offender with the loss of (part of the) collusive profits, once his misbehaviour is discovered. A common punishment is for the non-cheating cartel members to revert to the non-collusive price by raising output for some time (Osborne and Pitchik 1987). The longer a firm can cheat without being detected, though, the more profitable this becomes. Another problem with cheating is that the costs of punishment are regularly higher for the imposing cartel members than for the offender. However, if this method of punishment can be presented as a convincing strategy, it becomes possible to sustain the collusive equilibrium.

One way of ensuring punishment is by embracing a 'most favoured customer' clause (often to be found in combination with a 'meeting competition' clause). As cheating on a collusive price is generally profitable in the short run – until it is detected and punished – a 'most favoured customer' clause guarantees the buyer any discount offered to another buyer by the same seller under the terms of the contract. Thereby, uncertainty about rivals' prices is reduced, thus allowing firms to track just one or two buyers' prices to monitor rivals' reliability (Phlips 1995, 91–93). An alternative way of bolstering collusive agreements is by increasing cross-ownership among rivals, as this creates greater similarity of interests. Whether partial ownership actually hinders or facilitates collusion depends on the industry demand conditions, given that some of the penalty is borne by the rivals through their stake in the punished firm (Reitman 1994; Farrell and Shapiro 1990).

5.2.4 Efficiency savings from horizontal cooperation

Cooperation between firms may be motivated by goals that are beneficial to social welfare. Competition law should take into account these benign effects of competitor collaboration rather than solely focusing on the anti-competitive effects. Different types of cooperation can lead to a range of efficiencies, such as economies of scale and scope, better planning of production, advantages in marketing and distribution, and in research and development. In the following, the different types of efficiency savings will be discussed in turn. The discussion is not intended to be exhaustive, but only aims at giving the reader a general picture of the different categories of efficiencies.

Economies of scale

Economies of scale are reductions in average unit costs attributable to increases in the scale of output at the plant level. Generally, economies of scale exist when the production cost of a single product decreases with the number of units produced. These costs savings can accrue *inter alia* from a better division of labour within the production unit, the spreading of fixed costs and longer production runs. There can also be scale economies in functions such as transport, distribution, and research. Lowering costs gives the opportunity to increase profitability. The size of the economies achieved will depend on the slope of the average cost curve for outputs below the optimum scale. Besides these static scale economies, there is the creation of learning effects associated with the increasing experience of producing a good or service. This means that the cost of producing each extra unit decreases as the cumulative previous output increases. The minimum efficient scale is the size of a plant at which all economies of scale are exhausted and beyond which the long-term average costs curve either turns upward or remains flat (if returns to scale remain constant).

Typical economies of scale include: (i) indivisibilities: many costs are independent of the scale of output (fixed set-up costs); when output is increased, indivisible costs can be spread over larger numbers, reducing thereby the cost per unit;[22] (ii) increase in dimension: for many types of capital equipment both the initial and operating costs increase less rapidly than capacity; (iii) economies of specialisation: the larger the output of a product, plant or firm, the greater will be the opportunities for specialisation of the labour force and the machinery; (iv) economies of massed reserves: a larger-sized firm may profit from the statistical law holding that random events tend to cancel out if there are enough of them; through its diversity a large firm may be better placed to spread its risks, resulting in economies for emergency stocks of raw materials and spare parts as well as for certain types of labour and monetary resources; (v) superior organisation: from a certain size onwards, automatic machinery may be used instead of manually operated tools, thus guaranteeing more innovative production as scale increases; and (vi) the learning effect: the essence of 'learning by doing' is that one learns how to reduce production costs through actual production experience (for examples and further qualifications, see Camesasca 2000, 137–139).

Economies of scope

Economies of scope are another field where horizontal cooperation can be beneficial for firms that engage in different but complementary activities. These economies materialise if it is less costly for one firm to perform two activities than for two specialised firms to perform them separately.[23] Economies of scope imply that it is efficient to produce two or more different products together on the basis of the same input. This does not necessarily mean that these products should be produced in a single plant. Economies of scope may also arise in distribution, when producers and distributors combine their operations. Several types of goods (for example, frozen pizzas and frozen vegetables) can be distributed in the same vehicles (refrigerated trucks) and economies of scope may be substantial if there are customer groups that are largely similar. In complex goods industries, such as cars or computers, there are appreciable economies of scale in several aspects of sales promotion and product differentiation.

Better planning of production and distribution

Horizontal cooperation can serve to optimise the planning of production and distribution. The research and development, as well as the production

---

[22] In its Guidelines on Article 81(3) EC, the European Commission gives the example of the cost of operating a truck. This is virtually the same regardless of whether it is almost empty, half-full or full [2004] O.J. C 101/97, at 66.

[23] See Baumol, Panzar and Willig (1982) and compare Coase, who observed, 'the distinguishing mark of a firm is the suppression of the price mechanism' (Coase 1937, 389).

and distribution processes, can be divided into a number of stages. Before a final product reaches the consumer, several actions must be performed by one or more firms. At each stage, undertakings must make a choice between performing the activity themselves (or together with other undertakings) or outsourcing the activity. Several efficiencies can be realised by improving the planning of production and distribution.

First, transaction costs may be saved. If firms have to rely heavily upon each other, transaction costs tend to be high and each firm is liable to be exploited by its contract partner. A company may lower its transaction costs by integrating vertically. Such costs include the initial costs of negotiating an agreement as well as the ongoing costs of enforcing it. Because no agreement can specify all possible contingencies, modifying agreements to deal with unforeseen events also causes important transaction costs. Every time two unrelated parties agree to a transaction to be completed in the future, each may engage in opportunistic behaviour, taking advantage of the other whenever circumstances allow them to do so. If contracts are simple, such circumstances are unlikely; in complicated contracts, however, the threat is real. The incentive for opportunistic behaviour changes if activities are organised within a firm rather than between companies in the marketplace, as disagreements can be resolved differently. Transaction costs are likely to be high in cases of asset specificity and changing market conditions (see section 2.9.1).

Second, vertical cooperation may offer the means to correct market failures due to externalities by internalising those externalities. This provides management with more effective ways to monitor and improve performance, ensuring, for example, that customer service departments fulfil the firm's warranty commitments, or guaranteeing market-wide uniform quality by controlling all retail or restaurant outlets, as one bad store can harm the business of all distributors. A good example may be found in any big international hotel chain, where a consumer who likes the outlets knows that the others are similar.

Third, integration of existing assets may ensure supply and generate additional synergies. A common reason for integration is to guarantee the supply of important inputs, as timely delivery is of crucial concern to business, especially in markets where prices are not the sole device used to allocate goods. In times of supply shortages or rationing, good customers often get the product first. Just-in-time deliveries (i.e. an obligation on a supplier to continuously supply the buyer according to his needs) minimise inventory costs, while ensuring timely delivery. Under these circumstances, closer cooperation improves the probability of meeting the deadlines. In sum, synergies result from an integration of existing assets.

Advantages in marketing and distribution

Competitor collaboration may also confer advantages in marketing, for instance through the pooling and streamlining of sales forces, the ability to offer distributors a broader product line, the use of common advertising schemes and the sharing of advertising media discounts. Examples of efficiencies include: (i) the need to obtain a certain level of advertising messages before they reach their maximum effectiveness; (ii) multi-brand interaction when a favourable reputation from one set of products spills over to other products with the same brand name; and (iii) consumer advertising leading to more intense distribution, more prominent display of more sizes and fewer shortages (Boyder and Lancaster 1986). Promotional economies, however, pose severe analytical problems, especially as the element of chance plays an important part in sales promotion. A more streamlined advertising campaign might enable firms to charge higher prices than smaller firms with comparable products. Also, it is not quite clear to what extent market structure is affected by the private advantages of sales promotion.

Economies of research and development

Collaboration of competitors allows spreading costs and risks. R&D efforts are often expensive and almost always risky, so that arrangements spreading the costs and risks of the undertaking among two or more companies can be very attractive. These risks can arise because of the unproven nature of certain technologies, the uncertain nature of demand for unfamiliar products, and the short life cycle for many high-technology products. This point is closely related to Schumpeter's view, namely that a monopolistic surrounding may provide a more secure platform to engage in risky R&D investment, as a large firm's access to capital may be an advantage in obtaining the necessary financing for costly R&D.[24]

There are many situations in which companies have complementary assets but only partially overlapping technological abilities. It is highly unlikely that all firms are equal in the effectiveness of their innovative efforts. A company may possess private information about R&D opportunities or may have unique assets indispensable for innovative success. This type of synergy is commonplace when the venture participants are firms from different industries or

---

[24] Schumpeter (1950, 81–106). In attaining the requisite knowledge and putting it to practical use, extensive sunk costs may be encountered. See Baumol and Ordover (1992, 84).

different niches of an industry. Moreover, the transfer of technology among the various activities that constitute innovation is not without cost. This is especially true if the know-how to be transferred cannot easily be bundled; this will be the case for simultaneous development activity where knowledge has a high secrecy component. One solution would be the transfer of personnel which is easier to realise within a company than under a contractual relationship (Jorde and Teece 1990).

Competitor collaboration may eliminate redundant R&D efforts and thus lower costs without significantly reducing innovation.[25] Some firms fail to manage the complexities of the innovative race so that their disappearance will not slow the innovative pace; rather, the resources entangled in such obsolete projects will be freed for use elsewhere (Fudenberg 1983). Independent research activities often proceed down (near) identical technological paths (unnoticed because of the pressures of the competitive surroundings),[26] while a given research finding can be used for many applications at little extra costs. This duplication may be wasteful and can be minimised if research plans are coordinated (Shapiro and Willig 1990; Ordover and Baumol 1988; Nalebuff and Stiglitz 1983; Dasgupta and Stiglitz 1980). On the other hand, independent research programmes may hide important differences. Combining such programmes may risk the elimination of an alternative path of discovery. Nonetheless, the public good nature of information suggests that cooperation is more likely to promote efficiency. In this context, joint ventures can be seen as promoting the *ex post* dissemination of innovations, for example, if they include firms that otherwise would neither conduct the research independently nor purchase the requisite know-how through a licensing agreement. To the extent that diffusion is promoted, such cooperation increases downstream competition.

The transfer of technology among the various production stages that constitute innovation, development, manufacture and marketing is not costless. These expenses will increase considerably when the knowledge involved has a high tacit component; this is often the case in high-technology markets. Additionally, the combining activities proceed in part simultaneously. Both characteristics require a tighter basis than what can be offered by an arm's-length and non-exclusive contractual relationship on the marketplace (Winter 1987). Once innovation has occurred, consumers have to be willing to switch from their current appliance. Especially when network effects are

---

[25] Gilbert and Sunshine (1995, 594). This illustrates Schumpeter's hypothesis that the average productivity of R&D increases with firm size. See Fisher and Temin (1973).

[26] Leading to an over-investment in R&D relative to the social optimum; see Bhattacharya and Mookerjee (1986).

high, more concentrated market structures, such as joint ventures, can help to disperse new and beneficial technology.

5.3   European competition law

The Treaty on the Functioning of the European Union (TFEU) sets out the general rules relevant to horizontal restrictions in Article 101. According to Article 101(1) TFEU, all agreements, decisions of associations of undertakings or concerted practices between undertakings that restrict competition and affect trade between Member States are prohibited. The prohibition may, however, be declared inapplicable if the four cumulative conditions of Article 101(3) TFEU are fulfilled. To qualify for an exemption, the cartel agreement must achieve efficiencies benefiting consumers without imposing restrictions which are disproportionate to the advantages achieved or which eliminate competition in respect of a substantial part of the products in question. Article 101 TFEU does not differentiate as far as the legal consequences are concerned: clauses in agreements violating the prohibition and not qualifying for an exemption are null and void (Article 101(2) TFEU).[27] However, fines imposed on the basis of Regulation 1/2003 (up to a maximum of 10% of the turnover of the companies which infringe the cartel prohibition) and the Guidelines on fines[28] reflect the seriousness and duration of the infringement (see section 8.2.1 for further discussion).

The European Commission has issued several policy documents clarifying the scope and contents of the cartel prohibition contained in Article 101(1) TFEU. The 2014 Notice on agreements of minor importance (*De minimis* Notice) provides a safe harbour for agreements between undertakings that do not exceed the market share thresholds set out in this Notice and do not contain hard-core restrictions.[29] The European Commission's 2004 Notice on the application of Article 81(3) EC (now Article 101(3) TFEU) provides a general framework that should allow businesses to assess whether their respective practices are lawful.[30] Since this Notice contains general guidance (and is not restricted to an analysis of the conditions for exemption), this document is often referred to as the General Guidelines. The purpose of the 2011 Guidelines on horizontal cooperation is 'to provide an analytical framework for the most common types of horizontal cooperation', which is to be

---

[27] Whether the sanction of nullity affects the entire agreement is to be decided under the relevant rules of national private law.

[28] [1998] O.J. C 9/3; see also Chapter 8 on enforcement.

[29] Notice on agreements of minor importance which do not appreciably restrict competition under Article 101(1) of the Treaty on the functioning of the European Union, O.J. C 291, 30.08.2014.

[30] [2004] O.J. C 101/97.

'based on criteria that help to analyse the economic context of a cooperation agreement' (EU Horizontal Guidelines, at 7). In particular, the Horizontal Guidelines deal with research and development agreements, production agreements, purchasing agreements, agreements on commercialisation and standardisation agreements. In the remainder of this section, the constitutive elements of the cartel prohibition and the conditions for exemption will be discussed from an economic perspective. First, the notions 'agreements between undertakings' and 'concerted practices' are clarified. Second, the legal distinction between 'restrictions by object' (hard-core cartels, such as explicit collusive agreements to fix prices or share markets between producers and sellers of substitute products) and 'restrictions by effect' (soft cartels) are introduced. Article 101(1) TFEU specifically prohibits hard-core cartels; the range of soft cartels and other forms of competitor cooperation covered by the prohibition is unclear. Third, the conditions for exemption (Article 101(3) TFEU) are clarified. Lastly, the specific status of non-concentrative joint ventures is discussed.

5.3.1 Agreements between undertakings and concerted practices

Article 101(1) TFEU addresses both formal and informal agreements between undertakings.[31] It is sufficient for an agreement to exist 'if the undertakings in question have expressed their joint intention to conduct themselves on the market in a specific way'. The form in which this intention was expressed is irrelevant.[32] Documentation of explicit coordination can be established through direct material evidence or from evidence on firms' behaviour. In practice, direct evidence is deduced from documents, handwritten notes, confidential business information of one company found at another company and minutes of meetings. Often a cartel is organised under the cover of an ostensibly legitimate trade association.[33] The wording 'decisions of associations of undertakings' implies that participation in a trade association meeting with an opportunity to communicate about prices is generally insufficient for inferring a violation of Article 101(1) TFEU; a joint decision to increase prices taken at that meeting must be proven.

Proving the existence of illegal cartel agreements poses great difficulties when there is no explicit evidence of written or oral communication. Implicit

---

[31] On the notion of undertaking, see Jones and Sufrin (2014, 127); Wils (2000).
[32] Case T-7/89 *S.A. Hercules Chemicals NV v. Commission* [1991] ECR II-1711, at 2; Case T-9/99 *HFB and Others v. Commission* [2002] ECR II-1487, at 199; Case C-74/04 P *Commission v. Volkswagen* [2006] ECR I-6585, at 37.
[33] Recall the famous quote of Adam Smith that people of the same trade seldom meet together without trying to conspire against the public interest (see section 2.2.1).

coordination is difficult to substantiate. The concept of 'concerted practices' has been clarified in the case law of the Court of Justice of the European Union (CJEU). In the *Imperial Chemical Industries (ICI)* case, the CJEU decided that public announcements of price increases, which are put into effect over a very short period, eliminate all uncertainty between competitors regarding their future conduct (amount, subject matter, date and place of price increases) and eliminate a large part of the risk inherent in independent changes of market conduct. Under EU competition law, a concerted practice thus relates to coordination where firms 'without having reached the stage where an agreement properly so-called may have been concluded, (...) knowingly substitute practical cooperation between them for the risks of competition'.[34] In the *Wood Pulp* case (see Box 5.1), the European Commission fined 36 producers of bleached sulphate wood pulp used in paper manufacturing and three of their trade associations for parallel price movements. This case was built on evidence of parallel quarterly announcements of prospective price rises. The Commission justified the sanction by evidence of price transparency and information exchange. However, in spite of its broad definition of concerted practices in the *ICI* case, on appeal the CJEU reversed the Commission's decision. The Court noted that:

> Parallel conduct cannot be regarded as furnishing proof of concertation unless concertation constitutes the only plausible explanation for such conduct. It is necessary to bear in mind that, although Article 85 of the Treaty prohibits any form of collusion which distorts competition, it does not deprive economic operators of the right to adapt themselves intelligently to the existing and anticipated conduct of their competitors.[35]

In sum, the case law of the ECJ has clarified that providing evidence of a concerted practice requires: (i) contact between firms; (ii) subsequent behaviour on the market; and (iii) causality between the two.[36] Regarding the definition of concerted practices, the 2011 EU Horizontal Guidelines have reaffirmed:

> The concept of a concerted practice refers to a form of coordination between undertakings by which, without it having reached the stage where an agreement

---

[34] Case 48/69 *Imperial Chemical Industries Ltd. v. Commission (Dyestuffs – ICI)* [1972] ECR 619, at 64.

[35] Joined cases C-89/85, C-104/85, C-114/85, C-116/85, C-117/85 and C-125-129/85 A. *Åhlström Osakeyhtio and others v. Commission (Wood Pulp II)* [1993] ECR I-1307, at 71. The difference between parallel pricing and collusion has been confirmed in the T-Mobile case, which concerned a meeting where four mobile operators exchanged confidential information concerning dealer remunerations, see the preliminary ruling of the ECJ, Case C-8/08, *T-Mobile Netherlands BV, KPN Mobile NV, Orange Nederland NV and Vodafone Libertel NV v Raad van bestuur van de Nederlandse Mededingingsautoriteit*.

[36] Case C-49/92P *Commission v. Anic Partecipazioni SpA* [1999] ECR I-4125.

properly so-called has been concluded, practical cooperation between them is knowingly substituted for the risks of competition.

Horizontal Guidelines, at 60

The economic theory of collusion does not distinguish between collusive outcomes that result from explicit coordination and those from tacit collusion, as far as the welfare effects of collusion are concerned. Tacit collusion in the economic sense may occur without any communication or even without competitors being aware of it. Nevertheless, oligopolistic interdependence should not be equated with prohibited concertation and some evidence of communication or coordination (on prices, quantities or facilitating practices) makes economic sense (Motta 2004, 185–190). Economists stress the difficulties of drawing conclusions on the existence of tacit collusion with any certainty; the crucial variable is the self-sustainability of the illegal arrangement. In line with the above observations relating to the complications that firms encounter when trying to provide an adequate mechanism to enforce repeated interactions without knowing for sure each other's behaviour and motives (see section 5.2.3), the absence of a strict prohibition of tacit coordination seems economically justified. There is indeed a serious risk that firms' legitimate competitive interactions in the market are misconceived as behaviour that consciously tries to support a non-competitive market outcome. The (difficult) task for competition law is to frame an economically justified and legally administrable standard. EU competition law attempts to reach these goals in the following way. Implicit coordination that is solely based on the firms' observations of market interactions does not provide sufficient evidence of an infringement of Article 101(1) TFEU. A distinction must be made between competition (firms taking individual 'unilateral' decisions), allowed parallel conduct and concerted practices prohibited by EU competition law. The strict definition of concerted practices requiring that cooperation constitutes the only plausible explanation for parallel conduct may be justified because the costs of type I errors associated with the implementation of a broader standard are likely to be substantial. To avoid false convictions, the CJEU has implicitly accepted the economic logic and acknowledged that the law does not deprive firms of the right to 'adapt themselves intelligently to the conduct of their competitors'.[37] The backdrop of this definition is that anti-competitive horizontal restrictions may escape from the Article 101(1) TFEU prohibition (type II errors) and cause efficiency losses from the immunisation of tacit collusion. Therefore, to minimise the costs of type II errors, it is also crucial to limit the scope of the restrictions 'by object' to cases where forms of tacit

---

[37] Joined Cases 40-48/73, 50/73, 54-56/73, 111/73, 113/73 and 114/73 *Coöperative Vereniging 'Suiker Unie' VA and others v. Commission* [1975] ECR 1663.

agreement (such as information exchanges between rivals) to instances where the anti-competitive goal is the only plausible explanation and no outweighing efficiency benefits can be expected (see for further discussion section 5.3.2).

Given the absence of a distinction between explicit and implicit coordination in formal economic theory, economic evidence is not sufficiently specific to furnish the legally required proof of a concerted practice. However, economic evidence may justify the start of an investigation procedure (e.g. a dawn raid, in conformity with Article 20 of Regulation 1/2003). Even though econometric tools cannot furnish conclusive legal evidence for a violation of Article 101(1) TFEU, competition authorities may use economic tools helping them to draw the border line between parallel pricing and prohibited concerted practices. Hüschelrath (2010) suggests a three-step approach consisting of: (i) a structural analysis of the industries concerned; (ii) a behavioural test of industries identified as suspicious by the previous analysis; and (iii) a dawn raid executed by the competition authority to find hard evidence of the concerted practice. Concerning the structural indicators, the reader is referred to the above discussion of the market characteristics that facilitate collusion (see section 5.2.3). The behavioural screens include several methods: they may focus on structural breaks (e.g. caused by a price war) or exogenous shocks (e.g. changes in input costs). Even though these screens do not allow a final conclusion on the existence of illegal agreements (except when the outcome detected by the screen is highly unlikely unless it is the result of explicit coordination), they may justify enforcement actions by the competition authority according to Article 20 Regulation 1/2003.[38]

Box 5.1: *Wood Pulp* case

In 1985, the European Commission found that wood pulp producers from the United States, Canada and Finland had engaged in concerted conduct in violation of Article 81 EC Treaty.[39] The producers made quarterly price announcements, sometimes simultaneously and sometimes around the same date. The prices were almost always quoted in US dollars, which increased their comparability across the Member States. The prices and price changes tended to be uniform. The Commission considered that the parallel behaviour could not be explained as rational, independently chosen parallel conduct in an oligopolistic market. Interestingly, there were a large number of producers (40), customers and products, so that lack of both market concentration and price transparency

---

[38] Contrary to the more cautious approach of Hüschelrath (2010), some economic commentators support infringement decisions that are solely based on econometric evidence (if there is a history of barometric price leadership, see Devlin 2007).
[39] 1985 O.J. L 85/1.

seemed to make a collusive outcome unlikely. However, in the Commission's view, the market became transparent as a result of the quarterly price announcements. The parties sought annulment of the Commission's decision before the CJEU.

The CJEU stated that parallel conduct cannot furnish proof of a concerted practice 'unless concertation constitutes the only plausible explanation for such conduct'.[40] In the CJEU's view, this was not proven by the European Commission. First, the system of price announcements could be regarded as a rational response to the need felt by both buyers and sellers to limit commercial risks. Wood pulp was bought by paper manufacturers having long-term relationships with the suppliers. The price of wood pulp accounted for between 50% and 75% of the cost of paper; information about prospective maximum prices was thus considered crucial to estimate their costs, plan production and fix the prices of paper. The quarterly circle was a compromise between the manufacturer's desire for foreseeability and the producer's wish not to miss profit opportunities. The CJEU also disagreed with the Commission's arguments about market transparency. Far from being artificial, the transparency was considered the consequence of the well-developed network of business relations. A buyer was always in contact with several wood pulp producers, in order to diversify its sources of supply and not becoming overly dependent on a single producer. To protect themselves against the uncertainties of the market, paper manufacturers maintained close links with each other and exchanged information on prices of which they were aware. In conclusion, there was a legitimate business justification for the price announcements and the similarity in the dates of price announcements was the result of the high degree of market transparency. Finally, the CJEU added the general observation that 'the parallelism of prices and the price trends could be explained by the oligopolistic tendencies of the market'.[41]

The CJEU may be criticised for having underestimated the anti-competitive effects of the quarterly price announcements. Even though the buyers desired advance price information, this does not automatically imply that information must be given simultaneously by competing sellers and even less that price rises have to be uniform. Moreover, the ceiling prices restricted, at least partially, price competition and reduced uncertainty about future price behaviour. In the earlier *Dyestuff* case,[42] the elimination of uncertainty concerning the undertakings' reciprocal price behaviour on different markets was seen as sufficient to prove the common intention of the undertakings involved to limit competition. In contrast with the wood pulp case, the announcements were not made at the request of buyers but initiated by a price leader. Price increases were announced and supposed to take effect at a specified later date. The competitors usually followed suit, announcing within a few days their intention to increase prices by the same percentage.

---

[40] Cases C-89, 104, 114, 116–117, 125–129/85 [1993] ECR I-1307, at 64.
[41] Cases C-89, 104, 114, 116–117, 125–129/85 [1993] ECR I-1307, at 126.
[42] Case 48/69 *Imperial Chemical Industries Ltd. v. Commission (Dyestuffs – ICI)* [1972] ECR 619.

Taking into account the specific circumstances of the *Wood Pulp* case, it cannot be excluded that advance price announcements may, also in the future, be prohibited as concerted practices in the absence of a legitimate business justification and in less transparent markets. In spite of the reversal of the European Commission's decision in the *Wood Pulp* case by the CJEU, the Commission reiterates in its 2011 Horizontal Guidelines that price transparency can be considered to establish a prohibited concerted practice:

> Where a company makes a unilateral announcement that is also genuinely public, for example through a newspaper, this generally does not constitute a concerted practice within the meaning of Article 101(1). However, depending on the facts underlying the case at hand, the possibility of finding a concerted practice cannot be excluded, for example in a situation where such an announcement was followed by public announcements by other competitors, not least because strategic responses of competitors to each other's public announcements (which, to take one instance, might involve readjustments of their own earlier announcements to announcements made by competitors) could prove to be a strategy for reaching a common understanding about the terms of coordination.
>
> Horizontal Guidelines, at 63

5.3.2 Restrictions of competition as the object or the effect of cooperation

Under EU competition law, hard-core agreements such as price fixing, market sharing and output restrictions are considered having as their object the restriction of competition.[43] In such cases, no further evidence is required to show that an explicit agreement causes negative market effects. The prohibition thus applies without the need for taking into account the agreement's economic context. Consequently, the legal analysis will mainly entail enforcement-related issues such as leniency, fines and damages (for a discussion of these enforcement problems, see section 8.2). The discussion below proceeds in three steps: first, the concept of restriction of competition 'by object' is clarified; second, restrictions 'by effect' are analysed; third, a brief economic assessment of the distinction is provided.

---

[43] As shown by the recent cases these infringements are still a major part of the EU Commission's enforcement priorities. See e.g. Case COMP/ 39258, *Air Cargo*, 9 November 2010; Case COMP/38899, *Gas-Insulated Switchgear*, 24 January 2007; Case COMP/38823, *Elevators and Escalators*, 21 February 2007.

Restrictions of competition by object

The distinction between restrictions by object and restrictions by effect has been heavily disputed in the enforcement practice. The European Commission and NCAs applied an ever-expanding interpretation of restrictions by object, thus avoiding having to prove the anti-competitive effects of agreements or practices. In *Cartes Bancaires*, the CJEU put a halt to this evolution, clarifying the definition of infringements by object on the basis of its earlier case law.[44] According to the Court, certain types of collusive behaviour, e.g. horizontal price fixing, are so likely to have negative effects, in particular on the price, quantity or quality of the goods and services, that it may be considered redundant to prove their actual effects on the market. However, where the analysis of a type of coordination between undertakings does not reveal a sufficient degree of harm to competition, the effects of the coordination require a careful analysis. In order to determine a restriction by object, regard must be had to the content of the coordination's provisions, its objectives, and the economic and legal context of which it forms a part, the nature of the goods or services affected, as well as the real conditions of the functioning and structure of the market in question. The parties' intention is not a necessary factor, even though it can also be taken into account. In sum, the CJEU stresses that the concept of restriction by object should be interpreted restrictively.

Following the *Cartes Bancaires* judgment, the European Commission issued its Guidance on restrictions of competition by object for the purpose of defining which agreements may benefit from the *De minimis* Notice. This document lists the restrictions of competition that are described as 'by object' or 'hardcore' in the various Commission regulations, Guidelines and Notices, supplemented with examples taken from the CJEU's case law and the Commission's decisional practice. Horizontal agreements having as their object a restriction of competition are considered by the nature of the cooperation to indicate the applicability of Article 101(1) TFEU as they are presumed to have negative market effects.[45] The European Commission considers this to be the case even if such agreements fall under its *De minimis* Notice's less than 5% market share hurdle.[46] The European courts ruled that for agreements fixing prices,[47] market sharing,[48] quotas[49] and rigging bids,[50] it is unnecessary to take into account

---

[44] Case C-67/13, *P Groupement des Cartes Bancaires v. Commission*, ECLI:EU:C:2014:2204.

[45] Compare the EU Horizontal Guidelines, at 18; equally, see the US Horizontal Guidelines, at 3.1.

[46] Commission Notice on agreements of minor importance, [2001] O.J. C 368/13.

[47] Case 123/83 *Bureau National Interprofessionnel du Cognac (BNIC I) v. Guy Clair* [1985] ECR 391.

[48] Case 41/69 *ACF Chemiefarma NV v. Commission* [1970] ECR 661, para. 128.

[49] Case T-142/89 *Usines Gustave Boël SA v. Commission (Welded Steel Mesh)* [1995] ECR II-867, 871.

[50] Case T-29/92 *Vereniging van samenwerkende prijsregelende organisaties in de bouwnijverheid (SPO I) and others v. Commission* [1995] ECR II-289.

the actual effects of those agreements. As a result, the prohibition often ensues virtually *per se* with the issues at stake in prolonged hard-core cartel proceedings, thus evolving mostly around the standard of proof adhered to and the fines to be imposed.[51] The EU case law shows the imposition of high administrative fines even when the agreement was only partially implemented.[52] On top of this criminal proceedings in the Member States may be initiated and damage claims may be brought (for further discussion, see Chapter 8). Besides the three classical 'by object' restrictions (price fixing, market sharing, bid rigging), in the above-mentioned communication the Commission also bans information sharing about future prices and quantities, collective boycott agreements, and restrictions on the parties' ability to carry out R&D or use their own technology for further R&D.[53] In this way, the scope of the European prohibition is remarkably broader than the reach of the *per se* prohibitions under the US Sherman Act (see section 5.4 below).

The EU Horizontal Guidelines state that an exchange of strategic information can facilitate collusion by artificially increasing transparency in the market and lead to anti-competitive foreclosure if the exchange of commercially sensitive information places unaffiliated companies at a significant competitive disadvantage. Consequently, information exchanges between competitors of individualised data regarding future prices or quantities are considered a restriction by object (Horizontal Guidelines, at 72–74). When the information exchange concerns present data and not information on intended future prices or quantities, there is no restriction by object. However, in the Commission's view, also the latter type of information may be an efficient mechanism for monitoring deviations from a collusive outcome in a concentrated market, which is stable and non-complex. Therefore, a restriction by effect may be found and the cartel prohibition (Article 101(1) TFEU) will apply if it cannot be shown that consumers profit from the achieved efficiencies (Article 101(3) TFEU). Recently, the Court of Justice had the opportunity to assess the European Commission's practice. In the *Bananas* case, the Commission found a cartel in which banana suppliers engaged in bilateral pre-pricing communications during which they exchanged information on factors that influence the price-setting of bananas, discussed price trends or gave indications of future prices. The Commission held that these

---

[51] For a highly illustrative example, see the numerous appeals against the European Commission's decision in Case IV/33.833 *Cartonboard* [1994] O.J. L 243/1; see Cases T-295/94, T-304/94, T-308/94, T-309/94, T-310/94, T-311/94, T-317/94, T-319/94, T-327/94, T-334/94, T-337/94, T-338/94, T-339/94, T-340/94, T-341/94, T-342/94, T-347/94, T-348/94, T-352/94, and T-354/94 *Cartonboard* [1998] ECR II-813.

[52] In *Marine Hoses* total fines amounted to €132 million, with individual fines ranging from 0 (immunity for company profiting from leniency) to almost €60 million (Case COMP/39406, 28.01.2009).

[53] Guidance on restrictions of competition 'by object' for the purpose of defining which agreements may benefit from the *De Minimis* Notice, Commission Staff Working Document, 25.6.2014, SWD(2014) 198 final.

information exchanges were liable to influence pricing behaviour, concerned the fixing of prices and gave rise to a concerted practice having as its object the restriction of competition. Dole, one of the cartel participants, challenged the qualification of the pre-pricing communications as a restriction of competition by object before the CJEU.[54] In its judgment, the Court reiterates the principles set out in *Cartes Bancaires*. It recalls that information exchange between competitors should be understood in light of the notion that each competitor should independently determine its market behaviour. This strictly precludes exchanges of information which may influence competitors' behaviour, or disclosure of own intentions concerning market behaviour, where the object or effect of this information exchange is to create conditions of competition which do not correspond to the normal conditions in the market in question. In the Court's view, information exchanges which remove uncertainty between competitors as regards timing, extent and details of future modifications of market behaviour must be regarded as a restriction by object. This is the case even if there is no direct connection between the exchange of information and consumer prices. Furthermore, according to the CJEU, it may be presumed that undertakings taking part in the information exchange take account of this information in determining their own market conduct. It is up to the undertakings to rebut this presumption.

Box 5.2: Case law on horizontal restrictions in the BRIC countries
Box co-authored by Maria Fernanda Caporale Madi (Brazil)

China: Price fixing

In 2014, the National Development and Reform Commission (NDRC) found that eight Japanese auto parts manufacturers (Hitachi, Denso, Asian Industry, Mitsubishi Motors, Mitsuba, Yazaki, Furukawa and Sumitomo) had agreed to fix the prices of at least 13 products for the Chinese market, including starters and alternators, for a period of almost 10 years. Four bearing manufacturers (Fujio, Seiko, JTEKT and NTN) were found to have engaged in a monopoly agreement that effectively raised bearing prices in the Chinese market. During meetings in Japan and Shanghai they discussed price increases for China and other Asian markets. The NDRC imposed record breaking fines of 1.24 billion renminbi, including the largest-ever fine for a single company of 290.4 million renminbi. The Auto Parts investigation was the NDRC's second major international cartel investigation, after previously following global regulators in sanctioning six multinational LCD panel makers from Korea and Taiwan a total of 353 million renminbi.

---

[54] Case C-286/13 P *Dole v. Commission*, ECLI:EU:C:2015:184.

India: Bid rigging

In the Shoe Cartel case, the CCI fined 11 rubber shoe manufacturers approximately US$ 900,000 for bid rigging in the supply of rubber shoe soles to the Directorate General of Supplies and Disposals in 2011. The bids made by the shoe manufacturers were very similar, despite differences in their operations, production capacities, costs, geographies and profits. Most of the manufacturers had restricted the quantity they would supply, thus forcing the Directorate General to conclude contracts with all the bidders if it wanted to fill the terms of the contract. The Directorate General of Supplies and Disposals became suspicious and notified the CCI. The CCI examined the bidding pattern and found, in light of both the near-identical prices and the limited range in terms of quantities quoted by each of the manufacturers, collusion between manufacturers, using the industry's trade association as a platform for their meetings. Commercially sensitive performance statements in relation to the other accused were found in the possession of one of the accused, which led the CCI to infer the sharing and exchange of information among bidders prior to participating in the bid.

Brazil: Cement cartel

In 2014 the Brazilian Antitrust Authority, also known as CADE (*Conselho Administrativo de Defesa Econômica*, Administrative Council of Economic Defence), condemned six companies,[55] six individuals and three associations for being involved in a cartel that lasted from 2002 to 2006. The investigation began when a former employee of one of the involved cement companies made a leniency application with CADE, describing the whole dynamics of the cartel. The documents presented suggested that the cement companies, together with their sector associations, were: (i) fixing prices and quantity of cement and dividing the regional cement and concrete markets in Brazil; (ii) allocating clients and concluding agreements not to compete; (iii) raising barriers to entry for new competitors in the cement and concrete markets; (iv) dividing the concrete market through shares equivalent to the market shares in the cement market; and (v) coordinating control of the supply sources of cement. The main strategy of an engaged sector association (Brazilian Association of Portland Cement – ABCP) consisted of lobbying the Brazilian Association of Technical Standards (ABNT) to introduce new standards for the cement market. The proposed changes were aimed not at improving the quality of the product but at creating restrictions on the activities of smaller competitors, bringing them 'out of the norm.'[56] The fines imposed upon the cement cartel summed BRL 3.1 billion (approximately €800 million), one of the biggest penalties ever imposed by

---

[55] The companies involved in the 'cement cartel' were Holcim Ltd, Cimpor Cimentos de Portugal, Votorantim Cimentos SA, Camargo Correa SA, Itabira Agro Industrial SA and Cia de Cimentos Itambé SA.
[56] Administrative Proceeding 08012.011142/2006-79, vote of the Commissioner Alessandro Octaviani, § 595, 278 (free translation, original in Portuguese).

CADE in a cartel case.[57] Criminal procedures against the six individuals have also been initiated by federal and state prosecutors; these cases are still pending.

Restriction of competition as the effect of cooperation

Most competitor cooperation does not have as its object a restriction of competition. For gauging the applicability of Article 101(1) TFEU in such cases, an analysis of the agreement's effects is required. Thereto the agreement must be able to limit competition between the parties involved and it must be likely to affect competition in the market to such an extent that negative market effects as to prices, output, innovation or the variety or quality of goods and services can be expected. The Horizontal Guidelines explicitly admit that this depends on the economic context of the agreement, taking into account both (i) the nature and content of the agreement and (ii) the parties' combined market power, as this (together with other structural factors) determines the capability of the cooperation to affect overall competition (Horizontal Guidelines, at 19–20). The economic analysis thus prescribed by the European Commission is basically a two-tier test: first, one has to decide what characteristics the parties' cooperation has and, second, it must be investigated what amount of market shares the parties hold in their competitive surroundings.

The characteristics of a cooperation agreement relate to factors such as the business purpose of the cooperation, the competitive relationship between parties and the extent to which they intend to integrate their activities. Although no single element is found decisive for inferring whether, overall, the coordination will be likely to raise competitive concerns, the EU Horizontal Guidelines offer guidance on the different elements to be taken into account when assessing horizontal arrangements. Horizontal cooperation agreements can limit competition in several ways. They can be exclusive, thus limiting the possibility of the parties to compete against each other or third parties. They can also require the parties to contribute assets or affect their financial interests in such a way that their decision-making independence is appreciably reduced. The effect may be the lessening of competition between the parties. The reduced competitive pressure may also benefit competitors, who will be able to also profitably raise prices. Horizontal cooperation agreements can also lead to the disclosure of strategic information, or achieve commonality of costs, thus increasing the likelihood of coordination between the parties. Some horizontal cooperation agreements, e.g.

---

[57] Administrative Proceeding 08012.011142/2006-79.

production and standardisation agreements, may give rise to foreclosure concerns (Horizontal Guidelines, at 162–167 and 277–307).

If the content and nature of the agreement points towards a potential competitive worry, the second component of the test for deliberating whether the effect of a cooperation may serve to restrict competition (by raising prices, restricting output, hampering innovation, or limiting the quality or variety of goods and services available) requires an assessment of the market power of the parties involved. At least preliminarily, the market share of the firms is often considered determinative to make inferences about market power. Since the ECJ's ruling in *Delimitis*,[58] a full market analysis is already required under Article 101 TFEU in all those cases not representing *per se* infringements.[59] In the *Flat Glass* case, the Court of First Instance (now General Court) stated that the definition of the relevant market in a more systematic way is a 'necessary precondition of any judgment concerning allegedly anti-competitive behaviour.'[60] This position was further refined in *European Night Services* where it was held that 'in assessing an agreement under Article 81(1) of the Treaty, account must be taken of the actual conditions in which it functions, in particular the economic context in which the undertakings operate, the products or services covered by the agreement, and the actual structure of the markets concerned.'[61] For a long time, the market power of the parties involved was gauged according to the (negative) test of noticeability formulated in *Völk v. Vervaecke*[62] investigating whether the possible effect on competition was appreciable. The European Commission issued the *De minimis* Notice creating relatively safe harbours based on low market shares, to which the Horizontal Guidelines extend. Similarly, the Guidelines on Fines and Commission's practice in this field reflect that market impact is crucial to determine liability and the level of the fines if an infringement is found (see section 8.2 for further discussion). The EU Horizontal Guidelines create a range of relatively safe harbours, depending in scope on the nature of the agreement (as do most block exemptions). For example, if the parties together hold less than 25% of the market for agreements on R&D, less than 20% for production agreements, or less than 15% for purchasing agreements and commercialisation agreements, then a restrictive effect of the cooperation is considered unlikely.

---

[58] Case C-234/89 *Delimitis v. Henniger Bräu AG* [1991] ECR I-935.

[59] Made explicit in Case T-14/89 *Montedipe/Anic SpA v. Commission (Polypropylene – Montedipe)* [1992] ECR II-1155.

[60] Joined Cases T-68/89, T-77/89, T-78/89 *Societa Italiana Vetro SpA, Fabrica Pisana SpA, Vernante Pennitalia v. EC Commission (Italian Flat Glass)* [1992] ECR II-1403.

[61] Joined Cases T-374/94, T-375/94, T-384/94, T-388/94 *European Night Services Ltd. et al. v. Commission* [1998] ECR II-3141, at 136.

[62] Case 5/69 *Völk v. Vervaecke* [1969] ECR 295.

Economic assessment

Economic analysis stresses the need to examine the real-life consequences of all types of horizontal cooperation. Hence, it may be questioned whether a strict legal dividing line between anti-competitive restrictions 'by object' and anti-competitive restrictions 'by effect' can be justified. Ideally, competition rules should satisfy two criteria: prohibitions should be both economically justified and legally administrable. Since both requirements cannot be simultaneously satisfied to their full extent, competition law will not escape from a trade-off and should focus on minimising the sum of error costs. Price-fixing cartels are the most forward example of traditional agreements having as their object the restriction of competition. A fully fledged economic analysis could show that prices are not above competitive levels, making antitrust intervention redundant. Even in markets that lend themselves to successful cartelisation (homogeneous products, mature market, predictable demand, no huge advances in technology and high barriers to entry), price-fixing agreements may prove to be ineffective because of the presence of large buyers on the market and plenty of cheating on the cartel price. Even though their explicit objective is to raise prices, under these circumstances, cartels will be imperfect and thus not able to push through the prices agreed effectively.

Does this imply that EU competition law should entirely abandon the concept of restrictions by object? In spite of the potential ineffectiveness of hard-core cartels, a qualification of price fixing as a restriction by object (or a *per se* violation under US antitrust law, see section 5.4.2.) may still be justified since the administrative costs of enforcing the prohibition are likely to outweigh the gains resulting from lowering error costs (type I errors: false convictions). However, requiring evidence of actual price effects is warranted to minimise error costs whenever the sustainability of price cartels is low because of a high cheating risk. This necessitates a further distinction of different types of price-fixing agreements. The European Commission also classifies recommended minimum prices (for example, recommended minimum fees for architects)[63] in the category of 'by object' restrictions, since they would facilitate price co-ordination. In markets where the risk of cheating is high, devices that merely facilitate (but not prescribe) price coordination should not be condemned *per se*. Particularly in the sector of the liberal professions, the economic literature has warned against ill-conceived decisions in the absence of an effects based analysis. If the number of practitioners in these markets is high, cartel discipline will be difficult to maintain and cheating will be very attractive. The non-sustainability of price cartels in liberal professions markets is also confirmed

[63] Case 38549, *Architectes Belges*, cited in the Guidance on restrictions of competition 'by object' for the purpose of defining which agreements may benefit from the *De Minimis* Notice, SWD (2014) 198 final, at 6.

by empirical evidence (Stephen 1993). Current EU competition law pushes the relevant economic evidence aside if the objective to fix prices or control output can be proven and the (lack of) economic impact on the market is only taken into account when determining the ultimate fine.

Avoiding disharmonies between economic analysis and the EU legal competition regime and, at the same time, keeping the legal system administrable is also a recurrent challenge in the treatment of implicit agreements. Clearly, a prohibition of tacit collusion in the economic sense (which would avoid all welfare losses caused by collusion) is not administrable, since there is no enforceable legal remedy to prevent that competitors take each other's behaviour into account. Hence, illegal tacit coordination must be carefully defined in order to isolate anti-competitive behaviour (not generating efficiency gains) that can be effectively prohibited. Information exchange between rivals is a case in point. The economics of information stresses the public good characteristics of information, making it clear that information may generate pro-competitive benefits. Information exchanges allow rivals to solve coordination issues and eliminate duplicative investments in the assessment of market conditions. A careful assessment, which balances anti- and pro-competitive effects, is needed before any conclusions can be drawn (Nitsche and von Hinten-Reed 2004). The European Commission itself acknowledged the need for a case-by-case analysis in the *Fatty Acids* decision, the first time an agreement on the exchange of information in itself constituted an infringement of EU competition law.[64] Depending on the underlying facts, the exchange of information can also be seen as neutral (see, for example, the *UK Tractor* cases)[65] or benign (see, for example, *European Wastepaper Information Service*).[66] The qualification of implicit coordination as a restriction by object must be limited to cases where no efficiency advantages can materialise and the prohibition of the conduct can be effectively administered. The question whether 'information exchanges between competitors of individualised data regarding intended future prices or quantities' (Horizontal Guidelines, at 72–74) satisfy these criteria is further discussed below. To that end, a comparison with Section 1 of the Sherman Act is helpful. Also, US antitrust law is plagued by an ambiguous notion of 'tacit agreement' but it does not condemn

---

[64] Case IV/31.128 *Fatty Acids* [1987] O.J. L 3/17. On the legal treatment of information exchange agreements, see Morais and Feteira (2015); Wagner-von Papp (2013); Capobianco (2004); Gonzales Diaz, Kirk, Perez Flores, and Verkleij (1999).

[65] Cases IV/31.370 & IV/31.446 *UK Agricultural Tractor Registration Exchange* [1992] O.J. L 68/19; decision upheld in CFI and ECJ, Case T-35/92 *John Deere v. Commission* [1994] ECR II-957, upheld in C-7/95P [1998] ECR I-3111; and Case T-34/92 *Fiatagri and New Holland v. Commission* [1994] ECR II-905, upheld in C-8/95P [1998] ECR I-3175.

[66] *European Wastepaper Information Service* [1987] O.J. C 399/7.

price information exchanges *per se*, if no direct impact on consumer prices can be shown (see sections 5.4.1 and 5.4.2).

5.3.3 Pro-competitive effects of horizontal restrictions

Article 101(3) TFEU expressly endorses the efficiencies that collaboration among competitors may generate, if the following four cumulative[67] conditions are met: (i) the agreement must contribute to improving the production or distribution of goods (or services), or to promoting technical or economic progress; (ii) consumers must be allowed a fair share of the resulting benefits; (iii) any restrictions imposed must be indispensable to attaining the preceding objectives; (iv) the agreement must not be capable of eliminating competition in relation to a substantial part of the products in question.

It is important to stress that the assessment under Article 101(3) TFEU becomes relevant only if Article 101(1) TFEU determines an infringement of competition. In the absence of restrictions of competition, it is not necessary to determine the benefits of an agreement. Where in an individual case a restriction of competition within the meaning of Article 101(1) TFEU has been proven, Article 101(3) TFEU can be invoked as a defence. When the four cumulative conditions of Article 101(3) are fulfilled, it is assumed that the agreement enhances competition within the relevant market, because it leads the undertakings concerned to offer cheaper or better products to consumers, compensating the latter for the adverse effects of the restrictions of competition (EU General Guidelines, at 34 and 41). The strict illegality of hard-core cartels does not imply that they disqualify for an exemption through Article 101(3) TFEU because of their anti-competitive nature. Still, the European Commission and the Courts are quite wary of allowing agreements which are considered to carry few efficiencies, while being generally deemed most restrictive of competition, thus implying a decrease in welfare. It is for this reason that the conditions for exemption laid down in Article 101 (3) TFEU are interpreted strictly.

Article 101(3) TFEU can be applied either to individual agreements or to categories of agreements by way of a block exemption regulation.[68] When an agreement is covered by a block exemption the parties to the restrictive

---

[67] Joined cases 43/82 and 63/82 *VBVB and VBBB v. Commission* [1984] ECR 19, para. 61.

[68] Examples are contained in Commission Regulation (EU) No 1217/2010 of 14 December 2010 on the application of Article 101(3) of the Treaty on the Functioning of the European Union to certain categories of research and development agreements, O.J. L 335, 18.12.2010, p. 36–42; Commission Regulation (EU) No 1218/2010 of 14 December 2010 on the application of Article 101(3) of the Treaty on the Functioning of the European Union to certain categories of specialisation agreements, O.J. L 335, 18.12.2010, p. 43–47.

agreement are relieved of their burden under Article 2 of Regulation 1/2003 of showing that their individual agreement satisfies each of the conditions of Article 101(3) TFEU. They only have to prove that the restrictive agreement comes within the reach of the block exemption. The application of Article 101(3) TFEU to categories of agreements by way of block exemption regulation is based on the presumption that restrictive agreements that fall within their scope fulfil each of the four conditions laid down in Article 101(3) TFEU (General Guidelines, at 35). Where no block exemption applies, the Article 81(3) Notice indicates a methodology to assess the pro-competitive effects of an agreement.

Regulation 1/2003 makes both Article 101(1) and Article 101(3) TFEU directly applicable by the European Commission, National Competition Authorities (NCAs) and national courts.[69] It is for the undertakings themselves to assess the compatibility of their agreements with Article 101(3) TFEU.[70] To facilitate this self-assessment, the Article 81(3) Notice (also referred at as the EU General Guidelines) contains some general guidance on the application of Article TFEU. The framework of analysis relating to Article 101(3) TFEU is as follows. To start with, the General Guidelines determine that all efficiency claims must be substantiated so that the following can be verified: (i) the nature of the claimed efficiencies; (ii) the link between the agreement and the efficiencies; (iii) the likelihood and magnitude of each claimed efficiency; and (iv) how and when each claimed efficiency would be achieved. To do so, the Guidelines contain a detailed description of two 'types' of efficiencies: (a) cost efficiencies (including economies of scale and scope, as well as improved planning, General Guidelines, at 64–68); and (b) qualitative efficiencies (including dynamic efficiencies related to improvements in innovation and distribution, General Guidelines, at 69–72).

Next, the General Guidelines explain that the second condition of Article 81(3) EC implies a two-fold test: (i) the restrictive agreement as such must be reasonably necessary in order to achieve the efficiencies; and (ii) the individual restrictions of competition that flow from the agreement must also be reasonably necessary for the attainment of the efficiencies. According to the

---

[69] [2003] O.J. L 1/1, at Article 3. For a discussion of the new system of enforcement, see Chapter 8.

[70] Up to May 2004, the European Commission held the sole authority and broad discretion to grant exemptions under Article 9(1) of Regulation 17 by individual decisions or by block exemption regulations. By contrast, Regulation 1/2003 has introduced a system of self-assessment that leaves it mostly up to companies and their advisors to determine whether or not their agreements lead to anti-competitive effects under Article 101(1) TFEU, and, if so, whether pro-competitive effects – under the four cumulative conditions of Article 101(3) TFEU – can offset any welfare loss entailed.

European Commission, the decisive factor is whether or not the restrictive agreement and individual restrictions make it possible to perform the activity in question more efficiently than would likely have been the case in the absence of the agreement or the restriction concerned (General Guidelines, at 73–74).

Concerning the third condition for an exemption, the General Guidelines explain that the pass-on of benefits must at least compensate consumers for any actual or likely negative impact caused to them by the restriction of competition found under Article 101(1) TFEU. Moreover, the European Commission holds that society as a whole benefits where the efficiencies lead either to fewer resources being used to produce the output consumed, or to the production of more valuable products and thus to a more efficient allocation of resources. In line with the overall objective of Article 101 TFEU to prevent anti-competitive agreements, the net effect of the agreement must at least be neutral from the point of view of those consumers directly or likely affected by the agreement. If such consumers are worse off following the agreement, the third condition of Article 101(3) TFEU is not fulfilled. The positive effects of an agreement must be balanced against and compensate for its negative effects on consumers. When this is the case, consumers are not harmed by the agreement. A certain time lag between the emergence of the efficiencies and the pass-on to consumers is acceptable. However, the greater the time lag, the greater also must be the efficiencies to compensate for the loss to consumers during the period preceding the pass-on (General Guidelines, at 83–94).

In order to deal with the difficulties relating to the accurate calculation of the consumer pass-on rate, the General Guidelines refer to a number of characteristics to be taken into account as far as cost efficiencies are concerned (such as the market structure, the nature and magnitude of the efficiency gains, elasticities of demand and the nature of the restriction of competition). As far as qualitative efficiencies are concerned, the European Commission notes that it is difficult to attach a precise value judgement, and more generically states that it must be 'carefully assessed whether the claimed efficiencies create real value for consumers in that market so as to compensate for the adverse effects of the restriction of competition' (General Guidelines, at 103–104).

Finally, the General Guidelines deal with the fourth condition of Article 101(3) TFEU and focus on the various sources of (actual and potential) competition in the market, the level of competitive constraint that they impose on the parties to the agreement and the impact of the agreement on this competitive constraint. Entry, the presence of mavericks and the impact of product differentiation are singled out (General Guidelines, at 105–115).

5.3.4 The efficiency of coordination and joint ventures

Joint ventures provide a good illustration of the difficulties that may be caused by the system of self-assessment envisaged under Regulation 1/2003. Complex economic activities involving multiple firms (such as a joint R&D project), which are governed by individual contracts, encounter substantial transactional problems, especially when they run for an extended time period. Specifying the terms of the arrangement, bringing together the parties' disparate economic goals and fixing the rate of future contributions by participants will often pose insurmountable difficulties to the parties. One apparent solution thereto is to internalise all activities in one firm by way of a full merger. However, this may raise problems of its own in terms of the parties' differing desires for future development, as well as because of the antitrust implications mergers tend to raise.

As almost any agreement integrating two or more firms' operations could be described as a joint venture, the antitrust literature has focused on a number of factors discerning the distinctive efficiency advantages and particular anti-competitive risks. Brodley lists four conditions: (i) the enterprise is under the joint control of the parent firms which are not under related influence; (ii) each parent makes a substantial contribution to the joint enterprise; (iii) the enterprise exists as a business entity separate from its parents; and (iv) the joint venture creates a significant new business capability in terms of new productive capacity, new technology, a new product, or entry into a new market (Brodley 1982, 1526–1529). Similar contingencies have been developed by the CJEU in its *Philip Morris* judgment.[71] As a result, a joint venture is broader than a simple contractual arrangement, as it involves the creation of a new firm or business rather than being merely a cooperation between the parties. Yet it also differs from a merger because it typically involves the creation of a separate, limited-purpose firm, not a full union of two previously independent firms.

Reflecting their hybrid status situated in-between simple coordination and full merger, joint ventures are exposed to a special competition law regime. Since the 1997 amendments to the EU Merger Regulation came into force, all full function joint ventures are subject to a system which draws mainly from the procedures and timelines as instituted by the Merger Regulation – as indeed it does not make sense to treat joint ventures more harshly than the more far-reaching alternative of merger. The joint ventures' distinct organisational form and its characteristics are acknowledged by their special position, which is explicitly provided for in Article 2(4) of the Merger

---

[71] Joined Cases 142/84 and 156/84 *BAT and Reynolds v. Commission (Philip Morris)* [1987] ECR 4487.

Regulation. Article 101 TFEU remains applicable to cases of coordination of the parent companies' behaviour. The substantial provisions contained in Article 101(3) TFEU are well honed to deal with the efficiencies generated by joint ventures.

Joint ventures offer a means of achieving many of the transactional efficiencies related to integrating activities within a single firm, without encountering the disadvantages of mergers. Joint ventures can achieve economies of scale in research and distribution not reachable through single firm operations. Shared profits and managerial responsibilities alleviate the risk of opportunism and informational imbalance, while offering a means to monitor the use of the parties' input in the project. Valuating the parties' respective input to the project is mitigated, because this can await determination on the market over the course of the joint ventures' running time. Joint ownership also provides a way of spreading the costs of producing valuable information that is normally protected from appropriation only by contractual undertakings which are difficult to enforce. Joint ventures thus represent the tool of choice for projects involving high risk, high information costs, or innovation activities for which there are no equally efficient substitutes. From the foregoing, the obvious question arises if and how European competition law takes these efficiencies into account under Article 101(3) TFEU.

Under the self-assessment imposed by Regulation 1/2003, and the guidance contained in the Article 81(3) Notice, efficiencies have to counterbalance any anti-competitive effects that joint ventures may entail. The latter are similar to regular cases of coordinated behaviour, mainly related to collusion (see Brodley 1982). Hereinafter, the four requirements prescribed by Article 101(3) TFEU will be assessed in turn. To start with, all kinds of improvements in production, distribution, and technical and economic progress may be taken into account. Regarding joint ventures, the European Commission has held the following benefits as relevant:[72] (i) the likelihood of producing a new or greatly improved product resulting in increased choice for consumers; (ii) the contribution and sharing by the parents of complementary technology or experience; (iii) objective technical difficulties which are insurmountable for the individual parent companies; (iv) speeding up the entry of a new competitor, in comparison with the market situation without the joint venture, as well as the penetration of new markets; (v) the need to share the costs and risks of research and development, or where the capital costs of long-term investment are particularly high; (vi) the need to supply customers with a range of products or services as well as the joint venture's ability to provide

---

[72] For an overview of the relevant case law, see Morais (2013).

speedy and efficient after sales services in the case of large equipment manufacturers; (vii) the advantages of an associated specialisation arrangement; (viii) the lowering of prices; (ix) improved capacity utilisation, rationalisation and capacity reduction. Although the above listing of potential benefits associated with cooperative agreements (and joint ventures in particular) appears extensive, a study of the case law leads to the conclusion that such efficiencies are hardly ever quantified in practice. Given the limited practical feasibility of such quantification, it may suffice to point out that the resulting level of discretion the European Commission enjoys under Article 101(3) TFEU is substantial. Because of the restricted supervision exercised by the European Courts, the perception of some form of industrial policy meddling was never entirely subdued.

Article 101(3) TFEU requires that the restriction of competition resulting from the agreement must be indispensable for the synergies to materialise. Thereto the European Court of First Instance determined in *European Broadcasting Union*[73] that the provisions of the agreement in question must be 'objectively and sufficiently determinate so as to enable [its provisions] to be applied uniformly and in a non-discriminatory manner'. To decide whether the restrictive clauses contained in the joint venture agreement (such as non-competition clauses) are indispensable the Court's *Matra* ruling obliges the European Commission to consider whether the parent companies were capable of entering the market on their own and had substantial reason for doing so.[74] If similar or greater benefits would have been obtained if the parent companies had entered the market separately, or the adverse effects of competition are disproportionate, then the efficiency gains are to be refused as countervailing benefits. More generally, if less restrictive alternatives are economically feasible, then the European Commission may rule that close cooperation structures are unnecessary for reaching the stated goals.[75] Next, a fair share of the benefits associated with the joint venture is to be passed on to consumers, in line with the general goal of EU competition law as discussed in Chapter 2 of this book (see section 2.5.2). In the case of joint ventures falling under Article 101 TFEU, the European Commission assumes this to be the case if the relevant market is competitive or if the buyers are powerful and sophisticated companies.[76] Finally, Article 101(3) TFEU and Article 2(3) of the Merger Regulation state that no exemption may be given for an agreement which gives the parties the possibility of eliminating

---

[73] Joined cases T-528/93, T-542/93, T-543/93 and T-546/93 *Métropole Télévision and others v. Commission (Eurovision II)* [1996] ECR II-649.

[74] Case T-17/93 *Matra Hachette SA v. Commission and Ford-Volkswagen (Matra II)* [1994] ECR II-595, 637.

[75] Compare Case IV/32.006 *Alcatel/ANT* [1990] O.J. L 32/19, para. 20.

[76] European Commission, 14th Annual Report on Competition Policy (1994), para. 177 (1995).

competition over a substantial part of the products or services. As such the European Commission strives to ensure that there is still 'sufficient external competition to guarantee the maintenance of an effective competitive structure on the markets concerned'.[77]

5.4 US antitrust law

The US approach to horizontal restrictions varies from their treatment under EU competition law in a number of respects. Several hard-core restrictions under EU competition law are also regarded *per se* violations under the US antitrust rules. However, the analogy between the two systems is not complete, since US antitrust law has no exemption possibility. The crucial distinction under US antitrust law is whether restraints are prohibited *per se* or must be judged under the Rule of Reason. It has been written in the past that the EU system might allow for a similar approach, taking both pro- and anti-competitive effects into account for the analysis under article 101(1) TFEU (Ritter, Braun and Rawlinson 2000, 103–104; Faull and Nikpay 1999, para 2.98; Black 1997). However, the Rule of Reason approach has been explicitly rejected by the General Court in the cases *Métropole Télévision*, *Van den Bergh Foods* and *MasterCard*. According to the CJEU, pro-competitive effects of agreements can only be weighed within the framework of Article 101(3) TFEU. This article would 'lose much of its effectiveness if such an examination had already to be carried out under Article 101(1) TFEU'.[78] The remainder of this section provides an overview of the most relevant US case law and a summary of the relevant US Guidelines issued by the US enforcement agencies. The differences between US antitrust law and EU competition law are commented upon from an economic perspective.

5.4.1 Agreements in restraint of trade

Contrary to Article 101(1) TFEU, US antitrust law does not make a distinction between agreements and concerted practices. However, it results from the case law that the prohibition of Section 1 Sherman Act is not restricted to explicit agreements, i.e. an express preceding verbal agreement, written or oral. Hence, US antitrust practice is facing similar definition problems when the scope of the prohibition is extended to 'tacit agreements', the meaning of which is equally as ambiguous as the EU concept of concerted practices (see also Ghezzi and Maggiolino 2014). In the *Twombly* case, the Supreme Court stated that a sufficient complaint must allege 'an agreement, tacit or express'[79]

---

[77] Case COMP/36.253 *P&O Stena Line* [1999] O.J. L 163/61, at paras 67–135.

[78] *Métropole télévision* (n 645), para. 74; *Van den Bergh Foods* (n 646), para. 107.

[79] *Bell Atlantic Corp. v. Twombly*, 550 U.S. 544, 533 (2007).

and further clarified that conscious parallelism, defined as a common reaction of firms in a concentrated market that recognise their shared economic interests and interdependence with respect to price and output decisions, is 'not in itself unlawful'.[80] The meaning of what beyond mere interdependence constitutes a tacit agreement (without being mere tacit collusion in the economic sense) remains unclear. Lower courts require plaintiffs to show 'plus factors' such as 'proof that the defendants got together and exchanged assurances of common action or otherwise adopted a common plan even though no meetings, conversations or exchanged documents are shown'.[81] Commentators make a further distinction between 'plus factors', which are economic actions and outcomes above and beyond parallel pricing that are largely inconsistent with unilateral conduct, and 'super plus factors', which provide a strong inference of explicitly coordinated action. Examples of the latter include inter-firm transfers, rising prices, profits in an industry with excess capacity, sharing of sensitive competitive information, dominant firm conduct in an industry without a dominant firm, and actual prices that significantly exceed the but-for price (Marshall and Marx 2012).

In the internet age, company executives no longer need to organise secret meetings to fix prices or coordinate their competitive behaviour. Nowadays, technological advances enable more sophisticated ways of communication between companies. These forms of interaction may lead to a common understanding even if the specific goal of, for example, price fixing remains unspoken. The internet not only gives consumers the possibility to compare prices but also allows competitors easier monitoring of price policies and may thus facilitate collusion. Hence, removing the ambiguity concerning what constitutes a concerted practice (EU) or a tacit agreement (US) has became a major challenge for Law and Economics scholars. Page (2016) argues that a tacit agreement is a category of Sherman Act violations that may be distinguished from both simple interdependence in an oligopolistic market and express agreement. He defines a tacit agreement as 'interdependent conduct coordinated by prior communication of competitive intentions that lack any efficiency definition'. Also, in the absence of a preceding verbal agreement, rivals may demonstrate their accord with a communicated proposal or expressed intent by subsequent interdependent conduct. The challenge is to isolate the forms of interdependence that are economically inefficient and ultimately harm consumers.

To this end, Page (2016) suggests a distinction between private and public information and a further differentiation as to whether the information relates to present or future choices. Private communication (such as direct and secret price discussions among rivals) is less likely to benefit consumers than a public announcement. Also, if the communication is only about present pricing (or another competitive variable), firms will be less able to coordinate. Four scenarios can thus be distinguished. First, private communications about future competitive choices are most likely to violate Section 1 of the Sherman Act. Second, private communications about present prices should be analysed carefully under the Rule of Reason. Third, public communications about present prices do not prove a tacit agreement. Fourth, public communications about future prices usually benefit consumers, unless the communication is designed in a way to coordinate competitive behaviour and conveys no useful information to non-rivals. An example of the first scenario is the *Foley* case,[82] where rivals met privately to discuss the need for a price increase, never exchanged promises to raise prices and then acted consistently with the stated intentions. An efficiency justification could not be argued since no consumers were present at the meetings. Examples of the latter scenario include speeches at trade association meetings and statements in trade journals, followed by an unusual pattern of price increases. Page's proposal provides a clearer account of tacit agreement that builds upon earlier suggestions in economic papers[83] (for the US: Werden 2004; for the EU: Kühn 2001) and may reduce the efficiency losses from a legal immunisation of tacit collusion. For the comparative analysis of the EU and US systems, an important difference is that Page's proposal still requires evidence that the private communications between firms coordinated later oligopoly behaviour. A step towards *per se* illegality is not made, contrary to the European Commission's Horizontal Guidelines that define private exchanges of information about future prices a restriction by object (see section 5.3.2).

5.4.2 *Per se* illegality

The US Supreme Court has ruled that a practice is *per se* illegal and may be condemned without further inquiry when it would 'always or almost always tend to restrict competition and decrease output'.[84] In 1927, in *United States v. Trenton Potteries*,[85] the Supreme Court held that price fixing is illegal regardless of the reasonableness of prices. In 1940, in *United States v. Socony Vacuum*, the Court condemned as *per se* illegal combinations 'formed for the purpose and with the effect of raising, depressing, fixing, pegging, or

---

[82] 598 F.2d 1313 (4th Cir. 1979).

[83] For the US: Werden 2004; compare for the EU: Kühn 2001.

[84] *Broadcast Music, Inc. v. CBS*, 441 US 1, 19–20 (1979) (citing *United States v. United States Gypsum Co.*, 438 US 422, 441 n.14 (1978).

[85] 273 US 392 (1927).

stabilizing [prices]'.[86] This broad language casts a wide net of practices; it led to decisions branding a large number of antitrust violations as *per se* illegal. However, since the late 1970s, the Supreme Court has substantially narrowed the scope of agreements treated as *per se* illegal. In a series of decisions, it has ruled that *per se* treatment is inapplicable to vertical territorial restrictions,[87] blanket licences for copyrighted music,[88] concerted refusals to deal,[89] vertical maximum price fixing[90] and vertical price restraints.[91] In United States federal courts, all of these restraints are now analysed under the Rule of Reason.

Today, *per se* illegal treatment in the United States is reserved for hard-core cartel conduct; this includes horizontal price fixing,[92] bid rigging,[93] and market allocation agreements.[94] In 2004, the Supreme Court recognised collusion among competitors as 'the supreme evil of antitrust'.[95] *Per se* treatment also continues to apply to tying arrangements[96] and group boycotts[97] if certain conditions are met. Notably, several types of conduct – including vertical restrictions such as minimum resale price fixing and territorial limitations and horizontal competitor exchanges of future pricing information – that the European Commission treats as 'by object' infringements are analysed under the Rule of Reason.[98] Hub and spoke cartels, which have both horizontal and vertical linkages, create some uncertainty as to under which standard they have to be assessed. The *Apple/Amazon* case provides a clear example of these difficulties (see Box 5.3).

The Antitrust Division of the Department of Justice (DoJ) and the Federal Trade Commission (FTC) share responsibility for federal governmental

---

[86] 310 US 150 (1940).

[87] *Continental T.V. v. GTE Sylvania*, 433 US 36 (1977). See Chapter 6, section 6.3.2.

[88] *Broadcast Music v. Columbia Broadcasting System*, 441 US 1 (1979).

[89] *Northwest Wholesale Stationers, Inc. v. Pacific Stationery & Printing Co.*, 472 US 284 (1985).

[90] *State Oil Co. v. Khan*, 522 US 3 (1997). See section 6.3.1.

[91] *Leegin Creative Leather Products, Inc. v. PSKS*, 551 US 877 (2007). See section 6.3.1.

[92] *United States v. Socony-Vacuum Oil Co.*, 310 US 150, 223 (1940); *United States v. Trenton Potteries Co.*, 273 US 392, 397–98 (1927).

[93] *United States v. Heffernan*, 43 F.3d 1144 (7th Cir. 1994) (Posner, J) (bid rigging is a subset of price-fixing offences).

[94] *Palmer v. BRG of Georgia, Inc.*, 498 US 46, 49–50 (1990) (per curiam); *United States v. Topco Associates*, 405 US 596, 608 (1972).

[95] *Verizon Communications v. Law Offices of Curtis V. Trinko*, 540 US 398, 408 (2004).

[96] *Eastman Kodak Co. v. Image Technical Services, Inc.*, 505 US 451 (1992); *Jefferson Parish Hospital District No. 2 v. Hyde*, 466 US 2, 15–18 (1984).

[97] *FTC v. Indiana Federation of Dentists*, 476 US 447, 458 (1986); *Northwest Wholesale Stationers v. Pacific Stationery & Printing Co*, 472 US 284, 295–96 (1985).

[98] *United States v. United States Gypsum Co.*, 438 US 422, 441 n.16 (1978); *United States v. Citizens & National Bank*, 422 US 86, 113 (1975); *Maple Flooring Manufacturers Association v. United States*, 268 US 563, 582–83 (1925).

enforcement of the US antitrust laws. However, only the DoJ has the authority to bring criminal antitrust cases (see section 8.3.1 for further discussion). In theory, the government could charge *any* violation of the Sherman Act as a criminal offence. The line between criminal and civil violations of the law has shifted over time. In fact, for much of the law's history, the government failed to articulate clearly which violations would be subject to criminal prosecution. In addition, over the years, some enforcement officials made no attempt to limit criminal enforcement to the most egregious, hard-core antitrust violations. (Baker 1978). The DoJ did not articulate clear guidance on how it would exercise its prosecutorial discretion to charge antitrust violations criminally until the late 1970s and early 1980s (Baker 1978, at 414). Since then, the policy on criminal prosecutions has been fairly consistent: criminal prosecution has been reserved for the most serious hard-core cartel offences, i.e. agreements among horizontal competitors to fix prices, rig bids and allocate customers or territories.[99] Cases involving conduct that raises novel issues of law or fact or that could arise from confusion in the law or confusion caused by past prosecutorial decisions are handled civilly, not criminally.[100]

The DoJ does not criminally prosecute some violations that the European Commission labels restrictions 'by object'. For example, it would not have brought criminal charges in the information exchange case that the European Commission brought against banana importers[101] and the Court of Justice of the European Union upheld in *Dole Food Company v. Commission*.[102] There the violation was treated as cartel conduct even without proof that competitors agreed on prices or that their conduct affected prices. In fact, US enforcement authorities routinely forego prosecuting criminal cases in which they have developed substantial evidence that competitors regularly exchanged sensitive information about future prices, but have insufficient evidence to prove an agreement to fix prices. Moreover, the United States would not bring criminal charges against the vertical restrictions that the European Commission treats as 'by object' offences, e.g. vertical price restraints and territorial restrictions (see section 6.3 for further discussion).

---

[99] US Department of Justice, Antitrust Division Manual (5th ed. April 2015) at III-12, http://www.justice.gov/atr/division-manual; Federal Trade Commission and the US Department of Justice, Antitrust Guidelines for Collaborations Among Competitors (April 2000), at 8, https://www.ftc.gov/system/files/documents/public_statements/300481/000407ftcdojguidelines.pdf.

[100] See US Department of Justice, Antitrust Division Manual (5th ed. April 2015) at III-12, http://www.justice.gov/atr/division-manual.

[101] EU Commission Decision No. C(2008) 5955 (Case COMP/39 *Bananas*).

[102] Case T-588/08 [2013].

Box 5.3: The e-book case

In January 2010, Apple Inc was about to launch its first tablet computer, the iPad, and signed an agreement with five of the 'Big Six' US publishers to enter the e-book market. At that time, Amazon – selling nearly 90% of all e-books in the US market – largely dominated the sector. The Amazon agreement with the publishers was based on the traditional wholesale model, under which the books were sold to Amazon at a wholesale price, while the online store was free to set the retail price. Under this scheme, and in order to boost its Kindle e-book reader, Amazon defined an aggressive retail price strategy aimed at marketing the new releases and the bestselling books at $9.99, a price level below the wholesale price. The publishers were concerned about the consequences of Amazon's pricing strategy on their profits for the hardcover books and, in the long run, for their ability to continue to set profitable wholesale prices. For this reason, they attempted different strategies to influence Amazon's retail prices, but without any success.

Apple's entry in the market completely modified the scenario. The agreements between Apple and the publishers relied on three main components: the agency model, the price caps and the 'most-favoured nation' (MFN) clause. Under the agreement, the publishers were free to set the retail price of an e-book up to a maximum price related to the hardcover list price, while Apple received a flat 30% commission on the revenues. The MFN implied that if the retail price of an e-book was lower in another e-retailer bookstore, the publisher was forced to charge the same price for the Apple's e-bookstore. As a consequence, the agency model spread into the e-book market, Amazon's market share dropped to 60% and the retail prices increased.

In December 2011, the European Commission opened a formal proceeding to assess whether the international publishers had engaged in an anti-competitive practice affecting the sale of the e-books.[103] The Commission was concerned that the adoption of the agency model contracts represented part of a coordinated strategy aimed at raising the retail prices for e-books. Despite these concerns, the Commission closed the proceeding in December 2012 without finding any infringement. Instead, the Commission adopted a commitment decision that made the commitments proposed by Apple and by four publishers legally binding. They agreed to terminate all existing agreements and committed themselves not to enter in new agreements that included MFN clauses for five years.[104]

Conversely, the US antitrust enforcement showed a more complex development, involving different plaintiffs and claims. The civil suit was filed on April 2012 by the DoJ and separately by 33 States and US territories alleging the violation of Section 1

---

[103] European Commission, *Commission opens formal proceedings to investigate sales of e-books*, Brussels, Press Release, 6 December 2011.
[104] Case COMP/39.847, *E-books*, Commitment Decision, 2012.

of the Sherman Act and of different state antitrust statutes. Civil class-action lawsuits had also been filed and were consolidated with the DoJ and states' complaints before Judge Denise Cote, US District Court Judge for the Southern District of New York. In the judgment concerning the civil suit released in July 2013,[105] Judge Cote found that 'Apple directly participated in a horizontal price-fixing conspiracy. As a result its conduct is per se unlawful (para. 153)'. Apple appealed the District Court decision, arguing that as a vertical player its conduct would have to be judged under the Rule of Reason standard. Nevertheless, the Court of Appeals upheld the Second District ruling.[106] On the basis of the Apple's settlement with the class-action plaintiffs, the Court of Appeal's decision implied that Apple had to pay $400 million to consumers and up to $50 million in attorney fees.[107]

The decisions might be criticised under several respects. First, in the light of the previous case law, and relying on *Leegin*, the 'hub and spoke' scheme conducts would have been more properly analysed under the Rule of Reason standard, as the *per se* rule should be limited to the most severe restrictions of competition (for further discussion, see Chapter 6). From an economic perspective, it might be argued that Apple had adopted legitimate business practices, such as the agency agreements, whose pro-competitive effects were not carefully assessed under the *per se* rule. The analysis also seems to have largely overlooked the features of the e-book market structure at the time of Apple's entry, i.e. the dominance of Amazon and the fact that the $9.99 retail price set below the wholesale price constituted a barrier to entry. To conclude, as affirmed by Judge Jacobs in the dissenting opinion in the appeal judgment, the decision might be criticised as 'Apple's challenged conduct broke Amazon's monopoly' (...) 'immediately deconcentrated the e-book retail market', and encouraged innovation.[108] These arguments were resumed in Apple's petition for certiorari, although the US Supreme Court decided to deny the petition in March 2016.[109]

5.4.3 The Rule of Reason

Today, in the US the Rule of Reason is 'the prevailing standard of analysis'[110] and the approach taken in most antitrust cases. Under this rule, the court is required to weigh 'all of the circumstances of a case' in deciding whether a

---

[105] *United States vs Apple Inc.*, 952 F. Supp. 2d 638 (S.D.N.Y. 2013).

[106] *United States vs Apple Inc.*, 791 F3d 290, 2d Cir. 2015.

[107] US District Court, Southern District of New York, *In Re: Electronic Books Antitrust Litigation* (Final Judgment), 21 November 2014.

[108] *Ibid.*, dissenting opinion p. 28–29.

[109] In the Supreme Court of the United States, *Apple Inc. vs United States et al., On petition for a writ certiorari to the united states court of appeals for the second circuit*, 28 October 2015 and Supreme Court of the United States, Order List:577 US, 7 March 2016, *Certiorari Denied*, p. 20.

[110] *Continental T.V., Inc. v. GTE Sylvania Inc.*, 433 US 36, 49 (1977).

practice constitutes an unreasonable restraint on competition.[111] However, the Rule of Reason analysis has limits: it 'does not open the field of antitrust inquiry to any argument in favour of a challenged restraint that may fall within the realm of reason'.[112] Instead, the question is whether the conduct 'is one that promotes competition or one that suppresses competition'[113] and the analysis focuses on the 'market impact'[114] of the conduct at issue. Arguments unrelated to competitive impacts are irrelevant.[115] As the Supreme Court stated in *NCAA v. Board of Regents:* 'Under the Sherman Act the criterion to be used in judging the validity of a restraint on trade is the impact on competition.'[116]

Application of the Rule of Reason by courts

Courts in the US have 'structured' the Rule of Reason analysis in terms of shifting burdens of proof.[117] Initially plaintiffs bear the burden of proof that an agreement has or is likely to have a substantial anti-competitive effect. If a plaintiff meets this burden, the burden shifts to the defendant to produce evidence of the pro-competitive benefits of the conduct. If the defendant produces evidence of pro-competitive benefits, then the plaintiff must establish that the conduct is not reasonably necessary to achieve the stated goal or that the anti-competitive harm outweighs the stated pro-competitive effects.[118] The ultimate question is whether the restraint's anti-competitive harm substantially outweighs the competitive benefits for which the restraint is reasonably necessary.[119]

US courts have taken different approaches to balancing purported anti-competitive effects and pro-competitive benefits in Rule of Reason cases. Some cases have involved detailed market analyses, including market definition, assessments of defendants' market share and market power, and proof of how the challenged conduct impairs competition.[120] In some cases, courts have ruled that direct evidence of actual anti-competitive harm can eliminate the need for a detailed analysis of the market or defendants' market power.[121] In other cases, courts have found it unnecessary for plaintiffs to do

---

[111] *Continental T.V., Inc. v. GTE Sylvania Inc.*, 433 US 36 (1977).
[112] *National Society of Professional Engineers v. United States*, 435 US 679, 688.
[113] *Professional Engineers*, 435 US, at 691.
[114] *Ibid.*, at 691 n.17 (citing *Continental T.V. v. GTE Sylvania Inc.*, 433 US 36, 50–51 (1977)).
[115] See *FTC v. Superior Court Trial Lawyers Association*, 493 US 411, 424 (1990).
[116] *NCAA v. Board of Regents*, 468 US 85, 104 (1984) (footnote omitted).
[117] ABA (2012), at 62.
[118] *Ibid.*, at 62.
[119] *Ibid.*, at 62.
[120] *Ibid.*, at 70–73.
[121] *FTC v. Indiana Federation of Dentists*, 476 US 447, 460 (1986).

an in-depth, complete analysis of all relevant market factors. Instead, they have opted for a more truncated approach, sometimes referred to as a 'quick look' analysis, where 'an observer with even a rudimentary understanding of economics could conclude that the arrangements in question would have an anti-competitive effect on customers and markets.'[122] In sum, the US courts now approach the plaintiff's burden of proof in Rule of Reason cases along a spectrum, depending on the nature of the challenged restraint.

Once the burden shifts to defendants, courts have recognised a large number of possible justifications for restraints. They have recognised justifications that the challenged restraints increase output, create operating efficiencies, make new products available, enhance product or service quality and widen customer choice.[123] The Supreme Court has provided little guidance on how courts are to conduct the final step in the Rule of Reason analytical process: the balancing of pro- and anti-competitive effects. In fact, some lower courts have questioned the feasibility of such balancing. As Judge Bork stated in the *Rothery* case: '[T]hough it is sometimes said that (…) it is necessary to weigh procompetitive effects against anticompetitive effects, we do not think that is a usable formula if it implies an ability to quantify the effects and compare the values found.'[124] In fact, few courts have attempted this balancing, because most Rule of Reason cases turn on the plaintiffs' or defendants' failure to meet their initial burdens of proof.[125]

Application of the Rule of Reason by the US antitrust agencies

US enforcement officials have issued *Antitrust Guidelines for Collaborations Among Competitors*,[126] which, like the EU 2011 Horizontal Guidelines, articulate the enforcement agencies' approach to analysing competitor collaborations. The US Guidelines employ the US law's framework of treating agreements to fix prices or output, rig bids or divide markets as *per se* illegal and other types of competitor arrangements as subject to the Rule of Reason (US Horizontal Guidelines, at 1.2). *Per se* illegal agreements are deemed harmful to competition without further inquiry and are subject to potential criminal prosecution (US Horizontal Guidelines, at 3.1–3.2). All other agreements are analysed under the Rule of Reason, which focuses on the question of 'whether the relevant agreement likely harms competition by

---

[122] *California Dental Association v. FTC*, 526 US 756, 770 (1999).

[123] ABA (2012), at 74–75.

[124] *Rothery Storage & Van Co. v. Atlas Van Lines*, 792 F.2d 210, 229 n.11 (D.C. Cir. 1986).

[125] ABA (2012), at 79–80.

[126] US Department of Justice & Fed. Trade Comm'n, Antitrust Guidelines For Collaborations Among Competitors (2000) ('US Horizontal Guidelines') http://www.ftc.gov/os/2000/04/ftcdojguidelines.pdf.

increasing the ability or incentive profitably to raise price above or reduce output, quality, service or innovation below what likely would prevail in the absence of the relevant agreement' (US Horizontal Guidelines, at 3.1–3.3). The US Guidelines state that the Rule of Reason analysis involves a 'flexible inquiry and varies in focus and detail depending on the nature of the agreement and market circumstances' (US Horizontal Guidelines, at 1.2).

The US Guidelines prescribe that a Rule of Reason analysis begins with an examination of the nature of the relevant agreement and consideration of the agreement's purpose and any anti-competitive harm it may already have caused. If the nature of the agreement and absence of market power demonstrate the absence of anti-competitive harm, the conduct will not be challenged. Alternatively, if the likelihood of harm is evident from the nature of the agreement or the agreement has already caused harm, then the conduct will be challenged absent 'overriding benefits that could offset the anticompetitive harm' (US Horizontal Guidelines, at 3.3). This approach is similar to the 'quick look' analysis that US courts undertake in some Rule of Reason cases.

The US Guidelines also address how the enforcement agencies will address competitor agreements that raise possible competitive concerns but that require detailed market analyses (US Horizontal Guidelines, at 3.3). Typically the analysis will involve defining relevant markets and calculating market shares and concentration as a first step in determining whether the agreement may create or increase market power or facilitate its exercise. It will also include consideration of the degree to which the parties have the ability and incentive to compete independently and the prospects that entry would be timely, likely, and sufficient to prevent anti-competitive harms (US Horizontal Guidelines, *ibid.*). If this analysis identifies potential for competitive harm, it then will consider whether the agreement is reasonably necessary to achieve pro-competitive benefits that would likely offset anti-competitive harms (US Horizontal Guidelines, *ibid.*).

The US Guidelines walk through several factors that are relevant to full Rule of Reason inquiries. These include: the nature of the agreement, its business purpose and operation in the marketplace; whether the agreement limits independent decision making or combines control or financial interests; whether the agreement may facilitate collusion; the relevant markets affected by the collaboration, including goods markets, technology markets, and research and development (innovation) markets; market shares and market concentration; the ability and incentive of the participants to compete, including exclusivity, control over assets, the financial interests in the collaboration or in other participants, control over the collaboration's significant decision making, the likelihood of anti-competitive information sharing and duration of the collaboration; entry; and the pro-competitive benefits of the collaboration, including the efficiencies generated, the necessity for the collaboration and whether there are less restrictive alternatives that achieve the same end (US Horizontal Guidelines, at 3.31–3.36).

The US Guidelines provide a safety zone for agreements when market shares are no more than 20% of each relevant market and the agreements are not *per se* illegal, facially anti-competitive or subject to merger analysis (US Horizontal Guidelines, at 4.2). In addition, they create a second safety zone for research and development collaborations US Horizontal Guidelines, at 4.3). This safety zone requires that three or more independently controlled research efforts in addition to the subject agreement have the specialised assets or characteristics and the incentive to do R&D that is a close substitute for the subject collaboration's R&D. Factors relevant to determining the closeness of substitutes include: the nature, scope and magnitude of the R&D efforts; their access to financial support; their access to intellectual property, skilled personnel or other specialised assets; their timing; and their ability to successfully commercialise the innovation.

Box 5.4: Extraterritorial application of competition laws

With cartels becoming more and more international, questions have been raised about the extraterritorial reach of competition enforcement. For global conglomerates, the international trend towards farther-reaching enforcement against foreign commerce materially increases the risk that they will face financial penalties in multiple jurisdictions based on the same sales revenues. The past two decades have seen a dramatic increase in international cartel cases involving price-fixing agreements on components in global supply chains. Often US antitrust law has been applied when most of the collusive conduct and the direct sales of price-fixed components occurred outside of the US. In these cases, the components were incorporated into finished products overseas and then sold into the US. This has resulted in extensive litigation over the extraterritorial application of both the Sherman Act. Also, the scope for extraterritorial enforcement of EU competition law has raised intriguing questions. The CJEU has decided that component sales through transformed products in the EU reflect an EU infringement for regulatory enforcement and fining purposes. Below, the extraterritorial reach of both US antitrust law and EU competition law is further commented upon.

European Union

In *Innolux* the CJEU was called to examine for the first time the Commission's use of a novel – and extensive – approach to punish cartel conduct that took place abroad and concerned components largely manufactured outside of the EU, with limited direct imports of the cartelised components into the EU. The Commission took the view that sales in the EU of finished goods likely reflected some of the cartelised panel overcharge and thus likely harmed the EU market. It imposed fines on LCD panel manufacturers based on two types of commerce: (i) panels delivered directly by the LCD panel manufacturers into the EU, and (ii) panels that vertically integrated LCD panel manufacturers transformed themselves, intragroup, in Asia into finished products (e.g. TVs, monitors) and were then shipped to the EU where they would undertake the first external sale (through the sale of the – non-cartelised – finished good).

To back up its inclusion of the latter category of commerce, the Commission relied on the EU concept of what constitutes the relevant 'undertaking' for antitrust purposes, which essentially means that all companies that are part of the same corporate group are treated as one single entity. Using this concept, the Commission essentially assimilated sales through intra-group transformed products as direct EU shipments to third parties, taking the view that, in both scenarios, the first 'sale' of a LCD panel to third parties (whether as a stand-alone component or integrated into a TV or monitor) took place in Europe. In *Innolux*, the CJEU blessed this approach, stressing that cartelised LCD sales through intragroup transformed products may adversely impact the EU market. This ruling means that manufacturing activities that take place abroad can be subject to the EU's fining powers, which can increase financial exposure significantly if finished products end up in the EU.

United States

In 2004, the US Supreme Court issued an important ruling in *F. Hoffmann-La Roche Ltd. v. Empagran S.A,*[127] a case involving claims by foreign purchasers of vitamins subject to a global cartel agreement. In this case, the Court considered the Foreign Trade Antitrust Improvements Act of 1982 (FTAIA),[128] a complex and inartfully drafted statute that had received little attention for many years after its passage. In cases involving Sherman Act claims based on conduct outside of the United States, the FTAIA requires that the conduct either: (i) involves import trade or commerce; or (ii) has a 'direct, substantial, and reasonably foreseeable' effect on domestic commerce that must 'give rise to' a Sherman Act claim.[129] In *Empagran*, the Court ruled that while the conspiracy affected vitamin prices in the United States, those effects did not 'give rise to' the claims of

---

[127] 542 US 144 (2004).
[128] Pub. L. No. 97–290, title IV, § 402, 96 Stat. 1246 (1982) (codified at 15 U.S.C. § 6a).
[129] 15 U.S.C. § 6a(2).

purchasers that had bought vitamins outside of the United States.[130] The Court held that the non-US purchasers could not bring claims based on the Sherman Act.

Since the *Empagran* decision, US courts have puzzled over and parsed the language of the FTAIA. For example, courts have considered the meaning of 'direct' in the requirement that non-import commerce must have a 'direct, substantial, and reasonably foreseeable' effect on US commerce to be subject to the Sherman Act. Two cases have interpreted the direct-effect language to require a 'reasonably proximate causal nexus'.[131] Another court, in *United States v. Hui Hsiung*,[132] a case upholding convictions of defendants for their participation in a global cartel involving TFT-LCD panels, held that '[c]onduct has a "direct" effect for purposes of the domestic effects exception to the FTAIA "if it follows as an immediate consequence of the defendant[s'] activity."'[133] The court described this as a 'proximate causation' standard. Although a standard of 'immediate consequence' appears to be more exacting than one of 'reasonably proximate causal nexus', it's unclear what practical difference the standard made to the *Hsiung* court's analysis.

In *Hsiung* the court looked at 'the constellation of events' that surrounded the [TFT-LCD] conspiracy in ruling that the commerce in the TFT-LCD panel case was sufficiently 'direct' to meet the FTAIA's standard.[134] The court noted that the panels are a substantial cost component of the finished products (70–80% in the case of monitors and 30–40% for notebook computers). It also cited evidence that increases in panel prices directly affected finished product prices in the United States: 'The testimony underscored the integrated, close and direct connection between the purchase of the price-fixed panels, the United States as the destination for the products, and the ultimate inflation of prices in finished products imported to the United States.' And the court concluded: 'The direct connection was neither speculative not insulated by multiple disconnected layers of transactions.'

In *Minn-Chem v. Agrium*, a case involving an alleged global cartel in potash, the court found that the alleged conduct was sufficiently direct, observing that it was not a case in which 'action in a foreign country filters through many layers and finally causes a few ripples in the United States'.[135] And in *Motorola Mobility LLC v. AU Optronics*,[136] another case related to the TFT-LCD conspiracy, Judge Posner concluded that the conspiracy involved sufficiently direct effects to be reached under the FTAIA. In his ruling, Judge Posner observed that the effect of price-fixing components used in cellphones

---

[130] 542 US 144, 162 (2004).
[131] *Minn-Chem Inc. v. Agrium*, 683 F.3d, at 845, 857 (7th Cir. 2012); *Lotes Co. v. Hon Hai Precision Indus. Co.*, 753 F.3d 395, 411 (2d Cir. 2014).
[132] *United States v. Hui Hsiung*, 778 F.3d 738, 758–59 (9th Cir. 2015).
[133] *Ibid.*, at 758–59 (quoting *United States v. LSL Biotechnologies*, 379 F.3d 672, 680–681 (9th Cir. 2004)).
[134] *Hui Hsiung*, at 759–760.
[135] *Minn-Chem Inc. v. Agrium*, 683 F.3d, at 845, 857 (7th Cir. 2012) (en banc).
[136] 775 F3. 816, 819 (7th Cir. 2015).

(Motorola Mobility's claim) was less direct than the alleged effect of the potash cartel (Minn-Chem's claim). But he then referred to the language of the *Minn-Chem* case: 'This doesn't seem like "many layers," resulting in just a "a few ripples" in the United States cellphone market, though (...) the ripple effect probably was modest.'[137] Judge Posner assumed for purposes of the decision that the commerce at issue was sufficiently direct for FTAIA purposes.

The *Motorola Mobility* decision went on to dismiss the plaintiff's claims, finding that they failed to meet the FTAIA's requirement that the effect of anti-competitive conduct on domestic US commerce must 'give rise to' a US antitrust claim. This was the section of the FTAIA at issue in the *Empagran* case. Motorola's non-US subsidiaries purchased the price-fixed components. The court ruled that the subsidiaries must seek relief in the countries in which they or the defendants do business, but that they have no right to relief under US antitrust laws. Notably, the decision went on to distinguish between the ability of private claimants and the US Justice Department to seek redress under the FTAIA. The court ruled: 'If price-fixing by the component manufacturers had the requisite statutory effect on cellphone prices in the United States, the Act would not block the Department of Justice from seeking criminal or injunctive remedies.'[138]

5.5 Conclusions

Economic theory is helpful in explaining why competitors have incentives to cooperate and why cartels are formed. As soon as the number of suppliers is limited and the products sold are not homogeneous, perfect competition no longer exists. In game theory, models have been developed which describe behavioural choices of firms in an oligopolistic market, where they have to take the reactions by their competitors into account. Some cartels will succeed, while others will fail. The economics of collusion discuss three prerequisites for cartel success: (i) the potential for monopoly power, given the characteristics of the market; (ii) expected high gains; and (iii) the need to overcome the organisational problems of cartels. This chapter found that oligopolistic markets do not necessarily lead to collusive outcomes. At the same time, economic insights demonstrate that cooperation between firms may be motivated by goals that are beneficial to societal welfare. Different types of cooperation can lead to a range of efficiencies, such as economies of scale and scope, better planning of production, advantages in marketing and distribution, and in research and development. Competition law should

---

[137] *Ibid.*
[138] *Motorola Mobility*, at 825.

take into account these benign effects of competitor collaboration and weigh them against the anti-competitive effects.

Turning to the applicable laws, this chapter explained how European competition law seeks to restrain anti-competitive coordination of companies' behaviour. Article 101(1) TFEU bans cartel agreements, decisions of associations of undertakings, and concerted practices that harm competition. Article 101(3) TFEU grants an exemption when the benefits of the agreement in terms of efficiencies and consumer welfare are deemed to prevail without causing disproportionate restrictions or eliminating competition for a substantial part of the products in question. This is an exception rule, which provides a defence for undertakings against a finding of an infringement of Article 101(1) TFEU. This directly applicable exception system allows companies to self-assess whether they are caught by Article 101 TFEU. The Article 81(3) EC Notice (also called General Guidelines) provides more detailed guidance thereto.

EU competition law differentiates between agreements having restriction of competition as their object and agreements or concerted practices which, also implicitly, may have anti-competitive consequences. Economic analysis stresses the need to examine the real-life consequences of both explicit and tacit collusion. Even though restriction of competition may be the proven object of cooperation, market evidence may show that prices are not substantially above competitive levels, which makes antitrust intervention less compelling or even unnecessary. In general, agreements such as price fixing, market sharing, quotas, and rigging bids having as their object the restriction of competition will mainly entail enforcement-related issues such as leniency, fines, and damages. Horizontal agreements having as their object a restriction of competition are considered by the nature of the cooperation to indicate the applicability of Article 101(1) TFEU as they are presumed to have negative market effects, and current EC competition law seemingly allows economically relevant evidence to be pushed aside if the objective to fix prices or control output can be proven; (lack of) economic impact will be taken into account only when determining the ultimate fine. If competitor cooperation does not have as its object a restriction of competition, the applicability of Article 101(1) TFEU requires an analysis of the agreement's effects. The agreement must thus be able to limit competition between the parties involved and it must be likely to affect competition in the market to such an extent that negative market effects as to prices, output, innovation or the variety or quality of goods and services can be expected. The EU Horizontal Guidelines hold that this depends on the economic context of the agreement, taking into account both the nature and content of the agreement as well as the parties' combined market power. Together with other structural factors, this determines the capability of the cooperation to affect overall competition.

Under US antitrust law, the crucial distinction is between agreements (explicit or tacit) that are illegal *per se* and types of conduct to be judged under the Rule of Reason. Criminal prosecution remains limited to the hard-core restrictions. Not only explicit agreements but also tacit agreements may constitute antitrust violations. US antitrust law does not use the concept of concerted practices but also distinguishes between express coordination and mere interdependence in oligopolistic markets. In-between forms of conduct, such as meetings of competitors, may constitute an antitrust infringement if parallel pricing is joined by 'plus factors' that are inconsistent with competitive conduct. The range of hard-core restrictions (horizontal price fixing, bid rigging and market sharing agreements) is smaller than the practices that are regarded as restrictions 'by object' under EU competition law. Private exchanges of information about future prices may constitute a tacit agreement but it will also be required to show an ultimate negative impact on consumer prices. The Rule of Reason is the dominant approach under US antitrust law. The Courts have 'structured' the Rule of Reason in terms of shifting burdens of proof. Further clarification as how the reasonableness test is to be applied can be found in the Guidelines of the US enforcement agencies.

5.6   Bibliography

American Bar Association (2012), *Antitrust Law Developments* (ABA Book Publishing, 7th ed.)

Asch P, Seneca J (1976), 'Is Collusion Profitable?' 58 *The Review of Economics and Statistics* 1

Baird D, Gertner R, Picker R (1998), *Game Theory and the Law* (Harvard University Press, 2nd ed.)

Baker D (1978), 'To Indict or Not To Indict: Prosecutorial Discretion in Sherman Act Enforcement' 63 *Cornell Law Review* 405

Baumol W, Ordover J (1992), 'Antitrust: Source of Dynamic and Static Inefficiencies?', in T Jorde and D Teece (eds.), *Antitrust, Innovation, and Competitiveness* 82 (Oxford University Press)

Baumol W, Panzar J, Willig R (1982), *Contestable Markets and the Theory of Industry Structure* (Harcourt College Publishers)

Bhattacharya S, Mookerjee D (1986), 'Portfolio Choice in Research and Development' 17 *RAND Journal of Economics* 594

Black O (1997), 'Per Se Rules and Rules of Reason: What Are They?' 18 *European Competition Law Review* 145

Blair R, Harrison J (2010), *Monopsony in Law and Economics* (Cambridge University Press)

Boyer K, Lancaster K (1986), 'Are There Scale Economies in Advertising?' 59 *Journal of Business* 509

Brodley J (1982), 'Joint Ventures and Antitrust Policy' 95 *Harvard Law Review* 1523

Burkett J (2006), *Microeconomics: Optimization, Experiments, and Behavior* (Oxford University Press)

Camesasca P (2000), *European Merger Control: Getting the Efficiencies Right* (Intersentia)

Capobianco A (2004), 'Information Exchange under EC Competition Law' 41 *Common Market Law Review* 1247

Carlton D, Perloff J (2005), *Modern Industrial Organization* (Pearson, 4th ed.)

Clarke R (1983), 'Collusion and the Incentives for Information Sharing' 14 *Bell Journal Of Economics* 383

Coase R (1937), 'The Nature of the Firm' 4 *Economica* 386

Dasgupta P, Stiglitz J (1980), 'Industrial Structure and the Nature of Innovative Activity' 90 *Economic Journal* 266

Devlin A (2007), 'A Proposed Solution to the Problem of Parallel Pricing in Oligopolistic Markets' 59 *Stanford Law Review* 1111

Dick A (1996), 'When Are Cartels Stable Contracts?' 39 *Journal of Law and Economics* 241

Dick A, Knight M (1998), *Notes to Accompany Seminar on Tacit Collusion*, Internal seminar paper prepared for the Department of Justice, Washington

Farrell J (1987), 'Cheap Talk, Co-ordination, and Entry' 18 *RAND Journal of Economics* 34

Farrell J, Shapiro C (1990), 'Asset Ownership and Market Structure in Oligopoly' 21 *RAND Journal of Economics* 275

Faull J, Nikpay A (1999), 'Article 81', in J Faull and A Nikpay (eds.), *The EC Law of Competition* (Oxford University Press)

Fisher F, Temin P (1973), 'Returns to Scale in Research and Development: What Does the Schumpeterian Hypothesis Imply?' 81 *Journal of Political Economy* 56

Fonseca M, Normann H (2012), 'Explicit vs. Tacit Collusion. The Impact of Communication in Oligopoly Experiments' 56 *European Economic Review* 1759

Friedman J (1971), 'A Non-cooperative Equilibrium for Supergames' 38 *Review of Economic Studies* 1

Fudenberg D (1983), 'Pre-emption, Leapfrogging and Competition in Patent Races' 22 *European Economic Review* 3

Ghezzi F, Maggiolino M (2014), 'Bridging EU concerted Practices with U.S. Concerted Actions' 10 *Journal of Competition Law and Economics* 647

Gilbert R, Sunshine S (1995), 'Incorporating Dynamic Efficiency Concerns in Merger Analysis: The Use of Innovation Markets' 63 *Antitrust Law Journal* 567

Gonzalez Diaz F, Kirk D, Perez Flores F, Verkleij C (1999), 'Horizontal Agreements' in J Faull, A Nikpay (eds.), *The EC Law of Competition* 333 (Oxford University Press)

Haan M, Schoonbeek L, Winkel B (2009), 'Experimental Results on Collusion', in J Hinloopenand and H Normann (eds.), *Experiments and Competition Policy* 9 (Cambridge University Press)

Haddock D (1982), 'Basing Point Pricing: Competitive v. Collusive Theories' 72 *American Economic Review* 289

Hovenkamp H (1994), *Federal Antitrust Policy. The Law of Competition and Its Practice* (West Publishing Company)

Hüschelrath K (2010), 'How Are Cartels Detected? The Increasing Use of Proactive Methods to Establish Antitrust Infringements' 1 *Journal of European Competition Law and Practice* 522

Jones A, Sufrin B (2014), *EU Competition Law: Text, Cases and Materials* (Oxford University Press, 5th ed.)

Jorde T, Teece D (1990), 'Innovation and Cooperation: Implications for Competition and Antitrust' 4 *Journal of Economic Perspectives* 75

Kovacic W (1993), 'The Identification and Proof of Horizontal Agreements under the Antitrust Laws' 38 *Antitrust Bulletin* 5

Kühn K (2001), 'Fighting Collusion: Regulation of Communication between Firms' 16 *Economic Policy* 167

Kühn K, Vives X (1995), 'Information Exchanges among Firms and their Impact on Competition' (Office for Official Publications of the European Community, Luxembourg)

Malueg D, Tsutsui S (1997), 'Coalition-proof Information Exchanges' 63 *Journal of Economics* 259

Marshall R, Marx L (2012), *The Economics of Collusion. Cartels and Bidding Rigs* (MIT Press)

Morais L (2013), *Joint Ventures and EU Competition Law* (Hart Publishing)

Morais L, Feteira L (2015), 'The Chameleon in the Room: Transatlantic Views on Information Exchange in the Field of Competition Law' <https://ssrn.com/abstract=2657639>

Motta M (2004), *Competition Policy. Theory and Practice* (Cambridge University Press)

Nalebuff B, Stiglitz J (1983), 'Information, Competition and Markets' 73 *American Economic Review* 278

Nitsche R, von Hinten-Reed N (2004), *Competitive Impacts of Information Exchange* (Charles River Associates)

Ordover J, Baumol W (1988), 'Antitrust Policy and High Technology Industries' 4 *Oxford Review of Economic Policy* 13

Osborne M, Pitchik C (1987), 'Cartels, Profits and Excess Capacity' 28 *International Economic Review* 413

Page W (2016), 'Tacit Agreement Under Section 1 of the Sherman Act', University of Florida, Levin College of Law, Research Paper No. 16-45 <https://ssrn.com/abstract=2760524>

Page W (2010), 'Facilitating Practices and Concerted Action Under Section 1 of the Sherman Act', in K Hylton (ed.), *Antitrust Law and Economics* 23 (Edward Elgar)

Phlips L (1995), *Competition Policy: A Game-theoretic Perspective* (Cambridge University Press)

Pindyck R, Rubinfeld D (2005), *Microeconomics* (Prentice Hall, 6th ed.)

Posner R (1970), 'A Statistical Study of Antitrust Enforcement' 13 *Journal of Law and Economics* 365

Reitman D (1994), 'Partial Ownership Arrangements and the Potential for Collusion' 42 *Journal of Industrial Economics* 313

Ritter L, Braun W, Rawlinson F (2000), *European Competition Law: A Practitioner's Guide* (Kluwer Law International, 2nd ed.)

Schelling T (1960), *The Strategy of Conflict* (Harvard University Press)

Schumpeter J (1950), *Capitalism, Socialism and Democracy* (Harper & Brothers, 3rd ed.)

Selten R (1973), 'A Simple Model of Imperfect Competition, where 4 are Few and 6 are Many' 2 *International Journal of Game Theory* 141

Shapiro C, Willig R (1990), 'On the Antitrust Treatment of Production Joint Venture' 4 *Journal of Economic Perspectives* 113

Stephen F (1993), 'Effects of Deregulation in Professional Services Markets: Scottish Conveyancing Markets 1984–1989' *Strathclyde Papers in Economics no. 93/9*

Stigler G (1964), 'A Theory of Oligopoly' 72 *Journal of Political Economy* 44

Sugden R (1995), 'A Theory of Focal Points' 105 *Economic Journal* 533

Vives X (2001), *Oligopoly Pricing: Old Ideas and New Tools* (MIT Press)

Wagner-von Papp F (2013), 'Information Exchange Agreements', in I Lianos and D Geradin (eds.), *Handbook on EU Competition Law – Substantive Aspects* 130 (Edward Elgar)

Werden G (2004), 'Economic Evidence on the Existence of Collusion: Reconciling Antitrust Law with Oligopoly Theory' 71 *Antitrust Law Journal* 719

Wils W (2000), 'The Undertaking as Subject of EC Competition Law and the Imputation of Infringements to Natural or Legal Persons' 25 *European Law Review* 99

Winter S (1987), 'Knowledge and Competence as Strategic Assets', in D Teece (ed.), *The Competitive Challenge: Strategies for Industrial Innovation and Renewal* (Ballinger)

6

Vertical restrictions

Roger Van den Bergh

6.1   Introduction

Manufacturers may impose conditions on the distributors (wholesalers and retailers) with whom they deal beyond requiring them to pay the purchase price for the supplied products. For example, in contracts with retailers, manufacturers may specify the retail price at which the products must be resold. Apart from price restrictions, territorial restrictions limiting the places where distributors may resell the supplied products and customer restrictions limiting the group(s) of buyers to which the products can be resold are widespread in distribution agreements. Such contractual terms are commonly called 'vertical' restrictions. As agreements between two entities at different levels of the supply chain, they are contrasted with 'horizontal' restrictions. These are limitations placed in contracts between two entities at the same position in the chain.[1] Generally, vertical restrictions are considered less harmful for competition than horizontal agreements. The reason for this is that horizontal agreements are entered into by competitors, whereas vertical restrictions regulate the relationship between firms which usually do not compete with each other.

For the purposes of legal and economic analysis, vertical restrictions are commonly divided into price and non-price restrictions. Price restrictions can take different forms. Manufacturers may require retailers to charge a fixed price or limit their freedom to determine prices by setting a minimum or maximum retail price. This practice is variously termed resale price maintenance (in the US), vertical price fixing (in the EU) or fair trade (until the 1970s in the US).[2] An important variant of resale price maintenance is the

---

[1] The distinction between horizontal restrictions and vertical restrictions is not always easy to apply. Sometimes it leads to inaccurate and confusing descriptions of business relationships; in a number of cases (such as retailer boycotts) there is a combination of both horizontal and vertical restrictions. See Carstensen and Hart (2003).

[2] US state laws (dating from the 1950s) allowing resale price maintenance in a number of US states were called 'fair trade laws'.

communication by the manufacturer of non-binding recommended prices or advertised prices.

Non-price restrictions include: (i) requirements that distributors (wholesalers, retailers) do not locate near each other, so that each dealer enjoys some degree of territorial protection (exclusive distribution); (ii) requirements that retailers do not sell competing products (exclusive purchasing);[3] (iii) requirements that retailers sell a fixed quantity or a minimum number of units (quantity fixing); (iv) requirements that retailers satisfy a number of quality requirements (selective distribution); and (v) requirements that retailers operate within a standardised and highly detailed promotional framework (franchising).[4] Franchising is a distribution format, which bundles several types of vertical restrictions. In EU competition law, a franchise has been defined as:

> a package of industrial or intellectual property rights relating to trademarks, trade names, shop signs, utility models, designs, copyrights, know-how or patents to be exploited for the resale of goods or the provision of services to end users.[5]

Franchisors provide franchisees with a total system of doing business, thus decreasing the likelihood of failure compared to the bankruptcy risk of less experienced independent retailers. In order to protect the parties' specific investments, various clauses containing vertical restrictions are inserted into the franchise contracts. On the one hand, exclusive territories may be granted to franchisees to ensure that they will earn a sufficient return on the investments they sink. On the other hand, exclusive dealing provisions and non-competition clauses may be inserted into the contract to safeguard the franchisor's incentives to invest in know-how. Looking at the EU definition of franchising, it becomes clear that there are important parallels between intellectual property rights and vertical restrictions. Trademarks, which are an inherent part of franchise agreements, allow the manufacturer to police the retailers' investments in maintaining the quality signals contained in the trademarked

---

[3] Hereinafter also called 'exclusive dealing'.

[4] The terminology used is taken from the (old) EC Regulations, which were in force until 31 May 2000 (Regulation 1983/83 [1983] O.J. L 173/1; Regulation 1984/83 [1983] O.J. L 173/5). Exclusive distribution is also termed 'exclusive territories', whereas exclusive dealing is synonymous with exclusive purchasing. In this chapter these terms are used interchangeably.

[5] Article 1(3)(a) Regulation 4087/88 [1988] O.J. L 359/46. The Franchising Regulation was replaced by Regulation 2790/1999 on vertical agreements [1999] O.J. L 336/21, but continued to apply until December 31, 2001 for agreements already in force on May 31, 2000. Today franchising is covered by the most recent block exemption on vertical restrictions: Regulation 330/2010 on vertical agreements and concerted practices [2010] O.J. L 102/1.

brand. Minimum resale prices serve the same goal by curbing free-riding and guaranteeing promotional efforts and provision of sales services.

In the policy analysis of vertical restrictions, a further distinction is made between intra-brand competition and inter-brand competition. The manufacturer and its retail network may be considered as a unique vertical structure. If the brand name of a product offered by a vertical structure is attached to the corresponding manufacturer, intra-brand competition refers to competition between retailers offering the same product of a given manufacturer within a given vertical structure. Inter-brand competition involves the interaction between different vertical structures; it refers to competition between retailers offering different products. Intra-brand competition is typically limited by minimum resale price maintenance: retailers selling the same brand can no longer compete on price. However, resale price maintenance may increase inter-brand competition by giving retailers strong incentives to improve pre-sale and post-sale services in order to attract consumers away from products of competing manufacturers. Conversely, other vertical restrictions may limit inter-brand competition. If retailers are tied to manufacturers by means of exclusive purchasing agreements, in-store competition between competing brands will be weakened or eliminated (think of cars as an example).

Positive economic analysis seeks to explain why manufacturers establish vertical restrictions. Broadly speaking, there are both efficiency theories and theories advancing the anti-competitive effects of vertical restrictions. Even though in antitrust practice the dominant economic explanation (justification) has been the free-riding theory, at least equal attention should be given to broader theories focusing on the need to protect retailers' promotional efforts (also in the absence of free-riding) and insights from transaction cost theory (particularly in the case of franchising). Efficiency theories contrast with theories focusing on the anti-competitive effects of vertical restrictions. Collusive behaviour of either manufacturers or retailers may underlie resale price maintenance agreements. In the Law and Economics literature, vertical restraints are commonly explained as instruments to enhance the efficiency of distribution agreements between manufacturers and distributors. More generally, vertical restrictions can be economically rationalised as ways to achieve efficient distribution of consumers' goods by excluding free-riding (see section 2.6) and, more generally, to solve coordination problems between manufacturers and distributors. However, vertical restrictions may not only enhance economic efficiency; they may also limit competition.

The structure of this chapter is as follows. After this introduction, section 6.2 addresses the question why manufacturers may find it profitable to place vertical restrictions on the distributors' actions. Besides the efficiency theories, section 6.2 also discusses economic theories stressing the anti-competitive effects of non-price vertical restrictions: limitation of market entry (foreclosure), dampening competition at the upstream level and abuse of market power. After an overview of the relevant economic literature, sections 6.3 and 6.4 provide a comparative overview of the competition rules governing vertical restrictions. Both US antitrust law and EU competition law are described and contrasted with each other. A brief comparison with antitrust rules of emerging economies (China, India and Brazil) is included in a separate box. The history of US antitrust law, which is described in section 6.3, shows a gradual evolution of a strict *per se* prohibition of (certain types of) vertical restrictions to an assessment under the Rule of Reason. The evolution in the EU, which is described in section 6.4, is equally enticing: competition law has evolved from legal formalism to an effects-based approach, which pays more attention to the impact of vertical restrictions on economic efficiency. After the comparative assessment, section 6.5 concludes this chapter.

6.2   Economic analysis of vertical restrictions

6.2.1   Evolution of economic thinking

Initially, economists were uneasy about vertical restrictions because several restrictions, such as prohibiting retailers to lower prices or sell competing products, appear to limit competition and harm consumers by increasing product prices. At first blush, not only the suppliers but also the buyers seem to profit from price competition. Everything else equal, lower retail margins will increase product sales and, hence, manufacturers' profits. From the point of view of consumers, non-service supplying discount retailers will attract buyers who do not value additional services. Conversely, full-service retailers will be patronised by consumers valuing additional advice, demonstrations, and post-sale services. Hence, if manufacturers, retailers and consumers all profit from low prices, why not leave it all to the market when price competition increases manufacturers' profits and provides consumers with the level of services best adapted to their personal preferences? The answer to this intriguing question is that the early economic assessments of vertical restrictions ignored the costs of distribution. Obviously, the model of perfect competition that takes distribution as a costless activity does not provide good intuition for markets that rely on substantial sales expenditures. Every manufacturer must pay retailers for their sales efforts and monitor them to make sure that products are distributed in a manner that is best for the manufacturer's interests.

The evolution of economic thinking on vertical restrictions led to the emergence of more benign views. Nowadays economists describe the relation between a manufacturer and a distributor as a principal-agent dependency. The principal (manufacturer) hires the agent (distributor) to perform an action in a manner that the principal cannot fully control (Carlton and Perloff 2005, 414). Principal-agent problems create a variety of both horizontal and vertical externalities,[6] which can be addressed with vertical restrictions. Each vertical structure faces a number of decision variables: fixing of wholesale and retail prices, quantities to be purchased by distributors, quantities to be sold to consumers, sellers' efforts, location of stores and so on. Neither the manufacturer nor the distributor (wholesaler and/or retailer) can control all these variables directly: the manufacturer controls some, while the distributor monitors others. Some decisions affect the total profits of the vertical structure; other decisions affect the distribution of profits between the manufacturer and the retailer. The decentralisation of decision making generates externalities, since one firm's decisions affect the other firm's profits. It is thus natural for the manufacturer and the distributor to look for some means of aligning both parties' interests and, in that respect, vertical restrictions can help. A large part of the economic literature discusses vertical restrictions as instruments to solve coordination problems in vertical structures (Rey and Caballero-Sanz 1996, 11–21).

The transaction cost approach to problems of competition law (see section 2.9) has made it clear that the costs of distribution will determine the choice to be made by the manufacturer between setting up his own distribution system (a firm) or signing contracts with independent distributors (the market solution). If the latter option is chosen, vertical restrictions may cope with lock-in effects, which are the consequence of specific investments and the resulting risk of appropriating profits through opportunistic behaviour. Once a long-term investment that involves substantial sunk costs (for example in specialist equipment or training) is made, the investing firm's bargaining position is weakened. Accordingly, the firm will not want to make this investment before particular arrangements to avoid a hold-up by the other contract party are agreed upon. The transaction cost approach reaffirms and refines some of the insights flowing from the principal-agent models. Transaction-specific investments bind the manufacturer and the distributor closely together (small-numbers exchange). Therefore, the contract parties are highly vulnerable to shirking but vertical restrictions may limit the scope for opportunistic behaviour on either the manufacturer's or the distributor's side.

---

[6] An externality is a negative or positive consequence of an action by an individual (or firm) on another person (or firm).

The economic insights relating to vertical restrictions are further commented on below. First, economic theories on price restrictions are discussed. Thereafter, the focus shifts to non-price restrictions. In both sections, theories advancing anti-competitive effects are contrasted with efficiency theories. In the section on price restrictions, also an overview of empirical work is given as well as a brief account of the behavioural approach to minimum resale price maintenance. Recently, behavioural scholars have argued that resale price maintenance may be the result of systematic errors (cognitive biases) on the part of boundedly rational manufacturers. Therefore, resale price maintenance may be used excessively and inefficiently, also when there is no free-riding problem, and may harm consumers by reducing output.

6.2.2   Price restrictions

Suppliers or dealers have often hypothesised resale price maintenance (minimum vertical price fixing) to function primarily as an aid to collusion. However, there has been considerable development of other economic theories of vertical restrictions that recognise the principal-agent nature of the manufacturer-distributor relationship. In addition, current economic thinking on vertical price fixing carefully distinguishes between minimum retail prices and maximum retail prices. Whereas the former may enhance efficiency in distribution by preventing free-riding and solving coordination problems among manufacturers and distributors, the latter may serve the interests of both manufacturers and consumers by preventing the charging of successive monopoly profits. Before further exploring the efficiency savings brought about by resale price maintenance, it will be investigated whether vertical price fixing has any (important) potential to limit competition.

Collusion theories

Collusion theories refer to the possibility that minimum vertical price fixing may be used to sustain a dealers' cartel or facilitate upstream collusion by reducing the manufacturers' incentives to lower wholesale prices. There are two main effects of minimum retail prices on competition. First, the dealers can no longer compete on price and this leads to a total elimination of intra-brand price competition. Second, there is increased transparency on price and responsibility for price changes. The latter effect makes horizontal collusion easier, at least in concentrated markets.

In the manufacturer-collusion theory, minimum vertical price fixing is used to set retail prices that reflect the collusive wholesale price. Vertical price fixing is said to prevent cheating since retail price cuts are easier to detect. It also makes wholesale price cuts less desirable, since such a price cut at the upstream level cannot be passed on to the downstream level (Posner 1977). In the distributor-collusion theory, dealers acting as a group induce the supplier to enforce a collusive minimum price through vertical price fixing. The goal pursued is either to discipline price-cutting among the distributors (retailers) or to prevent the evolution of more efficient forms of distribution. Vertical restrictions are thus used to circumvent the prohibition of horizontal price fixing. Clearly, this is a misuse of vertical restrictions to be banned by competition law.

Competition lawyers sometimes tend to overemphasise the risk that manufacturers can be persuaded by retailers to introduce and monitor resale price maintenance. In this respect, economists are more sceptical. There are two reasons why the traditional emphasis on vertical price fixing as a mechanism to organise collusion may be misplaced (Utton 2003, 239–240). First, the collusive price desired by retailers conflicts with the manufacturer's interest of making maximum sales, given the wholesale price. The gain to a manufacturer of maintaining a resale price may not be worth the cost of losing the high-volume business of discount stores. Hence, a manufacturer may gain more by reporting collusion between dealers to the competition authorities than by enforcing minimum retail prices. Second, given that entry is relatively easy in many retail markets, abnormally high profits resulting from vertical price fixing are likely to attract new entrants. According to the traditional economists' view, it seems unlikely that dealers' collusion is a major explanation for minimum vertical price fixing, although there may be instances where retailers have put pressure on manufacturers to impose minimum resale prices.[7] The opposite conclusion is tenable only in as far as retailing markets are not competitive and fit the description of local small-numbers oligopolies (Sharp 1985, 37; Porter 1976, 13).

In recent literature, economists take a more cautious attitude and warn against negative horizontal effects of vertical agreements between manufacturers and distributors. Resale price maintenance may restrict both intra-brand and inter-brand competition when rival manufacturers distribute their goods through the same competing retailers. In a theoretical paper Rey and Vergé demonstrate that resale price maintenance, even as part of bilateral vertical contracts, can generate industry-wide monopoly prices and profits in the context of 'interlocking relationships'. The final impact on consumer prices depends on the degree of competition at the different stages of the supply chain as well as on the impact of manufacturers and distributors when the contract terms are defined (Rey and Vergé 2010). The analysis of 'interlocking

---

[7] An example is the Pioneer decision of the European Commission, *Pioneer Commission decision* 80/256/EEC [1980] O.J. L 60/21.

relationships' provides some theoretical support for a prohibition of 'hub and spoke' cartels. Manufacturers distributing their products through competing retailers may possess information about consumer prices charged by competing retailers and the communication of this information to a particular retailer may facilitate collusion at the downstream level of the supply chain.

Efficiency theories

Efficiency theories of (minimum and maximum) resale price maintenance include: (i) the double monopoly mark-up theory; (ii) the free-riding theory; (iii) the quality certification theory; (iv) the contract enforcement mechanism theory; (v) the outlets theory; (vi) the demand risk theory; and (vii) the optimal retail services theory. With the exception of the monopoly mark-up theory, which explains maximum vertical price fixing, all theories provide an economic rationale for fixing minimum resale prices.

Double monopoly mark-up theory

The successive monopoly mark-up problem offers an efficiency explanation for fixing maximum retail prices. If the manufacturer and the distributor both enjoy a monopoly position, each of them will want to add a monopoly mark-up to their cost (production cost of the manufacturer, input cost of buying goods of the distributor). Consequently, consumers will face two mark-ups instead of one. The manufacturer charges the distributor a wholesale price above his marginal cost. The distributor treats this price as his marginal cost and adds a second monopoly mark-up. The consequence of this double marginalisation[8] is a lower output and a higher price than in the case of a vertically integrated firm, which takes care of both manufacturing and distribution. Both consumers and manufacturers are worse off with successive monopolies. Consumers facing the double mark-up pay higher prices. Profits for manufacturers under successive monopolies are also lower, since output decreases (for a graphical presentation, see Carlton and Perloff 2005, 416). The coordination problem comes from the fact that each firm, when setting its own price, does not take into account the effect of this price on the other firm's profit. The distributor 'forgets' that reducing quantity adversely affects the manufacturer's profit; the latter is negatively affected by this vertical externality.

Vertical restrictions can be used to prevent losses due to successive monopoly mark-ups. If vertical price fixing is legal, the manufacturer may impose contractually a maximum retail price and thus prevent the distributor from

---

[8] Double marginalisation was the first coordination problem in vertical structures formally analysed. See Spengler (1950, 347).

raising his price too much above the wholesale price. Avoiding the successive addition of margins by the manufacturer and the retailer will ensure that the retail sales volume is as large as possible. Maximum resale price maintenance may serve to combat monopolistic pricing by single retailers in remote geographical areas.[9] In addition, a retailer may use it to curb price discrimination and limit opportunistic behaviour (Carstensen and Hart 2003). Maximum vertical price fixing used for the sole purpose of eliminating the problem of double marginalisation guarantees lower prices and protects manufacturers from output reduction. A benign antitrust treatment is warranted since the practice allows for price competition between retailers and generates reduced prices for consumers.

Free-riding theory: guaranteed provision of pre-sale services

The free-riding theory is the best known among all the economic theories providing an explanation for fixing minimum retail prices. In 1960, Lester Telser published an article on vertical restrictions that has since become a classic. In this essay, the free-riding problem plays a central role in explaining minimum resale price maintenance (Telser 1960). Free-riding, which is an example of a negative externality, occurs when one firm benefits from the actions of another without paying for it. This problem may need to be cured in the context of distribution agreements. It is important that a manufacturer's motives for imposing vertical restrictions are well understood. If the distributors' margins increase, retail prices will also rise and a drop in the number of products sold will ensue. A fall in the manufacturer's profits should therefore be expected. However, there are circumstances in which vertical price fixing improves the manufacturer's position because the long-term advantages arising from a more efficient distribution exceed the short-term disadvantageous consequences flowing from the reduction in demand resulting from the retailers' higher profit margins.

An increase in advertising and pre-sale services as a result of minimum vertical price fixing can enhance the value of the product to a more extensive group of consumers and should be able to generate increased demand. It should, therefore, be potentially advantageous for a rational manufacturer marketing differentiated products to fix minimum retail prices with a view to encouraging his retailers to offer such services. Sales promotion in the form of advertisements, displays of goods, knowledgeable sales help and customer demonstrations obviously add to the retail price. Here the free-riding problem may emerge. Consumers could go to a store providing a full service,

---

[9] This explanation fits the facts of the *Khan* case decided by the US Supreme Court; see the discussion in section 6.3.1.

where they get explanation of how to use the product, free tests, detailed information about alternative offers and so on. Having obtained the information and weighed the various available options, consumers could then go to the nearest discount store, which provides no service but offers the desired product at a cheaper price. Consumers would thus free-ride on the full service. Similarly, retailers who do not invest in the same promotion efforts can profit from the advertising and selling services of others and free-ride on the sales efforts of their competitors. Consequently, the retailers may decide to stop providing pre-sale services in order to remain profitable. If (too) many dealers, who suffer from free-riding, take this decision, consumers who value services will no longer find supplies. Minimum vertical price fixing imposed by the manufacturer cures the free-riding problem and the ensuing disappearance of dealers offering full service from retailing markets. It encourages retailers to offer an optimum level of sales services.

The limitations of the free-riding theory

Before jumping to the conclusion that it should be simply legal for manufacturers to fix minimum retail prices, the limits of the free-riding argument should be stressed. First, the free-riding theory is based upon a number of assumptions that may not fit the characteristics of real-life markets. Second, the age of the internet has fundamentally changed the underlying logic of the argument. Third, the welfare impact of resale price maintenance remains ambiguous. Hence, the free-riding argument does not allow easy normative conclusions.

First, the underlying assumptions of the free-riding argument should always be kept in mind. To start with, the free-riding theory is fundamentally grounded in the value of pre-purchase information and pre-sale services to consumers. Consequently, the argument will be stronger for expensive and complex products, which exhibit experience and credence qualities,[10] than

---

[10] The distinction between search goods, experience goods and credence goods is a familiar one in the field of information economics. The quality of search goods can be tested before buying (for example, most quality aspects of clothes). The quality of experience goods is learned only through the 'repeat purchase mechanism', after the goods were bought (for example, the quality of canned food). In contrast with search goods and experience goods, the quality of credence goods cannot be ascertained, so that the buyer has to 'trust' the supplier, for example buying medical treatment services based upon the reputation of the doctor (see Darby and Karny 1973). A market where information about the traded goods is not readily available is likely to fail because of 'adverse selection'. High-quality suppliers will not find buyers since the latter are not willing to pay more than an average price for goods, the quality of which they cannot know before buying. As a consequence, high-quality products are driven out of the market by average-quality products and these, in turn, are ousted by the lowest quality available. This process of adverse selection implies that in the long run only poor-quality goods are offered to consumers. Adverse selection in markets with asymmetric information may justify quality regulation (standards, licensing). See generally the seminal article by Nobel laureate George Akerlof (1970).

for simple goods, whose quality can be ascertained at low cost and for which no additional information and service by salespersons is necessary. For example: the free-riding theory may explain minimum retail prices for sophisticated audio and video equipment, for which showrooms, product demonstrations and knowledgeable sales assistance are important. By contrast, the free-riding rationale can hardly illuminate the need of minimum prices for cheap and simple products such as sweets, chocolate, coffee, pet foods, jeans, underwear, shoes or handbags. The free-riding problem should thus not be generalised to all kinds of goods and services but instead be limited to expensive experience goods that are not regularly bought and for which the consumer needs information provided by sales persons in non-convenience outlets. Next, for the free-riding theory to apply, consumers must be able to benefit from the services without purchasing the product. Hence, the free-riding problem occurs only in cases where services are necessarily linked to the product; it does not arise if retailers can sell the goods and services separately. The problem is based on two factors. Sales must be taken away from retailers who offer a complete service and must go, instead, to suppliers of low-grade services. Next, the provision of services, including those provided by the first category of retailers, must be reduced as a result of the free-riding.

Second, the internet has fundamentally changed the ways in which many consumers shop. This change also has an impact on the relevance of the free-riding argument, which has not yet been fully acknowledged by competition authorities (see for further discussion Box 6.4). Marina Lao takes a closer look at internet retailing and the issues it raises pertaining to the free-riding justification. She distinguishes three possibilities. First, the internet may increase the scope of free-riding on brick-and-mortar retailer services for sensory-experience products. Before the internet age a consumer had to visit multiple stores to find the cheapest price after (s)he had tested the product (for example, a perfume) in a physical services store. Today the information desired can be acquired by visiting a single brick-and-mortar store and then searching the internet for an identical item sold at a lower price by an online retailer. Second, for other products (not sensory-experience products), the internet may provide more information on different models and brands (for example, information on a navigation system) than a physical services store. In this case, the goal of protecting traditional, full-service retailers may no longer justify minimum retail prices. Third, in the internet age there may be free-riding in the opposite direction, harming online sales, and benefiting traditional retailers. Marketing research confirms that today it is more common that brick-and-mortar retailers take a free-ride on the services provided by internet retailers. After having gathered all necessary information from the internet, the consumer may purchase from a brick-and-mortar shop.

Lao argues that these developments invite a rethinking of the antitrust approach towards minimum resale price maintenance. In her view, free-riding can also be analysed as a positive externality, contrary to conventional theory that stresses its negative effects. Internet consumers (modestly) increase the crowd in a retail outlet and may thus stimulate sales by other consumers, which leads to a net gain for the brick-and-mortar storeowner (Lao 2010). In sum, in the internet age, the traditional free-riding argument needs further qualifications.

Third, the above analysis did not yet provide an answer to the question whether the free-riding argument may support the use of minimum resale price maintenance from a welfare point of view. If allocative efficiency is the goal to be reached, the free-riding argument cannot easily justify minimum prices because of its unclear welfare effects. William Comanor has powerfully argued that the welfare effects of minimum retail prices are ambiguous. In sharp contrast with the case of double marginalisation, solving vertical coordination problems by means of minimum resale price maintenance is not necessarily socially desirable. Firms and consumers may disagree on the optimal amount of retail services or, more precisely, on the right mix between retail services and prices. Since the interests of manufacturers and consumers may diverge, minimum vertical price fixing may be efficient from the manufacturer's point of view but not from a social welfare perspective.

Manufacturers are interested in the marginal consumers (consumers who decide to buy the product thanks to the additional pre-sale efforts of retailers) they can attract through increased sales efforts and they tend to neglect the impact of their decisions on infra-marginal consumers. Marginal consumers will purchase more products only if the value they derive from the services is higher than the increase in price. By contrast, infra-marginal consumers are relatively insensitive to a price increase caused by the provision of retail services and will continue to buy the product even if the additional services are valued less than the increase in price. As a result, manufacturers will profit from imposing minimum resale price maintenance when the marginal consumers value the additional services more than the costs of those services, and this regardless of the infra-marginal consumers' preferences. If marginal consumers are willing to pay more to benefit from additional services whereas infra-marginal consumers would prefer to have lower services and prices, then it may be in the interest of the vertical structure to increase the level of effort and the retail price, even though it hurts the majority of consumers and decreases total welfare (Comanor 1985).

In technical terms, the consequences of allocative efficiency depend on the shifts of the demand curve because of the provision of services. Increased demand may generate both additional profits for the manufacturer and an increase in consumer surplus, but this outcome is not guaranteed (for graphical presentations, see Scherer and Ross 1990, 541–548; Utton 2003, 235–238). The manufacturer's interest is congruent with the interest of marginal buyers only; these buyers will receive the pre-sale services they desire. However, the interest of the manufacturers and those of the infra-marginal consumers may diverge. The result of using minimum resale price maintenance may be overprovision of services to the latter group of consumers. The divergence between the objectives of the manufacturer and the dealer, on the one hand, and the objectives of the consumers, on the other, is likely to be important when the vertical structure enjoys market power. If potential buyers can easily switch to alternative solutions, minimum vertical price fixing is unlikely to hurt consumers.

Quality certification theory

Telser's original free-riding theory has been broadened to include other more general information services such as the fashion or quality certification implicit in high-reputation outlets carrying the product. According to the quality certification theory, formulated by Howard Marvel and Stephen Mc Cafferty, consumers decide to buy the product because they see it in a retail establishment that has a reputation for selling quality merchandise or stylish products.[11] If the retailer has developed a reputation for selling only fashionable products (for example, by being a fashion trendsetter), other dealers can free-ride on the investments made by the certifying store by stocking the same goods (Marvel and McCafferty 1984). This type of free-riding is different from the long-run reduction in demand because of price discounting.

The quality certification theory not only explains minimum vertical price fixing for complex and expensive goods, such as computers, audio and video equipment, and consumer durables, but also for simple products that fit the fashion and quality certification version of the theory. Examples include clothes,[12] cosmetics and perfumes. Particular quality aspects of some of these goods cannot perfectly be observed prior to purchase; when they are sold in high-reputation outlets information asymmetries on the part of consumers

---

[11] See also the opinion of the majority of the US Supreme Court in: *Leegin Creative Leather Products, Inc. v. PSKS, Inc.*, 551 U.S. 877 (2007), at 891.

[12] Compare *FTC v. Levi Strauss & Co.*, 433 U.S. 36 (1977). It is indeed questionable which kind of services can affect the demand for jeans but quality certification may very well explain the use of minimum resale price maintenance for this product.

may be overcome by quality certification. For example, in the case of clothes, shops that do not hire qualified sales persons who are able to spot trends in fashion and recognise high-quality clothes could free-ride on the reputation of high-quality stores. Minimum retail prices may prevent this.

Apart from curing information asymmetries, minimum vertical price fixing may also add to the prestige of the brand name, which may be a valuable asset to (some) consumers.[13] Manufacturers may wish to maintain prices as a means of ensuring that outlets with the highest reputation for quality carry their products. This view is connected to a traditional justification for limitations of price competition often found in the legal literature, namely that it prevents the practice of 'loss leaders'.[14] A distributor may decide to cut the price of a popular leading brand in order to attract customers to his store. Manufacturers may legitimately feel that, if consumers frequently judge quality by price, the widespread use of their products as loss leaders will negatively affect sales as consumers lose confidence in their quality (Utton 2003, 238).

Contract enforcement mechanism theory

Benjamin Klein and Kevin Murphy have advanced another efficiency theory, which sees minimum resale price maintenance as a contract enforcement mechanism. Whereas the special services theory is an example of a principal-agent problem created by horizontal externalities, the contract enforcement mechanism theory involves vertical externalities. For some products, the distributor can influence the final quality of the good received by the consumers. Examples include products for which post-sale services are important, such as cars and household appliances (think of washing machines and ovens as examples). In some circumstances, the dealers may have an incentive to

---

[13] A counter-argument is that minimum retail prices are less needed if the brand name is already well known, so that the manufacturer must not (or no longer) rely on retailers for certification. See also Marvel and McCafferty (1984, 349).

[14] In some European countries, such as France and Belgium, sales at loss prices are prohibited, even when practised by non-dominant firms (see Article L 442-2 of the French Code du Commerce and Article VI.116 of the Belgian Wetboek Economisch Recht). Traditionally, this prohibition was justified *inter alia* by the fear that large retail stores may attract consumers by lowering prices for popular brands, while at the same time keeping prices constant for other goods needed in everyday life. This practice is characterised as 'the island of losses in the ocean of profits'. Clearly, the French and Belgian prohibitions cannot be justified on consumer protection grounds but only serve the goal of protecting 'fair' competition between traders. From a competition law perspective, sales at loss prices could be problematic when they are practised by a dominant firm (see the discussion of predatory pricing in section 7.4). Interestingly, German competition law takes a mid-position between banning sales at loss prices by all traders and a prohibition addressed only to dominant firms. Undertakings that enjoy 'superior market power' (because of their financial strength or better access to supplies) may not practise sales at loss prices in a systematic way (§ 20 Absatz 4 *Gesetz gegen Wettbewerbsbeschränkungen*).

provide a lower quality level than the manufacturer would like, thus creating a vertical externality for the latter. Minimum retail prices, together with control over the number of dealers and the right to terminate dealers, can solve this problem (Klein and Murphy 1988).

Minimum vertical price fixing is thus used to create incentives for distributors to provide the quality of post-sale services that the manufacturer desires. The potential future flow of rents assures that retailers will not engage in shirking and will follow the manufacturer's wishes with respect to the nature and amount of services needed. For the theory to apply, the distributor must be able to affect the consumer's satisfaction in a non-trivial way. Cars may serve as an example to illustrate the relevance of the contract enforcement mechanism theory. Cheap repair services may increase short-run profits of car dealers but a poor-quality service will damage the reputation of the brand and harm the long-run economic interests of the vertical structure. Obviously, the contract enforcement theory does not offer an across-the-board justification for minimum retail prices. As is the case with the other efficiency explanations, dealer services must be crucial to the quality of the products sold. If the dealer's behaviour is unimportant to quality, such as is the case with gasoline, beer, ice cream, or cosmetics, other explanations for minimum resale price maintenance must be sought.

Outlets theory

According to the outlets theory, minimum vertical price- fixing is used to increase the number of outlets willing to carry the product (Gould and Preston 1965). If competition between retailers is very intense, the manufacturer may be confronted with the problem that too few retailers are willing to stock the product. In such a case, minimum resale price maintenance may function as a substitute for a direct limitation of the number of retailers. It can be added that the interests of manufacturers and retailers may also diverge with regard to the location of the outlets. For example, retailers may choose to locate sufficiently far from other retailers to ensure that they achieve high profits. By eliminating competition between retailers, minimum retail prices may contribute to an optimal density of the retail network. From the latter perspective, minimum vertical price fixing is an alternative to location clauses.

Demand risk theory

Patrick Rey and Jean Tirole have advanced the demand risk theory, which sees minimum vertical price fixing as a means of reducing the risk faced by differentiated distributors when consumer demand is uncertain. Exclusive distribution contracts have the effect of transferring all demand risk to distributors. If distributors are more risk-averse than the manufacturer, it may be optimal to share some of the risk between the parties. Minimum vertical price fixing, which limits the extent of discounting if demand turns out to be low, has this effect (Rey and Tirole 1986). Minimum resale price maintenance may protect retailers' income by reducing the extent to which their profits vary with sales. It should be added that, in spite of this potential efficiency benefit, the use of resale price maintenance might not be socially desirable due to its adverse effects on consumers.

Optimal retail services theory

More recently, Benjamin Klein has proposed an all-encompassing efficiency theory of resale price maintenance that builds upon the former theories but has a broader scope than the earlier economic justifications Klein explains resale price maintenance as an effective way for a manufacturer to make sure that dealers provide an optimal amount of retail services. Guaranteeing the provision of retail services is a valid economic concern that poses a number of challenging issues, also in the absence of free-riding. Klein argues that separate payments are not an efficient way to compensate retailers for the supply of promotional services. A manufacturer may thus choose resale price maintenance to assure retailers a sufficient expected return, so that they adequately promote and distribute the manufacturer's product (Klein 2012).

Klein's arguments can be summarised as follows. Consumers choose to shop at a retailer where they expect to receive the greatest consumer surplus, taking account of retail prices, good product selection, service quality, convenient location and other possible demand factors. Although retailing is highly competitive, retailers will often have a group of loyal consumers who receive greater satisfaction from shopping with them. Since consumer demand is not perfectly elastic, retailers will have some discretion in choosing the particular products they stock and actively promote. Manufacturers who wish that retailers effectively promote and sell their products must create distribution arrangements giving retailers the expectation to earn a sufficient return on their retailing assets, such as their shelf space and sales efforts. Prominently displaying a manufacturer's product will significantly affect demand for the promoted product; likewise, additional salespersons attention devoted to the sale of a particular product is very valuable for the manufacturer. Both product display and salespersons efforts have little inter-retailer demand effects but significant inter-brand demand effects. These effects occur also in the absence of free-riding (for example, persons convinced to buy a particular piece of clothing may not be likely to go to another store charging lower prices without providing point-of-sale assistance) and manufacturers may look for devices that may turn the retailers' discretion in their favour.

To make sure that their products are effectively promoted (adequate product display, information provision by sales personnel), manufacturers must compensate retailers for the supply of point-of-sale promotional services. Resale price maintenance is an efficient compensation mechanism for these services. Direct compensation of retailers' efforts will often not be feasible. In case of shelf space services, per unit time payments might be an option, but several aspects of retailers' performance (for example, increased salesperson efforts) cannot be easily specified in measurable units bought by the manufacturer. For this reason, more general agreements leaving it up to the retailer to determine the details of the promotional services may be more efficient. At this point, minimum resale price maintenance appears as the best way of guaranteeing an efficient distribution of consumer goods.

Empirical studies

Given the existence of diverging economic theories on minimum resale price maintenance, the question about the relative importance of these theories in real-life markets naturally emerges. In the US, both opponents and proponents of resale price maintenance quote empirical research. The first group points at studies showing that resale price maintenance results in higher consumer prices, even when there is no evidence of an upstream or downstream cartel. A study by Thomas Overstreet showed that, during the Miller-Tydings period (when resale price maintenance was allowed under US state laws),[15] in US states where resale price maintenance was legalised resale prices were 19–27% higher than in US states where the practise remained prohibited (Overstreet 1984). A recent study by MacKay and Smith confirms that resale price maintenance causes price increases and that a more favourable legal environment for resale price maintenance results in a loss in consumer welfare (MacKay and Smith 2014).

The second group argues that principal-agent theories have a greater potential to explain minimum vertical price fixing than collusion theories. Research by Ornstein found that less than a third of the resale price maintenance cases involved hints of a cartel. This author claims that further restrictions need to be imposed in order to sustain a cartel (Ornstein 1985). An investigation by Pauline Ippolito of US cases litigated between 1975 and 1982 revealed that only 13% of the overall sample and 10% in the private-case sample

---

[15] See for further explanation of the Miller-Tydings Act, section 5.3.11.a.

contained allegations of any horizontal collusion.[16] By contrast, the free-riding theory could provide an explanation for 65% of the private litigation sample (Ippolito 1991).

The available empirical evidence must be treated with caution. The study by Overstreet seems to show that price increases seem inevitable when resale price maintenance is allowed. Unfortunately, this study tells us very little about the causes of the price increase. As explained above, there are several pro-competitive explanations of higher prices. Hence, a differentiation is needed between complex goods for which the provision of sales services must be guaranteed (free-riding rationale) but also for more basic products that come within the reach of the quality certification rationale. If pro-competitive uses are not separated from anti-competitive uses, price increases alone do not allow conclusions on the welfare impact of resale price maintenance. The rival studies by Ornstein and Ippolito seem to show that a rule prohibiting minimum resale price maintenance is likely to deter the use of this type of vertical restraint to solve principal-agent problems between manufacturers and distributors. The question left unanswered by the latter studies is the ultimate welfare impact of minimum resale price maintenance. As long as it is unknown how many (marginal) consumers value the sales services, the economic benefits from resale price maintenance cannot be balanced against the costs suffered by (infra-marginal) consumers who do not wish to pay for those services.

A behavioural warning

All traditional economic theories of minimum resale price maintenance assume that manufacturers are rational decision makers who engage in profit-maximising price fixing. By contrast, behavioural theories argue that minimum resale price maintenance is often the product of systematic errors on the part of real world, boundedly rational manufacturers. The focus on cognitive biases provides explanations that differ from the efficiency approach. Avishalom Tor and William Rinner argue that behavioural biases may explain why a manufacturer wants to rely on resale price maintenance, even in cases when this is unnecessary to avoid free-riding. The loss aversion bias, the status quo bias, and the framing bias may illuminate why a manufacturer chooses minimum retail prices, even in the absence of an efficiency reason such as curing a free-riding problem (Tor and Rinner 2011). The arguments advanced by Tor and Rinner are summarised below.

---

[16] US antitrust laws are both publicly and privately enforced. Enforcement mechanisms are discussed in Chapter 8 of this book.

Due to loss aversion, individuals find the pain associated with the negative prospect of a potential loss far stronger than the pleasure of the prospect of a comparable gain. Hence, individuals are less likely to pursue a course of action with defined costs and undefined benefits, even when the risk is cost-justified. Loss aversion may explain why a manufacturer resists price-cutting by downstream retailers even when the expected gains from price-cutting meet or exceed the expected losses. Manufacturers who are already averse to price cutting and overestimate its expected harm will be prone to using resale price maintenance excessively and inefficiently. Plagued by a *status quo* bias individuals assess outcomes vis-à-vis their current position and thus are tempted to prefer the current state of things. Manufacturers who make use of resale price maintenance may engage in costly preventive efforts to preserve the *status quo* and prevent potential painful losses due to price competition. On top of the loss aversion and *status quo* biases, framing effects may exacerbate the use of resale price maintenance. Decision frames influence choices by making individuals prefer the alternative that is more directly compatible with a problem. For example, manufacturers who wish their dealers to provide adequate pre-sales services will resort more easily to minimum resale price maintenance than to other devices (such as territorial exclusivity, recommended prices, refusals to deal, and antitrust immune decisions to reward pre-sales services separately or take over the marketing efforts from the dealers). The reason is that resale price maintenance tackles the problem of price cutting directly, while the other arrangements only indirectly serve that purpose.[17] As a result of several cognitive biases, manufacturers may use resale price maintenance excessively and inefficiently. From a behavioural perspective, the resulting welfare losses may warrant an antitrust prohibition.

6.2.3 Non-price restrictions

As is the case with price restrictions, both theories arguing anti-competitive effects and efficiency theories are advanced to explain why manufacturers may wish to impose vertical restrictions upon their distributors. The first group of theories holds that vertical restrictions may be used to erect entry barriers or dampen competition at the upstream level. Conversely, principal-agent theories regard non-price restrictions as methods to cope with problems of successive monopolies or prevent free-riding. In addition, the transaction cost theory explains vertical restrictions as remedies to the

---

[17] Regarding this last argument, European competition lawyers will recognise the proportionality requirement of the cartel prohibition (Art. 101(3) TFEU), which requires that restrictions do not go further than necessary to improve the distribution of goods. Therefore, less intrusive instruments to guarantee the provision of services must be chosen: from the viewpoint of behavioural scholars because they are not affected by the framing bias; from the standpoint of competition lawyers because they unduly interfere less with the competitive process.

danger of opportunistic behaviour in cases where manufacturers and distributors are dependent upon each other because of the specific investments made to carry out the transactions (asset-specificity).

Vertical restrictions as anti-competitive practices

Theories arguing anti-competitive effects have been advanced to explain exclusive purchasing contracts. Exclusivity may pose two problems from a competition point of view: it raises search costs for consumers and it may cause market foreclosure. Exclusive purchasing arrangements, such as single branding arrangements, imposed upon retailers can raise search costs for consumers in relation to comparing prices of competing products and obtaining price information in the first place (Neven, Papandropoulos and Seabright 1998, 31). This adverse effect is particularly likely to be an issue for low value goods, such as impulse ice cream.[18] Professional buyers may afford specialist purchasing departments because their decisions relate to sizeable transactions. By contrast, for final consumers, search costs in time and effort will be often high relative to the value of the good and single branding contracts exacerbate this problem.

A more general argument is that exclusive purchasing contracts lead to market foreclosure. If some distributors agree to handle the products of only one supplier, those outlets are foreclosed to other manufacturers. A new supplier hoping to enter the market has no other choice but setting up its own distribution network, if this is at all feasible given the inherent costs and involved risks. In the competition economics jargon, long-term exclusive purchasing contracts foreclose markets by 'raising rivals' costs'. However, one should not immediately jump to the conclusion that exclusive purchasing arrangements create barriers to entry. First, exclusive purchasing arrangements must last for longer than the normal contractual period. Otherwise, competing manufacturers have equal opportunities to win distributors at contract renewal time. Second, to qualify exclusive dealing as an entry barrier, a close examination of the markets involved is needed. An incumbent with market power can make it difficult or impossible for a rival to enter by tying up scarce distribution channels (for a discussion, see Segal and Whinston 2000; Rasmusen, Ramseyer and Wiley 2000). However, if the manufacturer attempting to enforce exclusive dealing has a modest market share, the foreclosure effect is likely to be minimal. Even if the manufacturer has a substantial market share, an exclusive distribution contract is likely to have little effect on competition if entry into distribution is easy. In this respect, zoning or licensing laws are

---

[18] See *Langnese-Iglo GmbH* [1993] O.J. L 183/19.

particularly relevant.[19] Generally, strict requirements on entry set by public regulation are more worrisome for competition than attempts of private parties to create their own entry barriers. In short, as Michael Utton concludes: 'Exclusive dealing may be a means of applying pre-existing market power, but does not in itself create it' (Utton 2003, 242).

Not only exclusive purchasing agreements but also exclusive distribution agreements may limit inter-brand competition. Exclusive distribution contracts reserve a territory or a customer group to particular retailers. In the short run, exclusive territories can be used to dampen competition among rivals. In the long run, such restrictions may be used by incumbent firms to deter entry. In both cases, these anti-competitive effects rely on a strategic use of the delegation of price decisions to distributors.[20] If dealers possess market power, cuts in wholesale prices will only be partly passed on to consumers. In addition, if one manufacturer's dealer cuts its retail price following a reduction in the wholesale price, then the other dealers may also react by cutting their retail prices. Both of these effects reduce the expected increase in sales that can be generated by lower wholesale prices and discourage manufacturers from doing so. Reducing intra-brand competition through the use of exclusive territories thus makes the demand perceived by the manufacturer less elastic to its own wholesale price (Rey and Caballero-Sanz 1996, 18).

A related argument is that incumbent firms may use both exclusive purchasing and exclusive distribution agreements to commit themselves to a tough attitude in the event of entry by modifying the partners' attitude towards competitors (Rey and Caballero-Sanz 1996, 20). Exclusive purchasing agreements entered into for long periods induce the dealers to engage in fierce competition if competing products appear. Similarly, exclusive territories may be allocated to induce a tougher response on the part of the distributor in the event of geographically limited entry. In the absence of exclusive distribution agreements, manufacturers may be reluctant to engage in price wars that could also affect neighbouring areas. In contrast, an exclusive distributor would be likely to engage in tougher competition with the local entrant (for a formal analysis, see Rey and Stiglitz 1985). Finally, also franchising contracts may generate negative effects on inter-brand competition. In the short run, incumbents' know-how may reinforce their position, facilitate horizontal

---

[19] In some European countries the opening of retail stores of a certain size is subject to the holding of a licence (for example France: Loi 96-603, 5.07.1996 and Belgium: Loi 13.08.2004 sur les implantations commerciales/ Wet handelsvestigingen).

[20] As a consequence, resale price maintenance which rules out any freedom in the distributor's choices of prices cannot be used to dampen inter-brand competition. Vertical price fixing will favour rather than limit inter-brand competition.

collusion and dampen competition among existing rivals. In the long run, the existence of (networks of) franchise agreements may make it more difficult for potential competitors to enter the market (Rey and Caballero-Sanz 1996, 39).

The above theories stressing the anti-competitive effects of non-price vertical restrictions should not detract from the important insight that inter-brand competition may be equally stimulated by the use of such restrictions. The allocation of exclusive territories may induce manufacturers to enter new markets and persuade competent and aggressive retailers to make the investments required in the distribution of products not yet known to consumers. By raising profits and allowing greater efficiency to be achieved, exclusive territories (and also minimum vertical price fixing, see above) can attract more entrants. Franchise agreements, in turn, increase the incentives to invest in (commercial) know-how and promote the entry of innovative technologies. The positive effects of vertical restrictions on inter-brand competition deserve particular attention in a non-integrated market, where entrants need to make large investments to gain ground. This is an important economic lesson, which has not (yet) been absorbed fully by EU competition law (see section 6.4.2).

Efficiency theories

Efficiency theories of non-price restrictions may be loosely divided in two groups: on the one hand, principal-agent theories (including the double monopoly mark-up theory and the free-riding theory), and on the other hand, the transaction cost theory. Each of these theories is discussed in turn.

Double monopoly mark-up theory

If there are successive monopolies in manufacturing and distribution, the double monopoly mark-up theory may explain also vertical restrictions other than maximum resale price maintenance. Both minimum sales quotas and franchising may reduce inefficiencies flowing from successive monopolies in manufacturing and distribution (Carlton and Perloff 2005, 415). Manufacturers may require that distributors sell a minimum number of products. Such sales quotas induce distributors to expand their output by lowering their prices, so that the magnitude of the second monopoly mark-up is reduced. Also, franchising may serve as a device to cope with the double monopoly mark-up problem. As indicated above, a manufacturer may charge the distributor one price for the product and a second price for the right to sell the product. While charging the marginal cost for his product, the manufacturer may make positive profits from the payment of a franchise fee, which grants the right to sell the product under a brand name in the promotional framework set up by the franchisor. The problem of the double monopoly mark-up is thus overcome and profits will be equal to the ones earned by an integrated manufacturer-distributor (Carlton and Perloff 2005, 416).

Free-riding theory

The free-riding theory may explain also vertical restrictions other than minimum resale price maintenance. The argument has been extended by Chicago School commentators to different intra-brand restrictions, such as the reservation of exclusive sales territories and exclusive sales channels (selective distribution, franchising). From the manufacturer's point of view, the advantage of an exclusive territory arrangement is that the offer of a wider margin to the distributors will encourage them to maintain a high quality of service.

Protection against free-riding may equally explain inter-brand restrictions, such as exclusive purchasing. Exclusive territories address free-riding of one dealer on the efforts of another, whereas exclusive dealing addresses free-riding of one manufacturer on the efforts of a competitor. Exclusive purchasing agreements can be understood as means of protecting the manufacturer's property rights in cases in which he possesses informational advantages and is therefore better placed to organise the distribution of his own products (Marvel 1982). If a manufacturer conducts a massive advertising campaign to entice consumers to go to the distributor to buy his products, other manufacturers using the same distributor also benefit from the increased customer flow. The free-riding manufacturer who does not advertise has lower costs and can sell at a lower price. Customers may view the free-riding manufacturer's product as a better deal at a lower price. Other instances of free-riding among manufacturers using the same dealer occur when one manufacturer trains its dealers to repair or sell its product, or provides a list of potential customers to a dealer. In both cases, other manufacturers can take a free-ride on the training expenditures or on the first manufacturer's customer list. A common solution to these free-riding problems is an exclusive purchasing contract. If a manufacturer forbids his retailers to carry products of competing manufacturers, he will be able to obtain the full reward of his sales efforts (Carlton and Perloff 2005, 424).

A variant of the free-riding theory is the quality certification argument discussed above. Exclusive supply arrangements may protect the quality certification granted by specialised stores. A manufacturer willing to introduce a new 'premium' product needs to sell primarily through retailers who enjoy a reputation for selling only high-quality products. If discount stores also sell the product, its premium character will be undermined. To convince premium stores to sell the premium product, manufacturers may prefer exclusive contractual relationships for a certain period – even though these contracts should not last too long in order to enable large-scale distribution of the premium products afterwards (Geradin, Layne-Farrar and Petit 2012, 467–468). The quality certification theory is thus relevant for a proper understanding of the motives for both minimum resale price maintenance and exclusive supply contracts.

The free-riding justification also plays a prominent role in explaining vertical restrictions in franchising contracts. Know-how is very sensitive to free-riding: once it is transferred to a third party, this party may use it and even diffuse it at will. Franchisors' incentives to invest in know-how are, in general, insufficient if manufacturers cannot appropriate the full returns for their efforts. Hence, they may wish to stop franchisees from selling competing products (to prevent competitors gaining from the commercial training offered to the franchisees) or from opening stores outside the franchised network or starting up a similar business after the termination of the agreement.

Transaction cost theory

Vertical restrictions – not just territorial restrictions but also restrictions on the circle of purchasers, and also vertical price fixing – reduce transaction costs. Manufacturers may place vertical restrictions on distributors to approximate the outcome that would occur if the firms vertically integrated. The relevant concepts of the transaction cost approach, such as asset-specificity and opportunistic behaviour, have been explained in Chapter 2 of this book (see section 2.9). The reader is referred thereto for an analysis of how transaction cost theory may fundamentally change the qualification of vertical restrictions as a competition problem.

Franchising is an example of regularly repeated transactions for which moderate relationship-specific investments are needed. The investments lose much or all of their value if the franchise agreement is ended. Consequently, terms in franchising contracts must cope with the risk of opportunistic behaviour, which may lead both franchisor and franchisee to an underprovision of such investments. Collectively, all franchisees as well as the franchisor have a strong interest in ensuring that the reputation of the network remains untarnished. Individually, however, some franchise holders may seek to increase sales by reducing the quality of the product and saving on costs. The exclusive franchise provides the incentive structure needed to cope with this 'sub-goal pursuit' problem (Williamson 1986, 199–202). In return for a commitment by the franchisee that the product will always be provided according to the detailed conditions laid down in the contract, the franchisor guarantees that no one else will be granted a franchise in the territorial area specified. A franchisee would be reluctant to make specific investments if nothing prevents the franchisor from locating another franchisee next to him once the investment has been sunk. Territorial protection thus serves the efficiency goal by reducing the risk of opportunistic behaviour.

6.3   US antitrust law

This section discusses the treatment of vertical restrictions under US antitrust law.[21] A comparison with EU competition law follows in the next section. Summaries of the relevant provisions in the competition laws of emerging economies are contained in Box 6.1. This brief comparative overview informs the reader about how developing economies are dealing with competition problems caused by vertical restrictions.

Box 6.1: Vertical restrictions under the competition laws of emerging economies

China

The Chinese Anti-Monopoly Law (AML) draws a distinction between horizontal monopoly agreements (Article 13 AML) and vertical monopoly agreements (Article 14 AML). In agreements with trading parties, undertakings are prohibited from: (i) fixing the resale price to a third party; (ii) restricting the minimum resale price to a third party; or (iii) other monopoly agreements prosecuted by the Anti-Monopoly Enforcement Authority under the State Council. Apparently, Article 14 AML reduces the range of prohibited vertical agreements to a subset of price restrictions, with the *caveat* that the competent enforcement agency might investigate and discipline other practices. According to the current Chinese enforcement scheme, price restrictions fall under the exclusive jurisdiction of the National Development and Reform Commission (one of the administrative agencies enforcing the Chinese competition law). Article 14 AML forms a delicate interpretative knot. Does it make economic sense to condemn only vertical price restrictions, subject to a catch-all clause for non-price restrictions? In any case, limiting antitrust scrutiny to vertical price-fixing cases represents a unique solution in the antitrust

---

[21] A more extensive treatment of US antitrust law on vertical restrictions can be found in Baker (2013); Colino (2010), at 35 ff.; Hylton (2003, 252–278).

panorama. Interestingly, the reduced coverage of the prohibition makes it almost super-fluous to make recourse to EU-style block exemptions and safe harbours.

Is the Chinese approach towards vertical restrictions defensible? With respect to non-price restrictions, Article 14 AML comes close to the extreme positions of Chicago scholars, who pleaded for *per se* legality of vertical restrictions in the early 1980s (Posner 1981). Since there are powerful efficiency explanations for most of these restrictions (see section 6.2.1), problems may occur only in the case of serious limitations of inter-brand competition. As long as most downstream (retailing) markets are sufficiently competitive, antitrust scrutiny of non-price restrictions is likely to cause high administrative costs (block exemptions) without compensating benefits. A Chinese-style escape clause (Article 14 *in fine*) may be sufficient to catch the rare cases of welfare losses caused by vertical restrictions. With respect to price restrictions, the Chinese solution does not seem to swallow the Chicago wisdom as easily and it comes close to the EU approach. Article 15 AML provides for exceptions, partly similar to the EU possibility of exemptions under Article 101(3) TFEU. Ultimately, the welfare assessment of the Chinese rule will crucially depend on the willingness of the competent enforcement agency to grant an exemption in cases where price restrictions increase efficiency without substantially reducing the level of inter-brand competition.

India

The Indian Competition Act (2002) distinguishes between horizontal agreements and vertical agreements. The former category of agreements is treated more harshly than the latter. Horizontal price fixing, market sharing and bid rigging are practices that are presumed illegal; the burden of proof is on the defendant to show that the agreement in question is not causing an appreciable adverse effect on competition. This presumption does not apply to vertical agreements, which are subject to a Rule of Reason analysis. Both positive and negative effects of vertical restrictions will have to be taken into account before deciding on the legality of vertical restrictions. The distinction made by the Competition Act comes close to the treatment of vertical restrictions under US antitrust law. As explained in section 6.3.1, this approach may be defended by economic arguments. Whereas potential anti-competitive effects are not excluded, the efficiency potential of vertical agreements is explicitly recognised and this may have a decisive impact on the outcome of cases.

Brazil

Law No. 12.259 of November 30, 2011 structures the Brazilian system for the protection of competition. Most provisions concern enforcement issues: the working of the Administrative Council of Economic Defence (*Conselho Administrativo de Defesa Econômica*, CADE) and the administrative penalties. Concerning the 'violations of the economic order', Article 36 captures all restrictions of competition in a very broad and generic way. Acts that have as their objective or effect to limit, restrain or in any way injure free competition or free initiative are considered violations of the economic order if practised by an undertaking enjoying market power (which is presumed if the market share is 20% or higher). Article 36 specifically mentions 'to impose on the trade of goods or services to distributors, retailers and representatives, any resale prices, discounts, payment terms, minimum or maximum quantities, profit margin, or any other market conditions related to their business with third parties'.

The enforcement practice of CADE shows that – on top of a *de minimis rule* that applies if the market share of the company under investigation is below 20% – the broad prohibition is mitigated by a Rule of Reason. In the case of price restrictions, a distinction is made between maximum prices and minimum prices. Price caps are accepted if they are imposed unilaterally by the manufacturer, bring benefits to consumers (by preventing local retailers to charge monopoly prices) and leave a sufficient degree of price competition in the market. The view towards minimum prices is more critical. CADE fears that resale price maintenance is imposed upon the request of retailers, restricts price competition, and is likely to adversely affect consumers. Therefore, in the case of vertical minimum price fixing the burden of proof is reversed and the investigated company must show outweighing efficiencies that cannot be reached by less restrictive means (for a discussion of Brazilian cases, see Gonçalves 2015). As a result, Brazilian competition law resembles EU competition law, with the exception of the safe harbour provision for vertical minimum price fixing that is not available in the latter regime (for a critical discussion, see section 6.4.2).

Under Section 1 of the Sherman Act, 'every contract (combination ... or conspiracy) in restraint of trade' is illegal. In practice, this very broad prohibition is substantially relaxed, since only few types of conduct are deemed *per se* illegal and most antitrust claims are analysed under the Rule of Reason.[22] A chronological review of the case law of the US Supreme Court shows a changing attitude towards the desirability of *per se* rules with regard to vertical restrictions. First, this section analyses the case law on price restrictions. Not long after the enactment of the Sherman Act, in the *Dr. Miles* case (1911) the US Supreme Court established a *per se* rule against a vertical agreement between a manufacturer and his distributor to set minimum resale prices.[23] It would take almost 100 years for the US Supreme Court to overrule this early judgment by establishing a Rule of Reason regarding minimum resale

---

[22] For the explanation of the distinction between *per se* rules and the Rule of Reason, see Chapter 1, section 1.1.

[23] *Dr. Miles Medical Company v. John D. Park & Sons Company*, 220 U.S. 373 (1911).

price maintenance in the *Leegin* case (2007).[24] Ten years earlier, the Court had already endorsed such a lenient approach with respect to maximum re-sale prices in the *Khan* case (1997).[25] Second, the analysis shifts to the US case law dealing with other vertical restrictions, in particular territorial and customer restrictions. In this area, the Rule of Reason has established itself already since the 1970s (*Sylvania* case), at a time when the Chicago School started to exert a noticeable influence on the US Supreme Court's case law. The benign view towards non-price vertical restrictions found its clearest formulation in the Guidelines of 1985 issued by the Antitrust Division of the Department of Justice.[26] As mentioned above, it would take another 30 years after *Sylvania* to bridge the gap between economic theory and antitrust law with respect to vertical restrictions and to achieve overall consistency in the assessment of vertical restrictions.

6.3.1 Price restrictions

The period of the per se *prohibition*

For a very long time all price-fixing agreements were seen as *per se* illegal. Beginning with *Dr. Miles* in 1911, the US Supreme Court recognised the il-legality of agreements under which suppliers set the minimum resale price to be charged by their distributors. John D. Park, a distributor, refused to enter into a contract that established minimum prices at which Dr Miles's drug products had to be sold. The Supreme Court ruled that this pricing agree-ment was illegal because it suppressed competition among distributors and was equivalent to the fixing of price.[27] The Court relied on the old common-law rule that a 'general restraint upon alienation is ordinarily invalid'.[28] The Court then explained that the agreements would advantage the distributors, not the manufacturer, and were analogous to a combination among compet-ing distributors, a horizontal restraint that the Sherman Act treated as void.[29]

In 1911 the US Supreme Court had little experience with applying antitrust law; its decision was based more on legal formalism than on an analysis of the relevant economic justifications for resale price maintenance. Clearly, the

---

[24] *Leegin Creative Leather Products, Inc. v. PSKS, Inc.*, 551 U.S. 877 (2007).

[25] *State Oil Co. v. Barkat U. Khan and Khan & Associates Inc.*, 118 S.Ct. 275 (1997).

[26] 50 Fed. Reg. 62, 663 (February 14, 1985). The DoJ Guidelines outlined both the pro-competitive (increased inter-brand competition, new entry and elimination of free-riding) and anti-competitive (reduction of intra-brand competition, exclusion of competitors and facilitation of collusion) consequences. The DoJ then advocated a Rule of Reason balancing both effects.

[27] *Dr. Miles Medical Company v. John D. Park & Sons Company*, 220 U.S. 373 (1911), at 400.

[28] 220 U.S., at 404–405.

[29] *Ibid.*, at 407–408.

property law issues in *Dr. Miles* played a crucial role. Especially important was whether Dr Miles's right not to sell its medicines at all gave it the lesser right to sell under (price) conditions that bound all subsequent purchasers, even those not in 'privity' with the company. In a classic article, Edward Levi showed that courts were mostly concerned about the property rights of retailers who did not purchase directly from manufacturers (Levi 1960).

Legal formalism kept on playing a major role when only eight years later the US Supreme Court undermined itself the effectiveness of the *per se* prohibition by distinguishing between unilateral decisions of the manufacturer and concerted action with the distributor. In the *Colgate* case, the US Supreme Court decided that a manufacturer could unilaterally determine its retail price and refuse to sell to discounters.[30] Colgate refused to supply dealers who sold below suggested prices and cut off dealers who did so. However, there was no evidence of a contract or conspiracy between Colgate and its dealers.[31] The distinction between legal unilateral action and illegal mutual agreement was based on the rationale that a seller should be free to choose its own customers and that, absent any agreement, there could be no violation of Section 1 of the Sherman Act. In this way, the US Supreme Court in fact substantially softened the strict prohibition of minimum resale price maintenance. In practice, it is not always easy to show the difference between unilateral action on the side of the manufacturer and minimum resale price maintenance agreed upon (or even instigated) by dealers. Rather than contributing to consumer welfare, the real beneficiaries of the *Colgate* doctrine were competition lawyers. The unclear prohibition of unilateral price fixing served the interests of litigation-driven attorneys. It increased demand for legal advice on the intricacies of the prohibition and ways of action to avoid the finding of a mutual agreement on minimum prices between manufacturers and distributors.

A next episode in the US history of minimum resale price maintenance is the passage of state laws in the 1930s. Because of political pressure by retailers' trade associations, various US states passed minimum resale price maintenance laws, called Fair Trade Laws. Minimum retail prices were seen as a way of impeding the growth of large, low-cost, retail chains (Martin 1994, 511). In 1937, US Congress passed the Miller-Tydings Fair Trade Act,[32] which

---

[30] *United States v. Colgate & Co.*, 250 U.S. 300 (1919).
[31] More recent case law has confirmed the need to show a conspiracy. Complaints by dealers about price cutting by a discounter are no sufficient proof of a conspiracy. It must be shown that the manufacturer and others 'had a conscious commitment to a common scheme designed to achieve an unlawful objective'. *Monsanto Co. v. Spray-Rite Service Corp.*, 104 S.Ct. 1464 (1984), at 1469.
[32] 50 Stat. 693.

made resale price maintenance legal under the federal Sherman Act where it was legal under state law. In the early 1950s, minimum resale price maintenance laws were enforced in all states except Alaska, Missouri, Texas, and Vermont. The effect of the Miller-Tydings Act was strengthened in 1952 by the McGuire Act,[33] which reversed case law of the US Supreme Court and made it possible to enforce minimum retail prices even against dealers who had not signed the resale price maintenance agreement. The laws allowing 'fair' prices – that is minimum prices set by the manufacturer – were repealed in 1975.[34] At that time, the Consumer Goods Pricing Act[35] again placed minimum resale price maintenance within the ambit of Section 1 of the Sherman Act. Consequently, the *per se* illegality decided in the US Supreme Court's case law resumed its full force.

Up until 2007, the US Supreme Court kept the *per se* prohibition of minimum resale price maintenance intact. In 1984, it did not profit from the opportunity offered in the *Monsanto* case to reverse the *Dr. Miles* rule.[36] At the same time, the *Colgate* doctrine was revitalised, requiring 'a conscious commitment to a common scheme designed to achieve an unlawful objective'.[37] Consequently, unwilling compliance with a unilaterally announced policy was not seen as concerted action in the meaning of the Sherman Act. In a later case, the Supreme Court held that even in the presence of an explicit agreement between manufacturer and retailer, the manufacturer would not be charged with infringement of the Sherman Act unless a specific resale price was set.[38] Generally and gradually, while persisting with the *per se* prohibition, the range of practices that are judged to be resale price maintenance was substantially narrowed down and limited to concerted vertical price fixing. Dramatic changes in the law on vertical restrictions would not occur until 1997 with respect to maximum prices and 2007 with respect to minimum prices.

---

[33] 66 Stat. 632.

[34] It may be mentioned that, by the time of repeal of the Miller-Tydings Act and the related McGuire Act, 36 states had fair trade laws and the laws were not actively enforced in many of them (Carlton and Perloff 2005, 670).

[35] 89 Stat. 801.

[36] *Monsanto Co. v. Spray-Rite Service Corp.*, 104 S. Ct. 1464 (1984), at 1469–1470, footnote 7. Eleven years earlier, in *Sylvania*, the US Supreme Court declined to comment on the *per se* treatment of vertical price restrictions, noting that the issue involved significantly different questions of analysis and policy (*Continental TV, Inc. v. GTE Sylvania* (433 U.S. 36 (1977), at 51, footnote 18).

[37] *Monsanto Co. v. Spray-Rite Service Corp.*, 465 U.S. 752 (1984), at 1469.

[38] In the Court's words 'a vertical restraint is not illegal *per se* unless it includes some agreement on price or price levels' (*Business Electronics Corp. v. Sharp Electronics Corp.*, 485 U.S. 717 (1988), at 728).

The shift to the Rule of Reason for maximum retail prices

Back in 1951, the US Supreme Court condemned an agreement between two affiliated liquor distillers to limit the maximum resale price charged by retailers.[39] Remarkably, at that time the Court did not distinguish between minimum prices and maximum prices, even though the economic effects of these practices are different. The Court held that both types of restrictions limit the freedom of retailers to sell products in accordance with their own judgement, and this was considered sufficient to establish a *per se* violation. The wish to protect property rights of retailers was apparent. In the *Albrecht* case, the US Supreme Court again had to deal with price-fixing agreements. This case involved a newspaper publisher who had granted exclusive territories to independent carriers subject to their adherence to a maximum price on resale of the newspapers to the public. The Court decided that the imposition of a maximum price by a supplier upon his distributors was *per se* prohibited as well.[40]

It took almost 30 years until *Albrecht* was overruled. In 1997, the Supreme Court delivered its opinion in the case *State Oil v. Khan*.[41] Operators of a gas station had entered into an agreement with an oil company, which fixed maximum gasoline prices by making it worthless for the operators to exceed the suggested retail prices. Under the agreement, it was allowed to charge any amount for gasoline sold to the station's customers, but if the price charged was higher than the suggested retail price, the excess was to be rebated to the oil company. The Supreme Court found it difficult to maintain that vertically imposed maximum prices could harm competition to the extent necessary to justify their *per se* invalidation. The theoretical justification supporting *Albrecht*, such as the fear that resale price maintenance interferes with dealer freedom or the concern that maximum prices may be set too low for dealers to offer consumers essential or desired services, was considered insufficient. More importantly, the Court stressed that the *per se* rule could exacerbate problems related to the unrestrained exercise of monopoly power by dealers who have exclusive rights within certain territories. In this way, the double marginalisation argument was accepted. Maximum prices would avoid the charging of double monopoly mark-ups, since not only State Oil (because of market share and brand loyalty) but also Khan (being a distributor enjoying territorial exclusivity) possessed market power. If both the manufacturer and the distributor want to make monopoly profits, the outcome will not be profit maximising for them. Maximum prices protect both the actors in the

---

[39] *Kiefer-Stewart Co. v. Joseph E. Seagram & Sons, Inc.*, 340 U.S. 211 (1951).
[40] *Albrecht v. Herald Co.*, 390 U.S. 145 (1968).
[41] *State Oil Co. v. Barkat U. Khan and Khan & Associates Inc.*, 118 S.Ct. 275 (1997).

production-distribution chain and the final consumers. Hence, their legality will allow curing the double monopoly mark-up problem. As a consequence of the *Khan* rule, since 1997 in the US maximum resale price maintenance is judged under the Rule of Reason.

The shift to the Rule of Reason for minimum resale price maintenance

It took almost a century after *Dr. Miles* for the US Supreme Court to over-rule the *per se* prohibition of minimum resale price maintenance in the *Leegin* case.[42] Leegin manufactured leather goods and accessories; the company controlled the promotion and distribution of its products and suggested min-imum resale prices. Serious trouble between Leegin and a retailer emerged when the latter decided to mark down the entire Brighton belts line by 20%, in order to compete with other retailers. Leegin terminated the retailer and ceased supplying leather belts to the store.

In the district court, the retailer argued that Leegin had violated the *per se* prohibition of minimum resale price maintenance and won a $1.2 million judgment against the manufacturer. Leegin appealed the ruling all the way to the US Supreme Court. First, Leegin argued that it had established a lawful unilateral pricing policy, in line with the Supreme Court's *Colgate* doctrine. Later, in the Court of Appeal, Leegin's argument changed: it no longer dis-puted that it had entered into vertical price-fixing agreements with its retailers but that the Rule of Reason should apply to those agreements. The Court of Appeals rejected this argument. When the case reached the Supreme Court, the highest US judges got a unique opportunity to reconsider the old *per se* rule established in the *Dr. Miles* case. With a five to four majority decision, the Supreme Court decided to overrule the *per se* prohibition of minimum resale price maintenance.

The majority opinion in *Leegin*, written by Justice Kennedy, extensively cites the economic literature on vertical price fixing. It stresses that there are sever-al pro-competitive justifications for a manufacturer's use of resale price main-tenance. The US Supreme Court embraces the free-riding rationale and the quality certification argument. Next to emphasising these pro-competitive uses of resale price maintenance, the majority in *Leegin* reiterates that the pri-mary purpose of the antitrust laws is to protect inter-brand competition. In this way, the legality of minimum retail prices is linked to the leading mantra of antitrust that restrictions of intra-brand competition promote inter-brand competition. First, the free-riding argument stressing that retail services may

---

[42] *Leegin Creative Leather Products, Inc. v. PSKS, Inc.*, 551 U.S. 877 (2007).

be underprovided, absent vertical restrictions, is presented as a desirable restriction of intra-brand competition. Minimum resale price maintenance encourages retailers to invest in services or promotional efforts that aid the manufacturer's position against rival manufacturers. Consumers may learn about the benefits of products from product demonstrations or advice given by knowledgeable sales personnel. If consumers can then buy the product from discount retailers, the high-service retailers will lose business to the discounters. Second, the US Supreme Court adds that resale price maintenance can increase inter-brand competition by facilitating market entry. Manufacturers entering new markets can use the restrictions in order to induce competent and aggressive retailers to make the investments of capital and labour that is required to promote unknown products in new consumer markets. Conversely, the Supreme Court also acknowledges the potential anti-competitive effects of minimum resale prices. It states that resale price maintenance may facilitate a manufacturer cartel and might be used to organise cartels at the retailer level. Notwithstanding the risks of unlawful conduct, the majority sees the Rule of Reason as the appropriate standard to judge minimum resale price maintenance agreements. In the words of the majority of US Supreme Court judges:

> It cannot be stated with any degree of confidence that resale price maintenance always or almost always tend(s) to restrict competition and decrease output.[43]

Box 6.2: *Leegin*: Justice Breyer's dissent and further analysis

Justice Breyer wrote a spirited dissent signed by three other justices. Notwithstanding the sharply divided result (five to four), the US Supreme Court was actually in unanimous agreement that the relevant antitrust economics indicated that minimum resale price maintenance may generate both anti-competitive consequences and pro-competitive efficiencies. The dissent takes the position that, given the mixed economic theory, the case should have been resolved, not by the traditional test for deciding whether to apply *per se* scrutiny but rather by the empirical evidence and the doctrine of *stare decisis*.

The dissenting opinion in *Leegin* indicates two main reasons why the *per se* rule against resale price maintenance should have been kept intact. First, Breyer argues that the pro-competitive benefits of minimum retail prices, in particular the services argument, are overstated and that the empirical evidence supporting the free-riding argument is

---

[43] *Ibid.*, at 894.

weak. The question is whether the free-riding problem is serious enough to significantly deter dealer investment. The dissenting opinion admits that free-riding may occur in theory but that in practice the problem is limited: 'We do, after all, live in an economy where firms, despite Dr. Miles' per se rule, still sell complex technical equipment (as well as expensive perfume and alligator billfolds) to consumers.'[44] Second, the change in the law raises administrative costs. Regarding this effect, Justice Breyer's wording is particularly sharp: '(...) economics can, and should, inform antitrust law. But antitrust law cannot, and should not, precisely replicate economists' (sometimes conflicting) views. That is because law, unlike economics, is an administrative system the effects of which depend upon the content of rules and precedents only as they are applied by judges and juries in courts and by lawyers advising their clients. And that fact means that courts will often bring their own administrative judgement to bear, sometimes applying rules of per se unlawfulness to business practices even when those practices sometimes produce benefits.'[45] In light of the inconclusive empirical evidence, the dissent considers the burden of overturning a long established legal precedent as too high and favours the reduction of administrative costs (legal certainty) over uncertain pro-competitive benefits.

Commenting on the *Leegin* case, Ghosh (2010) argues that the source of the difference of opinion between the majority view and the dissenting judges are differing views of contract and competition. The majority envisions a realm of contractual freedom in which the manufacturer can use minimum resale price maintenance in order to guarantee the provision of services to consumers or allow retailers to compete over price. A Rule of Reason approach requires that the anti-competitive harms are clear and dominate any pro-competitive justifications. It fully respects the manufacturer's choice; at the same time, it vests strong proprietary rights upon the manufacturers that may run counter to traditional ideas of price competition. Whereas the majority's opinion extensively cites from the transaction costs economics literature, the dissenting opinion cites empirical evidence that resale price maintenance caused price increases during the Fair Trade Laws period. In a property rights approach, the manufacturer (principal) is entitled to take measures for ensuring that retailers (agents) distribute the manufactured products in an optimal way. From a price competition perspective, however, this right may be problematic.

Recent developments in the US show that, in spite of the *Leegin* rule, the debate on the desirability of minimum resale price maintenance has not stilled. Several bills were introduced in the Senate and the House of Representatives to reverse the Leegin doctrine and reinstate the *per se* ban. No less than 37 state attorneys general opposed the *Leegin* outcome. On the academic level, behavioural antitrust scholars have argued that

---

[44] *Ibid.*, at 916.
[45] *Ibid.*, at 914.

manufacturers who are victims of cognitive biases will make a too extensive use of re-sale price maintenance (see above). In practice, the real-life effects of the more positive attitude towards resale price maintenance hinge on the division of the burden of proof in litigation. The Department of Justice suggested a 'structured' Rule of Reason. If the plaintiff shows (i) the existence of resale price maintenance, and (ii) structural conditions that make the practice likely anti-competitive, then the burden of proof shifts to the defendant.[46] The Federal Trade Commission suggested a truncated Rule of Reason: market power in the relevant market must be a necessary element of any violation.[47] It may be added that the behavioural scholars Tor and Rinner have suggested that plaintiffs should demonstrate a reduction of output following the employment of resale price maintenance, 'a showing that would indicate its anti-competitive or boundedly rational and excessive nature' (Tor and Rinner 2011, 66). In the view of these scholars, bounded rationality should be sufficient in establishing the plaintiff's *prima facie* case. Consequently, the burden of proof for showing pro-competitive benefits would lie upon the defendant. The FTC's view seems close to the EU approach in the block exemption on vertical restrictions, which has introduced a presumption of legality if market shares are 30% or less (see section 6.4.2). However, vertical minimum price fixing does not have its place in this safe harbour; it remains *quasi per se* prohibited. It is indeed upon the party seeking leeway for using resale price maintenance in the distribution of complex products to prove the presence of efficiencies (overcoming free-riding problems) and the resulting benefits for final consumers. Because of the different divisions of the burden of proof, it seems likely that resale price maintenance may become widespread in the US, whereas it will remain a prohibited practice in the EU.

6.3.2 Non-price restrictions

The case law on non-price restrictions has equally evolved from *per se* prohibitions to treatment under the Rule of Reason. This part of US antitrust law did not cause similarly heated debates as the discussion on the legality of price restrictions and a Rule of Reason was accepted already in the 1970s. In 1963, the US Supreme Court addressed the issue of territorial restrictions for the first time in the case *White Motor Co.*[48] A truck manufacturer had limited the territory in which its distributors could sell the contract product. A majority of the Supreme Court held that too little was known about the impact

---

[46] Varney C, Assistant Attorney Gen., U.S. Department of Justice, 'Antitrust Federalism: Enhancing Federal/State Cooperation, Remarks before the National Association of Attorneys General' (October 7, 2009), http://www.usdoj.gov/atr/public/speeches/250635.pdf.

[47] *In re* Nine West Group, Inc., FTC Dkt. C-3937, Order Granting In Part Petition To Reopen and Modify Order Issued April 11, 2000, at 12, 2008 WL 2061410 (May 6, 2008).

[48] *White Motor Co. v. United States*, 372 U.S. 253 (1963).

of such vertical restrictions to warrant treating them as *per se* unlawful.[49] Four years later the Supreme Court suddenly changed direction and enunciated in *Schwinn*[50] a clear-cut, but formalistic, distinction between restrictions imposed by a manufacturer who retained ownership of the goods in question and those imposed by a manufacturer after parting with ownership. The first were to be judged under the Rule of Reason, whereas the latter would be illegal *per se*.

A renewed acquaintance with the *Schwinn* case is useful to understand the shift from legal formalism to economic analysis. The facts of the case were as follows: In an effort to combat the erosion of his market share, Schwinn, a manufacturer of bicycles, had set up a complex distribution system. Schwinn sold less than half of his bikes to distributors, each of whom was instructed to resell only within designated territories and only to retailers franchised by Schwinn. The manufacturer also consigned a small portion of his bikes to these distributors under similar restrictions. The rest of the bikes, more than half, were sold and shipped to franchised retailers upon orders taken by distributors acting as sales agents who received a commission on these sales. The Supreme Court decided that the Rule of Reason applied to the merchandise handled by distributors solely as consignees or as sales agents, whereas restrictions concerning the merchandise sold were held illegal *per se*. The latter restrictions were considered as obviously destructive of competition. If a manufacturer parts with ownership over his product or transfers risk of loss to another, he may not reserve control over its destiny or the conditions of its resale. The very same restrictions, unlawful as to bikes sold, were held valid when incident to consigned bikes or bikes for which the distributors acted as sales agents. Even though the Supreme Court acknowledged that some vertical restrictions may have pro-competitive effects by allowing smaller enterprises to compete and that such restrictions may avert vertical integration in the distribution process, it concluded that manufacturers may no longer control product marketing once dominion over the goods had passed to dealers.[51] It is striking that property issues played a leading role in *Schwinn*. They remind of the emphasis on the property rights of retailers in *Colgate* (see above). In both cases, loopholes were created that reduced the scope of the *per se* ban on vertical restrictions: the distinction between unilateral conduct and concerted practices in the analysis of price restrictions, and the consignment loophole, which also applies to sales agents, in the analysis of non-price restrictions.

---

[49] *Ibid.*, at 263.
[50] *United States v. Arnold, Schwinn & Co.*, 388 U.S. 365 (1967).
[51] *Ibid.*, at 379–380.

Under current US antitrust law, territorial restrictions and customer restrictions are no longer invalid *per se*. In 1977, Schwinn was overruled in the *Sylvania* case.[52] Sylvania, a TV manufacturer, imposed territorial restrictions on his distributors who were allowed to resell only from store locations approved by Sylvania. The restrictions imposed on the retailers were less strict than in *Schwinn*: retailers were left free to sell to any type of customer, including discounters and other non-franchised dealers. The majority, however, indicated that it could find no distinction between the customer restrictions in *Schwinn* and the territorial restrictions in *Sylvania*. To demonstrate the economic efficiency of exclusive territories, the US Supreme Court emphasised their desirable impacts on inter-brand competition in the long run:

> Vertical restrictions promote inter-brand competition by allowing the manufacturer to achieve certain efficiencies in the distribution of his products. These redeeming virtues are implicit in every decision sustaining vertical restrictions under the Rule of Reason. Economists have identified a number of ways in which manufacturers can use such restrictions to compete more effectively against other manufacturers. For example, newcomers and manufacturers entering new markets can use the restrictions in order to induce competent and aggressive retailers to make the kind of investment of capital and labour that is often required in the distribution of products unknown to the consumers.[53]

The Supreme Court then emphasised that 'departure from the Rule of Reason standard must be based upon demonstrable economic effect rather than (...) upon formalistic line drawing.' After having acknowledged that exclusive territories reduce intra-brand competition, the Supreme Court advocated a Rule of Reason because of the possible benefits of these restrictions on inter-brand competition.[54]

6.4   EU competition law

Ever since the landmark *Grundig* case (see Box 6.3) it has been clear that the prohibition of restrictive agreements contained in Article 101(1) TFEU covers both horizontal and vertical agreements. The harshest consequence of the decision of the CJEU was that conferring absolute territorial

---

[52] *Continental T.V. Inc. v. GTE Sylvania Inc.*, 433 U.S. 36 (1977).

[53] *Ibid.*, at 54–55.

[54] As decided in *Sylvania*, the Rule of Reason applies to all territorial restrictions, including the stricter variants of the *Schwinn* case (compare the dissenting opinion by Justice White).

protection upon a distributor became one of the 'mortal sins' of European competition law,[55] for which there is no chance of an exemption. Only in the late 1990s, this strict ban has been relaxed: distributors selling new brands or entering new markets and making substantial investments may be granted a limited territorial protection for a period not exceeding two years.[56] Next to equating vertical restrictions with horizontal collusion, the CJEU has interpreted the requirement that inter-state trade must be affected very broadly.[57] Also agreements between undertakings located in the same EU Member State may come within the scope of the prohibition. As a consequence of these sweeping prohibitions, exemptions became necessary to clear vertical restrictions that are not covered by the *De minimis* Notice.[58] Until 31 May 2000 different group exemption regulations covered specific types of agreements: exclusive distribution,[59] exclusive purchasing,[60] motor vehicle distribution and servicing,[61] and franchising.[62] In the late 1990s, the old Regulations were replaced by a general umbrella exemption for vertical restrictions (Regulation 2790/99).[63] The most recent block exemption for vertical restrictions is contained in Regulation 330/2010; the contents of this block exemption are clarified in accompanying Guidelines.[64]

---

[55] Another mortal sin is vertical price-fixing, even though the new block exemption has limited the strict ban on the setting of retail prices, allowing the possibility of maximum retail prices. See below, at section 6.4.2.

[56] In such case passive sales may be restricted during a maximum period of two years after the entry. For further discussion, see below at section 6.4.2.

[57] Case 23/67 *Brasserie de Haecht v. Wilkin-Janssens* [1967] ECR 407.

[58] Agreements of minor importance generally fall outside Article 101(1) TFEU. The relevant threshold is the parties' market share; it is set at 15% in a vertical case, while being only 10% for horizontal agreements; see Communication from the Commission, Notice on agreements of minor importance which do not appreciably restrict competition under Article 101(1) of the Treaty on the Functioning of the European Union (*De Minimis* Notice) O.J. C 291/1, 30.8.2014.

[59] Commission Regulation (EEC) No 1983/83 of 22 June 1983 on the application of Article 85(3) of the Treaty to categories of exclusive distribution agreements [1983] O.J. L 173/1; corrigendum [1983] O.J. L 281/24.

[60] Commission Regulation (EEC) No 1984/83 of 22 June 1983 on the application of Article 85 (3) of the Treaty to categories of exclusive purchasing agreements [1983] O.J. L 173/5; corrigendum [1983] O.J. L 281/24.

[61] Commission Regulation (EC) No 1475/95 of 28 June 1995 on the application of Article 81 (3) of the Treaty to certain categories of motor vehicle distribution and servicing agreements [1995] O.J. L 145/25.

[62] Commission Regulation (EEC) No 4087/88 of 30 November 1988 on the application of Article 85 (3) of the Treaty to categories of franchise agreements [1988] O.J. L 359/46.

[63] Commission Regulation (EC) No 2790/1999 of 22 December 1999 on the application of Article 81 (3) of the Treaty to categories of vertical agreements and concerted practices [1999] O.J. L 336/21.

[64] Commission Regulation 330/2010 on the application of Article 101(3) of the Treaty on the Functioning of the European Union to categories of vertical agreements and concerted practices, O.J. 23.4.2010, L 102/1; Guidelines on Vertical Restrictions, O.J. 19.5.2010, C 130/1.

Box 6.3: The landmark *Grundig* case

Any analysis of the legality of vertical restrictions under EU competition law must start with the landmark case *Grundig/Consten*.[65] Grundig, a German supplier of electronic equipment, decided to enter the French market in 1957 (before the creation of the common market) and agreed with the French distributor Consten to supply only Consten within France with specified products. Consten agreed not to handle competing goods and not to supply the contract goods outside its territory. The same restrictions, including the export ban, applied for dealers in Germany and distributors in other states, which became members of the newly established European Economic Community. Distributors in each country owned the trademark Gint, which was placed on each item, and were thus able to sue parallel importers for infringement of the mark. With the establishment of the common market and the entering into force of the European competition rules in 1963, price differentials across the Member States created scope for parallel imports. At first blush, imports from low-price countries into high-price countries can be seen as beneficial since they allow cheaper supplies to consumers who previously had to pay higher prices. However, parallel importers can be seen as free-riders because they profit from the efforts of the distributor in the import country without contributing to the promotional expenses incurred by this distributor and other dealer(s). The agreements between Grundig and its distributors aimed precisely at the exclusion of this free-riding. Nevertheless, the European Commission held the restrictions contrary to Article 101 TFEU without paying attention to the problem. The Commission's decision was clearly influenced by the primary purpose of the EU competition rules to prevent market segregation along national borders by private firms. The CJEU confirmed the Commission's decision.[66]

In reaching its decision, the European Commission adopted an *ex post* approach. When distributors are already active in different Member States, absolute territorial protection may hinder market penetration that seeks to take advantage of price differentials. The picture changes in an *ex ante* perspective, when the investments are not yet made and parties are still negotiating their agreements. In contrast to lawyers who tend to adopt an *ex post* approach, economists generally evaluate agreements from an *ex ante* perspective. The *Grundig/Consten* case could have had a rather different outcome if an *ex ante* perspective had been used. Would it have been possible for Consten to penetrate the French market without having been granted an exclusive sales territory, ensuring that the distributor would reap any harvest resulting from his investment? If lack of protection from free-riding deters firms from becoming distributors, EU competition rules may reach exactly the opposite effect of that for which they were

---

[65] *Grundig/Consten* [1964] O.J. 2545. It was the first decision on an issue of competition law to reach the European Court of Justice.
[66] Cases 56 and 58/64 *Consten and Grundig v. Commission* [1966] ECR 299.

enacted.[67] Counterproductive results may also occur when companies decide to integrate vertically (as happened later on between Grundig and Consten) to realise the same efficiencies that could have been achieved in a less anti-competitive way by means of vertical restrictions in distribution contracts.

6.4.1 The old Regulations and the introduction of the More Economic Approach

A short historical overview is instrumental for a proper understanding of the current legal regime. The old Regulations contained both a 'white list' of clauses, which could be inserted into contractual agreements without losing the benefit of the block exemption, and a 'black list' of clauses that, when inserted, had the effect of bringing the agreement within the scope of the cartel prohibition. The white list had a 'strait-jacketing' effect: to avoid problems of compatibility with the EU competition rules firms were given an incentive not to include 'grey clauses' that were not explicitly exempted. The overall picture was further complicated by judicial interventions, in which the CJEU dictated a schizophrenic discipline for selective distribution. Such a system was *per se* prohibited if based on quantitative criteria but remained outside the scope of Article 101(1) TFEU if inspired by qualitative criteria relating to the qualifications of the retailer and the appearance of its retail shop. Since the number of retailers could be limited by increasing the quality requirements, virtually indistinguishable relationships were given sharply divergent legal treatments.[68]

In an exercise of rationalisation and modernisation of its policy concerning vertical restrictions, the EU Commission adopted a new general block

---

[67] After the prohibition of their dual pricing system (different prices for home and export sales to take account of the additional promotional costs borne by foreign distributors), Scottish whisky manufacturers decided to withdraw their most popular brands from the UK market. See Korah (1978).

[68] A nice example of the old schizophrenia is the treatment of distribution networks for cosmetics and perfumes. Compare *Yves Rocher* [1987] O.J. L 8/49 on franchising; and *Yves Saint Laurent* [1992] O.J. L 12/24, as well as *Givenchy* [1992] O.J. L 236/11, on selective distribution. In the decision concerning the franchised network of Yves Rocher (a popular brand for cosmetics), the European Commission argued that making the opening of a new Yves Rocher Centre dependent on the results of a market study is not to be considered as a limitation of competition, because the choice of a bad location would lead to commercial failure and could damage the reputation of the franchised network. By contrast, in decisions concerning selective distribution of rival cosmetics (*Yves Saint Laurent* and *Givenchy*) a limitation of the number of retail outlets in function of the economic potential of the geographical area was not allowed. On the other hand, the Commission accepted substantial minimum supply figures because an unlimited recognition of dealers who are not able to buy minimum quantities (not exceeding 40% of the average turnover of all retail shops in an EC Member State) would destabilise the selective distribution system. The acceptance of minimum purchasing quantities comes very close to the degree of territorial protection granted to franchisees. Except from increasing income for competition lawyers, these distinctions brought no benefits.

exemption in 1999, replacing three of the previous block exemptions. This block exemption covered all vertical restrictions in distribution agreements, excluding only the distribution of motor vehicles.[69] The 1999 Regulation was generally characterised as a clear exponent of what has become known as the More Economic Approach to EU competition law. Even though several disharmonies between competition economics and competition law continued to exist, the EU Commission tried to fit insights from transaction cost economics and principal-agent theories into the existing legal framework. The 1999 Regulation rested on the basic economic premise that the ability of a vertical agreement to produce anti-competitive effects hinges predominantly on the market power of the supplier, which reveals the degree of inter-brand competition. As long as the latter type of competition prevails, concerns about intra-brand competition are less worrisome. The safe harbour mechanism, which was introduced by Regulation 2790/1999, benefited manufacturers provided their market share did not exceed 30%. If they did not make use of blacklisted clauses, such as resale price maintenance, the agreements benefited from the group exemption. In the case of a higher market share, agreements could be granted an individual exemption only after a full assessment of the conditions spelled out in Article 101(3) TFEU.

6.4.2 The current block exemption: Regulation 330/10

Currently, one broad umbrella block exemption (Regulation 330/10)[70] covers all vertical restrictions in distribution agreements for all goods and services. In the block exemption, the EU Commission works with two parameters: the level of market power involved and the nature of the vertical restrictions. Regulation 330/10 is largely tailored after the previous block exemption dating from 1999. The most striking innovation consists of the fact that, in order to profit from the safe harbour mechanism, not only the market share of the supplier but also the market share of the buyer must be 30% or less.

Market share criteria

In any assessment of the legality of vertical restrictions, the first question to ask concerns the market shares of the contracting parties on both the supply side and the demand side of the relevant market. Following the *De minimis* Notice, vertical agreements fall outside the scope of Article 101(1) TFEU when the market shares of the undertakings do not exceed 15%, provided

---

[69] Green Paper on vertical restrictions in EC competition policy, COM/96/0721 Final – executive summary, p. ii, footnote 2.
[70] O.J. 23.4.2010, L 102/1. The Regulation is clarified by the Guidelines on Vertical Restrictions, O.J. 19.5.2010, C 130/1.

that none of the so-called hard-core restrictions are included in the agreement and no cumulative effect issues arise.[71] Above the *de minimis* threshold, a double market share test must be applied. Regulation 330/2010 introduces a presumption of legality (safe harbour) if two conditions are met: (i) the manufacturer has a market share not exceeding 30% on the market where it sells the contract goods, *and* (ii) also the buyer has a market share of 30% or less on the market where it purchases the contract goods, again conditional upon the requirement that the manufacturer and the distributor do not include blacklisted clauses (hard-core restrictions) in their distribution agreements. Finally, it should be noted that the EU Commission has the power to withdraw the benefit of the group exemption, for instance where similar vertical restrictions cover more than 50% of the relevant market.

The black list

The block exemption does not apply to hard-core restrictions. These restrictions are included in a 'black list'; they do not profit from the benefit of the group exemption and it is unlikely that they will be permitted by way of individual exemptions. The black list mentions: (i) resale price maintenance; (ii) market partitioning by territory or customer group; (iii) restrictions of sales to end users by members of a selective distribution network; (iv) restriction of cross-supplies within a selective distribution system; and (v) restrictions preventing end users, independent repairers and service providers from obtaining spare parts directly from the manufacturer. Besides the black list, Regulation 330/10 mentions three kinds of obligations that are excluded from the coverage of the Block Exemption, but are deemed severable. This implies that the prohibited restrictions will be voided without invalidating the remaining part of the agreement. The severable restrictions are: (i) non-compete obligations exceeding a duration of five years; (ii) post-term non-compete obligations; and (iii) the obligation for dealers belonging to a selective distribution network not to buy products for resale from specific competing suppliers. The hard-core restrictions are further commented on below.

Price restrictions

Whereas price recommendations and maximum price fixing are admitted if the market shares of the participating parties (seller and buyer) do not exceed the market share threshold of 30% (Guidelines, at 226), Regulation 330/10 introduces a *quasi per se* ban of vertical minimum price fixing. The prohibition of resale price maintenance covers both direct agreements on

---

[71] In the case of a network of agreements also purely national distribution systems may come within the scope of the cartel prohibition.

fixed or minimum resale prices or agreements achieving resale price maintenance through indirect means, such as fixed distribution margins, maximum
discount levels, rebates dependent on the observance of a given price level
or the termination of deliveries as a response to a given (too low) price level.
These legal requirements are reminiscent of the US Supreme Court's *Colgate*
doctrine (see section 6.3.1). If there is no explicit agreement expressing the
concurrence of wills, it must be proven that a unilateral request of one party
received the acquiescence of another party. In the absence of explicit acquiescence, the competition authority may be able to prove the existence of tacit
acquiescence. For this purpose, it must be shown that one party explicitly or
implicitly requires the cooperation of the other party for the implementation
of its unilateral policy and the other party complies with this requirement
by implementing the unilateral policy in practice. Tacit acquiescence may
also be deduced from the level of coercion exerted by a party to impose its
unilateral policy on the other party, taken together with the number of distributors who are actually implementing in practice the unilateral policy of
the supplier. The European Commission clarifies that a system of monitoring
and penalties, set up by a supplier to penalise those distributors who do not
comply with its unilateral policy, points to tacit acquiescence if this system
allows the supplier to implement in practice its pricing policy.[72]

In its Guidelines, the EU Commission explains that the prohibition of minimum resale price maintenance is based on its serious anti-competitive effects: facilitation of collusion among sellers or buyers, softening competition
at different levels of trade, ensuing price increases, and foreclosure of smaller
rivals and reducing dynamism and innovation at the distribution level. Even
though the EU Commission states that it is unlikely that the conditions of
Article 101(3) TFEU can be fulfilled, the European competition authority
also accepts that supplier-driven resale price maintenance may lead to efficiencies. For example, in the case of experience and complex products, resale
price maintenance may help to prevent free-riding. However, the (heavy)
burden of proof that minimum retail prices achieve important distribution
efficiencies lies upon the manufacturer (Guidelines, at 225).

Territorial and customer restrictions

The second blacklisted clause regards territorial and customer restrictions. Market partitioning by territory can also be the result of both direct

---

[72] Guidelines, at 25(a). One may add the critical remark that the paragraph on coercion and tacit acquiescence
seems counterintuitive. Dealers who must be coerced will generally not agree with a given commercial policy,
such as resale price maintenance. Moreover, the Commission's view does not line up with the *Bayer* case. See
also Geradin *et al.* (2012).

obligations (such as the duty not to sell to certain customers in certain territories) and indirect measures (such as reduction of discounts and termination of supplies to dealers selling outside their appointed territory). There are, however, four exceptions to the hard-core restriction of market partitioning by territory or customer group. The first exception involves the prohibition of active sales by a buyer to a territory or customer group that has been allocated exclusively to another buyer. Whereas passive sales, i.e. responding to unsolicited requests from customers responding to general advertising or promotion, should always be allowed, actively approaching potential customers may be prohibited. The latter includes direct mail, unsolicited emails and actively approaching a specific customer group or customers in a specific territory (Guidelines, at 51). The prohibition of active sales poses new challenges in the internet age. This has led the EU Commission to formulate a number of specific guidelines, which are discussed in Box 6.4. The second exception is the restriction of direct sales to end users by a buyer operating at the wholesale level of trade. Third, resellers taking part in a selective distribution system may be prohibited to sell to unauthorised distributors within the territory reserved by the supplier to operate that system. However, cross-supplies between authorised retailers must remain possible.

It has been stressed that territorial and customer restrictions may achieve important efficiency savings, in particular as a remedy against free-riding. The European Commission is aware of the problem, but remains reluctant to accept its consequences to their full extent. On the positive side, a manufacturer may appoint an exclusive distributor in certain territories if 'passive sales' to such territories are permitted (Guidelines, at 51). This means that distributors must be free to sell and deliver goods in response to unsolicited requests from individual consumers, including, generally, over the internet. On the negative side, an absolute territorial protection excluding both active and passive sales to consumers without time limitation cannot be organised. Whereas absolute territorial protection remains on the blacklist of prohibited vertical restrictions, an exception can be made if substantial investments made to enter new markets require restrictions of passive sales and such protection is granted for a maximum period of two years (Guidelines, at 61).

Other blacklisted clauses

The third and fourth blacklisted clauses relate to selective distribution networks. Selective distribution is a retail structure whereby a manufacturer selects the distributors who will be allowed to resell his products. To be admitted to the selective distribution network, a number of qualitative criteria relating to the qualifications of the retailer and the retail shop (outside and inside appearance, adequate displaying of products and timely delivery of products) must be satisfied. In a selective distribution system, authorised dealers should be free to sell, both actively and passively, to all end users, also with the help of the internet. Selective distribution may not be combined with exclusive distribution, since that would lead to a hard-core restriction of passive sales. Restrictions of sales to end users are equally blacklisted. In addition, cross-supplies between appointed dealers within a selective distribution system should remain possible (Guidelines, at 56–58).

The fifth blacklisted clause regards restrictions imposed upon end users, independent repairers and service providers from obtaining spare parts directly from the manufacturer of those spare parts. Moreover, this last prohibition can be violated in both direct and indirect ways. Indirect violations may be the consequence of restrictions in supplying technical information and special equipment that is needed for using the spare parts. However, the original manufacturer may require dealers operating in his own repair and service network to buy spare parts from him (Guidelines, at 59).

Box 6.4: Vertical restrictions and the internet

The rapid growth of internet sales has posed new challenges to the design of a legal regime for vertical restrictions in distribution contracts. As discussed in the main text (see section 6.2.2), the free-riding argument must be re-assessed: it may create both negative externalities harming traditional traders and positive externalities benefiting brick-and-mortar stores. In the discussions preceding the enactment of Regulation 330/2010, internet players (such as eBay) argued that firms operating selective distribution systems were undermining online distribution through various means, such as prohibiting the setting-up of a website, requiring the observance of recommended prices and a cap on quantities sold. Sellers of branded products (cosmetics, jewellery, watches) argued that the provision of pre-sales and post-sales services is put at risk if consumers may first search online and then buy at 'brick and mortar shops' (Geradin *et al.* 2012, 491, with further references). The block exemption does not specifically address these issues but the European Commission has included a detailed assessment of internet sales in its Guidelines.

The Guidelines on vertical restrictions take a positive stance towards internet sales by extending the notion of passive sales. At the same time, measures to protect a selective distribution system are explicitly legalised. Setting up an internet website is considered a form of passive sale. Accordingly, sales via the internet to another territory or customer base cannot be subject to restrictions. The block exemption establishes a new catalogue of hard-core restrictions of passive sales: (i) agreeing that the exclusive distributor shall prevent customers located in another exclusive territory to view its website or shall put on its website automatic rerouting of customers to the manufacturer's or other exclusive distributors' websites; (ii) agreements whereby an exclusive distributor is required to terminate an internet transaction if the credit card details reveal an address that is not within his exclusive territory; (iii) agreeing that the distributor shall limit its proportion of overall sales made over the internet; and (iv) agreeing that the distributor shall pay a higher price for products intended to be resold by the distributor online than for products intended to be resold offline ('dual pricing'). In exceptional cases, internet sales may be considered a form of active sales and can thus be restricted. This is the case if a distributor sends emails to customers located in the exclusive territory of another distributor. Similarly, the Guidelines consider online advertisements specifically addressed to certain customers as a form of active sales to those customers.

The Guidelines state that within a selective distribution system, dealers should be free to sell to all end users, also with the help of the internet (Guidelines, at 56). Nonetheless, the supplier may set quality standards for the use of the internet websites to resell his goods. Just as quality standards for a shop or for selling by catalogue or for advertising and promotion in general may be required, quality requirements for internet sales may be imposed. This implies that the supplier may require his distributors to have one or more bricks-and-mortar shops or showrooms as a condition for becoming a member of his distribution system.

6.4.3   The lacking economics in the More Economic Approach

Clearly, there is no perfect harmony between competition economics and EU competition law. The European Commission argued that:

> economic theory cannot be the only factor in the design of policy. (...) Strict economic theory must take place in the context of existing legal texts and jurisprudence.[73]

At best, the EU competition rules may be seen as an unspoken compromise between the conflicting objectives of market integration and the desirability of efficiency enhancing vertical restrictions. As a consequence of the above, many of the long-standing economic criticisms directed towards the old regulations (Van den Bergh 1996; Hawk 1995) remain valid after the legal reforms. Within the scope of this book, a full analysis of the inconsistencies of the current block exemption is not possible. Below, only three major criticisms are elaborated: the continuing importance of technical legal distinctions, the different treatment of price and non-price restrictions, and the

---

[73] Green Paper on vertical restrictions in EC competition policy, COM/96/0721 Final, at para. 86.

inherent weaknesses of the market share criteria (see for further discussion Van den Bergh 2016).

Technical legal distinctions

Even though economic arguments are becoming increasingly important, technical legal distinctions remain and often determine the outcome of cases. This has the unfortunate consequence that economically similar practices are treated differently. Any manufacturer considering how to distribute products in the internal market or any of its Member States has a wide range of choice. The main decision to be taken relates to the extent to which its distribution system is to be integrated with the remainder of its organisation. The greatest degree of control is given by making use of its own employees. In many cases, however, direct representation may not be the best method of ensuring effective distribution in foreign countries. Local agents or distributors will be more familiar with local markets, languages, and selling conditions. Agents bring principals into contractual relations with customers and receive a percentage commission on sales. Distributors purchase goods at their own risk and resell them either directly to the public or through (selected) wholesalers and dealers. Under the current legal regime, the choice in favour of a particular distribution method may be distorted by a different legal treatment of alternative solutions that are all similar from an economic perspective.

Vertical integration

The block exemption applies to restrictions of competition contained in agreements or concerted practices entered into between two or more undertakings each of which operates at a different level of the production or distribution chain (Article 2(1) Regulation 330/10). If the manufacturer hires his own workers, Article 101(1) TFEU does not apply, since employees are not independent undertakings. Full vertical integration thus falls outside the scope of the cartel prohibition.[74] Under the old legal regime, firms had a strong incentive to integrate vertically rather than to appoint distributors. In this respect, it is most relevant to note that Grundig and Consten (see Box 6.3) ultimately integrated vertically. Also, after the legal reforms, the incentive for branded manufacturers to integrate vertically (and distribute their goods through wholly owned subsidiaries) remains a way to escape the prohibition of blacklisted clauses. The difference in legal status between full vertical integration and vertical restrictions in long-term contracts is not understandable from an economic point of view. It must not be forgotten that

---

[74] Agreements within a group are free from attack as long as they aim merely at an internal distribution of tasks. See Case 27/71, *Béguelin v. SAGL* [1971] ECR 949.

vertical restrictions are imposed by manufacturers on distributors with the aim of approximating the outcome that would occur if the firms vertically integrated. In the case of full vertical integration, a hierarchical structure is set up to minimise exactly the same costs vertical restrictions aim to reduce.[75] Control of opportunistic behaviour by dealers is possible either by inserting clauses into long-term contracts or by substituting an employer-employee hierarchy for the contractual relationship.

Parties who consider hard-core restrictions essential for the viability of their commercial relationship may decide in favour of a vertical merger if the costs of vertical integration are lower than the benefits of the blacklisted vertical restrictions. For this reason the trend to change the legal form of the trans-actions may continue. This is worrisome if distribution through employees (full vertical integration) is less efficient than the appointment of independ-ent distributors. If firms decide to integrate vertically rather than to appoint distributors, efficiency losses may be substantial: distributors may be more aware of local market conditions, costs to control and monitor the employ-ees may be high, and distributors may have better incentives to promote the products since they bear themselves the transaction risks. The current treatment of vertical restrictions not only carries the risk of inefficiencies but is also ineffective. Only where the cost of vertical integration is higher than the cost of imposing vertical restrictions does a ban on particular vertical restrictions, such as the prohibition of minimum resale price maintenance, effectively end such practices (Carlton and Perloff 2005, 430–431).

Distributors or agents?

Besides through integrating vertically, companies may circumvent the scope of the prohibitions by replacing agency agreements for distribution agree-ments. The appointment of an agent does not involve Article 101 TFEU. An agent negotiates and/or concludes contracts on behalf of a principal, either in the agent's own name or in the name of the principal, for the purchase or sale of goods.[76] In contrast with a distribution agreement, where property is transferred from the supplier to the buyer, property in the contract goods bought or sold does not vest in the agent. Since the agent does not acquire property in the contract goods, his operations form part of the principal's activities and the obligations imposed upon him fall outside Article 101(1)

---

[75] This basic insight is derived from Coase's seminal work. See Coase (1937). Coase's ideas have been further elaborated upon in Williamson (1975).

[76] In legal literature the term 'agent' has a meaning that is different from the one used in economic analysis. The economic concept is much broader than the legal concept: it covers all sales persons performing tasks for a manufacturer. Legally, only sales agents not bearing financial and commercial risks can be qualified as agents.

TFEU. Nonetheless, since the agent is a separate undertaking, the provisions concerning his relationship with the principal (single branding, post-term non-compete obligation) may infringe Article 101(1) TFEU. Moreover, if the agent bears financial and commercial risks (such as product liability claims, non-performance by customer, etc.),[77] the relevant agreement will be subject to the general prohibition. By contrast, if financial or commercial risks are incurred by the agent, the agent will be seen as an independent distributor. As a consequence, under EU competition law principals may control agents' behaviour (Article 101(1) TFEU does not apply) but limitations on a distributor's freedom are critically assessed.

The distinction based on the transfer of the property title is remarkably close to the old-fashioned American *Schwinn* rule.[78] According to the principle of alienation, which was the basis for the *Schwinn* decision of the American Supreme Court, an individual who relinquished possession of goods does not retain any rights whatsoever over the goods.[79] The Supreme Court ruled that vertical restrictions are illegitimate *per se*, because they violate the retailer's freedom by subjecting him to the manufacturer like an employee. The manufacturer cannot exercise any power over the resale of goods that have left the sphere of his ownership. Before the 1977 *Sylvania* judgment of the US Supreme Court,[80] which introduced an effects-based analysis, vertical restrictions imposed on independent dealers were seen as illegal *per se*, whereas restrictions in agency agreements were judged under the Rule of Reason.

Under current US antitrust law the distinction between distributors and agents has become largely irrelevant, since all vertical restrictions (customer and territorial restrictions, as well as minimum resale price maintenance) are judged under the Rule of Reason. In practice, this implies that those clauses are legal in most cases (as long as there is sufficient inter-brand competition) and this will give manufacturers less incentive to change the legal form of the transaction by substituting an agent for an independent dealer. The European Commission missed the opportunity to get rid of the old-fashioned distinction between distributors and agents. Consequently, similar conclusions as in the case of vertical integration emerge: the current rules are both inefficient

---

[77] Three types of risk are material to the definition of an agency agreement: (i) contract-specific risks directly related to the negotiated and/or concluded contracts; (ii) market-specific investments which are usually sunk; and (iii) risks related to other activities undertaken on the same product market. European Commission, Guidelines on vertical restrictions [2010] O.J. 19.5.2010, C 130/4–130/6.

[78] *United States v. Arnold, Schwinn & Co.,* 388 U.S. 365 (1967).

[79] If possession and ownership are not equated, the latter may be understood as a bundle of property rights. This bundle can be split up and only some of the rights can be exchanged with the physical transfer of the product into the hands of a downstream agent.

[80] *Continental T.V. Inc. v. GTE Sylvania Inc.,* 433 U.S. 36 (1977).

and ineffective. Agency agreements rather than distributorships may be used to circumvent the prohibitions of the black list. Distorted business decisions will follow if a legal form is chosen because of the more lenient treatment of a less efficient alternative.[81] Moreover, changes of the legal form mainly benefit specialised competition lawyers and significantly add to the indirect costs of the cartel prohibition.

Different legal treatment of price and non-price restrictions

One of the most important lessons for competition law that can be drawn from the economic analysis of vertical restrictions is that the nature of the restraint on its own does not allow any prediction on whether it will always have good or bad effects on economic efficiency and welfare. Consequently, there is no sound economic reason for a different treatment of price and non-price restrictions. The economic analysis applies, word for word, to both types of restrictions.

Vertical minimum price fixing is the first clause mentioned on the black list of Regulation 330/2010. Admittedly, the Guidelines create an opening for assessing efficiency benefits of minimum resale prices. More particularly, re-sale price maintenance is seen as helpful to induce better distributors' efforts when a manufacturer introduces a new product. The European Commission adds that the goal of protecting pre-sales services may be important when experience or complex products are sold. However, the parties must:

> convincingly demonstrate that the RPM agreement can be expected to not only provide the means but also the incentive to overcome possible free-riding between retailers on these services and that the pre-sales services overall benefit consumers as part of the demonstration that all the conditions of Article 101(3) are fulfilled.

> Guidelines, at 225

In spite of this opening, the starting point remains that minimum resale price maintenance is blacklisted and the heavy burden of proof makes it unlikely that firms will be able to successfully plead an efficiency defence. The result is a *quasi per se* prohibition.

Political reasons may explain why efficiency arguments relating to mini-mum prices fixed by manufacturers are not easily accepted. In contrast with

---

[81] The latter distribution structure causes efficiency losses if independent distributors are more aware of local market conditions, the costs to control and monitor the employees are high, and distributors have better incentives to promote the products since they bear themselves the risk of the transactions.

theories explaining minimum resale price maintenance, economic efficiency theories of maximum retail prices easily support a benign antitrust treatment of the practice. Minimum resale price maintenance causes higher consumer prices, which seems to prove the collusion theories rather than the efficiency approaches. Policy makers may be reluctant to accept arguments justifying minimum resale price maintenance, since the practice seems to have a direct negative effect on retail prices. Moreover, other vertical restrictions (selective distribution, franchising) may increase price levels, but that effect is indirect and its precise intensity may remain hidden to consumers. Additionally, in the European context setting of minimum prices at the retail level can be used as an instrument to achieve market partitioning along national borders. In such circumstances the market integration goal will again take precedence over efficiency considerations.

The weaknesses of the market share criteria

From a competition policy perspective, the crucial question is whether vertical restrictions cause restrictions of competition that are not made good by efficiency savings. This inevitably leads to a trade-off balancing the efficiency gains against the anti-competitive effects. Competition lawyers recognise this trade-off only to a limited extent. The 'mantra' of competition law evaluates a vertical restraint in terms of the promotion of inter-brand competition versus the restriction of intra-brand competition. However, this distinction does not capture the full balancing act. Benefits in terms of efficiency savings must be weighed against costs in terms of restrictions of competition. Even in the absence of inter-brand competition, sales efforts can stimulate trade and benefit consumers. From an economic perspective, an efficiency defence must therefore also be available for firms enjoying market power. Whereas, in principle, this is not excluded under US antitrust law, the block exemption is without prejudice to the application of Article 102 TFEU; individual exemption for practices considered an abuse of dominant position is not possible.

Regulation 330/2010 applies when the market shares of both the supplier and the buyer do not exceed 30%. The European Commission has chosen this market share cap both for reasons of legal certainty and to bring the legal treatment of vertical restrictions more in line with the economic approach. It is doubtful whether these goals have been reached. Admittedly, in the absence of horizontal market power it is unlikely that the issues of vertical restrictions are important. Unfortunately, as shown in Chapter 4 of this book, market shares are not a completely reliable indicator of market power (see section 4.3). A major problem is that relevant markets may be ill-defined and this will lead to biased conclusions. In addition, the proper relevant market depends on the type of anti-competitive allegation that is considered. A decision that a firm has a low market share might be relevant to restrictions that could permit prices to rise. However, it would not be relevant to restrictions that would raise entry barriers and prevent post-entry prices from falling (Salop 2001). By limiting the evaluation solely to market shares and ignoring other probative evidence, accurate outcomes cannot be guaranteed. In addition, the market share cap of 30% may be judged too static an approach for allowing a full-scale welfare analysis of dynamic distribution markets.

Limiting the economic analysis to suppliers having market shares exceeding 30% may not allow a full economic analysis of the vertical restrictions at hand. Vertical restrictions may affect several markets. Distributors may buy intermediate or final goods: whereas in the former case it may be sufficient to analyse the market where manufacturers and distributors meet, in the latter case it will usually be necessary to investigate also the competitive effects on the downstream market, where consumers buy. In short, an analysis of the effects on all relevant markets at each level of trade affected by the restrictions is necessary. The most striking innovation of Regulation 330/2010 is that also the market share of the buyer on the market where it purchases the contract products must be taken into account. One may, however, wonder whether it is wise bringing within the scope of the block exemption agreements involving buyers with market shares not exceeding 30% on the buying market, where they compete with other buyers. Should the analysis not rather focus on the market share on the downstream market, where the buyer resells the products to end consumers? Large retailers may dispose of both buying power and selling power. In many cases buying power and selling power are interlinked: a supermarket chain with selling power may also have an important buying power, as it becomes an important gateway for the suppliers willing to reach consumers.

Buying power exercised upstream vis-à-vis suppliers may be either harmful or beneficial (see for a discussion, Chen 2007). Harmful effects occur when a powerful buyer uses its power to induce its supplier into an exclusivity arrangement that will foreclose competing downstream buyers. By contrast, when the supplier enjoys market power, the 'countervailing power' of the buyer may solve competition problems that otherwise would have existed. For example, a large supermarket chain may put a limit on the ability of a market power-enjoying manufacturer of consumer goods to raise prices above competitive levels. If the discounts obtained thanks to buying power are passed on in downstream markets, also consumers will profit from lower prices. These beneficial effects of buying power will not materialise if the supermarket has a large market share (and may therefore limit competition) downstream. One would thus expect that the market share on the market where the buyer resells the goods is also relevant. However, in applying the block exemption, market shares must be calculated on the buying market, not on the selling market.

6.5   Conclusions

In the economic literature, different reasons have been advanced for explaining why firms make use of vertical restrictions in distribution contracts, such as price fixing, location clauses or customer clauses. On the one hand, there are efficiency explanations that analyse the relation between manufacturers and dealers as a source of principal-agent problems or regard vertical restrictions as instruments to reduce transaction costs. On the other hand, there are theories arguing that vertical restrictions may be used to support collusion, create entry barriers and restrict inter-brand competition. The empirical literature on vertical restrictions is limited and does not provide an unequivocal picture. Hence, the assessment whether in a particular case a vertical restraint, such as resale price maintenance, is anti-competitive or an instrument to achieve efficiency savings remains context specific.

A large part of the economic literature advances efficiency explanations for price restrictions by analysing them as instruments to solve coordination problems in vertical structures. Maximum prices prevent a double monopoly mark-up in cases of successive monopolies and thus increase the output of the distributor to the benefit of both the manufacturer, who will sell more products, and the consumers, who will pay lower prices. Minimum prices may achieve efficiency savings in different ways. First, they may prevent free-riding among distributors in cases where pre-sale services are important. Second, they may function as quality certification mechanisms for branded goods. Third, they may guarantee that contractual obligations will be respected if after-sale services are important. Fourth, vertical minimum price fixing may improve risk distribution if distributors are more risk-averse than manufacturers. Fifth, minimum prices may ensure a sufficient number and optimal density of sales outlets. Sixth, from a more general perspective, minimum resale price maintenance may assure an optimal provision of distribution services. In contrast with maximum prices, minimum prices are not unequivocally desirable from a global welfare perspective. If the gains of the marginal consumers, who particularly value the pre-sales services, are lower than the losses of infra-marginal consumers, who prefer lower prices to increased service, the overall effect on consumer surplus will be negative.

Also with respect to non-price restrictions, several efficiency explanations have been advanced. Exclusive distribution (territorial protection) prevents free-riding among distributors active in different geographical areas. In turn, exclusive purchasing prevents free-riding on the advertising or training expenditures of a manufacturer by a rival supplier. Also, the transaction cost approach may rationalise vertical non-price restrictions. If relation-specific investments are made, some degree of exclusivity will be necessary to protect the dealers from opportunistic behaviour (hold-up) by the manufacturer.

The efficiency explanations of vertical restrictions are challenged by an alternative view, which stresses their anti-competitive potential. It is argued that vertical restrictions may facilitate collusion between producers or dealers. Vertical restrictions may also restrict inter-brand competition by increasing higher search costs for consumers and causing price rigidity. Finally, vertical restrictions may create entry barriers, in particular in cases of exclusive purchasing agreements and franchised networks.

For a long time, both in the US and the EU, competition rules relating to vertical restrictions were dominated by technical legal distinctions rather than economic analysis. Nowadays economists plead in favour of an effects-based approach focusing on the potential anti-competitive effects and efficiency benefits of vertical restrictions. The following policy lessons may be advocated upon the basis of a fully fledged economic analysis. First, the economic consequences of vertical restrictions, and not their legal form, should be decisive in judging their conformity with the competition rules. This implies the rejection of simple rules such as *per se* (il)legality of (certain types of) vertical restrictions. Competition law should not hinder the achievement of efficiencies through vertical agreements; only if there is a serious risk of anti-competitive consequences should antitrust authorities and judges intervene. Second, different types of vertical restrictions can be substitutes for each other so that there is no economic reason for distinct rules. Hence, economic analysis does not provide a justification for the different treatment of price and non-price restrictions. The price to be paid for the unwillingness to revise the strict prohibition of vertical minimum price fixing is high: it excludes the design of a legal regime for vertical restrictions that is consistent with economic theory.

A substantial amount of new thinking has led to a substantial revision of the policy implications, but competition law has not been revised so rapidly (and frequently) as the economic theories on vertical restrictions. In addition, legal or political reasons may continue inhibiting a full reception of the economic analysis of vertical restrictions. The divide between antitrust economics and antitrust law has been better overcome in the US, where a general appreciation under the Rule of Reason takes away some of the frictions that still characterise EU competition law. After an evolution of almost an entire century, US antitrust law has achieved consistency in the legal treatment of vertical restrictions. The case law of the US Supreme Court evolved from *per se* prohibitions to a Rule of Reason, which applies to all types of vertical restrictions. With the judgment of the US Supreme Court in *Leegin* the different approaches in US case law on vertical restrictions have been reconciled with each other and reduced to a unitary regime. The Rule of Reason, which allows for taking into account the economic effects of practices challenged under the US antitrust laws, now governs all vertical restrictions. In this way, a different treatment of certain categories of vertical restrictions, for which there is no economic reason, is avoided.

The picture in Europe is different. In the past, the legality of vertical restrictions had to be judged on the basis of several group exemptions covering different types of vertical restrictions and the case law of the European Court of Justice on selective distribution. The old regime was heavily based on technical legal distinctions (form of the agreements), the exemptions had a 'straitjacketing effect' and the law contained a number of inconsistencies (such as the contrasting favourable treatment of franchising and the ban on quantitative selective distribution). The recent block exemptions have been presented as a More Economic Approach, which is effects-based rather than form-based. Regulation 330/2010 provides a safe harbour for manufacturers wishing to impose vertical restrictions provided their market share and the market share of the buyers do not exceed 30%. To profit from the group exemption, manufacturers may not use blacklisted clauses, such as vertical minimum price fixing and clauses guaranteeing an absolute territorial protection. If the market shares exceed 30%, a full economic analysis under Article 101(3) TFEU is required.

An economic analysis of the EU competition rules regarding vertical restrictions shows that there is no complete harmony between economic theory and competition law. First, legal distinctions remain a hindrance for a full integration of economic insights. Full vertical integration (through a merger) is an alternative for long-term contracts containing vertical restrictions, but not subject to the same legal treatment. Also, the preservation of the distinction between an agent and a distributor is form-based and not effects-based. Second, the strict prohibitions of minimum resale price maintenance and absolute territorial protection are equally inconsistent with economic theory. Different forms of vertical restrictions are mutually interchangeable, so that legal prohibitions create a substituting effect. If minimum prices are outlawed, other devices will be used to cope with free-riding: limitation of the number of dealers, exclusive territories, contractual obligations to provide services, refusals to deal, subsidising dealers' efforts or marketing by manufacturers. There is no economically sound reason for a different treatment of these interchangeable devices. Competition problems arise only when there is insufficient inter-brand competition in the affected markets. In conclusion, current US antitrust law is superior to EU competition law for reasons of efficiency and internal consistency.

6.6   Bibliography

Akerlof G (1970), 'The Market for "Lemons": Quality Uncertainties and the Market Mechanism' 84 *Quarterly Journal of Economics* 488

Baker J (2013), 'Exclusion as a Core Competition Concern' 78 *Antitrust Law Journal* 527

Carlton D, Perloff J (2005), *Modern Industrial Organization* (Pearson, 4th ed.)

Carstensen P, Hart D (2003), 'Khaning the Court: How the Antitrust Establishment Obtained an Advisory Opinion Legalizing "Maximum" Price-fixing' 34 *University of Toledo Law Review* 24

Chen Z (2007), 'Buyer Power: Economic Theory and Antitrust Policy' 22 *Research in Law and Economics* 17

Coase R (1937), 'The Nature of the Firm' 4 *Economica* 386

Colino S (2010), *Vertical Agreements and Competition Law: A Comparative Study of the EU and US Regimes* (Hart Publishing)

Comanor W (1985), 'Vertical Price-Fixing, Vertical Market Restrictions, and the New Antitrust Policy' 98 *Harvard Law Review* 983

Darby M, Karny E (1973), 'Free Competition and the Optimal Amount of Fraud' 16 *Journal of Law and Economics* 67

Geradin D, Layne-Farrar A, Petit N (2012), *EU Competition Law and Economics* (Oxford University Press)

Ghosh S, 'Vertical Restraints, Competition and the Rule of Reason', in K. Hylton (ed.) *Antitrust Law and Economics, Volume 4 Encyclopedia of Law and Economics* (Edward Elgar, 2nd ed.)

Gonçalves P (2015), 'Vertical Price Restrictions: Recent Developments in Brazilian Antitrust Policy Regarding Resale Price Maintenance (RPM) and Suggested Resale Prices', in C Zarzur, K Katona, and M Villela (eds.), *Overview of Competition Law in Brazil* (Editora Singular)

Gould J, L Preston (1965), 'Resale Price Maintenance and Retail Outlets' 32 *Economica* 302

Hawk B (1995), 'System Failure: Vertical Restrictions and EC Competition Law' 32 *Common Market Law Review* 973

Hylton K (2003), *Antitrust Law. Economic Theory & Common Law Evolution* (Cambridge University Press)

Ippolito P (1991), 'Resale Price Maintenance: Empirical Evidence from Litigation' 34 *Journal of Law and Economics* 263

Klein B (2012), 'Assessing Resale Price Maintenance After *Leegin*', in E Elhauge (ed.) *Research Handbook on the Economics of Antitrust Law* 174 (Edward Elgar)

Klein B, Murphy K (1988), 'Vertical Restrictions as Contract Enforcement Mechanisms' 31 *Journal of Law and Economics* 265

Korah V (1978), 'Goodbye Red Label: Condemnation of Dual Pricing by Distillers' 3 *European Law Review* 62

Lao M (2010), 'Resale Price Maintenance: The Internet Phenomenon and "Free Rider" Issues' 55 *Antitrust Bulletin* 473

Levi E (1960), 'The Parke, Davis-Colgate Doctrine: the Ban on Resale Price Maintenance' 1960 *Supreme Court Review* 258

MacKay A, Smith D (2014), 'The Empirical Effects of Minimum Resale Price Maintenance' <https://ssrn.com/abstract=2513533>

Martin S (1994), *Industrial Economics. Economic Analysis and Public Policy* (Macmillan Publishing, 2nd ed.)

Marvel H (1982), 'Exclusive Dealing' 25 *Journal of Law and Economics* 6

Marvel H, McCafferty S (1984), 'Resale Price Maintenance and Quality Certification' 15 *RAND Journal of Economics* 346

Neven D, Papandropoulos P, Seabright P (1998), *Trawling for Minnows: European Competition Policy and Agreements between Firms* (Center for Economic Policy Research)

Ornstein S (1985), 'Resale Price Maintenance and Cartels' 30 *Antitrust Bulletin* 401

Overstreet T (1984), *Resale Price Maintenance: Economic Theories and Empirical Evidence* (Bureau of Economics, Federal Trade Commission)

Porter M (1976), *Interbrand Choice, Strategy, and Bilateral Market Power* (Harvard University Press)

Posner R (1981), 'The Next Step in the Antitrust Treatment of Restricted Distribution: Per Se Legality' 48 *University of Chicago Law Review* 6

Posner R (1977), 'The Rule of Reason and The Economic Approach: Reflections on the Sylvania Decision' 45 *University of Chicago Law Review* 1

Rasmusen E, Ramseyer J, Wiley J (2000), 'Naked Exclusion: A Reply' 90 *American Economic Review* 310

Rey P, Caballero-Sanz F (1996), 'The Policy Implications of the Economic Analysis of Vertical Restrictions', European Commission, Economic Paper no. 119

Rey P, Stiglitz G (1985), 'The Role of Exclusive Territories in Producers' Competition' 16 *RAND Journal of Economics* 431

Rey P, Tirole J (1986), 'The Logic of Vertical Restrictions' 76 *American Economic Review* 921

Rey P, Vergé T (2010), 'Resale Price Maintenance and Interlocking Relationships' 58 *Journal of Industrial Economics* 828

Salop S (2001), 'Analysis of Foreclosure in the EC Guidelines on Vertical Restrictions', in B Hawk (ed.), *International Antitrust Law & Policy* (Juris Publishing)

Scherer F, Ross D (1990), *Industrial Market Structure and Economic Performance* (Houghton Mifflin Company, 3rd ed.)

Segal J, Whinston M (2000), 'Naked Exclusion: A Comment' 90 *American Economic Review* 296

Sharp B (1985), 'Comments on Marvel: How Fair is Fair Trade?' 111 *Contemporary Policy Issues* 37

Spengler J (1950), 'Vertical Integration and Antitrust Policy' 58 *Journal of Political Economy* 347

Telser L (1960), 'Why Should Manufacturers Want Fair Trade?' 3 *Journal of Law and Economics* 86

Tor A, Rinner W (2011), 'Behavioral Antitrust: A New Approach to the Rule of Reason after *Leegin*' 2011 *University of Illinois Law Review* 805

Utton M (2003), *Market Dominance and Antitrust Policy* (Edward Elgar, 2nd ed.)

Van den Bergh R (2016), 'Vertical Restraints: The European Part of the Policy Failure' 61 *Antitrust Bulletin* 167

Van den Bergh R (1996), 'Modern Industrial Organisation Versus Old-Fashioned European Competition Law' 17 *European Competition Law Review* 75

Varney C (2009), Assistant Attorney Gen., U.S. Department of Justice, 'Antitrust Federalism: Enhancing Federal/State Cooperation, Remarks before the National Association of Attorneys General' (October 7) <http://www.usdoj.gov/atr/public/speeches/250635.pdf>

Williamson O (1986), *Economic Organization: Firms, Markets, and Policy Control* (New York University Press)

Williamson O (1975), *Markets and Hierarchies: Analysis and Antitrust Implications* (Free Press)

7

Unilateral conduct of dominant firms

Andrea Giannaccari and Roger Van den Bergh

7.1   Introduction

This chapter discusses some types of behaviour often considered to be anti-competitive when practised by firms enjoying substantial market power (dominance). Freedom of contract is a fundamental principle of legal orders worldwide. Firms, even those enjoying significant market power, are generally free to negotiate and conclude contracts with the parties with whom they want to deal. However, when an undertaking with market power refuses to supply its products or services, denies access to its infrastructure or refuses to license its intellectual property rights (IPRs), competition law may be violated. Apart from refusals to deal, also tying and bundling practices, predatory pricing, price discrimination and the granting of discounts may be considered exclusionary practices prohibited by competition law. The main focus in this chapter is on Article 102 TFEU, which prohibits abuses by dominant firms, and on Section 2 of the Sherman Act, which outlaws monopolisation and attempts to monopolise.

From the economic theory of monopoly one could deduce that exploitative practices, most prominently charging too high prices, would be the major concern of the prohibition of abuses by dominant firms. Article 102(a) TFEU does indeed mention 'directly or indirectly imposing unfair purchase or selling prices or unfair trading conditions' as the first example of abuse. This formulation, which clearly expresses fairness as a policy consideration, stands in marked contrast with Section 2 of the Sherman Act, which focuses on monopolising conduct and thus more easily enables an economics-oriented welfare analysis. In practice, however, under EU competition law it is unclear which criteria have to be applied to assess whether a price is 'fair'. Competition authorities have been using comparisons with some measure of cost, prices charged by competitors or prices in other markets to challenge excessive prices. These attempts remained largely unsuccessful due to information problems[1] and difficulties of finding comparable markets where prices are not above competitive levels (Gal 2013). Conversely, the US legal regime does not recognise the exploitative abuse as an antitrust offence. Section 2 of the Sherman Act does not prohibit firms from setting a high price; the freedom of a seller to determine the conditions (including the price) upon which products or services are sold represents a central element of the free market as perceived in the US tradition. To complete the antitrust picture worldwide, it may be noted that also enforcement agencies in developing economies have assessed claims about high prices (for example, India and China, see Box 7.1). The main text of this chapter deals solely with exclusionary behaviour.

Exclusionary behaviour can take three different forms (EAGCP 2005). First, an incumbent firm may force the exit or prevent the entry of a rival firm, or discipline its competitive behaviour (exclusion within one market). Exclusion of this first type can be achieved through *inter alia* predatory pricing, targeted rebates and tying the sale of complementary products. Second, the exclusionary effects may materialise in a market which is related to the home market of the dominant firm. When the competitive conditions in the former market depend on the competitive conditions in the latter market, anti-competitive effects may result also in the non-dominated market (exclusion in adjacent markets). Exclusion of this second type can be achieved through a variety of practices, the most important of which are bundling and tying. Third, exclusion may take place at different stages of the production process, either upstream or downstream (exclusion in vertically related markets). A prominent example is a refusal to deal through which a dominant firm refuses access to a 'bottleneck', i.e. an input in the production process that is necessary for enabling upstream or downstream firms to perform their economic activity (essential facilities).

The assessment of exclusionary practices is the field of competition law where the integration of economic insights has been most slow and is so far only (very) partially completed. The Court of Justice of the European Union (CJEU) has defined an abuse as:

> an objective concept relating to the behaviour of an undertaking in a dominant position which is such as to influence the structure of a market where, as a result of the very presence of the undertaking, the degree of competition is weakened and which, through recourse to methods different from those which condition normal competition in products or services on the basis of the transactions of commercial

---

[1] Price-cost comparisons are also very costly to undertake. For this reason both firms and competition authorities may abstain from such exercises.

operators, has the effect of hindering the maintenance of the degree of competition still existing in the market or the growth of that competition.[2]

Apart from introducing the vague and slippery concept of 'normal competition', this definition has provided the basis for condemning so-called structural abuses, which exclude actual or potential rivals from the market (exclusionary behaviour) and it continues to represent the foundation of European case law (Akman 2012; Kallaugher and Sher 2004). In 2009, the EU Commission adopted its Guidance Paper on enforcement priorities in applying Article 102 TFEU.[3] This document represents the last step in the modernisation process aimed at introducing a More Economic Approach, also in relation to exclusionary abuses.[4] With the issuance of this soft law document, which is not binding for the EU courts, the Commission has attempted to overcome the tendency to judge unilateral practices according to their form, rather than in relation to the effects produced in the market. Contrary to the formalistic reading undertaken in the past, the attention has been focused on (the likelihood of) consumer harm. Furthermore, the Guidance Paper allows for the possibility that the dominant firm justifies its conduct on the basis of the efficiencies generated in the market. Of particular relevance is the 'as efficient competitor test', according to which the Commission intends to take action only if the practices are able to impair firms that are as efficient as the dominant undertaking. The Guidance Paper has undoubtedly surfaced as an important step in the transition process towards an effects-based approach (Witt 2010; Ezrachi 2009). However, in contrast with Article 101 TFEU, an economics-based approach does not seem in tune with the text of Article 102 TFEU. The formulation of the prohibition on abuse of dominance is inspired by ordoliberal thinking (see section 2.4; Möschel 1989) and fairness considerations. Consequently, the philosophy underlying the prohibition of abuse of dominance is very different from US antitrust law.

This chapter is structured as follows. In the next sections, the following practices are subsequently discussed: refusals to deal (and the essential facility doctrine), tying and bundling, predatory pricing, price discrimination and discount schemes. To start with, these types of conduct are analysed in light of the relevant economic theory, thus emphasising the effects that they are likely

---

[2] Case 85/76 *Hoffmann-La Roche v. Commission (Vitamins)* [1979] ECR 46, at para. 6.

[3] Communication from the Commission, O.J. [2009] C 45/7, *Guidance on the Commission's enforcement priorities in applying Article 82 of the EC treaty to abusive exclusionary conduct by dominant undertakings*, hereinafter referred to as 'Guidance Paper'.

[4] The previous steps are mainly represented by the study commissioned to EAGCP, 'An Economic Approach to Article 82' (July 2005); and DG Competition, 'Discussion Paper on the Application of Article 82 of the Treaty to Exclusionary Abuses' (November 2005).

to produce in markets and underlining when they may lead to harmful or, conversely, beneficial effects on competition. Thereafter, the economic analysis is contrasted with the current legal treatment of exclusionary practices both in the US and in the EU. In this regard, in addition to framing the conducts within the substantive laws of the different legal systems, the analysis critically investigates the decisional practice and the case law. The purpose of the comparative analysis is to show whether the evaluation of unilateral practices is carried out in accordance with the economic insights. For each type of conduct, a comparative law and economics analysis is undertaken to appreciate the prevailing similarities and differences between US antitrust law and EU competition law. Finally, several examples of abusive conducts are further discussed in boxes, in order to highlight specific features of unilateral conduct and to appreciate how they are judged in other legal systems (China, Russia).

Box 7.1: Excessive prices in new antitrust frameworks: the Chinese *Qualcomm* case

In 2013, the National Development and Reform Commission (NDRC),[5] one of the three competition authorities in China, opened an investigation of Qualcomm Inc.'s business practices. At the time, Qualcomm was the world's largest chipmaker and it held a number of standard-essential patents (SEP) in the communication industry. The NDRC investigated Qualcomm's excessive prices in licensing patents.[6] Controlling price levels is an extremely difficult exercise, which US and EU competition authorities are very reluctant to undertake.

Qualcomm held a dominant position in the SEP licensing markets for CDMA, WCDMA and LTE wireless communication standards (with 100% market share) and in the correspondent baseband chips markets (with 93%, 54% and 96% market shares, respectively). Qualcomm's licensing scheme for SEPs was based on a comprehensive licensing package, whose content resulted to be unknown by the customers. Qualcomm did not disclose the patents for which the royalties were charged and the package could also include expired patents. The business model provided that the royalties were applied to the net wholesale price of the mobile devices. Therefore, whenever the SEPs were incorporated in an expensive product, Qualcomm's royalties were higher than in the case of low-priced items. As part of the licensing agreement, Qualcomm also requested its customers to cross-license their own patents. Qualcomm argued, *inter alia*, that new patents had been constantly added to the patent portfolio and that the value of the expired ones was at least compensated by those newly added. The defendant also

---

[5] *NDRC v. Qualcomm Inc.*, February 10, 2015.
[6] NDRC also found that Qualcomm was tying, without justification, non-standard essential patents to SEPs and that unfair terms of sale were included in its baseband chip supply contracts.

claimed that the free cross-licensing was necessary to preserve its other customers from infringement prosecutions. Nevertheless, the combination of these business practices was considered unlawful under the Chinese antimonoply law because, according to the NDRC, it led to excessive licensing fees.

During the investigation, Qualcomm had offered a package of remedies committing itself to limit the licence fee to 65% of the wholesale net price of the devices sold in China, to disclose the patent list in negotiations with Chinese counterparts and to avoid free cross-licensing. However, Qualcomm was ordered to cease its abusive practices and it was fined RMB 6.088 billion (approximately US$975 million), corresponding to 8% of the firm's 2013 revenues generated in China. Notably, the fine was the highest ever imposed in China, where companies can be fined up to 10% of their annual revenues. In the same decision, Qualcomm's commitments were also approved by the NDRC.

The decision of the Chinese authority is not in line with the antitrust practice elsewhere. In particular, no economic analysis can be found: neither concerning the level of prices charged by Qualcomm related to, for instance, its investments costs, nor regarding the effects on consumer welfare. Furthermore, the decision neglects the long-run implications on the incentives to innovate stemming from the imposition of a price cap on royalties. As a consequence, the NDRC's assessment resembles an industrial policy intervention rather than an antitrust action banning exploitative conduct. For these reasons, the decision has raised marked criticisms in the US; Chinese antitrust enforcement has appeared as a tool to protect national companies by granting more favourable access conditions to Qualcomm's technologies.

7.2 Refusals to deal and the essential facility doctrine

The competitive assessment of refusals to deal is a difficult exercise, as it requires finding a balance between the general principle of freedom of contract, the protection of property rights and the aim to foster legitimate competition. A refusal to deal may lead to foreclosure if the dominant firm's behaviour deprives rivals of essential assets to compete in the market. However, a duty to deal may generate negative effects on innovation and consumer welfare, which can outweigh the short-run gains. For this reason, there is a substantial consensus among Law and Economics scholars that the duty to deal or to grant licences has to be limited (Cass and Hylton 1999; Easterbrook 1986). In addition, the literature has stressed the legal difficulties in identifying a coherent analytical framework for interpreting the duty to deal (Speta 2003; Hovenkamp 2000). Closely linked to refusals to deal is the essential facility doctrine. This theory originated in US antitrust law and has been later developed, although not in the same terms, within EU competition law. The underlying rationale is that a facility controlled or owned by a dominant firm represents a fundamental asset for a rival, usually active in a downstream market, and that its access or sharing is necessary to compete. From an economic perspective, the essential facility doctrine raises similar concerns as the duty to deal. Exclusionary effects have to be weighed against the potential negative impact on innovation and consumer welfare.

7.2.1 Economic analysis

A refusal to deal may allow the dominant firm to continue charging prices above marginal costs and restricting output, thus causing allocative inefficiency and damaging consumers in the short run (Frischmann and Waller 2008). Conversely, whenever a duty to deal with rivals is imposed on the dominant firm, the incentives to invest and innovate may be reduced. In the latter scenario, dynamic inefficiencies may appear in the long run and harm consumer welfare. As a consequence, the valuation of the net effect of a duty to deal is a complex exercise. In addition to the difficulties regarding a proper identification of the practice, it may involve a difficult balance of opposite effects between the short and the long run (Shelanski 2009).

The traditional economic rationale to justify a duty to deal is that this obligation may allow rival firms to dispose of an indispensable input to access the market and effectively compete with the dominant firm. Clearly, a first prerequisite for imposing a duty to deal is that the input, or the infrastructure, is truly fundamental for rival firms. In economic terms, this means that the input has to be shareable; its use must be possible by both the owner and its competitors. Second, the input must be essential: there should be no substitutes that allow the economic activities to be performed in the absence of the duty to deal. Third, it must be impossible to duplicate the input, since replication in a reasonable period is not cost-effective (Motta 2004, 66). Especially in network industries or in liberalised economic sectors, such as public utilities, the access to an infrastructure may allow rivals to compete effectively with incumbent firms. It is not accidental that, both in the US and in the EU, the first litigated cases concerned access to physical infrastructures in the transport sector (ports) and telecommunications. Moreover, the need to grant this access appeared stronger when the firm owning the asset was simultaneously active in the provision of the services. Under the above conditions, the refusal to deal may be motivated by the wish to exclude the entry of rival firms in the downstream markets (Whinston 1990).

When a dominant firm is vertically integrated and refuses to deal with a competitor in a downstream market, various factors that are contingent upon the characteristics of the industry involved affect the welfare analysis (compare OECD 1996; Werden 1987, 473). Economic theory teaches that vertical integration by a monopolist has no effect on welfare in a world of complete information and certainty, where the upstream monopoly is uncontested and sells to identical downstream buyers who use these inputs in fixed proportions and employ a constant return to scale production technology. It does not matter whether the monopolist charges prices at the stage of production or decides to integrate downstream; he will be able to appropriate all monopoly profits in either scenario (Ordover and Saloner 1989, 564). This insight is in accordance with the Chicago view that there is only one monopoly profit to be gained, without any utility for the monopolist to take recourse to foreclosing competitors in the downstream market (see section 7.3.1). This argument no longer holds, however, when there is scope for the monopolist to charge different profit-maximising prices to different customers. This will be the case when contracts are secret. The upstream monopolist may then use vertical restraints to reduce intra-brand competition downstream, even when the latter market is competitive (Hart and Tirole 1990). The effects on social welfare can then only be determined through a case-by-case assessment.

Further negative effects can result if the antitrust enforcement agencies are easily inclined to provide competitors the access to facilities or the sharing of the inputs held by dominant firms. The possibility that competitors might rely on a lenient rule concerning the duty to deal, or to license IPRs, creates disincentives in terms of independent development of their own inputs or assets. In such case, consumer welfare may be damaged because new products, for which there could be a potential demand, will not be offered, thus hampering desirable product differentiation. From a dynamic perspective, it may be argued that granting access through essential facilities should be limited to natural monopolies (Werden 1987). In other industries, the application of the essential facilities doctrine may undermine the incentives to innovate. Giving its competitors access to the bottleneck is an expropriation of the return on the dominant firm's efforts. If the bottleneck is due to an intellectual property right, competition authorities should be even more reluctant to intervene (EAGCP 2005).

7.2.2 US antitrust law

US courts have displayed a marked reluctance to impose on economic actors obligations to deal with their rivals. Since the 1919 ruling in *Colgate*,[7] the

---

[7] *United States v. Colgate & Co.*, 250 U.S. 300 (1919). The Supreme Court held that '[i]n the absence of any purpose to create or maintain a monopoly, the [Sherman Act] does not restrict the long-recognised right of a trader or manufacturer engaged in an entirely private business, freely to exercise his own independent discretion as to parties with whom he will deal' (*ibid.*, at 307).

Supreme Court has consistently reaffirmed the right for a firm to independently choose its commercial partners. The Court rarely applied the competition rules to force dominant undertakings to provide access to or share their infrastructures with competitors. Rather, the decisions in which a duty to deal was imposed – such as *Otter Tail*,[8] *Aspen Skiing*[9] and *Kodak*[10] – did not exhibit a disposition to restrict the dominant firms' right to choose the parties with whom they want to deal. The essential facility doctrine has not received better support. Although the Supreme Court has never recognised a distinct 'essential facilities doctrine', its origin is conventionally traced back to the 1912 decision in *United States v. Terminal Railroad Ass'n*.[11] In this case, the Court found that a bottleneck facility that could not be duplicated had to be shared with competitors on a non-discriminatory basis. However, since the ruling in *United States v. Terminal Railroad Ass'n* the federal courts applied the doctrine with caution, recognising the general principle that the freedom of contract can be constrained only in exceptional circumstances (Pitofsky, Patterson and Hooks 2002).

Some lower courts have applied the essential facility doctrine in the extraordinary circumstance in which an undertaking used the control of a bottleneck to foreclose actual or potential rivals. In *MCI Communications v. AT & T Co.*,[12] the Court of Appeals for the Seventh Circuit outlined a four-pronged test to define the conditions under which a firm with market power may be found liable for a violation of Section 2 of the Sherman Act. In order to establish liability under the essential facility doctrine, a plaintiff has to show: (i) the control of the essential facility by a monopolist; (ii) a competitor's inability to practically or reasonably duplicate the essential facility; (iii) the denial of the use of the facility to a competitor; and (iv) the feasibility of providing the facility.[13] This test has been constantly adopted by US courts to evaluate essential facility claims (Hovenkamp 2008; Waller 2008). Worth noting is that its practical application hardly led to the finding of antitrust liability. It has been difficult to prove that the facility controlled by the dominant firm is truly essential to competition and that it is not possible to have it replicated by competitors. The exact definition of what represents an essential facility has appeared as one of the most problematic issues of the *MCI* test. However, the disputes have shown that both tangible assets as well as IPRs could be scrutinised under its heading, even though the latter have been treated

---

[8] *Otter Tail Power Co. v. United States*, 410 U.S. 366 (1973).
[9] *Aspen Skiing Co. v. Aspen Highlands Skiing Corp.*, 472 U.S. 585 (1985).
[10] *Eastman Kodak Co. v. Image Technical Services, Inc.*, 504 U.S. 451 (1992).
[11] *United States v. Terminal Railroad Ass'n*, 224 U.S. 383 (1912).
[12] *MCI Communications v. AT&T Co.*, 708 F.2d 1081 (7th Cir. 1983).
[13] *Ibid.*, at 1132–1133.

as essential facilities in a very small number of cases (Meadows 2015; Lao 1999). In this respect, the courts have agreed that a facility – to be qualified as essential – has not merely to be useful to rivals but its denial must place the competitors 'at a severe handicap'.[14] Moreover, in a number of judgments – including *Aspen Skiing*[15] – particular emphasis was put on the requirement that the refusal to deal must be driven by the anti-competitive intent to harm consumers.

The last step toward a (very) restrictive interpretation of the duty to deal (and the essential facilities doctrine) under US antitrust law is represented by the judgment of the Supreme Court in *Trinko*.[16] This case concerned the failure by a telecommunications firm, Verizon, to grant other rival carriers non-discriminatory access to its infrastructure. The plaintiff, a client of one of Verizon's competitors, had brought a class action alleging that the firm's refusal to provide its competitors access to the network represented an infringement of Section 2 of the Sherman Act. The Supreme Court, with an opinion delivered by Justice Scalia, concluded that Verizon was not liable for the refusal to deal. The opinion made extensive use of economic arguments to limit the circumstances in which a refusal to deal may give rise to antitrust liability, highlighting the risks and the negative effects related to a dominant firms' obligation to deal or to share its resources with rivals. The Supreme Court stated that monopoly is an important element of free-market systems. In particular, it noted that the ability to impose monopoly prices is what 'attracts business acumen';[17] this explains why the risks concerning innovation are incurred in the first place. The most important part of the opinion is the one immediately following; it is worth quoting it in its entirety:

> Firms may acquire monopoly power by establishing an infrastructure that renders them uniquely suited to serve their customers. Compelling such firms to share the source of their advantage is in some tension with the underlying purpose of antitrust law, since it may lessen the incentive for the monopolist, the rival, or both to invest in those economically beneficial facilities.[18]

The Supreme Court thus joined the line of reasoning of those opposing the essential facilities doctrine by requiring a rigorous economic assessment of the negative effects in terms of dynamic efficiency that a lenient application

---

[14] *Twin Labs., Inc. v. Weider Health & Fitness*, 900 F.2d 566, 568 (2d Cir. 1990).
[15] *Aspen Skiing Co. v. Aspen Highlands Skiing Corp.*, 472 U.S. 585 (1985).
[16] *Verizon Communications Inc. v. Law Offices of Curtis V. Trinko, LLP*, 540 U.S. 398 (2004).
[17] *Ibid.*, at 405.
[18] *Ibid.*, at 407–408.

could generate.[19] Furthermore, the Court held that a duty to deal would require antitrust institutions to act as central planners, supervising the terms of commercial contracts (prices and quantities) between the monopolist and its rivals, a role for which they are ill-suited.

After *Trinko*, it may be concluded that the refusal to deal and the essential facilities doctrine do not play a meaningful role in current US antitrust enforcement. The Supreme Court has rejected to a large extent a duty to deal by the monopolist firm, thus disavowing the inclination of inferior US courts to impose obligations to grant access to the firm's essential facilities (Lao 2009). The general principle according to which a dominant firm does not have any duty to deal with its competitors has been reaffirmed, with the clarification that the exception to this general rule can occur only exceptionally (Hay 2005; Douglas Melamed 2005). The Court also departed from the essential facility doctrine, pointing out that it had never recognised the theory, thus limiting its practical strength (Shelanski 2009). A breach of Section 2 of the Sherman Act may be found only when the undertaking discontinues a previous and profitable dealing with another party, to achieve an anti-competitive end in an unregulated market. This restrictive interpretation excludes antitrust liability, in the absence of previous dealings. Even though not directly concerning IPRs, this ruling has also particular significance with respect to this domain (Veel and Katz 2013). The restrictive interpretation of the duty to deal in *Trinko* has been confirmed in the *linkLine* case.[20]

7.2.3 EU competition law

In early decisions based upon Article 102 TFEU, the European Commission seemed willing to impose an obligation to grant access to a physical infrastructure in a host of industries, ranging from telecommunications and transmission of energy to transport (Temple Lang 1994). Notwithstanding lack of consensus even on which cases constituted an essential facility – the term was used for the first time in 1992, in *Sealink*[21] – the Commission advanced a broad principle holding that companies in a dominant position must not refuse to supply their goods or services to either competitors or customers if the refusal would have a significant effect on competition, which cannot

---

[19] Areeda 1989; see also Hovenkamp (2008, 4), who has emphasised that: '[t]he "essential facility" doctrine is both harmful and unnecessary and should be abandoned'. The same author argues that '[t]he so-called "essential facility" doctrine is one of the most troublesome, incoherent, and unmanageable bases for Sherman § 2 liability. The antitrust world would almost certainly be a better place if it were jettisoned, with a little fine tuning of the general doctrine of refusal to deal to fill any gaps' (Hovenkamp 2011, 336).

[20] *Pacific Bell Telephone Co. v. linkLine Communications Inc.*, 555 U.S. 438 (2009).

[21] *Sealink/B&I Holyhead* (interim measures), [1992] 5 CMLR 255.

be legitimately justified.[22] Essential facilities thus became an acronym for forcing access by new competitors on deregulated markets, often based on competitors' complaints alleging that their economic survival was at risk.

Frequently, the factual analysis – starting with the definition of the relevant market – was conducted in a rather patchy manner; this resulted in an overtly summary appraisal of the essential character of the facility at hand. The *Sea Containers vs. Stena Sealink*[23] case may serve as an example. Concerning the Holyhead harbour in Wales, the Commission concluded that Stena Sealink had abused its dominant position 'in the provision of an essential facility' as the harbour's operator by refusing access without objective justification or by granting other companies access only on terms less favourable than those given to its own services. In so doing, Stena Sealink protected its position as a ferry operator from Holyhead. Unfortunately, picking a particular route as the relevant market following Sea Container's contentions, without conducting an in-depth analysis, artificially narrowed down the assessment to start off with. As a result, the EU Commission's approach found itself open to allegations of protecting competitors rather than competition (Venit and Kallaugher 1994, 333). Nevertheless, the Commission relied on this precedent in disputes concerning similar facilities in other Member States.[24] In the initial application phase of the essential facilities doctrine, the exact legal conditions for identifying whether an infrastructure or network is essential, as to consequently impose a duty to grant access to the competitors, were not clearly defined. The expansive interpretation of the essential facility concept conflicted with economic insights, because the negative effects in terms of dynamic efficiency and incentives to invest were mostly underestimated.

The occasion to accomplish the necessary fine-tuning emerged in *Bronner*, a preliminary reference from an Austrian court, where the CJEU developed a test limiting the scope of the essential facility doctrine under Article 102 TFEU.[25] The Bronner conditions for a facility to be essential can be

---

[22] In Case IV/34.689 *Sea Containers v. Stena Line* [1994] O.J. L 15/8, the Commission stated that the facility has to be considered essential where access is necessary for competitors to provide services to their customers, imposing an 'insuperable barrier to entry' or creating a 'serious, permanent and inescapable handicap' to their activities and that, in the absence of legitimate business reasons, access could not be denied or granted on terms less favourable than those which the dominant firm gave to its own services (*Sealink/B&I* 9 C.M.L.R. 255 (1992)).

[23] Case IV/34.689 *Sea Containers v. Stena Line* [1994] O.J. L 15/8.

[24] Commission Decision 94/119/EC, 1994 O.J. L 055/52 (concerning a refusal to grant access to the facilities of the Port of Rødby, Denmark).

[25] Case C-7/97, *Oscar Bronner GmbH & KG v. Mediaprint Zeitungs- und Zeitschriftenverlag GmbH & Co KG, Mediaprint Zeitungsvertriebsgesellschaft mbG & Co KG and Mediaprint Anzeigengesellschaft mbH & Co KG* [1998] ECR I-7791. The facts of the latter case can be briefly summarised as follows. Mediaprint had a very large share of the daily newspaper market in Austria (46.8% of in terms of circulation and 42% in terms of

summarised as follows: (i) the facility is controlled by a monopolist; (ii) the facility is indispensable in order to compete on the market with the controller of the facility; (iii) access is denied or granted only on unreasonable terms; (iv) no legitimate business reason is given for objectively justifying the denied access; (v) a competitor is unable (practically or reasonably) to duplicate the essential facility. In *Bronner,* the CJEU has emphasised the indispensability of the requested facility for the competitors, making it also an important element in the analysis of cases concerning duties to deal. In weighing the indispensability character, the judgment stressed the need to make a rigorous assessment in relation to the technical, legal, and economic obstacles that rivals face in developing alternative facilities. Compared with earlier case law, the CJEU found that it was no longer sufficient to rely on the mere fact that the dominant firm is the owner of the facility to impose an obligation to deal, but rather that the asset in question has to be indispensable. More generally, the Bronner test reflects an attempt to align the case law with economic theory, trying to depart from the interventionist approach that characterised the initial duty to deal enforcement practice (Evrard 2004).

In the following years, the case law mainly focused on disputes concerning intellectual property rights. Although neither the EU Commission nor the courts have explicitly linked the term essential facility to intellectual property rights, their decisions have relied upon the precedents dealing with duty to deal cases concerning physical property. The leading case for assessing the duty to license IPRs is *Magill.*[26] The CJEU found that the mere refusal to license an IPR did not constitute a breach of Article 102 TFEU. To find an illegal conduct, 'exceptional circumstances' must be identified (Ahlborn 2004). In *Magill,* they were recognised in the facts that: (i) the refusal to grant the licence prevented access to the market of a new product, a comprehensive

---

advertising revenues) and operated the only nationwide newspaper home-delivery scheme in that country. Bronner, the publisher of a rival newspaper, which, by reason of its small scale (3.6% in terms of circulation and 6% in terms of advertising revenues), was unable either alone or in cooperation with other publishers to set up and operate its own home-delivery scheme in economically reasonable conditions, asked to have access to Mediaprint's scheme for appropriate remuneration. The Court held that refusing access did not constitute an abuse of a dominant position within the meaning of Article 102 TFEU.

[26] Three television broadcasters (BBC, ITV and RTE) published weekly television guides exclusively for their own TV programmes and claimed copyright protection on their respective programme listings under the UK and Irish law. Magill, an Irish publisher, attempted to compile these listings into one comprehensive television guide, a product that was not yet available in the market. The three broadcasters refused to license their listings to Magill, preventing the publication of the new guide. Magill then filed a complaint against the broadcasters. The European Commission held that the refusal by the television stations was an abuse of dominant position, thus ordering the compulsory licence of the copyright on the TV listings. The decision was upheld by the General Court and by the Court of Justice. Joined cases C-241/91 P and C-242/91 P, *RTE and ITP v Commission* [1995] ECR I-743; on appeal from Cases T-69-70/89, 76/89, *RTE, ITP, BBC v. Commission* [1991] ECR II-485, on appeal from Case COMP IV/31.851 *Magill TV Guide/ITP, BBC and RTE* [1989] 4 CMLR 757.

TV guide, for which there was a potential consumer demand; (ii) there was no objective justification for the refusal to license; and (iii) the refusal to license copyrighted work allowed the dominant firms (i.e. the broadcasters) to foreclose competition in the secondary market. In view of these exceptional circumstances, the CJEU upheld the Commission's and the General Court's decisions to condemn the refusal under the rubric of Article 102(b) TFEU. It is worth questioning whether the CJEU has underestimated the economic arguments put forward by the broadcasters to justify their refusal. The defendants claimed that the imposition of a licence would produce negative welfare effects by reducing their incentives to innovate. However, the CJEU ruled that the information protected by copyright must be considered as basic information and that it was not possible to accept this justification because the copyrighted goods did not involve huge investments.

The principles set out by the CJEU in *Magill* have been restated in *IMS Health*.[27] This case concerned the refusal to grant the licence on a set of pharmaceuticals sales data, referred to as the 1860 brick structure, on which IMS Health held a copyright. The European Commission had closed the proceeding in 2001, with an interim decision ruling that the brick structure had become a *de facto* industry standard in the German pharmaceutical sector, similar to an essential facility, and consequently forced IMS to license the use of the structure to its rival, NDC Health.[28] The case also spurred litigation in the German courts since IMS had brought a legal action for copyright infringement against NDC Health. The Landgericht Frankfurt am Main decided to ask a preliminary ruling from the CJEU concerning the legal conditions for granting a compulsory license under Article 102 TFEU. The CJEU reiterated the principle according to which the simple refusal to grant access to IPRs does not constitute in itself an abuse of a dominant position. Rather, to identify an abuse in relation to the refusal to license IPRs, three cumulative conditions have to be satisfied: (i) the refusal has to be likely to prevent the appearance of a new product for which there is a potential and unsatisfied consumer demand; (ii) the refusal has to be unjustified; and (iii) the refusal should be able to foreclose actual or potential competition in the secondary market.[29] Additionally, in order to find the indispensable character of the brick structure, the CJEU pointed out that – similarly to the approach followed in *Magill* – it did not represent a creation with a high degree of innovativeness. In *IMS*, the Court linked the abuse consisting in the refusal to deal with its ability to prevent the emergence of a new product in a secondary

[27] Case 418/01, *IMS Health v NDC Health*, [2004] ECR I-5039.
[28] Case COMP/D3/38.044—*NDC Health/IMS Health*, Commission Decision, 2002 O.J. L 59/18 (interim measures).
[29] Case 418/01, *IMS Health v NDC Health*, [2004] ECR I-5039, paras 44–52.

market. In so doing, it attempted to find a balance between the need to protect intellectual property with the public interest in competitive markets. However, the proper categorisation of what can be considered to represent a new product and the exact identification of the upstream and downstream markets remain issues of complex evaluation, which are potentially able to foster an expansive interpretation of compulsory licensing (Lim 2007).

Although the CJEU did not explicitly refer to the essential facility doctrine to compel dominant firms to license their IPRs, there is a general consensus that the above judgments constitute the continuation of the doctrine. In this perspective, the decisions to apply this theory to IPRs may be criticised for its potential negative effects on the incentives to innovate. Since the right to exclude others (particularly competitors) constitutes the very subject matter of IP protection, the obligation to grant the licence through the antitrust enforcement cannot only represent an interference in the scope of intellectual property laws. It also creates *ex ante* uncertainty, which is likely to reduce the incentives to make socially optimal investments. Undoubtedly, the number of cases in which dominant firms have been forced to share their IPRs with rivals is limited. In addition, the scope for imposing a duty to license has been made subject to (even though not fully and consistently) defined exceptional circumstances. From a comparative perspective, however, the EU institutions have shown to be more prone than their US counterparts to consider the refusal to deal or to license IPRs among the list of abusive conducts. The former seem less concerned to chill, through the resulting obligations to deal or licence, the incentives to innovate.

In the controversial *Microsoft* case, the European Commission[30] and the General Court[31] adopted a somewhat different approach, to impose the firm a duty to provide the protocol specifications relating to its workgroup server operating systems (see the case discussion in Box 7.2). The Commission and the Court imposed a compulsory licensing duty on Microsoft's copyrighted works, specifying that the criteria defined in *Magill* and *IMS* to enforce a duty to license do not constitute an exhaustive list. Moreover, the obligation was imposed while highlighting that the firm' s refusal to provide rivals with the interoperability information was likely to lead to a limitation of 'technical development', which was in turn able to harm consumers. The requirement defined in *Magill* and *IMS* that the refusal to license an IPR has to prevent the appearance of a new product was neglected in *Microsoft*. Also, the decisions have made clear that the protection of intellectual property may not

[30] Case COMP/C-3/37.792—Microsoft Corp., Commission Decision, 2007 O.J. L 32/23 (March 24, 2004).
[31] Case T-201/04, *Microsoft Corp. v. Commission*, 2007 ECR II-3601.

be considered as an objective justification (Economides and Lianos 2010). Ultimately, the test adopted in *Microsoft*, in addition to exhibiting some differences with respect to the criteria previously defined, seems to reflect an idea of competition favouring the protection of competitors and is much less prone to protect intellectual property in case of conflict (Veel and Katz 2013).

In its 2009 Guidance Paper, the European Commission confirmed that a refusal to deal covers a wide range of practices and does not distinguish the refusal to license IPRs from other refusals.[32] Such a refusal infringes Article 102 TFEU when the licence is necessary to provide interface information or grant access to an essential facility or network (Guidance Paper, at 78). The Commission has further indicated to concentrate its enforcement efforts on cases where the following three conditions are satisfied: (i) the refusal relates to a product or service that is objectively necessary to be able to compete effectively on a downstream market; (ii) the refusal is likely to lead to the elimination of effective competition on the downstream market; and (iii) the refusal is likely to lead to consumer harm (Guidance Paper, at 81). Even though the number of cases in which dominant firms have been forced to share their IPRs with rivals is still limited, the current state of the case law is unsatisfactory. The scope of the duty to license has taken the form of not fully consistent 'exceptional circumstances' and may continue to chill the incentives to innovate.

Box 7.2: Microsoft and the duty to grant competitors (the same level of) interoperability information

In September 2007, the General Court upheld the European Commission's decision in the *Microsoft Corp.* case.[33] The Commission imposed on Microsoft a €497 million fine for having infringed Article 102 TFEU by tying its Windows Media Player to its operating system (see section 7.3.3 for a discussion of tying) and by refusing to supply interoperability information for the purpose of developing and distributing products competing with Microsoft's own products in the work group server operating systems market.[34] The case originated from a complaint lodged by Sun Microsystem, Microsoft's competitor in the workgroup server operating systems market (WGSOS), which

---

[32] See Guidance paper, at 78. According to the Commission, '[t]his concept covers many practices, such as a refusal to supply products to existing or new customers, refusal to license intellectual property rights, including when the licence is necessary to provide interface information, or refusal to grant access to an essential facility or a network'.

[33] Case T-201/04 *Microsoft v Commission* [2007] ECR II-3601.

[34] Case COMP/C-3/37.792—*Microsoft Corp.*, Commission Decision, 2007 O.J. L 32/23 (March 24, 2004).

accused the US firm of having abused its dominant position by refusing to provide the interoperability information needed by Sun to develop its products. At that time, Microsoft had an over 90% market share in the client PC operating systems market. The Commission found that the firm held a dominant position also in the market for work group server operating systems, where its market share was around 60%.

The case displayed an emblematic conflict between the protection of intellectual property rights and the access to the (alleged) essential information for competition purposes. From an economic perspective, Microsoft's behaviour could have had several justifications. The firm claimed that the information requested by Sun was protected by IPRs and it also highlighted that being forced to share such information would have reduced its incentives to innovate. Furthermore, Microsoft argued that the minimum level of interoperability to guarantee effective competition was already available in the market. Nevertheless, the Commission embraced a different notion of interoperability. It stated that, in order to compete in the WGSOS market, Microsoft's competitors needed full compatibility of their products with the Microsoft operating system. Therefore, the interoperability information requested by Sun was deemed essential to achieve effective competition. The refusal to supply such information was considered an abuse of dominant position.

Microsoft appealed the Commission's decision, arguing that, since the interoperability information was protected by IPRs, the refusal to supply could not be considered a violation of Article 102 TFEU. Microsoft also argued that the 'exceptional circumstances' requirement, which has been established in *Magill* and *IMS Health*, had not been properly satisfied. Neglecting to a large extent the economic arguments that suggest caution in granting access to IPRs, the General Court lowered the requirements previously set in the case law. First, the Court held that the mere protection of IPRs does not constitute an objective justification for the refusal to supply, thus dismissing the arguments relating to the reduced incentives to innovate by stating that they simply represent 'vague and theoretical arguments'.[35] To satisfy an objective justification plea, Microsoft would have had to prove a significant negative impact on its incentives to innovate, if forced to disclosure the information. Moreover, the Court reduced the burden of proof concerning the elimination of competition in the market, affirming that it is not '(...) necessary to demonstrate that all the competition on the market would be eliminated', but that 'the refusal at issue [was] liable to or likely to eliminate all effective competition'.[36] The Court also ruled that, in order to ascertain whether a refusal to license IPRs is capable of causing a prejudice to consumers, preventing the appearance of a new product '[could not] be the only parameter'.[37] In so doing, the General Court testified that the list of exceptional circumstances set in the previous

---

[35] Case T-201/04 *Microsoft* v *Commission* [2007] ECR II-3601, at para. 698.
[36] *Ibid.*, at para. 563.
[37] *Ibid.*, at para. 647.

case law is not exhaustive, suggesting that other criteria might be taken into account when deciding a duty to deal case, even when IPRs are at stake.

The judgment of the General Court may be criticised because it has embraced a form-based approach, which concentrates on the structure of the market by looking at the market shares of the actors involved. Furthermore, the Court inferred the prejudice to consumers merely from the disadvantages of Microsoft's competitors. In other words, it seems that the Court was more concerned with the injury to the competitive structure and interests of individual competitors than the real harm suffered by consumers as a result of the refusal to supply the same level of interoperability information.

7.3 Tying and bundling

Practices of dominant firms may generate anti-competitive effects in related or adjacent markets. A dominant firm may establish a link between its home market and a horizontally related market through bundling and tying. Bundling may be pure or mixed. In the case of pure bundling, two or more products are sold together for a single price (for example, fixed-price menus). Pure bundling may be achieved through contractual agreements or through technological links, which make it physically impossible for the consumer to buy the products separately (technological bundling; a well-known example is Microsoft's technological integration of its browser Internet Explorer with its operating system Windows). In a pure bundle the products are offered only in fixed proportions, such as A-B or 2A-2B. In mixed bundling, consumers have the choice of buying the products separately or as a package (the bundle), which is sold at a discount (for example, all-in holiday packages).

With respect to tying, a distinction can be made between a static tie and a dynamic tie. The static tie can be considered as half of a mixed bundle or an exclusivity arrangement. In such a case, the customer who wants to buy product A must also buy product B, although it is possible to acquire product B separately. Consequently, the products offered for sale are B or A-B as a package. Hence, in the case of a static tie, the sale of the 'tying product' is contingent on the purchase of the 'tied product', both products belonging to different relevant product markets.[38] The difference between pure bundling and a static tie is that under the latter the tied product may be bought alone. The difference between mixed bundling and a static tie is that in the former case both products are available separately. The second type of tying is a dynamic form of a pure bundle, i.e. a dynamic tie. In order to be able to buy product A, a customer is also required to buy product B, but the quantity of

---

[38] Commission Guidelines on Vertical Restraints [2000] O.J. C 291/1, at 106.

product B may differ from customer to customer. The combinations for sale may be A-B, A-2B, A-3B and so on. Hence, a dynamic tie has the feature of exclusivity of a static tie, but the amount of the tied product may differ. The products are sold in variable proportions. A dynamic tie is also labelled 're-quirements tying'; an example is the sale of a photocopier on the condition that the purchaser also buys toner and paper from the same manufacturer. The older legal and economic literature uses tying as a general denominator for each of the described practices.

7.3.1 Economic analysis

Tying and bundling are anti-competitive if these practices exclude competitors and harm consumers. Conversely, tying and bundling are benign if they increase efficiency. The Chicago School criticised the traditional leverage argument, according to which a monopolist in the market for product A (home market) may use tying in order to reduce competition for a complementary product B (adjacent market) and thus achieve two monopoly profits. More recent theoretical economic research has revealed the limitations of the Chicago critique and has shown that dominant firms may strategically use bundling or tying in order to leverage market power in adjacent markets. However, given the strict assumptions of the new theories, the number of cases where the practice is anti-competitive is likely to be low. By contrast, bundling and tying may generate different types of efficiencies (cost savings, quality assurance) and can also be used as a price discrimination device. The different economic explanations for bundling and tying are successively presented below.

Tying and bundling as an anti-competitive practice: leveraging market power

The overwhelmingly negative attitude towards tying in competition law has its origin in the 'leverage theory', which was popular in the early days of antitrust. The basic argument is that a firm having a dominant position in the market for the tying product (possibly as the consequence of patent protection) uses tying arrangements to extend its dominant position into the market for the tied product. As a consequence, there are two deadweight losses and a dominant firm obtains a monopoly profit twice. In the 1970s Chicago economists attacked this theory and argued that it is not possible for a firm to leverage monopoly power from one activity into another. Even if the firm is a monopolist in the market for the tying product, it cannot achieve a second monopoly profit in the market for the tied product (single monopoly profit theorem). The following example may illustrate the Chicago reasoning. Assume two complementary products: the first product is sold at the profit-maximising monopoly price of €200 and the second product is competitively priced at €30. To achieve a double monopoly profit, the sale of the first product must be made contingent upon the purchase of the second product and the price for the latter product must be increased to, for example, €50. However, if the price of the tied product is higher than the competitive price, consumers will perceive the package price as too high and will buy less of the tying product (Posner 2001, 197; Bork 1993, 365). Since consumers are not willing to pay €250 for the first product sold in combination with the second product, which they value at €30, the firm will have to reduce its package price to maximise its profits; in the example this is €230. Hence, achieving a double monopoly profit through tying is not possible. By contrast, the dominant firm will profit from competition in the market of the second product since any monopoly profit earned by others will reduce its own (Evans and Padilla 2005, 77).

Recent research in industrial organisation has clarified that the Chicago approach is only valid on its own assumptions. The Chicago critique applies only if the tied market is perfectly competitive. Obviously, a crucial assumption is that consumers are perfectly informed: if they are not able to calculate the full package price, the risk that they may be exploited cannot be excluded. This is the reason why the US Supreme Court decided in the *Kodak* case that buyers of photocopying machines, who are required to purchase maintenance services from the same manufacturer, may be exploited if they cannot calculate the lifetime cost of using the machine (see the case discussion in Box 7.3).

Box 7.3: Leveraging market power and aftermarkets: the US *Kodak* case

The facts of the *Kodak* case[39] can be summarised as follows. Kodak sold photocopiers in competition with numerous other sellers. At the time of the litigation, Kodak had a 23% share of the high-volume copier market and less than a 20% share of the micrographic equipment market. Kodak effectively tied sales of machinery and repair and maintenance services by refusing to supply independent service organisations with spare parts. The latter complained that Kodak had limited the availability of its proprietary spare parts in order to monopolise the market for the servicing of Kodak photocopiers and other equipment. The independent service organisations conceded that Kodak did not have market power in the original equipment markets, but claimed that the tying product was Kodak replacement parts. Kodak was alleged to have used its monopoly

---

[39] *Eastman Kodak Co. v. Image Technical Services, Inc.*, 112 S.Ct 2072 (1992).

power in the Kodak parts aftermarket, where it essentially had a 100% market share, to gain control of the Kodak service aftermarket by means of illegal tying. Kodak's defence was primarily based on the argument that if there is competition in the primary market of the equipment, aftermarket power cannot negatively affect consumers. The Supreme Court, however, ruled that it was possible for a manufacturer to have monopoly power in the servicing of its equipment even if it did not have market power in the original sale of that equipment. The Supreme Court recognised that the manufacturer's ability to raise prices in aftermarkets will in all cases be constrained by the possibility of consumers purchasing alternative equipment from another manufacturer. However, if consumers lack the necessary information to calculate the likely lifetime costs of competing producers' machines, they may find themselves locked into a particular brand of equipment after they have made their initial equipment purchase. Consumers should look at the package price covering the initial purchase price of the machine and all maintenance costs during its lifetime. If consumers are fully informed at the time of the initial purchase decision, manufacturers can raise the price of the maintenance services only at the expense of lowering the initial purchase price of the equipment. Conversely, information deficits on the part of the consumers enable manufacturers to raise prices in aftermarkets, thus exploiting consumers who are locked into the original products due to high switching costs.

The Supreme Court rejected the defendant's economic theory of fully informed consumers considering full package prices before making purchases and accepted the plaintiff's economic theory of an aftermarket hold-up of imperfectly informed consumers. This view has been criticised in the academic literature. Klein (1998) argues that an aftermarket hold-up is not possible even if consumers are totally uninformed, as long as there is competition among informed sellers in the primary market. Sellers know that they will be able to increase aftermarket prices up to the amount of the consumers' switching costs (not by a higher amount since consumers will switch to competing suppliers after they learn about the high repair parts and maintenance prices). Vigorous competition in the primary market will force manufacturers to reduce equipment prices to avoid loss of sales to competing suppliers. In the view of Klein, hold-ups require that sellers also possess imperfect information of future market conditions. Unanticipated changes in market conditions determine whether a manufacturer will find it profitable to engage in a hold-up. Opportunism will be in the private interests of a manufacturer if the benefit to be gained from exploiting locked-in consumers by asking super-competitive prices for maintenance services exceeds the resultant loss of future demand for the primary good. Short-term gains from opportunistic behaviour may exceed long-term reputational costs caused to the brand name, if there is an unexpectedly large increase in demand for services or an unexpectedly large decrease in demand for equipment. In the former case, hold-ups are profitable given the substantial gains from a strategy of installed base opportunism. In the latter case, long-run reputational disadvantages become less important and the costs of a hold-up may become less than the gains of such an action. This is particularly true for firms that have decided to exit the primary market. In a 'last period' situation, the brand name cost associated with the lost premium on future sales becomes an unimportant constraint on seller behaviour. Klein stresses that hold-ups, even if they do occur, are not evidence of market power. Manufacturers may decide to engage in a hold-up even if they face competition from many alternative suppliers. Many contract disputes are the consequence of changes in market conditions not anticipated when the original contractual agreement was reached. Contract law is superior to antitrust law in hold-up cases because it explicitly takes account of the contractual environment (Klein 1998).

The *Kodak* case bears close resemblance to the older European *Hugin* case.[40] A manufacturer of cash registers refused to supply spare parts to competing suppliers of servicing, thus tying the supply of maintenance and repair services to the purchase of spare parts for the machines. Even though Hugin's market share in the market for cash registers was low (not exceeding 13%), the refusal to supply independent service organisations was qualified as an abuse. In the European Commission's view, the refusal to supply had the result of removing a major competitor (Liptons) in the market of service, maintenance, repair and supply of reconditioned machines. In the early days of EU competition law, the relevant competition problems of aftermarkets were not touched upon. The CJEU annulled the decision for a different reason, namely the absence of impact on interstate trade.

In the theoretical economic literature, a number of models have been developed showing that – contrary to the Chicago learning – dominant firms may strategically leverage market power in adjacent markets. Within the scope of this book, a complete overview of this literature cannot be provided. Two different scenarios of anti-competitive effects will be briefly presented. First, bundling may lead to entry deterrence in the market of the bundled product if this market is subject to economies of scale. Second, tying and bundling may affect the future competitiveness of rivals in the market of the tied/bundled product and deter them from competing in the home market. The first scenario involves independent products (Nalebuff 1999; Whinston 1990). By credibly committing itself to sell the products only as a bundle (for example, technological tying), the dominant firm signals to competitors in the market of the bundled good that pricing will be aggressive. Fierce competition in the bundled good market may decrease the rivals' profits and force them to exit. By using its monopoly position in the home market to capture a sufficiently large share in the adjacent market, bundling can deny the rivals

---

[40] Case 22/78 *Hugin Kassaregister AB v. Commission (Hugin)* [1979] ECR 1869.

the requisite scale that they require to compete. Once the rival has left the tied market, the dominant firm may recoup the lost profits through increased prices. However, if the dominant firm is unable to commit itself to the bundling strategy (if it cannot credibly threaten to refuse supplies to customers who do not want to purchase the bundle), re-entry may be expected if the price of the bundled good is increased.

The second scenario involves complementary products. Bundling (technological tying) can be a profitable strategy in markets where firms compete through upfront R&D investments and entry is, therefore, risky. By tying the two products, the prospects of recouping an investment (by new entrants) are made less certain. The reason is that innovations by newcomers must be simultaneously successful in both markets because the tying and tied good are complements. In the first period the dominant firm offers both products whereas the rival offers only the second good; in the second period the rival can also produce the first good. In the first period, tying may prevent entry or induce exit in the market for the complementary good, since the prospects of recouping investment costs are made less certain. The reason is that newcomers must be simultaneously successful in both markets. As a consequence, in the second period bundling may preserve the dominant position in the home market. Since successful entry requires that newcomers enter two markets instead of one, the entrants' incentives for investment and innovation will be reduced (Carlton and Waldman 2002; Choi and Stefanadis 2001). These models show under which conditions tying and bundling may cause anti-competitive effects, but their practical value is limited because the available data are rarely adequate to determine whether the practice will actually reduce welfare (weighing any potential efficiencies with possible losses due to foreclosure).

Efficiency explanations of bundling and tying

If the only purpose of bundling and tying was to hinder the entry or to induce the exit of an equally efficient competitor, a flat prohibition would be defensible. In reality, however, market foreclosure is not the entire story. The foreclosure explanation is challenged by efficiency theories. Bundling and tying may reflect consumers' preferences, achieve cost savings and/or be used for reasons of quality assurance. Other explanations for tying include the wish to practise price discrimination or to increase the sales of the tying product. Firms may thus advance several reasonable business rationales for tying in order to defend themselves against the 'abuse of dominance' or monopolisation claim.[41]

Tie-in sales are benign if they generate efficiencies. Many products are naturally and efficiently tied together or bundled. There is no reason for antitrust intervention when consumers desire assembled products such as laced shoes, radios, cars or PCs with software already installed. Besides reflecting consumer preferences, bundling and tying may generate cost efficiencies. Cost savings resulting from economies of scope arise if consumers purchase complementary goods from the same producer. Also, the suppliers' costs of producing and distributing those products are reduced through bundling or tying.

Another reason to engage in tying is quality assurance and the related protection from opportunistic behaviour (Bork 1993, 379–380). Generally, a firm may assure quality by forcing customers to buy another of its products or services and not to use substitutes. A manufacturer of durable goods may decide to operate through a network of exclusive dealerships, forcing customers to purchase servicing from the network. The refusal to supply independent service organisations may be motivated by the concern that the low quality of the servicing provided by the latter may harm the reputation of the network.

A prominent explanation for bundling and tying is that it permits profitable price discrimination (Motta 2004, 462; Tirole 1998, 146).[42] Once an intermediate durable good is sold, control of its rate of utilisation passes to the downstream purchaser. Manufacturers of durable goods may tie the purchase of relatively low-valued commodities to the sale of the primary goods. Hence, tying arrangements (in particular a dynamic tie or 'requirements tying') may be motivated by the goal of gaining control over the rate of utilisation of durable goods (Bowman 1957, 24). Tied sales of machines and complementary products may enable manufacturers to charge higher prices to high-intensity users.[43] The same is true for tied sales of machines and maintenance services.

---

[41] Another non-benign reason of tie-in sales is to evade price regulation. If the price for the tying product is regulated, a high price for tied products can circumvent the price regulation unless the price for the latter products is also fixed. In most European countries price controls for consumer goods have been abolished. The hypothesis of evasion of price regulation, which is not further elaborated upon in the text, may remain relevant as long as price controls exist (e.g. in the sector of utilities) and tie-in sales are commercially feasible.

[42] Stigler (1963) explained a single-package price for films (block booking) as a method to price discriminate according to the implicit valuation of different films within the package by individual buyers.

[43] A clear example is the *Vaessen-Moris* case decided by the European Commission in 1979 (Case IV/29.290 *Vaessen-Moris* [1979] O.J. L 19/32). A firm acquired a patent on a machine to make sausages. The use of the machine was free for users who agreed to buy skins from the supplier of the machine. A competing skin manufacturer complained that he was foreclosed from the market of the secondary product. The EU Commission argued that the patent owner had extended monopoly power into a second market, without

If the purpose of the tying firm is to discriminate in price, other alternatives, such as attaching a meter to measure the intensity of use, are available. These alternatives may, however, involve greater policing and monitoring costs than a tying scheme. The welfare effects of price discrimination are discussed below (see section 7.5).

The foreclosure explanation of tying is also challenged by the possibility to use tying arrangements for repair parts in order to increase the sales of the original equipment. By increasing prices for maintenance services and reducing the prices of the original equipment,[44] manufacturers may wish to prevent customers from opportunistically extending the useful lives of the machines and, hence, buying fewer of them than would be consistent with the firm's profit-maximising objectives. The welfare effects of such arrangements are ambiguous. A larger output of high-quality durable goods must be balanced against a reduction of the output of repair parts below competitive levels.

7.3.2   US antitrust law

In the old days of US antitrust, judges regarded tying as merely anti-competitive. In *Standard Oil*, Justice Frankfurter wrote that tying agreements 'serve hardly any purpose beyond the suppression of competition'.[45] In the *Northern Pacific* case (1958) the Supreme Court held that tying denies competitors free access to the market for the tied product, not because the party imposing the tying requirements has a better product or a lower price but because of his 'power leverage in another market'.[46] In *Jefferson Parish*,[47] the majority decided to keep the *per se* prohibition intact, but required that the tying allegation has to pass several screens before being considered illegal. This test (modified *per se* illegality) consists of four steps: (i) the tying and tied goods are two separate products; (ii) the defendant has market power in the tying product market; (iii) the defendant forces consumers to purchase the tied product; and (iv) the tying arrangement forecloses a substantial volume of commerce. However, even though the Supreme Court decided to preserve the *per se* rule, it has to be noted that the minority opinion of four Justices pointed out that it was appropriate to overrule the prohibition, thus privileging a Rule of

---

checking whether the package price for the machine and the skins was higher than the sum of the prices when the goods were sold separately. High-intensity customers who place a relatively high value on the particular features of the specific manufacturer's product were willing to pay relatively high prices for the use of the machine (on the welfare effects of price discrimination, see section 7.5.1).

[44] In competitive markets overpricing of service implies the corresponding underpricing of equipment.

[45] *Standard Oil Co v. United States*, 337 U.S. 293, 305–306 (1949).

[46] *Northern Pacific Railway Company v. United States*, 356 U.S. 1 (1958).

[47] *Jefferson Parish*, 46 U.S. 9 (1984).

Reason analysis. Lastly, in *Independent Ink*,[48] the Supreme Court expressed further doubts on whether the *per se* rule represents the appropriate legal standard to evaluate tying. The Court clarified that the mere existence of a patent does not support any presumption of market power, and that tying arrangements involving patented goods may be deemed unlawful only upon proof of substantial market power. More importantly, although the Court did not countermand the *per se* illegality of these practices, the judges seemed to believe that such a strict prohibition is not the most suitable way to assess the potential efficiencies that tying practices can generate. This reading of the Supreme Court's judgment has led some authors to believe that it was a missed opportunity to formally reject the *per se* prohibition (Kobayashi 2008; Wright 2006).

Over time, the lower courts have expressed a clear willingness to approve tying arrangements. Already in the 1960s, some decisions stated the lawfulness of tying conducts. In *Jerrold Electronics*[49] – a case concerning a tying arrangement between a TV broadcasting system with the installation and maintenance service – the manufacturer's argument was that services provided by persons lacking the necessary skills were likely to cause serious malfunctions. The judges held that the tying of the receiving system with the installation and assistance services was justified because of the innovative nature of the technology and in order to ensure the necessary level of quality.

The most representative example of a more lenient approach to tying is the *US Microsoft* case (2001). The leverage theory does not appear in the D.C. Circuit Court of Appeals' opinion. Rather, the Court caused a Copernican revolution in the antitrust treatment of tying by endorsing a Rule of Reason approach to technological tying (bundling). The lower Court of the Columbia District held that the tying of the Microsoft operating system with Internet Explorer had foreclosed the rival software, Netscape Navigator, from the browsers market. On the basis of the previous case law, the judges decided that, since Microsoft has a dominant position in the operating systems market, the tie of the operating system to another product amounted to a conduct prohibited *per se*.[50] On appeal, Microsoft argued that the software industry is characterised by highly integrated products, emphasising also that the type of competition emerging in such settings creates competition 'for' the market rather than within the market ('tipping'). The player who wins the competitive battle obtains a monopoly position; however, this position is only temporary until another innovative product is able to replace the

---

[48] *Illinois Tool Works Inc. v. Independent Ink, Inc.*, 547 U.S. 28 (2006).
[49] *United States v. Jerrold Elecs. Corp.*, 187 F.Supp 545 (E.D. Pa. 1960).
[50] *United States v. Microsoft Corp.*, 97 F. Supp. 2d 59 (D.D.C. 2000).

previous one. The Court of Appeals shared these arguments and concluded that the tying arrangements in the software industry must be analysed according to the Rule of Reason.[51] It highlighted that the precedents on which the Supreme Court's case law had been developed were grounded on economic sectors exhibiting different characteristics from those pertaining to the new economy markets.[52] The Court considered that a mechanical application of the traditional *per se* rule in relation to highly innovative platform software would lead to welfare enhancing and pro-competitive forms of tying being condemned. In sum, the Court decided to develop a 'technology exception' to the *per se* prohibition. Henceforth, under a Rule of Reason standard it must be shown that tying harms the competitive process and thereby hurts consumers; in addition, there is scope for the monopolist to argue a pro-competitive justification (for example, greater efficiency or enhanced consumer appeal).[53] The Rule of Reason allows the assessment of whether the integrated product is more valuable to end users than the sum of its parts. Technological bundling can be accepted if it leads to an increase of consumer welfare. Among academic scholars, there is now a broad consensus that the *per se* standard no longer represents an appropriate rule to evaluate tying and bundling (Elhauge 2009; Areeda and Hovenkamp 2007, para 1729e2).

7.3.3   EU competition law

The American Supreme Court's view that tying agreements serve hardly any purpose beyond the suppression of competition has inspired EU competition law and has laid the basis for a sceptical treatment of tying, which has come close to a *per se* prohibition. The formulation of Article 102(d) TFEU, which qualifies as an abuse the 'acceptance of supplementary obligations which (...) have no connection with the subject of (...) contracts', remains a major obstacle to an analysis focusing on allocative efficiency and consumer welfare. The idea of a superficial link between products is more hospitable to the protection of competitors from (unsubstantiated) leveraging of market power than to a careful analysis of competitive harm damaging consumers.

The leverage argument was prominently present in the *Hilti* and *Tetra Pak* cases. In *Hilti*,[54] a manufacturer supplying nail guns to the construction industry was found to have abused its dominant position by tying the purchase of nails and cartridges to the purchase of guns. Both the Hilti nail gun and its cartridge strips were protected by patent. Hilti had a 55% market share

---

[51]   *United States v. Microsoft Corp.*, 253 F.3d 34 (D.C. Cir. 2001).
[52]   *Ibid.*, at paras 90–97.
[53]   *U.S. v. Microsoft*, 253 F.3d 34 (D.C. Cir.2001), at 95–97.
[54]   Case IV/31.488 *Eurofix-Bauco/Hilti* [1988] O.J. L 65/19.

in the market for nail guns, but a much lower market share in the market for Hilti-compatible nails and cartridge strips. The EU Commission's decision, upheld by the CJEU, found Hilti guilty of abusing its dominant position by commercial practices that hindered the entry into the market for Hilti-compatible nails of independent nail producers. The *Tetra Pak* case[55] concerned the world leader in the field of packaging liquid foods (such as milk and fruit juices) in cartons. Tetra Pak produced both packaging machinery and cartons. At the time of the decision, Tetra Pak's market share in aseptic packaging (i.e. for long-life products) was between 90% and 95%, while its market share in non-aseptic packaging (i.e. for fresh products) was between 50% and 55%. Tetra Pak required exclusive use of Tetra Pak cartons on its machines. Moreover, Tetra Pak sold cartons on the Italian market for non-aseptic packaging at prices below average variable costs. The first practice was condemned as illegal tying and the price reductions were seen as evidence of 'predatory pricing' prohibited by Article 102 TFEU (see section 7.4.3).

In the evaluation of the two cases, the European Commission condemned the conduct of both companies without carrying out a thorough market analysis. After having found dominance in their respective markets, the Commission established that the products were different and declared that an objective justification was missing. The tying practices were held illegal without performing an economic assessment of their potential pro-competitive character. Both decisions were confirmed by the General Court and by the CJEU, which rejected the various justifications advanced by the parties. In *Hilti*, the CJEU did not accept the argument that tying guns with nails was needed to solve safety concerns.[56] In *Tetra Pak*, the CJEU held that even if the tying could have been justified on the grounds of commercial usage (machines and cartons), the conduct represented an infringement of Article 102(d) TFEU.[57] In both cases, the main concern of the Commission and the EU courts was to preserve the competitive structure of the market, attempting to protect the ability of smaller firms to compete.

The *Microsoft*[58] case can be seen as the first attempt by the EU Commission to dismiss the formalistic approach followed in the past by evaluating the effects of tying in the software market. The Commission found that Microsoft

---

[55] *Elopak Italia/Tetra Pak* [1991] O.J. L72/1.

[56] Case C-53/92 P, *Hilti AG v. EC Commission* [1994] ECR I-667; Case T-30/89 *Hilti v. Commission* [1991] ECR II-1439.

[57] Case C-333/94 P, *Tetra Pak International SA v. Commission* [1996] ECR I-5951; Case T-83/91, *Tetra Pak International v. Commission* [1994] ECR II-755.

[58] Case COMP/C-3/37.792, *Microsoft Corp.*, Commission Decision, 2007 O.J. L 32/23 (March 24, 2004) (Commission Decision 2004).

had abused its dominant position on the client PC operating systems market, where it held a market share of approximately 90%, by tying its Windows Media Player to the Windows operating system. More specifically, the Commission outlined four conditions under which it considered tying as incompatible with Article 102 TFEU: (i) the tying good and the tied good are two separate products; (ii) the company concerned is dominant in the tying product market; (iii) the company does not give customers a choice to obtain the tying product without the tied product; and (iv) tying forecloses competition. Comparing this approach with US antitrust law, these requirements boil down to a modified *per se* illegality test. In the US Microsoft case, such a test was rejected in favour of a Rule of Reason approach (see section 7.3.2). Conversely, on the basis of the above criteria, the EU Commission concluded that Microsoft had illegally tied the sale of its operating system with that of its streaming media software. Compared with the analysis of tying in the older EU competition practice, the most notable change is the analysis of the potential foreclosure effects that the tying was likely to produce, especially in terms of its impact on software developers and market development (for an elaborate critical discussion of the *Microsoft* case, see Pardolesi and Renda 2004).

In spite of the Commission's focus on the economic effects of technological tying, on appeal the General Court has again halted the transition towards a More Economic Approach. The *Microsoft* judgment can be criticised because it largely focused on the market structure and advanced the view that the tying of the operating system and the media player granted Microsoft an 'unfair advantage', which was suitable *ipso facto* to generate exclusionary effects. Scholars have censored the Court's findings, considering that it has refused to embrace an effects-based analysis, thereby underestimating to a large extent the insights of modern economic theory that tying can lead to anti-competitive effects only in particular circumstances (Ahlborn and Evans 2009).

In its 2009 Guidance Paper, the European Commission has again clarified when tying may trigger enforcement actions. The relevant conditions are the following: (i) an undertaking is dominant in the tying market; (ii) the tying and tied products represent distinct products; and (iii) the tying practice is likely to lead to anti-competitive foreclosure. The last requirement represents the clearest signal of the willingness not to consider tying and bundling arrangements as *per se* unlawful. Although the evidence of the anti-competitive foreclosure represents one of the constitutive elements in the assessment of tying and bundling, the Guidance Paper does not provide further guidance on how such effects have to be established in practice. In addition, the Guidance Paper formulates restrictive conditions under which the Commission may consider efficiency claims, such as savings in production and distribution or reduced transaction costs for customers and suppliers.[59] Up until today, there are no cases of tying or bundling in which an objective justification was accepted; this may be largely due to the substantial difficulties to successfully implement an efficiency defence. In the only case concerning tying since the issuance of its Guidance Paper, the Commission concluded the proceeding through a commitment decision, without performing the full assessment that characterises an economic approach.[60]

Box 7.4: The Russian *Google* case: a different attitude towards bundling?

The *Yandex vs Google* case[61] originated from the complaint submitted to the Federal Antimonopoly Service of the Russian Federation (FAS) by Yandex LLC, the largest Russian search provider. The case concerned Google's conduct with respect to the Android operating system and its applications. It resembles the EU Microsoft case with regard to the bundling between its operating system and the Windows Media Player.

Google's Android was the dominant mobile device operating system worldwide and it held a prominent role also in the Russian market for smartphones and tablets. Google also owned the Google Play app store, an application allowing searching for other software developed for devices operated by Android. Significantly, Google Play's features made it commercially important for smartphones and tablet manufactures to have it pre-installed on their devices. Google provided Google Play under a mobile application distribution agreement, which bundled it with other mobile applications (Google Mobile Services, GMS), including a number of Google's applications and services (such as Google Search or Google Chrome). In order to obtain Google Play, manufactures had to compulsorily pre-install all the GMS applications on their devices. Additionally, they had to set some of them as default options and they were also prevented from pre-installing any other application produced by Google's competitors.

The FAS found that Google held a dominant position in the market for pre-installed app store for the Android operating system in Russia, with a market share exceeding 50%. The commercial practices were considered anti-competitive especially with

---

[59] The *Guidance Paper* clarifies, at para. 30, that the dominant firm has to demonstrate, with a sufficient degree of probability, and on the basis of verifiable evidence, that the following cumulative conditions are fulfilled: (i) the efficiencies have been, or are likely to be, realised as a result of the conduct; (ii) the conduct is indispensable to realise these efficiencies; (iii) there must be no less anti-competitive alternatives to the conduct that are capable of producing the same efficiencies; (iv) the efficiencies must benefit consumers; and (v) the conduct may not eliminate all or most existing sources of actual or potential competition.

[60] Case COMP/39230, *Rio Tinto Alcan*, Commission Decision of 20 December 2012.

[61] Federal Antimonopoly Service of the Russian Federation, *Resolution on case no. 1-14-21/00-11-15*, September 18, 2015.

respect to the mobile search market, since Google required the pre-installation of its own search engine as an exclusive search option by default. Google appealed against the decision, but the Court upheld the FAS judgment, including the fine of 438 million rubles (around US$6.8 million) which was imposed for the infringement.

Google's defence was primarily based on the fact that the bundling of applications, an ordinary business practice, was both commercially and technically justified, that it was not addressed against Google's competitors and that it generated efficiency benefits, due to the full compatibility of the preinstalled applications on users' devices. Google also highlighted that Android allowed end users to disable pre-installed software, change the initial settings and download and install competing applications.

Merely relying on the circumstance that each application would continue to run even if users had self-installed and used alternative applications, the FAS established that the technological reasons for bundling Google Play with GMS applications were lacking. Moreover, the Russian authority considered in its investigation neither any possible positive impact on consumer welfare produced by the bundling of the applications offered by Google, nor any other economic justification of Google's business practices. Also, the possibility that users were free to use different products was not considered a sufficient condition for the market's contestability, as Google was in any event able to reach a considerable penetration of adjacent markets through its bundling strategy.

The FAS may be criticised for not having undertaken a detailed analysis of consumer harm and rapidly dismissing the efficiency defence advanced by the US firm. The decision has not proven that Google's practices reduced effective competition in the market, thereby harming consumers. As a consequence, the FAS appears to protect Google's competitors, in particular Yandex, rather than to foster competition or increase long-run consumer welfare.

7.4   Predatory pricing

Predatory pricing involves conduct by a dominant firm, called the predator, which incurs short-term losses in a particular market in order to induce the exit or deter the entry of a rival firm, called the prey, so that super-normal profits can be earned in the future, either in the same market or in other markets. In the long antitrust history, the definition of predatory pricing has proven to be problematic (Spector 2001). The minimum consensus is that predation involves a temporary reduction in prices to harm competition and to achieve higher profits in the long term.[62] However, since low prices are also a virtue of the competitive process, competition authorities face a difficult task in distinguishing predatory pricing from healthy price competition. The elimination of inefficient firms is the natural consequence of competition; the competitive process will be damaged only if rivals who are also efficient are driven out of the market through price reductions by dominant firms.

Economic models on predation analyse predation as a two-stage process. In the predation phase, the predator practises low prices to hinder the prey from reaping enough profits to remain in the market.[63] In the post-predation phase, when the prey is forced out of the market, the predator will be able to increase prices up to the level that compensate the losses incurred during the first phase.[64] There are two related debates on predatory pricing: a theoretical debate focusing on the question whether it may actually occur and a policy debate concerning the optimal legal rule for predatory pricing. Chicago scholars have questioned the rationality of the practice and concluded that predation should not cause antitrust worries. Modern economic literature has relaxed some of the (strict) Chicago assumptions and has developed theories showing the conditions under which predatory pricing may be rational. However, the various theories differ on the exact conditions under which the predatory campaign can be successful. The second part of the debate concerns the optimal legal rule. It can be extremely difficult for enforcement agencies and courts to distinguish between harmful predatory pricing and desirable competitive price cutting. An optimal legal rule should deter harmful predatory pricing and avoid to overly deter legitimate price cuts. At the same time, the required evidence of an illegal predatory conduct should not be too strict, in order to avoid under-deterrence of undesirable predatory strategies.

---

[62] For a legal definition of this practice in the U.S. *see Transamerica Computer Co. v. IBM*, 698 F.2d 1377, 1384 (9th Cir. 1983), where it is noted that 'Predatory pricing occurs when a company that controls a substantial market share lowers its prices to drive out competition so that it can charge monopoly prices, and reap monopoly profits, at a later time.'

[63] It has to be noted that predatory conduct may harm competition in other ways: they may deter market entry, discipline a rival as to enforce cartel pricing, or reduce the value of the competitor and of its assets with a view to acquire (or merge with) the prey.

[64] Predatory pricing is mostly discussed as the strategy of firms to reduce prices in the pre-predation phase, with an exclusionary intent, and to increase them in the post-predation phase. However, there are models explaining predation with respect to quantities. In the latter scenario, the predator increases output and the post-predation phase is characterised by a restriction of production instead of an increase in price (Tirole 1988).

7.4.1 Economic theories

McGee and the Chicago School: predatory pricing as an irrational strategy

In the famous *Standard Oil* case,[65] which is still controversial more than a century later (Leslie 2012; Page 2012; Dalton and Esposito 2011), the US Supreme Court ruled that the firm had illegally monopolised the market through the adoption of unfair methods of competition, like '(…) local price-cutting at the points where necessary to suppress competition.'[66] In reaching this decision, the Supreme Court did not take into account a specific cost measure to judge the legality of the price level. Neither the profitability of the predatory strategy nor its effects in terms of consumer welfare was analysed. In 1958, John McGee wrote a seminal contribution on the *Standard Oil* case, which had a considerable influence on both the economic theory of predation and the antitrust practice. He advanced several arguments to discredit the idea that a firm is able to exclude its competitors by an aggressive pricing policy in several local markets. According to McGee, firms do not adopt predatory strategies because it is inherently unprofitable or more convenient for the predator to merge with the prey (McGee 1958). Following McGee's analysis, the belief that predation is unlikely to occur gradually paved its way among Chicago scholars.

According to the Chicago view, there are (at least) three fundamental reasons why firms do not engage in predatory pricing. First, a dominant firm cutting prices below costs will lose money in the short run (even though it may hope to drive rivals out of business and increase its power to control prices afterwards). The predator may lose substantially more than the target firm: as a consequence of the low prices, market demand for the products may significantly increase and the costs of the overall price reductions may be larger than the losses incurred by the prey to meet competition. The magnitude of the losses will depend on how long the predatory campaign must last to induce the exit of the prey. If the assets employed in an industry are sunk, the costs to a new entrant of leaving the market are greater and the price war will be of long duration (Martin 1993, 454–458). Generally speaking, the losses from predation do not make predatory pricing a profitable strategy.[67]

Second, even if the predator succeeds in driving the target firm out of the market, in the absence of barriers to entry a monopolist will not be able to

---

[65] *Standard Oil Co. of New Jersey v. United States*, 221 U.S. 1 (1911).

[66] *Ibid.*, at 43.

[67] It should be added, however, that the predator might be able to lower prices selectively in particular regions or for particular types of customers, thus targeting predatory discounts at the market segments in which the prey is most heavily committed. Under the latter scenario losses will be lower and can be recouped more easily.

earn super-competitive profits. If markets are contestable, the target firms will re-enter or new firms will be attracted by the prospect of creaming off monopoly profits. If it is profitable for the target firm to re-enter, it will, so it is argued by Chicagoans, be able to find the financial resources needed to survive the price war (Bork 1993, 147–148). Also, customers who are the ultimate victims of the predator's future monopoly prices will come to the aid of target firms. The prey may offer long-term contracts at a price which will be lower than the price the predator would charge if it obtained a monopoly (Easterbrook 1981, 270–271). In short, predatory pricing is a profitable strategy only if the monopoly profits from predation in the second stage of the predation process exceed the losses during the first stage of predation when prices were below costs. To make predation credible, there must thus be the possibility of recoupment, which precludes predatory pricing in markets that are relatively easy to enter.

Third, even if – because of the existence of entry barriers – the strict condition of recoupment is satisfied, predatory pricing is not necessarily the most profitable alternative. From a profit-maximising point of view, mergers may be a better alternative since the revenues to be gained during the predatory price war will always be less than those that could be obtained immediately through merger and will not be higher after the war is concluded (McGee 1958, 140). The latter point needs a qualification, however. Acquiring a competitor may be unlawful under the provisions on merger control, so that the purchase of a rival firm is ruled out as an option. If mergers are illegal, a predator will have to carry the price war to the bitter end, and this is more costly (both in terms of incurred losses and risk of being detected by antitrust authorities) than instigating a price war to drive down the purchase price of a rival (Saloner 1987). If there is a good chance that the merger will be cleared, the latter strategy may be the driving motive for predatory pricing. Indeed, mergers and predatory pricing need not be mutually exclusive. Predatory pricing or other predatory tactics could soften up a potential acquisition, making the prey more willing to deal or to lower the acquisition price.

Alongside these theoretical arguments aimed at emphasising the irrationality of predatory pricing, several empirical studies undertaken in the 1970s have contributed to increase the perception of the scarce occurrence and profitability of the practice. Besides McGee's assessment in relation to *Standard Oil*, studies that reviewed court cases found few instances of successful predation (Koller 1971). Other scholars emphasised that many of the alleged victims of predatory strategies had not suffered any harm and that there was no conclusive evidence showing the opposite (Elzinga 1970; Adelman 1966). All these considerations suggested that the predatory strategy should be regarded with great scepticism concerning its rationality, probability of success and frequency (OECD 1989).[68] As it was metaphorically synthesised by Judge Easterbrook, the occurrence of predatory pricing is akin to the appearance of dragons (Easterbrook 1981, 264). For others, it is as rare as white tigers or unicorns.[69]

If the Chicago School's arguments are accepted, the antitrust offence of predatory pricing may simply be forgotten. However, there are good reasons to think that predatory pricing can be entirely rational and the threat of it credible. In addition to the possibility of price discrimination making price wars less costly, two crucial assumptions of the Chicago analysis warrant careful consideration: free entry and perfect information. First, entry is rarely completely free. If barriers to entry (in particular, high sunk costs) exist, the dominant firm will be able to raise prices after eliminating competition. The extent to which super-normal profits can be extracted will be directly related to the height of the entry barriers. Even if entry barriers are low, the expectation of low profits due to vigorous competition in the market place will deter entry if the associated costs are seen as irrecoverable (Bishop and Walker 2010, 60). Second, and even more importantly, the Chicago theory holds only in markets characterised by perfect information. If this assumption is relaxed, it becomes possible to show that predatory pricing may be an entirely rational strategy. Under conditions of imperfect information, victims of predatory pricing will not easily receive financial aid in the capital market or convince customers, who are the ultimate victims of the predator's future monopoly prices, to support them. The prey may give a too optimistic picture of his chances of surviving the price war. Potential financial lenders, who are aware of this danger, may therefore ask a higher risk premium, disadvantaging the target firm. Long-term contracts between the prey and its customers may also be difficult to agree upon because of the high transaction costs involved (Martin 1993, 463). Therefore, contrary to what is assumed by Chicago scholars, financial markets and coalitions of customers will not always provide support to firms that are targets of predatory campaigns. This implies that predatory pricing cannot be ruled out as a rational strategy.

---

[68] Even today there is wide disagreement about the frequency of predation. The discussion is largely theoretical and few empirical analyses have been carried out. Regarding the latter, some authors believe that evidence on predation demonstrates that the conduct is frequent and not merely an occasional phenomenon (Vaheesan 2015). Other authors are more sceptical and do not generalise the results of the empirical studies, questioning the real-life cases advanced as proof of predation and the methods used to derive this conclusion (Kobayashi 2010).

[69] Federal Trade Commission, Hearing Before the Subcommittee on Consumer Protection, Product Safety, Insurance, and Data Security of the Senate Committee on Commerce, Science, and Transportation, 100th Cong. 29 (1987) (statement of Commissioner Mary Azcuenaga).

Game theory: predatory pricing as a rational strategy

Modern economic literature has relaxed the Chicago assumptions and clarified under what conditions predatory pricing may be a rational and profitable strategy (Ordover 1998). Stimulated by the growing number of observed instances of predation and the emergence of game theory providing the necessary tools to analyse complex strategic situations, the economic discipline has developed new theories of predatory pricing. In its early days, game theory seemed to provide support for the Chicago School's reasoning. Nobel prize winner Reinhard Selten developed a formal model showing that accommodating new entrants is a rational strategy for a dominant firm operating in several geographical markets; in equilibrium, threats of predation are not credible (Selten 1978). He called this a 'paradox' because logical game-theoretical reasoning did not seem to coincide with intuition and observations of reality. Later studies, however, showed that the paradox may be resolved by relaxing Selten's assumptions of perfect information on the prey's side and studying a finite number of markets. Predatory pricing can be rationalised for its demonstration effect, insulating the dominant firm from competition in all or some of the markets in which it operates. In a dynamic world of imperfect and asymmetric information, the predator seeks to influence the expectations of rivals by convincing them that continued competition or future entry into the market would be unprofitable.

Three main types of formal economic models have been constructed in which predatory behaviour emerges in equilibrium as a rational strategy for the predator: deep pocket models, signalling models and reputation models. All these models share a common feature: predation is a phenomenon that can be explained when there is imperfect information. The game-theoretical models do not mean that predatory pricing is widespread. The contribution to competition policy from these models is to recognise the strategic and dynamic nature of predation. They lead to the important insight that the traditional Chicago analysis is correct only under conditions of perfect information.

Deep pocket models (capital market imperfections)

The traditional deep pocket model contrasts a dominant firm having easy access to capital or able to cross-subsidise from other markets, where it meets relatively little competition ('deep pocket' or 'long purse'), and a rival facing tighter financial constraints. The former (the predator) can decrease prices below the level of the latter's variable costs and thus exhaust the financial resources of the prey, outlasting it from the market. If the losses of the price war can be recovered by monopoly profits afterwards, the deep pocket scenario shows predatory pricing as a feasible and rational strategy (Benoit 1984; Telser 1966). However, in game-theoretical terms, instigating a price war is not an equilibrium strategy since the informed prey will leave the market after the first signs of predation or not enter in the first place. In such circumstances, price reductions must not even be effectuated to deter rivals. More recent theoretical research has overcome this problem by relying on developments in the theory of finance discussing situations of imperfect information. In its newer version, the deep pocket models – or more appropriately, the capital market imperfection models – present predatory pricing as a rational and profitable strategy under equilibrium.

Deep pocket models rest upon imperfections in the capital market. Capital market imperfections are the consequence of principal-agent problems, for instance when lenders cannot observe the level of effort or risk chosen by borrowers. Under conditions of imperfect information, target firms will not receive funds or, at least, will face higher interest rates because the risk of bankruptcy is greater. Incumbents facing potential entrants may exacerbate existing capital market imperfections. Predatory pricing in the first period may impair the target firm's access to capital in the second period (LeBlanc 1996; Bolton and Scharfstein 1990). If the prey depends on outside financing (banks, shareholders, other financial institutions), capital providers must know that the victim's losses are due to predation and not to poor management or unfavourable market conditions. In addition, suppliers of financial capital will have only limited information about the prey's ability to survive a period of predatory pricing and about the predator's resources and the determination of its management to pursue a predatory strategy to the bitter end. In another model, it is shown that under imperfect information predatory pricing can raise rivals' costs by reducing their equity and hence raise their capital costs (Tirole 1988, 378). As a consequence, a predatory campaign by a dominant firm may cause rival firms to exit the market in order to escape from bankruptcy.

Reputation models

In reputation models of predatory pricing, the predator develops and maintains a reputation for preferring to fight entry (Kreps and Wilson 1982; Milgrom and Roberts 1982b). The reputation acts as an entry barrier because it leads potential entrants to the belief that entry would be vigorously resisted and so is unlikely to be profitable. Reputation motives for predatory behaviour are particularly important if the incumbent operates in many markets, because predation in one market can spill over into a reputation for aggressive

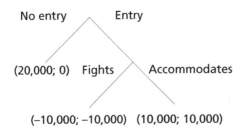

No entry   Entry

(20,000; 0)   Fights   Accommodates

(–10,000; –10,000)   (10,000; 10,000)

Figure 7.1 Reputation game: rational firm

responses against entry in all markets. The following example illustrates the game-theoretical reasoning (see Figure 7.1).[70] An incumbent monopolist owns a chain of stores in many towns and faces potential entrants in each town. The different towns make up separate geographical markets. In the first market, prior to the entry of competition the firm was making monopoly profits amounting to €20,000. Following entry it has the choice between price cutting to resist the entrant (deterrence strategy) or cooperating (i.e. accommodating the entrant). In the former case both the incumbent and the entrant will lose €10,000. In the latter case, when the potential entrant enters and the incumbent firm accommodates entry, both will make profits of €10,000 (see Figure 7.1).

Faced with these pay-offs, the entrant will enter and the incumbent will cooperate. The entrant believes at the start that the incumbent accommodates when the former enters. Clearly, a strategy to deter entry will not work in the final market. It would cost the incumbent a pay-off of €10,000 with no possibility of a later gain; thus the incumbent would certainly cooperate in the final market. Selten showed that, when this game is repeated a finite number of times, this outcome holds for each of the geographical markets. Selten called this a paradox because, he argued, in reality the incumbent firm would be much more likely to adopt a deterrence strategy from the beginning in the first market (Selten 1978). The main condition for this result is that the entrants know with certainty that the incumbent has an incentive to accommodate entry.

However, the outcome may be entirely different if the entrant is only slightly uncertain about the incumbent's pay-offs from predating or accommodating entry. There may be different types of incumbents. Most incumbents are rational and evaluate only the monetary returns from accommodating. A few,

---

[70] The example is based on Bishop and Walker (2002, 222–223).

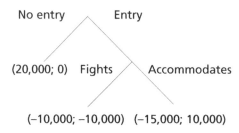

No entry   Entry

(20,000; 0)   Fights   Accommodates

(−10,000; −10,000)   (−15,000; 10,000)

Figure 7.2 Reputation game: irrational firm

however, may be aggressive: they may suffer a loss of face if they fail to carry out a threat and the profits from cooperating are not sufficient to make up for it. In the case of an irrational incumbent, the pay-offs in case of cooperating are different and the solution of the game will be that the incumbent predates and the entrant decides to stay out. An irrational incumbent, who wants to develop a reputation for aggressive responses to entry, may prefer losses if the negative consequences of not fighting outweigh the gains of accommodating the entrant. To the irrational incumbent, accommodating may cause a cost that, due to loss of face, amounts to €15,000. If the incumbent resists entry (since a loss of €10,000 is lower than a loss of €15,000), the entrant has a choice between losing €10,000 in case of entry and losing nothing if he stays out. Consequently, the entrant will stay out (see Figure 7.2).

With no possibility of recouping losses in the last market, a rational incumbent will cooperate in all markets. If the entrant in the penultimate market knows that he should not take the warning seriously, both competitors will again face each other in the last market. By contrast, an irrational and aggressive incumbent will adopt a stop-at-nothing approach to eliminate competition. The aggressive predator will also resist in the last market and the entrant, who knows this, will decide not to enter the previous markets. Given this result, rational incumbents as well may choose to predate in early rounds in order to deter future entry by making potential entrants think that they will have to face an aggressive incumbent. Entrants may thus be confronted with an apparently irrational incumbent who is mimicking the actions of the aggressive type. A key element of this argument is that a rational incumbent need not bear the full costs of predation in all markets, since entry will be deterred in some of them. In the example given, accommodating entry in ten markets brings the incumbent profits amounting to €100,000 (10 × €10,000). Predatory pricing in three markets (losses of 3 × €10,000 = €30,000) and being a monopolist in the other seven markets (gains of 7 × €20,000 = €140,000) leads to a higher profit of €110,000 (€140,000 − €30,000 = €110,000).

If the incumbent wants to develop a reputation for aggressive responses to competition, the entrant must be certain whether the incumbent is rational or not. Entrants observe the previous actions of the incumbent. When there is some uncertainty in the pay-offs, predation may be a sensible strategy for both rational and aggressive incumbents. Even a tiny amount of fear on the part of potential entrants that the incumbent might be aggressive could make it rational for incumbents of all types to fight entry to deter future entrants. Aggressive incumbents will predate because they suffer a loss of face if they fail to carry out a threat, but also rational incumbents may choose to predate in early rounds in order to deter entry by making potential entrants believe that they are aggressive incumbents (Baird, Gertner and Picker 1994, 178–183). Mimicking behaviour of an irrational firm may lead to higher profits. Whether predation is a successful strategy thus depends very much on whether the predator and the prey believe it is a successful strategy. Even though apparently irrational, predatory pricing may be rewarding if entry in a number of markets is prevented in some of them. In conclusion, the inability of entrants to distinguish different types of incumbents may deter entry and, contrary to what Chicago economists believed, predatory pricing may be a rational strategy.

Signalling models

Signalling models also lead to the conclusion that predatory pricing can be a profitable strategy. These models start from the assumption that the predator has an informational advantage over the prey and is, therefore, able to influence the target firm's expectations about future profits. It is possible that an entrant does not have complete information about the production costs of the predator or is unable to predict whether demand for his (new) product will be either high or low. Under such circumstances, a better-informed incumbent firm has an incentive to charge low prices. In this way, the predator signals that competing with him will not be profitable, perhaps by conveying false information that market demand is low or that he has lower costs than the prey. By signalling to rivals that the predator has low costs, firms may be induced to exit. If the predator signals its low costs, staying in or entering a market requires that the prey perceives the price as predatory and not as normal price competition.

Signalling models have been developed by Milgrom and Roberts, who assume better information about costs and market demand on the side of the predator (Milgrom and Roberts 1982a; see also Roberts 1986), and by Saloner, who shows that signalling may lower the acquisition costs of the target firm (Saloner 1987). Apart from the above assumption, these models also suppose that the less informed prey deduces the incumbent's information advantage from its price and output decisions and correctly interprets the predator's choices. Even if the latter assumption is not satisfied, predation will cause the prey's exit and, therefore, warrant antitrust scrutiny. Related game-theoretical approaches towards predatory pricing, which are known as signal-jamming models, assume no better information on the part of the predator but rather his ability to exert an impact on prices or demand which cannot be correctly observed by the prey (Fudenberg and Tirole 1986; Riordan 1985).

Behavioural approaches

Advocates of behavioural antitrust widely endorse the view that firms rely on predatory schemes much more often than believed by Chicago scholars. Predatory pricing is explained outside the rational profit maximisation framework, by relying on insights from (experimental) psychology. Different from rational choice theory, these studies explain the conduct of firms as the result of subjective choices made by individuals who bear responsibilities in taking business decisions. Cognitive limitations (heuristics and biases) of company directors may help in explaining firms' behaviour, also when this includes illegal practices under the antitrust laws.

Harry Gerla was among the first authors to make use of behavioural insights in explaining predatory conduct. His analysis emphasises that (individuals taking decisions within) companies are affected by a loss aversion bias (see Chapter 2, Box 2.2). Since firms perceive disproportionately negative effects from losses, they are disposed to engage in risky predatory behaviour to limit the harm suffered. As a result, dominant firms fearing a reduction of their market shares may resort to predation in an attempt to avoid suffering this loss (Gerla 1985). Other scholars rely on empirical evidence to suggest that managers of dominant firms are disposed to adopt a risky predation strategy under different scenarios: when their company faces a high (or average) probability of suffering losses or when the firm is incurring a persistent reduction of its market share. This outcome is also likely when the high risks or the achievement of short-term losses occur in a competitive environment that does not rationally permit to predict a sufficient likelihood of recoupment (Tor 2003; Guthrie 2003).

Behavioural economics also claims that the directors' choices are often affected by cognitive biases, which make firms more likely to engage in predation. Several authors have pointed out that managers are subject to an optimism bias, which leads them to overestimate the success of the predatory campaigns and make them persist in these strategies, even when it is clear that they cannot be profitable (Stucke 2012; Leslie 2010). Moreover, bounded rationality may equally cause preys to overestimate the real risks associated with predation, discouraging them from efficiently addressing this conduct. Finally, the confirmation bias may affect the judiciary. Due to the impact exerted by the Chicago school, judges may underestimate the risks and the chances of successful predation and, consequently, reject antitrust liability of the firms engaged in predatory pricing. Even though the literature on behavioural antitrust is expanding in recent years, it has not yet been able to successfully permeate antitrust practice. Behavioural antitrust has been criticised both from a theoretical point of view and also for its lacking consistency on empirical grounds (Van den Bergh 2013; Wright and Stone 2012).

7.4.2   US antitrust law

Although no federal statute expressly outlaws predatory behaviour, US antitrust law entails different standards of liability applying in predation cases. First, the conduct may infringe Section 2 of the Sherman Act if it is undertaken by a dominant firm in order to acquire or maintain market power in a relevant market. Second, predation may violate Section 1 of the Sherman Act when it is jointly pursued through a collusive agreement between competitors that results in an unreasonable restraint of trade. Finally, the conduct may fall under the forms of price discrimination prohibited by the Robinson–Patman Act.[71]

Notwithstanding the many causes of action and the impressive literature on predation, there is not a significant track record of cases in the long US antitrust history. This is due mainly to the impact exerted by the Chicago School on US courts. Originally, predatory pricing cases were infrequent (*Standard Oil*[72] being a noticeable exception) until after the passage of the Robinson–Patman Act in 1936. According to the latter Act, discriminatory price cutting by large inter-state sellers injuring small local businesses was made virtually *per se* unlawful. The most dramatic example of the strong enforcement efforts in the old days of US antitrust law is the *Utah Pie* case.[73] The plaintiff sold frozen pies and had over 65% market share in one regional market. Three national firms entered into that market and constantly sold at lower prices than in other regional markets. Even though during a period of four years Utah Pie's sales and profits increased considerably, its market share fell to about 45%. The Supreme Court held that a firm operating in two or more markets cannot engage in price competition in one of those markets without

---

[71] 15 U.S.C. § 13(a).
[72] *Standard Oil Co. v. United States*, 221 U.S. 1 (1911).
[73] *Utah Pie Co. v. Continental Baking Co.*, 386 U.S. 685 (1967).

doing so in all. The *Utah Pie* decision was heavily criticised for not considering consumers' interest in low prices (Elzinga and Hogarty 1978; Bowman 1968).[74] More generally, at least until 1975, the legal standard used by the courts to infer predation was based on the finding of two elements: a structural requirement of market power and the unfair use of the pricing policy with the intention to exclude rivals (Brodley and Hay 1981). If they were found, the courts condemned the defendant without devoting particular care to the relationship between costs and prices (Giocoli 2013).

The enforcement climate changed radically with the publication of the seminal Areeda–Turner article in 1975. Their rule suggesting the illegality of prices below average variable costs (used as a proxy for marginal costs) had an immediate and dramatic impact on the courts. In the five years following the publication of this article no plaintiff prevailed. Given the latter effect and the difficulties of cost determination, the courts augmented the Areeda–Turner rule with other factors, including market structure and intent. While there were variations, most courts held that a price below average variable costs (AVC) was presumptively unlawful, while a price above average total costs (ATC) was conclusively lawful. A price falling between both benchmarks was presumptively lawful, but the presumption could be rebutted by evidence of intent and market structure.

In the 1980s Chicago analysts gained a noticeable influence upon American case law on the subject of predatory pricing. In the *Matsushita* case, which was based on Section 1 of the Sherman Act, US manufacturers of consumer electronic products accused Matsushita of combining with other Japanese manufacturers to monopolise the American market through predatory pricing. The Supreme Court quoted a number of publications by disciples of the Chicago view in support of its rejection of predatory pricing as a rational (i.e. profit-maximising) economic strategy.[75] The Supreme Court emphasised that a campaign of predatory pricing can be rational only if, after the elimination of the target, there remains sufficient market power to raise prices and thus generate additional income. Given that it was improbable that the purpose of the predatory pricing could be achieved, the majority concluded that the firms 'competed for business rather than to implement an economically senseless conspiracy'.[76] In *Matsushita*, the Supreme Court

---

[74] In the end, the Robinson–Patman Act turned out to be an ineffective instrument for protecting competitors. Utah Pie went bankrupt in 1972 because of poor management (Elzinga and Hogarty 1978).

[75] The Court claimed that 'There is a consensus among commentators that predatory pricing schemes are rarely tried, and even more rarely successful'; see *Matsushita Elec. Indus. Co. v. Zenith Radio Co.*, 475 U.S. 574, 598 (1986).

[76] *Ibid.*, at 597–598.

majority shared the Chicago view and expressed its scepticism on the rationality of predation, also questioning its plausibility. Furthermore, the opinion argued that, in order for the alleged conduct to be profitable, the defendant would have to recover its losses through cartel pricing. This possibility was considered unlikely, given the inherent instability of collusive agreements.[77] The requirement of recoupment was formulated a few years later by Judge Frank Easterbrook in assessing another case of predation.[78] Since then, the *Matsushita* reasoning and the proof of recoupment have represented the characterising elements of US case law.

The US Supreme Court analysed predatory pricing again in the iconic *Brooke Group* case.[79] This judgment represents the Supreme Court's most important predatory pricing decision in modern times. The alleged predation occurred in response to the plaintiff's introduction of non-branded, low-cost cigarettes. The defendant, who had only a 12% market share, introduced its own, similar non-branded cigarettes and undersold its rival in a series of ever-steeper price cuts. For 18 months it held prices below AVC, thus sustaining losses of millions of dollars. At the end of this period, the plaintiff raised the price and the price war came to an end. The Supreme Court rejected the possibility of predatory pricing. Since the defendant was relatively small, predation could occur only through the joint action of the leading firms engaged in oligopolistic price coordination. The latter was considered implausible given the market conditions on the oligopolistic manufacturers' market.

Importantly, the Supreme Court specified in *Brooke* the two necessary requirements to prove a predatory pricing allegation: (i) plaintiffs must prove that the defendant has charged prices below some appropriate cost benchmark; and (ii) there must be a 'dangerous probability' (under Section 2 of the Sherman Act) or a 'reasonable possibility' (under the Clayton Act and the Robinson–Patman Act) of a sufficiently high probability of recoupment. As to the former, the Court did not clearly specify how costs have to be measured. In the majority opinion's terminology, a price cannot be predatory unless it is below 'some measure of cost' or even 'some measure of incremental cost'.[80] Concerning the proof of recoupment, the Court used the *Brooke* case to impose this requirement for all predatory pricing claims falling under Section 2 of the Sherman Act. More precisely, the plaintiff must prove that the predator will be (or has been) able to raise price above the competitive level

---

[77] 475 U.S., at 590–592.

[78] *A.A. Poultry Farms, Inc. v. Rose Acre Farms, Inc.*, 881 F.2d 1369, 1399–1401 (7th Cir. 1989).

[79] *Brooke Group Ltd. V Brown & Williamson Tobacco Corp* 509 U.S. 209 (1993). It may be noted that Robert Bork argued the case before the Supreme Court on behalf of Brown & Williamson, the prevailing defendant.

[80] *Ibid.*, at 222.

(the so called 'recoupment capability') and that such increase will be (or has been) sufficient to compensate the predator for its predatory investment (the so called 'recoupment sufficiency'). In addition, in order to prove the actual or prospective profitability of predation, the plaintiff must demonstrate that the structure of the market makes recoupment possible. This implies taking into account whether the predator can absorb the market shares of the prey, the existence of entry barriers and the degree of concentration in the market. Clearly, the *Brooke* decision has attributed a central role to the recoupment requirement: it considers this element as the ultimate object of an unlawful predatory scheme, since it represents the means through which the predator is able to profit from predation.[81]

Recently, the Supreme Court relied on the *Brooke* framework to assess the *Weyerhaeuser* case,[82] which concerned predatory bidding allegations. The defendant had been found guilty by lower courts to have made a predatory buying of an input (alder logs). It purchased about 65% of the goods available in the region by bidding up its price in order to exclude the rival firm, Ross-Simons, from the market. The Supreme Court reversed the Ninth Circuit's verdict, stating that the two practices – predatory pricing and predatory bidding – have to be considered 'analytically similar'. Hence, the two-pronged Brooke test must be applied also in relation to predatory bidding claims. The Supreme Court's judgment has been criticised because the defendant (Weyerhaeuser) occupied only a monopsonistic position in the acquisition of inputs and was subject to fierce competition in the downstream market (with a 3% market share in the domestic market of the output). In addition, the analogy between predatory pricing and predatory bidding has caused scepticism among commentators, who noted that successful monopsony predation is probably as unlikely as successful monopoly predation (Blair and Lopatka 2008; Hylton 2008).

To conclude, the requirements defined by the Supreme Court in *Brooke*, paired with the opinion in *Matsushita*, testify as to the huge impact of the Chicago School on the adjudication of predatory conduct (Elzinga and Mills 2014). By making recoupment a constitutive element of predation, the Court has put on plaintiffs a burden of proof that is particularly difficult to satisfy. It is not accidental that, from 1993 to 2000, no plaintiff won a predation case at the federal court level (Bolton, Brodley and Riordan 2000, 2258–2259). In the following years, few predation cases were successful, thus making

---

[81] The Court stated that 'The plaintiff must demonstrate that there is a likelihood that the predatory scheme alleged would cause a rise in prices above a competitive level that would be sufficient to compensate for the amounts expended on the predation, including the time value of the money invested in it', *ibid.*, at 225–226.

[82] *Weyerhaeuser Co. v. Ross-Simons Hardwood Lumber Co.*, 549 U.S. 312 (2007).

predatory pricing a *de facto* legal practice in the US. This outcome has often been justified as it helps reducing the risks and effects of false positives that harm consumer welfare. Furthermore, the ability for the dominant firm to recoup its losses represents a proxy for inferring whether the company would have undertaken a predatory price-reduction strategy. US courts are keen to believe that, whenever the likelihood of recoupment is missing, it is unlikely that companies will start a predatory campaign (Leslie 2013, 1708). The result is that courts and agencies often dismissed allegations of predation, precisely because the plaintiffs failed to meet the burdensome proof of recoupment. The assessment standard emerged in *Brooke* has often been applauded by the agencies (Antitrust Modernization Commission 2007)[83] but it has also fuelled the criticism that the Supreme Court's requirements represent an excessive burden to evaluate the anti-competitive nature of price cuts (Vaheesan 2015; Leslie 2013; Kirkwood 2008). Finally, it is noteworthy that the game theoretic approaches have been neglected in the US courtrooms, not at least because of their difficult judicial administrability and practical implementation (Giocoli 2013; Hovenkamp 2005, 159).

7.4.3 EU competition law

The first predation case under EU competition law involved the strategy implemented by Akzo, a dominant supplier of benzoyl peroxide, against its rival ECS in the UK. Akzo granted selective, high discounts to the major customers of ECS, in order to incite ECS to withdraw as a supplier from the plastics market.[84] To conclude in favour of predation in breach of Article 102 TFEU, the EU Commission heavily relied on the proven intent of Akzo to eliminate ECS and also pointed to previous predatory episodes (the elimination of another competitor, Scado, after which Akzo raised prices again). Both assessments were based solely on internal documents of Akzo. The Commission did not refer to the Areeda–Turner test (see section 7.4.2) and refrained to define a criterion to assess when prices had to be considered predatory, suggesting that even prices higher than ATC could have been abusive.

---

[83] See Antitrust Modernization Commission, Report and Recommendations, April 2007, 89, where the Supreme Court's opinion in *Brooke* is applauded for being 'clear, predictable in application and administrable'.
[84] ECS/AKZO [1985] O.J. L374/1. The case can be summarised as follows. Akzo was the major European producer of organic peroxides, one of which benzoyl peroxide, was used as a flour additive in the United Kingdom and Ireland. There were three large buyers (flourmills) of roughly comparable size with a combined market share of 85%, next to a number of smaller flourmills. Most sales of organic peroxide were in the European plastics market where Akzo was a dominant supplier. ECS, a British firm, which was initially one of Akzo's customers, began to produce benzoyl peroxide for its own use and, later on, started to expand into the plastics market. Akzo responded with threats of overall price reductions and price cuts targeted at ECS's main customers in order to induce its rival to exit the plastics sector.

On appeal the CJEU defined both the criteria to establish predation as well as, more generally, the conceptual framework to assess predation cases, which has been in use since then. Next to correcting the classification of some costs (by qualifying as fixed some costs that the Commission had identified as variable), the CJEU specified the cost-based criteria to establish an abuse of dominant position. The two-tier test set out by the CJEU relies on two cost criteria: average variable costs (AVC) and average total costs (ATC). First, it states that an abuse of dominant position must be presumed once prices fall below the level of AVC. According to the Court's reasoning, a firm in a dominant position will always suffer losses if it charges such prices and it has an interest in doing so only if it aims at excluding competitors. Later, it has been clarified in *France Télécom* that the presumption can be rebutted if other reasons justify pricing below AVC.[85] Nevertheless, rebutting this presumption is very difficult in practice.[86] Second, the test developed by the CJEU implies that prices higher than AVC but lower than ATC must be considered unlawful if they are part of a strategy to eliminate competitors. According to the CJEU, such prices can exclude from the market firms that are just as efficient as the dominant firm but do not possess sufficient financial resources to enter a price war.[87] Once prices are higher than AVC but lower than ATC, it is not presumed that they are predatory but it is necessary to adduce supplementary evidence to establish incontrovertibly the existence of a strategy aimed at the exclusion of competitors.

The proof of exclusionary intent has appeared to be a complex task and poses serious difficulties to both the European Commission and other plaintiffs. It is far from easy to determine the strategic motivations of a firm in a dominant position in a market where a plurality of subjects operate. To start with, the intent to exclude competitors through a pricing policy constitutes a natural aim for companies operating in competitive markets. In this regard, the CJEU has clarified that distinguishing between lawful and unlawful intent requires to rely on 'sound and consistent evidence', which can be direct or indirect.[88] Usually, direct evidence is substantiated through internal documents, for example information exchanges between the management that clearly show a predatory strategy. In *Akzo*, for instance, the intent was inferred from records of meetings between Akzo and ECS directors that showed the Akzo threats against its rival. In *France Télécom*, the Commission relied on internal documents that indicated a plan to pre-empt the broadband market to prove

---

[85] Case C-202/07, *France Télécom v. Commission* [2009] ECR I-2369, at para. 109.
[86] See the Opinion of AG Mazák of 25 September 2008 in Case C-202/07 P France *Télécom v. Commission*, at para. 95.
[87] Case 62/86 *AKZO v. Commission* [1986] ECR 1503, at paras 71–72.
[88] Case T-83/91 *Tetra Pak International v. Commission* [1994] ECR II-755, at para. 151.

the intent to exclude competitors in the ADSL market.[89] Indirect evidence is often based on an analysis of the market conditions and the position of the dominant undertaking and its competitors in the market.[90] In *Tetra Pak II* (see section 7.3.3), where directly incriminating evidence was not available, the General Court clarified that the exclusionary intent can be derived from a number of convergent factors: the duration of the period in which the losses were incurred, their amount and the firm's strategy to sell products at a loss only in some geographical areas.[91] Generally, the decisional practice has displayed a wide (for some scholars, excessive) discretion concerning the type of evidence used to prove the exclusionary intent. Some scepticism is justified: it is sufficiently known that firms tend to exaggerate in their own documents the success of their destruction campaigns. A rule based on proven improper intent is often a function of luck and of the defendant's legal sophistication: firms with executives sensitive to antitrust problems will not leave any documentary trail of predatory intent. Hence, applying the *Akzo* rule will often boil down to a discussion of indirect evidence.

The CJEU had the opportunity to reconsider the recoupment element in *Tetra Pak II*.[92] In the latter case, the Commission concluded that the company had implemented a predatory conduct in the sale of non-aseptic cartons in the Italian market by fixing prices below AVC. Tetra Pak challenged the Commission's findings before the General Court and the CJEU, relying on the economic theory accepted in US case law. In particular, the firm complained that the Commission had found a predatory behaviour without proving that there was a reasonable prospect of subsequently recouping the losses incurred in the first predation phase. This line of argument was rejected by the CJEU, which held that the Commission has no obligation to prove the likelihood of recoupment. The Court emphasised that 'in the circumstances of the case'[93] it was not appropriate to require further proof of the ability for the company to recover its losses. Rather, in accordance with the assessments made by the Commission, the conduct had to be outlawed as it posed the risk to eliminate competitors. However, since the CJEU had narrowed down the recoupment requirement to the specific circumstances of the case, it was argued that the Court had left open the possibility to change its approach over time. Also, in *Compagnie Maritime Belge*, the Advocate General had argued that the proof of recoupment represents a central element of the predation

---

[89] Case C-202/07, *France Télécom SA v. Commission* [2009] ECR I-2369.

[90] See Guidance Paper, at paras 20, 65–66, where the Commission has enlisted what has to be considered has 'cogent and convincing evidence', specifying the factors that it takes into account to operate such assessment.

[91] Case T-83/91 *Tetra Pak International v. Commission* [1994] ECR II-755.

[92] Case C-333/94 P, *Tetra Pak International SA v. Commission* [1996] ECR I-5951.

[93] *Ibid.*, at para. 41.

test.[94] However, in the most recent *France Télécom* case (see the discussion in Box 7.5), both the General Court and the CJEU have excluded any interpretative doubts by confirming that the recoupment test is not a condition or part of the predatory pricing test.[95]

The *Akzo* test has been embraced by the Guidance Paper. The European Commission does not make any reference to the possibility of recoupment as a part of the determination of predation. This does not mean that the EU competition agencies do not carry out any assessment on the possibility that the dominant firm may eventually recover its losses. The analysis of dominance (including an assessment of entry barriers) takes into account the prejudice that the conduct may cause as a result of increased market power. However, the administrative practice and the case law do not require proof that the losses suffered in the first phase of predation may be recouped in order to find an abuse under Article 102 TFEU. Compared with the case law, the Guidance Paper mentions different cost benchmarks that the Commission is likely to use in assessing the losses deliberately incurred by the dominant firm in pursuing the predatory conduct. These are average avoidable costs (AAC) and long-run average incremental costs (LRAIC) rather than AVC and ATC. The failure to cover AAC indicates that the dominant firm is sacrificing its short-term profits and that an equally efficient competitor cannot serve the customers without incurring a loss.[96]

From a Comparative Law and Economics perspective, the EU case law on predation is very different from its US counterpart as a result of its refusal to take on board relevant economic insights. The focus is put on the first phase of predation, i.e. the reduction of prices below some level of cost, and lack of recoupment does not represent a real concern. The weakest point both in the European Commission's reasoning and in that of the CJEU is that in neither of them was it adequately demonstrated that the so-called 'predatory pricing' could have succeeded. Even though Chicago economists may have underestimated the danger of predatory pricing (as was later shown in game theoretical analyses), economists generally agree that any approach to the identification of predation must begin with an analysis of whether predation is a feasible strategy. The facts of the *Akzo* case do raise some serious doubts as to the feasibility of the alleged predatory pricing campaign. After a two-year price war, the market share of ECS decreased from 35% to 32%;

---

[94] Opinion of Advocate General Fennelly, *Compagnie Maritime Belge* [2000] ECR I-1365, at para. 136.
[95] Case T-340/03, *France Télécom SA v. Commission* [2007] ECR II-117, at paras 224–228; Case C-202/07, *France Télécom SA v. Commission* [2009] ECR I-2369, at para 110.
[96] See *Guidance Paper*, at paras 26–27.

in the same period the share of Akzo increased only by 2%.[97] The withdrawal of ECS and the potential recoupment must be doubted because of low entry barriers (Rapp 1986) and the possibility of the large buyers in the oligopolistic market to elaborate a counterstrategy aiming at keeping ECS in the market. To safeguard their discounts in the long run, large buyers could have entered into long-term contracts with ECS (Utton 1986, 113). Taking into account these facts, the only indisputable conclusion seems to be that Akzo was guilty of behaviour aiming at causing commercial harm to ECS. There is also an alternative explanation of the Akzo case, which explains the facts as the breakdown of a cooperative oligopoly (Phlips and Moras 1993). If undertakings in dominant positions can be accused of abusing their power merely when they put competitors at a disadvantage, Article 102 TFEU will outlaw much more than anti-competitive predatory pricing.

Box 7.5: The *Wanadoo* case:[98] is recoupment a precondition to a finding of predation?

In 2003, the European Commission imposed a fine of €10.35 million on France Télécom for having abused its dominant position (through its 72% owned subsidiary, Wanadoo) by charging predatory prices in the market for ADSL-based internet access services. The Commission concluded that Wanadoo had been offering its ADSL services at prices below AVC between March 2001 and August 2001 and at prices approximately equal to AVC but below ATC between August 2001 and October 2002. At that time, the supply of high-speed internet access was an emerging market and the conduct was held abusive for impeding France Télécom's competitors access to the market. In assessing the case, the Commission undertook an analysis of the recoupment issue, even though noting that it was not obliged to do so. Looking at the market structure and at the economic literature, the Commission concluded that 'the recoupment of losses is rendered plausible in the present case by the structure of the market and the associated revenue prospects'.[99] In making this assessment, the Commission revealed its commitment towards a More Economic Approach. Clearly, this was an attempt to make the proof of recoupment a requirement under Article 102 TFEU.

Conversely, both the General Court and the CJEU followed the traditional formalistic approach. In assessing the case, the General Court fully relied on the precedents and held that 'it was not necessary to establish in addition proof that [Wanadoo] had a realistic chance of recouping its losses'.[100] On appeal, France Télécom claimed, contrary

---

[97] Case IV/30.698 ECS/*Akzo Chemie* [1985] O.J. L 374/1, at paras 91–94.
[98] Case C-202/07 P, *France Télécom v Commission* [2009] ECR I-2369.
[99] Case COMP/38.233, *Wanadoo Interactive*, Commission Decision, 2003 O.J., at para. 336.
[100] Case T-340/03, *France Télécom v Commission*, [2007] ECR II-107, at para. 227.

to the Commission's interpretation, that the case law required proof of a possibility of recouping losses and that the General Court had failed to provide adequate reasoning for the conclusion that the proof of recoupment was unnecessary. Interestingly, Advocate General Mazák was persuaded by this argument and rejected the approach of the General Court in relation to the recoupment issue. He argued that 'the case law requires the possibility of recoupment of losses to be proven.'[101] Consequently, in his view, 'the Court of First Instance failed to explain why it considered that proof of the possibility of recoupment of losses was not necessary in the light of the specific facts of the instant case.'[102] According to the Advocate General's interpretation, the conclusions of *Tetra Pak II*[103] on the unnecessary proof of recoupment were related to the specific circumstances of the case and could not be considered as a general rule. Notwithstanding these arguments, the CJEU dismissed the appeal, upholding the conclusion that the recoupment of losses does not represent a necessary precondition to a finding of predatory pricing.[104]

The judgments of the General Court and the CJEU in *Wanadoo* have clarified the case law's attitude towards the recoupment issue. However, they may be criticised for not being in line with the economic insights on predatory pricing, which stress that predation cannot be considered a rational economic behaviour if recoupment is not possible. As a reply to this criticism, it is usually argued that, under Article 102 TFEU, the requirement of recoupment is basically satisfied by the finding of dominance. However, the two assessments are rather different: dominance is assessed taking into account the historical market conditions, whereas proving the possibility of recoupment is a forward-looking exercise.

7.5   Price discrimination

The approaches of economists and lawyers towards price discrimination vary because of their different methodologies. Whereas economists analyse price discrimination from an economic welfare perspective and stress its potential efficiency benefits, lawyers are mostly sceptical about the distributional consequences and the 'unfair' advantage that price discrimination may cause to individual competitors. Hence, different views may be observed starting from the conceptualisation of the practice to the weight given to the effects produced in the market.

---

[101] Opinion of Mr Advocate General Mazák, delivered on 25 September 2008, in Case C-202/07 P, *France Télécom SA v Commission of the European Communities*, at para. 69.
[102] *Ibid.*, at para. 58.
[103] Case C-333/94 *Tetra Pak International SA v Commission* [1996] ECR I-5951.
[104] *Ibid.*, at 110–113.

7.5.1 Lessons from economic theory

Price discrimination occurs when identical products are sold at different prices under identical cost conditions or when non-identical but similar goods are sold at prices which are in different ratios to their marginal costs (Armstrong 2008; Posner 2001, 79–80; Stigler 1966, 299). At the same time, price discrimination in an economic sense occurs if identical units of a product are sold at a common price under different cost conditions. It must be stressed that different prices for identical or similar goods do not necessarily imply price discrimination. A bulk buyer obtaining large quantities of goods will be charged lower prices than a small-scale customer. This should not be labelled discriminatory pricing if cost savings (administrative costs, costs of transportation and other handling costs) can justify price differences. Moreover, to avoid hasty conclusions on the existence of price discrimination, persistent cost differences in marketing should also be taken into account. A final introductory remark is appropriate. The central concern of competition law must be systematic price discrimination by firms with substantial market power. Sporadic price discrimination is characteristic of the adjustment of competitive markets towards equilibrium.

Three conditions must be satisfied to enable a firm to engage in price discrimination and make it a profitable strategy (Scherer and Ross 1990, 489). First, the firm must possess some market power.[105] In perfectly competitive markets, firms have to take the market price as given and cannot practise price discrimination. It must be stressed that price discrimination requires power only over one's own prices, not necessarily a monopoly. Discriminatory prices on their own are not evidence of antitrust market power. All that is necessary is that the firm faces a negatively sloped demand for its products, as do all firms selling unique products (monopolistic competition). Second, the firm must be able to sort its customers as to be able to apply a higher price to those having a higher valuation. Therefore, the supplier must have information about the maximum prices (different groups of) consumers are willing to pay (i.e. information about the reservation prices). Clearly, the degree of information available to the firm in relation to its clients defines the form of discrimination which it can implement. If the undertaking has only imperfect information about the willingness to pay of its customers, it will not be able to practice perfect price discrimination. Third, arbitrage must be prevented. Buyers paying low prices must not be able to easily transfer the products to other groups of buyers paying higher prices, since this would

---

[105] However, according to some authors, price discrimination can occur even if market power is missing. See e.g. Levine (2002), who discusses the prevalence of highly differentiated price structures in competitive economic contexts.

prevent the producer from maintaining price differences between classes of buyers. Price discrimination will be a profitable strategy only if a firm is able to group consumers together around their different reservation prices and to prevent resale by low price consumers to high price consumers. For this reason, price discrimination often occurs for goods that cannot be stored (such as electric power) and for services (for example, in the sector of the liberal professions). Similarly, price discrimination will be possible if the resale of goods is virtually impossible because of transportation and transaction costs or in circumstances where companies are able to impose a resale ban in their sales conditions (Carlton and Perloff 1999, 279).

Following the seminal work of Pigou (1920), it is common to distinguish three types of price discrimination: first, second, and third degree. The common goal of the different types of discrimination is to 'capture as much as consumer surplus as possible' (Carlton and Perloff, 1999, 280). First-degree price discrimination occurs when each single unit of output is sold at the highest possible price. It is difficult to imagine a situation in which this type of price discrimination could be implemented, and it is generally considered to be of theoretical interest only (Motta 2004, 493).[106] Perfect price discrimination leads to an outcome which is allocatively efficient, since the firm is able to sell its entire output at prices covering marginal costs and each unit of output is sold at its maximum demand price (given that different consumers have different reservation prices). Under monopoly without price discrimination, some of the consumer surplus is transferred to the producer and there is a deadweight loss which causes a true decrease in welfare (see section 2.3.3). By contrast, if the monopolist can perfectly price discriminate, consumers with high reservation prices will be charged more than consumers with lower reservation prices. First-degree price discrimination thus eliminates the deadweight loss associated with single-price monopoly. If the goal of competition policy is the minimisation of the deadweight loss, first-degree price discrimination is clearly a good thing. Compared with the situation of a monopolised market where a single price is charged, consumers with higher reservation prices are offered additional output and consumers with lower reservation prices are better off since they can now afford to buy the good. However, consumer surplus is entirely captured and transferred to the monopolist. Even though the sum of producer and consumer surplus is maximised, this result does not eliminate other objections to monopoly, such as the distributional effects and the social costs resulting from rent-seeking (Posner 1975).

---

[106] An example of first-degree price discrimination might be '(...) something like a small-town doctor who charges his patients different prices, based on their ability to pay' (Varian 1987, 431).

Whereas first-degree price discrimination is mainly a theoretical case, both second- and third-degree price discrimination regularly occur in practice, since they require less information about demand. Second-degree price discrimination takes place when a firm sells different units of output for different prices, even though every individual buying the same amount of the goods pays the same price. Output is divided into successive batches that are sold for the highest price customers are willing to pay. Hence, prices differ across the units of the goods but not across people, so that some buyers enjoy a consumer surplus. Block pricing (i.e. charging a decreasing average price with increasing use), often practised by public utilities, or quantity discounts related to large purchases (for example, family packs sold in supermarkets) represent two forms of second-degree price discrimination. To increase welfare, block pricing may be encouraged if average and marginal costs decrease by expanding output. Consumer welfare can thus be increased, even though allowing greater profit to the company (Pindyck and Rubinfeld 1998, 381; id. 2017). Second-degree discrimination is likely to increase welfare if it allows firms to supply goods or services to specific groups of consumers, which would not have had the ability to purchase without price discrimination. However, its welfare effects must be assessed on a case by case basis, paying attention to whether price discrimination results in an increase or a decrease of total output.

Lastly, third-degree price discrimination occurs when a firm segregates consumers into distinctive groups characterised by different elasticities of demand that are explained by exogenous criteria such as location, age, sex or occupation. Different (groups of) buyers pay different prices, but every unit of output sold to a given buyer (or a given group) is sold at the same price. Thus, prices do not differ across the units of the good (as is the case under second-degree price discrimination) but between individual (or groups of) consumers. Third-degree price discrimination is the most common form of discriminatory marketing. It obviously requires that firms are able to identify and separate the market segments having different elasticity of demand. Firms charge different prices in different segments of their markets; deviations of prices from marginal costs will be highest in markets with the least elastic demand. In various industries, pricing above marginal costs is needed to recover fixed costs and provide incentives for firms to make investments in the future (Ridyard 2002). Examples of third-degree price discrimination permeate a large variety of industries, ranging from cement producers to record companies and law firms; they include student discounts, cheaper train tickets for aged people, cheaper theatre tickets for young customers, and the sale of identical or virtually identical products under different brands in various EU Member States. Clearly, the practice is not confined to dominant firms.

The welfare analysis of third-degree price discrimination is not as clear-cut as the above analysis of first-degree price discrimination. In a classic article, Schmalensee shows that the impact of third-degree price discrimination by a monopolist on welfare is indeterminate. Welfare may increase if price discrimination succeeds in increasing the output level, for example by allowing the firm to enter a new market segment. In general, however, unless a prohibition of price discrimination results in a substantial reduction in output, price uniformity will be superior to price discrimination (Schmalensee 1981). In non-monopolised markets, price discrimination may raise concerns about competition at the downstream level (for example, if retailers who are customers of a price discriminating supplier compete on the basis of different input costs) and predatory pricing (see section 7.4). However, most commentators agree that it must be possible for cost differences to be reflected in price differentials and that price discrimination may have beneficial effects in oligopolistic markets. Rigid oligopolistic price structures may be enlivened by secret rebates (Scherer and Ross 1990, 308). Secret price cuts are the Achilles' heel of tacit collusion. If price discrimination is prohibited, price discipline in oligopolistic markets may be tighter than it might otherwise have been. Apart from this beneficial effect, the welfare analysis of third-degree price discrimination in general leads to ambiguous results.

The ambiguity of the economic analysis also makes the results of the removal of price discrimination ambiguous. The most important lessons for competition law seem to be the following. First, price discrimination is not a phenomenon confined to firms with dominant market power and is as such not anti-competitive. From an efficiency perspective, intervention of competition authorities to guarantee price uniformity may be defended only if the firm engaged in price discrimination possesses substantial market power. Second, in fixed cost recovery industries, firms must be able to charge prices in excess of marginal costs, in order to keep incentives to invest intact. Third, if a result of the introduction of uniform pricing is that a large group of low-price consumers no longer receive supplies, price discrimination is preferable from a welfare point of view. It must be noted that uniform prices may have adverse distributional effects if lower income groups are forced to pay higher prices. To conclude, a *per se* prohibition of these practices, or conversely their lawfulness, cannot be justified on the basis of economic theory. Depending on the specific elements characterising the cases at hand, price discrimination may or may not generate economic benefits. The effects in terms of consumer welfare are ambiguous and can be fully assessed only with regard to single cases.

7.5.2 US antitrust law

Section 2 of the Clayton Act prohibits practices that are likely to cause price discrimination if their effect is the reduction of competition or the strengthening of monopolistic positions.[107] In 1914, at the time when the Clayton Act was enacted, its main target was to outlaw price differences that dominant companies practised in different geographical markets. They charged lower prices where there was greater competitive pressure and subsidised these prices with profits realised in other markets. In 1936, in the midst of the Great Depression, the Congress decided to strengthen the provisions on discrimination through the enactment of the Robinson–Patman Act.[108] The aim of the Congress was to protect small retailers from the tough competition by large chain stores. Because of their larger bargaining power, the latter were able to obtain better buying conditions than the smaller retailers. This enabled the chain stores to start price wars in downstream retailing markets that threatened the survival of small stores. The Congress intended to reduce the 'unfair' competitive advantage that the large retail chains held with respect to the traditional stores (Gifford and Kudrle, 2010). Until the early 1970s, the Robinson–Patman Act was enforced by the Federal Trade Commission when suppliers applied different prices to their customers, with the aim of protecting small retailers even when this came at the consumers' expenses. For this reason, the attempt to assess price discrimination under the Robinson–Patman Act has been labelled 'surely antitrust's least glorious hour' (Bork 1993, 382).

Since the mid-1970s, the enforcement of the Robinson–Patman Act has witnessed a progressive decline. The goal to protect individual competitors has been replaced by assessments focusing on efficiency and consumer welfare. Price discrimination is still challenged, but only when the practice embodies a predatory nature, subject to the antitrust rules on predatory pricing (see section 7.4.2). In contrast, US antitrust law no longer focuses on the exploitative abuse that price discrimination may cause. It recognises the freedom of the monopolist firm to set the price level, including the charging of 'high' prices in particular markets (OECD 2016b). The Robinson–Patman Act has become basically unenforced by the US antitrust authorities, with only one case taken by the FTC in the last 25 years. This outcome has recently induced

---

[107] Clayton Act, Ch. 323, § 2, 38 Stat. 730 (1914).
[108] 15 U.S.C., at paras 13–13a.

the Antitrust Modernization Commission to recommend its repeal (AMC 2007, 317).

7.5.3   EU competition law

Article 102(c) TFEU states that firms having a dominant position are prohibited to apply 'dissimilar conditions to equivalent transactions with other trading parties, thereby placing them at a competitive disadvantage'. For this prohibition to apply, four conditions have to be satisfied. First, the transactions have to be equivalent. In order to assess the equivalency, the product or service provided must be substitutable taking into account all relevant market factors.[109] The products or services have thus to be similar in terms of physical qualities or in a functional sense.[110] Moreover, the commercial transactions have to take place within a similar commercial context[111] and within a proximity in time. However, if substantial differences arise in terms of costs, quality and type of service provided, services are not equivalent.[112] Also the trading parties must be equivalent (i.e. comparable).[113] Second, whether or not trading conditions are dissimilar can be assessed by reviewing (i) the nature of the transaction; (ii) the differences in the nature of the products (or services) sold; and (iii) the cost of supply.[114] Third, a competitive disadvantage must be shown. Unfortunately, the assessment of this condition has been unclear in EU competition law. The case law clarified that the parties must be in competition among themselves, but several aspects concerning this condition (for instance, the proximity of such competition between favoured and disfavoured parties, the size and extent of the competitive disadvantage, and how it has to be evidenced) have received little consideration by the European Commission, thus leaving their exact interpretation without clear-cut answers (O'Donoghue and Padilla 2013, 789). Fourth, there may be objective justifications for the different treatment: for example, technical or commercial grounds, taxation or custom duties, transportation costs,

---

[109] Case IV/33.941 *HOV-SVZ/MCN* [1994] O.J. L 104/34, at para. 47. See also, for what concerns services, Case T-301/04, *Clearstream Banking AG and Clearstream International SA v Commission* [2009] ECR II-3155.

[110] See Case 27/76, *United Brands v. Commission* [1978] ECR 207, in which the CJEU recognised that the bananas had the same origin and were basically of the same quality. See also Case T-229/94, *Deutsche Bahn AG v Commission* [1997] ECR II-1689.

[111] Case C-95/04 P *British Airways Plc v. Commission* [2007] ECR I-2331; Case C-52/07 *Kanal 5 and TV 4 AB v Föreningen Svenska Tonsättares Internationella Musikbyrå (STIM) upa* [2008] ECR I-9275.

[112] Case 27/76 *United Brands v. Commission* [1978] ECR 207, at para. 302. See also the Opinion of Advocate General Jacobs in Case 395/87 *Ministère Public v. Tournier* [1989] ECR 521.

[113] Case C-62/86 *AKZO Chemie v. Commission* [1991] ECR I-3359.

[114] Cases IV/34.621 and IV/35.059 *Irish Sugar* [1997] O.J. L 258/1, at para. 138; Case 13/63, *Italy v Commission* [1963] ECR 165.

currency fluctuations and others. The burden of proof lies on the dominant company.[115]

Article 102(c) TFEU has been applied in relation to different categories of price discrimination: primary line injury, secondary line injury and geographical price discrimination. Primary line injury concerns discriminatory conduct undertaken by the dominant firm towards its customers, which may create exclusionary effects on its horizontal competitors. Two examples of discrimination falling in this category are the *Irish Sugar*[116] and *Compagnie Maritime Belge*[117] cases. In both cases, the dominant firms were condemned for having used selective discount schemes, with the aim of excluding their competitors from the market. Secondary line injury occurs when the dominant undertaking engages in price discrimination with its trading partners, thereby producing adverse effects for the latter. The effect of the discriminatory practice manifests itself between the dominant firms' customers in the downstream market. This kind of discrimination appears semantically more in line with the wording of Article 102(c) TFEU. Finally, geographical price discrimination occurs when the dominant firm sells the same product (or provides the same service) at a different price in various EU Member States. This form of discrimination has been often accompanied by various facilitating measures, aimed at reducing arbitrage. Geographical discrimination has been one of the major competitive concerns in the EU, since charging different prices in different Member States has been constantly perceived as an obstacle that damages the achievement of the internal market (Geradin and Petit 2006).

From an economic perspective, many criticisms can be formulated regarding the European case law on price discrimination. First, consumer harm is not sufficiently taken into account in applying Article 102 TFEU. As explained above, the different forms of discrimination may generate positive effects in terms of consumer welfare, for instance by giving some end users the ability to purchase goods or services that they could not acquire if prices were uniform. However, neither the Commission nor the EU courts have fully addressed the role of consumer harm as a necessary element in assessing price discrimination cases (Temple Lang 2012). The formulation of Article 102(c) TFEU makes no reference to consumers. It merely compels an analysis to verify if a trading party was treated differently from another. The expansive interpretation of the discrimination concept, which includes also primary

---

[115] Case 311/84 *CBEM v CLT and IPB (Télémarketing)* [1985] ECR 3261, at para. 26.

[116] See Case T-228/97 *Irish Sugar v Commission* [1999] ECR II-2969, in particular paras 140 and ff.

[117] Joined Cases C-395/96 P and C-396/96 P, *Compagnie Maritime Belge and Others v. Commission* [2000] ECR I-1365.

line injury, and the decision of the CJEU stating that it is not necessary to rigorously apply the conditions defined in the provision[118] have further diluted the need for a full economic analysis. Lastly, in *Tetra Pak II*, the CJEU has specified that the finding of an abusive conduct does not require evidence concerning the anti-competitive effects.[119] As a result, the focus in Article 102(c) TFEU cases is on the harm suffered by individual competitors and much less attention is given to the (indirect) damage suffered by consumers (O'Donoghue and Padilla 2013).

Second, EU institutions have failed to take into consideration defences based on objective justifications, specifically when grounded on economic arguments emphasising the pro-competitive effects of price discrimination. In *British Airways*,[120] the European Commission and the CJEU condemned the scheme of bonus commissions practised by the dominant firm to reward the travel agencies for the increase in sales with respect to those previously realised. This scheme was deemed illegal because different bonuses could be granted in cases where different travel agents realised the same amount of sales. The mechanism was aimed at enhancing the sales efforts of single agents, rewarding the increase generated in relation to the previous period and not on the absolute amount of sales made. The EU competition agencies did not take into account that the scheme provided a set of incentives for contract performance between the principal (British Airways) and the agents (the travel agencies). More generally, the Commission's decisional practice and the case law of the EU courts have not undertaken rigorous evaluations to verify the potential pro-competitive effects of price discrimination, particularly the increase in output and its impact on consumers.

Third, market integration seems to be pursued as a goal in itself without paying attention to the potential adverse effects of banning geographical price discrimination, in terms of both efficiency and equity. A well-known example is the classic *Chiquita* case.[121] United Brands Corporation (UBC) imported bananas from Latin America and was selling bananas under the brand name Chiquita to distributors at different prices in various Member States. This case offers a school example of third-degree price discrimination. First, UBC enjoyed sufficient market power to be able to control prices: the popular brand name Chiquita is a unique product feature. Second, consumers were

---

[118] Case 85/76 *Hoffmann- La Roche & Co AG v. Commission* [1979] ECR 461.
[119] Case C-333/94 P *Tetra Pak International SA v. Commission* [1996] ECR I-5951; Case T-83/91 *Tetra Pak International v. Commission* [1994] ECR II-575.
[120] C-95/04 P *British Airways v Commission* [2007] ECR I-2331; European Commission, Decision IV/D-2/34.780 *Virgin/British Airways* [2000] O.J. L 30/1.
[121] Case 27/76 *United Brands v. Commission* [1978] ECR 305.

grouped together around the highest price they were prepared to pay. The highest prices were charged in Belgium, Denmark and Germany, whereas the lowest prices were charged in Ireland. The Irish consumers were willing to pay less because of their lower incomes, whereas the Belgian, Danish and German consumers – because of their higher willingness and ability to pay – were charged higher prices. Lastly, arbitrage was prevented by prohibiting the distributors in various EU Member States from reselling green bananas. In sum, the economic requirements for third-degree price discrimination were neatly satisfied. Nevertheless, the prohibition of the practice under Article 102(c) TFEU may be criticised for its counterproductive effects on both allocative efficiency and distributive goals. Uniform prices, which may result from a prohibition of price discrimination, are at odds with the goal to increase trade across borders. Moreover, when a dominant firm must supply the goods at the same import prices and demand conditions in various Member States differ, the only result will be that retailers will discriminate. This may provoke non-integrated firms to make inefficient integration decisions in order to practise price discrimination without incurring antitrust penalties. Another objection relates to the concern for equity, which was adversely affected. In the *Chiquita* case, uniform prices came at the expense of a more equitable income distribution. Price uniformity implied price increases in a poor country and price decreases in richer countries. Poor consumers who could afford to buy bananas at lower prices may be unable to do so if prices are uniform, but higher (Geradin and Petit 2006; Bishop 1981).

7.6 Discounts and rebates

Discount and rebate schemes are widely adopted in consumer, intermediate or retail markets. In essence, they represent the sign of healthy and legitimate price competition. Even though the terms are often used as synonyms, discounts entail a reduction with respect to a price list, whereas rebates imply a refund that is granted retrospectively. Quantity discounts (or rebates) are granted if sales exceed a particular objective amount and are available to all customers. Loyalty (or fidelity) rebates are paid to customers in return for exclusivity requirements, i.e. the duty to buy a specific product from the dominant supplier. Target rebates are granted on the basis of the volume of purchases made during a given reference period, agreed upon with the supplier. When the target is reached, the discount is usually retroactively applied on all the purchases made during the reference period. Notwithstanding the differences between these categories, the common element is that all discounts and rebates are conditional upon achieving a certain purchasing target in relation to a specified period (Jones and Sufrin 2014, 455). At first blush, the competitive assessment of discounts and rebates set by dominant

firms should be positive because they can be perceived as instruments leading the dominant firm to share its profits with its commercial counterparts.
However, similarly to other price-reducing practices such as predatory
pricing, their antitrust evaluation in not an easy task. On the one hand, the
granting of discounts and rebates may be the result of the greater efficiency
enjoyed by dominant firms. On the other hand, they may be inspired by the
intent to exclude rival suppliers (market foreclosure) or to exploit trading
parties and consumers (Temple Lang 2012).

7.6.1   Lessons from economics

Economic analysis has highlighted the pro-competitive benefits associated
with fidelity rebates and the conditions under which they are likely to generate exclusionary effects harming the competitive process and ultimately consumers. However, similarly to other abusive practices, there is no clear rule
to assess *ex ante* whether loyalty discounts are pro-competitive and when,
conversely, they must be presumed unlawful. The dividing line between anti-
competitive conduct (likely to exclude the competitors and harm consumers) and a legitimate practice (able to generate efficiencies) is particularly
thin (O'Donoghue and Padilla 2013, 471).

Pro-competitive effects

Economic theory has advanced several reasons why companies, including
dominant firms, offer loyalty rebates to their customers, agents or distributors. First, such schemes may prove useful in solving moral hazard problems
that typically occur in the context of vertical relationships between producers
and distributors. Discounts granted to retailers may provide the necessary incentives to ensure that they increase their efforts in view of advertising, sales
promotions or other commercial terms, to the benefit of end users (Spector
2004). Second, further efficiencies are associated with the reduction of the
double marginalisation problem (compare section 6.2.2). If market power
exists both upstream and downstream, suppliers and buyers will apply their
mark-ups, which will lead to higher prices for consumers. In this respect,
loyalty discounts (but also target and quantity discounts) constitute a classical form of nonlinear pricing, implying that the price paid by a customer is
not strictly proportional to the quantity purchased. Economic models suggest that the profits for both parties can be increased, while the price paid by
consumers is lower than the one resulting if loyalty discounts are not adopted
(Kobayashi 2005).

Next to curing moral hazard and avoiding double marginalisation, two additional benefits can be mentioned. Loyalty discounts can help reducing hold-up problems between manufacturers and retailers when there is a risk that potential investments by producers (such as those in education) are subject to free-riding. The adherence to loyalty schemes may provide the optimal level of incentives for the manufacturer to make such investments, by ensuring that the retailer does not exploit these efforts to promote the sale of rival products (OECD 2002). Finally, fidelity discounts can increase welfare when products are characterised by high fixed costs. In such circumstances, producers must define a price level above marginal costs, which may result in prices much higher than consumers are willing to pay. Price discrimination may overcome this problem. By charging a lower price to consumers with a higher elasticity of demand and setting a higher price for the product units purchased by consumers with a lower demand elasticity, producers will be able to sell more units of their products (Elhauge 2009). In this way, output will increase by enabling consumers with a lower willingness to pay to buy goods.

Anti-competitive effects

There are many instances in which discounts and rebates may create exclusionary effects and harm consumers. First, loyalty discounts can be defined with the aim to exclude rivals of the dominant firm or to hamper their access to the market, with the consequence of reducing consumer choice and decrease total welfare (Tom, Balto and Averitt 2000). The anti-competitive effects result from the requirement that the grant of the discount is subject to the buyer's commitment to obtain its supplies primarily from the dominant firm. Loyalty discounts can thus display incentives that are likely to produce effects similar to exclusive purchasing arrangements. Under specific conditions, even equally efficient rivals may not be able to compete with the dominant firm. Loyalty discounts create switching costs whenever the customer intends to turn to other suppliers, leading to or increasing lock-in effects (Kobayashi 2005). If customers want to deal with other suppliers, they must forgo the fidelity discounts calculated retroactively on the entire volume of the purchases made and on those applied to the additional units to be acquired from the dominant undertaking.

Moreover, economic theory has shown that a suction effect may emerge. When a customer reaches a level of purchases close to the target, a marginal increase in sales leads to the application of the discount on all the units previously acquired. In this scenario, the incremental price (i.e. the price that the customer has to pay for the marginal units needed to reach the threshold) may be lower than both the list price and the discounted one. Economic studies suggest that the suction effect is likely to emerge whenever a customer willing to deal with a dominant firm's rival is facing the risk of losing the rebate for the units already purchased and/or the future ones. Put differently, loyalty rebates may create strong disincentives to purchase from more than one (dominant) seller. However, the economic literature emphasises that the anti-competitive effects arise only when several cumulative conditions are satisfied. The firm setting the discount scheme must have market power, which affects a considerable portion of its customers' requirements (inelastic demand). To contest the share of elastic demand (the contestable part), rival firms should award high discounts on limited quota, in order to compensate buyers for the loss of the financial benefits deriving from the dominant firm's loyalty discounts. In such circumstances, rivals could be forced to offer negative prices to reward buyers for the loss of the loyalty discounts. Next, the anti-competitive effect will be stronger if the dominant firm can rely on an assured base of sales, that is to say when the dominant company is certain that its customers are willing to buy the majority of their requirements from it. This raises additional difficulties for competitors: they will have to set even higher discounts for the incremental units of goods, above the defined threshold. Finally, when it is necessary to have a minimum efficient scale to enter or compete in the market, loyalty discounts are more likely to produce anti-competitive effects by not allowing rivals to offset the suction effect (Faella 2008).

7.6.2 US antitrust law

US courts have adopted a particularly cautious approach in the assessment of discount practices, crafting a presumption of substantial lawfulness for different types. The case law (mostly at the lower courts level) focuses mainly on two categories: loyalty/fidelity rebates and bundled discounts. In addition, the Department of Justice (DoJ) has recently filed a number of lawsuits[122] and expressed greater attention than before regarding forms of above-cost pricing (Department of Justice 2008, 58).

Loyalty discounts

Fidelity discounts can be scrutinised under Sections 1 and 2 of the Sherman Act, under Section 3 of the Clayton Act (which prohibits discount practices conditional upon an obligation not to purchase from competitors) or under

---

[122] Intel Corporation; Analysis of Proposed Consent Order to Aid Public Comment, 75 Federal Register 48338 (Aug. 10, 2010); *United States and State of Texas v. United Regional Health Care System*; Proposed Final Judgment and Competitive Impact Statement, 76 Federal Register 13209 (March 10, 2011).

Section 5 of the Federal Trade Commission Act (which aims at assessing unfair methods of competition).[123] In spite of the different legal standards, US courts have censured the use of loyalty discounts in only a small number of cases, mainly under the laws of predatory pricing and exclusive dealing. When the claims focused on price irregularities, the proceedings were to a large extent closed without finding any infringement. Importantly, the courts have considered the price reductions resulting from the granting of discounts as pro-competitive elements. In *Henry v. Chloride*, for instance, the Court of Appeal for the Eight Circuit stated that '(...) non-predatory price cuts are to be encouraged under the antitrust laws', pointing out that '(...) prices above average total cost are legal per se'.[124] Similarly, in *Concord Boat v. Brunswick*,[125] a case concerning loyalty discount programmes offered by Brunswick to boat builders to make them purchase its engines, the Court of Appeals reaffirmed that price rebates constitute the very essence of competition. In this perspective, it was argued that if the discounted price is higher than AVC '(...) the plaintiff must overcome a strong presumption of legality by showing other factors indicating that the price charged is anticompetitive'.[126] Since it has been recognised that discount practices entail a high pro-competitive potential, the general rule is that above-cost discounting is not anti-competitive.

Furthermore, also the evaluation of loyalty discounts under the test of predation has generally affirmed their lawfulness. In this regard, the US judges referred to the Supreme Court's decisions in *Brooke Group*[127] and *Matsushita*[128] (see section 7.4.2) and demanded the same degree of enforcement accuracy. Consequently, the US courts considered below-cost discounting rarely successful, requiring plaintiffs to satisfy the two-pronged test defined in *Brooke* as to below-cost pricing and recoupment. Usually, proceedings involving the adoption of the predation test were decided rejecting the plaintiffs' claims. A notable case, especially if compared with the identical EU proceeding closed with the imposition of a fine, is *British Airways*.[129] The Court of Appeals for the Second Circuit held that the agreements entered into with travel agents were lawful under both Section 1 and Section 2 of the Sherman Act. The loyalty rebates were assumed suitable to produce pro-competitive effects, recognising that a mechanism aimed at rewarding costumer loyalty promotes 'competition on the merits'. Additionally, it was underlined that the conduct

---

[123] It has to be noted that plaintiffs have occasionally looked for relief under the Robinson–Patman Act (15 U.S.C. Section 13). However, there are few precedents addressing the legality of rebates under this Act.

[124] *Henry v. Chloride, Inc.*, 809 F.2d 1334, 1344–1346 (8th Cir. 1987).

[125] *Concord Boat Corp. v. Brunswick Corp.*, 207 F.3d 1039 (8th Cir. 2000).

[126] *Ibid.*, at 1061, quoting *Morgan v. Ponder*, 892 F.2d 1355, 8th Cir. 1989.

[127] *Brooke Group Ltd. v. Brown &Williamson Tobacco Corp.*, 509 U.S. 209 (1993).

[128] *Matsushita Elec. Indus. Co. v. Zenith Radio Corp.*, 475 U.S. 574 (1986).

[129] *Virgin Atl. Airways Ltd. v. British Airways PLC*, 257 F.3d 256 (2d Cir. 2001).

had not caused adverse effects in terms of output reduction. In relation to the predation test, the Court held that it was not proven that the price was below the incremental costs, that there was a reasonable possibility of recoupment and that BA's incentive scheme had harmed consumers.[130]

Even the attempt to trigger antitrust liability under the law of exclusive dealing has not yielded different results, since courts revealed some reluctance to assimilate this type of discounts to exclusive purchasing agreements. In *NicSand*,[131] the Sixth Court *en banc* found that whenever discounts do not exhibit a predatory nature, they do not infringe the antitrust laws, even when they are aimed at fostering exclusive dealings. In this case, the Court concluded that the discount schemes had to be interpreted as entry-inducing conducts.[132] Identical findings were expressed by the District Court in *Natchitoches*,[133] by the Court of Appeals for the Ninth Circuit in *Allied Orthopedic Appliances*,[134] by the Court of Appeals for the Eight Circuit in *Southeast Missouri Hospital*[135] and, in 2016, by the Third Circuit in *Eisai Inc. v. Sanofi-Aventis U.S.*[136] In all the proceedings, the courts rejected the allegations that loyalty discounts – even when linked to high purchasing volumes – have exclusionary effects. The freedom of buyers to choose other suppliers was considered not affected by the schemes and a substantial market foreclosure was not considered proven.

Summing up, there has been only slight judicial success in attacking loyalty discounts as either predatory pricing or exclusive dealing. Practices leading to lower prices are generally assumed to benefit consumers. Furthermore, in the case of loyalty rebates it has been often found that they are likely to produce pro-competitive effects in the vertical relationships between producers and suppliers, thus mirroring the economic insights. Even though the Department of Justice has recently pointed out that these types of discounts can produce exclusionary effects under specific conditions, it has nonetheless been specified that the standard of assessment is the predation test (Department of Justice 2008). This conclusion is in line with the Supreme Court's ruling in *linkLine*, which has asserted the pivotal role of this method in the evaluation of all pricing practices.[137] Nevertheless, commentators

---

[130] *Ibid.*, at 265–269.

[131] *NicSand, Inc. v. 3M Co.*, 507 F.3d 442 (6th Cir. 2007).

[132] *Ibid.*, at 453–454.

[133] *Natchitoches Parish Hospital Service District v. Tyco International*, No. 05-12024 PBS, 2009 WL 4061631 (D. Mass., Nov. 20, 2009).

[134] *Allied Orthopedic Appliances, Inc. v. Tyco Health Care Group, LP*, 592 F.3d 991 (9th Cir. 2010).

[135] *Southeast Missouri Hospital v. C.R. Bard, Inc.*, 643 F.3d 608 (8th Cir. 2011).

[136] *Eisai Inc. v. Sanofi-Aventis U.S., LLC*, No. 14-2017, 2016 WL 2600321 (3d Cir. May 4, 2016).

[137] *Pac. Bell Tel. Co. v. linkLine Communications, Inc.*, 129 S. Ct. 1109 (2009).

conclude that the debate is not yet exhausted: neither on the definitive legal standard by which to review these practices, nor on the definition of the most appropriate test to identify whether the discounts are more likely to produce exclusionary effects (OECD 2016a; Dorsey and Jacobson 2015; Moore and Wright 2015).

Bundled discounts

Bundled discounts represent the second category that has received particular attention from the US courts. This practice occurs when different products are sold together in a package at a single price, granting the buyers a discount for the purchase. It is a common practice, which nevertheless raises some antitrust concerns. Although it is beneficial for consumers in terms of price reduction, the use of bundled discounts can lead to market foreclosure, even when the joint price of the goods is not predatory. Furthermore, this conduct is relatively new to the courts, which have expressed some uncertainty on how to proceed (Moore 2012). That said, it might be argued that bundled discounts do not benefit from the same presumption of legality enjoyed by fidelity discounts. In particular, in *LePage's*,[138] the Court of Appeals for the Third Circuit decided not to adopt the price test defined in *Brooke*, thus outlawing the bundled discounts for their ability to foreclose access to the market by rivals who did not produce a range of products comparable to that of the dominant firm.

More recently, several lower courts have questioned the *LePage's* standard, by adopting stricter criteria based on the predatory nature of the bundled price and refraining from taking action when this price was not below cost (Faella 2012). In the most recent *Cascade* case,[139] the Ninth Circuit affirmed the centrality of the predation criteria defined in *Brooke*, suggesting the application of a specific price test ('the discount attribution' test), and thereby adopting a more cautious attitude in the interpretation of these schemes (Weber 2009). For this reason, it is difficult to affirm the precise state of the art. The limited number of precedents concerning bundled discounts revealed disagreement among circuit courts as to when anti-competitive effects emerge. This uncertainty has raised a lively debate in an attempt to define the most appropriate (price) test (Moore 2012; Hovenkamp and Hovenkamp 2009).

---

[138] *LePage's v. 3M*, 324 F.3d 141 (3d Cir. 2003).
[139] *Cascade Health Solutions v. PeaceHealth*, 515 F.3d 883 (9th Cir. 2008).

7.6.3   EU competition law

In EU competition law, the treatment of discounts and rebates has been characterised by marked legal formalism. These practices have been evaluated without paying particular attention to the effects that they are likely to produce. Originally, the European Commission and the CJEU distinguished between quantity rebates and loyalty discounts. The former were perceived as non-discriminatory and legal. Conversely, loyalty discounts were assimilated to exclusive purchasing agreements used by the dominant undertaking, with the aim to exclude rivals. Loyalty discounts were considered abusive and the ability of companies to successfully invoke objective justifications was limited. The different legal treatment of quantity and loyalty discounts led dominant firms to adopt increasingly complex discount schemes – developing hybrids of the previously mentioned typologies – to escape from the prohibition of Article 102 TFEU. For this reason, the Commission and the CJEU have progressively tightened the assessment of discount schemes, on the assumption that they represent instruments to enhance customer loyalty. To this end, EU courts have often used the concepts 'loyalty-inducing' or 'fidelity-building' in relation to discounts schemes that originally did not fit within the fidelity rebates category (Jones and Sufrin 2014, 456).

Quantity discounts versus loyalty discounts

Quantity discounts are presumptively legal. Although the case law has not explicitly and consistently clarified the reasons and (more importantly) the exact conditions under which they benefit from a favourable treatment, it may be concluded that quantity discounts do not constitute an abuse when they reflect economies of scale, cost savings and other efficiencies.[140] In particular, the European courts agree that this category of discounts is not fidelity inducing.[141] Since it is difficult for the sales thresholds defined by the dominant firm to match the total requirements of different customers, quantity discounts will not induce a strong loyalty. In most cases, these discounts are not individualised but based on objective amounts offered on equal terms to all customers. If they are not discriminatory, they can hardly generate exclusionary effects. With the exception of the *Michelin II* case, in which the abusive character was found on account of the long duration of the discounts and their loyalty inducing character,[142] quantity rebates were declared legal.

---

[140]   Case T-203/01 *Michelin v. Commission* [2003] ECR II-4071 ('Michelin II'), at para. 58.

[141]   Case 322/81 *Nederlandsche Banden-Industrie-Michelin v. Commission* [1983] ECR 3461, at paras 71–72; Case 85/76, *Hoffmann-La Roche & Co. AG v. Commission* [1979] ECR 461, at para. 90.

[142]   Case T-203/01, *Manufacture Française des Pneumatiques Michelin v. Commission* [2003] ECR II-4071.

Their lawfulness was recognised in *Hoffmann-La Roche*,[143] *Michelin I*[144] and more recently in *Solvay*[145] and *Post Denmark II*.[146]

By contrast, fidelity rebates are generally held unlawful. In the seminal *Hoffmann-La Roche* case, the CJEU stated that fidelity rebates granted by a dominant firm have to be regarded as incompatible with Article 102 TFEU. The reason is that they tend to restrict or deprive the freedom of purchasers to choose between different sources of supply, thus hampering market entry and the competitive process. Since then, the CJEU has constantly emphasised the anti-competitive character of these schemes, highlighting that their main purpose is to grant a financial benefit to customers, with the sole goal to prevent them from obtaining supplies from competing producers.[147] This view has led to a qualification of fidelity rebates coming close to a *per se* abuse. The Commission and the EU courts regularly held that in order to outlaw these rebate schemes, it is sufficient to prove the simple tendency to create customer loyalty. In some circumstances, the jurisprudence went even further, considering that the intent to exclude rivals or discourage market entry was sufficient to establish their illegality. The unlawfulness was found not only in relation to pure loyalty rebates resulting from legal obligations imposing on customers a full or a partial exclusivity but also when the rebates were made conditional on the customer's duty to purchase all or most of his supplies from the dominant firm.[148] Since *Hoffmann-La Roche*, the basic presumption is that a dominant firm wants to exclude its competitors when it offers a financial benefit to its customers on the condition that the latter do not turn to other suppliers. In many circumstances, the analysis of economic effects was superficial, if not totally ignored (Zenger 2012). Also, the most recent cases, such as *Solvay*[149] and *Tomra*,[150] largely focused on the form of the rebates and essentially presumed the existence of anti-competitive effects.

---

[143] Case 85/76, *Hoffmann-La Roche & Co. AG v. Commission* [1979] ECR 461.

[144] Case 322/81, *NV Nederlandsche Banden-Industrie Michelin v. Commission* [1983] ECR 3461.

[145] Case T-57/01 *Solvay v Commission* [2009] ECR II-4621, at para. 318.

[146] C-23/14 *Post Danmark A/S v. Konkurrencerådet*, (Judgment of the Court), 6 October 2015, at para. 27.

[147] Case 85/76, *Hoffmann-La Roche & Co. AG v. Commission* [1979] ECR 461, at para. 90.

[148] Case T-203/01 *Michelin v. Commission* [2003] ECR II-4071; Case T-65/89, *BPB Industries and British Gypsum v. Commission* [1993] ECR II- 389; Case 85/76, *Hoffmann-La Roche & Co. AG v Commission* [1979] ECR 461; Joined Cases 40–48, 50, 54–56, 111, 113 & 114/73 *Cooperatieve vereniging Suiker Unie UA & Others v. Commission* [1975] ECR 1663.

[149] Case T-57/01 *Solvay v. Commission* [2009] ECR II-4621.

[150] C-549/10 P, *Tomra Systems ASA v. European Commission*, 19 April 2012.

Hybrid discount schemes

The last category of discounts includes schemes where the financial incentive is not directly linked to an exclusive supply from the dominant firm, but the mechanism for granting the rebate may have a fidelity-building effect.[151] In this residual category, one finds target discounts and rebate systems related to the attainment of individual sales objectives. Traditionally, in EU practice and case law, the various discount mechanisms falling in this residual category have been perceived to be likely to induce customer loyalty. As a consequence, the discount practices are deemed unfair when the following features are found: (i) the individualisation of the discounts granted to customers; (ii) the more than proportional progression of the discount rates compared to the sales target;[152] (iii) the adoption of long reference periods regarding the objectives to be achieved; (iv) the retroactive application of discounts to the entire amount of purchases;[153] and (v) the lack of transparency of the discount system.[154] Generally, these discount schemes were found illegal under the assumption that they tend to limit the freedom of customers to choose the sources of supply, thus hindering the access to the market by rival firms. The emphasis of the decisional practice and the case law has been placed on the loyalty-inducing potential, considering that these systems exert pressure on buyers to make purchases from the dominant firm, especially at the end of the reference period. The case law has clarified that the loyalty-inducing potential requires an analysis of all relevant circumstances, in particular the 'buyer's freedom to choose his sources of supply, to bar competitors from access to the market, or to strengthen the dominant position by distorting competition'.[155] However, in *Michelin I*, *Michelin II* and *British Airways*, little attention was paid to the actual or potential anti-competitive effects or the harm suffered by consumers.

The Guidance Paper and recent case law

In its Guidance Paper, the European Commission acknowledges that discounts can generate efficiencies and benefit consumers. Importantly, the Commission also advances an innovative and complex methodology to assess when discount and rebate schemes are likely to foreclose equally efficient competitors (Zenger 2012). To this end, the Guidance Paper suggests

---

[151] Case T-286/09 *Intel Corp v. European Commission* [2014] (GC, 12 June 2014), at para. 78.

[152] Case T-203/01 *Michelin v. Commission* [2003] ECR II-4071 ('Michelin II').

[153] European Commission, Decision IV/D-2/34.780 *Virgin/British Airways* [2000] O.J. L 30/1.

[154] *Irish Sugar* [1997] O.J. L258/1, [CMLR] 666, at para. 150.

[155] Case 322/81 *Nederlandse Banden-Industrie-Michelin v Commission* [1983] ECR 3461 ('*Michelin I*'), at para. 71–73, C-95/04 P *British Airways v Commission* [2007] ECR I-2331, at para. 65–67; Case C-549/10 P *Tomra Systems and Others v. Commission*, 19 April 2012, at para. 71.

as a benchmark the price that an equally efficient competitor should set to reward the customer for the loss of the discount offered by a dominant firm, as a result of the shift of a portion of its demand (i.e. the relevant range, estimated on the basis of the contestable portion) from the dominant firm to the rival (Guidance Paper, at 42). The Commission's concern is that the market may be foreclosed if the discounts granted by the dominant undertaking discourage customers from switching even small amounts of their contestable portion of demand. The suggested methodology for assessing the legality of the discount schemes consists of two steps. In a first step, law enforcers must estimate the price that an equally efficient competitor should offer its customers to compensate for the loss of the discount. The effective price that the competitor has to match is thus represented by the list price minus the rebate lost by switching, calculated over the relevant range of sales and in the relevant period of time (Guidance Paper, at 41). In a second step, the effective price must be compared with the dominant firm's costs. If this price is above the dominant firm's LRAIC (long-run average incremental costs), the practice would normally not be considered anti-competitive because an equally efficient rival would be able to compete. However, if the effective price is below AAC (average avoidable cost), the discount is deemed likely to produce a foreclosure effect by excluding an efficient competitor (Ridyard 2014). Finally, if the effective price is between AAC and LRAIC, the Commission will investigate whether other factors may lead to the conclusion that entry or expansion by equally efficient competitors is affected (Guidance Paper, at 44).

Certainly, the Guidance Paper has proposed an innovative methodology, which is theoretically convincing and grounded on a sound economic rationale. In this way, the Commission has tried to overcome the formalistic approach adopted by EU judges, by introducing an assessment criterion largely based on the effects generated by discounts and rebates (Ezrachi 2009). However, the case law emerged after the publication of Guidance Paper has downsized the prospects of a substantial change in the evaluation of discount practices. Especially in *Tomra*,[156] a case concerning fidelity discounts on reverse vending machines used by supermarkets to collect empty containers of drinks, the CJEU upheld the findings of the General Court[157] and reaffirmed the old principles. In order to establish the unlawful nature of a discount scheme, it is sufficient to show that it tends to restrict competition or that it is capable of having such effect. According to the Court, loyalty discounts carry incentives that produce anti-competitive outcomes. Hence, there is no

---

[156] C-549/10 P, *Tomra Systems ASA and Others v European Commission*, 19 April 2012.
[157] T-155/06, *Tomra Systems and Others v Commission* [2010] ECR II-4361.

need to adopt a price test (as the one put forward in the Guidance Paper) to ascertain whether an equally efficient competitor can make a competitive offer.[158] Notwithstanding the fact that the EU judges made extensive use of the terminology and of the conceptual framework proposed in the Guidance Paper, their decision to reject the use of the price test seems at odds with the guiding principles of the Guidance Paper (Federico 2011; Peeperkorn and Rousseva 2010).

In the most recent *Post Denmark II* case,[159] the CJEU has again showed reluctance to embrace the economic approach. The judgment originated from a preliminary reference submitted by a specialised Danish Court and concerned the status of rebates adopted by the incumbent postal operator in Denmark. The decision is important because it gave the Court the possibility to provide general guidance for the assessment of discount practices and to clarify various aspects concerning the role of economic analysis. First, the CJEU has confirmed the categorisation emerged in the previous case law, lastly in *Intel*.[160] The distinction is kept between three categories: (i) quantity rebates; (ii) rebates granted by the dominant firm under the condition that the customer purchases all or most of its requirements from it (i.e. fidelity rebates within the meaning of *Hoffmann-La Roche*); and (iii) discounts where the grant of a financial incentive is not directly linked to a condition of exclusive or quasi-exclusive supply from the undertaking in a dominant position.[161] Consequently, the EU courts will continue classifying discount schemes depending on their form and apply the legal standards emerged in the old case law. Second, the CJEU has clarified the role to be granted to the 'as efficient competitor' test in the evaluation of discount practices. It stated that this test is not a necessary pre-condition to the finding that a rebate is anti-competitive and therefore illegal under Article 102 TFEU. According to the CJEU, the 'as efficient competitor test' merely represents 'one tool amongst others' to assess whether there is an abuse of a dominant position in the context of a rebate scheme.[162] The CJEU has not denied, at least in principle, that the test can be a proxy for the evaluation of discount practices, but it has taken a critical position regarding the methodology proposed in the Guidance Paper. While not dismissing any potential usefulness, as conversely noted by Advocate General Kokott in the same case,[163] the CJEU has restated

---

[158] C-549/10 P, *Tomra Systems ASA and Others v European Commission*, 19 April 2012, at paras 68–80.

[159] C-23/14, *Post Danmark A/S v Konkurrencerådet*, (Judgment of the Court), 6 October 2015.

[160] Case T-286/09 *Intel Corp v European Commission* [2014] (GC, 12 June 2014), at paras 75–79.

[161] C-23/14 *Post Danmark A/S v Konkurrencerådet*, (Judgment of the Court), 6 October 2015, at paras 23–29.

[162] *Ibid.*, at para. 61.

[163] C-23/14 *Post Danmark A/S v Konkurrencerådet*, Opinion of Advocate General Kokott, delivered on 21 May 2015, at 4, where it is noted – referring to the price-cost test and to the appreciable impact of the exclusionary effects that '[t]hese questions are particularly important at a time when there are mounting calls for European

in a general perspective its lack of confidence in the test, as it was already evidenced in *Tomra*[164] and *Intel*.[165]

A critical assessment

The principles emerged in the EU case law are not in line with the relevant economic insights. The European approach to discounts and rebates can be criticised for considering (almost *per se*) abusive various types of discounts according to their form. Rather than using sophisticated economic tools to enable a full welfare analysis of discounts and rebates, EU judges appear much more concerned with the quest for legal certainty. Even though form-based rules may be easily administrable, the rejection of an economic methodology also imposes potentially high costs. First, to a large extent a formalistic approach underestimates the pro-competitive effects that discounts and rebates may generate. Second, further inefficiencies result when there is no obligation to prove the seriousness and appreciable nature of the anti-competitive effects. In restating the old case law, the CJEU has not required a high standard of proof. It suffices that a discount scheme is likely to produce exclusionary effects. The evidence accepted by the Court appears as weak, presumptively inferred or completely missing. Third, the wide use of the concepts 'fidelity-building' and 'loyalty-inducing' is ambiguous. It is unfit to detect the exact conditions under which a rebate scheme represents either a form of legitimate competition on the merits or an unlawful exclusion of rivals from the market. From an economic point of view, it is likely that a discount system aims at achieving customer loyalty, but this does not seem a strong proxy to assess its lawfulness. Fourth, a final gap between the case law and the economic approach relates to the assessment of the discriminatory nature of discounts. As explained above, price discrimination may be welfare-enhancing (see section 7.5.1). However, the EU courts have opposed the discriminatory nature of discount schemes by objecting to the fact that the individualised character of the purchase thresholds causes two firms to receive different discounts for the same volume of sales.[166]

---

competition law to adopt a more economic approach. It is my view that, in its replies, the signal effect of which is likely to extend well beyond the present case, the Court should not allow itself to be influenced so much by current thinking ("Zeitgeist") or ephemeral trends, but should have regard rather to the legal foundations on which the prohibition of abuse of a dominant position rests in EU law.'

[164] C-549/10 P, Tomra Systems ASA and Others v European Commission, 19 Aril 2012, at paras 74, 80.

[165] Case T-286/09 *Intel Corp v European Commission* [2014] (GC, 12 June 2014), at paras 140–166.

[166] In relation to fidelity discounts, see Case 85/76, *Hoffmann-La Roche & Co. AG v Commission* [1979] ECR 461, at para. 90; Commission decision 91/299/EEC, *Soda Ash – Solvay*, L 152/21 (1991), at para. 62; concerning the target discounts, see Court of First Instance, December 17, 2003, Case T-219/99, *British Airways plc/Commission*, in ECR, 2003, II-5917, at para. 228; Commission decisions of May 14, 1997, Case IV/34.621, 35.059/F-3, *Irish Sugar plc*, O.J. L 258/1 (1997).

In sum, the transition process towards an economic approach in the antitrust treatment of discounts in the European Union still seems (very) long. The publication of the Guidance Paper, paired with the Commission's approach in assessing these conducts, represents a positive attempt to reduce the gap between the enforcement practice and the economic insights. Also, the tendency to employ economic concepts and arguments in the decisions has to be appreciated. However, the Guidance Paper does not provide more than a theoretical background, without being able to permeate the case law. The latter keeps formal distinctions intact without confronting them with the economic rigour of the economic tests. In this respect, it has also to be noted that the standard of proof in relation to the anti-competitive effects is still modest (likely effects) and that the traditional narrow interpretation of an objective justification remains in place. In addition to the application problems of the 'as efficient competitor' test (Kjølbye 2010; Temple Lang 2009), the major critical element seems to be the difficulties faced by EU judges to metabolise a change in perspective as to favour a fully coherent effects-based analysis.

Box 7.6: The *Intel* case: a formalistic or an effects-based analysis?

With its judgment in the *Intel* case,[167] the General Court upheld the decision of the EU Commission, which found that Intel had abused its dominant position in the worldwide market for microprocessors based on the x86 architecture ('CPUx86'). The Commission imposed a fine of €1.06 billion, the highest fine ever inflicted upon a single firm. Specifically, Intel was condemned for having adopted a complex strategy to foreclose market access to its main competitor (AMD), through two distinct abusive conducts: (i) the granting of discounts to major original equipment manufacturers (OEMs) – Dell, HP, NEC, Lenovo; and (ii) making direct payments to computer manufacturers in order to prevent or delay the sale of rival products. In particular, the abusive discount schemes were conditional on the duty of OEMs to purchase their CPUs exclusively or almost exclusively from Intel.

The Commission's decision relied on both a formal and an effects-based analysis. On the one hand, the Commission argued that the granting of discounts was conditional upon an exclusive purchase obligation. On the basis of the existing and settled case law, it was not required to provide evidence of actual foreclosure. On the other hand, the analysis was focused on whether the loyalty rebates were capable of causing or likely to produce anti-competitive foreclosure. While declaring that it was not necessary to undertake the effects-based analysis, the Commission decided to use the 'as efficient

---

[167] Case T-286/09 *Intel Corp v European Commission* [2014] (GC), 12 June 2014.

competitor (AEC)' test defined in the Guidance Paper. It took into account the size of the rebates, the contestable share, the time horizon and a relevant cost measure (AAC). In this respect, it is worth noting that the practical application of the AEC test in relation to the discounts charged by Intel required huge resources, coupled with extensive investigation powers, and appeared remarkably complex. A significant part of the decision focused on the comparison between the Commission's methodologies with those presented by the company's consultants, in order to define whether some costs had to be counted as average avoidable costs. In concluding its assessment, the Commission considered to have proven that Intel's discount policy had produced an exclusionary effect since an equally efficient competitor, in order to offset the dominant firm's offer, would have had to set a price lower than AAC. However, the practical application of the test exhibited a particularly high level of complexity. More than 150 pages of the decision are devoted to the AEC test. Importantly, the significant elements of the methodology – such as the relevant range, the contestable portion of demand, the internal costs necessary to calculate AAC and others – are characterised by a high level of discretion. Even small differences in the estimations of these parameters seem likely to overturn the results of the test (Rosenblatt and Armengod 2012; Lande 2009).

The General Court, in upholding the Commission's findings, released a formalistic judgment. First, the opinion confirmed the taxonomy based on the form of the discounts (quantity discounts, exclusivity/fidelity rebates and the third residual category) and concluded that Intel's discount scheme belonged to the second category. In this regard, the Court stated that – since *Hoffmann-La Roche* – this type of discount is presumptively unlawful. It is thus not necessary to perform an analysis of the circumstances of the case to establish a potential foreclosure effect, since loyalty discounts are by their very nature likely to restrict competition.[168] Furthermore, clearly neglecting the importance of an economic approach, the Court argued that is not required to prove a causal link between the rebate scheme and the actual effects produced in the market.[169] In relying on settled case law, the Court reaffirmed that it is sufficient to prove the existence of a loyalty mechanism.[170] Concerning loyalty discounts and rebate schemes falling into the third category, the Court contended the irrelevance of the AEC test to establish the abusive nature of the conduct. According to the EU judges, the AEC test allows to assess whether the discount system may force an equally efficient competitor to define negative prices, but not to decide whether the discounts make it more difficult, or impossible, for a competitor to be present in the market.[171]

From the foregoing, it is clear that the General Court has rejected the usefulness and the theoretical strength of the AEC analysis in relation to discount cases. This

---

[168] *Ibid.*, at paras 80–81, 85.
[169] *Ibid.*, at paras 102–115.
[170] *Ibid.*, at paras 144–145.
[171] *Ibid.*, at paras 149–153.

holding appears largely based on the previous case law, thus continuing a formalistic approach.[172] What seems to matter most to the EU judges is that loyalty discounts are able to restrict competition, not only when access to the market is impossible but also when it is made only more difficult. The outcome of the *Intel* case represents a setback in the transition process towards a More Economic Approach and seems to have set even stricter limits to the possibility for dominant firms to adopt discount schemes other than quantity ones (Rey and Venit 2015; Wils 2014).

7.7 Conclusions

This chapter analysed several types of exclusionary behaviour by dominant firms. It has shown that the welfare effects of these practices are inherently difficult to assess. All forms of so-called 'exclusionary behaviour' may generate efficiencies and benefit consumers. This leaves competition authorities and judges, who take economic analysis seriously, with a difficult task: they have to carefully analyse the reasons why firms engage in such practices and assess their effects on allocative efficiency and consumer welfare in real-life markets.

The assessment of the net welfare effects of a refusal to deal is a complex exercise, since it involves a trade-off between short-term and long-term effects, taking into account both static and dynamic concerns. US antitrust law enforcement has exhibited a marked reluctance, formally recognised in *Trinko*, to use the antitrust regime for imposing a duty to deal on dominant firms. Conversely, EU competition law has been more prone to ensure rivals access to the dominant firm's assets, even when protected by intellectual property rights. In the early case law, it was decided that a dominant firm may be obliged to provide access to its networks or infrastructures. The essential facility doctrine emerged as a functional legal construct to enhance competition in liberalised markets. In these early cases, economic analysis was largely missing. In the *Bronner* case, the CJEU has adopted a more rigorous test, defining the conditions for a facility to be deemed essential, thus embracing an approach more open to economic insights. In recent years, the focus has shifted to the duty to license intellectual property rights. In this

---

[172] But see the Opinion of Advocate General Wahl, 20 October 2016, Case C-413/14 P, *Intel Corporation Inc. v. European Commission*, who noted, in particular, that: (a) the General Court erred in finding that 'exclusivity rebates' constitute a separate and unique category of rebates that requires no consideration of all the circumstances in order to establish an abuse of dominant position; (b) the General Court erred in law in its alternative assessment of capability by failing to establish that the rebates and payments offered by the appellant had, in all likelihood, an anti-competitive foreclosure effect; and (c) the General Court failed to assess whether the anti-competitive effects stemming from certain agreements between Intel and Lenovo had the capacity to produce any immediate, substantial and foreseeable anti-competitive effect in the EEA.

area, a clear and consistent rationale for finding an abuse of dominant position is still missing. EU competition law is not fully in line with insights from economic theory, which stress the need to limit the duty to share resources with competitors because of its negative impact on innovation.

Tying and bundling may both cause competitive harm and serve legitimate business goals, which enhance efficiency. Again, an effects-based analysis is necessary to distinguish among beneficial and harmful effects. Economic analysis had not yet produced robust studies to highlight the conditions under which tying and bundling produce welfare-enhancing effects that are sufficiently general and easily administrable by the courts. In US antitrust law, pro-competitive arguments advanced by modern economic theory have started to permeate the case law, the *Microsoft* case being the most paradigmatic example. The US Supreme Court might be on the verge of adopting a Rule of Reason analysis, as already done by some lower courts, but the *per se* prohibition has not yet been overruled. In EU competition law, there is less willingness to reject the formalistic approach followed in the past. The recent practice of the European Commission, paired with the issuance of the Guidance Paper, has signalled a positive trend towards the reception of a more economic approach. However, it remains to be seen whether the case law of the European Courts will be open to a more careful analysis of the anti-competitive effects and fully consider the efficiency gains benefiting consumers.

The welfare effects of low prices practised by dominant firms (predatory pricing) are ambiguous since they may be a sign of both healthy competition and predation. Contrary to the learning of the Chicago School, modern economic theories have shown that predatory pricing can be a rational and profitable strategy. An economically sound competition law should carefully analyse whether anti-competitive effects (exclusion) materialise in real-life markets. Also concerning predatory pricing, the decisional practice is different under the two major competitive frameworks analysed in this book. Under the US Sherman Act, plaintiffs face a higher burden of proof: they must show that losses suffered during the price war may be recouped in the post-predation phase. While this requirement appears consistent with economic theory, EU competition law continues to focus only on the first phase of predation. A dominant firm infringes Article 102 TFEU if it reduces prices below average variable costs or below average total costs provided the intent to exclude competitors may be proven.

Price discrimination can be beneficial if it reduces the deadweight loss by increasing output, in particular when the practice allows the dominant firm to serve additional market segments. Price discrimination no longer causes serious antitrust worries in the US, since the Robinson–Patman Act is no longer actively enforced. By contrast, EU competition law remains to a large extent indebted to formalistic assessments, rather than focusing the analysis on the effects of price discrimination and the (likely or effective) harm suffered by consumers. In the case of geographical discrimination, the goal of the EU market integration continues to exert much more prominence than an effects-based economic analysis. The gap between economic insights and EU case law is also evidenced in relation to the ability for the parties to pursue a defence strategy. The objective justifications focused on the incentives for and effects of price discrimination have not received particular consideration in the various proceedings.

Also discount and rebates schemes may produce both beneficial and harmful effects on competition. A sound economic approach requires proof of anticompetitive effects (exclusion of rivals) and harm to consumers (increased prices, reduced output). The assessment of discount practices carried out by the US antitrust agencies and courts is much more cautious than that followed in the EU. Their pro-competitive nature is generally acknowledged in terms of benefits directly achievable by consumers or because of the efficiencies that arise between producers and distributors. Together with the traditional disfavour towards false positives, these assessments have sparked a presumption of lawfulness regarding loyalty discounts and a cautious approach regarding bundled discounts. In contrast, European competition law often considers as abusive, basically *per se* and according to their form, various types of discounts. In this way, the pro-competitive effects that these schemes may generate are underestimated. The CJEU has recently confirmed the three-fold categorisation of discounts: (presumptively legal) quantity discounts, (illegal) loyalty discounts and (likely illegal) loyalty inducing discounts. In spite of the debate on the role of economic analysis and the publication of the Guidance paper by the European Commission, which has suggested an 'as efficient competitor' test, the reluctance of the CJEU to adopt a fully fledged economic approach has not changed.

At a more general level and in a comparative perspective, it may be concluded that the greatest degree of convergence between competition economics and competition law has been reached at the administrative enforcement level. Both the US antitrust agencies and the EU Commission are more committed to enhance an economic approach than the judges deciding competition cases. In particular, the European Commission follows a more economic approach in its Guidance Paper, trying to discharge a formalistic reading of cases concerning abuses of dominant position. The differences between the two legal systems are most pronounced at the judicial level. The US Supreme Court, as well as lower courts, are much more prone to assess unilateral conduct by looking at the economic effects produced in real-life markets. By contrast, the General Court and the CJEU are to a large extent still committed to formalistic analyses. In this respect, the EU case law exhibits a much wider gap with the economic insights. More importantly, the EU judges have appeared rather reluctant, sometimes assuming a reactive stance, to fully embrace an effects-based approach. This reluctance can be explained by concerns about legal uncertainty and because of the practical difficulties (lack of administrable rules) that the new methodologies pose. This attitude seems to have slowed down the transition process favoured by the EU Commission, especially after the issuance of the Guidance Paper.

7.8 Bibliography

Adelman M (1966), *A&P: A Study in Price-Cost Behavior and Public Policy* (Harvard University Press)

Ahlborn C (2004), 'The Logic & Limits of the "Exceptional Circumstances Test" in Magill and IMS Health' 28 *Fordham International Law Journal* 1109

Ahlborn C, Evans D (2009), 'The Microsoft Judgment and its Implications for Competition Policy Towards Dominant Firms in Europe' 75 *Antitrust Law Journal* 887

Akman P (2012), *The Concept of Abuse in EU Competition Law: Law and Economic Approaches* (Hart Publishing)

Antitrust Modernization Commission (2007), 'Report and Recommendations' (April 2007) <http://govinfo.library.unt.edu/amc/report_recommendation/amc_final_report.pdf>

Areeda P (1989), 'Essential Facilities: An Epithet in Need of Limiting Principles' 58 *Antitrust Law Journal* 841

Areeda P, Hovenkamp H (2007), *Antitrust Law: An Analysis of Antitrust Principles and their Application* (Aspen Publishers)

Armstrong M (2008), 'Price Discrimination', in P Buccirossi (ed.), *Handbook of Antitrust Economics* 433 (MIT Press)

Baird D, Gertner R, Picker R (1994), *Game Theory and the Law* (Harvard University Press)

Benoit J (1984), 'Financially Constrained Entry into a Game with Incomplete Information' 15 *RAND Journal of Economics* 490

Bishop S (1981), 'Price Discrimination under Article 86: Political Economy in the European Court' 44 *Modern Law Review* 282

Bishop S, Walker M (2010), *Economics of E.C. Competition Law: Concepts, Application and Measurement* (Sweet & Maxwell, 3rd ed.)

Blair R, Lopatka J (2008), 'Predatory Buying and the Antitrust Laws' 2 *Utah Law Review* 415

Bolton P, Brodley J, Riordan M (2000), 'Predatory Pricing: Strategic Theory and Legal Policy' 88 *Georgetown Law Journal* 2253

Bolton P, Scharfstein D (1990), 'A Theory of Predation Based on Agency Problems in Financial Contracting' 80 *American Economic Review* 93

Bork R (1993), *The Antitrust Paradox. A Policy at War with Itself* (Basic Books)

Bowman J (1957), 'Tying Arrangements and the Leverage Problem' 67 *Yale Law Journal* 19

Bowman W (1968), 'Restraint of Trade by the Supreme Court: The *Utah Pie Case*', 77 *Yale Law Journal* 70

Brodley J, Hay G (1981), 'Predatory Pricing: Competing Economic Theories and the Evolution of Legal Standards' 66 *Cornell Law Review* 738

Carlton D, Perloff J (2005), *Modern Industrial Organization* (Pearson, 4th ed.)

Carlton D, Waldman M (2002), 'The Strategic Use of Tying to Preserve and Create Market Power in Evolving Industries' 33 *RAND Journal of Economics* 194

Cass R, Hylton K (1999), 'Preserving Competition: Economic Analysis, Legal Standards and Microsoft' 8 *George Mason Law Review* 1

Choi J, Stefanadis C (2001), 'Tying, Investment and the Dynamic Leverage Theory' 32 *RAND Journal of Economics* 52

Dalton J, Esposito L (2011), 'Standard Oil and Predatory Pricing: Myth Paralleling Fact' 38 *Review of Industrial Organization* 245

Department of Justice (2008), 'Competition and Monopoly: Single-Firm Conduct Under Section 2 of the Sherman Act' <http://www.justice.gov/atr/public/reports/236681.pdf, 2008>

DG Competition (2005), 'Discussion Paper on the Application of Article 82 of the Treaty to Exclusionary Abuses' <http://ec.europa.eu/competition/antitrust/art82/discpaper2005. pdf>

Dorsey E, Jacobson J (2015), 'Exclusionary Conduct in Antitrust' 89 *St. John's Law Review* 101

Douglas Melamed A (2005), 'Exclusionary Conduct Under the Antitrust Laws: Balancing, Sacrifice, and Refusals to Deal' 20 *Berkeley Technology Law Journal* 1247

Easterbrook F (1986), 'On Identifying Exclusionary Conduct' 61 *Notre Dame Law Review* 972

Easterbrook F (1981), 'Predatory Strategies and Counterstrategies' 48 *University of Chicago Law Review* 263

Economic Advisory Group for Competition Policy (2005), 'EAGCP Report on An Economic approach to Article 82 EC' <http://ec.europa.eu/dgs/competition/economist/eagcp_ july_21_05.pdf>

Economides N, Lianos I (2010), 'A Critical Appraisal of Remedies in the E.U. Microsoft Cases' 2010 *Columbia Business Law Review* 346

Elhauge E (2009), 'Tying, Bundled Discounts, and the Death of the Single Monopoly Profit Theory' 123 *Harvard Law Review* 397

Elzinga K (1970), 'Predatory Pricing: The Case of the Gunpowder Trust' 13 *Journal of Law and Economics* 223

Elzinga K, Hogarty T (1978), '*Utah Pie* and the Consequences of Robinson-Patman' 21 *Journal of Law and Economics* 427

Elzinga K, Mills D (2014), 'Antitrust Predation and The Antitrust Paradox' 57 *Journal of Law and Economics* 181

Evans D, Padilla J (2005), 'Designing Antitrust Rules for Assessing Unilateral Practices: A Neo-Chicago Approach' 72 *University of Chicago Law Review* 73

Evrard S (2004), 'Essential Facilities in the European Union: *Bronner* and Beyond' 10 *Columbia Journal of European Law* 491

Ezrachi A (2009), 'The European Commission Guidance on Article 82 EC – The Way in Which Institutional Realities Limit the Potential for Reform' (Oxford Legal Studies Research Paper No. 27/2009) <https://ssrn.com/abstract=1463854>

Faella G (2012), *Politiche di Sconti delle Imprese Dominanti* (Giappichelli)

Faella G (2008), 'The Antitrust Assessment of Loyalty Discounts and Rebates' 4 *Journal of Competition Law and Economics* 375

Federico G (2011), '*Tomra* v Commission of the European Communities: Reversing Progress on Rebates?' 32 *European Competition Law Review* 139

Frischmann B, Waller S (2008), 'Revitalizing Essential Facilities' 75 *Antitrust Law Journal* 1

Fudenberg D, Tirole J (1986), 'A "Signal-jamming" Theory of Predation' 17 *RAND Journal of Economics* 366

Gal M (2013), 'Abuse of Dominance-Exploitative Abuses', in I Lianos and D Geradin (eds.), *Handbook on European Competition Law* 385 (Edward Elgar)

Geradin D, Petit N (2006), 'Price Discrimination Under EC Competition Law: Another Antitrust Doctrine in Search of Limiting Principles?' 2 *Journal of Competition Law and Economics* 479

Gerla H (1985), 'The Psychology of Predatory Pricing: Why Predatory Pricing Pays' 39 *Southwestern Law Journal* 755

Gifford D, Kudrle R (2010), 'The Law and Economics of Price Discrimination in Modern Economies: Time for Reconciliation?' 43 *UC Davis Law Review* 1235

Giocoli N (2013), 'Games Judges Don't Play: Predatory Pricing and Strategic Reasoning in US Antitrust' 21 *Supreme Court Economic Review* 271

Guthrie C (2003), 'Prospect Theory, Risk Preference, and the Law' 97 *Northwestern University Law Review* 1115

Hart O, Tirole J (1990), 'Vertical Integration and Market Foreclosure', in *Brookings Papers on Economic Activity, Microeconomics* 205 (Brookings Institution Press)

Hay G (2005), '*Trinko*: Going All The Way' 50 *Antitrust Bulletin* 527

Hovenkamp H (2011), *Federal Antitrust Policy: The Law of Competition and Its Practice* (West, 4th ed.)

Hovenkamp H (2008), 'Unilateral Refusals to Deal, Vertical Integration, and the Essential Facility Doctrine' (U Iowa Legal Studies Research Paper No. 08-31) <https://ssrn.com/abstract=1144675>

Hovenkamp H (2005), *The Antitrust Enterprise: Principles and Execution* (Harvard University Press)

Hovenkamp H (2000), 'The Monopolization Offense' 61 *Ohio State Law Journal* 1035

Hovenkamp H, Hovenkamp E (2009), 'Complex Bundled Discounts and Antitrust Policy' 57 *Buffalo Law Review* 1227

Hylton K (2008), 'Weyerhaeuser, Predatory Bidding, and Error Costs' 53 *Antitrust Bulletin* 51

Jones A, Sufrin B (2014), *EU Competition Law: Text, Cases and Materials* (Oxford University Press, 5th ed.)

Kallaugher J, Sher B (2004), 'Rebates Revisited: Anti-Competitive Effects and Exclusionary Abuse under Article 82' 25 *European Competition Law Review* 263

Kirkwood J (2008), 'Controlling Above-Cost Predation: An Alternative to Weyerhaeuser and Brooke Group' 53 *Antitrust Bulletin* 369

Kjølbye L (2010), 'Rebates Under Article 82 EC: Navigating Uncertain Waters' 31 *European Competition Law Review* 66

Klein C (1998), 'Market Power in Aftermarkets', in F McChesney (ed.), *Economic Inputs, Legal Outputs: The Role of Economics in Modern Antitrust* 47 (Wiley)

Kobayashi B (2010), 'The Law and Economics of Predatory Pricing', in K Hylton (ed.), *Antitrust law and Economics* 116 (Edward Elgar)

Kobayashi B (2008), 'Spilled Ink or Economic Progress? The Supreme Court's Decision in Illinois Tool Works v. Independent Ink' 53 *Antitrust Bulletin* 5

Kobayashi B (2005), 'The Economics of Loyalty Discounts and Antitrust Law in the United States' 1 *Competition Policy International* 114

Koller R (1971), 'The Myth of Predatory Pricing: An Empirical Study' 4 *Antitrust Law and Economics Review* 105

Kreps D, Wilson R (1982), 'Reputation and Imperfect Information' 27 *Journal of Economic Theory* 253

Lande R (2009), 'The Price of Abuse: Intel and the European Commission Decision' (GCP: The Online Magazine for Global Competition Policy) <https://ssrn.com/abstract=1434985>

Lao M (2009), 'Access and "Essential Facilities": From Terminal Railroads to Microsoft' 62 *SMU Law Review* 557

Lao M (1999), 'Unilateral Refusals to Sell or License Intellectual Property and the Antitrust Duty to Deal' 9 *Cornell Journal of Law and Public Policy* 193

Leblanc G (1996), 'Predatory Price Wars' 29 *The Canadian Journal of Economics* 293

Leslie C (2013), 'Predatory Pricing and Recoupment' 113 *Columbia Law Review* 1695

Leslie C (2012), 'Revisiting the Revisionist History of *Standard Oil*' 85 *Southern California Law Review* 573

Leslie C (2010), 'Rationality Analysis in Antitrust' 158 *University of Pennsylvania Law Review* 261

Levine M (2002), 'Price Discrimination without Market Power' 19 *Yale Journal on Regulation* 1

Lim D (2007), 'Copyright Under Siege: An Economic Analysis of the Essential Facilities Doctrine and the Compulsory Licensing of Copyrighted Works' 17 *Albany Law Journal of Science and Technology* 481

Martin S (1993), *Industrial Economics. Economic Analysis and Public Policy* (Macmillan Publishing, 2nd ed.)

McGee J (1958), 'Predatory Price Cutting: The Standard Oil (N.J.) Case' 1 *Journal of Law and Economics* 37

Meadows M (2015), 'The Essential Facilities Doctrine in Information Economies: Illustrating Why the Antitrust Duty to Deal is Still Necessary in the New Economy' 25 *Fordham Intellectual Property, Media and Entertainment Law Journal* 795

Milgrom P, Roberts J (1982a), 'Predation, Reputation and Entry Deterrence' 27 *Journal of Economic Theory* 280

Milgrom P, Roberts J (1982b), 'Limit Pricing and Entry under Incomplete Information: An Equilibrium Analysis' 50 *Econometrica* 443

Moore A (2012), 'Anticompetitive Bundled Discounts: A Way Out of the Wilderness' 37 *Journal of Corporation Law* 951

Moore D, Wright J (2015), 'Conditional Discounts and the Law of Exclusive Dealing' 22 *George Mason Law Review* 1205

Möschel W (1989), 'Competition Policy from an Ordo Point of View', in A Peacock and H Willgerodt (eds.), *German Neo-Liberals and the Social Market Economy* 142 (Macmillan Publishing)

Motta M (2004), *Competition Policy. Theory and Practice* (Cambridge University Press)

Nalebuff B (1999), 'Bundling as an Entry Barrier' 114 *Quarterly Journal of Economics* 283

O'Donoghue R, Padilla J (2013), *The Law and Economics of Article 102 TFEU* (Hart, 2nd ed.)

OECD (2016a), 'Roundtable on Fidelity Rebates – Note by The United States' DAF/COMP/WD(2016)20

OECD (2016b), 'Price Discrimination' DAF/COMP(2016)15

OECD (2002), 'Loyalty and Fidelity Discounts and Rebates' DAFFE/COMP(2002)21

OECD (1996), 'The Essential Facilities Concept' OCDE/GD(96)113

OECD (1989), 'Predatory Pricing' <http://www.oecd.org/dataoecd/7/54/2375661.pdf>

Ordover J (1998), 'Predatory Pricing,' in P Newman (ed.), *The New Palgrave Encyclopedia of Economics and the Law* 77 (Palgrave Macmillan)

Ordover J, Saloner G (1989), 'Predation, Monopolisation and Antitrust', in R Schmalensee and R Willig (eds.), *The Handbook of Industrial Organization I* 537 (North Holland)

Page W (2012), 'Standard Oil and U.S. Steel: Predation and Collusion in the Law of Monopolization and Mergers' 85 *Southern California Law Review* 101

Pardolesi R, Renda A (2004), 'The European Commission's Case Against Microsoft: Kill Bill?' 27 *World Competition* 558

Peeperkorn L, Rousseva E (2010), 'Article 102 TFEU: Exclusive Dealing and Rebates' 2 *Journal of European Competition Law and Practice* 36

Phlips L, Moras I (1993), 'The AKZO Decision: A Case of Predatory Pricing?' 41 *Journal of Industrial Economics* 315

Pigou A (1920), *The Economics of Welfare* (Macmillan)

Pindyck R, Rubinfeld D (2017), *Microeconomics* (Pearson, 9th ed.) (to be published)

Pindyck R, Rubinfeld D (1998), *Microeconomics* (Prentice Hall, 4th ed.)

Pitofsky R, Patterson D, Hooks J (2002), 'The Essential Facilities Doctrine Under United States Antitrust Law' 70 *Antitrust Law Journal* 443

Posner R (2001), *Antitrust Law* (University of Chicago Press, 2nd ed.)

Posner R (1975), 'The Social Costs of Monopoly and Regulation' 83 *Journal of Political Economy* 807

Rapp R (1986), 'Predatory Pricing and Entry Deterring Strategies: The Economics of AKZO' 7 *European Competition Law Review* 233

Rey P, Venit J (2015), 'An Effects-Based Approach to Article 102: A Response to Wouter Wils', 38 *World Competition* 1

Ridyard D (2014), 'Interpreting the As-Efficient Competitor Test in Abuse of Dominance Cases' 10 *Competition Law Review* 125

Ridyard D (2002), 'Exclusionary Pricing and Price Discrimination Abuses under Article 82 EC: An Economic Analysis' 23 *European Competition Law Review* 286

Riordan M (1985), 'Imperfect Information and Dynamic Conjectural Variations' 16 *RAND Journal of Economics* 41

Roberts J (1986), 'A Signalling Model of Predatory Pricing' 38 *Oxford Economic Papers* 75

Rosenblatt H, Armengod H (2012), 'The Commission's Approach to Conditional Discounts: A Look at Tomra and Intel' 2012 *European Antitrust Review* 49

Saloner G (1987), 'Predation, Mergers, and Incomplete Information' 18 *RAND Journal of Economics* 165

Scherer F, Ross D (1990), *Industrial Market Structure and Economic Performance* (Houghton Mifflin Company, 3rd ed.)

Schmalensee R (1981), 'Output and Welfare Implications of Monopolistic Third-Degree Price Discrimination' 71 *American Economic Review* 242

Selten R (1978), 'The Chain Store Paradox' 9 *Theory and Decision* 127

Shelanski H (2009), 'Unilateral Refusals to Deal in Intellectual and Other Property' 76 *Antitrust Law Journal* 369

Spector D (2004), 'Loyalty Rebates and Related Pricing Practices: When Should Competition Authorities Worry?', in D Evans and J Padilla (eds.), *Global Competition Policy. Economic Issues and Impacts* 317 (LECG)

Spector D (2001), 'Definitions and Criteria of Predatory Pricing' (MIT Department of Economics, Working Paper No. 01-10)

Speta J (2003), 'Antitrust and Local Competition Under the Telecommunications Act' 71 *Antitrust Law Journal* 99

Stigler G (1966), *The Theory of Price* (Macmillan, 3rd ed.)

Stigler G (1963), 'United States v. Loew's Inc: a Note on Block Booking' 1963 *The Supreme Court Review* 152

Stucke M (2012), 'Is Intent Relevant?' 8 *Journal of Law, Economics and Policy* 801

Telser L (1966), 'Cutthroat Competition and the Long Purse' 8 *Journal of Law and Economics* 259

Temple Lang J (2012), 'How Can the Problems of Exclusionary Abuses under Article 102 TFEU Be Resolved?' 37 *European Law Review* 136

Temple Lang J (2009), 'A Question of Priorities – The European Commission New Guidance on Article 82 is Flawed' 8 *Competition Law Insight* 2

Temple Lang J (1994), 'Defining Legitimate Competition: Companies' Duties to Supply Competitors and Access to Essential Facilities' 18 *Fordham International Law Journal* 437

Tirole J (1988), *The Theory of Industrial Organization* (MIT Press)

Tom W, Balto D, Averitt N (2000), 'Anticompetitive Aspects of Market-Share Discounts and Other Incentives to Exclusive Dealing' 67 *Antitrust Law Journal* 615

Tor A (2003), 'Illustrating a Behaviorally Informed Approach to Antitrust Law: The Case of Predatory Pricing' 18 *Antitrust* 52

Utton M (1986), *The Economics of Regulating Industry* (Blackwell)

Vaheesan S (2015), 'Reconsidering Brooke Group: Predatory Pricing in Light of the Empirical Learning' 12 *Berkeley Business Law Journal* 81

Van den Bergh R (2013), 'Behavioral Antitrust: Not Ready for the Main Stage' 9 *Journal of Competition Law and Economics* 203

Varian H (1983), *Intermediate Microeconomics: A Modern Approach* (W.W. Norton)

Veel P, Katz A (2013), 'Beyond Refusal to Deal: A Cross-Atlantic View of Copyright, Competition and Innovation Policies' 79 *Antitrust Law Journal* 139

Venit J, Kallaugher J (1994), 'Essential Facilities: A Comparative Law Approach', in B Hawk (ed.), *International Antitrust Law & Policy: Fordham Corporate Law 1994* 319 (Juris Publishing)

Waller S (2008), 'Areeda, Epithets, and Essential Facilities' 3 *Wisconsin Law Review* 359

Weber J (2009), 'Backing Bundled Discounts after Brooke Group: Analyzing the Debate over the Legality of Above-Cost Bundled Discounts' 94 *Iowa Law Review* 775

Werden G (1987), 'The Law and Economics of the Essential Facilities Doctrine' 32 *Saint Louis University Law Journal* 433

Whinston M (1990), 'Tying, Foreclosure, and Exclusion' 80 *American Economic Review* 837

Willard K, Balto D, Averitt N (2000), 'Anticompetitive Aspects of Market-Share Discounts and Other Incentives to Exclusive Dealing' 67 *Antitrust Law Journal* 615

Wils W (2014), 'The Judgment of the EU General Court in Intel and the So-Called "More Economic Approach" to Abuse of Dominance' 37 *World Competition* 405

Witt A (2010), 'The Commission's Guidance Paper on Abusive Exclusionary Conduct – More Radical than it Appears?' 35 *European Law Review* 214

Wright J (2006), 'Missed Opportunities in Independent Ink' 5 *Cato Supreme Court Review* 333

Wright J, Stone J (2012), 'Misbehavioral Economics: The Case Against Behavioral Antitrust' 33 *Cardozo Law Review* 1517

Zenger H (2012), 'Loyalty Rebates and the Competitive Process' 8 *Journal of Competition Law and Economics* 717

8

Enforcement

Roger Van den Bergh

8.1 Introduction

In a significant number of industries, cartels continue to form and succeed in maintaining discipline over a long period. A major problem of the cartel prohibition thus seems to be an enforcement issue. In economic terms, the enforcement of competition law may be qualified as optimal if welfare-reducing anti-competitive practices are properly punished and deterred, no enforcement errors are made and enforcement costs are minimised. Full deterrence is achieved when all firms abstain from engaging in welfare-reducing anti-competitive practices, since the gains from doing so are lower than the costs of the sanctions that are imposed for violating the competition rules. Error costs may occur when practices that do not harm economic welfare are falsely prohibited (type I errors/false positives) or harmful practices are allowed (type II errors/false negatives). Enforcement costs are not minimised when the benefits of the competitive processes that are preserved do not outweigh the administrative costs of detection (information costs) and sanctioning violations of the competition rules. These administrative costs include both the expenses of the public sector (costs of competition authorities and courts) and the costs borne by the businesses or individuals concerned (management costs, costs of external lawyers and experts). Full deterrence will not be efficient if the enforcement costs are higher than the benefits resulting from prohibiting harmful practices. An optimal enforcement system minimises the sum of social costs resulting from the infringement and the costs of enforcement.

In designing enforcement mechanisms, policy makers face difficult choices. All decisions made will have an impact on the level of deterrence and on the risks that errors are made or that enforcement costs are not minimised. The relevant policy questions are even more complex since, besides the deterrence objective, goals of retributive and corrective justice have to be taken into account as well. Retributive justice requires that offenders get a punishment that adequately reflects the societal disapproval of their behaviour. Corrective justice requires that the harm done is properly corrected, by forcing the offender to pay a just compensation to its victims. This chapter highlights the relevant insights on the enforcement of competition rules from an economic perspective, without neglecting their relation with the justice goals. It will be shown that it is difficult to pursue all the above goals simultaneously, so that policy makers will not be able to escape from difficult trade-offs.

The structure of this chapter follows Shavell's distinction of the three basic dimensions according to which methods of law enforcement can differ: the form of the sanctions, the role of private parties versus public agents in enforcement, and the timing of the legal intervention (Shavell 1993). In a federal or quasi-federal context, such as the EU, a fourth dimension must be added: the division of competences between the central competition authority and decentralised enforcement agencies (NCAs: national competition authorities of the Member States). The 'modernisation' debate on the enforcement of EU competition law around the turn of the century[1] was largely limited to the third and fourth dimensions of the choice between different enforcement systems. This discussion was focused on the following two questions: first, should there be an *ex ante* control of anti-competitive practices or is it sufficient to perform an *ex post* control? Under a notification regime, firms may be required to inform the competition authorities on practices they are contemplating, so that antitrust authorities may screen agreements before they are put into practice. The alternative regime tries to achieve deterrence by imposing sanctions if competition is harmed and no exception to the prohibition of anti-competitive practices applies. Second, should enforcement of the competition rules be decentralised by giving more powers to NCAs and judges, thereby alleviating the burden of a single central enforcement agency (European Commission)? Because of the modernisation, from May 2004 onwards, EU competition law has shifted from an *ex ante* notification and authorisation system to an *ex post* legal exception regime, which is directly applicable. At the same time, the enforcement of the competition rules has been decentralised largely.

---

[1] This debate started with the publication of the White Paper on Modernisation of the Rules Implementing Articles 81 and 82 (formerly Articles 85 and 86) of the EC Treaty ([1999] O.J. C 132/1) and resulted in the enactment of Regulation 1/2003 on the implementation of the rules on competition laid down in Articles 81 and 82 of the Treaty [2003] O.J. L 1/1). This Regulation replaced the old enforcement system contained in Regulation No. 17, enacted back in 1962 (Council Regulation No. 17 [1962] O.J. 13/204). Together with Regulation 1/2003, the Commission has published a total of six Notices: two on cooperation (within the Network of Competition Authorities [2004] O.J. C 101/43 and between the Commission and the courts of the EU Members States [2004] O.J. C 101/54), one on the handling of complaints [2004] O.J. C 101/65, one on informal guidance relating to novel questions concerning Articles 81 and 82 [2004] O.J. C 101/78 and two Guidelines on the interpretation of concepts of competition law: the effect on trade concept [2004] O.J. C 101/81 and the application of Article 81(3) of the Treaty [2004] O.J. C 101/97.

Even though the importance of the modernisation debate should be acknowledged, the first two questions on the type of sanctions and the role of private parties in the enforcement of the competition rules have gained prominent importance in more recent years. Comparing EU competition law with US antitrust law, the main policy issue is the choice between administrative fines or criminal sanctions (fines, imprisonment sentences) as instruments to enforce the prohibitions. For reasons of clarity, it should be stressed at the outset that competition law is not a tool of active policy intervention. Competition authorities should not be confused with price regulators. Competition law is based on the principle that competition itself is the best mechanism for avoiding welfare losses. Competition authorities can punish and deter certain agreements and certain practices by imposing fines but should not try to determine actively how market participants must behave by setting prices or prescribing particular forms of conduct. The fines can be imposed on companies only, but it is also possible to complement them with individual penalties imposed on the responsible decision makers within the companies. The latter sanctions may include: fines inflicted upon individuals, imprisonment, or disqualification of directors who committed an antitrust violation. Decisions to impose fines interact with the implementation of leniency programmes. The latter are used to enhance the detection of cartels. By granting full or partial immunity to companies confessing their participation in a prohibited conspiracy, cartel participants get incentives to admit the illegal agreement and cooperate with the investigation started by the competition authority. Not only public agents but also private parties can play an important role in the enforcement of the competition rules. In the case of public enforcement, antitrust authorities may put an end to infringements in administrative law procedures. Private enforcement involves actions to obtain injunctive relief or damages brought by private parties in civil courts. By claiming damages for the harm suffered as a consequence of the violation of the competition rules, private parties may contribute to the achievement of both deterrence and compensation (corrective justice).

The structure of this chapter is as follows. Section 8.2 discusses the sanctions for infringement of the cartel prohibition. The merger review process is not described in this chapter; enforcement issues relating to merger control are discussed in the next chapter (see sections 9.3.2 and 9.4.5). The sanctions contained in both EU competition law and US antitrust law are discussed from a Comparative Law and Economics perspective. Section 8.2 also assesses the different sanctions from the viewpoint of retributive and corrective justice and pays attention to requirements of procedural justice (legal certainty, proportionality). Section 8.3 discusses the question relating to the enforcement agents. Whereas private parties so far have played a rather modest role in enforcing the EU competition rules, they have been much more active in the US. This has had an impact on both the number and type of cases under antitrust investigation. Section 8.3 discusses the advantages and disadvantages of both public and private enforcement. It is asked whether and to what extent, from an efficiency perspective, private court actions are an alternative for – or a desirable supplement to – enforcement by administrative agencies. The role of private enforcement in reaching corrective justice is also assessed. Particular attention is devoted to the 2014 Damages Directive,[2] which is supposed to facilitate and encourage private enforcement of EU competition law. The question discussed in section 8.4 relates to the timing of the legal intervention. It may be assumed that firms react differently to divergent enforcement regimes and that this will have an impact on the type of agreements entered into. If the system change from *ex ante* notification to *ex post* control of legality entails the risk that more harmful agreements are implemented or that some beneficial agreements are no longer signed (type I and type II errors), the new regime will be far from optimal. Section 8.4 gives an overview of the theoretical economic literature, which sheds some light on these questions, and attempts an economic evaluation of the system change. In section 8.5, the question is asked whether a decentralised enforcement system, as introduced in the EU from May 2004 onwards, is superior to a centralised control. Economic arguments for and against (de)centralisation are presented and an assessment of the system change is provided. Finally, section 8.6 concludes.

8.2 The choice of sanctions

8.2.1 Comparison of EU and US sanctions

This section subsequently discusses different types of sanctions, their legal form and severity. Thereafter, the enforcement practice of competition authorities is illuminated by an overview of the relevant Guidelines published by these agencies. The last part of this section discusses the conditions for granting leniency to antitrust offenders. Throughout the entire section, EU competition law is compared with US antitrust law.

Differences in types, legal form and severity of sanctions

As far as sanctions for infringement of competition rules are concerned, there are remarkable differences between EU competition law and US antitrust law (Wils 2002). These differences relate to the range of antitrust offenders that

---

[2] Directive 2014/104 on certain rules governing actions for damages under national law for infringements of the competition law provisions of the Member States and of the European Union [2014] OJ L 349/1.

can be fined, the type and legal form of the sanctions, and their magnitude. The first difference is that EU competition law – at European Commission level – is enforced by imposing fines on undertakings, whereas in US antitrust law such penalties are combined with fines on individuals as well as imprisonment. The Court of Justice of the European Union (CJEU) has defined undertakings as economic units, even if in law the economic unit may consist of several natural or legal persons.[3] In practice, for reasons of enforceability, the European Commission imposes fines on companies (or other legal persons), to which the violation committed by the undertaking is imputed. The situation in the US is different, since antitrust law is also enforced by means of sanctions imposed on individuals, including corporate directors, officers and employees. It may be added that recently individual fines have been introduced in the competition law of some EU Member States.[4] Hence, from the perspective of individual liability, the contrast between the two major competition law systems is diminishing.

A second difference relates to the legal form of the sanctions. If an infringement decision is taken[5] under Article 7 Regulation 1/2003, the European Commission may impose an administrative fine. In the US, criminal prosecution of hard-core cartels (price fixing, bid rigging and market allocation agreements) may be initiated by the Department of Justice. Comparing US antitrust law and EU competition law, one notices that fines can be either criminal or administrative. Criminal fines carry a stigma effect, showing that society morally disapproves infringements of the cartel prohibition. Whereas such a censure is clearly present in US antitrust law – both at the federal and state level – with respect to the most serious violations of the Sherman Act (price fixing, market sharing and bid rigging), the fines imposed under EU competition law for similar infringements are not of a criminal law nature (Article 23(5) Regulation 1/2003). It should be added, however, that the competition laws of an increasing number of EU Member States also allow for criminal sanctions, which can be imposed on both companies and individuals (see Box 8.1). The parallel provisions of administrative-type sanctions

---

[3] Case 170/83 *Hydroterm v. Compact* [1984] ECR 2999, para. 11.

[4] For example, the following maximum fines may be imposed on individuals: €450,000 in the Netherlands, €1 million in Germany, €75,000 in France and unlimited criminal fines in the United Kingdom.

[5] An infringement decision (Article 7 Regulation 1/2003) must be distinguished from a commitment decision (Article 9 Regulation 1/2003). The finding of an infringement may lead to a 'cease and desist' order, a termination of the practice (if not already ended), behavioural remedies (e.g. contractual obligations), structural remedies (divestitures) and fines. A commitment decision is not a final decision on the infringement and is available only for violations characterised by a lack of gravity. Commitments may be proposed by the parties; the practice is similar to the consent decrees under US antitrust law. The choice between an infringement decision and a commitment decision is a trade-off between procedural efficiency and deterrence. The latter may be cheaper to implement (even though monitoring is time consuming and costly, and the case may have to be reopened) but they lack the deterrent effect of fines imposed by an infringement decision.

at EU level and criminal-type sanctions at Member State level may lead to tensions in determining the appropriate level of fines and the desirability of leniency applications (see below).

Box 8.1: Criminal sanctions in national competition laws of EU Member States

The United Kingdom may serve as a primary example of the obstacles that may be encountered when competition law infringements are criminalised at the EU Member States' level. The apparent success of US criminal cartel convictions was a driving force behind the adoption of criminal penalties in the UK. However, if there is no competition culture similar to the one in the US, public support for criminalisation is weak and competition authorities face legitimacy issues when they start criminal proceedings. The Enterprise Act 2002 introduced prison sanctions, individual fines and director disqualifications. Section 188 of the Enterprise Act is formulated as a separate crime and applies only to obvious, hard-core agreements (price fixing, limitation of supply or production, market sharing, bid rigging). Conversely, the UK cartel offence does not apply to vertical agreements. In addition, abuses of a dominant position are not criminalised. Individuals who are found guilty of a cartel offence may be penalised with prison sanctions of up to five years and unlimited individual fines. Criminalised cartel offences are the subject of a trial by a jury in a criminal court. Aside from the cartel offence, the Enterprise Act also introduced company director disqualification for any infringement of the national competition law (Section 200).

To impose criminal sanctions, the legal system requires a narrowly focused prohibition. Hence, the cartel offence cannot be a copy of Article 101 TFEU, since the wording of this article (referring to all restrictions of competition) is much too broad and not appropriate for criminalisation. According to the original text of Section 188 of the Enterprise Act, the commission of the cartel crime required 'dishonesty'. This concept had two elements. As an objective matter, it had to be assessed whether the defendant acted dishonestly according to the standards of reasonable people. As a subjective matter, it had to be investigated whether the defendant realised that his behaviour was dishonest by those standards. The application of Section 188 remained far behind expectations: until 2016 fewer than ten cases (of which only three successful) were brought and not a single director disqualification order was decided. In order to make it easier to prosecute cartels, the Enterprise and Regulatory Reform Act 2013 removed the dishonesty requirement from the original text. To avoid an overly broad criminal offence, several statutory exclusions were inserted. These exclusions include notification of the cartel to customers, publication in an official public record, lack of intent to conceal the cartel and, remarkably, obtaining legal advice before the making or implementation of a cartel agreement. It may be doubted whether the latest legal reform will overcome the above problems and increase the use of criminal sanctions to deter cartelisation in the UK. Critics have argued that poor drafting and flawed exercise of enforcement powers are responsible for the failure to earn and secure the legitimacy of the criminalised cartel offence (Galloway 2016; Calvani and Carl 2013).

Infringements of competition have been (partly) criminalised also in other EU Member States. In Ireland, price fixing and related hard-core cartel behaviour are subject to criminal sanctions (Massey 2004). Conviction on indictment may result in a maximum corporate and individual fine of €4,000,000 or 10% of the turnover during the prior financial year. Individuals may also be sentenced to a maximum of ten years' imprisonment (Section 8 of the Irish Competition Act 2002). Ireland is the EU country which has imposed the highest number of imprisonment sentences but they have all been suspended (Marvão and Spagnolo 2016). As is the case in the UK, judges are not eager to impose criminal sanctions on cartel members (Calvani and Kaethe 2013). In Germany, restrictions of competition in relation to tenders (bid rigging) are punished with criminal sanctions and professional disqualifications (paragraph 298 *Strafgesetzbuch*, the German Penal Code). Criminal sanctions have been introduced also in France (up to 4 years' imprisonment for fraudulent and decisive participation in cartels, Article L 420-6 French Commercial Code), Denmark (imprisonment for between 18 months and 6 years), Austria (bid rigging), Italy (imprisonment of up to 5 years for bid rigging, Article 353 Codice Penale) and Estonia (see for more details the contributions in Cseres, Schinkel and Vogelaar 2006).

The third aspect in a US–EU comparison is the severity of the sanctions. The European Commission is empowered to impose on undertakings or associations of undertakings fines not exceeding 10% of the worldwide turnover in the preceding business year of each of the undertakings participating in the violation. In the US, corporations risk heavy criminal penalties. After two amendments of the Sherman Act (in 1974 and 1990) and the passing of an Alternative Fine Statute, the maximum fine has been further increased by the Antitrust Criminal Penalty Enhancement and Reform Act of 2004. The fine that can be imposed on an organisation now amounts to $100 million or, alternatively, twice the gross gain to the offender or twice the gross loss to the victims of the conspiracy.[6] The maximum sentence for individuals is ten years' imprisonment and a fine that is the greatest of $1 million, twice the gain to the cartel or twice the loss suffered by the victims.

---

[6] Antitrust Procedures and Penalties Act of 1974 § 3, Pub. L No. 93-528, 88 Stat. 1706; Antitrust Amendments Act of 1990 § 4, Pub. L No. 101-588, 104 Stat. 2879, 18 U.S.C. § 3571(d).

To avoid conclusions flowing solely from a 'law in the books' comparison, it must be empirically investigated how the legal differences work out in real-life antitrust practice. Available figures show an increase in fine levels over the past ten years in both the US and EU. In the period 2000–2003, the fines obtained by the Antitrust Division of the Department of Justice (DoJ) exceeded $150 million, $280 million, $75 million and $107 million, respectively. The fines obtained in 2004 totalled over $350 million.[7] Recent figures covering the last ten years provided by the DoJ indicate ever-increasing fines (with the exception of the fiscal years 2010 and 2011). Total criminal fines and penalties amounted to $338 million (2005), $473 million (2006), $630 million (2007), $701 million (2008), $1 billion (2009), $555 million (2010), 524 million (2011), $1.1 billion (2012), $1 billion (2013), $1.3 billion (2014) and $3.6 billion (2015). The picture in Europe shows fines that varied in magnitude in the period 2007–2013 but constantly reached higher levels than in the US. Giannaccari and Landi (2014) report the following data concerning total fines imposed by the European Commission: €809 million (2007), €2.2 billion (2008), €2.6 billion (2009), €2.8 billion (2010), €741 million (2011), €1.7 billion (2012) and €2.1 billion (2013). Obviously, to avoid the hasty conclusion that the EU enforcement is harsher than its US counterpart, the availability of criminal sanctions imposed on individuals (fines and imprisonment) in the latter system must be accounted for. In the reported fiscal years, the number of cases brought against individuals has always been larger than the number of corporations charged: for example, the proportion was 82/27 in 2011, 34/21 in 2013 and 66/20 in 2015. Since companies conspire to fix prices through individual employees (and the employer cannot reimburse the prison penalty), over the past 30 years the DoJ has sought longer incarcerations, rather than larger individual fines.[8] In the 1990s the average actual prison term was 8 months; this average increased to 20 months in the years 2000–2009 and 24 months in the period 2010–2015 (see http://www.justice.gov/atr for regular updates on the enforcement actions). It should be noted that the absence of individual criminal sanctions in the EU enforcement system is not corrected by imposing the highest possible administrative fines on companies. In fact, the vast majority of the fines imposed are below 1% of the firm's turnover and only 12% of the fines are close to the cap of 10% of the total turnover in the previous business year (Giannaccari and Landi 2014).

---

[7] See Hammond S, 'An overview of recent developments in the Antitrust Division's Criminal Enforcement Program' (Speech), Kona (Hawaii), January 10, 2005. For figures on total fines obtained in the years 2001–2003, see Magney and Anderson (2004).

[8] In January 2009, a 69-year-old executive was sentenced to 48 months in jail. This is the longest incarceration ever imposed for a single antitrust violation. US DoJ, 'Former Shipping Executive Sentenced to 48 Months in Jail for His Role in Antitrust Conspiracy', Press Release 09-075 (30 January 2009).

Guidelines on imposing fines

The European Commission enjoys large discretionary powers for setting fines in cases of intentional or negligent infringements of the EU competition rules (Article 23(2) Regulation 1/2003). The only limit provided for by law is that the imposed fine does not exceed 10% of the total turnover in the preceding business year of the infringing undertaking(s). For a long time, the Commission's fining policy was not based on specific criteria. Starting from the imposition of the first fines in the 1969 *Quinine* case[9] until the publication of the first Guidelines in 1998, no precise indications as to how particular factors were used in reaching specific fine levels were provided. In practice, a certain percentage of the turnover in one year of the different participants in the relevant market (usually the sales of the product in the European Community) was taken as the basis for administrative fines in cartel cases. In 1992, one author found that the fines varied roughly between 2% and 4% of the turnover in the European Community (Reynolds 1992). Heavier fines were imposed in cases of hard-core infringements (price fixing, market sharing); for example, in the 1994 *Cartonboard* case the fines amounted to 9% for the ringleaders and 6% for the foot soldiers.[10] In 1998, to ensure 'transparency and impartiality', the European Commission published its first Guidelines for calculating fines.[11] These Guidelines took a qualitative rather than a quantitative approach and were criticised for their opaque character. From a viewpoint of deterrence, the lack of reference to the quantity of goods affected by the price increase created the risk that fines were chosen regardless of the position of companies in the relevant market (Joshua and Camesasca 2004). In addition, the CJEU censured decisions of the European Commission that did not take account of the affected commerce and reduced the fines imposed.[12]

As a response to these criticisms and also to align the EU sanctions with the US enforcement system (plea bargains),[13] in 2006 the European Commission refined the old Guidelines and issued a new policy document. The 2006 Guidelines make clear that the European Commission follows a two-step methodology. In a first step, a basic amount of the fine is fixed and in a second step, this amount is adjusted upwards or downwards. The basic amount reflects

---

[9] Case IV/26623 *Quinine* [1969] O.J. L 192/5.

[10] Case IV/C/33.833 *Cartonboard* [1994] O.J. L 243/1.

[11] Guidelines on the method of setting fines [1998] O.J. C 9/3.

[12] Case T-61/99 *Adriatica di Navigazione SpA v. Commission* [2003] ECR-5349. The decision of the Court of First Instance in *Lysine* added that the relevant criterion is the overall impact on the market and not on an individual firm's conduct, Case T-224/200 *Archer Daniels Midland Company v. Commission* [2003] ECR II-2597.

[13] In US criminal proceedings parties may plead guilty in return for reduced fines.

the gravity and duration of the infringement. In fixing the basic amount, the European Commission refers to the value (before tax) of the undertaking's sales of goods or services to which the infringement relates in the affected geographical market. As a rule, the proportion of the value of sales taken into account is set at a level of up to 30% of the value of sales. The basic amount will be close to this maximum figure in case of hard-core infringements (price fixing, market sharing and output-limiting agreements). In choosing the percentage of the value of sales (up to a maximum of 30%), a variety of factors may be considered: the nature of the infringement, the combined market shares of the parties concerned, the geographical scope of the infringement and its degree of implementation (Guidelines, at 22). Next to the gravity of the infringement, the Commission adjusts the fine base to mirror the duration of the infringement. The value of sales is multiplied by the number of years of participation in the infringement. For example, the amount set for gravity may be increased up to 50% for infringements of between one and five years. Finally, in cases of hard-core infringements, the Commission also includes in the basic amount a sum of between 15% and 25% of the value of sales (so-called entry fee) in order to deter undertakings to entering into such practices. In the second step, the basic amount may be adjusted upwards for aggravating circumstances or downwards for attenuating circumstances. The Guidelines contain a non-exhaustive list of such circumstances. Aggravating circumstances include repeated infringements, refusal to cooperate or the role in a cartel as leader or instigator (Guidelines, at 28). Attenuating circumstances are, for example, the passive role in a cartel set-up or termination of the infringement as soon as the Commission intervenes (Guidelines, at 29). Further adjustments may have to be made to ensure that the imposed fine does not exceed the maximum ceiling of 10% of the worldwide turnover of the company involved in the conspiracy. In addition, in exceptional cases, the Commission may reduce the fine because of the inability to pay in a specific social and economic context. This requires objective evidence that imposition of the normal fine would irretrievably jeopardise the economic viability of the undertaking concerned and cause its assets to lose all their value (Guidelines, at 35). Eventually, the last step in the calculation of the fine is the application of the percentage reduction as provided for in the Leniency Notice if the requirements of the latter (see next section) are satisfied.

In contrast with the older EU enforcement policy, figures relating to the volume of the affected commerce have been always crucial for calculating fines in US antitrust law. The US Sentencing Guidelines use 20% of the volume of affected commerce as the base fine level for convicted organisations.[14]

---

[14] See US Sentencing Commission, *Guidelines Manual*, November 2003, § 2R1.1 (d) 1, p. 275. For a complete description of the application of the US Sentencing Guidelines, see Wise (2004).

In drafting these Guidelines, the Sentencing Commission has relied on estimates that the average overcharge from price fixing is 10% of the selling price.[15] Since the Sentencing Commission believes that the loss to society is larger than the excess profits gained by the cartel members, this percentage is doubled to set the start point for the fine calculation. Depending on culpability factors and other circumstances, the fines for organisations may be increased up to 80% of the volume of affected commerce and thus reach a level that is eight times the assumed overcharge from price fixing.

Leniency programmes

Public enforcers often lack sufficient evidence to prove a violation of the competition rules. This is particularly worrisome in the case of hard-core cartels (such as price fixing and agreements to share markets), which may result in increased prices and reduced choices for consumers without any redeeming virtue. Leniency programmes aim at increasing the rate of detection by granting favourable treatment to companies willing to inform the antitrust authorities about serious infringements and to put an end to their participation in secret cartels. In order to improve the chances that hidden cartels are detected and punished, the Antitrust Division of the DoJ started an amnesty programme in 1978. Under that programme, cartel members who reported their illegal activity before an investigation was under way were eligible for complete immunity from criminal sanctions. The grant of amnesty, however, was not automatic and the Antitrust Division retained a large margin of discretion in the decision-making process. This first programme was not successful: only a few amnesty applications were filed and no single international cartel was detected.

In 1993, three major revisions were made to the US Leniency Programme. First, amnesty has become certain when a corporation comes forward prior to an investigation and meets the programme's requirements. These conditions include duties to terminate promptly the participation in the illegal activity, to cooperate fully with the Antitrust Division and to make restitution to injured parties. Amnesty will be granted only if, at the time the corporation comes forward with evidence, the Antitrust Division had not yet received information about the illegal activity from another source. Second, amnesty may still be available even if cooperation with the Antitrust Division starts after the investigation is under way. Third, if a corporation qualifies for automatic amnesty, then all officers, directors and employees who cooperate are equally protected from criminal prosecution.

---

[15] Recent research has shown that this figure may seriously underestimate the price increases caused by cartels. See section 8.3.3.

US antitrust law does not require that the applicant meets an evidential burden to be conditionally admitted to the DoJ's Programme, provided the illegal activity is reported with candour and completeness. To grant leniency before an investigation has begun, six conditions must be met. These conditions are the following: (i) the Antitrust Division has not received information about the illegal activity from any other source; (ii) the corporation took prompt and effective action to terminate its part in the activity; (iii) the corporation reports the wrongdoing with candour and completeness and provides full cooperation; (iv) the confession is truly a corporate act, as opposed to isolated confessions of individual executives or officials; (v) where possible, the corporation makes restitution to injured parties; and (vi) the corporation did not coerce another party to participate in the illegal activity and clearly was not the leader or originator of the activity. Leniency may also be granted, after an investigation has begun, to the corporation that is the first to come forward at the time when the Antitrust Division does not yet have evidence that is likely to result in a sustainable conviction and granting leniency is not unfair to others. In the latter case, most of the above conditions (ii)–(v) equally apply.[16]

In 1994, the US corporate leniency programme was complemented by a leniency policy for individuals which renders them immune from criminal charges.[17] In addition, the Antitrust Criminal Penalty Enhancement and Reform Act of 2004 further increased the effectiveness of the leniency programme by excluding the possibility that if the conditions for amnesty are satisfied, individual claimants may collect treble damages for infringements of the antitrust laws. This 'detrebling' provision in the case of a company that cooperates with private litigants against other members of a cartel has removed a major disincentive for submitting amnesty applications. The revised US leniency policy had an enormous impact on the incentives of companies and individuals to report illegal conspiracies. In recent years, the US Corporate Leniency Programme has been responsible for detecting and cracking many hard-core violations, in particular international price-fixing cartels.

The European leniency programme started in 1996.[18] In spite of the US experience that was already available at that time, the European amnesty programme took a timid start. Under the first Leniency Notice, full immunity from fines was not guaranteed. Even the first firm willing to cooperate with

---

[16] US Federal Department of Justice, Corporate Leniency Policy, available at: https://www.justice.gov/atr/corporate-leniency-policy.

[17] US Federal Department of Justice, Leniency Policy for Individuals, available at: https://www.justice.gov/atr/leniency-program.

[18] Commission Notice on the non-imposition or reduction of fines in cartel cases, [1996] O.J. C 207/4. For a detailed analysis on this first Notice, see Wils (1997).

the European Commission by providing information about the infringement could nevertheless be penalised up to 25% of the otherwise imposed fine. It was also required that the leniency applicant came forward with 'decisive evidence' proving the existence of the cartel. The 2002 Leniency Notice[19] made cooperation with the Commission much more attractive by making it possible to grant full immunity from fines for the first company which cooperates with the Commission, and by replacing the 'decisive evidence' requirement by two different evidential thresholds for obtaining full leniency in different situations. In addition, firms that were not the first to come forward with the required evidence and, therefore, cannot profit from full immunity are still eligible for a reduction of the fine. In 2006 the European Commission again amended its Leniency Notice, mainly to clarify the information to be provided by leniency applicants and the duty of cooperation.[20]

Under the current Leniency Programme, the European Commission will grant an undertaking immunity from any fine if the undertaking is the first to submit information and evidence which may enable the Commission to carry out a targeted inspection in connection with the cartel (commonly a surprise investigation: a so-called dawn raid) and if, at the time of the application for immunity, the Commission did not yet have sufficient evidence to carry out an inspection. The immunity applicant must provide the Commission with a leniency corporate statement, which must provide a detailed description of the cartel arrangement and other evidence related to the alleged cartel. A number of additional requirements must be met to qualify for immunity. These include the following: (i) the company must cooperate fully and continuously with the Commission; (ii) it must have ended its involvement in the cartel at the time when it submitted the required evidence; and (iii) it may not have coerced other undertakings to join the cartel.

A peculiar characteristic of the EU Leniency Programme, which does not exist under the US system, is the sliding scale, whereby companies that do not qualify for full amnesty are still eligible for reduction in fines ranging from 20% to 50%. In contrast with the US 'winner takes it all' approach, undertakings may be granted a reduction of fines if they submit evidence which represents 'significant added value' with respect to the suspected infringement, provided they fulfil the conditions that apply to immunity applicants (i.e. ending their involvement in the cartel no later than the time at which the evidence is submitted and genuine, full cooperation with the Commission's investigation). The reductions in fines may reach a maximum of 50%. The timing is crucial: the first company willing to cooperate may

---

[19] Notice on immunity from fines and reduction of fines in cartel cases [2002] O.J. C 45/3.
[20] Commission Notice on immunity from fines and reduction of fines in cartel cases [2006] O.J. C 298/17.

obtain a reduction in fines of between 30% and 50%, the second will be able to obtain a reduction of between 20% and 30%, and the reduction for all others is limited to a maximum of 20%. The precise percentage reduction a company will obtain within the category to which it is allocated depends on the nature and the level of detail of the submitted evidence – the Commission prefers evidence originating from the period to which the facts pertain to evidence subsequently established or to circumstantial evidence – and the extent and continuity of the cooperation. It may be added that the Commission introduced a cartel settlement procedure in 2008, under which undertakings can obtain an additional fine reduction of 10% if they make a formal settlement submission, which recognises the infringement, the undertaking's liability for the infringement and the acceptance of a range of likely fines and a waiver of some procedural rights.[21]

8.2.2 Economic assessment

Different enforcement goals and the concept of optimal enforcement

The effectiveness of (the level of) fines can be judged in different ways, depending on the goal(s) that sanctions are supposed to achieve. Economic analysis cannot offer clear guidance if it must be judged whether the offender is adequately punished, since economic parameters (such as the gains achieved) are no reliable indicator of the degree of moral disapproval that society wishes to signal (retributive justice). From an economic point of view, the most relevant goal to be assessed is the ability of the enforcement system to deter violations of competition law. Consequently, the economic analysis below provides an assessment of whether the sanctions imposed are effective in preventing future infringements, both by the punished offender(s) and other companies active in the market. The European Commission's 2006 Guidelines on the method of setting fines subscribe to the deterrence goal: fines should impose a pecuniary sanction on undertakings that violated competition law and deter future infringements by those and other firms.[22] Fines imposed for reasons of deterrence should be sufficiently high to make it unprofitable for firms to engage in anti-competitive practices. For antitrust

---

[21] Commission Regulation (EC) No 622/2008 of 30 June 2008 amending Regulation (EC) No 773/2004, as regards the conduct of settlement procedures in cartel cases [2008] O.J. L 171/3. For a comment on the settlement procedure, see Wils (2008). This article clarifies that plea bargaining in the US can be seen as a combination of reductions of fines and settlements.

[22] 'Fines should have a sufficiently deterrent effect, not only in order to sanction the undertakings concerned (specific deterrence) but also in order to deter other undertakings from engaging in, or continuing, behaviour that is contrary to Articles 81 and 82 of the EC Treaty (general deterrence)' (Guidelines, at 4). See also the early ECJ judgment in the *ACF Chemiefarma* case, where the Court held that fines 'have as their objective to suppress illegal conduct as well as to prevent it being repeated'.

conspiracies of which the probability of detection is low (such as price fix-ing), traditional deterrence theory teaches that it is imperative to require the payment of the multiple of profits to achieve efficiency. If a multiplier in inverse proportion to the probability of detection and punishment of the violation needs to be applied, the resulting fine may exceed the ability to pay of the antitrust offender. When such a judgment-proof problem arises, competition law may provide alternative sanctions, such as imprisonment of the individual decision makers (e.g. directors of companies) who decided to commit an antitrust violation.

Besides the focus on deterrence, the analysis below investigates whether the current sanctioning policy achieves corrective justice and equally respects legal due process requirements (procedural fairness, proportionality). This extension of the analysis is necessary to obtain a more complete understand-ing of the current enforcement mechanisms, which are not exclusively based on deterrence goals. Sending corporate managers to jail may seem a very harsh sanction in countries lacking a competition culture. Even though such an ap-proach may be necessary to achieve deterrence, it may conflict with other no-tions of adequate punishment, such as the legal proportionality requirement. Under the latter approach, only (administrative) fines may be considered appropriate sanctions. These fines may be lower than the amount required for effective deterrence if their only purpose is to guarantee corrective justice, implying that a committed wrong is corrected by forcing the wrongdoer to pay a sum of money that is an adequate compensation for the harm caused. Alternatively – from a perspective of corrective justice – one may consider it 'just' to disgorge the profits realised by the infringement of the law. Again, this will have an impact on the amount of the monetary sanction, implying that it may be lower than the sum needed to achieve deterrence. A simple example can illustrate that fines imposed for reasons of deterrence may be (much) higher than sanctions imposed for reasons of corrective justice. If the profit achieved by a price-fixing cartel equals 10, the harm caused to society in terms of deadweight loss amounts to 20 and the probability of detection is 15%, the fine to achieve deterrence should be at least 67.[23] Conversely, the fines to compensate for the harm (20) or to make sure that profits are disgorged (10) are both considerably lower. The problem with deterrence-based amounts of punishment is that they create a gap between the sanction imposed and the offending conduct in individual cases. As formulated by Yeung, such sanctions are 'prone to generating counter-intuitive outcomes which may appear at odds with the community's perception of fairness and

---

[23] The fine will need to be even higher if the goal is to internalise the full social costs of cartels. Victim groups include direct buyers, indirect buyers (firms downstream in the supply chain, end consumers) and suppliers of a cartel. On top of these losses, costs of rent-seeking must be accounted for.

morality' (Yeung 2004, 70). In sum, the deterrence goal may conflict with justice goals. Policy makers must make a number of choices, depending on the goals they are willing to achieve. In making these choices, they should realise that different policy goals may be inconsistent with each other and should find ways to reduce the ensuing tensions or carefully make inevitable trade-offs.

Turning back to the deterrence goal, a crucial insight to be kept in mind when judging different enforcement mechanisms is that full deterrence cannot be achieved. Not only will companies constantly find new creative ways to obstruct the detection of illegal conspiracies; prevention of all cartel agreements is simply too costly. The policy choices relating to the type and severity of sanctions and the resources to be spent on detection should fully account for the resulting enforcement costs. These include administrative costs (costs of detection, prosecution and punishment) and the costs of legal and economic advice for both law enforcers and offenders. From an economic perspective, the latter costs are a pure deadweight loss. An optimal enforcement regime will investigate possible antitrust violations only as long as the goal of deterrence is worth the costs of attaining it (Elzinga and Breit 1976, 9; Souam 2001). Optimal enforcement requires an efficient mix of enforcement expenditures and fines (and/or imprisonment). Similar conclusions will be reached when the goal of enforcement is corrective justice through compensation; again, the presence of enforcement costs will imply that full compensation is not optimal.

Enforcement mechanisms to achieve deterrence

In a deterrence approach, the sanctions imposed for infringements of competition rules must achieve a genuine dissuasive effect and ensure that firms have an incentive to avoid any kind of unlawful anti-competitive agreement or practice. In a seminal contribution, Nobel prize winner Gary Becker has shown that criminal fines can be understood as prices attached to certain forms of undesirable conduct. If the price is too high, rational people will refrain from engaging in such behaviour. Alternatively, crimes will be committed if the expected benefits exceed the expected costs, which equal the statutory fine discounted by the probability of detection and punishment (Becker 1968). Becker's view on criminal sanctions is most relevant for the enforcement of the cartel prohibition. Whereas the assumption of rational behaviour may be criticised with regard to irrational crimes (such as murder), calculating behaviour seems a rather realistic scenario for white-collar crimes. Antitrust violations generally result from calculating business decisions.[24] Firms will engage in price fixing if the gains derived from this activity are higher than the costs, both adjusted for the probability that they will materialise in case of detection and punishment. In cases of *per se* prohibitions and easy qualification of the act as an infringement of the law, the main enforcement problem is the detection of the infringement. In other cases, the standard of proof allowing the imposition of punishment will be more burdensome. For the latter reason, it seems that the Becker model of the rational criminal is most suitable for hard-core cartels. The costs of colluding consist not only of fines (F) imposed by competition authorities but also of damages (D) awarded by the courts multiplied with the probability of detection and punishment (p). The costs expected by the colluding firm must exceed the gains (π) expected by the potential law infringer. This can be rewritten as:

$$\pi < p(F+D)$$

The other side of the coin is the cost of different enforcement mechanisms. Both the choice of the sanction and the way in which it is determined are relevant here. Clearly, imprisonment is more costly than imposing fines. Next, for the calculation of the fines it is easier to estimate the gains of an antitrust violation than to assess the harm caused. Gains are a function of increased consumer prices that may be estimated econometrically, whereas the calculation of the deadweight loss is fraught with great difficulties. The upper ceiling of the enforcement costs is given by the deadweight loss and the losses of dynamic efficiency and rent-seeking (see section 2.3.4); beyond this limit the enforcement of antitrust rules is welfare-reducing. Consequently, a low level of collusive activity will always remain and should not be challenged by the enforcement agencies because it would be too costly compared with the social benefits that can be obtained.

A standard argument in the Law and Economics literature is that a combination of a low probability of detection and high fines is best in terms of efficiency (Eide 1999, Block and Sidak 1980). According to Becker's model, which assumes that monetary sanctions can be increased without cost (since they simply amount to a transfer of wealth from the offender to the society), fines should be increased up to the highest feasible level, which is up to the ability to pay of the offender. By keeping at the same time the probability of detection at the lowest level, the highest level of deterrence can be reached with the lowest use of scarce resources. For competition authorities, it is

---

[24] The results of a survey by Feinberg (1985) confirm that disregard for the law in pursuit of profits is an important source of EU antitrust violations.

indeed very costly to control all kinds of behaviour in order to detect infringements, and important resources can be saved by keeping the probability of detection low. Moreover, the scope for raising the enforcement resources is limited in practice, since enforcement budgets are fixed and cannot be easily changed. It follows from traditional deterrence theory that optimality can still be achieved when fines are increased in order to compensate for a low probability of detection. However, three problems remain. First, it is difficult to choose an increase in fines that is exactly proportionate to the decrease in the optimal amount of resources spent on detection. Second, fines may create distortive effects. For example, if fines are calculated based on a share of the affected commerce, firms have an incentive to increase the cartel price above the monopolistic price (for this and other distortions, see Bageri *et al.* 2013). Third, behavioural studies suggest that, at least for some crimes, an increase in sanction severity does not act as a deterrent but an increase in the probability of sanction does. If the perceived likelihood of detection contributes more to compliance behaviour than the severity of the sanction, the basic deterrence matrix of low probability and high severity of punishment (including criminalisation) becomes questionable (Beaton-Wells and Parker 2013).

The next question relates to the amount of the efficient fine. To set this fine, information is needed about both the probability of detection and the amount of the gains in cases of competition law infringements. It is clear that cartels cause more harm to society than gains for the participants, since only part of the losses are recovered through transfer to the cartels. The harm of such antitrust infringements is difficult to assess, since it does not simply equal the consumer surplus transferred to the producer but also consists of the additional loss of consumer welfare (deadweight loss), the harm in terms of productive and dynamic efficiencies as well as the costs of the rent-seeking efforts. To achieve deterrence, however, it is sufficient to know the size of the gains, since this amount multiplied in inverse proportion to the probability of detection and punishment enables the enforcement agency to set the fine above the expected profit (Polinsky and Shavell 1994). A different approach originating in Chicago School thinking is based on the need to internalise the full social costs of cartels. Companies confronted with this socially optimal sanction will commit only 'efficient' violations of antitrust law (Landes 1983; Becker 1968). The former approach may be preferred to the latter since the calculation of gains is more amenable to everyday antitrust practice than the calculation of the deadweight loss. Compared with the problems in determining the harm (which *inter alia* requires information on the elasticity of demand and supply and the size of the rent-seeking efforts), the determination of the gain (even though difficult enough in its own right) is easier to assess. This explains why with regard to the determination of sanctions more attention is paid to the financial benefits of the infringement than to the harm caused (Van Oers and Van der Meulen 2003).

The comparison of the EU and US enforcement regimes has shown that fines can be calculated either based on figures about turnover, or by referring to the gains of the lawbreakers or the losses caused by the infringement of the competition rules. From a deterrence perspective, it is crucial to estimate both the gains of a cartel and the detection rate.

Taking a price cartel as an example, the gains that the cartel members obtain will depend on the sales volume of the products concerned by the violation, the price increase caused by the cartel, the price elasticity of demand faced by the cartel members and the duration of the cartel. The gains equal the mark-up times the volume of the affected commerce. Figures on sales are not difficult to obtain given the broad availability of market studies. It is more difficult to determine the mark-up, since this requires either econometric calculation or the identification of a benchmark of the competitive price in the absence of collusion. The first method requires data on costs, prices and quantities that must be interpreted by using a credible model of interaction without collusion. The second method requires the use of reference prices, like foreign prices (corrected according to national differences in the level of costs) or historical prices (before and after method). Both methods pose theoretical difficulties and empirical complexities. While acknowledging these problems, reference can be made to a couple of papers that have tried to estimate the size of the cartel overcharge. Connor and Bolotova (2006) found that the overcharge is 17–19% for domestic US cartels and 30–33% for international cartels. Combe and Monnier (2011) identified an overcharge of 34%. The second element needed to set an efficient fine is the rate of detection. From the 1980s onwards, several studies were published that estimate the percentage of detected cartels. Generally, estimates range between 10% and 17%.[25]

Bringing the estimates of the rate of detection and the size of the overcharge together, it becomes possible to calculate the efficient fine. Examples in the literature are based on the assumptions that, on average, cartels raise prices by 10% and that the cartel duration is five years.[26] If a price increase of 10% leads to an increase in profits of 5% of turnover, the cartel lasts five years and

---

[25] See Werden and Simon (1987, 917): probability lower than 10%; Bryant and Eckard (1991, 531): probability between 13% and 17%; Combe and Monnier (2011, 256): probability of 15%.

[26] These figures are based on American studies. Figures on road building bid-rigging cases suggest that the conspiracies increased price by at least 10%. See Wils (2002), with further references. Own-price elasticity of demand is supposed to be −2.

the probability of detection and punishment is 16%,[27] a fine in the order of no less than 150% of the annual turnover would be needed to effectively deter a price cartel from being implemented (Wils 2002, 201). The research mentioned above shows that the appropriate multiplier might be much higher than the last figure. Connor and Lande found that the overcharge is between 15% and 16% for domestic US cartels and 25% for international cartels. In addition, they note that cartel duration is likely to be longer than five years: cartels may last between seven and eight years. If only the adjustment for the underestimated overcharge is made, fines would have to be in the range of 225–375% of annual turnover to deter (Lande and Connor 2007). Finally, Werden estimates that a deterrent fine should be set around 200% of the annual turnover of the firm in the relevant market (Werden 2009). Such high fines are far above the percentage figures that can be deduced from the European Commission's sanctioning practice. Up until 1998, fines were in the range of between 2% and 9% of the turnover in the products concerned by the violation. Fines have considerably increased after the publication of the Guidelines,[28] but – since the maximum level of 10% of the annual worldwide turnover has not been adjusted upwards – may still be too low to effectively deter serious infringements of the European competition rules.

Do antitrust fines achieve deterrence? A comparison of US antitrust law and EU competition law

Several reasons may be advanced why the current enforcement of EU competition rules is not economically optimal and its US counterpart scores better on the deterrence scale. First, the level of fines in absolute terms is higher in the US than in the EU. The changes to the Sherman Act, increasing the fines up to $100 million or twice the gain/loss resulting from the conspiracy, clearly reflect a goal of deterrence.[29] The US Sentencing Guidelines accept that it is possible to estimate the gains achieved by a cartel as a percentage of the selling price. The gains to the cartel can be estimated as the product of the volume of sales and the price increase. The US Federal Sentencing Commission model takes as the start point 20% of the total volume of

---

[27] This figure is based on an American study, estimating the probability of a successful prosecution of a price cartel at most between 13% and 17%. See Bryant and Eckard (1991).

[28] Record fines have been imposed for hard-core cartels, such as Case IV/31.149 *Polypropylene* [1986] O.J. L 230/1, Case IV/33.833 *Cartonboard* [1994] O.J. L 243/1, and Case COMP/37.512 *Vitamins* [2003] O.J. L 6/1.

[29] The goal of deterrence was also clearly embraced by the American Congress: 'The committee believes that increasing the maximum fines for criminal violations of section 1 is necessary and appropriate to deter the most flagrant and abusive forms of antitrust crimes (…) Particularly with respect to corporate offenders, fine levels are simply too low to deter effectively antitrust conspiracies and courts have been reluctant to impose maximum fines even for wilful violations' (Senate Report to the Antitrust Amendments Act of 1990, Senate Report No. 101-287, 1990 U.S. Code Congress and Admin. News, at 4111).

affected commerce, but allows adjusting this figure upwards to no less than 80%. This is ten times the percentage of turnover that was imposed by the EU Commission in the period before the 2006 Guidelines were issued. An increase in the level of sanctions has been left out of the European debate on the revision of the enforcement system. There is no guarantee that the fines that can be imposed on multi-billion-euro corporations within the limit of 10% of total turnover will be sufficiently high to achieve deterrence.

Second, US antitrust law allows imposing sanctions upon individuals (decision makers within the company) whereas the administrative fines in the EU can be inflicted upon undertakings only. In a critical evaluation of the EU enforcement system, Wils proposes to make use of individual penalties, including imprisonment, in combination with corporate sanctions. Even increasing the fines on companies above the current limit of 10% of the worldwide turnover would not cure the problem of under-deterrence, for the following reasons. First, profits are usually not retained and, in any case, would count for only a fraction of the fine. Moreover, liquidating the assets would not generate sufficient revenues if the annual turnover exceeds the assets. Second, imposing very high fines would force companies into bankruptcy, causing undesirable social costs (losses to, among others, employees, creditors and tax authorities). Third, the imposition of high fines may have undesirable side effects. Creditors will suffer a diminution in the value of their securities, salaries of employees may be cut down, tax receipts will be reduced and the costs may be passed on to consumers in the form of higher prices (Wils 2005; Wils 2002). According to Wils, deterrence can be best increased by threatening the accountable decision makers within the firm with individual fines.

Third, the European enforcement regime does not provide a remedy for the judgment-proof problem. There is indeed a risk that the financial position of firms which violated the competition rules will not allow them to pay the fines imposed.[30] The deterrence goal will not be achieved if no alternative sanctions to cure the judgment-proof problem, such as imprisonment, are available. In addition, prison sanctions overcome the problem that firms may compensate managers *ex ante* for taking the risk of committing antitrust violations or indemnify them *ex post*, thus taking away the deterrent effect of fines. Imprisonment avoids such circumventing behaviour (Wils 2002). The judgment-proof problem has gained particular prominence in the aftermath of the financial crisis. Spagnolo neatly characterises the immunity of banks as a 'too big to fine' problem; this makes banks more judgment-proof than other firms. If governments and regulators are unwilling to let large banks bear the

---

[30] In fact, the Guidelines on fines already provide for a possible reduction of the fine to take into account a company's (in)ability to pay.

consequences of their mistakes, in order to prevent bankruptcy and the need to recapitalise banks, large banks may have more incentives to misbehave. The (in)famous *LIBOR* case[31] shows that price fixing by banks is a realistic scenario. To deter cartels in the banking industry, sending CEOs of large banks to prison may be the only solution for the 'too big to fine' problem (Marvão and Spagnolo 2016). A final remark is appropriate. Even though prison sanctions may be a very effective deterrent and carry a strong moral message, they should be used only for hard-core infringements (horizontal price fixing, bid rigging and market allocation schemes). Imprisonment should not be used for other horizontal agreements, vertical restraints and infringements because of the risk of type I errors.

Fines from a justice perspective

In EU competition law fines serve two goals: punishment (retributive justice) and deterrence.[32] Contrary to the US vision of things, the justice goal may be given more importance than the deterrence goal. Regulation 1/2003 seems to reflect requirements of proportional justice rather than deterrence. As explained above, the upper ceiling expressed as 10% of the worldwide turnover of the undertaking, which committed an antitrust violation, is ill-suited to achieve deterrence. Its only function seems to be the determination of the limit above which the size of the fine is deemed to be dangerous for the existence itself of the undertaking and, hence, not proportional. The maximum fine reflects the degree of disapproval of the behaviour. In Europe there is not (yet) a competition culture comparable to the US one and people still tend to consider infringements of competition rules less serious than other forms of disapproved conduct sanctioned by criminal fines (although reference must be made to criminalisation of competition law in a number of EU Member States, see Box 8.1). Very high fines (such as 200% of the annual turnover of the products concerned by the violation) imposed to achieve deterrence may be disproportionate to the degree in which society disapproves of the harm caused and thus conflicts with goals of proportional justice (Article 49(3) TFEU).

A similar concern seems to underlie the use of leniency programmes. The tension arises between the principle of equal treatment and the immunity of fines needed to provide incentives for self-reporting. There may be concerns about lack of retributive justice if an antitrust offender escapes punishment

---

[31] Case AT.39924 — *Swiss Franc Interest Rate Derivatives*) (CHF LIBOR), O.J. C 72, 28.2.2015, p. 9–11.

[32] Case 41-69, *ACF Chemiefarma NV v Commission of the European Communities*, at paras 171–174; Joined cases 100 to 103/80, *SA Musique Diffusion française and others v Commission of the European Communities*, at paras 105–108; European Commission, Guidelines on the method of setting fines, at 4.

and if the application of the leniency programme leads to unequal treatment of the cartel participants. In an extreme case, where a cartel has only two members, one firm is immunised and the other condemned to pay the maximum (eventually, criminal) fine. Such vastly different treatments conflict with perceptions of retributive justice and fairness (requirement of proportionality) in jurisdictions where law enforcers are expected to be unbiased pursuers of justice (see for further discussion: Harding, Beaton-Wells and Edwards 2015).

Economic assessment of leniency programmes

Leniency programmes may significantly contribute to the efficiency of law enforcement. Competition authorities may try to detect and punish cartels by using their investigatory powers (requests for information and inspections) but requirements of procedural justice may limit the use of these instruments to cases where there are already relatively precise indications about a suspected cartel agreement. The most severe infringements of competition law (horizontal price fixing, bid rigging) are commonly the result of secret agreements and the involved companies or their staff may be the only ones holding the necessary evidence to prove the violations. By guaranteeing a lenient treatment for the cheaters and making it profitable to deviate from the collusive path, leniency programmes aim at destabilising cartels. Leniency programmes bring not only direct benefits, resulting from lowering the costs of detection in cases of hard-core violations, but also indirect benefits. Since antitrust authorities can devote more resources to cartels that are not revealed, the detection rate of the latter may also increase.

The leniency programme has a clear underlying economic logic: it increases the probability of detection and punishment by placing the cartel members in a prisoner's dilemma (see section 5.2). All cartel members have an interest that the cartel cannot be proven (not to confess) but mistrust among the cartel members creates a race to be the first to confess. In a prisoner's dilemma, each player can be better off by defecting from the 'not confess' to the 'confess' strategy. Hence, the cartel members may decide to confess, even though it is in their common interest not to do so. Consider the very common situation when a cartel first learns that it is under investigation. Each member of that cartel knows that any of its co-conspirators can be the first to come forward in exchange for total immunity from fines. Such a decision will seal the fate of all other cartel members. Clearly, it would be in the common interest of the cartel members that nobody decides to cooperate with the antitrust authority, thus depriving the latter of the evidence needed to prove an infringement.

However, the amnesty for the first one through the antitrust authority's door creates tension and mistrust among the cartel members.

Legal commentators argue that the experience with the US amnesty programme teaches that leniency programmes are successful when three conditions are met (see the discussions by Sandhu 2007; Riley 2002). First, antitrust laws must provide the threat of firm sanctions for hard-core infringements. Second, antitrust offenders must perceive a significant risk of detection by antitrust authorities if they engage in illegal conspiracies. Third, antitrust authorities must publish clear and transparent leniency programmes so that prospective cooperating parties can predict with a high degree of certainty whether they will get immunity. Since the first two conditions are met to a lesser extent in Europe, the European Commission's leniency programme risks being less successful than its US counterpart is. Exposure to criminal sanctions may be the driving factor in the decision of US firms to cooperate with the antitrust authorities. In addition, if competition law infringements are not of a criminal law nature, a number of investigative techniques will not be available, thus reducing the perceived risk of detection. With respect to the third requirement, the heavy evidential burden of 'decisive evidence' contained in the first European leniency programme has been replaced by less stringent requirements that bring the European programme more in line with its US counterpart. An evidential hurdle continues to exist for partial amnesty (granted to firms not qualifying for full immunity from fines), which can be granted only if the evidence submitted represents 'significant added value'. In both US and EU systems of enforcement, the clarity and transparency of the leniency programme are still reduced by fairness arguments. In Europe, companies that did 'take steps to coerce other undertakings to participate in the infringement' (see the Leniency Notice, at 11c) do not qualify for full immunity. In the US, a similar restriction applies if leniency is required before an investigation has begun and no information about the illegal activity has been reported from any other source. In other cases and after an investigation has begun, the Antitrust Division may decide not to grant leniency if this would be 'unfair' to others. Discretionary powers to assess the role of companies in the offence may be defensible for corrective justice reasons. However, if companies cannot predict how 'coercion' will be interpreted, they may decide against cooperation and existing cartels may remain unreported and unpunished. It may be added that the lesson that leniency programmes must be clear, transparent and predictable is also very relevant for the design of leniency policies in developing countries. For example, the lack of success of the Chinese leniency programme has been attributed to its ambiguity and inconsistency (see for further discussion: Oded 2013).

Turning to the theoretical economic literature, several useful insights for designing optimal leniency programmes can be found (for a survey on the economics of leniency programmes in antitrust, see Spagnolo 2008). Motta and Polo have demonstrated that it can be efficient to reduce fines even when an antitrust investigation is already under way but the competition authority has not yet obtained evidence of an infringement. Reduced fines are a second-best instrument in cases where the budget of the competition authority is not sufficiently high to conduct investigations and intervene often enough to fully deter collusion (Motta and Polo 2001). The Leniency Programme of the European Commission is in line with this theoretical insight, since it admits cartel members to join the leniency programme even after an investigation has started, when the incentive to cheat is stronger and the cartel more unstable. The economic literature also shows that positive rewards may deter collusion in a more effective way than reduced fines by increasing the incentives to self-report, even though apparently reducing deterrence. Spagnolo assumes that cartels are convicted after detection and focuses on cartels that are not already under investigation. He shows that an efficient outcome is reached when the competition authority offers a positive award equal to the sum of the fines paid by the convicted firms to the first party that reports (Spagnolo 2004). If the maximum fine is high enough, such a reward policy can achieve full deterrence at no cost. Aubert, Rey and Kovacic demonstrate that positive rewards have a larger deterrence effect than reduced fines and that rewards for individuals be more effective than corporate ones. In particular, positive rewards to employees can be very effective, provided they are high enough to compensate the employee for the anticipated reduction in future earnings, since being a whistle-blower is likely to end the insider's career with his employer and possibly with the entire industry. These authors also discuss remedies for potential adverse effects of reward programmes, such as introducing fines for false denunciations in order to avoid restrictions of efficient exchanges of information between competing firms (Aubert, Rey and Kovacic 2006). Also, recent experimental studies have shown that the use of rewards may have a stronger effect on cartel detection than fine reductions (Bigoni 2012). The latter insights from economic theory have not generated much enthusiasm from antitrust enforcers. Even though whistle-blower rewards become increasingly popular in the fight against fraud, competition authorities have been extremely reluctant to give rewards to whistle-blowers and, if they do (e.g. in the US, UK and Ireland), the amounts are typically too low to compensate for potential retaliation costs imposed by the convicted firm (Marvão and Spagnolo 2016).

A persisting problem of leniency programmes is their potential counter-productive effect, which manifests itself in three forms: the lowering of the average fine, an excessive reliance on leniency as a substitute for investigative efforts and the potential strategic use of leniency programmes by cartelists. As a consequence of granting leniency to cartels, the overall fines will be lower since companies that come forward with relevant evidence will get (full or partial) immunity. There is a negative impact on deterrence *ex ante* since the overall expected fines will be lower, given the possibility of a fine reduction for law offenders who have cooperated with the antitrust authorities (Motta and Polo 2001). Possible negative effects on deterrence may be mitigated by raising the level of sanctions and through limiting conditions for immunity. Experimental research shows the importance of the absolute level of fines and suggests that the combination of severe sanctions and a well-managed leniency policy allows reducing the costs of random inspections (Bigoni *et al.* 2015). On both points, the US leniency programme seems to score better than its EU counterpart. First, EU competition law is in need of stiffer sanctions (in particular imprisonment) to effectively deter. Even though the European Commission increased the fine level concomitant with the adoption of the Fining Guidelines, the absence of individual penalties and prison sentences puts a limit on the use of instruments to increase the overall level of deterrence. Second, the combination of full immunity for the first confessing firm and the sliding scale of fine reductions for firms that cooperate with the European Commission in a later stage entails a serious risk of excessive leniency. Ideally, only one firm should be granted leniency in exchange for important information to be used against the other cartel members. Every additional leniency grant reduces the overall sanctions imposed on cartels and the incentive to report first, since also firms stepping forward later may receive fine reductions (Marvão and Spagnolo 2016). Next, a warning is needed concerning an excessive use of leniency programmes. If competition authorities rely too much on the success of leniency programmes, cartelists may start doubting their ability to detect cartels. This would have the perverse effect of stabilising cartels and put the continuity of leniency programmes at risk. Figures on the enforcement practice of the European Commission indicate that in recent years the number of cartels that had not been detected through leniency has dropped substantially: from 15 cases in the period 2001–2005, 9 cases in the period 2006–2010 to only 2 cases in the period 2011–2015. It is thus important that the European Commission strengthens its investigative efforts to detect cartels, in particular by signalling that it welcomes information from informants (employees, trade associations) in order to guarantee the sustainability of the leniency programme (Wils 2016). A final concern is the potential strategic use of leniency programmes. Successful cartels are sophisticated organisations that may try to exploit leniency policies to facilitate the creation and maintenance of cartels. If companies participate in several cartels they could take turns to apply for leniency; also they could use leniency as a mechanism to punish deviations from the cartel agreement. Wils (2016) considers these risks to be limited (in the absence of convincing examples from the case law) and argues that the current EU leniency programme limits the scope for strategic abuse by granting full immunity only to the first cooperating cartel participant.

8.3   Public or private enforcement

8.3.1   The choice between public and private enforcement

There are two basic approaches to deter socially harmful behaviour: enforcement by public agencies and litigation by private parties. In the field of competition law, most countries use both enforcement systems in varying degrees. Private litigation is common in the US (and to a lesser extent in the United Kingdom and other common law jurisdictions). Section 7 of the Sherman Act and Section 4 of the Clayton Act entitle any firm to bring a lawsuit against a competitor for three times the damages suffered from any violation of the antitrust laws. In practice, 90% of antitrust cases in the US are private actions at both federal and state levels.[33] In contrast, public enforcement has traditionally played a dominant role in the enforcement of EU competition law. In recent years, important steps have been taken to strengthen the role of private enforcement.[34] These efforts ultimately resulted in the adoption of Directive 2014/104 on damages actions for infringement of the EU competition rules. The recent change of the European enforcement system seeks to increase the role of private parties in several ways: among others, by facilitating access to evidence, lowering the burden of proof and introducing the principle of joint and several liability. However, the impact of private enforcement through national courts in the EU will probably remain far behind the effect of private actions in the US. Important institutional differences continue to exist between the two legal systems (in particular the possibility to bring class action suits and the prospect of treble damages), which makes private damages claims in the US much more attractive. In the

---

[33] Since 1975 private antitrust actions have accounted for a very large percentage, varying between 83.4% and 96.6%, of all antitrust actions filed in the US. In 2004, 95.7% of all antitrust cases were brought by private plaintiffs. In 2008, there were 1287 private antitrust actions in federal courts, accounting for 96.1% of the total number of antitrust cases. According to the last available data, the percentage of private damages actions is currently around 90%.

[34] In 2005 the Commission published a Green Paper on damages actions for breach of the EU antitrust rules in order to 'set out different options for further reflections and possible action to improve damages actions'. The adoption of the Green Paper was followed by a public consultation. In 2008 the Commission adopted the White Paper on damages actions for breaches of antitrust rules, which contained a set of proposals (policy choices and specific measures) which would propitiate better opportunities of full redress for the victims of antitrust violations. The White Paper was supported by a Staff Working Paper and an impact assessment, elaborated on the basis of an external report (Renda *et al.* 2008).

remainder of this section, the differences between the EU and US systems of enforcement are further explained and an economic assessment of the respective strengths and weaknesses of both systems is provided.

Besides the preference for private litigation, also the way in which public enforcement of the competition rules is organised varies. At the European (quasi) federal level, a single administrative body (the European Commission) has been empowered to enforce the competition rules. After the modernisation of the system of enforcement introduced by Regulation 1/2003 (which entered into effect on 1 May 2004), the competition rules are also enforced by a network of national competition authorities (NCAs) and judges.[35] The procedures for the application of the EU competition rules by NCAs are largely governed by national law, so that there is no uniform set of litigation rules. In the US, the competences to enforce federal antitrust law are shared by the Antitrust Division of the Department of Justice (DoJ) and the Federal Trade Commission (FTC). A striking difference between the enforcement of US antitrust law and EU competition law is the combination of investigative, prosecutorial and adjudicative powers in the latter system. Conversely, in the US, the DoJ must seek a court judgment to prohibit a violation of Sections 1 and 2 of the Sherman Act. The FTC combines prosecutorial and adjudicative powers, but a complex system of internal checks and balances has been built into the decision process. A more detailed analysis and economic assessment of these differences follows below.

8.3.2 Public enforcement: the combination of investigative, prosecutorial and adjudicative powers

In Europe all stages of the procedure (investigation, negotiation, decision and political review) are assigned to the European Commission. The European Commission enjoys great autonomy and is largely independent of courts to bring enforcement actions. In US antitrust terms, 'the Commission combines the functions of prosecutor, judge and jury' (Van Bael 1986). It is to be noted that at the Member States level, several laws contain specific safeguards to ensure the independence and impartiality of the NCA. Partly as a response to the desire of greater uniformity in enforcement systems and in reaction to complaints about an improper combination of functions, a Hearing Officer has been appointed within the European Commission (DG COMP). In this way, the combination of prosecutorial and adjudicative powers has been mitigated, but the extent of the latter has remained unchanged. The European

---

[35] The NCAs form the European Competition Network (ECN), which has been a catalyst in promoting greater convergence of enforcement systems.

Commission enjoys relatively large discretionary powers when deciding on the substance of the infringement, the level of the fines and the fine discount granted through a leniency application. The Commission's ultimate decision is subject to an appeal before the General Court (previously Court of First Instance), and it may be noted that in cartel cases the Court tends to limit its in-depth review to points of process rather than substance.

In the US, the DoJ has extensive powers to investigate potential violations of Sections 1 and 2 of the Sherman Act but has no power to adopt decisions finding an infringement and imposing sanctions. To that effect suits must be brought in court; district courts may impose fines on companies or fines and prison sentences on individuals. Unlike the DoJ, which has only investigative and prosecutorial functions, the FTC has also adjudicative powers. Under the FTC Act, it can issue cease-and-desist orders to stop unfair methods of competition, including violations of Sections 1 and 2 of the Sherman Act. The initial decision, which is taken by an administrative law judge, may be appealed to the FTC. When deciding on the appeal, the FTC's Commissioners sit as judges and hear directly both sides of the case. This is different from the European enforcement system, since in the latter jurisdiction there is no independent initial adjudicator and the European Commissioners decide on the proposal of the Competition Commissioner, who has been briefed by the DG Competition officials dealing with the case.

The question whether it is preferable to separate the adjudicative function from the investigative and prosecutorial functions may be discussed by assessing the strengths and weaknesses of the alternative systems in terms of accuracy and administrative costs. Since the European Commission combines all functions, enforcement errors caused by overly active competition officials may be more frequent than in a system in which Community judges would take the ultimate decision. Conversely, administrative costs may decrease by combining the investigative, prosecutorial, and adjudicative functions. Wils (2004) argues that, theoretically, there are three possible sources of prosecutorial bias. First, competition authorities may hold the initial belief that a violation is likely to be found and search for evidence, which confirms rather than challenges this belief (confirmation bias). Second, officials may be psychologically motivated to avoid discovering that there is no case for a prohibition decision (hindsight bias) or may desire to justify past efforts, thus pre-empting complaints about inefficient use of scarce resources. Third, competition authorities may wish to show a record of numerous infringements and high fines, in order to demonstrate that they are fulfilling their task well (desire to show a high level of enforcement). All these risks can be contained by internal checks and balances (such as a peer review panel or the setting up of a separate entity, which plays the role of the devil's advocate) and frequent judicial review. However, such controlling mechanisms will decrease the savings in administrative costs. Wils (2004) concludes that an alternative system in which the European Commission would prosecute before the Community courts seems superior for cartels and abuse of dominance cases.[36]

8.3.3   The role of private parties in enforcing competition law

A comparison: US antitrust law and EU competition law

In the US, the attractiveness of private actions is due to peculiarities of tort law (treble damages) and several procedural tools, such as contingency fees, class actions and easy access to evidence. First, successful plaintiffs are entitled to claim three times the actual damage (Section 4 Clayton Act). Such private antitrust lawsuits are likely after a successful criminal prosecution, since a criminal conviction constitutes *prima facie* evidence that the defendant violated the antitrust laws in any subsequent civil litigation.[37] The prospect to collect treble damages is a powerful incentive for private parties to take legal action against their competitors. Second, in the US contingency fee arrangements are legal. Attorneys at law may conclude an agreement with their clients stating that the lawyer receives payment only if (s)he wins the case. The fee is usually a fraction of the awarded damages, but the lawyer receives nothing if the case is lost. Under a contingency fee system, the client thus bears no trial risk. On top of this, it may be noted that in most EU countries the losing party has to bear the trial costs of the winning party. Generally, more law suits will be brought if trial costs are shared. Third, the possibility of antitrust class action suits may be an appropriate remedy if private parties lack incentives to sue because their individual damages are relatively small compared with the costs of litigation (e.g. in price-fixing cases). Class actions allow plaintiffs to obtain damages not only for the harm they suffered themselves but also for the harm suffered by other victims.[38] Finally, procedural law mitigates problems of proof faced by private parties. US courts generally order the defendant to supply all relevant information in a pre-trial discovery procedure. In the case of global cartels, this also covers documents submitted

---

[36] In merger cases, only the hindsight bias seems relevant. There is no risk for a confirmation basis or a too high level of activity, since the parties concerned must notify mergers and most mergers are judged unproblematic. See Chapter 9.

[37] See §5(a) Clayton Act, §16(a) 15 U.S.C.

[38] The first attempt in Europe to achieve results similar to a class action concerned the cement cartel. A number of direct purchasers in Germany pooled their resources in a Belgian company to enable the filing of a suit in Germany and to gain access to their mutual pricing data for assessment by economic experts as evidence of the alleged overcharge.

to other agencies, such as the European Commission.[39] The pre-trial discovery requests are not subject to strict procedural safeguards (no requirement of proportionality) and thus may seem very intrusive for European observers.

Unlike the Sherman Act and the Clayton Act in the US, the TFEU is silent on the question as to whether victims of competition law violations are entitled to compensation. Neither does the TFEU include any express provision on the size of damages that successful plaintiffs may receive. Since all parts of Articles 101 and 102 TFEU are directly applicable in the Member States and create rights that individuals may enforce, decisions on the concrete contours of private enforcement are left to secondary EU law and European and national case law. Regulation 1/2003 has facilitated the invocation of the nullity defence by empowering national courts to apply the four conditions of Article 101(3) TFEU, instead of having to suspend their proceedings and wait for a decision of the European Commission. However, this Regulation contains no rule that directly encourages the development of damage actions. In the past, EU competition law was invoked largely as a 'shield' to justify non-performance of a contractual obligation on the ground that the contractual provision in question infringed the cartel prohibition (so-called Euro defence). The use of competition law as a 'sword' to obtain injunctive relief to prevent harm or to obtain damages remained limited. In 2001, the CJEU removed the uncertainty as to whether individuals harmed by a breach of the European competition rules have any right to claim damages. In its *Courage* judgment, the CJEU enunciated a Community law-based right to damages.[40] The Court stated that private actions for damages before the national courts will help to ensure the full effectiveness of the competition rules, and in particular the practical effect of the cartel prohibition. Private enforcement can thus 'make a significant contribution to the maintenance of effective competition in the Community'.[41] Since there is no harmonisation of sanctions or remedies at the national level, it remains for the domestic legal systems of each Member State to determine the remedies and procedures for claiming damages, provided these rules meet the requirements of equivalence and effectiveness.[42] Requirements to successfully claim damages for harm caused by infringements of EU competition law should not be more strict than for infringements of national law (principle of equivalence) and the national procedures must allow full protection of the individual rights based on directly applicable provisions of the TFEU (principle of effectiveness).

---

[39] For an economic analysis of this mechanism, see Polinsky and Shavell (2000).
[40] Case C-453/99 *Courage Ltd. v. Bernard Crehan* [2001] ECR I-6297. For a comment, see Komninos (2002).
[41] *Ibid.,* para. 34.
[42] *Ibid.,* para. 26.

Compared with US law, the underdevelopment of damages actions in Europe[43] is understandable if one takes into account the lack of incentive mechanisms as far as private enforcement of the competition rules is concerned. Civil damages actions have remained the preserve of national jurisdictions. The European Union's courts, based in Luxembourg, are only entitled to hear cases arising out of decisions or actions of EU institutions or Member States. Hence, plaintiffs who have suffered harm on a pan-European level must bring individual claims in accordance with the rules of tort law and procedural law that apply in all concerned jurisdictions.[44] Even though compensation of antitrust damages is deemed fundamental since the *Courage* judgment of the CJEU, several characteristics of the European system of enforcement continue to limit the potential impact of damages claims on reaching both goals of deterrence and compensation. Directive 2014/104 has been a long-awaited step forward in facilitating private damages claims for infringement of European competition law, but it has not been able to deal satisfactorily with all complexities of private enforcement.

On the positive side, Directive 2014/104 improves the position of victims of antitrust infringements in several ways. First, Article 3 introduces an obligation for Member States to grant all victims of competition law infringements standing to claim full compensation. Standing may not be limited to direct victims (purchasers) but must also include indirect victims (end consumers). Full compensation covers actual loss, loss of profit and payment of interest from the time the harm occurred until compensation is paid. Second, the Directive contains new rules on disclosure of evidence. According to Article 5(1), courts can order a process party (claimant or defendant) or a third party to disclose relevant evidence which lies in their control where 'a claimant (…) has presented a reasoned justification containing reasonably available facts and evidence sufficient to support the plausibility of its claim for damages'. Article 5 further states that the pieces of evidence or relevant categories of evidence to be disclosed must be specified as precisely and as narrowly as possible by the courts and subjects disclosure of evidence to a proportionality test (Article 5 (2) and (3)). Article 6 contains special rules on evidence in the file of a competition authority: some categories of evidence, mentioned in Article 6(5), can be disclosed only after the investigation is closed. Article

---

[43] The Ashurst study on private enforcement (2004) found only 60 cases involving damages claims and 23 damage awards based on both national and EU competition laws since their adoption. These findings, together with the analysis of the conditions to claim damages, supported the statement of 'astonishing diversity and total underdevelopment' of antitrust private enforcement in Europe (Ashurst 2004, 1).

[44] There is some scope for forum shopping, since claims can be brought in the jurisdiction where the defendant has its domicile or in the jurisdiction where the harmful event occurred (Articles 4 and 7(2) of the Brussels Regulation No 1215/2012). Hence, claimants can freely choose the jurisdiction as long as the defendant has some anchor therein.

8 empowers national courts to impose effective, proportionate and dissuasive penalties in case of parties' failure to comply with the disclosure rules. Third, the Directive lowers the burden of proof for private parties. Article 9(1) brings the legal effect of NCA decisions in line with the European Commission's decisions by extending their probative effect to judgments of national courts. Article 9(2) requires national courts to treat infringement decisions of a NCA or a review court of another Member State at least as *prima facie* evidence. In this way, it becomes easier for victims of cartels to claim compensation based on Article 101(1) TFEU decisions of NCAs and national courts, even when they were rendered in another Member State. The Directive further reduces the burden of proof for victims to receive compensation by introducing a rebuttable presumption that cartel infringements cause harm. However, two problems remain: (i) quantification of harm may remain difficult and the practical guide on quantifying harm issued by the European Commission[45] may pose problems when it is to be applied by non-specialised courts; and (ii) the claimant is still under an obligation to provide the evidence of a causal link between the infringement and the harm suffered. Fourth, Article 11(1) introduces a very significant change regarding tort liability. Member States are required to move from individual to joint and several liability, according to which each of the infringing undertakings is bound to compensate the harm in full. An infringing undertaking, which is liable for damages through joint behaviour, may recover a contribution from any other infringing undertaking. According to Article 11(5), the amount of contributions between the co-infringers is to be determined in light of their relative responsibility. The criteria to be used in such assessment (for example, market share, turnover or role in the cartel) are left for national law.

On the negative side, Directive 2014/104 has not removed the factors that may reduce the number of private damages claims below the socially optimal level. First, the prospective damages award may be too small: there is no right to treble damages and punitive damages are generally considered to be against the public order (*ordre public*) in civil law jurisdictions.[46] Even though punitive damages may be a significant contribution to the deterrence of hard-core cartels (since they may correct for the low risk of detection), it has not been possible to overcome problems posed by long-standing European legal traditions. Article 3(3) clarifies that full compensation may not lead to overcompensation, such as punitive or multiple damages, known from US antitrust law. Second, the risk of losing the case may act as a further deterrent,

---

[45] Communication from the Commission on quantification of harm in actions for damages based on breaches of Articles 101–102 TFEU, O.J. 13.6.2013, C 167/9. See for further discussion Box 8.3.
[46] In England and Wales exemplary damages may be awarded under the conditions spelled out in the case *Rookes v. Barnard* [1964] 1 All ER 367.

since procedural costs cannot be spread over several victims and information costs to cure problems of proof (in particular quantifying harm and proving causation) may be prohibitively high. Contingency fees that contribute to risk spreading are not generally available as a way of financing damages claims. Third, the Directive does not contain any provision concerning collective redress mechanisms (collective actions, representative actions). Out of fear of US-like class actions, preference was given to the option of a broadly applicable (not competition law-specific) EU Recommendation,[47] which has turned out to be a weak political compromise. Box 8.2 summarises the current legal status of collective redress mechanisms in the EU and highlights the remaining problems of under-deterrence and under-compensation. A (partial) market solution to the enduring regulatory problems is being provided by firms specialised in the pooling of claims on a commercial basis (for example, Collective Damages Claims/CDC Brussels and Claims Funding Europe). These so-called 'special purpose vehicles' can play an important role by offering specialist help in preparing complex litigation (problems of proof, difficulties in calculating damages) and providing risk spreading for plaintiffs with little or no financial means. Pooling of claims is also the only remaining route to compensation if collective actions or representative actions are not possible. Finally, the information asymmetry to the detriment of the victims of cartelisation is not fully corrected. Directive 2014 has created easier access to evidence for private parties in order to better align the EU enforcement system with its US counterpart, but the extent to which information gathering is facilitated remains far behind the possibilities offered by the pre-trial discovery procedure in the US.

Box 8.2: The persisting collective action problem: an EU–US comparison

In the European discussion on private enforcement of competition law, US-style class actions are heavily criticised for their excesses and abuses. For political reasons, the collective action problem has been left out of the scope of Directive 2014/104 and only a Recommendation favouring European-style procedures has been issued.[48] The negative view on the US system runs the risk of throwing away the child with the bathwater and losing important insights on optimal private enforcement of competition law. Even though a class action creates principal-agent problems, it must be acknowledged

---

[47] Commission Recommendation on common principles for injunctive and compensatory collective redress mechanisms in the Member States concerning violations of rights granted under Union law [2013] O.J. L 201/60.

[48] At the time of writing, the impact of the Recommendation has remained limited. A few EU countries introduced legislation to facilitate collective actions: United Kingdom, France and Belgium.

that such procedure also may bring important advantages as an instrument to cure the rational apathy problem, overcoming free-riding and providing adequate funding. These results are not necessarily achieved when preference is given to alternatives, such as representative actions by consumer organisations, which would better fit with the European legal culture. Hereinafter a more nuanced overview of the costs and benefits of US class actions is given and the European alternatives are critically assessed (for a more elaborate discussion, see Van den Bergh 2013, with further references).

In a seminal paper, Kalven and Rosenfield (1941) argued that a major advantage of class actions is their potential to overcome the problem of rational apathy. Private parties will bring law suits only if the private benefits of doing so (expected outcome of the legal proceedings) are higher than the private costs (litigation costs, costs of hiring lawyers). This private cost-benefit calculus has no systematic relation with the social costs and benefits. The social costs also comprise the harm suffered by individuals who do not sue and other losses that cannot be attributed to the litigating parties. To align the private motive and the social motive to sue, all monopoly losses should be compensated to force the firms infringing competition law to internalise the full negative welfare effects of their behaviour. The extent to which collective actions will be able to overcome the rational apathy problem crucially depends on their legal design. Opt-in collective actions require an explicit approval by affected victims to join the action, whereas an opt-out scheme leaves them the choice not to be bound by the outcome of the litigation. Opt-in collective actions may face difficulties in attracting sufficient participation but opt-out collective actions are likely to score better in terms of deterrence. If group members act rationally, it is not in their interest to opt out of the proceeding. Given the larger group of victims, larger cost savings and better risk sharing will become possible. Especially in cases of small damage amounts, victims are unlikely to opt out and start their own proceedings. The rational apathy problem, which may remain pervasive under opt-in schemes, may thus be better overcome.

The most prominent cause for concern about US-style class actions arises from the principal-agent problem. Typical for a principal-agent relationship is that the interests of the agent (attorney) do not coincide with the interests of the principal (victims). The class action is controlled by an attorney, who acts like an entrepreneur. The attorney, who initiates the procedure, is willing to make a substantial investment, hoping to obtain a generous fee[49] in the event that a judgment is rendered or the case settles. The principal-agent problem is exacerbated by the opt-out scheme. Under an opt-in scheme a minimum of effort and interest by the represented parties may still be expected. Conversely, under an opt-out scheme, the group of silent plaintiffs is larger and more heterogeneous, and many victims may not even be aware of the damages action. The resulting agency problems are twofold: frivolous suits may be brought and the attorney

---

[49] Under a contingency fee arrangement, the attorney receives a percentage (20% is not uncommon) of the total amount of awarded damages.

may spend too little effort in securing the victims' rights (shirking) or conspire with the corporate wrongdoer through a collusive settlement (sweetheart deal). Frivolous suits may be brought to extract settlements when for firms the costs of defending themselves in court are larger than the costs of the expected damage payments. Early settlements are another risk: it is appealing for the attorney, who receives a percentage of the damages award as a fee, to settle the case if the private costs of pursuing the claim outweigh the expected increase in the fee to be received. Settlements in US class actions that resulted in gains to attorneys at the expense of the class are found in several studies. A prominent example of deficient representation are class action settlements providing the victims with low-value coupons for price reductions on further purchases from the (price fixing) defendant, which in practice are never redeemed. In these cases, high lawyers' fees were calculated on basis of the total value of coupons (Bronsteen 2005; Rosenfield 1976).

The principal-agent problem in US class actions has been tackled in different ways. The perceived abuse of coupon settlements to the detriment of the class was one of the reasons for the Class Action Fairness Act, which was enacted in 2005. Even though the use of coupons in settlements is not prohibited, this Act restricts the fees paid to class attorneys to the value of the redeemed coupons. In addition, it makes coupon settlements less attractive by enabling the court to require that a portion of the value of unclaimed coupons flows to charitable organisations or governmental bodies. As an alternative to regulation, judges may be asked to conduct a preliminary test of the merits of the case to prevent unmeritorious claims. However, judicial review implies higher judicial costs; opposition to a skilfully designed class action settlement may be prohibitively expensive. Courts may lack the information to be able to properly monitor the attorney who is leading the class action. Moreover, judges may not favour a reopening of the case, which would result in increased workload with no corresponding reward. Judges may thus have powerful incentives to approve class action settlements and such settlements are very difficult to evaluate.

Because of the bad press suffered by US class actions, European policy makers have advanced opt-in collective actions and representative actions by consumer associations as promising alternatives. The former should curtail the risk of inadequate representation by requiring an opt-in procedure, which also respects rules of national procedural laws requiring explicit consent from represented victims (recall, for example, the French adage 'nul ne plaide par procureur' and the German constitutional right to a day in court). The latter are presented as a genuinely European solution that is rooted in the cultural and legal traditions of the EU Member States. (In many EU countries, consumer associations are entitled to obtain cease-and-desist orders if consumer protection rules are infringed). However, there are several reasons for doubting the effectiveness and efficiency of the European-style alternatives. First, if the rational apathy problem is not cured and the risk of free-riding behaviour is not contained, collective actions and representative actions will not sufficiently deter competition law infringements. The preference given to opt-in procedures is likely to keep the number of damages claims low and will not overcome the problem that participation rates are affected by rational apathy. Also, compared to opt-in procedures, opt-out group actions may better limit free-riding behaviour. This problem may be particularly serious if consumer associations cannot attract a sufficiently high number of members paying their dues. Second, representative actions by consumer associations are no easy way to overcome the principal-agent problem. In both US-style class actions and representative actions brought by consumer associations, the main challenge is to design a collective redress mechanism that ensures that the representative optimally defends the rights of the group of harmed victims. Whether this is an individual lead plaintiff, an attorney, or an association is in principle irrelevant. Distorted representation must be prevented by ensuring democratic control of the association by the members, control of the acting lawyer and immunity from ideological and political pressure. The risk that associations are captured by private interests is exacerbated by allowing *ad hoc* certification following a particular infringement. Standing may be restricted to consumer associations that are designated in advance or certified by courts; in addition individual consumers should be given sufficient possibilities of 'voice' and 'exit'. Third, the problem of funding representative actions by consumer associations cannot be solved easily in the absence of contingency fee arrangements. Membership dues may not provide the consumer association a budget that is sufficiently large to cover the costs of court proceedings. Also, government funding cannot be provided without limits.

On top of the problems discussed above, Directive 2014/104 struggles with finding the right balance between compensation of victims and protecting leniency incentives. Two legislative changes may create adverse effects on the leniency programme. First, the disclosure provisions substantially facilitate the burden of proof in damages actions. Since immunity of fines does not include protection from follow-on damages actions, members of a hard-core cartel may be disincentivised to step forward. Second, the rule of joint and several liability creates a high burden for immunity recipients, given that they are likely to be the primary target of follow-on damages actions. The Directive tries to overcome these problems and keep leniency incentives intact. According to Article 6(6), leniency corporate statements enjoy an absolute protection from disclosure. However, this prohibition does not restrict the disclosure of such statements under the conditions of the Transparency Regulation.[50] The Directive also introduces a general ceiling for damages actions filed against immunity recipients. The amount of the contribution due by those undertakings shall not exceed the harm it caused to its direct or

---

[50] Regulation 1049/2001, O.J. 31.5.2001, L 145/43.

indirect purchasers (Article 11(4)). However, the exception does not apply to immunity recipients if it would make it impossible for victims to obtain full compensation from the co-infringers, particularly in cases of insolvency of a cartel member. It may be doubted whether these provisions are able to enhance private damages claims while keeping leniency incentives intact. An alternative solution could have been chosen, according to which cooperating undertakings that have received immunity or reduction from fines would be granted the same protection against damages liability. Following this alternative solution, the non-cooperating members of the cartel would then have to compensate the victims for the harm caused by the cartel. Using a game theoretical approach, Kirst and Van den Bergh (2016) show that, under certain conditions, this alternative is a superior approach to resolve the conflict between optimal leniency incentives and compensation for all victims.

Economic analysis: do we need private enforcement?

In a perfect public enforcement system, competition authorities initiate an optimal number of proceedings in all types of cases and impose optimal sanctions. In the real world, which is far from perfect, private enforcement may be a useful complement to public enforcement. First, private actions draw private resources into the enforcement process and thus complete public enforcement, which may be unable to deal with all attention-worthy cases. This is particularly important when private parties have better access to information than the public authority: for instance, with respect to the harmful effects of vertical restraints (Di Federico and Manzini 2004, 158). However, it must be noted that private parties are not protected from retaliation (such as exclusion from a selective distribution system) and may, therefore, be reluctant to initiate proceedings. Apart from this *caveat*, enabling courts to deal with competition law cases increases the number of law enforcers. Private enforcement may thus generate an additional deterrent effect, particularly if companies are more likely to avoid infringements of the competition rules when they risk having to pay damages to their competitors.

It should be clear that public enforcement and private enforcement are not mutually exclusive options. Both enforcement models have their own strengths and weaknesses. The challenge for policy makers is to find an optimal mix of public and private enforcement, the contents of which will differ depending on the type of infringement: horizontal agreements (hard-core cartels), vertical agreements or abuse of a dominant position (to be further differentiated between exploitative abuses and exclusionary abuses). Criteria for making a choice between public and private enforcement include the type of sanction that is deemed appropriate, the existence of information advantages and the difference between the private and social motive to sue. Also, the focus on the compensation goal rather than the deterrence goal will have an impact on the design of the optimal enforcement system. A preliminary requirement to achieve optimal deterrence and/or compensation is that indirect buyers are given the right to claim damages. For example, in cases of price fixing, overcharges are usually passed on along the supply chain: from manufacturers to wholesalers, from wholesalers to retailers and from retailers to end consumers. If the latter have no standing, the law-breaking firms will not be confronted with the total size of the harm caused. Below, the arguments in favour of either public or private enforcement will be elaborated. Thereafter, the desirability of giving standing to indirect buyers will be addressed.

Criteria for choosing between public and private enforcement

Choice of sanctions

When focusing on sanctions, public enforcement of competition law appears to score better in terms of deterrence. In cases of hard-core cartels (such as price fixing) private parties may not even realise that they are harmed. They may also face difficulties in proving the size of the damage and the causal link between the infringement and the harm. Competition authorities are better at discovering and proving antitrust infringements since they have wider investigative powers than private parties.[51] Without the investigative powers of competition authorities, very serious infringements may remain undiscovered and unpunished. Moreover, even if it was possible to identify all victims – including not only consumers who paid above competitive prices but also those who would have bought the product at a lower price – problems of under-deterrence would persist. Private actions for damages do not exhibit detection advantages and a variety of sanctions to fine-tune the enforcement levels. Damages are not related to the offender's gain and the level of compensation due is typically too low to achieve the deterrence goal. Damages awarded to private parties will be computed by reference to lost profits, which bear no relationship to the offender's gain. Also, multiple damages would be needed to offset the problem that only a limited number of victims decide to go to court. The trebling of damages in the US could be considered as trying to address this problem, but it remains doubtful that three is the correct multiplier. Applying a multiplier in inverse proportion to the probability of

---

[51] The European Commission and national competition authorities can threaten to impose a fine in case not all or incorrect information is supplied; see Art. 23(1) of Regulation 1/2003. Furthermore, competition authorities have the right to collect evidence by entering the premises of an undertaking without its consent; these are so-called 'dawn raids' (see Arts 17–22 of Regulation 1/2003).

detection and punishment is always difficult in practice, but could be done more easily by public authorities. Public enforcement is better able to design sanctions that capture the full size of the welfare loss. Competition authorities may choose the resources devoted to detection and the level of fines to be imposed. By controlling these variables they may pick the optimal enforcement level (Polinsky 1980). Finally, public enforcement enables the use of a wide variety of sanctions: besides administrative or criminal fines, prison sanctions may be used to achieve the deterrence goal. Imprisonment may cure the judgment-proof problem[52] in case of the offender's insolvency; it also adds a strong moral message that supports the efforts of public bodies to effectively enforce the prohibition of hard-core cartels.

Information advantages

The information advantages of private parties depend on the type of the victim, the type of infringement and the moment when information becomes available. Since they are closer to the law-breaking firms, traders (suppliers and buyers) may be better aware of the existence of hard-core cartels than final consumers. The former may thus play a more active role in enforcing the cartel prohibition, even though public enforcement remains clearly superior to achieve deterrence. More importantly, buyers (importers, wholesalers) have an information advantage – not only over consumers but also over public authorities – in discovering prohibited vertical restraints contained in contractual agreements with manufacturers. Next, the type of infringement has an impact on the availability of information. When the law is ambiguous, it is more difficult for private parties to draw accurate conclusions on the legality of their business partners' actions. *Per se* rules reduce uncertainty, whereas a Rule of Reason (US) or a fully fledged analysis of the conditions for exemption (Article 101(3) TFEU) makes it difficult for private parties to establish violations of competition rules. Also, public authorities are better placed to assess foreclosure effects in cases of exclusionary abuses (Section 2 Sherman Act, Article 102 TFEU). Lastly, the moment of information availability plays a role in assessing the effects of private enforcement. If information on infringements must still be gathered, public enforcement will be superior.

Difference between the private and social motive to sue

Private interests diverge from the general interest. Private parties will initiate proceedings only if the private benefits of doing so are higher than the private costs. The private costs consist of the information costs that must be borne

---

[52] The judgment-proof problem occurs if the damages to be paid are higher than individual wrongdoer's wealth. See Shavell (1986).

to discover the infringement, the costs of the court procedure, and the costs to prove the size of the damage and the causal link between the infringement and the harm. The private benefits consist of the sanction imposed on the law offender (assuming that there is no judgment-proof problem), as far as this will improve the financial situation and/or the competitive market position of the private claimant. This private cost-benefit calculus has no systematic relation with the social costs and benefits. The social costs also comprise the harm suffered by victims who do not sue and other losses (rent-seeking) that cannot be attributed to individual victims. Since potential plaintiffs are driven only by the private gains and expenses of their claims, they will have insufficient incentives to invest in detecting and litigating meritorious cases. Private enforcement may thus lead to under-deterrence. Private parties will not bring suit if the expected damages fall short of the litigation costs. This problem is known as rational apathy; it may be mitigated by appropriate forms of group litigation (see the discussion in Box 8.2). Private parties may also wish to reduce their own expenditures by relying on the efforts of other victims. Every victim of an antitrust infringement has an interest to leave the enforcement efforts to other victims, so that profits can be obtained without having to spend own resources. The free-riding problem will reduce the number of private actions below the level of enforcement that would be socially optimal. Also, this deficiency of private enforcement may be mitigated by relying on group litigation (see Box 8.2).

It is not only under-deterrence that causes inefficiency; private enforcement may also provoke the opposite effect of over-deterrence. Competition law may be used strategically by firms wishing to curtail the market opportunities of their rivals. In the US experience, the problem of unmeritorious actions has been identified as the major counterproductive consequence of private antitrust enforcement (Posner 2001, 275; Snyder and Kauper 1991). Plaintiffs are often competitors or take-over targets of defendants; they may have an incentive to sue even if they know that there is no violation of competition law. Strategic use of private enforcement through suits and counter-suits may prevent rivals form competing vigorously, extract funds from successful rivals (particularly by using the threat of treble damages), improve contract terms, enforce tacit collusive agreements and prevent hostile takeovers (McAfee, Mialon and Mialon 2008). The risk of unmeritorious claims (frivolous suits) is particularly serious when the formulations of competition law are unclear and the welfare impact of the business practices is ambiguous. Examples include the (il)legality of tying and predatory pricing. Tying may lead to foreclosure but it may also generate efficiencies if buyers prefer bundled goods. Low prices may be predatory if they aim at excluding a competitor from the market but they are, at the same time, also the main virtue of the competitive process (see the discussion of tying and predatory pricing in sections 7.3 and 7.4). Distinguishing anti-competitive from pro-competitive uses of these practices is difficult and provides scope for frivolous suits, which mainly aim at damaging the reputation of a competitor rather than protecting competition itself. Such an abuse of litigation should not be expected from public enforcers. Since their proclaimed goal is to maximise allocative efficiency and consumer welfare, it may be hoped that competition authorities are committed to a deterrence policy and that they will bring only meritorious suits. Unfortunately, public authorities are not always behaving as agents of the public interest. Employees of public enforcement authorities might wish to economise on their efforts, further their own career or pursue political objectives that collide with the efficiency goal of competition law (see section 3.7).

Corrective justice goal

Finally, the role of private enforcement in achieving justice goals must be considered. In this respect, it is important to distinguish between goals of social justice and corrective justice in individual cases. Public enforcement mechanisms may target (a large part of) the total social costs of antitrust infringements, whereas enforcement by private parties will be concerned only with the much smaller costs in individual cases. Private enforcement is not able to guarantee that law offenders must pay back the excess profits achieved or must compensate the losses caused to society at large. Competition authorities may be better able to disgorge profits than private parties. The latter sanction implies that excess profits achieved by infringements of competition law must be transferred to the state budget. National competition laws, which allow for such a sanction, do not leave this task to private parties but provide for specific enforcement mechanisms (Jones 2004). Damages awarded to victims do not cover the entire harm caused by restrictive practices: at most, harm to individual consumers is compensated and the deadweight loss remains outside of the calculation of the damage award. The emphasis put by the ECJ on private enforcement as a significant contribution to maintaining effective competition in the European market can be explained better by the need to provide for corrective justice in individual cases than by the broader social justice goals discussed above (principle of direct effect; *Individualschutzfunktion*).

Calculating damages from the perspective of corrective justice is not an easy task. Compensation of the harm suffered by individual victims poses serious difficulties: both the identification of all victims and the calculation of damages constitute major challenges for courts (on the methods of quantifying harm, see Box 8.3). The primary victims are those who would have bought the product at a lower price; the costs of identifying these buyers may be prohibitive. It is also difficult to identify the secondary victims, who bought at the cartel price, and the customers of these purchasers. There may be several tiers in the distribution chain between the manufacturer and the ultimate consumers and particular buyers should be awarded compensation only if the overcharge was passed on to them.[53] Often this is not an easy inquiry. Not only buyers of the high-priced goods but also suppliers of a cartel may be harmed. These tertiary victims should also be entitled to compensation if they can show that they are injured as a result of decreased sales associated with the reduction in output. In sum, compensation of persons injured will be difficult to implement in practice.

Box 8.3: Quantification of damages
Peter Camesasca and Phil Warren

EU competition law

With the increased focus on private enforcement, economic evidence of damages resulting from competition law infringements has gained importance in the EU. To assist the parties and national judges with the difficult exercise of calculating damages, the European Commission has issued the Communication on quantifying harm in antitrust damages actions, accompanied by a more comprehensive and detailed Practical Guide.[54] This Practical Guide gives an overview of methods and techniques used to quantify harm. Furthermore, it sets out the possible types of harm caused by anti-competitive practices. With respect to cartels, actions for damages usually deal with overcharges resulting from a price increase. To quantify the exact harm caused to individual customers, one should: (i) quantify the overcharge; and (ii) calculate how much of this overcharge has been passed on along the supply chain. To quantify the overcharge, the actual price paid by the customer is usually compared with the hypothetical price that would have been paid in the absence of the cartel (comparator-based methods). The hypothetical competitive price can be determined on the basis of the pre- and post-cartel prices or the price in a different geographical market (provided that this market was not affected by the cartel). In a next step, the pass-on effect should be determined.

---

[53] It should be added that Landes and Posner (1979) argued that, from a deterrence perspective, it may be preferable to deny standing to indirect purchasers and thereby increase the potential payoffs to direct purchasers who will thus have greater incentives to initiate private enforcement actions. For further discussion, see section 8.3.3.

[54] Communication from the Commission on quantifying harm in actions for damages based on breaches of Article 101 or 102 of the Treaty on the Functioning of the European Union, C(2013) 3440, 11.6.2013; Commission Staff Working Document – Practical Guide on Quantifying Harm in Actions for damages based on breaches of Article 101 or 102 of the Treaty on the Functioning of the European Union, SWD(2013) 205, 11.6.2013.

This is a particularly difficult exercise. Passing-on leads to a volume effect: an increase in price leads to a decrease in demand. As a consequence, the positive financial effect caused by (partially) passing on the overcharge is offset by a decrease in sales. In practice, EU competition law softens the demands of a strict economic approach to the quantification of harm, to the advantage of the claimant. The Damages Directive introduces a rebuttable presumption that cartels cause harm, and allows judges to estimate the harm (see section 8.3.3).

US antitrust law

A plaintiff must establish that it was injured in its business or property as a direct and proximate result of an antitrust violation.[55] The anti-competitive conduct must be a material and substantial cause of the injury.[56] The plaintiff is only entitled to damages that it has proven to a jury. As the Supreme Court has stated, 'even where the defendant by his own wrong has prevented a more precise computation, the jury may not render a verdict based on speculation or guesswork.'[57] But the Court has also stated that plaintiffs seeking recovery for antitrust harm should not face unduly high burdens for establishing their injuries.[58] It has observed that 'damage issues in [antitrust] cases are rarely susceptible of the kind of concrete, detailed proof of injury which is available in other contexts.'[59]

US law does not prescribe one formula for calculating damages in antitrust cases. Methodologies for calculating harm will vary from case to case and depend on such factors as the alleged violation and injury and the data available to the plaintiff. US courts have accepted several different methodologies. For example, the 'before and after' approach compares a plaintiff's profits, sales or prices paid during the alleged violation with a period before or after that time period.[60] The 'yardstick' approach compares the plaintiff's performance in the affected market with its performance in other markets or with the performance of benchmark firms in markets not affected by the alleged violation.[61] These methodologies invariably require use of expert witnesses. Judges play important gatekeeper functions in assessing the reliability of expert testimony and have the authority to exclude expert testimony based on a methodology that is obviously deficient.[62]

---

[55] *Lexmark International v. Static Control Components*, 134 S. Ct. 1377, 1390 (2014).

[56] *Zenith Radio Corp. v. Hazeltine Research*, 395 US 100, 114 (1969).

[57] *Brunswick Corp. v. Pueblo Bowl-O-Mat*, 429 US 477, 489 (1977); *Bigelow v. RKO Pictures, Inc.*, 327 US 251, 264 (1946).

[58] *Story Parchment Co. v. Paterson Parchment Paper Co.*, 282 US 555, 562 (1931).

[59] *Zenith Radio Corp. v. Hazeltine Research*, 395 US 100, 123 (1969).

[60] *Bigelow v. RKO Pictures*, 327 US 251, 264 (1946); *Story Parchment Co. v. Paterson Parchment Paper Co.*, 282 US 555, 562 (1931).

[61] *Bigelow v. RKO Pictures*, 327 US 251, 266 (1946).

[62] *Daubert v. Merrell Dow Pharmaceutical, Inc.*, 509 US 579 (1993); *Kumho Tire Co. Ltd. v. Carmichael*, 526 US 137 (1999).

While plaintiffs in the US seek damages for all types of antitrust violations, suits seeking damages for price fixing have grown significantly in the last two decades. 'In the 1970s and 1980s, antitrust class actions occasionally achieved large damage recoveries, but in recent decades recoveries have been larger and more frequent' (Werden, Hammond and Barnett 2012). This is also due to the increase in governmental enforcement actions against huge international cartels.[63] Plaintiffs in price-fixing cases often establish damages by comparing the prices they paid during the conspiracy period with the prices they paid before the conspiracy began and after it ended. The difference between the two prices, adjusting for other factors such as changes in demand or costs that could affect prices, constitute the price-fixing overcharge and form the basis for the damages calculation. Defendants invariably prepare alternative damages studies and attack plaintiffs' overcharge studies on such grounds as they relied on critical assumptions that were contrary to the evidence or inconsistent with economic reality or failed to consider essential facts related to plaintiffs' alleged injury.[64]

The right of standing for indirect buyers

In many cases the negative effects of competition law infringements committed by firms further up the supply chain (manufacturers, importers, wholesalers) manifest themselves downstream (retailers, end consumers). In the case of a price-fixing agreement, the question then arises as to whether indirect buyers (end consumers) should be entitled to bring a claim for damages if manufacturers (importers, wholesalers, retailers) have passed on the overcharges downstream to final consumers. A related question is whether firms upstream may invoke a passing-on defence if they are confronted with (multiple) claims of downstream buyers, in order to avoid overcompensation (in legal terms, unjust enrichment) of the latter. The US Supreme Court answered both questions negatively.[65] These judgments relied on two rationales: increasing deterrence, assuming that private parties would have little incentive to sue; and avoiding the complex litigation that pass-through calculations would entail for the courts. The Supreme Court's judgments were met with criticism and a majority of US states subsequently enacted laws permitting the passing-on defence and indirect purchaser standing.[66] In Europe, Directive 2004/104 has given a positive answer to both questions, even though the burden of proof remains high for companies wishing to

---

[63] See Antitrust Division, US Department of Justice, Criminal Enforcement Trends Charts, 2015, available at www.justice.gov/atr/criminal-enforcement-fine-and-jail-charts (2005–15 figures).

[64] See ABA (2012, 788).

[65] *Hanover Shoe Inc. v. United Shoe Machinery Corp.*, 392 U.S.481 (1968); *Illinois Brick Co. et al. v. Illinois et al.*, 431 U.S. 720 (1977).

[66] This has led to diverging rules, which create room for forum shopping. A famous example of follow-on litigation (more than 100 actions before state courts) is the *Microsoft* case. See Tomlin and Giali (2002, 163).

invoke the passing-on defence. The discussion below explains why indirect claims are needed for an efficient enforcement of competition rules.

The major argument is that precluding indirect purchasers' claims is likely to have a negative impact on deterrence. Optimal deterrence requires that the cartel participants are confronted with the full cost caused by the violation of the competition rules. If they must compensate only the harm suffered by direct buyers, the total harm caused by the cartel will not be internalised. Prominent economists have argued that the harm caused by a price cartel tends to be significantly underestimated. An exclusive focus on the price increases decided by first-line manufacturers neglects important additional economic losses. Measuring antitrust damages using the overcharge on the number of products that have been directly purchased from the law infringers is doomed to lead to under-deterrence of violations of the cartel prohibition. Both the volume effect and the additional inefficiencies resulting from passing-on must come on top of the direct overcharges (price effect). According to Basso and Ross (2010), the common practice of looking only at the direct loss of consumer surplus may result in underestimations amounting to more than 50% of the total harm. Against this background, the criticism that allowing indirect buyers the right to sue for damages may lead to multiple recoveries against the same defendant seems pointless. In the absence of multiple damages (for example, treble damages in the US) or punitive damages, no multiplier can be used to correct for the underestimation of the harm caused by price fixing if the volume effect (deadweight loss) is neglected. Allowing indirect claims may be the only practical way to increase deterrence and contribute to the reduction of welfare losses caused by price cartels.

The counter-argument, which supports the undesirability of indirect damages claims, is that the information costs of identifying an antitrust violation are lower for the direct buyers, since they are closer to the violation (Landes and Posner 1979). The scope of this argument must be limited to stand-alone actions, i.e. damages claims brought by private parties before the intervention by the competition authority. In follow-on cases, which are initiated after the discovery of a violation by the competition authorities, also indirect purchasers hold the relevant information. Lande and Davis (2008) provide some empirical evidence that seems to prove the superiority of direct claims from a deterrence perspective. Their survey finds that in 29 successful private antitrust cases, direct actions have led to a recovery that was five times greater ($11.2 billion) than the one generated by indirect actions ($2.1 billion). However, both from a theoretical and an empirical viewpoint, the arguments in favour of excluding indirect damages claims need further qualifications.

The key question is not who has the lowest information costs but rather who is most likely to investigate and sue the violator. Presumably because they are close to the violators, direct buyers may fear the risk of retaliation and the forced end of advantageous commercial relationships with their suppliers. On the empirical level, information about successful claims by direct purchasers does not provide conclusive evidence about the average impact on deterrence if there is no information about the overcharges that, because of the exclusion of indirect claims for damages, have not been detected or convicted (Renda *et al.* 2008, 471–472). In sum, allowing damages claims by indirect purchasers seems to fare better on the deterrence scale than the alternative option of restricting the right of standing to direct buyers.

Box 8.4: Enforcement of competition law in developing economies

Antitrust law in developing countries (BRIC and other emerging economies) has an immense potential. These are large economies with a gigantic consumer market and an equally important economy. In these countries concentrated markets are common, often as a remainder of a previously state controlled economy, and an effectively enforced competition law may substantially contribute to economic growth (see section 3.1). However, competition culture in new emerging economies is poorly developed, even among large firms, and the importance of competition law is only vaguely understood in most portions of the population. This poses difficult challenges to competition authorities: enforcement of competition rules in previously state controlled parts of the economy may meet political resistance and a lot of resources have to be spent on competition advocacy in order to gain legitimacy across the population. An important political obstacle follows from the legacy of the formerly planned economy. In China, it is still unclear if and, if yes, to what extent, administrative monopolies and state-owned companies are fully subjected to the provisions of the AML (Marquis 2013). A further obstacle is the lack of specialised knowledge (legal and economic expertise), which inhibits the speedy development of a competition law informed by economic analysis. Within the scope of this book, only a few illustrations can be given to illustrate the enforcement difficulties in developing economies. For further analysis the reader is referred to other publications (Zarzur, Katona and Villela 2015; Faure and Zhang 2013).

China

Also in developing countries, private damages claims may contribute to deterrence and guarantee compensation for victims of competition law infringements. China has a dual enforcement system: the competition rules are enforced by antitrust agencies as well as private parties. At the administrative level, the Chinese Anti-Monopoly Law

(AML) is enforced by three separate authorities: the National Development and Reform Commission (NDRC, responsible for price fixing), the State Administration for Industry and Commerce (SAIC, responsible for abuse of dominance and non-price agreements) and the Ministry of Commerce (MOFCOM, responsible for merger review). Next to cases initiated by NDRC and SAIC, the AML is enforced by private civil litigation. Article 50 AML provides a comprehensive cause of action to private parties harmed by anti-competitive conduct: 'If an undertaking engages in monopoly conduct and causes losses to others, it shall assume civil liability in accordance with the law.' This broad formulation includes cease-and-desist orders, payment of compensation and other civil responsi-bilities as potential remedies. More than 40 private actions were already filed in the first two years of the AML's existence, the vast majority of which were abuse of dominance claims. Private enforcement has been further enhanced by the Supreme People's Court, which issued a judicial interpretation (JI 2012) clarifying the scope and conditions of private action. It is now well-established that private parties can start legal proceedings independently of the administrative agencies and that also indirect victims are entitled to compensation (Farmer 2013). Interestingly, as is the case under US law, the prevailing plaintiffs are also entitled to compensation of attorneys' fees (Article 14 JI: 'reasonable expenses incurred in the investigation and prevention of monopolistic conduct').

Regarding the issue of (de)centralisation, China represents an interesting case for international comparisons. Besides the central level, there are several regional and local levels of government (autonomous provinces, municipalities). Given this *de facto* federal structure, it is remarkable that the AML is centrally enforced by NDRC, SAIC and MOFCOM. Marquis (2013) argues that the AML may have been a tool of re-centralisation of economic decision-making powers that the central government had gradually lost to lower-level authorities. Remarkably, private litigation also is relatively centralised, since only a limited number of courts can judge private claims. The latter part of the centralisation has been justified by the complexity of competition law cases and the need of consistency (Farmer 2013, 29). However, as the discussion in section 8.5.1 will illustrate, centralisation may lose several benefits of decentralisation, includ-ing information advantages and learning processes. Centralisation is also problematic when, compared with decentralised enforcement, political distortions at the central level are more worrisome. In the Chinese context, it may impede an effective control of anti-competitive practices by administrative monopolies and state-owned enterprises.

Brazil

Private antitrust litigation is entrenched in the Brazilian judicial culture, which is evi-denced by some remarkable differences with private damages claims in EU jurisdictions. Brazilian civil law judges enjoy an autonomous role, since they are not bound by decisions of the competition authority (CADE). Consequently, follow-on damages actions are less common than stand-alone claims. Also, collective actions may be brought by the state (mainly federal branches of the Prosecution Office) and private associations satisfying criteria of representativeness, technical expertise and financial capability. These actions are not be equated with US class actions, since the members of the association must opt in to receive payment of damages that cannot be trebled to increase deterrence. However, courts have decided that the full social costs of cartels must be compensated, which can be seen as treble damages in disguise. In sum, the Brazilian system is more hospitable to private enforcement of competition law than its European counterpart (for further discussion, see Magalhães *et al.* 2015).

Russia

Several obstacles to effective enforcement of competition law in developing economies remain. Several developing countries have invested important resources to train officials of competition authorities. However, the case of Russia shows that even if young competition authorities are well staffed with trained scientific personnel, the use and quality of economic analysis may lag behind if the competition authority is not sufficiently autonomous and its decisions are subject to appeal before relatively inexperienced judges. The Russian Federal Antitrust Service (FAS) has very broad competences that include not only the usual competition domains but also unfair competition, advertising, regulation of natural monopolies, investment in strategic companies and even price regulation. Avdasheva *et al.* (2016) show that the FAS has incentives to concentrate its enforcement efforts on cases that do not require intensive economic analysis. Moreover, these authors empirically demonstrate that the use of economic evidence affects the probability that infringement decisions are annulled by the courts. Since the reputation of FAS depends more on legal quality than sound economic analysis, the Russian competition authority does not have sufficient incentives to engage in detailed economic analysis.

In conclusion, developing economies have taken important steps to enable an effective enforcement of newly enacted competition laws. As is the case in the EU and the US, they have a dual enforcement system that strives to find the optimal mix of public and private enforcement. The comparative analysis above shows that efficient outcomes are still hindered by different causes: the legacy of formerly state-controlled economies, lack of expertise and a too-strong centralisation of enforcement powers.

8.4 *Ex ante* or *ex post* control: authorisation regime or legal exception regime?

According to general principles of European law, the competition rules contained in Articles 101 and 102 TFEU produce direct effects in relations between individuals and thus create direct rights in respect of the individuals concerned that the national courts must safeguard.[67] This implies that, together with the European Commission, national courts have jurisdiction to apply these Articles, with European law taking precedence over national law. Under the old enforcement regime, which was in force until May 2014, undertakings could notify their agreements to the European Commission, thereby seeking either a negative clearance and/or an individual exemption. Negative clearances were formal decisions (without conditions and obligations) certifying that, on the basis of the facts in its possession, the Commission saw no grounds under Article 81(1) EC for action on its part in respect of an agreement or practice. Negative clearances did not protect the firms concerned from later contrary decisions by national competition authorities or courts, or even by the European Commission itself when new facts emerged. If a restriction of competition within the meaning of Article 81(1) EC was found, the only way to escape from the prohibition was by benefiting from an exemption, provided that the four cumulative conditions of Article 81(3) EC were satisfied. In the absence of group exemptions for specific types of agreements, which were contained in Block Exemption Regulations, companies were obliged to notify their agreements to the European Commission and ask for an individual exemption. Exemption decisions could not take effect at a date earlier than the date of notification. Only the European Commission had the power to grant exemptions in individual cases. The Commission had full discretion to grant a decision and was – contrary to the strict time schedules that apply in merger cases – not bound by time limits. Exemptions were binding on national courts and national competition authorities. Judicial review of the Commission's decisions was possible before the European Courts.

The 'modernisation' of the enforcement regime, which is contained in Regulation 1/2003 that entered into force on May 2004, introduced important changes in the enforcement system. First, the notification and authorisation system is replaced by a system of legal exception. Article 1(1) of Regulation 1/2003 states: 'Agreements, decisions and concerted practices caught by Article 81(1) of the Treaty which do not satisfy the conditions of Article 81(3) EC shall be prohibited, no prior decision to that effect being required.' The last part of this sentence introduces the legal exception system. Consequently, from May 2004 on, the system of prior control under which agreements and restrictive practices are prohibited unless expressly permitted by the European Commission has been replaced by a regime under which firms are freed from the necessity of notifying agreements to ensure their legality. In other words, a switch from an *ex ante* to

---

[67] Case 127/73 *BRT v. SABAM* [1974] ECR 51, para. 16.

ex post control has been implemented. Second, the Commission has lost its monopoly to grant exemptions. All NCAs and national judges are now empowered to apply Article 101 TFEU in its entirety, including its third paragraph. Regulation 1/2003 is based on a system of parallel competences in which all competition authorities have the power to apply the current Articles 101–102 TFEU and are responsible for an efficient division of work. Together the NCAs and the Commission form a network called the European Competition Network (ECN). Under this system of parallel competences, cases can by dealt with by a single NCA, several NCAs acting in parallel or the European Commission. Also, national judges can apply the European competition rules in full. Third, the European Commission's and the national competition authorities' powers of investigation have been extended. Besides requests for information (Article 18), the Commission may take statements from employees during company visits (Article 19) and conduct all necessary inspections (Article 20), including premises different from those of the investigated company and inspections in private homes (Article 21). The competition authority of a Member State may in its own territory carry out investigations on behalf of and for the account of the competition authority of another Member State in order to establish infringements of European competition law.

In contrast with the cartel prohibition, enforcement of Article 102 TFEU has always been essentially *ex post*; exemptions from the ban on abuse of a dominant position are not possible. Undertakings enjoying a dominant position decide, eventually after having sought legal advice, whether they engage in a certain practice or not. If the European Commission is of the opinion that the action constitutes an abuse, it can order its termination and impose substantial fines. Also, national competition authorities and judges can enforce Article 102 TFEU to its full extent.

The major argument supporting the system change was the heavy workload it created for the European competition authority, forcing the Commission to spend resources on cases raising only minor if any competition concerns (Wils 2002, 212). However, lower administrative costs on their own cannot justify the conclusion that a legal exception regime is more efficient. A full-blown economic analysis of the switch from a centralised notification and authorisation system to a system of legal exception (with decentralised enforcement) also requires an investigation of its effects on two different types of costs: information costs and incentive costs. If the sum of the latter exceeds the savings of administrative costs, the system change will not be efficient. The remainder of this section analyses the information costs and incentive costs to allow for an appraisal of the overall efficiency of the switch from a notification system to a legal exception regime. A first set of questions relates to the impact on information costs: how does the system change affect the information about the existence of harmful cartels? What is the effect on the level of legal certainty available to the affected parties? A second set of questions relates to the impact on incentive costs. How does the switch affect the incentives of companies to enter into agreements? Does an *ex post* control sufficiently deter welfare-reducing agreements? Does the system change encourage welfare-improving agreements to be signed? Clearly, the effects on information costs and incentive costs are interrelated, and the introduction of a more decentralised enforcement system has an effect on the overall costs of the system reform as well.

8.4.1 Information costs

By abolishing the system of notification, the European Commission has lost a potentially important source of information on competition in particular markets. There exists an information asymmetry between, on the one hand, competition authorities and cartel participants and, on the other hand, third parties such as competitors and consumers. In both cases, the information asymmetry does not concern only the precise contents of the agreements but also other issues, such as market characteristics and the availability of substitutes, which may have an impact on the assessment of the legal validity of the concluded agreements. Since most substantive legal rules are not clear-cut, costly information-gathering and information-processing procedures must be conducted in order to assess whether a certain practice constitutes an infringement or not and whether it may profit from an exemption. These costs fall on both the companies and the law enforcers. The latter may commit two types of error: either they prohibit a practice that satisfies the conditions for an exemption (type I error) or they erroneously grant an exemption (type II error). Since these errors have a negative impact on the incentives to engage in welfare-improving behaviour or abstain from welfare-reducing conduct (incentive costs), optimal law enforcement should reduce the different types of information costs.

What are the effects of the modernisation of the enforcement system on the information costs indicated above? A distinction must be made between hard-core cartels and other anti-competitive practices. A notification system leads to lower costs of information gathering for the law enforcers if the undertakings voluntarily reveal the existence and contents of restrictive practices. Since this will not occur in cases of hard-core cartels, a switch from *ex ante* monitoring to *ex post* control has no detrimental effect on the information about the existence of those cartels. In addition, in the case of hard-core restraints, *ex post* intervention may be defended since the public authority already has information about their actual effects: horizontal restraints normally produce anti-competitive consequences without redeeming virtues. The picture is different in the grey area, where a great deal of uncertainty exists about whether or not a practice infringes competition law. Whereas hard-core cartels will be kept secret, companies may wish to reveal the existence of agreements, the legality of which is difficult to assess in order to obtain legal certainty. Vertical restraints are a good example: their legality is difficult to assess without having access to information about their likely effects. This information may become more readily available under a notification system. If the competition authority has limited information about the actual effects of a certain type of conduct, *ex ante* intervention seems more appropriate since it permits the authority to acquire the relevant data for such an appraisal. A notification system may reveal important information to the competition authorities that is very costly (or impossible) to acquire under a legal exception regime. This loss of information also affects competitors and consumers. If they are informed about the existence of welfare-reducing agreements, they can take action against such harmful practices in a more timely and effective manner (Pirrung 2004).

In the legal literature, the system change has been criticised because of the loss of legal certainty for undertakings (see for example Möschel 2000). In economic terms, this argument may be rephrased as an increase in information costs. Under a notification and authorisation regime, undertakings do not have to assess themselves whether anti-competitive agreements satisfy the requirements for exemption. If the antitrust authority grants a formal exemption, companies are entirely freed from the risk that the agreement may be considered illegal. Obviously, experience has shown that an authorisation system creates a workload that a competition authority cannot manage. Formal decisions were taken in only a very limited number of cases. However, under the previous regime, companies could at least acquire a relative certainty by obtaining a comfort letter from the European Commission. An additional loss in terms of legal certainty follows from the risk that within the ECN opinions on the legality of agreements and restrictive practices may differ. Since NCAs may act in parallel, there is a risk of conflicting decisions in the same case. Under the new system, also national judges may apply Article 101(1) TFEU in its entirety, and this further increases the risk of divergent decisions.

For assessing the impact of the system change on legal certainty, again the distinction between hard-core cartels and other anti-competitive practices (which may have redeeming virtues) is useful. In the former case, companies know that they commit a clear violation of the competition rules and risk heavy fines. In the latter case, clear answers as to the legality of the agreements are not easily available. The publication of Notices by the European Commission, which are not binding for national judges, may leave many questions unanswered. Under the new regime, companies no longer have the right to obtain an official evaluation and they have to rely purely on their own assessment of their practices. Given the parallel competences of the European Commission and NCAs, this is a serious problem for conducting business, especially in dynamic industries with high rates of innovation. The external information concerning market characteristics affecting the effects of their practices on each of the conditions for exemption may be difficult to acquire for private parties who have no investigative powers and may need costly external advice by economic experts. The validity of a restrictive practice will be checked only when it is challenged by a competition authority or by third parties before a court. Even the best legal and economic experts may have difficulties predicting how law enforcers will evaluate whether the restrictive practice infringes competition law. The legal certainty provided by an individual exemption cannot be perfectly substituted by expert advice. As a consequence, information costs will be higher under a legal exception regime than under a notification and authorisation system. The system change from *ex ante* control to *ex post* assessment may be better supported in the old Member States than in the new Member States. In the latter states, companies face greater uncertainty with respect to the legality of agreements and decentralisation, which goes hand in hand with a move from *ex ante* to *ex post* control, may create serious inefficiencies. This negative impact may be worsened by an increase in error costs (type I and type II) if the quality of the competitive assessment is not sufficiently high.

8.4.2   Incentive costs

To assess the efficiency of the alternative regimes (*ex ante* notification versus *ex post* assessment), the decisive question is under which system an optimal number of agreements will be signed. A preventive policy (notification) makes it possible to stop harmful agreements at an early stage. By contrast, in a repression regime with fines (legal exception) the competition authority analyses the agreements after they were signed and partially implemented. An *ex post* enforcement regime reduces the overall number of controls by competition authorities and therefore requires higher sanctions to compensate for the lower probability of detection of antitrust infringements (Di Federico and Manzini 2004). Regulation 1/2003 has left the maximum amount of the fine unchanged. When the level of sanctions is not increased, efficient outcomes can be reached only if detection efforts are intensified in a way that is proportional to the reduction of the expected fines perceived by potential infringers. The system change will decrease welfare if it leads to a higher number of harmful agreements, which are not scrutinised by the competition authorities. Moreover, the switch to a legal exception regime will decrease welfare if beneficial agreements are no longer entered into. A rise of incentive costs, i.e. under-deterrence of harmful agreements and over-deterrence of beneficial agreements, may (partly or entirely) offset the savings in administrative costs that were the main reason for the system change.

Theoretical economic literature, which models the behaviour of firms, allows for a better understanding of the possible outcomes of the system reform. This literature focuses on the impact of the modernisation on the type of agreements that firms might implement. Under the strong assumption that cartel authorities do not commit errors, Hahn shows that the system of *ex ante* control is superior to *ex post* control because the law enforcement has a greater deterrent effect when notification is required (Hahn 2000). Barros considers identical firms and focuses on the impact of the reduced legal certainty created by the removal of the notification and authorisation regime. He shows that, on the one hand, firms might be tempted to sign more restrictive agreements, since the probability of audit is reduced in the *ex post* regime. On the other hand, as legal uncertainty increases, firms may take less risk. Barros shows that the latter effect is more likely to prevail, implying that the reform should result in a lower number of restrictive agreements (Barros 2003). Neven considers heterogeneous firms and focuses on the incentives created by the elimination of the notification regime. *Ex post* monitoring leads to higher information costs, thus inducing firms to sign agreements that are more likely to be cleared by the competition authority. The consequence is that some beneficial agreements are no longer implemented. The consequence of the reform may be that beneficial agreements are no longer signed, for lack of legal certainty. Moreover, Neven argues that the removal of the notification regime induces some anti-competitive agreements, which would otherwise have been notified, to be implemented and not monitored. The level of *ex post* enforcement should be high to limit these errors (Neven 2002).

Loss *et al.* (2008) start from different assumptions: firms are aware of the status of the agreement and the audit gives the competition authority an imperfect signal on this status. They show that the notification regime dominates only when the quality of the assessment by the competition authority is fairly poor. The competition authority has prior beliefs concerning the impact of agreements on welfare, which it may revise when it analyses a case after having received information (signal). Priors may be good (e.g. joint research and development agreements) or bad (e.g. horizontal market sharing or resale price maintenance). The signal may be more or less accurate: when the signal is weakly accurate, the decision of the competition authority will be based on its prior beliefs. The authors show that the notification regime is preferred for intermediate values of the priors when the signal is not accurate, whereas the exception regime dominates when the priors are not too high and the signal is sufficiently accurate. When the priors reach extreme values, either a block exemption regime is preferred when the priors are extremely good or a black list regime dominates when the priors are extremely bad and the signal is not accurate. On the basis of these findings, the authors explain a possible motivation for the change from *ex ante* to *ex post* control. When prior beliefs are not extreme and the signal's accuracy increases, a move away from an authorisation regime to an exception regime is justified. It is reasonable to assume that the European Commission has improved its knowledge and that the quality of the decisions is much higher than in 1962. After this learning period, an *ex post* control may thus be efficient. This is due to the fact that if the signal is sufficiently accurate, the legal exception regime reaches an equilibrium, in which only beneficial agreements are signed.

8.5 Centralisation or decentralisation?

EU competition law shows a remarkable combination of centralised rule-making and decentralised enforcement. Regulation 1/2003 has consolidated a system of harmonised substantive rules and decentralised enforcement. Since the European Commission no longer enjoys an enforcement monopoly, different NCAs and judges compete with each other in the implementation of the cartel prohibition and the assessment of abuse of a dominant position. Economic analysis offers several criteria to judge the efficiency of the enforcement system's change.

On the one hand, decentralisation and the resulting competition between enforcement agencies may be supported by three economic criteria: (i) the ability of satisfying a greater number of preferences; (ii) the importance of learning processes; and (iii) the correction of information asymmetries between competition authorities and supervised undertakings. On the other hand, three different economic criteria favour centralisation: (i) externalities in other jurisdictions; (ii) the risk of a 'race to the bottom' caused by forum shopping; and (iii) the achievement of scale economies. The above analysis may be complemented by a Public Choice approach. Both regulated industries and enforcement agencies may prefer a level of enforcement that favours their own interests, rather than the general welfare of the EU. Also, the danger of 'regulatory capture' will be dependent on the level of enforcement: decentralised competition authorities may be too close to the firms to be supervised and risk losing their independence.

8.5.1 Arguments in favour of decentralisation

The first argument favouring decentralisation may be derived from the economic literature on federalism. It is based on the seminal theoretical article by Tiebout (1956), who showed that an optimal supply of public services can be guaranteed if people with similar tastes cluster together in communities providing their preferred bundle of public services.[68] If there is a sufficiently large number of communities, which offer diverging packages of local public services and people can freely move – or 'vote with their feet' – an optimal organisation of public services will follow. For such competition to take place, it is not needed that people physically move but it suffices that a 'free choice of law' rule enables them to decide which legal rule will apply to situations affecting their well-being. An important advantage in comparison with regulatory competition requiring factors of production to move across jurisdictions is that free choice of law allows choices of particular rules without having to accept the whole bundle of regulations of the respective jurisdiction. This may lead to very intense regulatory competition (Kerber and Budzinski 2003).

The discussion relating to the goals of competition law in Chapter 3 of this book has shown that preferences about the contents of the substantive rules vary substantially across jurisdictions, depending on the choice of the normative standard (total welfare, consumer welfare or the protection of the competitive process). In the field of enforcement, the same diversity may exist regarding the type of sanctions and the choice between public and private enforcement. Decentralised enforcement in the EU enables the Member States to honour the (potentially divergent) preferences of their citizens concerning heavily debated issues, such as criminalisation of cartel offences (to enhance deterrence and/or signal strong moral disapproval) and the

---

[68] Tiebout's theory is valid only if the following assumptions are satisfied:

- There must be a sufficiently large number of providers of public goods (local communities).
- There must be no restraints inhibiting perfect mobility between communities.
- There must be no information deficiencies.
- There must be no externalities.
- Municipalities must be able to exclude 'free riders' from the services offered.
- There must be no scale economies which necessitate cooperation between communities to profit from efficiency savings.

If the above conditions are not satisfied, centralisation may be warranted to improve upon efficiency.

resources to be spent on private enforcement dependent on the effectiveness of public enforcement.

The second argument in support of decentralisation finds its basis in the work of Nobel laureate Friedrich van Hayek, who stressed the benefits of competition as a learning process (von Hayek 1978, 66–81). Differences in rules allow for different experiences and may improve an understanding of the effects of alternative legal solutions to similar problems. This advantage relates both to the formulation of the substantive rules and their enforcement. Given the fundamental limitations of human knowledge, it cannot be assumed that policy makers know the best legal rules in advance. The quality of the performance of legal rules and systems of enforcement in a given jurisdiction is revealed by comparing it with the performance of different legal rules and systems of enforcement in other jurisdictions. The Hayekian concept of 'competition as a discovery procedure' entails parallel experimentation with new problem solutions and the imitation of the successful solutions by others through learning. This Hayekian concept is closely linked to the idea of 'yardstick competition', implying that information about the quality of the performance of governments and enforcement agencies is revealed by comparing it with the performance of others. Hayek's ideas are also close to the Schumpeterian concept of competition as a process of 'creative destruction', implying continuous innovation and imitation (see section 2.7.2). Many examples may be given why learning processes in the field of antitrust enforcement are particularly important. Given the debates on the deterrent effects of public fines, the principal-agent problems with private enforcement and many other uncertainties, the EU potentially represents a laboratory of 28 Member States that could choose different methods to optimise enforcement results. Centralisation resulting in far-reaching harmonisation would destroy these learning processes.

The third argument favouring decentralisation is the need to cope with informational asymmetries between regulatory agencies and regulated firms. Decentralisation is the more efficient the more valuable local information is for appropriate rule-making and enforcement. The asymmetry of information between competition authorities and supervised firms may be analysed as a principal-agent problem. Competition authorities (both national and supranational) have an information disadvantage vis-à-vis the firms they have to control; the former may be seen as the principals and the latter as the agents. Out of self-interest, the agents may be unwilling to reveal all the information needed by the principals. A related danger is the communication of false information. It may be argued that it is more difficult for firms to hide or misrepresent information to decentralised agencies than to a more remote agency.

In the field of competition law, information provided by firms may be cross-checked against information from competitors, consumer organisations and official sources. If such cross-checking is difficult, local agencies will still have a better view of the market than a supranational agency. Decentralisation may thus be advocated because it reduces the agency problem. There are, naturally, also intermediate solutions between full decentralisation and full centralisation. First, decentralised information gathering can help to remove much of the information asymmetry faced by central regulatory agencies. A second alternative for the choice between centralisation and decentralisation is the co-existence of national and supranational procedures. The European system of enforcement has moved from the former to the latter alternative and now consists of parallel competences combined with a division of work that leaves the most important cases to be decided by the European Commission.

8.5.2 Arguments in favour of centralisation

In the economic literature on federalism, the major argument in favour of centralisation is the need to internalise interstate externalities. Also, parallel enforcement of competition law prohibitions may generate externalities across jurisdictions. National competition authorities may not take into account the effects of their decisions on other national authorities. Positive externalities occur when action of all competent competition authorities is necessary to give full effect to the activity of a single competition authority. Suppose that a restrictive agreement causes harm in three Member States and that one of the competent competition authorities establishes an infringement of Article 101 TFEU. If this decision is not sufficient to end the entire infringement or sanction it adequately, the decision of the acting authority will cause a positive externality by increasing the value and exploitable rents to the other two competition authorities. Positive externalities will be underprovided because competition authorities that produce the externalities only account for the effect of their action on themselves. Negative externalities occur when the action of one competition authority reduces the value and exploitable rents of another authority. For example, an exemption by one competition authority dissipates the value of a second exemption by a competition authority in another Member State. Similarly, a leniency fine reduction from one national competition authority dissipates the value of a subsequent fine reduction by another national competition authority. Negative externalities will be overprovided because individual competition authorities do not account for the negative effects of their decisions on other authorities. Drawing upon these theoretical insights, one may expect that the direct applicability of the exemption provision will increase the overall amount of exemptions (Parisi and Depoorter 2005).

The adequate answer to the positive and negative regulatory externalities described above is centralised enforcement. The European system of parallel enforcement provides only partial solutions to the externalities problem. If the costs of either non-enforcement or a too-lenient enforcement of competition law in one of the Member States are borne by businesses and consumers in other Member States, centralised enforcement may be needed to ensure that these interstate externalities are internalised. The European Commission retains exclusive jurisdiction if a restrictive agreement or practice affects competition in cross-border markets covering more than three Member States. In this way, the underprovision of positive externalities by competing national competition authorities is overcome. If the agreement or practice has substantial effects on competition in two or three domestic markets, the European Commission's Notice provides for parallel action by the national competition authorities involved.[69] Also, in the latter case, centralised enforcement may be favoured to avoid opportunistic behaviour of one or two of the competent authorities. The exclusive jurisdiction of the Commission in cases where competition is affected in more than three Member States is also a way to avoid the negative externalities of the system of parallel enforcement. If the targeted agreement or practice affects competition in two or three Member States, only coordination of regulatory action may minimise the distortions described above. In this respect, it may be deplored that the Guidelines on cooperation within the network of competition authorities (ECN) are not legally binding. National competition authorities may suspend a proceeding when another national competition authority is dealing with a case, but they have no obligation to do so.[70] Consequently, there remains scope for negative externalities across jurisdictions.

A second argument supporting centralisation is the risk of a race to the bottom, causing a destructive competition between jurisdictions leading to 'bad' law.[71] A related argument in the political discussion is the need to guarantee a 'level playing field' for companies, which prevents market participants from gaining an unfair competitive advantage over their competitors because they are not subject to the same (stricter) legal rules. The theoretical basis for this

---

[69] Commission Notice on cooperation within the Network of Competition Authorities, para. 12.

[70] Commission Notice on cooperation within the Network of Competition Authorities, O.J. C 1012, 27.4.2004, at paras 20–22.

[71] Fear that destructive competition between states might produce undesirable results in the form of 'bad law' has often served as an argument for centralising certain areas of law. American scholars have advanced the argument in the contexts of corporate law and environmental law. However, with respect to corporate law, the view that states would engage in a race for the bottom in which they would attempt to outdo each other for the favour of corporate managers to the ultimate detriment of shareholders has been sharply criticised; see Romano (1985) and Romano (1993). Similarly, with respect to environmental law, it has been shown that the fear of a race to the bottom is both theoretically unsound and without empirical proof; see Revesz (2000).

fear is the existence of prisoner's dilemmas between jurisdictions. States may wish to outbid each other in lenient enforcement of competition law, in order to attract businesses to locate in their jurisdiction. However, a state will gain in the struggle to attract business only by choosing in favour of laxness when other states do not act in the same way. If all other states follow, only the businesses will gain. Although all jurisdictions could be better off with appropriate competition laws that are effectively enforced, a suboptimal equilibrium with an insufficient level of protection of competition may ensue. If jurisdictions compete with each other under the conditions of a prisoner's dilemma, there will be a race to the bottom and centralisation will then be required to generate efficient outcomes.

A deterioration of the quality of competition law may occur in different ways, depending on the type of regulatory competition (Kerber and Budzinski 2003). Three scenarios can be distinguished: the adoption of strategic competition policies to increase international trade, changing competition laws to attract mobile production factors, and enabling a free choice of the applicable competition rules. First, strategic competition policies deliberately protecting market power in domestic markets may attract foreign investment. Market power on domestic markets could be tolerated to support the attainment of market power on international markets. Examples of such strategies include the exemption of export cartels and the strategic use of merger control to support the creation of national champions. Second, the prospect of attaining market power in domestic markets (without effects on international trade) can make it attractive for firms to move into another jurisdiction. Firms may have incentives to locate in 'cartel paradises', either because they think that market power in domestic markets will improve their competitiveness on international markets or because they want to reap profits from domestic markets. States may provide incentives for firms to locate within jurisdictions if they value the freedom to form cartels and reap monopoly profits higher than the protection against those types of conduct if performed by their competitors. Third, a prisoner's dilemma emerges when firms enjoy the freedom to decide under which competition rules they want to do business in a particular market. The latter type of regulatory competition leads to forum shopping and may ultimately reduce overall enforcement of competition law below the socially optimal level. Although companies may be interested in being protected from anti-competitive behaviour by other market players, firms trapped in a prisoner's dilemma will choose lenient competition laws that do not restrict their business decisions on the market.

With the exception of forum shopping, the arguments about destructive competition on the market for competition laws seem mainly theoretical and lack sufficient empirical proof. Indeed, there are several counter-arguments why such destructive forms of competition are unlikely. Firms may decide to relocate their businesses not because of the prospect of a lax antitrust jurisdiction but primarily for different reasons, such as the level of taxes, the degree of unionisation of the labour force and the quality of the infrastructure in the state of establishment. There is also the counter-argument that competition between jurisdictions may cause a race to the top rather than a race to the bottom. Generally speaking, antitrust laws do not seem to hinder worldwide competitiveness in the light of the fact that no such laws bind business people in other countries. Successes in international trade are achieved through technological leadership, which is not necessarily due to monopoly power but may be the consequence of strong competitive pressures on the home market. Hence, competition policy may improve international competitiveness, contrary to the arguments in favour of an industrial policy favouring big enterprises through lax merger control or allowing anti-competitive practices. In this context, it must be added that a race to the top does not necessarily lead to efficient outcomes. A rush towards overzealous competition authorities may result in a too-high number of unnecessary prohibitions (type I errors). In discussing whether competition between jurisdictions causes either a race to the bottom or a race to the top, one should always bear in mind that the optimal level of antitrust enforcement is not necessarily the 'top' reached by unlimited regulatory competition.

8.5.3   A Public Choice perspective

So far, the discussion has proceeded on the assumption that regulatory powers are allocated in such a way as to maximise social welfare. However, private politics rather than global welfare may be the driving force behind (de)centralisation. It is well known that private interests may have an important impact on the contents of legal rules. The same is true with respect to decisions about whether to regulate at central or decentralised level(s). Interest groups prefer rules being formulated at the level at which their strength is greatest relative to that of other groups with divergent interest in the same area (Noam 1982). Hence, the question arises which interest groups may succeed in rent-seeking at the expense of the public at large.

Interest groups may be strong enough to pervert regulatory agencies. When not all interests are equally well represented, regulatory capture becomes possible. A general lesson from Public Choice is that industry groups will be more powerful lobbies than consumer groups. To be a powerful lobby, the interests represented must be homogeneous and benefits from lobbying should not flow to outsiders who do not pay for the benefits generated.

Some industry interests are represented by well-organised pressure groups that are able to cope with the free-riding problem easily through compulsory membership. For example, this argument is used to support the claim that the professions (medical doctors, attorneys) have been successful in generating rents for existing practitioners (Van den Bergh 1999, 89–130). Large firms will also be powerful lobbyists: they may gather information about the substantive and procedural issues concerned at low cost (as a by-product of their other activities); they may also have more at stake and may therefore be better able to spread the fixed costs of information acquisition (Neven, Nuttall and Seabright 1993, 175). Centralisation may weaken the power of some interest groups (e.g. middle-class retailers), but other groups may gain when competition policy is centralised (e.g. farmers). Some interest groups (e.g. insurance companies) appear to be equally powerful both at the supranational and at the national levels, although there may be some differences across Member States. The history of the block exemption for cartels on insurance markets illustrates how centralisation may even cause costs of market power in market states where competitive markets existed before.[72]

Attention must also be drawn to the bureaucrats' self-interest in power and prestige and to the behaviour of utility maximising judges. According to Public Choice analysis, the behaviour of bureaucrats may be explained by assuming that they pursue their self-interest, which includes salary, reputation and power. Contrary to managers of private firms in competitive markets, bureaucrats must not assess the marginal costs and benefits of their actions. Therefore, the budget of the bureau will be maximised regardless of the quality of bureaucrats' performance and productive inefficiency will ensue (Niskanen 1971). However, the extent of the welfare losses may be reduced by competition between different departments that have to compete for budget allocation (Ogus 1994, 69). This is the case with the different Directorate Generals within the European Commission. In addition, the bureaucrats' self-interest in power and prestige may be secured better by high status and agreeable work tasks, rather than budget maximisation (Dunleavy 1991).

The possibilities of regulatory capture have their limitations in the design of regulatory institutions. Although appropriate institutional design will not prevent regulatory capture altogether, it may nevertheless limit its scope. Neven, Nuttall and Seabright indicate three different responses to the problem of regulatory capture: accountability, independence and transparency. Mobility is one of the best guarantors of accountability: firms and individuals

---

[72] See Faure and Van den Bergh (1995). At the time of writing the European Commission is considering whether to withdraw this group exemption.

who are unhappy with substantive rules of law and/or their enforcement may simply move to another jurisdiction. When mobility is limited, other devices are necessary to guarantee that regulatory agencies are held to account through the political process to the general public. The argument for political independence rests on the fact that compared with the voting public at large, special interest groups can more easily influence politicians. Finally, transparency may reduce the informational asymmetries, aid regulatory agencies to commit themselves to a given regulatory policy and cope with unequal costs of gathering information (Neven, Nuttall and Seabright 1993, 164–165).

Centralised enforcement may be preferred if the risk of regulatory capture at lower levels of government is higher. National competition authorities may be inclined to favour national interests. Officials of a central antitrust authority are more remote from the firms they have to control and may thus act in a more independent way, making them less vulnerable to regulatory capture. However, the achievement of these advantages at the central level requires that several conditions are satisfied. Competition authorities should be responsible for the consequences of their decisions; they should be independent from the interest groups they are supposed to control and decision processes should be transparent to outside observers. Accountability implies that competition authorities must be politically responsible for their decisions. If accountability is limited, devices to guarantee independence and transparency become of crucial importance.

Profiting from Public Choice insights, the European system of enforcement may be criticised in several respects. European Commissioners are politicians. Although they are required to forswear national allegiances on joining the Commission, it would be naive to think that there is no risk of national capture. This risk has been institutionalised in the enforcement procedures. Before taking formal decisions, the European Commission is required to consult the Advisory Committee on Restrictive Practices and Dominant positions. This Committee is composed of representatives of the Member States' competition authorities. The meetings of the Committee are not open to the public. The Committee's opinion is attached to the draft decision when it is sent up to the Commissioners for approval, but it is not published or made available to the defendants. Although the Committee's opinion is not binding, it is clear that the decision procedure has many features which allow for capturing by national interests. In addition, all stages of the procedures (notification, investigation, negotiation, decision and political review) are assigned to the European Commission, subject to the qualifications on internal checks and balances and recourse to the European Courts discussed above (section 8.3.2). This unification of roles may improve the efficiency of the procedure and its clarity and predictability to the parties concerned, but it reduces transparency from the point of view of the general public.

The main weakness of the EU enforcement procedures is that political arguments will be considered even though they are supposed not to be referred to. It would be naive to think that political arguments will not be contemplated if they are not explicitly mentioned in the relevant competition law provisions. A competition authority can only be truly independent if it is not forced to take account of political arguments in the assessment of anti-competitive practices. Real independence requires that political modifications of decisions are taken by a separate agency. A division between the decision stage and the stage of political review may contribute to the independence of the competition authority. Such a functional division of powers may also contribute to transparency. The advantage of a division of functions is that political modifications can be made only after the decision by the competition authority. If this decision is previously published, the political arguments for changing the decision will have to be spelled out clearly. This transparency may reduce the informational asymmetries and aid a competition authority to commit itself to a given policy. In a number of Member States the scope for regulatory capture is limited in three ways: (i) rules improving political accountability; (ii) a division between the decision stage and the stage of political review; and (iii) rules on incompatibilities. If political distortions can be better reduced at the Member States' level, this may strengthen the case for decentralisation.

8.6 Conclusions

In this chapter, an economic framework has been used to compare US and EU rules on enforcement of competition law. Optimal enforcement of the competition rules requires that companies are deterred from engaging in welfare-reducing restrictive practices and that they keep incentives to sign agreements that are socially desirable. In other words, enforcement can be optimal only if no type I or type II errors are made. Moreover, enforcement costs must be minimised. These costs include the information costs of all relevant actors (companies that agree on restrictive practices, antitrust enforcers and third parties, in particular competitors and consumers) and the costs of the legal proceedings (lawyers' fees and expenses of antitrust authorities and judges). On top of the efficiency objectives, enforcement systems must also comply with requirements of justice. The punishment should adequately reflect the societal disapproval of the anti-competitive behaviour (retributive justice), the harm done must be compensated (corrective justice) and requirements of procedural justice (legal certainty, proportionality) must be respected. Since (some of the) efficiency goals and justice goals may conflict with each other, policy makers may not be able to escape from difficult trade-offs but should try to minimise the tensions between different policy goals.

Four dimensions of law enforcement have been discussed in this chapter: the type and severity of sanctions, the choice between public and private enforcement, the timing of the enforcement actions and the degree of (de) centralisation. A comparison of EU competition law and US antitrust law shows remarkable differences as far as the choice of sanctions and the importance of public vis-à-vis private enforcement are concerned. US antitrust law has opted in favour of criminal fines and imprisonment of individuals, whereas EU competition law relies mainly on administrative fines imposed on companies. A comparison of the EU and US systems further reveals that the dominant role of private enforcement in the latter system is due to a number of institutional differences. US antitrust law encourages private claims by allowing treble damages, contingency fees, class actions and pre-trial discovery procedures. Up until now, enforcement of competition law in Europe has largely remained a public task. Directive 2014/104 aims at facilitating private claims in different ways (*inter alia*, by allowing claims brought by indirect victims, lowering the burden of proof for private parties and introducing joint and several liability of cartel members) but has not solved the collective action problem. Consequently, it is not to be expected that private enforcement will soon gain an equally important role as it has in the US (due to the absence of class actions and illegality of contingency fees).

Three economic criteria determine the choice between public and private enforcement: the imposition of a sanction that deters anti-competitive behaviour, information advantages of the enforcer, and the difference between the private and social motive to sue. The costs of private parties to enforce the prohibition of hard-core cartels may be prohibitively high: they face significant information deficiencies about their existence and serious difficulties to prove the size of the harm as well as the causal link with the damage incurred. Even though private parties may have better information about the existence of vertical restraints and their possible anti-competitive effects, they may fear retaliation by the accused firms and decide not to initiate legal proceedings. Importantly, private claims will not generate payments that adequately compensate the harm to society. Damage awards to private parties will not cover the deadweight loss caused by cartels, the losses in terms of dynamic efficiencies and the costs of rent-seeking. The enforcement level will remain too low since the private cost-benefit calculus, which is decisive for the decision to sue, differs from the social costs and benefits of enforcing the cartel prohibition. Compared with private litigants, competition authorities enjoy far-reaching investigative powers to overcome information deficiencies and can tailor sanctions more effectively to reach the deterrence goal. In addition, leniency programmes may be designed to destabilise cartels and facilitate their detection and the punishment of antitrust violators. Both theoretical and empirical research shows that the efficiency of competition law enforcement can be improved by strengthening sanctions and improving the management of leniency programmes, while at the same time saving on investigation costs of random inspections by competition authorities.

The economic evaluation of the switch from an authorisation system to a legal exception system crucially depends on the availability and quality of information possessed by both companies and competition authorities. Regulation 1/2003 has increased the information costs for antitrust authorities, companies and third parties in the grey area of agreements, which have both anti-competitive and beneficial effects. Generally, a notification and authorisation system (*ex ante* enforcement) will be preferable if firms have limited knowledge about whether or not the action they are contemplating violates the competition rules. Under such circumstances, a legal exception regime (*ex post* enforcement) imposes information costs on firms, which may prevent the conclusion of beneficial agreements. On the contrary, if firms are well informed, *ex post* enforcement may be superior if the quality of the assessment by the competition authority is high. To improve upon efficiency, two requirements must thus be satisfied. First, there should be sufficient information on the side of companies that envisage signing agreements. Second, the quality of the assessment of the competition authority must be sufficiently high so that enforcement errors will be minimised. It may be doubted whether these requirements are satisfied in all Member States of the enlarged EU.

Economic analysis is equally helpful in assessing the efficiency of the decentralisation of enforcement brought about by Regulation 1/2003. A general lesson from economics is that decentralisation is the more efficient the more valuable local information is for appropriate decision making. Other arguments in favour of decentralisation are different preferences across jurisdictions (for example, concerning the desirability of criminal sanctions) and the importance of learning processes. By contrast, the achievement of scale economies, the need to internalise significant inter-state externalities and the prevention of a race to the bottom (forum shopping) plead in favour of centralisation. In sum, only an optimal mix of centralised and decentralised enforcement can achieve efficiency.

Regulation 1/2003 has aligned the European rules on enforcement with their US counterparts as far as the timing of the intervention is concerned. In addition, the increased role of national judges brought about by the decentralisation of the enforcement system is another feature that has reduced the differences between EU competition law and US antitrust law. Today, the important role of private enforcement and the imposition of criminal sanctions, including imprisonment of individuals, remain the principal differences between both systems of enforcement. It may be doubted whether single system components of one regime can simply be exchanged with the other regime's counterparts without adjusting the other components as well. *Ex post* enforcement reduces the number of controls by antitrust authorities and may lead to under-deterrence if the level of sanctions is not simultaneously increased.

8.7   Bibliography

American Bar Association (2012), *Antitrust Law Developments* (ABA Book Publishing, 7th ed.)

Ashurst (2004), 'Comparative Report - Study on the Conditions of Claims for Damages in Case of Infringement of EC Competition Rules' <http://ec.europa.eu/competition/antitrust/actionsdamages/comparative_report_clean_en.pdf>

Aubert C, Rey P, Kovacic W (2006), 'The Impact of Leniency and Whistle-blowing Programs on Cartels' 24 *International Journal of Industrial Organization* 1241

Avdasheva S, Katsoulacos Y, Golovanova S, Tsytsulina D (2016), 'Economic Analysis in Competition Law Enforcement in Russia: Empirical Evidence Based on Data of Judicial Reviews', in F Jenny and Y Katsoulacos (eds.), *Competition Law Enforcement in the BRICS and in Developing Countries* 263 (Springer)

Bageri V, Katsoulacos Y, Spagnolo G (2013), 'The Distortive Effects of Antitrust Fines Based on Revenue' 123 *Economic Journal* 545

Barros P (2003), 'Looking Behind the Curtain: Effects from Modernisation of European Competition Policy' 47 *European Economic Review* 613

Basso L, Ross T (2010), 'Measuring the True Harm from Price-Fixing to Both Direct and Indirect Parties' 58 *Journal of Industrial Economics* 895

Beaton-Wells C, Parker C (2013), 'Justifying Criminal Sanctions for Cartel Conduct: A Hard Case' 1 *Journal of Antitrust Enforcement* 198

Becker G (1968), 'Crime and Punishment: An Economic Approach' 76 *Journal of Political Economy* 169

Bigoni M (2012), 'Fines, Leniency, and Rewards in Antitrust' 43 *RAND Journal of Economics* 368

Bigoni M, Fridolfsson S, Le Coq C, Spagnolo G (2015), 'Trust, Leniency and Deterrence' 31 *Journal of Law, Economics, & Organization* 663

Block M, Sidak J (1980), 'The Cost of Antitrust Deterrence: Why Not Hang a Price Fixer Now and Then' 68 *Georgetown Law Journal* 1131

Bronsteen J (2005), 'Class Action Settlements: An Opt-In Proposal' 2005 *University of Illinois Law Review* 903

Bryant P, Eckard W (1991), 'Price-fixing: The Probability of Getting Caught' 73 *Review of Economics and Statistics* 531

Calvani T, Carl K (2013), 'The Competition Act 2002, Ten Years Later: Lessons from the Irish Experience of Prosecuting Cartels as Criminal Offences' 1 *Journal of Antitrust Enforcement* 296

Calvani T, Kaethe M (2013), 'The Competition Act 2002, Ten Years Later: Lessons from the Irish Experience of Prosecuting Cartels as Criminal Offences', 1 *Journal of Antitrust Enforcement* 296

Combe E, Monnier C (2011), 'Fines Against Hard-core Cartels in Europe: The Myth of Overenforcement' 56 *Antitrust Bulletin* 235

Connor J, Bolotova Y (2006), 'A Meta Analysis of Cartel Overcharges' 24 *International Journal of Industrial Organization* 1109

Cseres K, Schinkel M, Vogelaar F (eds.) (2006), *Criminalization of Competition Law Enforcement* (Edward Elgar)

Di Federico G, Manzini P (2004), 'A Law and Economics Approach to the New European Antitrust Enforcing Rules' 1 *Erasmus Law and Economics Review* 143

Dunleavy P (1991), *Bureaucracy and Public Choice: Economic Explanations in Political Science* (Harvester Wheatsheaf)

Eide E (1999), 'Economics of Criminal Behaviour', in B Bouckaert and G De Geest (eds.), *Encyclopedia of Law and Economics* 8100 (Edward Elgar)

Elzinga K, Breit W (1976), *The Antitrust Penalties. A Study of Law and Economics* (Yale University Press, 2nd ed.)

Farmer S (2013), 'Recent Developments in Regulation and Competition Policy in China: Trends in Private Civil Litigation', in M Faure and X Zhang (eds.), *The Chinese Anti-Monopoly Law* 15 (Edward Elgar)

Faure M, Van den Bergh R (1995), 'Restrictions of Competition on Insurance Markets and the Applicability of EC Antitrust Law' 48 *Kyklos* 65

Faure M, Zhang X (eds.) (2013), *The Chinese Anti-Monopoly Law* (Edward Elgar)

Feinberg R (1985), 'The Enforcement and Effects of European Competition Policy: Results of a Survey of Legal Opinion' 23 *Journal of Common Market Studies* 373

Galloway J (2016), 'Securing the Legitimacy of Individual Sanctions in UK Competition Law' 40 *World Competition*, https://papers.ssrn.com/sol3/papers.cfm?abstract_id=2884418

Giannaccari A, Landi C (2014), 'Le Sanzioni Antitrust nella Prassi Applicativa: Si Va Ne La Città Dolente' 16 *Mercato Concorrenza Regole* 201

Hahn V (2000), 'Antitrust Enforcement: Abuse Control or Notification?' 10 *European Journal of Law and Economics* 69

Harding C, Beaton-Wells C, Edwards J (2015), 'Leniency and Criminal Sanctions in Anti-Cartel Enforcement: Happily Married or Uneasy Bedfellows?', in C Beaton-Wells and C Tran (eds.), *Anti-Cartel Enforcement in a Contemporary Age: The Leniency Religion* 240 (Bloomsbury Publishing)

Jones C (2004), 'Private Antitrust Enforcement in Europe: A Policy Analysis and Reality Check' 27 *World Competition* 13

Joshua J, Camesasca P (2004), 'EC Fining Policy against Cartels after the Lysine Rulings: The Subtle Secrets of X' 2004 *European Antitrust Review* 6

Kalven H, Rosenfield M (1941), 'The Contemporary Function of the Class Suit' 8 *University of Chicago Law Review* 684

Kerber W, Budzinski O (2003), 'Towards a Differentiated Analysis of Competition of Competition Laws' 1 *Journal of Competition Law* 411

Kirst P, Van den Bergh R (2016), 'The European Directive on Damages Actions: A Missed Opportunity to Reconcile Compensation of Victims and Leniency Incentives' 12 *Journal of Competition Law and Economics* 1

Komninos A (2002), 'New Prospects for Private Enforcement of EC Competition Law: *Courage v. Crehan* and the Community Right to Damages' 39 *Common Market Law Review* 447

Lande R, Connor J (2007), 'Cartel Overcharges and Optimal Cartel Fines' <https://ssrn.com/abstract=1029755>

Lande R, Davis J (2008), 'Benefits from Private Antitrust Enforcement: An Analysis of Forty Cases' 42 *University of San Francisco Law Review* 879

Landes W (1983), 'Optimal Sanctions for Antitrust Violations' 50 *University of Chicago Law Review* 652

Landes W, Posner R (1979), 'Should Indirect Purchasers Have Standing to Sue Under Antitrust Laws? An Economic Analysis of the Rule of *Illinois Brick*' 46 *University of Chicago Law Review* 602

Loss F, Malavolti-Grimal E, Vergé T, Bergès-Sennou F (2008), 'European Competition Policy Modernization: From Notifications to Legal Exception' 52 *European Economic Review* 77

Magalhães C, Nogueira Dias G, Del Debbio C, Niclos Negrão F (2015), 'Private Antitrust Damages', in C Zarzur, K Katona and M Villela (eds.), *Overview of Competition Law in Brazil* 395 (Editora Singular)

Magney J, Anderson R (2004), 'Recent Developments in Criminal Enforcement of US Antitrust Laws' 27 *World Competition* 101

Marquis M (2013), Abuse of Administrative Power to Restrict Competition in China: Four Reflections, Two Ideas and a Thought', in M Faure and X Zhang (eds.), *The Chinese Anti-Monopoly Law* 73 (Edward Elgar)

Marvão C, Spagnolo G (2016), 'Should Price Fixers Finally Go to Prison? Criminalization, Leniency Inflation and Whistleblower Rewards in the EU' <http://www.cresse.info/uploadfiles/2016_pa5_pa2.pdf>

Massey P (2004), 'Criminal Sanctions for Competition Law: A Review of Irish Experience' 1 *Competition Law Review* 23

McAfee R, Mialon H, Mialon S (2008), 'Private v. Public Antitrust Enforcement: A Strategic Analysis' 92 *Journal of Public Economics* 1863

Möschel W (2000), 'Change of Policy in European Competition Law' 27 *Common Market Law Review* 495

Motta M, Polo M (2001), 'Leniency Programs and Cartel Prosecution' 21 *International Journal of Industrial Organization* 347

Neven D (2002), 'Removing the Notification of Agreements: Some Consequences for Ex Post Monitoring', in A von Bogdandy (ed.), *European Integration and International Co-operation. Studies in International Economic Law in Honour of Claus-Dieter Ehlermann* 351 (Kluwer Law International)

Neven D, Nuttall R, Seabright P (1993), *Merger in Daylight. The Economics and Politics of European Merger Control* (Centre for Economic Policy Research)

Niskanen W (1971), *Bureaucracy and Representative Government* (Transaction Publishers)

Noam E (1982), 'The Choice of Governmental Level in Regulation' 35 *Kyklos* 278

Oded S (2013), 'Leniency and Compliance: Towards an Effective Leniency Policy in the Chinese Anti-Monopoly Law', in M Faure and X Zhang (eds.), *The Chinese Anti-Monopoly Law* 142 (Edward Elgar)

Ogus A (1994), *Regulation Legal Form and Economic Theory* (Clarendon Press)

Parisi F, Depoorter B (2005), 'The Modernisation of European Antitrust Enforcement: The Economics of Regulatory Competition' 13 *George Mason Law Review* 309

Pirrung M (2004), 'EU Enlargement Towards Cartel Paradise? An Economic Analysis of the Reform of European Competition Law' 1 *Erasmus Law and Economics Review* 77

Polinsky A (1980), 'Private Versus Public Enforcement of Fines' 9 *Journal of Legal Studies* 110

Polinsky A, Shavell S (2000), 'The Economic Theory of Public Enforcement of Law' 38 *Journal of Economic Literature* 45

Polinsky A, Shavell S (1994), 'Should the Liability Be Based on the Harm to the Victim or the Gain to the Injurer?' 10 *Journal of Law, Economics, & Organization* 427

Posner R (2001), *Antitrust Law* (University of Chicago Press, 2nd ed.)

Renda A *et al.* (2008), 'Making Antitrust Damages Actions More Effective in the EU; Welfare Impact and Potential Scenarios' <http://ec.europa.eu/comm/competition/antitrust/actionsdamages/files_white_paper/impact_study.pdf>

Revesz R (2000), 'Federalism and Environmental Regulation: An Overview', in R Revesz, P Sands and R Stewart (eds.), *Environmental Law, the Economy, and Sustainable Development* 37 (Cambridge University Press)

Reynolds M (1992), 'EC Competition Policy on Fines' 3 *European Business Law Review* 263

Riley A (2002), 'Cartel Whistleblowing: Toward an American Model?' 9 *Maastricht Journal of European and Comparative Law* 67

Romano R (1993), *The Genius of American Corporate Law* (Aei Press)

Romano R (1985), 'Law as a Product: Some Pieces of the Incorporation Puzzle' 1 *Journal of Law, Economics and Organization* 225

Rosenfield A (1976), 'An Empirical Test of Class-Action Settlement' 5 *Journal of Legal Studies* 113

Sandhu J (2007), 'The European Commission's Leniency Policy: A Success?' 3 *European Competition Law Review* 148

Shavell S (1993), 'The Optimal Structure of Law Enforcement' 36 *Journal of Law and Economics* 255

Shavell S (1986), 'The Judgment-proof Problem' 6 *International Review of Law and Economics* 43

Snyder E, Kauper T (1991), 'Misuse of the Antitrust Laws: The Competitor Plaintiff' 90 *Michigan Law Review* 551

Souam S (2001), 'Optimal Antitrust Policy with Different Regimes of Fines' 19 *International Journal of Industrial Organization* 1

Spagnolo G (2008), 'Leniency and Whistleblowers in Antitrust', in P Buccirossi (ed.), *Handbook of Antitrust Economics* 259 (MIT Press)

Spagnolo G (2004), 'Divide et Impera: Optimal Deterrence Mechanisms against Cartels and Organized Crime' <http://www.cepr.org>

Tiebout C (1956), 'A Pure Theory of Local Expenditure' 64 *Journal of Political Economy* 416

Tomlin J, Giali D (2002), 'Federalism and the Indirect Purchaser Mess' 11 *George Mason Law Review* 157

Van Bael I (1986), 'The Antitrust Settlement Practice of the EC Commission' 23 *Common Market Law Review* 61

Van den Bergh R (2013), 'Private Enforcement of European Competition Law and the Persisting Collective Action Problem' 20 *Maastricht Journal of European and Comparative Law* 12

Van den Bergh R (1999), 'Self-Regulation of the Medical and Legal Professions: Remaining Barriers to Competition and EC Law', in B Bortolotti and G Fiorentini (eds.), *Organised Interests and Self-Regulation* 89 (Oxford University Press)

Van Oers M, Van der Meulen B (2003), 'The Netherlands Competition Authority and its Policy on Fines and Leniency' 26 *World Competition* 28

Werden G (2009), 'Sanctioning Cartel Activity: Let The Punishment Fit The Crime' 5 *European Competition Journal* 19

Von Hayek F (1978), 'Competition as a Discovery Procedure', in F Von Hayek, *New Studies in Philosophy, Politics, Economics, and the History of Ideas* 179 (University of Chicago Press)

Werden G, Hammond S, Barnett B (2012), 'Deterrence and Detection of Cartels: Using All the Tools and Sanctions' (National Institute on White Collar Crime) <www.justice.gov/atr/file/518936/ download>

Werden G, Simon M (1987), 'Why Price Fixers Should Go To Prison' 32 *Antitrust Bulletin* 917

Wils W (2016), 'Private Enforcement of EU Antitrust Law and Its Relationship with Public Enforcement: Past, Present and Future' 40 *World Competition*, http://ssrn.com/paper=2865728

Wils W (2008), 'The Use of Settlements in Public Antitrust Enforcement: Objectives and Principles', 31 *World Competition* 335

Wils W (2005), 'Is Criminalization of EU Competition Law the Answer?' 28 *World Competition* 17

Wils W (2004), 'The Combination of the Investigative and Prosecutorial Function and the Adjudicative Function in EC Antitrust Enforcement: A Legal and Economic Analysis' 27 *World Competition* 205

Wils W (2002), 'Does the Effective Enforcement of Articles 81 and 82 EC Require Not Only Fines on Undertakings but also Individual Penalties, in Particular Imprisonment?', in C Ehlermann and I Atanasiu (eds.), *European Competition Law Annual 2001: Effective Private Enforcement of EC Antitrust Law* 411 (Hart Publishing)

Wils W (1997), 'The Commission Notice on the Non-Imposition or Reduction of Fines in Cartel Cases: A Legal and Economic Analysis', 22 *European Law Review* 125

Wise M (2004), 'The System of Sanctions and Enforcement Co-operation in US Antitrust Law', in G Dannecker and O Jansen (eds.), *Competition Law Sanctioning in the European Union. The EU Law Influence on the National Law Systems of Sanctions in the European Area* 197 (Kluwer Law International)

Yeung K (2004), *Securing Compliance: A Principled Approach* (Hart Publishing)

Zarzur C, Katona K, Villela M (eds.) (2015), *Overview of Competition Law in Brazil* (Editora Singular)

9

Merger control

Roger Van den Bergh, Peter Camesasca and Andrea Giannaccari

9.1 Introduction

Previous chapters of this book dealt with contractual agreements coordinating the interaction between independent firms and unilateral behaviour of dominant firms or monopolisation. In this chapter the attention shifts to mergers, which cause structural changes to a market implying that firms integrate their operations more completely and permanently than was the case under the contractual settings discussed in Chapters 5 and 6. Due to internal pressures (recall the prisoner's dilemma), cartels tend to disintegrate after a while. By their very nature, however, concentrations[1] eliminate competition permanently between the participating firms. Since mergers are more intrusive than cartels, one might expect that the former are condemned by a simple *per se* rule. However, closer study of the motives that lead firms to concentrate suggests a more cautious approach. Concentrations – whether mergers, acquisitions of control or full-function joint ventures – may have detrimental as well as beneficial results for social welfare. On the one hand, there are possible anti-competitive effects of concentrations resulting from an augmentation of market power (transfer of consumer surplus to producers) and the related deadweight loss to society (allocative inefficiency). On the other hand, concentrations potentially generate benefits to society through a net welfare gain, which can materialise thanks to the efficiencies mergers may generate. The pro-competitive effects of mergers include rationalisation, better access to capital and more favourable buying conditions, economies of scale and scope (productive efficiencies), technological progress (dynamic efficiencies) and reduction of X-inefficiencies (managerial slack). More often than not, a particular concentration may combine anti-competitive and pro-competitive effects. Competition law attempts to distinguish between concentrations accordingly. This is not an easy exercise.

---

[1] In EU competition law, the term 'concentration' is a broad concept that covers mergers, acquisitions of control power and full-function joint ventures. See section 9.4.

Merger assessment is very different from the scrutiny of agreements and abuses. The latter imply illegal behaviour: types of conduct that are, or should be, *ex ante* known to firms, which therefore have a duty to abstain from it. Firms contemplating a merger are not called to evaluate whether their choice is legal or illegal. They must only notify their decision to merge and wait for the authorisation of the competition authority to implement it. The antitrust agency has to perform a prospective analysis, as concentrations determine future structural changes of the market. Based on information and data available prior to a merger, competition authorities need to project its impact, which will become clear only after the transaction is implemented. Both the anti-competitive consequences and the potentially outweighing efficiency savings are hard to predict for both the parties and the competition authorities. Due to its forward-looking nature, merger control is characterised by a high level of complexity, as well as discretion.

Both in the US and in the EU, merger control was added (as a third ingredient) to competition law at a later stage, after the antitrust agencies had realised that the assessments of mergers as monopolisation practices or abuses of dominant position were defective instruments to cope with the anti-competitive effects of concentrations. Today, the EU and the US have comparable systems of merger control: both the substantive test for the merger assessment and the institutional set-up are similar. In the US, the Clayton Act prohibits mergers if their effect 'may be to substantially lessen competition or tend to create a monopoly'. Initially, EU merger control focused on unilateral dominance since the criterion for assessment was phrased as the 'creation or strengthening of a dominant position'. After the revision of the EU control of concentrations (Regulation 139/2004), the test applied in EU competition law to assess whether or not a concentration warrants regulatory intervention is newly formulated in Article 2(3) of the Merger Regulation. This Article reads as follows:

> A concentration which would significantly impede effective competition in the common market or in a substantial part of it, in particular as a result of the creation or strengthening of a dominant position, shall be declared incompatible with the common market.

The SIEC (significantly impede effective competition) test is different from the old dominance test, which gave too much weight to market shares over economic effects.

Together with a similar substantive test (in spite of a seemingly semantic variation), both US antitrust law and EU competition law follow a similar two-step procedure to scrutinise mergers. In the first step (Phase I in the EU/ Initial Phase in the US), triggered by the parties' required merger notification, the antitrust authority makes a preliminary assessment of the merger's likely competitive effects. In most cases, the merger will be cleared at the end of this review. If required, the antitrust authority moves to the second step (Phase II in the EU/Second Request in the US) and performs a more detailed investigation. This step ends with a formal enforcement decision. The proposed merger may be either cleared or allowed under certain conditions. It is common practice in both the US and the EU to make the implementation of the merger conditional upon structural remedies, in particular the divestiture of specific assets (such as branded goods or retail stores) by the merged firm. Despite the similarity in the overall processes, certain features that are unique to either of both systems still cause differences between US and EU merger control. The European Commission's enforcement powers are limited to reviewing relatively large transactions, leaving smaller deals to the competition authorities of the Member States (NCAs). The delineation of national and Community control powers is based on worldwide turnover and Community turnover figures. The US merger control captures a broader size range in its regulatory net and, consequently, the number of notifications of mergers to the federal antitrust authorities is substantially higher.

As could be learned from Chapter 2 of this book, the early contributions by economists to the study of merger control were rooted in the Structure-Conduct-Performance (SCP) paradigm (see section 2.5.1). By analysing a number of industries with different degrees of concentration (measured by the CR8 and CR4 indexes), researchers found a correlation between market power and profit rates. The conclusion reached in many Harvard studies that concentration enables collusion and ultimately harms consumers came under attack by Chicago scholars, who stressed the efficiency savings of mergers. Modern industrial organisation theory accepts that concentrations may at the same time create market power and generate efficiencies, so that antitrust agencies cannot escape from difficult trade-offs in their assessment. In recent years, game theory has decisively advanced the study of imperfect competition, thus enabling the identification of the conditions under which concentration enables stable (tacit) collusion. Besides these anti-competitive coordinated effects of a merger, economic theory also stresses the risk of non-coordinated effects. A merger eliminates competitive constraints from substitute products and this may give the post-merger firm the power to unilaterally increase prices. Both coordinated effects (tacit collusion) and non-coordinated effects (unilateral price increases) economically justify the need for merger control. Besides the theoretical advances, in recent years a significant effort has been made in industrial organisation economics to provide empirical support for the assessment of market power and the likely effect of concentrations. Improved computer technology has enabled the collection of wider data sets at lower handling costs and econometric techniques have leapfrogged since the 1980s. Consequently, both theoretical economic analysis and empirical methods may be instrumental in improving the quality of merger control.

This chapter is structured as follows. Subsequent to this introduction, section 9.2 summarises the economics of merger control. It focuses on the economic insights that are relevant in assessing both the anti-competitive and pro-competitive effects of mergers. Attention is successively drawn to qualitative and quantitative evidence that may be useful in solving real-life cases. Section 9.3 discusses the current legal framework of merger control in the US. A similar analysis of EU merger control is provided in section 9.4. Sections 9.3 and 9.4 sequentially discuss the relevance of market shares and concentration indices, the analysis of the anti-competitive effects of mergers, and efficiency considerations. These sections thus attempt to answer the question of whether and, if so, to what extent, current US antitrust law and EU competition law in the field of merger control are consistent with economic principles. Besides a discussion of the substantive rules, sections 9.3 and 9.4 include a comparison of the respective enforcement systems: the administrative enforcement procedure of Regulation 139/2004 and the judicial control system in the US. With regard to EU competition law, this chapter also provides an economic analysis of the delineation of the control powers of the European Commission and those of the competition authorities in EU Member States. Throughout the chapter, by way of illustration, several case examples from both US antitrust law and EU competition law are discussed in separate boxes. The cases illuminate the anti-competitive effects that may be raised by horizontal concentrations (*Volvo/Scania*) and vertical mergers (*Nokia/Navteq*). The *GE Honeywell* case demonstrates the differences between the US approach and the EU control system. All cases illustrate the increasing economic sophistication in assessing concentrations. Other boxes discuss the specificities of merger control in developing economies, including China, India and Brazil. Section 9.5 concludes.

9.2 The economics of merger control: qualitative and quantitative analyses

This section faces the daunting task of summarising an almost unmanageable bulk of theoretical and empirical economic literature on merger control. This literature is very broad and an overview, with applications to either US merger control or the control of concentrations in the EU, easily justifies the publication of separate books (see for example Gore *et al.* 2013; Schwalbe and Zimmer 2009). In a search for headlines, the discussion below takes the following steps. First, some important distinctions are introduced. Mergers are divided into three categories: horizontal mergers, vertical mergers and conglomerate mergers. The next distinction is between anti-competitive effects and pro-competitive effects of mergers. Anti-competitive effects are further divided into two groups: non-coordinated effects and coordinated effects. Pro-competitive effects include different forms of efficiency savings: economies of scale and scope (productive efficiency), reduction of transaction costs and innovation (dynamic efficiency). In a second step, the discussion proceeds with a summary of the theoretical economic literature on horizontal mergers; both the anti-competitive effects and the pro-competitive effects are examined. Third, non-horizontal mergers are discussed along the same lines. In a fourth and last step, the empirical techniques to analyse the competition effects of mergers are introduced. Throughout the entire discussion, references are provided to the interested reader who is willing to familiarise themselves with the more technical and specialised literature.

9.2.1 Three categories of mergers and two types of anti-competitive effects

According to the competitive relationships between the parties involved, mergers can be grouped in three categories: horizontal mergers, vertical mergers and conglomerate mergers. In a horizontal transaction, one firm merges with or acquires another firm that produces or distributes identical or similar products at the same level of the supply chain in the same geographical area. In antitrust terms, the firms are active in the same relevant market and the merger eliminates competition between them. Horizontal mergers have two effects on market structure. First, they reduce the number of competing firms. Second, they increase market concentration, as the post-concentration market share is larger than either of the parties' share prior to the concentration. Horizontal mergers entail most competitive problems: they may dampen the competitive process by reducing the number of effective competitors, by softening competition, by impeding entry and by reducing the incentives to innovate. Hence, horizontal mergers are subject to the closest scrutiny by competition authorities.

In the case of non-horizontal mergers, the undertakings concerned are active on distinct relevant markets. The absence of a direct competitive constraint is the key feature that sets non-horizontal mergers apart from horizontal mergers. Two broad types of non-horizontal mergers can be distinguished: vertical mergers and conglomerate mergers. Vertical mergers involve companies operating at different levels of the supply chain. In a vertical merger, one firm acquires either a customer (forward integration) or a supplier (backward integration). Vertical mergers may be motivated by a desire to minimise transaction costs and cure principal-agent problems. They may also cause competitive concerns, though, which justify antitrust scrutiny. Conglomerate mergers occur between firms that are in a relationship, which is neither purely horizontal nor vertical. They include: (i) pure conglomerate transactions where the merging parties have no evident economic relationship (unrelated products); (ii) geographical extension mergers where the buyer makes the same product as the target firm, but does so in a different geographical market; and (iii) product extension mergers where a firm producing one product buys a firm which makes a different product that requires the application of similar manufacturing or marketing techniques (complementary or neighbouring products). Whatever form it takes, a conglomerate merger involves firms that operate in separate markets and thus has *prima facie* little direct effect on competition. However, in spite of the generated efficiencies, conglomerates may cause concerns about anti-competitive behaviour. For competition law purposes, conglomerate mergers are subject to control when the companies are active in closely related markets.

Two types of anti-competitive effects may be distinguished (Baker 1999). The first threat to competition comes from non-coordinated effects that arise when market concentration is sufficiently high for anti-competitive outcomes to result from the individual profit-maximising responses of firms to market conditions (without any of the firms involved being individually dominant). The second threat to competition comes from coordinated effects. Both effects are instances of oligopolistic behaviour. Their difference lies in the way that the firms involved take into account their competitors' behaviour. Non-coordinated effects are a consequence of individual rivalry, implying that firms decide their competitive strategy (price and quality decisions) individually and take their competitors' behaviour as given. Market power may nevertheless arise if some or all of the firms are able to raise prices profitably above competitive levels. Coordinated effects have as a necessary condition that firms act with the intention of affecting the future actions of their competitors. The wilful coordination of competitive behaviour may involve prices, output, division of territories or customer groups, and the choice of marketing strategies (advertising, set-up of distribution systems). Even though non-coordinated effects imply that firms do not expect to influence their competitors, firms in such a setting remain responsive to market conditions and take their decisions regarding prices and other competitive parameters in a way that corresponds therewith (i.e. to market conditions being the result of the decisions of other firms). Hence, another way of identifying the conceptual difference with coordinated effects is the passive nature in which firms subject to non-coordinated effects adapt to market conditions.

Horizontal mergers commonly cause both types of anti-competitive effects. The post-merger firm may be able to unilaterally increase its prices, without needing to coordinate its behaviour with the rival firms that remain active in the same relevant market. Alternatively, collusion may become easier after a merger has been implemented because the number of competitors has decreased or the symmetry between firms has increased. Non-horizontal mergers warrant antitrust scrutiny mainly because of non-coordinated effects. The most common concern is that the merger lessens the competitive pressure on the merged entity by reducing the ability and incentive to compete of rival firms. If actual or potential rivals have reduced access to supplies or markets, this foreclosure may result in consumer harm if prices increase or quality is reduced. Even though anti-competitive foreclosure is the major concern of non-horizontal mergers, coordinated effects may also arise, as a by-product of the concentration. In the next sub-sections, the anti-competitive effects of the three categories of mergers are discussed in more detail. Thereafter, it is examined whether pro-competitive effects (efficiency savings) may outweigh the merger's disadvantages.

9.2.2 Horizontal mergers

It follows from the Structure-Conduct-Performance paradigm (see section 2.5) that concentrated markets perform poorly and, hence, that structural remedies (prohibition of a concentration, divestitures) may improve market performance. This structuralist approach has come under attack for different reasons. Apart from the neglect of efficiency savings (powerfully voiced by the Chicago School, see section 2.6), the implementation of the SCP paradigm in practice has turned out to be far from easy. Even if economists agree that there is a relationship between concentration and size of firms on the one hand, and the cost-price margins in a particular market on the other hand, they disagree about the relevant numbers. The calculation of concentration indices is not a straightforward exercise and, more importantly, this approach may leave important competitive distortions untouched. Anti-competitive effects may also arise at lower concentration levels in markets with differentiated goods. By eliminating the competitive pressure from substitute products (in technical terms, internalising the negative effect of a price increase), the post-merger firm may unilaterally increase its prices.

As indicated above, the anti-competitive effects of mergers may be classified into two categories: non-coordinated and coordinated effects. The former are the consequence of the unilateral action of the merged firm that operates in a changed environment where competitive pressures of substitute products have decreased. The latter may materialise since, after the merger, the remaining firms can more easily coordinate their behaviour and tacitly agree on prices (tacit collusion). For the purposes of assessing the likelihood of anti-competitive effects that could arise out of a proposed concentration, in an expert study written for the European Commission, Ivaldi *et al.* (2003) suggest the following approach. First, one needs to establish how a given concentration may affect prices, output and other features of a market if firms respond individually to market conditions, without increasing the likelihood of tacit collusion. Anti-competitive effects may result because the merged firm will enjoy market power (single firm dominance) or may unilaterally increase its prices in a lasting and profitable way (non-coordinated effects). The second task is to assess what the impact of the concentration may be on the incentives for tacit collusion (coordinated effects). The discussion below proceeds in three steps: first, the measures of market concentration are discussed; second, attention is paid to non-coordinated effects; third, the discussion closes with an analysis of coordinated effects.

Market concentration

Market concentration is a function of the number of firms in a market and their respective market share. In the early SCP studies, market concentration was measured by the CR8 and CR4 indices. The CR8 index is obtained by summing up the market shares of the eight largest firms in an industry; the CR4 uses the same technique but limits the number of firms to four. The more recent Herfindahl–Hirschman Index (HHI) differs from the CR8 and CR4 indices in two respects: it includes all firms and takes account of the distribution of market shares. The HHI is obtained by summing up the squares of the market shares of all firms active in the industry. The HHI ranges from close to zero (atomistic market) to 10.000 (monopoly). Compared with the older CR8 and CR4, more weight is given to the shares of the larger firms in measuring concentration levels. The HHI gives a complete picture of the whole market and the dispersion of market shares, indicating whether they are evenly spread out or relatively equal. For example, a market containing five firms with respective market shares of 40%, 20%, 15%, 15% and 10% has an HHI of 2.550. The acceptance of the HHI was probably brought about by Stigler, who suggested that the HHI is an appropriate measure of concentration 'if we wish concentration to measure the likelihood of effective collusion' (Stigler 1950, 55).

The obvious drawback of the HHI index is that its use requires information about the market shares of all individual firms. However, if this information is available, the HHI is able to detect differences that would go unnoticed if market concentration were measured by the CR8 or CR4. For example, if only two firms are active in the market, the CR4 gives the same outcome irrespective of the relative strength of each firm. If these firms have market shares of 50% each, this implies a CR4 of 100. The same outcome is reached when the market shares are unevenly spread; if they are 70 and 30 respectively, the CR4 is again 100. By contrast, the HHI would be 5.000 (50^2 + 50^2) in the first scenario of equal market shares, whereas if the shares are respectively 30% and 70%, the HHI increases up to 5.800 (70^2 + 30^2). The latter figure indicates that the anti-competitive effects of the second merger are more serious than those of the first. As will be explained in the discussion of US and EU merger control below, competition authorities on both sides of the Atlantic currently make use of the HHI index to decide whether mergers should be subject to antitrust scrutiny (even though the use of the HHI is not mechanical, see below, sections 9.3. and 9.4).

Non-coordinated effects

When there is a limited number of firms remaining post-concentration, anti-competitive outcomes may arise if products are imperfect substitutes (product differentiation), even while belonging to the same antitrust market. Expert studies commissioned by the European Commission helpfully set out the theoretical underpinnings of non-coordinated effects (Ivaldi *et al.* 2003) and provide a detailed assessment of product differentiation and its impact on the review of concentrations (Epstein and Rubinfeld 2004). The basic insight is that ignoring the incentives of competitors to react to a proposed concentration in a non-coordinated setting will tend to produce a biased assessment of the likely impact of the concentration.

For the analysis of anti-competitive effects, industrial organisation theory distinguishes Bertrand price competition and Cournot quantity/output competition.[2] A substantial difference to market outcomes arises depending on whether firms react to each other's prices or quantities. When firms react to each other's prices, the presence of some reasonable close substitute is crucial for establishing competitive conditions. In other words, it is most important that there is some close competitor, not how many close competitors there are. When firms react to each other's quantities, the numbers of competitors count as well as the extent to which their products are substitutes. In other

---

[2] Depending on the nature of the industry, longer-term decisions such as investment, product choices and R&D may also play a role.

words, it matters not only that there are competitors but that there should be a sufficient degree of competition. Irrespective of whether firms compete on prices or quantities, market concentration increases the remaining firms' market power. Mergers have an impact on both the newly created entity and the remaining competitors. The impact on the remaining competitors depends on the type of competition. A concentration in either a Bertrand or a Cournot setting limits the competitive pressure on the other firms (i.e. through an increase in the newly created firm's prices, viz. reduction in their output). However, the competitors' likely reaction differs. When firms compete on price, these prices are often strategic complements. An increase in the price by the newly created entity will typically lead competing firms to also increase their own prices, although to a slightly lesser extent. Such a (from the newly created entity's perspective) positive reaction will encourage the concentration to further raise prices. Because of strategic complementarity of prices, the price effect is exacerbated. When firms compete on quantities, these quantities are often strategic substitutes. A reduction of output by the newly created entity will typically lead competing firms to expand their own output, although not fully compensating the initial output reduction. Still, this often attenuates the incentives of the newly created entity to reduce its output (for further discussion, see Hovenkamp 2017).

The non-coordinated (unilateral) effects of mergers consist of both direct (first order) effects and indirect (second order) effects. The direct impact of the concentration is that the merged firm does not have to fear that a part of its customers divert to the products of the former competitor. Prior to the concentration, each firm needed to consider the potential loss of business to its rival as a 'cost' of raising its own price. The concentration removes this cost and, hence, creates the incentive to raise price and/or reduce output. The second order effect is that non-merging firms in the same market can also benefit from the reduction of competitive pressure resulting from the merger, since the merged firm's price increase may switch some demand to rival firms. Close competitors of the merged firm may anticipate a price increase post-merger, which would give also those firms the possibility to increase their prices (or to worsen the quality of their product offerings). The combined effect of the responses of the merged company and its competitors may thus cause significant competitive distortions.

A simple example may illustrate the above insights (see Table 9.1). Assume that in a small town there are four independent grocery stores (A, B, C and D). Each store sells 100 units of a good at the price of €100. Competition constrains the market power of each store. If one of them tries to increase its prices in a significant way, many of its current customers may start shopping at one of the other stores. For example, a price increase of 5% by retail store A will divert sales to its competitors: 15 units will go to store B, 3 units to store C and 2 units to store D. This will decrease the turnover for store A from €10,000 to €8400 and will bring additional profits to its competitors: an increase in turnover of €1500 for store B, €300 for store C and €200 for store D. Anticipating this consumer switching behaviour when considering the price increase, retail store A will refrain from doing so. Its market power, i.e. its ability to charge consumers a high price, is limited by the presence of the rival stores. However, the degree of market power increases if two or more stores merge and create a chain of grocery stores. A simultaneous price increase by the merged stores may then become profitable, because the number of rival stores is reduced and the size of lost sales will be lower. After the merger of stores A and B, a price increase of 5% will lead to a turnover of €20,475 for the post-merger firm. This increases its turnover by €475 compared to the turnover of €20,000 under the pre-merger conditions. After the merger, a price increase will be profitable since only five units will be lost to the rival stores: three units are diverted to store C and two units to store D. In other words: the post-merger firm (A+B) is able to unilaterally increase its prices and thus earn higher profits. In addition, the local stores C and D that are not part of the merger may also decide to increase their prices, as they are protected under the price umbrella of the newly formed retail chain. Consumers will have to travel greater distances to find a store offering lower prices and those not willing to travel will have to pay higher prices at their usual store.

Table 9.1 Unilateral price increases

Units and prices before merger	Price increase of 5% by A before merger	Units and prices after merger A + B	Price increase of 5% after merger A + B
A: 100 × 100 = 10,000	A: 80 × 105 = 8,400	A + B: 200 × 100= 20,000	A + B: 195 × 105 = 20,475
B: 100 × 100 = 10,000	B: 115 × 100 = 11,500		
C: 100 × 100 = 10,000	C: 103 × 100 = 10,300	C: 100 × 100 = 10,000	C: 103 × 100 = 10,300
D: 100 × 100 = 10,000	D: 102 × 100 = 10,200	D: 102 × 100 = 10,000	D: 102 × 100 = 10,200

The above example explains why competition authorities carefully scrutinise mergers of large retail stores (see, for example, the investigations by the UK,

Belgian and German competition agencies).[3] Concentration in the grocery trade may create market power in local markets (even though larger than the small town in the above example, but still limited by the distance that shoppers are generally willing to travel) to the detriment of consumers.

Different factors affect the extent to which a merger creates unilateral market power. A non-exhaustive list of factors includes the degree of market concentration, the availability of substitutes and the possibility of entry. First, structural market factors may determine whether significant non-coordinated effects are likely to result from a merger. Other things equal, the larger the number of independent firms operating in the post-merger market, the less likely the anti-competitive effects will be. The larger the market share, the more market power a firm may possess. In particular, the larger the increase in market share, the more likely it is that a merger will lead to a significant increase in market power. In addition, the larger the increase in the sales of the higher-priced products, the more likely it is that the merged entity will find a price rise profitable, despite the accompanying output reduction. Second, the extent of the price increase and/or output decrease depends on the degree of substitutability between the respective products and the remaining ones. The higher the degree of substitutability between the merging firm's products, the more likely it is that a significant price increase will follow post-merger. A concentration between firms that produce close substitutes is more apt to raise prices than a concentration between firms producing imperfect substitutes. A newly created entity will raise prices to a lesser extent if other competitors produce close substitutes, Here again the type of competition (Bertrand or Cournot) matters. In Bertrand price competition settings, the elimination of competition between substitutes will be of greater significance. Third, the firm's ability to raise prices after a merger is limited by the existence of potential entrants. Firms which would find it unprofitable to enter the market at pre-merger prices might decide to become competitors if the merger brings about higher prices or lower quantities. By anticipating this effect, post-merger prices might not rise at all or, if they do, the price increase would be transitory. The extent to which potential entrants restrain the market power of firms, which consider a merger, crucially depends on the size of the sunk costs. The higher the costs that entrants cannot recover

---

[3] For the UK see: Competition Commission, *The Supply of Groceries in the UK Market Investigation* (April 2008), available at: http://webarchive.nationalarchives.gov.uk/20140402141250/www.competition-commission.org.uk/our-work/directory-of-all-inquiries/groceries-market-investigation-and-remittal/final-report-and-appendices-glossary-inquiry. A summary of the most important conclusions of this investigation is provided by Davis and Reilly (2010); For Germany, see: Monopolkommission, *Neunzehntes Hauptgutachten der Monopolkommission*, Berlin: Bundestag, Drucksache 17/10365, 368–375. For Belgium, see FOD Economie, *Prijsniveau in supermarkten*, Brussel, 2012, available at http://economie.fgov.be/nl/modules/publications/analyses_studies/etude_niveau_de_prix_dans_les_supermarches.jsp.

if they decide to exit the market, the higher the scope for price increases by the actual market participants. To the list of above factors, the existence of capacity constraints and the size of consumers' switching costs may be added. The larger the unused capacity of rivals, the less likely it is that the merged entity will enjoy market power. In addition, in industries characterised by high switching costs, consumers do not easily change their supplier, who will therefore enjoy market power.

Coordinated effects

Game theory has decisively advanced our understanding of collusive behaviour (the relevant literature is very extensive; see for an overview Kovacic *et al.* 2006; Compte, Jenny and Rey 2002). However, the theoretical results are crucially dependent on the assumptions made. It is extremely difficult to derive reliable and generally applicable criteria for predicting whether a merger will give rise to coordinated effects or make such effects more likely. Nevertheless, the following insights are helpful to assess whether coordination is sustainable (see also section 5.2). Coordinated effects (tacit collusion) can arise when firms interact repeatedly. They may then be able to maintain higher prices by tacitly agreeing that any deviation from the collusive outcome will trigger some retaliation. This implies that the coordinating firms must be able to monitor to a sufficient degree whether the terms of coordination are being adhered to. In addition, there must be a credible deterrence mechanism that can be activated if deviation from the collusive price is detected. For being sustainable, the retaliation must be sufficiently likely and costly to outweigh the short-term benefits from cheating on the collusive price. The short-term benefits, as well as the magnitude and likelihood of retaliation, depend, in turn, on the characteristics of the industry. The reactions of outsiders, such as current competitors not participating in the coordination (maverick firms) and future rivals, as well as customers, should not be able to jeopardise the results expected from the coordination.

Ivaldi *et al.* (2003) set out the theoretical underpinnings of tacit collusion. The authors helpfully outline the industry characteristics, which may be relevant in the assessment of coordinated effects that may arise from concentrations:

- Number of participants: A concentration that eliminates one of the significant competitors contributes to make collusion more sustainable.
- Entry barriers: Collusion is more of a concern in markets with high entry barriers (for a discussion of what may constitute an entry barrier, see section 4.7). This has two implications. First, a concentration that raises entry barriers (e.g. by uniting two potentially competing technologies) tends

to facilitate collusion. Second, collusion should be a concern for merger control only in those markets where there are significant entry barriers in the post-merger scenario.

- Frequency of interaction: Collusion is easier when firms interact more frequently. This factor is relevant to assess whether collusion is an important concern, since it affects the possibilities of monitoring and activating deterrence mechanisms.
- Market transparency: Collusion is easier when firms observe each other's prices and quantities. Some concentrations may have a direct impact on market transparency. For example, a vertical merger between a manufacturer and a distributor may allow the manufacturer to have better access to its rivals' marketing strategies (for further discussion, see 9.2.3).
- Demand characteristics: Collusion is easier in growing markets (taking as given the number of competitors that is ignoring the possible positive effect of demand growth on entry) than in declining markets and in stable markets than in fluctuating markets.
- Innovation: Collusion is easier to sustain in mature markets where innovation plays little role than in innovation-driven markets. In addition, a concentration that enhances the new entity's R&D potential may contribute to make collusion more difficult to sustain.
- Symmetry: It is easier to collude among equals, that is, among firms that have similar cost structures, similar production capacities, or offer similar ranges of products. Concentrations that tend to restore symmetry can facilitate collusion, whereas those who create or exacerbate pre-existing asymmetry are more likely, all things equal, to hinder collusion.
- Product homogeneity: This factor has a more ambiguous impact on the likelihood of collusion, since it affects both the incentives to undercut the rivals and their ability to retaliate. Product differentiation can contribute to introduce asymmetry between firms (e.g. when firms offer goods or services of different qualities), whereas product homogeneity can make the market more transparent.
- Multi-market contact: Collusion is easier to achieve when the same competitors are present in several markets. In addition, a concentration can increase significantly the number of markets on which the same firms are competing, in which case it may reinforce the possibility of collusion.
- Demand elasticity and buyer power reduce the profitability of collusion. In addition, large buyers have more latitude to break collusion. In bilateral oligopolies, price discrimination (secret discounts granted to large buyers) may be the only way to break-up a collusive equilibrium (Blair and Harrison 2010, 106).
- Other relevant factors include the existence of structural links or of a 'maverick' firm. Therefore, a concentration or a concentration remedy that

would create such links or remove a maverick is more likely to facilitate collusion. Finally, the particular organisation of some markets (e.g., auction design for bidding markets)[4] can be relevant to assess the plausibility of collusion.

Overall, the assessment of coordinated effects remains inherently complex. Some of the factors listed above may partially offset each other, in both theory and practice. Given the complexity of the assessment needed to find anti-competitive effects, a simple checklist approach to identify cases for antitrust intervention is not suited. This ill-founded and widespread belief among European competition lawyers was corrected when the Court of First Instance overturned the EU Commission's *Airtours* decision.[5] It is crucial to understand why (or why not) every single dimension is relevant in the concentration under review (see section 9.4).

Pro-competitive effects

Efficiency arguments pose a number of difficult questions to any competition authority wishing to engage in a coherent review of concentrations. From a Kaldor–Hicks perspective, a potential negative effect on social welfare in the form of higher consumer prices may be outweighed by efficiency gains. The start point for a proper theoretical understanding of this welfare trade-off is a seminal article by Nobel Prize winner Oliver Williamson (1968). Later theoretical literature further investigated the conditions that must be fulfilled for both the private profitability of mergers and their positive impact on social welfare. It has been shown that impressive synergies are required in order to allow efficiencies to outweigh the costs on consumers. This scepticism gets support from a behavioural perspective: both in the Behavioural Law and Economics literature and in marketing studies, the assumption that firms maximise profits through consummating a merger is abandoned. Instead, cognitive biases of company directors and different types of irrational behaviour (such as the desire for empire building) are advanced as the driving forces to merge.

Williamson's welfare trade-off

In 1968, Oliver Williamson published a seminal article, in which he contrasted the anti-competitive and beneficial effects of a merger (Williamson 1968; Williamson 1969). This trade-off is illustrated by Figure 9.1.

---

[4] For an overview of the competition problems to be tackled by an appropriate auction design, see Klemperer (2004); for an example relating to spectrum auctions, see Klemperer (2002).
[5] Case T-342/99, *Airtours v. Commission* [2002] ECR II-2585.

This graph depicts a common merger situation, namely an amalgamation that yields economies of scale, but at the same time increases market power. AC_1 represents the level of average costs of the two merging firms before the combination, while AC_2 shows the level of average costs after the merger. The price before the merger is given by P_1 and is equal to AC_1 as an index of pre-merger market power. The price after the merger is given by P_2 and is assumed to exceed P_1. If this were not the case, the merger would be strictly positive. The welfare effects of the merger are given by the different areas in the figure. The area designated A is the deadweight loss that results if price is increased from P_1 to P_2, assuming that costs remain constant. However, since average costs are actually reduced by the merger, the area designated S, which represents cost savings, must also be taken into account. In the graph, the area S is larger than the area A, so that the effect of the merger on total welfare is positive. Williamson concluded that for the net allocative effects to be negative, a merger that yields non-trivial economies must produce substantial market power and result in relatively large price increases.

Notwithstanding the theoretical justification for an efficiency defence in merger control provided by the above analysis, its application in competition law remains problematic. The ability to conduct the Williamsonian welfare trade-off depends on knowledge that is internal to the merging firms, thus making it a cumbersome tool under real-life antitrust constraints. The determination of the insiders' profits depends on knowing the internal cost savings which are 'easy to promise, yet may be difficult to deliver' (Farrell and Shapiro 1990, 109). The exact location of any of the triangles and rectangles used in the original Williamsonian diagram remains vague, making it

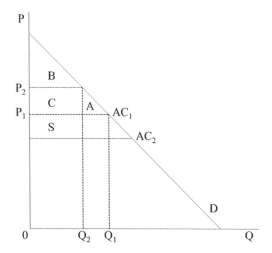

Figure 9.1 Welfare trade-off

impossible to calculate their areas mathematically. Competition enforcement agencies can rarely determine either the actual demand curve or the location of the initial cost curve, the distance this cost curve will shift or the amount the output will change. Apart from the well-known practical difficulties in the application of this approach to merger policy (for further discussion, see Camesasca 2000, 53–58), a major problem arises from the neglect of distributional consequences. Because of the merger, consumer surplus given by the area ABC is reduced to area B. Area C indicates a wealth transfer from consumers to producers. From a competition policy perspective, it may be unacceptable to clear a merger that benefits shareholders but harms consumers. If also consumers must gain, a Kaldor–Hicks improvement as contained in the Williamsonian trade-off will be insufficient to give green light to the merger. On top of these problems, the Williamsonian analysis depicts the effect of market power only as a static snapshot of the market in equilibrium, without taking into account the temporal effects of an increase in market power that may be more negative than positive (Kassamali 1996, 93; Fisher and Lande 1983, 1634–1638). If competition is to be preserved as a dynamic process, the concern in practice lies with the future development of the market and market power enduring over a long period.

Private profitability of mergers and their impact on consumer welfare

The impact of a merger on private profitability is not always clear. A concentration increases the output that the newly created entity can produce at a given average cost. Consequently, the post-merger firm faces a different maximisation problem because of the altered cost function and new strategic considerations. Salant, Switzer and Reynolds (1983) developed a theoretical model, which shows that exogenous concentrations may induce losses for the firms involved. This may happen even when the concentration creates such large efficiency gains through scale economies that it would be socially advantageous. Confirming Stigler's earlier finding (Stigler 1950), their model shows that the parties to a concentration do not capture all the profits resulting from the transaction. Therefore, concentrations that increase total industry profits need not be privately profitable.[6]

For the analysis of the impact on social welfare, Farrell and Shapiro (1990) developed a model that is broad enough to explain the adjustments of prices and quantities, in response to a concentration in an oligopolistic industry,

---

[6] In the theoretical literature, additional models have been developed that analyse the incentives to merge for both differentiated goods markets (Davidson and Deneckere 1984) and homogeneous products (Perry and Porter 1985). These models identify the principal conduct as well as structural characteristics that will give rise to merger activity.

under Cournot competition.[7] Instead of trying to distinguish some hard-to-prove effects of the concentration that are internal to the firms involved, they emphasise the external welfare effect of the concentration on consumers. If non-participant firms reduce their output, the concentration may lower welfare, even though it is profitable. This outcome will be more likely if collusion is facilitated, if oligopolists offering differentiated products compete in price, or if the combined market share of the firms involved is large, relative to the shares of the firms outside the concentration (Farrell and Shapiro 1990, 114–120, see also Jacquemin 1990, 543). On the contrary, if the outsiders expand their output considerably in response to the concentration, a significant welfare gain can be realised.[8] Few real-life industries, however, are compatible with the Farrell and Shapiro assumptions. Still, the following implications for competition law can be drawn. From an efficiency perspective, a large increase in HHI levels should be viewed with suspicion, but there is no reason to be more concerned about whether concentration levels as such are high or low (Willig 1991, 286). By focusing on the external welfare effects of a concentration, the competition authority is not making any evaluation of its profitability. Accordingly, approving a merger on the basis that it has no adverse external effects on the interests of third parties would leave private agents free to pursue their own advantage without regulatory intervention (Seabright 1994, 93).

The next step in the theoretical analysis is the quantification of efficiencies. If competition authorities require immediate consumer benefits through lower prices, mergers would require enormous cost savings. Two papers have demonstrated the latter result: the first paper discusses markets for homogeneous goods; the second focuses on differentiated goods markets. Froeb and Werden (1998) developed a test for welfare-enhancing concentrations among sellers of a homogeneous product under Cournot competition. With neither entry nor efficiencies, an amalgamation causes the merged firm to reduce output as a result of which total industry output falls (causing prices to increase) – even though remaining competitors will respond by increasing their own output. If, however, the concentration also reduces the merging firms' marginal costs, this tends to offset the anti-competitive effect of the concentration on prices. A sufficient reduction of the newly created firm's marginal costs would then result in an actual increase of total industry output

---

[7] Farrell and Shapiro's Cournot model may be extended to allow for tacit collusive behaviour, as is shown by Verboven (1995).

[8] Under Cournot competition, the presence of small firms with little market power is not desirable, as large mark-ups are associated with large market shares and large firms have lower marginal costs. This leads Farrell and Shapiro (1990, 119) to conclude that more concentration among the non-merging firms makes it more likely that the merger will be externally welfare enhancing.

and a related decrease in industry price. Froeb and Werden provide a table enumerating the sufficient reduction-condition for plausible elasticities of demand under various changes in concentration. They find that: (i) the necessary marginal cost reductions are quite sensitive to the elasticity of demand; (ii) modest marginal cost reductions (e.g. 5%) prevent price increases following concentrations of modest size; and (iii) implausibly large cost reductions (e.g. 20%) are necessary to prevent very large mergers from raising prices.[9]

With respect to differentiated goods markets, Werden (1996) developed an additional theoretical model considering an industry under Bertrand price competition. The paper shows that the compensating marginal cost reduction required to offset the anti-competitive effects induced by mergers depends on pre-merger product prices, diversion ratios[10] among products and profit margins. By estimating the compensating marginal cost reduction for different levels of pre-merger profit margins and diversion ratios, Werden reached the conclusion that 'if the products are highly differentiated and the merging firms compete intensively, large typically implausible cost reductions are necessary to restore pre-merger prices'.[11] When demand is elastic and pre-merger competition lively, synergies of 25% to 60% would be necessary to prevent prices from rising and antitrust from intervening under the consumer welfare standard. From these theoretical papers, it follows that the inclusion of the redistribution effect, including all or part of the wealth transfer, will greatly reduce, or even eliminate, the possibility of successfully conducting an efficiency defence.

Behavioural studies

The scepticism regarding the achievement of efficiencies, which might benefit consumers, gets further support from theories that abandon the rationality assumption. Bounded rationality and behavioural biases of managers may lead to merger decisions that destroy value rather than creating economic benefits to shareholders and ultimately consumers (for an overview of the vast theoretical and empirical literature, see Bhattacharya 2016). Behavioural studies suggest that not only the external environment (reactions of competitors) but also internal characteristics of the firm have an impact on merger

---

[9] By way of example, if the merging firms' market shares are 20% each, a 0.5 elasticity of demand would require a 66.67% compensating marginal cost reduction, while a higher elasticity, say 1, would require a 25% reduction in marginal cost (Froeb and Werden 1998).

[10] Diversion ratios measure the proportion of sales diverted from one product to another, as a consequence of a price increase. High diversion ratios imply fierce pre-merger competition.

[11] For example, for a 25% diversion ratio and 0.7 profit margin, the compensating marginal cost reduction would even need to be 77.78% (Werden 1996).

decisions. Managers taking these decisions may be boundedly rational: to simplify the processing of all relevant variables and data involved in an acquisition decision, they may make use of heuristics. As a result, the decision to merge is not the outcome of a rational choice but influenced by different factors, such as managers' former experiences or organisational routines (Jemison and Sitkin 1986). The behavioural theory of the firm sees the firm as a collection of sub-units with different and conflicting goals. A decision to merge thus requires coalition building, bargaining and conflict resolution (Powell, Lovallo and Fox 2011, 1375). In the aftermath of this decision process, when the conflicting goals re-emerge, the implementation of the merger may cause problems reducing the potential efficiencies of the transaction.

Besides bounded rationality, different types of managerial biases may affect merger decisions: overconfidence, hubris and empire building (on hubris, see Roll 1986). Overconfident CEOs are more likely to take merger decisions, even at the risk of destroying the value of the company. Managers who suffer from hubris believe that they are better than others in identifying target firms and extract value from mergers. Hubris arises from the power and prestige of CEOs and may lead them to pay too much for an acquisition. Finally, managers may be motivated by empire building. Their behaviour may be coined as managerial growth maximisation: they do not maximise the company's wealth but its growth as a method for satisfying personal ambitions. Empirical studies measuring the distribution of gains and losses across the acquiring and acquired firms found little evidence that mergers are carried out to achieve efficiencies but more evidence to show that merger decisions result from managerial discretion and hubris (Mueller and Sirower 2003).

9.2.3   Non-horizontal mergers

Non-horizontal mergers are generally less likely to create competition concerns. Unlike horizontal mergers, vertical or conglomerate mergers do not entail the loss of direct competition between the merging firms in the same relevant market. Due to the absence of substitutability between the products of the merging parties, the standard concern regarding the potential for horizontal mergers to generate anti-competitive effects does not apply. By contrast, if the activities and/or the products of the companies involved are complementary to each other, the integration of both companies within a single firm may produce significant efficiencies. Nevertheless, in some cases non-horizontal mergers also can cause competitive harm. The most common concern is that the merger gives rise to anti-competitive foreclosure by hampering rivals' access to supplies or markets, thus reducing price (or quality) competition and ultimately harming consumers. Below the anti-competitive effects and pro-competitive effects of vertical mergers and conglomerate mergers are further discussed.

Pro-competitive effects

In the case of vertical mergers, the integration of complementary activities or products may be pro-competitive in two different ways. At this point, the discussion of vertical restraints may be recalled (see section 6.2.2). Vertical mergers create similar efficiency savings: they eliminate double monopoly mark-ups and allow savings in transaction costs. First, a vertical merger involving complementary products may give rise to an incentive for the merged entity to reduce its prices. This pro-competitive effect results from the elimination of double marginalisation. Contrary to what the unilateral effects theory teaches regarding horizontal mergers (i.e. the profitability of a price increase), a related logic explains the profitability of a price reduction. A horizontal merger between two firms allows the internalisation (post-merger) of the negative effect from reducing price by one firm on the profits of the other firm (post-merger). Efforts to increase sales at one level may benefit sales at the other level (by lowering price or by speeding up innovation). In the case of a vertical merger, lowering the mark-up downstream may lead to increased sales not only downstream but also upstream and the other way around. Hence, a vertical merger between two firms allows the positive effect of reducing price by one firm on the profits of the other firm to be internalised (Gore *et al.* 2013, 382). Second, a vertical merger may decrease transaction costs and allow for better coordination in terms of product design, the organisation of the production process and the way in which the products are sold. In particular, self-interest-oriented behaviour inherent in short-term contracts may be overcome by full vertical integration. If a firm supplies an input to another firm enabling the latter to sell a higher quality end-product, the supplier of the input will be tempted to renegotiate input price to appropriate the entire surplus generated by the investment. If the downstream firm has significant bargaining power, the upstream firm may not make the initial investment. This hold-up problem may be eliminated by a vertical merger and initiate an investment that otherwise would not be made (Gore *et al.* 2013, 383–384).

Conglomerate mergers generate efficiencies similar to the ones discussed above. Mergers involving goods belonging to a range of products that are generally used by the same set of customers may give rise to customer benefits, such as one-stop shopping. In addition, conglomerate mergers may give rise to economies of scope that reduce costs or enable quality improvements.

Anti-competitive effects

In spite of their pro-competitive effects and potential to achieve important efficiencies and transaction cost savings, non-horizontal mergers may equally produce anti-competitive effects. As is the case with horizontal mergers, both non-coordinated effects and coordinated effects may arise. The former result when non-horizontal mergers lead to foreclosure by discouraging entry or expansion of rivals, or encourage their exit. Two forms of foreclosure can be distinguished. Vertical mergers may give rise to input foreclosure or customer foreclosure. Input foreclosure may occur when the merged entity is able to raise the costs of downstream rivals by restricting their access to an important input through price increases or a degradation of quality, or by excluding such access by a simple refusal to supply. Customer foreclosure may be the consequence of restricting the access of upstream rivals to a sufficient customer base. Input foreclosure and customer foreclosure may be welfare-reducing if a number of conditions, which are further discussed below, are satisfied. Coordinated effects may come about as a by-product of foreclosure, because of the reduction in the number of effective competitors in the market or the increase of the degree of symmetry between firms remaining active in the market. As explained above, a lower number of rivals and an increased symmetry between them make it easier to reach a common understanding on the terms of coordination and make collusion more stable (see section 9.2.2).

Three conditions must be satisfied for anti-competitive foreclosure to arise (see Gore *et al.* 2013, 393). First, the merged firm must have the ability to engage in input foreclosure. This requires significant market power in the upstream market, enabling the post-merger firm to affect the terms of supply to downstream firms. The supplied input must represent an important component of the downstream product, because it accounts for a large percentage of the total production cost or is critical to the production process of the downstream firm. If these conditions do not hold, a worsening of the terms on which the input is supplied will not materially affect competition in the downstream market. Second, the merged firm must have the incentive to increase the downstream rivals' costs; this will depend on the effect of the foreclosure strategy on the profits of the merged entity. On the one hand, input foreclosure has a negative effect on the profits of the upstream firm since it involves the sacrifice of sales to downstream rivals. On the other hand, input foreclosure positively affects downstream profits to the extent that downstream rivals increase their prices and sales are diverted to the downstream division of the merged firm (or allow it to raise prices charged to final consumers or a combination of both). The merged entity will have an incentive to foreclose only if, depending on the relative sizes of profit margins, the positive effect on downstream profits will outweigh the negative effect on upstream profits. Third, input foreclosure must give rise to higher prices in the downstream market, because the firms that are the subject of foreclosure form a significant part of the market and represent an important source of competition. By contrast, if the foreclosure affects only a small part of the downstream market or there are potential entrants (new non-integrated firms upstream or firms integrating downstream), there will be no lessening of competition. Finally, the analysis should be complemented by an assessment of efficiency savings. Vertical mergers may allow the elimination of double marginalisation. If this effect is merger specific, the efficiency savings may outweigh the anti-competitive effects. The discussion of the legal framework below will show that the Guidelines for merger assessment used by the competition agencies in the US and the EU invite a careful analysis of the above conditions (see the discussion of the *Nokia/Navteq* case in Box 9.4).

9.2.4 Quantitative techniques

Important advances in the development of quantitative methods have led to an exponential growth in the use of empirical methods in antitrust cases (Baker and Rubinfeld 1999). A main antitrust area where quantitative analysis is applied is the definition of relevant markets (see section 4.5). Each of the available techniques can be applied for the more general purpose of measuring market power and assessing the competitive effects of concentrations. New econometric tools enable the analysis of mergers to move away from structural presumptions and take a more direct approach by analysing whether the removal of price constraints would lead to an increase in consumer prices. Merger simulations attempt at answering the central question as to what would happen to prices if the merger was allowed unconditionally. In this respect, the wider availability of data is crucial. Contemplated mergers may be broken down into finely parsed product categories, such as stock-keeping units for products sold at retail (Baker 1997). If one can estimate own-price and cross-price elasticities over a period of time, highly sophisticated economic models of competition may be developed.

The implications for the control of concentrations are far-reaching (Hausman, Leonard and Zona 1992). A direct approach to assessing the competitive effects of a concentration yields additional information beyond the traditional standards. The reason is that changes in post-merger prices are captured, which may differ widely depending on particular economic conditions in a given industry. Economic models can also include expectations of reduced marginal costs, so that efficiencies in the form of cost reductions may be incorporated into the analysis of a proposed merger. This may make the structural market share-based analysis partly redundant for mergers in differentiated products markets (Hausman and Leonard 1997, 338; Baker 1997, 351; Werden 1997, 384). From an economic point of view, it is fair to say that quantitative techniques are fundamental to merger appraisal, in particular to assess unilateral effects. However, such a statement is still an open invitation for controversy in the antitrust world. Antitrust lawyers have argued that such a shift in the analytical paradigm is dangerous when the reliability of the models is hampered by limiting assumptions and/or data availability, as it can lead to 'unpredictable and unsound enforcement' (Rill 1997, 402–409). A similar aversion may be encountered in the case law.[12] Finally, warnings to make a cautious use of quantitative techniques have been voiced also by economic commentators (Bishop 2013).

Ivaldi *et al.* (2003) distinguish two segments of quantitative techniques: (i) empirical reduced-form analysis; and (ii) empirical structural-form analysis. Empirical reduced-form analysis includes statistical techniques that can be used to provide empirical evidence on issues of proof raised in antitrust cases. Numerous examples exist, such as regressions, factor analysis, correlations, Granger causality and cointegration tests. Using these techniques, the relationship that can be established between the facts of a specific case and economic models is either indirect, incomplete or informal. More useful for benchmarking purposes is the so-called empirical structural-form analysis. Here, the quantitative analysis is driven by an economic model, serving as a tool to interpret the relations that exist among the data measuring the competitive effects at hand. Two points are to be kept in mind. First, the relevance for the antitrust case under investigation is not always clear-cut. Second, the availability and quality requirements of the data are tough. In practice, the choice between a reduced-form and a structural-form analysis, or a combination of the two, is often a matter of data availability.

Structural-form analysis

The setting of a structural-form analysis is generally a static oligopoly with differentiated products, since this case underlies most modern industrial organisation analyses. Structural-form analysis starts from the presumption that market power does not result from the small number of competitors only; it also depends on the degree of substitutability among products. A first step is to define a demand model to approximate the behaviour of consumers. In a second step, it is necessary to specify supply, which comprises a cost function

---

[12] *Moore Corp. Ltd. v. Wallace Computer Services, Inc.,* 907 F. Supp. 1545 (D. Del. 1995).

and an objective function. The third step in a structural-form analysis uses statistical methods for fitting the economic model to the observed data, in order to obtain values for the demand and cost models, which, in turn, determine the equilibrium relationship between prices and market shares. There are various techniques and applications, including, among others – almost ideal demand system (AIDS) models, logit models, models testing for efficiency gains, market conduct tests using conjectural variations and dynamic models, and bidding market analyses. All require relatively detailed data sets and face a variety of theoretical and/or technical complications (for further discussion, Bishop and Walker 2010; Verbeek 2004). Frequently quoted examples where structural-form analysis was applied include *Kimberly-Clark/ Scott Paper* (see the case discussion in Chapter 4, Box 4.2) and *Volvo/Scania* (see the case discussion in Box 9.2).

Reduced-form analysis

Empirical reduced-form analysis, on the other hand, may deal with situations where data availability is low. The main techniques (for an overview, see Bishop and Walker 2010) are listed below; they may be helpful to prove non-coordinated effects.[13]

- Price correlation analysis, using (straightforward) time series of prices. When the prices of two products move together, the coefficient of correlation between the two series of prices is positive and high. This fact may be relevant for both market definition and evidence of collusion and, consequently, the popularity of price correlation tests in antitrust practice seems to be quite high. However, the interpretation of price correlations should be done with utmost care. The problem with this technique often lays in spurious correlations caused by, for example, a common component or raw material input. This and other intricacies of price correlations are further discussed in the box below.
- Hedonic price analysis can be used to exhibit or invalidate the existence of price differentials (while controlling for potential changes in product quality), based on price data and product characteristics. Here the problem lies with covering all potential sources of variability: as changes in price reflect both demand and supply-side effects, just controlling for changes in product quality might not be sufficient. Hedonic price analysis also played a role in *Volvo/Scania* (see the discussion in the separate box).

---

[13] Testing coordinated effects is much more difficult. In the absence of reliable economic models, establishing the link between structure and conduct in tacit collusion-type transactions requires more prospective and qualitative analysis.

- Closer to economic theory is residual demand analysis, a powerful tool based again on relatively limited data sets (time series on price and quantity for one firm or a small subset of firms in an oligopoly, and data on some cost shifters). The residual demand function subsequently derived from any differentiated-products model is the relationship between one firm's price and quantity, taking into account the supply responses of all other firms. The higher the elasticity of the residual demand curve (i.e. the more competitive its market surrounding), the lower is the capacity of the firm to raise its prices. The problem with residual demand analysis lays in observing the costs of other firms, which more often than not will require the use of proxies that could introduce sources of measurement error. Conversely, with data available from all firms, this technique would equal performing a structural-form analysis.

- Price-concentration studies evaluate the relationship between price and concentration in a given industry, based on the SCP paradigm (see section 2.5). If one accepts that market structure measured by the level of concentration affects market performance measured by the level of price, then – where regressions show a strong positive correlation between price and concentration – a merger which impacts significantly on concentration levels should raise anti-competitive concerns. This econometric technique is particularly useful in a cross-section analysis (for example, comparison of price levels in different geographical markets) where one market is under scrutiny. If higher concentration levels are associated with higher prices, this suggests that a merger will lead to higher prices.[14] In addition, econometric studies relating price to the degree of concentration in a certain industry can be useful to check a proposed market definition. If the relevant market is well defined, prices must be higher when market shares are elevated. If, by contrast, prices are higher in markets with a lower degree of concentration, high prices must be caused by other factors.[15] Notwithstanding the useful insights offered by price-concentration studies, a remaining difficulty is the endogeneity problem[16] when the test is performed at firm level. The level of concentration measured by the firm's market share is usually not independent of the level of price itself. Also,

---

[14] An example is the *Kleenex* merger case, discussed in Box 4.2. Another example is the investigation of the FTC into the effects of the merger between Staples and Office Depot, see section 9.3.2.

[15] For example, suppose that firms complain about high prices for advertisement space in regional newspapers. The latter will not constitute a relevant market if prices are higher in regions where these newspapers have a lower market share and meet substantial competition by national newspapers. High prices will then not be caused by exploitation of market power by regional newspapers, but rather by other factors such as the population density of the geographical area. This example also illustrates that it may be crucially important to define the relevant product market and geographical market simultaneously. Since the relevant market is precisely the area where profitable price increases are possible, in the given example, limiting the market to regional newspapers and excluding national newspapers is an ill-conceived decision.

[16] An endogeneity problem arises when a change in a variable occurs within a model or a system.

price-concentration analysis does not take account of efficiency gains and the existence of differentiated products. These complications make its application questionable.

Box 9.1: Price correlations: a popular but problematic empirical tool

To conduct a price-correlation analysis, time series data are essential. Correlation coefficients express quantitatively the scale of the relationship between the two price series. A correlation coefficient can take any value between +1 (perfect positive correlation: the prices series move perfectly together) and −1 (negative correlation: the price series move perfectly inversely to one another). High positive correlations may indicate that two products belong to the same relevant product market and pose competitive constraints upon each other. Price correlation studies are widely used as a tool for market delineation and the assessment of the collusion risk in EU merger cases. This is due to the simple intuition behind the technique and the relatively modest data requirements. A prime example is the *Nestlé/Perrier* case, in which price-correlation analysis played a central role in reaching the conclusion that different water brands were in the same relevant product market, because their prices were highly correlated with one another (between 0.85 and 1), regardless of whether the waters were still or sparkling. Correlations between the water brands and soft drinks appeared to be much weaker and sometimes negative, which seemed to justify the conclusion that soft drinks and waters constitute different product markets.[17]

How should the use of price-correlation studies in competition cases be assessed? According to the demands of modern empirics, price-correlation analysis as a sole means for defining relevant antitrust markets is not considered a robust tool. Price correlation tests suffer from a number of inherent shortcomings that may undermine their reliability. While looking at prices of goods over a period of time may have obvious advantages over investigating demand elasticities because of higher availability of information, the causality between price movements and the relevant market as presupposed may be unrelated. In fact, the risk of 'spurious' correlations must be overcome: parallel prices are neither a necessary nor sufficient condition for products being substitutes or regions being in the same geographical market. Spurious correlation results when the relationship between two price series is not driven by competitive interaction but caused by common factors that are not held constant in the analysis. For example, similarity in price movements may arise because firms have the same input costs so that price decreases or increases reflect the changing input costs, rather than competitive

---

[17] Case IV/M.190 *Nestlé/Perrier* [1992] O.J. L 356/1. For another example, see Case IV/M.1939 *Rexam/American National Can* [2001] O.J. C 325/11.

interaction between products or regions. Prices of petrol and toothbrushes might display high correlation because both are produced using oil, thus falsely suggesting that the products compete with each other (see Bishop and Walker 2002, 392). An alternative cause for a distorted price correlation analysis can be seasonality; for example similar price movements for ice creams and bathing suits, both sold independently of one another but at similar times. Likewise, low correlations need not always indicate that two products are not in the same market. To avoid spurious correlations, the price series should be adjusted to remove the common costs or take account of other common components in prices. More sophisticated econometric techniques, such as Granger causality and cointegration tests, can be used to complement the analyses and may solve the problem of spurious correlations. Granger causality is used to assess the degree of causality between the variables under investigation. A variable X is said to Granger-cause a variable Y, if taking into account past values of variable X leads to improvements in the predictions of variable Y (Granger 1969). Cointegration analysis examines whether two variables have a stable long-run relationship by comparing two price series and checking whether they are stationary (Engle and Granger 1987). The European Commission seems to be well aware of the problem of spurious correlation. In a number of merger cases the Commission dismissed the price correlation analysis presented by the parties because of the presence of common input costs into the production of the final product.[18]

Another problematic issue with price correlation studies is how high the correlation coefficient needs to be to trigger off the conclusion that different products or regions are within the same relevant market. Economic theory does not provide a clear benchmark against which the level of correlation must be assessed. There are indications in the case law that a correlation coefficient of 0.8 is sufficiently high to justify the conclusion that two regions are within the same relevant geographical market. Conversely, levels of 0.56 and 0.64 as well as correlation coefficients ranging from between −0.32 and 0.5 were considered too low for concluding that the price movements indicated a relevant product market.[19] Clearly, there is some arbitrariness in the above decisions that may be unsatisfactory from a viewpoint of procedural justice (lack of clarity and predictability, legal uncertainty). An arguably preferable alternative is starting from a potentially high correlation coefficient between two products, which are accepted as being in the same relevant market (for example Coca-Cola and Pepsi Cola). This figure may then be used as a benchmark against which lower correlation results (for example, other colas or soft drinks) are estimated. However, also in this alternative scenario some degree of subjectivity will remain in the final assessment and biased decisions cannot be totally excluded.

---

[18] For example, milk as a common input cost in the production of cheese (see Campina decision, Case COMP/M.5046, *Friesland Foods/Campina*, Commission decision of December 17, 2008).
[19] Case IV/M.190 *Nestlé/Perrier* [1992] O.J. L 356/1.

Ultimately, price-correlation analyses are an imperfect method of market definition because they focus on the boundaries of economic markets rather than relevant antitrust markets (see 4.3.3). In the case of a price increase of product A, a competing firm with a high elasticity of supply can expand production and render the price increase unprofitable. Yet, if the price of the substitute product is not raised, price correlation analysis will indicate a low correlation coefficient. Price correlation studies thus define economic markets instead of relevant antitrust markets, since supply substitution is not taken into account. For example, producers of soft drinks (cola, lemonade, fruit juices) could find it profitable to enter the market for mineral water in cases of price increases for the latter product. A price correlation analysis, which excluded soft drinks from the market definition because of correlation coefficients that were too low, will not provide an adequate foundation upon which the competitive effects of an agreement or a merger can be assessed. Given the limitations discussed above, price correlation tests should not be used in isolation but together with other evidentiary material. Also, it seems more defensible to exclude the existence of a single relevant antitrust market because of low correlation coefficients than to prove the opposite in case of high correlation coefficients (Gore *et al.* 2013).

9.3   US antitrust law

A brief historical overview is useful for a proper understanding of the current economic approach to merger control in the US. Therefore, this section starts with a description of the evolution in the US case law and the subsequent revisions of the Merger Guidelines by the US antitrust authorities. Thereafter, the current joint Horizontal Merger Guidelines (2010) of the Department of Justice (DoJ) and the Federal Trade Commission (FTC) are discussed. The section ends with a short note on enforcement.

9.3.1   Evolution of US merger control

In 1914 the Clayton Act was passed and the assessment of mergers was assigned to a newly created agency, the Federal Trade Commission (FTC Act). Section 7 of the Clayton Act[20] stipulates that:

> no person (...) shall acquire the whole or any part of the assets of another person (...) where (...) the effect of such acquisition may be to substantially lessen competition, or tend to create a monopoly.

---

[20] 15 U.S.C. 18 (1973 & Supp. 1995).

The wording of the Clayton Act makes it clear that the threshold for anti-trust scrutiny is not the creation of a dominant position (as it was originally the case in EU competition law, see section 9.4), but that mergers may be prohibited as soon as they 'substantially lessen competition'. In 1957 the Supreme Court explicitly confirmed the broad coverage of merger control by stressing its forward-looking nature. In *du Pont*, the Court decided that 'Section 7 is designed to arrest in its incipiency (...) the substantial lessening of competition'.[21] The case law of the 1960s gave a (very) broad interpretation of the requirement that mergers must substantially lessen competition, which was inspired by the structuralist approach that was popular in those days. In *Philadelphia National Bank*, the US Supreme Court found that a high degree of concentration established a rebuttable presumption of illegality. The Court stated that:

> a merger which produces a firm controlling an undue percentage share of the relevant market and results in a significant increase in concentration of firms in that market is inherently likely to lessen competition

and that

> it must be enjoined in the absence of evidence clearly showing that the merger is not likely to have such anti-competitive effects.[22]

Interestingly, the Court referred to publications by Harvard scholars to support the link between concentration and competitive effects. In its (in)famous judgment in the *Brown Shoe* case, the Court referred to market share data as 'one of the most important factors to determine the probable impact on effective competition in the relevant market'.[23] As explained in Chapter 4 (see section 4.3.2), a structuralist approach based on market shares calculated on ill-defined markets may lead to excessive interventionism that cannot be economically justified. In the 1960s the US Supreme Court formally condemned mergers between horizontal competitors with only minimal market shares of the combined firm: 30% in *Philadelphia National Bank*,[24] 5% in *Brown Shoe* and 7.5% in *Von's Grocery*. In the latter case, the Supreme Court pushed the structuralist approach to its extreme by creating an 'efficiency offence'. The Court ruled that incipient market power should be blocked, even

---

[21] *United States v. E.I. du Pont de Nemours & Co.*, 353 US 586 (1957), at 589.

[22] *United States v. Philadelphia National Bank*, 374 US 321 (1963), at 363.

[23] *Brown Shoe Co., Inc. v. United States*, 370 US 294 (1962), at 343.

[24] *United States v. Philadelphia National Bank*, 374 US 321 (1963), at 364–365: the Court was 'clear the 30% presents [a threat of undue concentration]', and that an increase in the market share from 44% to 59% 'plainly (...) must be regarded as significant'.

if the transaction was efficient.[25] In a later case, concerning the aluminium industry, the Court stated that:

> it would seem that the situation in the aluminium industry may be oligopolistic. As that condition develops, the greater is the likelihood that parallel policies of mutual advantage, not competition, will emerge.[26]

The Supreme Court retreated from its (extreme) structuralist approach in 1974, when it held in its *General Dynamics* judgment[27] that non-market share issues had to be examined as well. To determine whether there is a reasonable probability of a substantial lessening of competition, the US courts have subsequently focused on whether such mergers will cause the merged entity to have enough market power so that it could profitably increase prices.[28]

The strict merger policy of the 1960s was institutionalised by the initial 1968 Merger Guidelines issued by the DoJ. These Guidelines applied the CR4 index for determining the degree of market concentration (for a discussion of the drawbacks of this approach, see section 9.2.2; Weinstock 1982). Several passages of the 1982 Guidelines reflected an extreme interventionist approach. For example, Section 5 stated that a firm with a share of 15% in a highly concentrated market (with a CR4 index over 75%) could not buy a rival with a share exceeding 1%. Following the original version of the SCP paradigm (see section 2.4), conduct was given less weight than structure. A single sentence in the Guidelines affirmed that a concentrated market, where a few firms account for a large share of the sales, tends to discourage vigorous price competition by the firms in the market and to encourage other kinds of conduct, such as use of inefficient methods of production or excessive promotional expenditures of an economically undesirable nature (Section 2). The US Merger Guidelines were revised several times (1982, 1984, 1992, 1997 and 2010); the more recent versions reflect the evolving insights of modern industrial organisation theory. Thanks to the development of game theory, conduct is now given appropriate consideration in merger assessments and an efficiency defence has equally been accepted.

The modern US enforcement programme started with the 1982 revision of the Merger Guidelines, which revolutionised the antitrust analysis. The HHI

---

[25] *United States v. Von's Grocery*, 384 US 270 (1966). As the dissenting opinion to the latter case shows, 'the Court makes no effort to appraise the competitive effects of this acquisition'. See *ibid.*, at 282 (Stewart, J, dissenting).

[26] *United States v. Aluminum Co. of America (Alcoa)*, 377 US 271 (1964), at 280.

[27] *United States v. General Dynamics Corp.*, 415 US 486 (1974). See Coate (1992, 1009–1010).

[28] *United States v. Mercy Health Services, Inc.*, 902 F. Supp. 968 (N.D. Iowa 1995), at 975; *vacated as moot*, 107 F. 3d 632 (8th Cir. 1997).

index was introduced as a better way of measuring market concentration (Section 3 A). Market power was defined in economic terms as the ability of one or more firms to maintain prices profitably above competitive levels for a significant period of time. The Guidelines expressed concern with respect to both single-firm conduct and multi-firm behaviour. While the core of the Guidelines addressed the oligopoly problem (coordinated effects or collusion), the concept of unilateral effects was introduced under the heading of dominant firm. The concern for multi-firm exercise of market power was explained as follows:

> where only a few firms account for most of the sales of a product, those firms can in some circumstances co-ordinate, explicitly or implicitly, their actions in order to approximate the performance of a monopolist.

Sections 1 and 3 A II 1982 Merger Guidelines

Concentration remained a crucial factor in the assessment of mergers, because it was found to be much easier to raise prices above a competitive level and keep them there in a highly concentrated market.

The 1992 Horizontal Merger Guidelines were issued jointly by the DoJ and the FTC. They retained the focus and definition of market power of the earlier US Guidelines, but the discussion of the potential adverse competitive effects (the means by which market power may be exercised and the circumstances in which such conduct is likely to be successful) was substantially revised. Coordinated interaction and unilateral conduct of the merged entity were placed on an equal footing. Market concentration, while still a significant component of the analysis, became less determinative than under previous Guidelines. The 1992 Guidelines provided an analytical framework for determining whether a merger is likely to have adverse competitive effects, consisting of five steps: (i) market definition, measurement and concentration; (ii) competitive effects; (iii) entry analysis; (iv) efficiencies; and (v) failure or exiting assets (Section 0.2 of the 1992 Horizontal Merger Guidelines). The Guidelines used the HHI as their primary market concentration guide, with concentration levels of 1,000 and 1,800 as the two key levels. Any merger in a market with a post-merger HHI below 1,000 was considered unlikely to be challenged. A merger in a market with a post-merger HHI above 1,800 was likely to be challenged if the parties to the merger had market shares that would cause the HHI to increase by more than 100 unless mitigating factors (such as ease of entry) existed. Mergers in the in-between markets with moderate post-merger concentration levels between 1,000 and 1,800 required further analysis before a decision whether or not to challenge could be made. While the numbers of the HHI look pretty much the same in the 1992 Guidelines as they did in the earlier versions, the role assigned to market concentration, however, was altered substantially. No longer were the US enforcement agencies likely to make a challenge based on market concentration data alone. Instead, at the highest levels of concentration adverse effects were presumed, but this could be overcome by showing that the factors set forth in the remainder of the Guidelines made it unlikely that the merger would create or enhance market power or facilitate its exercise. By adopting such presumptive approach, the 1992 Guidelines underscored the importance of other market factors in the agencies' assessments and endorsed the richer analysis of the Supreme Court's decision in *General Dynamics*.[29]

9.3.2 The 2010 Merger Guidelines

The joint 2010 Merger Guidelines of the DoJ and the FTC constitute a remarkable policy document, for many reasons. They emphasise that the effects of mergers are context-specific and reject a single methodology for assessing mergers, which should no longer strictly follow the five-steps approach of the earlier 1992 Guidelines. Most remarkably, the 2010 Guidelines no longer adhere to the structural framework of analysis, with market definition as its cornerstone. The following passage is most striking:

> The Agencies' analysis need not start with market definition. Some of the analytical tools used by the Agencies to assess competitive effects do not rely on market definition, although evaluation of competitive alternatives available to customers is always necessary at some point in the analysis.
>
> Evidence of competitive effects can inform market definition, just as market definition can be informative regarding competitive effects. For example, evidence that a reduction in the number of significant rivals offering a group of products causes prices for those products to rise significantly can itself establish that those products form a relevant market. Such evidence also may more directly predict the competitive effects of a merger, reducing the role of inferences from market definition and market shares.
>
> Section 4, 2010 Merger Guidelines

The discussion below subsequently focuses on the role of market shares and concentration levels, the assessment of anti-competitive effects and outweighing efficiencies.

---

[29] *United States v. General Dynamics Corp.*, 415 US 486 (1974); compare the rigid structuralist approach of *United States v. Philadelphia National Bank*, 374 US 321 (1963).

Market concentration: a useful indicator of the competitive effects

Since the 1992 Guidelines, the stated antitrust concern of the US agencies is market power, with market concentration being rated as a 'useful indicator' of the likely competitive effects of a merger (Section 1.51). Therefore, careful attention is paid to the initial level of concentration and the predicted change in concentration due to the merger (Section 0.1 and 1.0 of the 1992 Guidelines). This reflects the view that anti-competitive harm is an increasing function of concentration. In principle, however, concentration has not functioned as a presumption of guilt. Instead, it has served to determine which cases should be investigated, concentration being a necessary, but on its own an insufficient, condition for a merger challenge (Coate and McChesney 1992, 291–292). The most recent 2010 Horizontal Merger Guidelines provide an analytical framework for evaluating whether a merger is likely to enhance market power. While the previous version of the Guidelines established a compulsory methodology consisting of five steps (see 9.3.1), the new approach rejects the idea of a single methodology. Rather, it proposes:

> a fact-specific process through which the Agencies, guided by their extensive experience, apply a range of analytical tools to the reasonably available and reliable evidence to evaluate competitive concerns in a limited period of time.

> Section 1, 2010 Merger Guidelines

Whereas, in the past, measuring market concentration was the crucial step in the analysis of competitive effects, it has become merely a part of the merger assessment. The 2010 Guidelines make it clear that market shares and concentration are considered in conjunction with other reasonably available and reliable evidence for determining whether a merger may substantially lessen competition.

As explained above, the 1992 Merger Guidelines used different thresholds to decide whether mergers would be challenged. The three-tier approach to industry concentration was conceived to rule out regulatory challenges of certain mergers based on the HHI alone (Greenfield 1984, 232). However, the enforcement practice made it clear that the HHI was not sufficient to determine the effects of concentration on anti-competitive behaviour. Indeed, no sound economic reason exists for picking out particular levels of the HHI as danger point, even though they seem fairly consistent with the available evidence (Schmalensee 1987, 49). On the one hand, setting the trigger levels of the HHI too high entails the risk of leaving too many anti-competitive mergers unchallenged. On the other hand, the consequence of setting these levels too low would be a substantial number of cases claiming offsetting efficiency effects with a fairly good chance of success.[30] It is important to note that in the US, the application of the set levels of HHI has never been overtly mechanical. As the evidence from the case law shows, US courts have 'hardly validated the Guidelines' wording of challenge in all but extraordinary circumstances' (Coate 1992, 116). Overall, a lack of entry barriers makes it hard for the enforcement agencies to convince the courts of the dangers that collusion is immanent,[31] and even merger to near monopoly may be allowed if sufficient evidence exists to support the inference of no anti-competitive effect.[32] In fact, the HHI levels as identified in the 1992 Guidelines were well-below actual enforcement trends. In a high-profile speech, then-Deputy Assistant Attorney General Kolasky (2002) provided statistics showing that successful merger challenges were generally brought by the DoJ in cases were the post-merger HHI levels are in the 2000–3000 range (often grounded on the risk of coordinated effects). For example, in 1990–91, the average post-merger HHI was 3801, with an average HHI change of 1798. Remarkably, in 2000–01, these numbers had risen to average post-merger HHI levels at 5215, with average HHI changes of 1729.

The 2010 Guidelines constitute the final step in the relaxation of concentration indices. Three types of markets are identified depending on the size of the HHI: (i) unconcentrated markets, HHI below 1500; (ii) moderately concentrated markets, HHI between 1500 and 2500; and (iii) highly concentrated markets, HHI above 2500. On the basis of these higher levels of concentration (compared with the 1992 figures), the Guidelines formulate the following standards. Mergers involving an increase in the HHI of less than 100 points are unlikely to have adverse effects and ordinarily require no further analysis. The same holds for mergers resulting in unconcentrated markets. Mergers resulting in moderately concentrated markets that involve an increase in the HHI of more than 100 points potentially raise significant competitive concerns and often warrant scrutiny. Mergers resulting in highly concentrated markets that involve an increase in the HHI of more than 200 points will be presumed (rebuttal is admitted) to be likely to enhance market power. At any rate, the Guidelines explicitly state that the purpose of the above thresholds is not to provide a rigid screen to separate competitively benign mergers from anti-competitive ones. Rather:

---

[30] This setting becomes even more realistic if the relevant market is defined too narrowly; see Fisher 1987, 32.

[31] See, e.g., *FTC v. Promodes*, 1989-2 Trade Cas. (CCH) para. 68,688 (N.D. Ga. 1989); *Waste Management v. United States*, 743 F.2d 976 (2d Cir. 1984).

[32] *United States v. Syufy Enterprises*, 712 F.Supp. 1386, *aff'd*, 903 F.2d 659 (9th Cir. 1990).

they provide one way to identify some mergers unlikely to raise competitive concerns and some others for which it is particularly important to examine whether other competitive factors confirm, reinforce, or counteract the potentially harmful effects of increased concentration.

Section 5.3 , 2010 Merger Guidelines

The end of market definition?

Beyond the adoption of a more integrated and less mechanistic approach, the most striking innovation of the 2010 Horizontal Merger Guidelines is the reduced emphasis on market definition. The Guidelines move away from structural presumptions towards an effects-based analysis, by introducing two quantitative techniques: merger simulation models and diversion ratios. Both techniques directly focus on the effects of mergers on consumer prices, bypassing the need to define relevant markets and calculating the HHI index. In addition, the Guidelines also endorse critical loss analysis as an empirical measure (Section 4.1.3). However, as explained in Chapter 4, the latter approach is a means for improving the quality of the market definition exercise, by linking it to the SSNIP test, rather than evading it altogether (see 4.5.3).

Merger simulation models analyse unilateral effects, i.e. post-merger (non-collusive) price increases that commonly arise as the consequence of mergers in differentiated goods markets. By utilising pre-merger data the effect on post-merger prices is predicted. Section 6.1. of the 2010 Guidelines reads:

> Where sufficient data are available, the Agencies may construct economic models designed to quantify the unilateral price effects resulting from the merger (...) These merger simulation methods need not rely on market definition.

The simulation models use information on prevailing prices and marginal costs together with estimated elasticities of demand to calculate the joint profit-maximising price for the merging parties. Moreover, the models examine further reactions of competitors to price increases, since the latter boost demand for products of competing suppliers giving them incentives to equally raise their prices. Finally, and importantly, the models also integrate the effect of merger-specific efficiencies (such as marginal cost reductions) that may affect prices positively. If carried out carefully, simulation models generate reliable predictions about profits achieved by the merging firms, post-merger prices (weighing both negative and positive effects) and the ultimate impact on consumer welfare. They directly focus on the impact of mergers on consumer prices, bypassing the need for market definition and the calculation of market shares (HHI index). A good illustration of this approach can be found in the *Staples/Office Depot* merger. The FTC investigated the effects of the merger between Staples and Office Depot, two superstores selling office products. The FTC collected data on concentration and prices in different geographical areas and used different econometric studies, which tried to assess market power directly. It resulted from these studies that Staples and Office Depot could charge significantly higher prices in the monopolised markets than in markets with two or three competitors (respectively 13% and 15%). These results were an important factor in the ultimate decision to reject the merger.[33]

Next to merger simulation models, the 2010 Guidelines propose the use of diversion ratios to assess the price effect of a merger between producers of substitutable products. Even though not by name, upward pricing pressure (UPP) analysis is proposed as a more accurate test of unilateral effects than the HHI index. The UPP index is derived from the work of Carl Shapiro (DoJ, see Shapiro 1996) and Joe Farrell (FTC). The UPP index measures the upward pricing pressure imposed by a merger as a function of diversion ratios, profit margins and efficiencies. Mergers with a positive UPP coefficient would require a detailed analysis without need to define a market because the UPP proxies demonstrate the unilateral effect of the merger on the prices charged by the post-merger firm. The economic logic behind the use of diversion ratios makes UPP analysis particularly useful if producers of two close substitute products merge. Since much of the sales forgone by the product whose price increased will be captured by its substitute, these producers have a strong incentive to unilaterally raise prices after the merger. The diversion ratio quantifies the fraction of sales lost by product 1 that is captured by product 2 and thus conveys information on the degree of substitution between the products of the merging firms. For example, if the diversion ratio equals 1, all sales lost by product 1 are shifted to product 2 and the firm selling both products post-merger can profitably impose a unilateral price increase. As stated by the 2010 Guidelines, high diversion ratios (e.g. 0.7) indicate a greater likelihood of unilateral effects, whereas such effects are unlikely if the value of diverted sales is proportionately small (Section 6.1). Again the 2010 Guidelines confirm that the finding of unilateral effects based on the value of diverted sales must not rely on market definition or the calculation of market shares and concentration (*ibid*). Diversion ratios can be estimated accurately if the relevant figures on cross-price elasticity of demand and own-price elasticity of demand are known. In the absence of these data, use can be made of evidence from consumer surveys; the *Vail Ski/Ralston Resorts* case provides a

---

[33] The merger was abandoned after a federal judge sided with the FTC in May 2016. See: https://www.ftc.gov/enforcement/cases-proceedings/151-0065/staplesoffice-depot-matter.

good illustration of the use of such measure.[34] Together with information on price-cost margins, which may be derived from accounting documents, the expected unilateral price increase by the post-merger firm may be estimated.

To predict the impact of a merger (unilateral price increase) between producers of substitute goods in a differentiated products market on prices, the analyst needs information about the diversion ratio, the price-cost margin (percentage mark-up above marginal cost) and the size of achievable efficiencies. In a first step, the unilateral price increase may be calculated as a function of the diversion ratio and the pre-merger mark-up. The following formula expresses this:

$$\frac{\left(P^{*}-P\right)}{P}=\frac{mD}{\left(1-m-D\right)}$$

If the pre-merger price for product 1 is 50 and the cost per unit is 30, then the pre-merger mark-up (m) equals $(50 - 30)/50 = 0.4$. If the diversion ratio is known to be $D = 0.2$, then the anticipated post-merger price increase is $(0.4 \times 0.2)/(1 - 0.4 - 0.2) = 0.2$. This means that the merged entity will likely maximise is profits by raising price by 20%. Generally, the profit-maximising post-merger price increase will be larger, the greater the diversion ratio, which indicates the volume of sales captured by a substitutable product.

In a second step, the efficiencies that reduce the marginal cost of product 1 must be taken into account. In the presence of efficiencies, the post-merger firm may increase its profits by reducing the price, in order to generate additional sales. The profit-maximising post-merger price decrease will be larger the greater the number of sales generated. A merger with efficiencies, therefore, creates both an incentive to increase price and an incentive to decrease price. The comparative strengths of these effects depend on the underlying profit margins for each product, the diversion of demand from product 1 to product 2 and the magnitude of the efficiencies. In essence, UPP requires these three separate pieces of information. If the price increase effect exceeds the price decrease effect, the merger is said to exhibit UPP and signals a need for further analysis (Rubinfeld and Epstein 2010).

---

[34] *US v. Vail Resorts, Inc.*; see https://www.justice.gov/archive/opa/pr/1997/January97/003at.htm. In this case, consumers were asked to rank different ski resorts under different price and snow conditions, in order to assess their willingness to shift between alternative ski destinations. For a critical discussion, see Nevo (2013, 318–319).

In spite of their apparent advantages (directly assessing the impact of mergers bypassing the cumbersome market definition exercise), merger simulation models pose problems of their own. First, the empirical techniques are data-intensive and highly technical. Quantitative analysis will not help antitrust investigations when the collected data are insufficient or inappropriate to predict the price effect of the merger under scrutiny. To prevent ostensibly sound but contradictory analysis and in order to convey credible simulation results, the quantitative analysis must be performed by a researcher with expertise in structural modelling. Also, the analyst must use estimation methods that are considered sound by experts in industrial organisation. Second, as is the case with all economic models, merger simulations rely on assumptions concerning the type of competition and the structural form of consumer demand. When the model does not fit the reality of the industry under review or the facts of the case, merger simulation can do little to inform an antitrust investigation. Simulation models typically presume that firms compete in price (Bertrand competition) and that each firm prices its branded goods to maximise its profits while considering any possible actions of its competitors (leading to a Nash non-cooperative equilibrium). If the market displays a different mode of competition, the empirical results of the simulation model are not robust, because the underlying economic theory does not adequately describe the type of competition in the market under investigation. Also, assumptions about consumer demand, which are needed to estimate the relevant own-price and cross-price demand elasticities, affect the predicted post-merger price increase. Again, if these assumptions do not fit the industry under investigation, simulation models cannot credibly forecast the impact of mergers on consumer welfare (Nevo 2013).

Also the use of diversion ratios is subject to potential pitfalls. For reasons of manageability, the antitrust authorities might prefer UPP analysis to merger simulations, since the former quantitative test requires only the measurement of diversion ratios and profit margins without needing assumptions about the shape of the demand curve. However, neither the calculation of diversion ratios nor the measurement of profit margins is a straightforward exercise. The simple diversion ratio equation also rests on a number of very restrictive assumptions: elasticity of demand is held constant; the competing firms are assumed to be symmetric and supposed to sell a single product. If these assumptions must be relaxed to fit the facts of the merger under investigation, the attractiveness of UPP as the 'easier' available technique clearly diminishes. In addition, the UPP analysis ignores the dynamic aspects of competition: if there is new entry or product repositioning after the merger, any predicted price increase will be overestimated (Bishop 2013).

As a final note, it must be added that US courts may continue to be reluctant and less willing to endorse the DoJ and FTC's view that antitrust analysis must not start with market definition. A drawback of the advanced economic approach is that it imposes analytical concepts and techniques to evaluate business behaviour, which do not easily fit with requirements of administrative efficiency (Kovacic 1997). Therefore, the case law may continue to require a stepwise approach in which market definition (and measurement of market shares and concentration) precedes the analysis of competitive effects. Consequently, the US antitrust authorities may fail to prohibit mergers when they do not meet the burden of proving distinct relevant product and geographical markets.[35] This does not imply that simulation models and diversion ratios become redundant. Instead, the quantitative tests may accompany a conventional structural merger analysis in the second stage of the assessment when, after the structural analysis (HHI index), the competitive consequences of the merger must be assessed. Instead of abandoning market definition altogether, quantitative tests may thus accompany and support traditional merger assessment schemes.

Analysis of anti-competitive effects and outweighing benefits

Concerning the evidence of adverse competitive effects, Section 2 of the 2010 Horizontal Merger Guidelines gives the antitrust agencies significant flexibility in how to prove their cases. In order to address the central question of whether a merger may substantially lessen competition, any reasonably available and reliable evidence may be submitted, including (but not limited to): (i) actual effects observed in consummated mergers; (ii) direct comparisons based on experience; (iii) market shares and concentration in a relevant market; (iv) substantial head-to-head competition; and (v) the disruptive role of a merging party. Evidence will be collected from all available sources (merging parties, customers, other industry participants and observers). The business community has voiced concerns that the new Guidelines provide less valuable guidance and increase legal uncertainty. This concern is probably unwarranted. As shown above, the enforcement practice had already departed from the 1992 Guidelines, so that the new version increases transparency on how the agencies assess proposed mergers. Moreover, the supposed simplicity and predictability of outcomes based on market shares and concentration indices is more apparent than real (see the discussion in Chapter 4, sections 4.3 and 4.4). Lastly, a trade-off between simple rules (legal certainty) and accuracy (reduction of enforcement errors) is inherent in any antitrust review. In the evaluation of proposed mergers, simplicity

---

[35] *U.S. v. Oracle Corporation* 331 F. Supp. 2d 1098 (2004), at 1158–1161. The Court decided that the prevailing methodology for assessing mergers requires market definition.

may have to be sacrificed to achieve greater accuracy and improve overall efficiency.

The 2010 Merger Guidelines contain additional sections that address a number of specific issues: price discrimination, buyer power and acquisition of minority positions. Special attention is given to adverse competitive effects stemming from discrimination of targeted customers. In this respect, Section 3 shows an explicit preference for narrow relevant product markets that capture the conditions for price discrimination. If the merger enhances market power over some customers but not others, differential pricing may be profit maximising if arbitrage between the different customer groups can be substantially limited or excluded. The Guidelines address the danger that mergers may harm some customers more than others, if the merger enhances market power over the former group and makes a discriminatory price increase profitable. Therefore, it is stated: 'When discrimination is reasonably likely, the Agencies may evaluate competitive effects separately by type of customer' (Section 3). Furthermore, the Guidelines acknowledge that mergers may enhance buying power. In such a case, the same framework (as described for the selling side of the market) must be used for evaluating whether a merger is likely to enhance market power on the buying side of the market. Lastly, the Guidelines address partial (minority position) acquisitions that do not confer control over the target to the acquirer. These acquisitions may cause significant competitive concerns by giving the acquiring firm the ability to influence the competitive conduct of the target firm or by reducing the incentive of the acquiring firm to compete.

In the assessment of a merger, the US antitrust agencies may have to carefully assess factors that could outweigh the anti-competitive effects of increased market power. In this respect, the 2010 Guidelines of the DoJ and FTC discuss the role of efficiencies and provide scope for a failing firm defence. The US antitrust agencies will not challenge a merger if cognisable efficiencies are of a character and magnitude such that the merger is unlikely to be anti-competitive. Cognisable efficiencies are merger-specific efficiencies that have been verified and do not arise from anti-competitive reductions in output or service. It is up to the merging parties to substantiate efficiency claims, so that their likelihood and magnitude can be verified. Generally, reductions of the marginal cost of production are more susceptible to verification than efficiencies relating to research and development. The merging parties must also show how efficiencies enhance the merged firm's ability to compete, by offering either lower prices or better quality products. In addition, the efficiencies must be merger-specific, i.e. likely to be achieved by the proposed merger and unlikely to be accomplished in the absence of the proposed merger (2010 Merger Guidelines, Section 10).

A concentration may involve a failing firm, i.e. a firm that would, in the absence of a merger, not be able to survive. In such a case, the *ex post* concentration situation should be compared not with the *ex ante* one but with the situation occurring after the failing firm would have exited the industry. Section 11 of the 2010 Guidelines accepts a failing firm defence if three conditions are satisfied. First, in the absence of a merger, the failing firm would be unable to meet its financial obligations in the near future. Second, the failing firm would not be able to reorganise successfully under Chapter 11 of the Bankruptcy Act. Third, the failing firm was not successful in good faith efforts to elicit reasonable alternative offers that would keep its tangible and intangible assets in the relevant market and pose a less severe danger to competition than does the proposed merger. The first two conditions require that the firm invoking the defence must not only have short-run problems but be unlikely to be viable in the medium to long term. The other conditions require that the proposed merger is the only or the best way to keep the assets of the firm in productive use.

9.3.3 Enforcement

The Hart–Scott–Rodino Act (1976) has focused the antitrust enforcement on reviewing mergers before they are consummated, rather than by undoing the market structure ('unscrambling the eggs') and policing monopoly prices directly. This prophylactic approach implies that parties must notify a proposed merger and that enforcement agencies must forecast potential anti-competitive effects before they occur. The proposed merger may be either cleared or allowed under certain conditions. It is common practice to make the implementation of the merger conditional upon structural remedies, in particular the divestiture of specific assets by the merged firm.

In the US, the decision to investigate and challenge a merger lies with the federal antitrust agencies. Initial contacts between the parties and the agencies are relatively informal. Only if competitive concerns surface does the review process start and parties must submit extensive data to enable the assessment of the potential anti-competitive effects of the proposed merger. Each time the agency wishes to obtain further information, it needs to go to court and have a judge sanction its request for further action. The antitrust agencies follow a two-step procedure to scrutinise mergers. In the first step (initial phase), triggered by the parties' required merger notification, the antitrust authority makes a preliminary assessment of the merger's likely competitive effects. In most cases, the merger will be cleared at the end of this review. If required, the antitrust authority moves to the second step (second request) and performs a more detailed investigation. This step ends with a for enforcement decision.

As will be explained below, the EU enforcement system is largely administrative. At the outset, this is clearly different from the US process, which is in essence judicial. The last say is always with the courts but the final decisions of the competent agencies (DoJ, FTC) are rarely challenged. Consequently, also in the US, the law in action is mainly agency enforcement policy. In fact, the US Supreme Court has not decided a merger case since 1976. The rather odd result is that old-fashioned judgments condemning mergers that are now routinely approved by the agencies are still, from a formal standpoint, good law. The absence of judicial control does not imply that enforcement decisions can be taken easily; the US enforcement scheme provides for immediate checks and balances to the regulatory intervention. However, the review process may also become open-ended and make it difficult for the parties to predict when final relief is in sight. From the latter perspective, the strict time lines in the EU provide a greater degree of legal certainty (see section 9.4.3 for further discussion).

Box 9.2: Merger control in China
Yingyuan Ma

The Chinese Anti-Monopoly Law (AML), including the provisions on merger control, entered into force in August 2008. The enforcement agency – the Ministry of Commerce Anti-Monopoly Bureau (MOFCOM) – was established in 2003; it is responsible for the implementation of the Interim Provisions for Foreign Investors to Merge Domestic Enterprises, an administrative regulation on mergers and acquisitions. In June 2011, an Anti-Monopoly Commission office under the supervision of the State Council was established within MOFCOM (website: http://fldj.mofcom.gov.cn). This office undertakes several tasks, including receiving concentration notifications, reviewing, investigating and assessing concentrations, as well as guiding domestic enterprises overseas in antitrust litigations, and facilitating international cooperation on multilateral and bilateral competition policy.

Chinese merger control policy has adopted a mandatory pre-merger notification system. On 3 August 2008, the State Council released the Provisions on Thresholds for Prior Notification of Concentrations of Undertakings. A prior notification must be filed when: (i) the participating undertakings' combined worldwide turnover exceeds RMB 10 billion, and at least two participating undertakings' turnover within China exceeds RMB 400 million in the previous accounting year; or (ii) when the participating undertakings' combined turnover within China exceeds RMB 2 billion, and at least two participating undertakings' turnover in China exceeds RMB 400 million in the previous accounting year. The notification procedure has to comply with the Guiding Opinions of the Anti-Monopoly Bureau of the Ministry of Commerce on the Declaration Documents and Materials of the Concentration of Business Operators, which was issued by MOFCOM in January 2009. Failure to notify is sanctioned by administrative fines.

According to Articles 25 and 26 AML, the Phase I review that starts after MOFCOM has accepted the notification should be completed within 30 days. The investigation may be continued within a Phase II review lasting 90 days. This procedure can be further extended with a maximum of 60 days. Article 27 AML lists six factors that MOFCOM should take into account when assessing the anti-competitive effects of a merger: (i) the participating undertakings' market share in the relevant market; (ii) the level of concentration in the relevant market; (iii) the concentration's technological impact; (iv) the concentration's effects on consumers and other business operators; (v) the concentration's effects on national economic development; and (vi) other elements considered by the authority.

After going through the assessment procedure, MOFCOM issues orders on the merger, which include three options: prohibition, approval and approval with conditions. The merger may be allowed only under restrictive conditions that include structural remedies, behavioural remedies or combined remedies. A written decision is delivered only when the merger is prohibited or approved with conditions. The publication of an official document containing the assessment of the economic effects of approved mergers is rare. After the Guiding Opinions of the Anti-Monopoly Bureau of the Ministry of Commerce on Streamlined Declaration of Market Concentration Cases has become effective on 31 December 2014, a simplified procedure on merger assessment has been adopted. A list of unconditionally approved transactions is published every month on the MOFCOM's website. Based on Article 53 AML, objections to MOFCOM decisions are subject to administrative reconsideration or administrative lawsuits.

Since merger policy in China came into force, more than 90% of the notifications have been unconditionally approved. Most conditionally approved mergers were between foreign companies. The published merger cases cover a large number of industries, ranging from consumer goods to pharmaceutical products. Most involved foreign companies are global players, which produce and sell products both in China and in the global market. When comparing the economic analysis present in Chinese merger decisions with the enforcement in the US and the EU, the following picture emerges. MOFCOM tends to rely more on the dominance test, the use of market concentration ratios and the imposition of behavioural remedies. Empirical studies showed that the use of behavioural remedies by MOFCOM was significantly more frequent than in the EU. The extensive use of behavioural remedies has been criticised for prioritising non-economic goals. In several cases, the merging parties were either required to maintain the price and quantity level for a given product in the market, such as in *Uralkali/ Silvinit, Henkel Hong Kong/Tiande*, or they were prohibited from increasing the market power of this product by acquiring other producers or by building new plants, such as in *InBev/Anheuser-Bush, Walmart/Newheight, Novartis/Alcon* and *Mitsubishi Rayon/ Lucite*. Some conditionally approved cases by MOFCOM, were unconditionally cleared by antitrust authorities in the US and the EU, such as *InBev/Anheuser-Busch, Mitsubishi Rayon/Lucite, General Motors/Delphi, Seagate/Samsung,* and *Google/ Motorola*. The conditionally approved case *Uralkali/Silvinit, Penelope (AlphaV)/Savio,* and *Henkel Hongkong/Tiande Chemical* did not even meet the notification requirement in the US and the EU.

MOFCOM's decisions to prevent a merged firm from entering an area of business or from expanding its operation line indicate a clear tension resulting from mixing competition policy with industrial policy. In *Mitsubishi Rayon/Lucite* and *General Motors/ Delphi*, MOFCOM mentioned that the increased 'competitiveness' of the merging party would restrict the access to a product market for other competitors. In *Coca-Cola/Huiyuan*, MOFCOM claimed that Coca-Cola holds a dominant position in the carbonated soft drink market, and that it may 'leverage its dominance' from the carbonated soft drink market to the fruit juice market. In particular, the merged firm would squeeze out market space for domestic small and medium-sized fruit juice producers. In *Seagate/Samsung* and *Western Digital/Hitachi*, MOFCOM investigated in detail how the hard disk drive (HDD) market functions, such as the issue of how large computer manufacturers bid for the order in HDD procurement, as well as how market entry, capacity usage, and innovation affect the development of the HDD industry. In both cases, MOFCOM explicitly mentioned the transaction's impact on consumers because China is one of the major consuming countries of personal computers. From the wording of the MOFCOM, it seems that the welfare impact on consumers and the domestic market was assessed from a broader picture, and it was taken as one of the issues to understand the function of an industry.

In some cases, domestic market considerations have also been extended to markets relying on international trade. In *Glencore/Xstrata* and *Marubeni/Gavilon* two global mergers, MOFCOM specifically focused on the effects of the transaction on the import market. In *Glencore/Xstrata*, MOFCOM mentioned that China is the major copper importing country and constitutes 50% of the global copper demand. In 2011, imported copper comprised 68.5% of the total supply of copper in China. In both cases, MOFCOM focused on the analysis of the transaction on the import supply of major natural resources. In *Glencore/Xstrata*, as a remedy to mitigate the anti-competitive effects, MOFCOM imposed a detailed trade requirement on the long-term contract (from 2013 to 31 December 2020) between Glencore and the Chinese buyers. In *Marubeni/Gavilon*, MOFCOM put emphasis on the merger's effects on the import market of soya beans. MOFCOM's investigation showed that 99% of the soya beans operated by Marubeni are exported to China. In 2012, 80% of the supply of soya beans in China relied on import. As the bargaining power from domestic firms is low, MOFCOM imposed behavioural remedies to require Marubeni and Gavilon to keep their business in soya beans independent. MOFCOM expressed similar concerns in *Uralkali/Silvinit*, and mentioned that the merger may negatively affect the agricultural development in China.

It results from the foregoing analysis that non-economic goals, in particular industrial policy considerations, have been incorporated into Chinese merger policy. The goal of protecting domestic enterprises has been supported by the general public. Nevertheless, it would be a significant step forward in the future development of Chinese merger policy if the economic analysis focusing on consumer welfare would play a more important role. Without the support of strong economic evidence, regulating the activities of merging entities may be criticised as a form of protectionism. Moreover, the written decisions published by MOFCOM show room for improvement by taking into account economic theories and modern empirical techniques, such as merger simulation. This will require a wider participation of economic experts and professionals in merger investigations.

9.4   EU competition law

Economic analysis is the cornerstone of the substantive analysis under the EU Merger Regulation and the Merger Guidelines.[36] In 2002, the European Courts rendered a number of important judgments that highlight the role of economic analysis. The Court of First Instance (now General Court) confirmed that the substantive rules of the Merger Regulation confer on the European Commission a certain discretion, especially with respect to assessments of an economic nature. At the same time, however, the Court required the European Commission to conduct 'a particularly close examination of the circumstances which are relevant for an assessment of the [competitive] effects' supported by 'convincing evidence' of economic and empirical nature. In addition, given the necessarily prospective nature of the assessment of dominance in the merger context, the Court pointed out that if the anticipated dominant position would emerge only after a certain lapse of time, the European Commission's analysis of the merging companies' future position must be 'particularly plausible'. Failure thereof

---

[36] Regulation 139/2004 [2004] O.J. L 24/1.

will result in a 'manifest error of assessment' and consequently lead to the annulment of the European Commission's decision.[37] The second revision of the Merger Regulation (after its coming into force in 1990 and a first review in 1997) in 2004 (Regulation 139/2004) is to a large extent coloured by the grievous losses the European Commission suffered at the hands of the Court of First Instance in *Airtours*,[38] *Schneider/Legrand*,[39] and *Tetra Laval/Sidel*.[40] The annulment of these three high-profile decisions (because of unsound substantive analysis) not only prompted an institutional shake-up of the Commission's Merger Task Force,[41] but the changes also resulted in a much-welcomed focus on an economic analysis of the competitive effects caused by concentrations and the issuance in 2004 of Horizontal Merger Guidelines.[42] Three years later, in 2007, the European Commission published additional Guidelines dealing with non-horizontal concentrations.[43] Both sets of Guidelines contain a detailed description of assessment standards, consistent with the principles of economic analysis. Below, the current European regime of merger control is further analysed; examples of the application of economic principles in real-life cases are provided in separate boxes.

Regulation 139/2004 defines two categories of concentrations: a merger between (parts of) previously independent undertakings and an acquisition of control of one or more (parts of) undertakings. A merger within the meaning of Article 3(1) (a) of the Merger Regulation occurs when two or more independent companies cease to exist as separate legal entities and a new company is established. Acquisitions occur when one company or several

---

[37] See Case T-5/02 Tetra Laval v. Commission [2002] ECR II-4381, at paras 119, 155, 162, 308, 336–337; as confirmed in Case C-12/03P Commission v. Tetra Laval [2005] ECR I-987.

[38] Case T-342/99 Airtours v. Commission [2002] ECR II-2585.

[39] Case T-310/01 Schneider v. Commission [2002] ECR II-4071.

[40] Case No COMP/M.2416 – *Tetra Laval/Sidel*, O.J. 2004 L43, p 13.

[41] When Mario Monti took office as Commissioner for Competition, he advanced the development of an economic interpretation of EU competition rules as one of his main objectives. A first step towards appreciating the relevance of economic arguments in competition cases was the publication of the Commission's Notice on the definition of the relevant market, which introduced new techniques of market definition based on economic analysis (see section 4.4.2). It must be emphasised that some parts of this Notice still raise economists' eyebrows but, compared with the old legal formalistic regime, important progress was certainly made. Today, in the area of merger control, the role of economic analysis is most advanced. The European Commission's increasing focus on economic analysis has been complemented by reinforcing the economic capabilities and resources of its administration. The apogee of this evolution has been the appointment of a Chief Economist at the Directorate General for Competition. The creation of this post is a significant step towards ensuring that EU Commission decisions will be supported by rigorous economic analysis. In this respect, attention should also be drawn to the internal Best Practice Guidelines aiming at checks and balances for its decision-making practice, available on the DG Comp website at: http://ec.europa.eu/competition/mergers/legislation/disclosure_information_data_rooms_en.pdf.

[42] Horizontal Guidelines [2004] O.J. C 31/5.

[43] Guidelines on the assessment of non-horizontal mergers under the Council Regulation on the control of concentrations between undertakings, O.J. C 265 of 18/10/2008.

companies acting jointly purchase all or part of the stock or assets of another company (Article 3(1)(b)). The acquisition must result in a stable control over (the whole or parts of) a company, which is defined as the possibility of exercising decisive influence (Article 3(2) Merger Regulation). The most common means for the acquisition of control is the purchase of shares or assets, but control can also be acquired on a contractual basis (long-term contracts resulting in a structural change of the market) and by any other means (creation of a situation of economic dependence on a *de facto* basis). In EU competition law, the control of concentrations also includes full-function joint ventures, where two (parent) companies pool (some of) their assets into a new entity which will operate on the market. Pursuant to Article 3(4) of the Merger Regulation, a concentration occurs by the creation of a joint venture, which performs on a lasting basis all the functions of an autonomous economic entity. For the criterion of full-functionality to be satisfied, it is sufficient that the joint venture is autonomous in operational respect, as requiring strategic autonomy would never satisfy the condition laid down in Article 3(4) of the Merger Regulation. If a joint venture has no operational autonomy, it will be analysed as a horizontal agreement and need to undergo full scrutiny under Article 101 TFEU (see section 5.4).

The European Commission assesses the anti-competitive consequences of a concentration through a two-step process. As a first step in this assessment, the market structure is analysed. If the market structure is such that it seems to require an in-depth analysis, the Commission will move to the second step of the assessment and evaluate the anti-competitive effects of the concentration. Following insights from economic analysis, the Commission considers two potential competitive concerns caused by the structural changes arising from horizontal concentrations. First, by eliminating the competition which exists between the parties prior to the concentration, the amalgamation may weaken to a significant degree the strength of the overall competitive constraint acting on one or more of the parties. Second, post-concentration the nature of competition may have changed in such a way that firms that were previously not coordinating their behaviour are post-concentration more likely to coordinate, or that firms which were already coordinating prior to a concentration find this easier and more stable. Efficiencies flowing from concentrations may counter or even outweigh potential anti-competitive effects. Below, the structural analysis, the anti-competitive effects of concentrations and potential efficiencies are subsequently discussed. Thereafter, the enforcement procedure and the centralisation of merger control are analysed.

9.4.1 Market shares and concentration levels: useful first indicators for reviewing concentrations

Market shares and concentration levels are generally found to 'provide useful first indications'[44] – no more, no less – of the market structure and of the competitive importance of both the parties to a concentration and their competitors. Market shares and concentration levels are calculated on previously defined relevant markets (see Chapter 4). All early merger decisions, in which the proposed concentration generated high market shares, led the European Commission – as later confirmed by the Court of First Instance in *Gencor*[45] – to define what may be understood by a dominant position in the merger context:[46] 'the ability to act to an appreciable extent independently of its competitors, customers, and, ultimately, its consumers'.[47] This definition is not materially different from the definition of dominance applied under Article 102 TFEU. In *Boeing/McDonnell Douglas*,[48] the Commission refers quite explicitly to the relevant definition, as:

> [t]he market power of Boeing allowing it to behave to an appreciable extent independently of its competitors, is an illustration of dominance as defined by the Court of Justice of the European Communities in its judgment in *Michelin*.[49]

The connection between the substantive test contained in the Merger Regulation and economic analysis was made in the 1990 *Renault/Volvo* case.[50] In this decision, the European Commission indicated its belief that there exists a very close link between the ability to act independently and the ability to increase prices without losing market shares.[51] Today it is fully acknowledged that market share figures make a good starting point for the analysis under the Merger Regulation, but should be used with caution. The assessment of market shares has consequently moved from an almost mechanical measurement towards taking into account the context of a market's

---

[44] See EC Horizontal Merger Guidelines, at para. 14; and also US Horizontal Merger Guidelines, at 1.51.

[45] Case T-102/96 *Gencor v. Commission* [1999] ECR II-753, at para. 200.

[46] See, e.g., Case IV/M 004 *Renault/Volvo* [1990] O.J. C 281/2, at para. 22; Case IV/M 053 *Aérospatiale Alenia/de Havilland* [1991] O.J. L 334/42, at para. 56.

[47] This is confirmed in the Commission Notice on the definition of the relevant market for the purposes of Community competition law [1997] O.J. C 37/1, at para. 10, explicitly referring to the definition given by the CJEU in Case 85/76 *Hoffmann-La Roche v Commission (Vitamins)* [1979] ECR 461. Dominance is thus 'less' than monopoly or quasi-monopoly.

[48] Case IV/M 877 *Boeing/McDonnell Douglas* [1997] O.J. L 336/16, at para. 37.

[49] At the same time, the Court of First Instance made it clear in *Tetra Laval/Sidel* that the assessment of potential *abuse* is the exclusive domain of Article 102 TFEU and should not play a part in the merger review context.

[50] Case IV/M 004 *Renault/Volvo* [1990] O.J. C 281/2.

[51] *Ibid.*, at para. 14.

characteristics and the nature of competition in it.[52] In a mature market, a high market share is more likely to confer market power than it would in a dynamic market subject to innovation and rapid change.[53] It follows that market shares represent an important factor as evidence of a dominant position, provided they not only reflect current conditions but are also a reliable indicator of future conditions. The dynamical aspects of a market as indicated by entry and exit, fluctuations of market share and the pace of technological change and innovation have come to play a prominent part in the European Commission's approach, pointing towards the need to make some sort of prediction about future developments when assessing mergers. This is probably what the Commission implied when it stated in *Renault/Volvo* that the test of dominance is to be understood as an appreciable freedom of action unlimited by actual or potential competition.[54] The CJEU's *Kali and Salz* ruling may be quoted to confirm these earlier findings, obliging the European Commission to assess dominance using a prospective analysis of the reference market[55] and concluding that '[a] market share of approximately 60% (...) cannot in itself point conclusively to the existence of a collective dominant position on the part of those undertakings'.[56] In *Gencor*, the Court of First Instance re-confirmed that market shares play a 'highly important' role, immediately putting its findings into perspective, however, by corroborating this finding as limited to a case-by-case approach, not binding the European Commission in subsequent cases. At best 'the view may legitimately be taken that very large market shares are in and of themselves evidence of the existence of a dominant position, save in exceptional circumstances'.[57]

Regulation 139/2004 has replaced the old dominance test by the SIEC test. The modified language – now referring to 'significantly impeding effective competition' – will ultimately affect the assessment of anti-competitive effects in this regard. According to the Horizontal Merger Guidelines, 'very large market shares' (defined as 50% or more) may be in themselves evidence

---

[52] In Case IV/M 068 *Tetra Pak/Alfa-Laval* [1991] O.J. L 290/35, at para. 23, the EU Commission said that a 'market share as high as 90% is, in itself, a very strong indicator of the existence of a dominant position. However, in certain rare circumstances even such a high market share may not necessarily result in dominance. In particular, if sufficient active competitors are present on the market, the company with the large market share may be prevented from acting to an appreciable extent independently of the pressures typical of a competitive market.'

[53] See, e.g., Case IV/M 206 *Rhône-Poulenc/SNIA* [1992] O.J. C 212/23.

[54] European Commission (1992), XXI Annual Report on Competition Policy 1991, 362.

[55] Joint Cases C-68/94 and 30/95 *French Republic and Société Commerciale des Potasses et de l'Azote (SCPA) and Entreprise Minière et Chimique (EMC) v. Commission* ECR, 1998, I-1375, at para. 221.

[56] Joint Cases C-68/94 and 30/95 *French Republic and Société Commerciale des Potasses et de l'Azote (SCPA) and Entreprise Minière et Chimique (EMC) v. Commission* ECR, 1998, I-1375, at para. 226.

[57] Case T-102/96 *Gencor v. Commission* 4 C.M.L.R., 1999, 971, at para. 199–216.

of the existence of a dominant market position.[58] The Horizontal Merger Guidelines also confirm (at 17–18) that the presumption of dominance based on such 'very large market shares' may be rebutted (if, for example, smaller competitors have the ability to act as a sufficient constraint through their incentives to increase production). Moreover, lower market shares may still raise competitive concerns in view of other factors (such as, for example, the strength and number of competitors, the presence of capacity constraints or the level of substitution between the products of the parties to the concentration). Finally, where market shares remain below 25%, it is presumed that the concentration will not bring about any anti-competitive effects (see also Recital 32 of the Merger Regulation).

Market shares are not to be detached from the effect the merger has on concentration. Prior to the issuance of the Horizontal Merger Guidelines, only general inferences could be drawn from the precedent case law (for an overview, see Camesasca 2000, 95–108). The Guidelines now offer a standardised approach similar to the one applied by the US antitrust agencies. The European Commission clearly points out that 'market shares and concentration levels provide useful first indications of the market structure' and that although current market shares are the norm, past or future market shares may be useful in dynamic industries (Horizontal Merger Guidelines, at 14–16). In terms of HHI, the relevant levels are the following: (i) any merger in a market with a post-merger HHI below 1000 is considered unlikely to be challenged; (ii) any merger in a market with a post-merger HHI between 1000 and 2000 is considered unlikely to be challenged if the increase in HHI is below 250 – except in 'special circumstances'; and (iii) any merger in a market with a post-merger HHI above 2000 is considered unlikely to be challenged if the increase in HHI is below 150 – except in 'special circumstances'. These low HHI levels are not more than an initial indicator of the absence of competition concerns. The 'special circumstances' listed concern concentrations involving entrants, important innovators, cross-shareholdings, mavericks, evidence of past or ongoing coordination or facilitating practices, and one party's pre-merger market shares in excess of 50%.

9.4.2 Competitive assessment of horizontal concentrations

The Horizontal Merger Guidelines state the following:

> A concentration may significantly impede effective competition in a market by removing important competitive constraints on one or more sellers, who

---

[58] See Case T-102/96 *Gencor v Commission* [1999] ECR II-753, at para. 205.

consequently have increased market power. The most direct effect of the merger will be the loss of competition between the merging firms. (…) Non-merging firms in the same market can also benefit from the reduction of competitive pressure that results from the merger, since the merging firms' price increase may switch some demand to the rival firms, which, in turn, may find it profitable to increase their prices.

Horizontal Merger Guidelines, at 24

The Guidelines then go on to explain that non-coordinated effects can emerge in settings of single-firm dominance, as well as in oligopolistic markets. The Guidelines discuss a number of factors, which may influence whether or not non-coordinated effects are likely to result from a concentration. Relevant circumstances are whether firms have large market shares, merging firms are large competitors, customers have limited possibilities to switch suppliers, competitors are unlikely to increase supply if prices increase, the newly created entity would be able to hinder expansion of competitors, and concentration eliminates an important competitive force (Horizontal Merger Guidelines, at 24–38).

Box 9.3: Case *Volvo/Scania*: potential market power for heavy trucks

One of the first examples of an in-depth review of non-coordinated effects is offered by the European Commission's prohibition of the proposed *Volvo/Scania* concentration.[59] The Commission found that this deal would cause serious competition law concerns by creating or strengthening dominant positions in a number of national markets for heavy trucks (Finland, Ireland, Norway and Sweden), touring coaches (Finland and the UK), inter-city buses (Denmark, Finland, Norway and Sweden) and city buses (Denmark, Finland, Ireland, Norway and Sweden).[60] The case provides a classic example of a horizontal merger creating single firm dominance in a number of differentiated product markets.

In finding that the concentration would create single firm dominance, the Commission gave strong weight to the merged company's high market share in the relevant markets (ranging from 50% to 90%). Moreover, Volvo and Scania were each other's closest competitors, with a long history of significant competition between them. Furthermore, the barriers to entry were high, requiring large investment over a significant period.

---

[59] Case COMP/M. 1672 *Volvo/Scania* [2001] O.J. L 143/74.
[60] *Volvo/Scania*, at paras 213 and 331.

Critics from the industry argued that the Commission failed to take sufficient account of the globalisation of the markets, the existence of potential competitors and the fact that European companies must grow in order to face competition from huge competitors outside Europe.[61] Subsequently, the proposed *Volvo/Renault* concentration[62] was approved, which raised concerns about the Commission's impartiality. In light of these criticisms, this case illustrates well the advantages of an analysis supported by quantitative evidence over an analysis based purely on qualitative argumentation.

The core issue in this case boiled down to the definition of the relevant geographical market, which turned out to be national in scope. In its assessment the Commission relied on sophisticated econometric simulation analysis,[63] most illustrative of which is the heavy trucks market (to which the remainder of the discussion will be limited).

In the published decision, the product market description is rather short and does not refer to the SSNIP test,[64] subdividing the truck market into three categories: light-duty trucks (less than 5 tons), medium-duty trucks (5–16 tons) and heavy-duty trucks (more than 16 tons). In the heavy truck market (the only category where the parties' market shares were substantial), a further sub-segmentation is noted between rigid trucks (integrated vehicles from which no semi-trailer can be detached) and tractor trucks (vehicles from which the semi-trailer can be detached). Although full substitution between these two sub-segments is not possible, the Commission still found that switching production from the supply point of view does not involve substantial costs. 'Heavy trucks' thus constituted the relevant product market.

The analysis of the geographical market is done in more detail, resulting in the conclusions that the markets were national in scope.[65] The available evidence showed that Volvo and other suppliers of heavy trucks had applied significantly different prices and margins for comparable products in different Member States. This, as well as non-price evidence (models and technical configurations differed considerably because of local consumer preferences and national technical requirements, the importance of profits from after-sales services may have induces dealers to charge higher prices to foreign customers and there were large variations in market shares across countries), warranted the conclusion that conditions of competition in the heavy truck market differed from one Member State to another.

---

[61] S.O. Spinks, *Recent cases under the Merger Regulation*, Speech held at Brussels, October 10, 2000.
[62] Case COMP/M. 1980 *Volvo/Renault V.I.* [2001] O.J. C 301/23. It should be noted that Volvo committed to sever all remaining links with Scania, which then established a strategic alliance with the Volkswagen group.
[63] A public version is available as a CEPR working paper (Nr. 2697); see Ivaldi and Verboven (2005).
[64] See *Volvo/Scania*, at para. 13–30. On the SSNIP test, see Chapter 4, section 4.4.
[65] *Volvo/Scania*, at paras 31–75.

To get to this conclusion, the European Commission relied in part on the aforementioned simulation analysis describing the price setting in the market for heavy trucks. In short, this econometric method refines the outcome commonly obtained by using more indirect concentration indices by taking into account not only differences in average price between different markets (as in a classic price concentration study) but also differences in the quality of the product sold and differences in the pricing strategy of the different manufacturers. This type of analysis requires high-quality data from both the parties to the merger, as well as from competitors, while also necessitating some restrictive assumptions to be made.

The starting point is a so-called hedonic price analysis, which compares the price of products whose quality changes over a period or over product space, due to either technological or subjective factors, or other services and optional equipment. Clearly this is the case in differentiated product markets, such as trucks that come in many different configurations (different body types, engine sizes, axle configurations, cab sizes and different carrying capacities). Furthermore, customer requirements differ across Europe (e.g. Nordic customers are allowed a larger carrying capacity; customers located in hilly areas need larger engines). In such circumstances price analysis has to be adjusted to account properly for quality differences or quality changes, purging the appraisal that pure price differences between standardised products can be isolated.

Using regression techniques it was possible to estimate the price position of the different manufacturers in each country, while allowing for the variations in the configurations of the trucks sold. These purged prices can be used to carry out other price tests based on which the inter-substitutability of the different trucks can be estimated. The study thus found that a hypothetical price increase of 5% was profitable in almost all countries under scrutiny (except Austria, Germany, Italy and Luxembourg). A different picture emerged for a hypothetical price increase of 10%. On the one hand, such a price increase was unprofitable for nine countries. On the other hand, for markets where the price increase was profitable, it was frequently more profitable than the 5% increase. This was most notable in Sweden, Norway, Finland and Denmark. The following table illustrates this result.

Price increase	Profit change of merging firms from alternative price increases		
	5	10	25
Austria	−0.70	−5.96	−35.09
Belgium	1.05	0.49	−8.63
Denmark	1.63	2.09	−2.25
Finland	251	2.98	−4.89
France	0.18	−1.40	−13.86
Germany	−0.23	−2.79	−19.70
Greece	1.39	−0.02	−14.49
Ireland	2.12	170	−10.02
Italy	−1.14	−7.63	−41.79
Luxembourg	−0.07	−1.51	−11.86
Netherlands	0.77	−2.47	−26.70
Norway	2.74	358	−2.37
Portugal	1.16	−0.12	−13.37
Spain	0.23	−2.05	−18.65
Sweden	2.95	491	567
United Kingdom	1.28	0.49	−11.04
European Union	1.00	49	−14.32

Source: Ivaldi and Verboven (2000).

The results contained in the above table may also be interpreted in terms of the market definition based on the SSNIP test. Following the rule that the relevant market is the minimum number of firms that can profitably raise prices by 5%, heavy trucks manufactured by the merged entity by itself would constitute the relevant market in 12 out of 16 countries. Under a 10% increase, the merged entity constituted the relevant market in 7 out of 16 countries.

Although these impressive numbers are still considered 'conservative' by the authors of the study (Ivaldi and Verboven 2000, 19), the European Commission, in the end, chose not to use it and based its decision on the more traditional evidence available. The reason for this lies in data shortcomings. Due to the time constraints imposed by the Merger Regulation, the study relied on list prices for one type of truck in the various countries. These prices, however, are far from the economic reality and the true transaction prices actually paid (taking into account discounts). Moreover, transaction prices differ substantially across Europe (list prices only serve as the starting point for the bargaining ploy). Furthermore, the type of truck chosen was not sold in all countries. In sum, one might say that the result was that the study gave 'information on products which no-one bought at prices that no-one paid'.[66] However, this case shows that econometrics, if applied carefully, can play an important role in merger control proceedings.

---

[66] Bishop S (2001), 'Economic aspects of recent merger cases' (Speech held at Brussels, April 27).

In its *Gencor* decision (1996), the Court of First Instance explained the conditions under which a horizontal merger may cause coordinated effects, at that time called 'collective dominance'. The Court stated:

> A merger in a concentrated market may significantly impede effective competition through the creation or strengthening of a collective dominant position, because it increases the likelihood that firms are able to coordinate their behaviour in this way and raise prices, even without entering into an agreement or resorting to a concerted practice within the meaning of Article 81.[67]

The Horizontal Merger Guidelines elaborate that a concentration may make coordination easier, more stable and more effective for firms that were already coordinating before the concentration. Such coordination may involve: keeping prices above competitive level, limiting production or the amount of new capacity brought into the market, dividing the market, or allocating contracts in bidding markets (Horizontal Merger Guidelines, at 24–38).

Coordination is more likely to emerge in markets where it is relatively simple to reach a common understanding on the terms of coordination. In *Airtours*, the Court of First Instance added that three conditions are necessary for coordination to be sustainable. The relevant circumstances are the following: (i) each member of the dominant oligopoly must have the ability to know how the other members are behaving in order to monitor whether or not they are adopting the common policy; (ii) there must be adequate deterrents to ensure that there is a long-term incentive in not departing from the common policy; and (iii) the foreseeable reaction of outsiders, i.e. current and future competitors, as well as of consumers, must not jeopardise the results expected from the common policy.[68]

9.4.3 Non-horizontal mergers

The Guidelines on the assessment of non-horizontal mergers indicate how the European Commission will assess the possible anti-competitive effects. In the case of vertical mergers, the major concern is anti-competitive foreclosure: either input foreclosure or output foreclosure. According to the Guidelines, foreclosure results where the access of actual or potential rivals to supplies or markets 'is hampered or eliminated as a result of the merger, thereby reducing these companies' ability and/or incentive to compete' (Non-Horizontal Guidelines, at 29). The foreclosure is regarded as anti-competitive when the

---

[67] Case T-102/96 *Gencor v. Commission* [1999] ECR II-753, at para. 277.
[68] Case T-342/99 *Airtours v Commission* [2002] ECR II-2585, para. 62.

post-merger firm (and possibly some of its competitors) will be able to profitably increase prices charged to consumers.

In its individual decisions on input foreclosure, the Commission examines: (i) whether the post-merger firm would be able to foreclose access to inputs; (ii) whether it would have the incentive to do so; and (iii) whether a foreclosure strategy would have a significant detrimental effect in the downstream markets. The Non-Horizontal Merger Guidelines point to three conditions, which are necessary for the merged entity to have the ability to foreclose its downstream competitors: the existence of a significant degree of market power, the importance of the input and the absence of timely and effective counterstrategies. The incentive to engage in foreclosure depends on the trade-off between the profits lost in the upstream market due to a reduction of input sales and the profit gained on the downstream market by raising rivals' costs. The relevant factors in this assessment are the level of profits that the merged entity obtains upstream and downstream, the extent to which downstream demand is likely to be diverted away from foreclosed rivals and the share of the diverted demand that the post-merger firm can capture (Non-Horizontal Guidelines, at 42). A concrete example of an assessment of a vertical merger, which follows the above criteria, can be found in the *Nokia/Navteq* case discussed in Box 9.4.

Box 9.4: Vertical merger: case *Nokia/Navteq*

In 2008, the European Commission approved the acquisition of Navteq, one of two providers of navigable digital map databases, by Nokia, at that time the largest manufacturer of mobile telephones in the world. This was a transaction of a purely vertical nature and an example of backward vertical integration, whereby a producer of a good acquires its main provider of an important input. Mobile telephone manufacturers and software providers had expressed concerns that the post-merger firm could foreclose them from the market of navigable digital map databases by increasing prices, providing degraded map sets, delaying access to latest maps or by reserving innovative features to Nokia. After having defined the relevant antitrust market,[69] the European Commission focused on Nokia's ability and incentives to raise competitors' costs by increasing the price of navigable digital map databases. In addition, the Commission analysed the merged entity's

[69] The Commission distinguished several relevant product markets: two relevant upstream markets (the provision of non-navigable digital map databases and navigable digital map databases respectively), an intermediate relevant market for the provision of navigation software and two relevant downstream markets (provision of navigation applications for mobile handsets and mobile phones). The relevant geographical upstream markets were considered to be world-wide and the relevant geographical downstream markets were defined to be at least EEA-wide.

incentives to limit competitors' access to such databases and the possible impact on consumers. As an integral part of its in-depth investigation, the Commission carried out an empirical analysis of the post-merger firm's incentives to engage in vertical fore-closure. The Commission concluded that such a strategy was unlikely, since the merged firm's ability and incentives to close off supplies of digital map databases to its competitors was deemed unprofitable. Consequently, the merger was approved since it would not significantly impede effective competition. Below, the Commission's analysis of the merged firm's ability and incentive to foreclose is further discussed.

First, the European Commission investigated whether Nokia, after the acquisition of Navteq, would have the ability to implement a strategy of anti-competitive foreclosure against non-integrated downstream rivals (software providers, mobile handset manu-facturers). Taking account of the existence of a significant degree of market power, the importance of the input for downstream competitors and the absence of timely and effective counterstrategies, this question was answered positively (Commission's Decision, at 270–330). The Commission argued that the post-merger firm would have market power with a market share of 50% and only one competitor (Tele Atlas) able to offer a similar quality product. It also remarked on the high gross margins achieved (ability to set prices well above marginal cost) and the importance of the input for downstream competitors. Next, the Commission noted the importance of the input for downstream competitors, either because of its cost or because it is a critical component of the downstream product. The Commission found that digital maps accounted for a significant share of the costs of navigation software providers. Even though digital maps make up only a limited share of the costs of mobile handsets, these maps were considered a critical input since they constitute a component without which naviga-tion services could not be proposed on mobile handsets. Concerning the possibility of counter-strategies, the Commission did not reach a firm conclusion. Mobile network operators could counter a foreclosure strategy from Navteq and a contract between Garmin and Navteq created a third market player, which could sell navigation solutions to mobile handset manufactures. However, this counter-strategy would protect neither navigation software providers nor providers of navigation services on websites. A final answer to this question was left open, since the merged firm would have no incentive to engage in a foreclosure strategy (see the arguments below).

Second, the Commission investigated whether the merged entity would have an in-centive to engage in input foreclosure even if this comes at the cost of profits on the upstream market (see Commission's Decision, at 270–354). Post-merger, Nokia and Navteq must take into account how the sales of map databases to Nokia's competitors will affect profits on both upstream and downstream markets. The Commission con-ducted a detailed analysis of the trade-off between profits lost in the upstream market for digital maps due to a reduction of input sales and the profits earned on the down-stream market as a result of increases in the costs of rivals. Thanks to the availability of data in the market of mobile handsets, a quantitative analysis (econometric estimation of the demand for mobile handsets) was possible. The Commission identified a number of factors suggesting that the actual increase in downstream demand would be low. Since map databases account for a small proportion of mobile handset costs, under any reasonable assumption regarding own-price elasticity and diversion rates, small price increases would lead to very few additional sales. Navigation services are only one feature among many that determine consumers' choices and rivals could enhance other features of their handsets to win customers. The possibility that a third firm (Garmin's agreement with Samsung) would be protected from foreclosure further limited the possibility to engage in input foreclosure. Supported by econometric estimation showing that the merged entity would capture only a limited volume of downstream sales, the Commission concluded that the merged entity would have no incentive to increase the price of the upstream product.

Even though not strictly necessary because of the absence of proven anti-competitive effects, the Commission also discussed a potential efficiency defence (see Commission's Decision, at 364–376). It accepted the problem of double mark-ups, since the marginal cost of map databases is close to zero and consequently gross margins are high. The Commission illustrated the reduction of the double mark-up with regard to the price of mobile handsets. Given that similar benefits are unlikely to be achieved by vertical agreements (volume discounts), the Commission further concluded that the elimination of the double marginalisation had be considered merger-specific to a large extent. By contrast, non-price efficiencies relating to improvements of products and new production processes were considered unlikely.

9.4.4 Efficiencies

In the early days of EU merger control, the European Commission appeared to be hostile to efficiency-enhancing mergers. The underlying logic was a by-product of the dominance test: a merger that not only combines market shares but also forms an efficiency base for extending those shares creates a dominant position twice. Rather than accepting an 'efficiency defence', the analysis of the positive economic effects of mergers thus resulted in establishing an 'efficiency offence'. As explained in Chapter 2 (see 2.5), this negative attitude to mergers ('big is bad') was heavily criticised by the Chicago School. However, the more benign US policy view, which balances anti-competitive effects and pro-competitive efficiency savings, had no impact on the early enforcement of the EU Merger Regulation. The traditional difference between the US and EU approaches to merger control can be understood by taking full account of the different policy perspectives. A total welfare approach, based on the Kaldor–Hicks criterion, necessarily implies that efficiencies are accepted as a reason to clear a merger which creates a dominant position. If the gains to shareholders (productive efficiencies, higher profits) outweigh the losses to consumers (higher prices), a Williamsonian trade-off suggests to clear the merger (see above, at 9.2.2). Whereas total welfare became a decisive normative goal in the Chicago analysis of the 1980s, EU competition law in general, and merger control in particular, was originally justified by the market integration goal and scope was made to include non-efficiency objectives in the overall assessment of mergers. In the past, the European Commission accepted efficiencies as an argument when the merger would create no dominant position. Consequently, the efficiency defence was accepted in cases where there was no need for it (Camesasca 2000). In its Guidelines the European Commission declares that the relevant benchmark in assessing efficiency claims is the absence of consumer harm (Horizontal Merger Guidelines, at 79). This is a clear rejection of the total welfare standard and Kaldor–Hicks improvements. A later passage of the Guidelines reaffirms this conclusion by pointing out that:

> Cost reductions, which merely result from anti-competitive reductions in output, cannot be considered as efficiencies benefiting consumers.

Horizontal Merger Guidelines, at 80

The solution opted for in the Horizontal Merger Guidelines is to acknowledge efficiencies as a potential counterbalance as part of the overall competitive appraisal within the meaning of Article 2(2) and (3) Merger Regulation.[70] This will be the case if the European Commission is in a position to conclude on the basis of sufficient evidence that the efficiencies generated by the concentration enable the newly created entity 'to act pro-competitively for the benefit of consumers, thereby counteracting the adverse effects on competition' (Horizontal Merger Guidelines, at 77). Thereto, the efficiencies have to (i) benefit consumers; (ii) be specific to the concentration; and (iii) be verifiable. Each of these requirements is further explained below.

For efficiencies to benefit consumers, they should be substantial and timely, and should in principle benefit consumers in those relevant markets, where it is otherwise likely that competition concerns would occur (Horizontal Merger Guidelines, at 79). The Commission lists the following examples: (i) cost savings in production, leading to a reduction in variable or marginal costs; reductions in fixed costs are considered less likely to result in lower prices for consumers, while cost reductions resulting from anti-competitive

---

[70] EC Horizontal Merger Guidelines, para. 76, referring also to Recitals 4 and 29 Merger Regulation, as well as Article 2(1)(b) Merger Regulation.

reductions in output are excluded; (ii) R&D and innovation efficiency gains leading to new or improved products; (iii) in the context of coordinated effects, cost savings leading to increased production and reduced prices, thereby reducing the newly created entity's incentive to coordinate its market behaviour (Horizontal Merger Guidelines, at 80–82). Timeliness and the incentive on the part of the newly created entity to pass efficiency gains on to consumers is often related to the existence of competitive pressure. The Guidelines thereto apply something like a sliding scale approach: the greater the possible anti-competitive effects, 'the more the EC Commission has to be sure that the claimed efficiencies are substantial, likely to be realized, and to be passed on, to a sufficient degree, to the consumer'. It is, as such, 'highly unlikely' that mergers to monopoly would be accepted based on efficiency claims (Horizontal Merger Guidelines, at 84).

For efficiencies to be specific to the concentration, they need to be a direct consequence of the concentration and impossible to achieve to a similar extent by less anti-competitive alternatives. The firms involved have the onus to demonstrate that there are no less anti-competitive, realistic and attainable alternatives (such as licensing arrangements, or a cooperative joint venture, see Horizontal Merger Guidelines, at 85).

For efficiencies to be verifiable, the European Commission must be reasonably certain that the efficiencies are likely to materialise and substantial enough to counteract a concentration's potential harm to consumers. If quantification is impossible, 'it must be possible to foresee a clearly identifiable positive impact on consumers' so that 'the longer the start of the efficiencies is projected into the future, the less probability is assigned to them' (Horizontal Merger Guidelines, at 86 and 88, the latter listing the type of evidence that can be relied on).

The Non-Horizontal Merger Guidelines accept the insights from economic theory that vertical mergers may overcome problems of double marginalisation and reduce coordination costs between different levels of the supply chain (see 9.2.3). They state that a vertical merger allows the merged entity to internalise any pre-existing double mark-ups, which result from both parties setting their prices independently pre-merger (Non-Horizontal Merger Guidelines, at 55). In addition, the Commission acknowledges that vertical mergers may align the incentives of the parties with regard to investments in new products, new production processes and the marketing of products (Non-Horizontal Merger Guidelines, at 57).

A final remark seems appropriate. Overall, the guidance provided by the Guidelines is relatively vague and it may be expected that the Commission will leave it to the parties to come up with a convincing efficiency rationale.[71] It may be expected that the occurrence of a successful efficiency defence will be rare. This is also in line with what economic theory teaches and empirical research demonstrates (see section 9.2.4).

Box 9.5: Conglomerate mergers and the US/EU divide: *GE/Honeywell*

The merger between General Electric Co. (GE) and Honeywell Inc. remains one of the most remarkable merger cases, not only due to the value of the operation (US$ 42 billion) but also for the different approaches followed by the US and EU enforcement agencies. At the time of the antitrust proceedings, GE was the largest corporation worldwide and the leading producer of jet engines for both commercial and military aircraft. Its market shares in the different relevant markets accounted for more than 50% (up to over 70%) in relation to different types of aircrafts. Honeywell was the major producer of a large cluster of aerospace products, including engine starters and engines for corporate jets, but also avionic and non-avionic products. The firm was the largest worldwide supplier of aerospace equipment, with market shares between 50% and 60% in relation to avionics products and between 60% and 70% in the market of engines for medium-sized corporate jets. A main goal of the operation was to combine the complementary product lines of the parties in these different economic clusters.

In October 2000, GE and Honeywell filed their merger notification with the US antitrust authorities. The Antitrust Division of the Department of Justice (DoJ) raised only minor concerns to the proposed merger. In particular, the DoJ pointed out that the concentration would create business overlapping in relation to military helicopter engines and for the maintenance and servicing of small jet engines. However, in May 2001, the DoJ reached an agreement with the two companies that solved the antitrust concerns: GE and Honeywell committed themselves to undertake (small) divestitures of the overlapping businesses. The merger was cleared without imposing other requirements or further spin-offs.[72] In the same period (May 2001), the Canadian Competition Bureau, too, informed the parties that it would not take any initiative to challenge the operation.

---

[71] It is to be noted that the Commission's DG Enterprise has come up with two expert studies on the topic of efficiencies. See de la Mano (2002) and Bishop *et al.* (2005).

[72] United States Department of Justice, Justice Department Requires Divestitures in Merger Between General Electric and Honeywell (May 2, 2001).

Conversely, a few months later (in July 2001) the European Commission decided to prohibit the acquisition of Honeywell by GE, declaring that it was incompatible with the common market.[73] The Commission emphasised the huge financial resources of the post-merger firm. It concluded that the merger would have significantly strengthened the dominance of GE in the markets of jet engines for large commercial and regional aircrafts and was likely to create a dominant position in the avionics, non-avionics and corporate jet engines sectors. First, the Commission was concerned that the merger would have eliminated the competition through the horizontal overlap in engines for large regional and corporate (large and small) regional jets. Second, since Honeywell was an important supplier of some engine parts, the proposed operation would have caused the vertical foreclosure of the other engine manufacturers. Third, the merger was likely to enhance products' bundling. In this regard, the Commission relied on the so-called 'portfolio theory', stating that whenever a company owning a series of prod-ucts acquires another firm owning complementary products, the merged entity has the incentive to provide a bundle of products (thus causing foreclosure through 'packaged offers'). Lastly, the Commission noted that the resulting entity would have had the ability to leverage its market power through strategic price cuts, thus strengthening its dominant position in the different relevant markets.[74]

The conflicting assessments by the DoJ and the European Commission feature two important issues. The first stems from the acknowledgment made by both authorities that the merger between GE and Honeywell would have led to a decrease in short-term prices. In this regard, the DoJ argued that this price reduction would have benefited the customers of the merging parties and increased the competition in the various sectors affected by the operation. Conversely, for the European Commission the decrease in prices was deemed to be likely only in the short term, while the products' bundling and the strategic price cuts would have damaged the competitive structure of the market in the medium term. This difference in the assessments shows that the intervention of the US authorities, also with respect to conglomerate mergers, aims at protecting consumers. Therefore, the expected decline in the products prices and the alleged bun-dling strategies were considered pro-competitive. In a rather opposite way, the decision taken by the Commission appears more prone to protect individual competitors and the competitive structure of the markets affected by the operation. The *GE/Honeywell* case has revealed a marked tension between the different authorities and in the transat-lantic debate (Grant and Neven 2005; Fox 2002). The second aspect to be highlighted is the problems that may arise from the application of national rules in relation to concentrations that occur in global markets. Competition authorities and courts evalu-ate the operations according to national rules and balance the costs and benefits at the

---

[73] Case COMP/M.2220, *General Electric/Honeywell v. Commission* (2001).

[74] In 2005, the General Court has upheld the Commission's decision primarily on the basis of the horizontal overlap issues. Cases T-209/01 and T-210/01, *Honeywell and General Electric v Commission* [2005] ECR II-5527.

national level. However, this may not be the most appropriate level to assess an international merger. As shown by the *GE/Honeywell* case, national antitrust rules – paired with a different reliance on economic theories and reasoning – may produce different outcomes in relation to a global merger. This result exemplifies the problem of national antitrust frameworks confronted with worldwide economic actors and transactions.

9.4.5   Enforcement

Procedural rules

The European procedure for reviewing concentrations can be characterised as largely administrative. The same officials from the Competition Directorate General (DG Comp) review the concentration, engage with the parties and draft a final decision to be taken by the college of European Commissioners. Only after the European Commission has taken its final decision can the parties take recourse to judicial review before the European Courts (General Court, CJEU). In the following, the European enforcement procedure is described; subsequently, the checks and balances of this process are presented.

The 2004 review of the Merger Regulation has maintained the system of mandatory notifications for concentrations reaching the turnover thresholds contained in Article 1 of the Merger Regulation. Notification is done by completing a Form CO, an exercise requiring detailed legal and economic analysis. The result of notification is that the timeline for review begins to run; in the meantime, the proposed concentration is suspended. Hence, implementation of the concentration before clearance by the European Commission is not possible and preliminary contacts or exchange of information between the parties' businesses is not allowed.

Prior to the notification, parties to a concentration often engage in informal discussions with DG Comp to address jurisdictional issues (for example, referral) and legal issues (for example, market definition, remedies), as well as the scope and preparation of the notification (Form CO). After the notification, phase 1 of the review starts (Article 6 Merger Regulation), during which the European Commission (through its officials at DG Comp) undertakes a preliminary review of the concentration. The deadlines to undertake this preliminary review are fixed: 25 working days for a normal review, extended with ten working days in case of remedy discussions (to alleviate competitive concerns) or a referral request pursuant to Article 9 of the Merger Regulation. At the end of phase 1, the European Commission decides either that the concentration does not raise competitive concerns and is cleared to proceed (eventually subject to remedies), or that further investigation is necessary. If the outcome of a phase 1 review is that the Commission needs further information to take a final decision, an in-depth review is opened in phase 2 (Article 8 Merger Regulation). The deadline to undertake this in-depth review is 90 working days, which can be extended to 105 working days in case of remedies. For complex cases, the deadline for decision can be extended by an additional 20 working days (but only at the parties' request or with their consent). After this extension, a final decision must be taken that results in clearance, possibly with remedies, or a prohibition.

During the European Commission's investigation, a number of meetings with both the notifying parties and third parties may take place. Such meetings can be informal *ad hoc* meetings, state of play meetings or triangular meetings (involving DG Comp, the notifying parties and third parties). In phase 2, the statement of objections, access to file provisions and the oral hearing (under the direction of a neutral hearing officer) formalise this exchange of views. Additional checks and balances of the Commission's internal process are contained in the Best Practice Guidelines, available on the DG Comp website. They also include a peer review system (the so-called devil's advocate panel), in which the DG Comp officials leading the investigation present and defend their findings and preliminary conclusions to a number of (uninvolved) colleagues. In sum, the European control of concentrations is basically a front-loaded administrative notification process. This is different from the US process, which is in essence judicial (see section 9.3.2).

Centralisation of merger control

The EU Merger Regulation contains a detailed framework for delineating the competences of the European Commission and the competition authorities of the EU Member States (NCAs). Industry interest groups are worried about lack of legal certainty when mergers have to be supervised several times, especially when the appraisal criteria differ across countries. When the Merger Regulation was introduced in 1989, a one-stop-shop review system was introduced. This ensures that the concentration is controlled either at the community level or at national level(s). Centralised review is reserved for concentrations with a community dimension, providing exclusive competence to the EU Commission. The jurisdictional thresholds for determining whether or not the centralised authority will review concentrations are contained in Article 1 of the Merger Regulation, which has introduced a number of turnover thresholds.

After the 2004 review of the Merger Regulation, the current thresholds are as follows. A merger has a community dimension if two positively formulated conditions and one negatively worded requirement are met. Positively, the (i) combined aggregate worldwide turnover of all the undertakings concerned must exceed €5000 million; and (ii) the aggregate Community-wide turnover of each of at least two of the undertakings concerned must be more than €250 million. Negatively, (iii) even if these thresholds are reached, the merger will not be supervised by the European Commission if each of the undertakings concerned achieves more than two-thirds of its aggregate Community-wide turnover within one and the same Member State (Article 1 (2) of the Merger Regulation).[75] Since the 1997 amendments to the Merger Regulation, additional turnover criteria apply in order to reduce the risk of multiple filings. The Commission must be notified of concentrations satisfying all following thresholds: the (a) combined aggregate worldwide turnover of all the undertakings concerned exceeds €2500 million; (b) in each of at least three Member States the combined aggregate turnover of all the undertakings concerned is more than €100 million; (c) in each of the same three Member States identified for the purpose of (b) above, the aggregate turnover of each of at least two of the undertakings concerned exceeds €25 million; and (d) the aggregate Community-wide turnover of each of at least two of the undertakings concerned is more than €100 million.

To allow better allocation of cases between the European Commission and the Member States, Regulation 104/2004 has fine-tuned the referral system. Practice had shown that national filings with multiple Member State authorities were a regular occurrence. Often, the relatively high turnover thresholds in the Merger Regulation were not met, while the much lower national thresholds were quite easily breached. The revised referral system enables referrals before and after notification. Requests can be made by both the European Commission and the Member States. A pre-notification referral from the European Commission to the Member States concerns a transaction with Community dimension of which parties believe that it may significantly affect competition within distinct national markets. A pre-notification referral from the Member States to the European Commission is possible for a concentration without a community dimension that must be reviewed in three or more Member States. A post-notification referral from the European Commission to the Member States can be submitted if a concentration threatens to significantly affect competition within a distinct

---

[75] Exceptions to these rules are contained in the so-called German (Article 9 Merger Regulation) and Dutch (Article 22 (3) Merger Regulation) clauses: the first clause allows for national merger control even if the thresholds are reached, whereas the second clause provides for the possibility of European merger control below the thresholds mentioned in Regulation 4064/89.

market. A post-notification referral from the Member States to the European Commission concerns a concentration that threatens to significantly affect competition within a national market and affects inter-state trade.

How can the current rules delineating jurisdiction between European and national competition authorities be assessed? The economic analysis of (de)centralisation advances two major arguments in favour of centralisation: the need to internalise interjurisdictional externalities and the risk of a race to the bottom. Starting from the insight that externalities are a powerful argument in favour of centralisation, the case for control under European competition law will be stronger, the more significant is the externalities' problem. Under competing national competition laws, mergers having extra-territorial effects must be scrutinised by the competition authorities of all Member States involved. This combined application of several national control procedures may cause problems of coordination and increase legal uncertainty. Under the EU Regulation, the scale of the parties to the transaction is crucial for determining whether the merger will be supervised by the European Commission. Neven, Nuttall and Seabright argue that it would have been more natural to let the absolute size of the spillovers determine whether the EU Merger Regulation should apply. Small transactions may have substantial spillovers, which will not always be considered appropriately by national antitrust authorities. To avoid this kind of distortion they suggest a threshold requiring that of the worldwide annual turnover half of the turnover within the EU must take place outside the Member State with the largest share of the combined turnover (Neven, Nuttall and Seabright 1993, 198). Such a rule would better enable the European Commission to investigate transactions that give rise to significant international spillovers. The 2004 modifications to the referral system provide for a viable corrector to the turnover-based thresholds for determining jurisdiction in cases where turnover does not clearly identify cross-border effects.

The race-to-the-bottom argument finds its theoretical basis in the existence of prisoner's dilemmas between Member States. The Merger Regulation provides scope for forum shopping, which gives parties the possibility to choose their preferred jurisdiction. The Merger Regulation has defined the division of powers between competition authorities and the free choice of the controlling agency (regulatory competition through free choice of law) has consequently been limited. However, in practice, firms may still seek to change the contents or the form of the contemplated transactions in order to have them controlled by a preferred competition authority. Although the prospect of alternative jurisdictions will presumably be a relatively minor consideration in the majority of deals, where the commercial rationale dominates, these considerations may matter at the margin. If control of a merger by the European Commission is preferred to control by national antitrust authorities, a (presumably large) minority partner may be added to increase the turnover of the undertakings concerned and make the merger a matter for the European Commission. When national competition authorities treat potentially anti-competitive mergers more strictly, firms may wish to change the contemplated merger in order to have it controlled in Brussels. It is, for instance, remarkable that German firms seem to have preferred the EU system to that of the German authority (*Bundeskartellamt*).[76]

Changing the form of the contemplated transaction is another example of forum shopping. With respect to joint ventures there is some evidence that firms changed the form of the joint venture because they wanted it to count as concentrative and thus be subject to the EU Merger Regulation (Neven, Nuttall and Seabright 1993, 195). The procedure under Article 101 TFEU, which applies to non-concentrative joint ventures, is more cumbersome than the control of concentrations. It is open-ended and tends to be lengthy; its implementation is perceived to be rather inflexible and decisions have limited duration, whereas there is no such time limit under the Merger Regulation. The incentives for parties to change the form of their transaction increases the indirect costs of merger control. There is thus a risk that the race-to-the-bottom will be won by central rules. The EU rules induce firms to engage in concentrations which tend to be durable, rather than in cartel agreements which are unstable by their very nature. Since the one-stop-shop principle excludes control of mergers by Member States above the Community thresholds, substantial increases of the concentration ratios in many European industries might be feared. To counteract these adverse effects, Article 2(4) of the revised Merger Regulation incorporates the Article 101 TFEU-type analysis into the assessment of compatibility under the Merger Regulation in the case of structural joint ventures having coordination effects. This avoids the difficulty of determining coordination effects at the jurisdiction stage, while subjecting all structural joint ventures to the same stage one and stage two timetables applicable to concentrations. Firms' incentives to engage in more durable concentration-style transactions for purely procedural reasons thus have been diminished.

---

[76] The German competition authorities have expressed concern from the outset that the Merger Regulation may be too lax. Officials from the *Bundeskartellamt* indicated that their assessment would probably have been different in cases, such as *Varta/Bosch*: see Neven, Nuttall and Seabright (1993, 81).

Box 9.6: Merger control in Brazil

Maria Fernanda Caporale Madi

The first Brazilian antitrust law (Law No. 8884/94) created the Brazilian Antitrust Agency (*CADE, Conselho Administrativo de Defesa Econômica*) and introduced a mandatory *ex post* merger control. Under this system, companies used to notify their merger *after* its conclusion, which compromised CADE's ability to decide cases on their merits. Law No. 12539/2011 introduced important structural changes in the Brazilian antitrust system. CADE was reorganised into three departments: the Tribunal, the General Superintendency (SG) and the Department of Economic Studies. The SG has the most important role in the merger review process, as its officials have the power to clear transactions in fast-track procedures or challenge them before the Tribunal. Importantly, Law No. 12539/2011 introduced the *ex ante* notification of mergers. Hence, since May 2012, Brazil ceased being one of the few countries in the world with an *ex post* merger control.

According to Article 90 of Law No. 12539/2011, a transaction must be notified when: (i) two or more previously independent companies merge; (ii) one or more companies acquire, directly or indirectly, by purchase or exchange of stocks, shares, bonds or securities convertible into stocks or assets, whether tangible or intangible, by contract or by any other means or way, the control or parts of one or more companies; (iii) one or more companies incorporate one or more companies; or (iv) two or more companies enter into an associative contract,[77] consortium or joint venture. Moreover, a merger shall be subject to CADE's pre-merger control if (i) it has effects in Brazil; (ii) at least one of the groups involved in the transaction has gross revenues in Brazil of at least BRL 750 million (equivalent in December 2016 to €220 million); and (iii) at least one other group involved in the transaction has gross revenues in Brazil of at least BRL 75 million (equivalent in December 2016 to €22 million).

After notification, there is a maximum waiting period for reviewing the transactions of up to 240 days, depending on the complexity of the case. Fast track procedures are usually decided by the SG, whereas non-fast track procedures require the approval of CADE's Tribunal. The latter procedure is similar to Phase I and II of European merger control (see section 9.4.5). CADE regards fast-track procedures adequate for: (i) transactions that result in horizontal overlaps with a combined market share lower than 50% as long as the market share increase is insignificant (e.g. variation under 200 HHI points); (ii) transactions resulting in vertical integration, as long as the parties do not control a share superior to 30% of any relevant market affected by the transaction. In the period between 2012 and 2016, 1738 merger cases were notified to CADE; 84% of these cases were analysed under the fast-track procedure. Moreover, more than 95%

---

[77] Resolution No. 17/2016 removed the vertical relationships, for instance supply and distribution agreements. According to the new rules, only arrangements between competitors must be reported to CADE.

of all cases were unrestrictedly approved by the authority.[78] Brazilian antitrust law has vested upon CADE very broad powers, allowing it to take whatever measures are deemed necessary to remedy the harm caused by a transaction, including the dissolution or break-up of a company.

By way of illustration, two recent cases are discussed below. The first case concerned the steel-making industry and was related to the acquisition of *Usinas Siderúrgicas of Minas Gerais S.A. (Usiminas)* by CSN, the two greatest companies in the steel market in Brazil. Although the operation was cleared by the antitrust authority, the approval was made conditional upon the reduction of CSN's stake in Usiminas. Through successive acquisitions of stock exchange, CSN became the sole owner of a great part of Usiminas's shareholdings. CSN now holds 17.43% of the social capital: 14.13% are ordinary shares and 20.71% are preferential shares. The current controlling block of the company, composed by Grupos Nippon, Techint and Caixa dos Empregados da Usiminas, holds 63.86% of the voting capital. The Reporting Commissioner of the case stated that the absence of control does not exclude the possibility of anti-competitive effects derived from this operation, since the incentives for the companies to compete change. The Commissioner also highlighted that limiting CSN's participation in Usiminas is necessary, since both steel industries are rivals on the 'extremely concentrated flat steel market' (Merger File no. 08012.009198/2011-21).

In December 2015, another important international transaction was approved with remedies. CADE allowed the acquisition of *Rexam PLC* by *Ball Corporation*, conditional upon the adoption of structural remedies (such as divestiture of plants and related tangible and intangible assets) and behavioural measures (for instance, the termination of certain supply agreements). According to the reporting Commissioner, the merger would constitute the tie-up of the two biggest producers of metal cans for beverages in Brazil. In the post-merger scenario, the market shares of both companies would be significant in all country regions (Merger Review No. 08700.006567/2015-07).

Box 9.7: Merger control in India
Sahib Singh Chadha

The Indian Competition Act of 2002 (Act), which became fully operational in June 2011,[79] is the principal legislation governing merger control in India. Any acquisition of control, shares, voting rights or assets and any merger and amalgamation exceeding the jurisdictional thresholds (based on asset and turnover computation) must

---

[78] Data available at: http://cadenumeros.cade.gov.br.
[79] By virtue of Competition Commission of India (Procedure in Regard to the Transaction of Business Relating to Combinations) Regulations, 2011 (Combination Regulations).

be mandatorily notified to the Competition Commission of India (CCI) and can be consummated only after due approval by the CCI. There are no exceptions to the compulsory notification requirement, except a *de minimis* rule and an exemption for the banking sector. Schedule 1 of the Combination Regulations also provides that notification with the CCI is not required for certain combinations that are ordinarily not likely to cause appreciable adverse effects on competition. Furthermore, intra-group transactions are also exempted, provided that such transactions do not result in acquisition of sole or joint control.

The CCI has not restricted its examination to any one specific industry, but has reviewed all transactions exceeding the thresholds. The Government of India vide amendment to the Combination Regulations of 5 March 2016 has revised the asset/ turnover threshold by 100%, in order to ensure that small transactions are kept outside the CCI's scrutiny. Up to the current day, most of the combinations reviewed by the CCI were cleared after conclusion of the Phase I review. However, the CCI subjected three transactions to an in-depth Phase-II investigation, since the market share of the parties was very high, and proposed divestiture remedies because of anticipated competitive concerns. The CCI has not yet prohibited or voided any transaction, which shows a very liberal approach in examining proposed amalgamations. In 2016, the total number of combinations notified to the CCI was 127, out of which 87 were approved and the remaining 40 are still under review.

The CCI conducted its first Phase-II investigation relating to the merger between Sun Pharmaceutical Industries Ltd. (Sun Pharma) and Ranbaxy Laboratories Ltd. (Ranbaxy). The CCI delineated the relevant product market at the molecule level, i.e. medicines/formulations based on the same active pharmaceutical ingredients.[80] This is in line with the internationally accepted practice of identifying competition concerns at the molecular level, rather than taking the broader therapeutic level. The CCI cleared the merger subject to the companies' duty to divest seven brands.[81] The key factor considered by the CCI during its investigation was the market share; the CCI stated that there would possibly be a major horizontal overlap in terms of the molecules offered by the combined entity.

The second Phase-II examination concerned the *Holcim/Lafarge* merger. In this case, the CCI relied on the Elzinga–Hogarty test and catchment area analysis to delineate the relevant geographical market (see section 4.5.2 for a discussion of this test). The use of

---

[80] The CCI stated that: 'The various generic brands of a given molecule are chemical equivalents and are considered to be substitutable (...) pharmaceutical drugs within a group may not be substitutable because of differences in the intended use, mechanism of action of the underlying molecule, mode of administration, contra-indications, side effects etc.' See para. 14 at page 5, available at http://www.cci.gov.in/sites/default/files/C-2014-05-170_0.pdf.

[81] Available at http://www.cci.gov.in/sites/default/files/C-2014-05-170A_0.pdf.

empirical tools has signalled that the CCI is taking steps to evaluate more data-based/ quantitative evidence in order to define the relevant market. However, it is interesting to note that while applying these tests, the CCI did not rely on any specific threshold level and laid emphasis on the fact there should be 'sufficient cause in terms of the competitive constraints for inclusion of an additional state/area in the relevant geographical market.'[82] The CCI analysed several factors, including: the level of concentration (using the Herfindahl–Hirschman Index, HHI), entry barriers, countervailing buying power, constraints exerted by competitors, the pre-combination degree of competition between the parties and the prevailing market structure (using the four-firm concentration ratio, CR4). After having revealed the likelihood of appreciable adverse effects on competition, the CCI recommended structural commitments: the divestiture of two assets coupled with the requirement of finding an upfront buyer not having any links with existing cement producers in the relevant market.

In 2016, PVR Limited (PVR) filed a notice with the CCI about its proposed acquisition of an undertaking of DLF Utilities Limited (DUL) comprising 39 movie theatre screens on a slump-sale basis. The CCI sent a show cause notice, requiring PVR to explain why Phase-II investigation should not be initiated. In its response, PVR proposed certain remedies to counteract CCI's concerns (for example, reduction of the period of non-compete obligations, doing away with the proposed cooperation agreement between the parties, and terminating the establishment of new projects in certain markets). The CCI, however, initiated a Phase-II investigation, inviting public comments. PVR later presented a revised remedies package, which incorporated certain structural and behavioural remedies, such as monetary caps on the rates of admission and of food/beverages, a freeze on expansion of business and terminating the establishment of new projects. The CCI analysed the market concentration using the HHI, the change in concentration/incremental market shares, the constraints exerted by competitors and the level of efficiency. The CCI found that the combination in question could lead to an appreciable adverse effect on competition. It, however, did approve the combination,[83] subject to the modifications proposed by PVR. It also proposed an additional structural remedy, i.e. divesting either 11 or 13 properties as identified by the CCI post-acquisition.

Since the Act adopts a suspensory regime, the consequences of not notifying or belated notification of a combination (gun jumping) entails a penalty, which may extend to 1% of the total turnover or assets of the combination.[84] In 2016 alone, the CCI recorded nine transactions to be in contravention of the provisions relating to gun jumping. The penalty imposed by the CCI lies in the range from INR 0.5 million to 30 million. When it comes to gun jumping, most contraventions regard the interpretation of the

---

[82] Para. 15.9, p. 8, available at http://www.cci.gov.in/sites/default/files/C-2014-07-190_0.pdf.

[83] Available at http://www.cci.gov.in/sites/default/files/event%20document/C-2015-07-288.pdf.

[84] Section 43A, Competition Act, 2002.

meaning of consummation or part of consummation. The CCI, however, while dealing with contravention attempts to provide interpretational guidance. One such example is in the Hindustan Colas and Shell proposed merger (Combination Registration No. C-2015/08/299), where the CCI observed that pre-payment of consideration (even a refundable deposit) has the effect of consummating a part of the combination and does not eliminate the statutory requirement of filing notice.[85]

All in all, the remedies imposed by the CCI for conditionally approving deals are not harsh and have an insignificant effect on the valuation of such deals. Besides, the CCI has taken several measures to ensure that the merger process is not only simple and efficient but also consistent with the global best practices. The latter measures include: informal and verbal discussions with the CCI staff prior to the filing of a combination notice, gathering information from local[86] and international authorities,[87] hearings prior to invalidation of the notice, no requirement for verification of documents, and so on. With an amendment in 2016, the CCI has provided clarity regarding the trigger for filing a notice by stating that a public announcement made in terms of securities regulation for acquisition of shares, voting rights and control will be considered as such. However, the period within which CCI tends to review a combination is something to be concerned about. The Sun–Ranbaxy merger took almost a year since its announcement, while in the Holcim case the CCI took almost 18 months to finish the inquiry. Further, the engagement of the CCI with stakeholders and members of the industry is not time bound and lengthens the inquiry period. The burdens of divestiture, finding an upfront buyer, getting the buyer pre-approved by the CCI all fall on the proposers of the merger and thus inordinately add to the delay of the entire transaction.

9.5 Conclusions

Mergers may harm competition by reducing the number of competitors, softening competition, impeding entry and reducing innovation. However, mergers may also generate efficiencies: productive efficiencies as a result of restructuring, more efficient allocation of resources and dynamic efficiencies resulting from increased innovation. Competition authorities face the

---

[85] Also see SCM Soilfert & Ors v. CCI (Appeal no. 59 of 2015) where the COMPAT held that even if the consideration amount was transferred to an escrow account and the buyer undertook to abstain from exercising any rights typically held by an acquirer of shares, such acquisition without the prior permission of the CCI would be seen as an instance of gun jumping.

[86] Illustratively, the CCI sought information from the Rubber Board Ministry of Commerce and Industry in acquisition of the chloroprene rubber business of E.I. du Pont de Nemours; available at: http://www.cci.gov.in/sites/default/files/C-2015-01-239_0.pdf.

[87] The CCI has signed a Memorandum of Understanding (MoU) on cooperation in the field of competition with competition authorities of several countries including Brazil, Russia, China, Australia, South Africa, Canada, United States of America and the European Union.

difficult task of assessing the anti-competitive effects of mergers and balance them against their potential benefits in terms of higher (productive, allocative and dynamic) efficiency. The US Clayton Act, which was passed in 1914, prohibits mergers if their effect may be to 'substantially lessen competition'. Conversely, there were no merger provisions in the text of the European Treaties and merger control was introduced only in 1989. The Merger Regulation has created a 'one-stop-shop' for mergers with a 'community dimension': mergers meeting certain turnover thresholds are controlled only by the European Commission. The substantive test for merger control has been reformulated by Regulation 139/2004, which has introduced the SIEC criterion.

Horizontal mergers combine firms active in the same selling or buying market. The competitive harm is likely to be serious if barriers to entry are high, but horizontal mergers may also generate important offsetting efficiencies. Vertical mergers combine firms acting at different levels of the supply chain or opposite sides of the market. They have a large potential of efficiencies, which may benefit both traders and consumers, but they may also foreclose competitors, either upstream or downstream. Conglomerate mergers refer to a combination not pertaining to either of the above categories. Mergers in different, but related, product markets may be justified by efficiencies (such as risk sharing) but may also raise antitrust concerns (for example, by the use of bundling practices).

Mergers produce two types of anti-competitive effects: coordinated effects and non-coordinated (unilateral) effects. In concentrated markets, firms are more likely to reach coordination, since their number is reduced and it is easier to coordinate their actions after the merger. But, also in the absence of coordination between firms in the post-merger market, mergers may harm competition by removing important competitive constraints on one or more sellers. In the case of unilateral effects, these sellers enjoy increased market power after the merger enabling them to restrict competition. Since the 2004 revision of EU Merger Control, both US antitrust law and EU competition law allow the control both of types of anti-competitive effects. The language of the Clayton Act 'substantially lessening competition' (Section 7) has always been sufficiently broad and the concept of unilateral effects has been introduced and further elaborated on in several versions of the US Merger Guidelines (starting in 1982 up until 2010). In the EU, Regulation 139/2004 defines the anti-competitive effects as a 'significant impediment to effective competition, in particular as a result of the creation or strengthening of a dominant position'. Henceforth, in both jurisdictions, not only coordinated effects (facilitated collusion after the merger) but also the effects that result from reducing the competitive pressure on the post-merger firm are part of the antitrust analysis.

In recent years, quantitative tests have become increasingly important for assessing the economic effects of mergers. Simulation models estimate post-merger price increases, starting from pre-merger prices; they use pre-merger market factors – prevailing prices and marginal costs together with estimated demand elasticities – to calibrate inter-firm competitive interaction. A simulation model may also account for transaction synergies: merger-specific efficiencies (such as reductions of marginal costs) which carry the potential to reduce prices and increase consumer welfare. They may inform the competition authorities about both the unilateral price effects and the efficiency gains that are likely to result from the merger. Diversion ratios measure the proportion of sales diverted from one product to another in case of a price increase. They are useful to assess unilateral effects of mergers in markets for differentiated goods.

In the US a proposed merger must be notified to the federal enforcement agencies, which will scrutinise the merger under Section 7 of the Clayton Act. Today, the application of the substantive test that the merger must substantially lessen competition necessitates the use of advanced economic analysis. The structural approach of the old days, when mergers were blocked even if the market shares of the merging firms were relatively low, has been replaced by a broad economic assessment in which many factors may play a role and that is conducted on a case-by-case basis. The DoJ and the FTC have issued joint Merger Guidelines, which provide clarification on merger assessment to the notifying parties. Market shares are seen as a first indicator of the competitive effects, not more, not less. Of particular importance is the view of the US antitrust agencies that the analysis must not start with market definition. The Merger Guidelines endorse several quantitative techniques, which allow the competitive effects to be assessed directly, including merger simulation models and diversion ratios. The UPP index measures the upward pricing pressure imposed by a merger as a function of diversion ratios, profit margins and efficiencies. However, US courts may continue to be reluctant towards quantitative approaches (mainly because of reasons related to legal certainty and administrative efficiency). As a consequence, sophisticated economic techniques may accompany a conventional structural merger analysis without replacing it altogether.

Economic analysis has equally become the cornerstone of the substantive analysis under the EU Merger Regulation. Consequently, with the exception of the assessment of conglomerates (see the *GE/Honeywell* case, discussed in Box 9.5), merger control on both sides of the Atlantic has become largely similar. As is the case in the US, market shares and concentration levels are seen as useful first indicators for reviewing concentrations. In addition, the European Commission's practice shows openness towards the use of quantitative methods that complement conventional structural analyses. This does not imply that there is no further scope for improvements. Data problems or subjective choices made by the competition authorities, in cases where economic models do not properly reflect the competitive conditions of the industry under investigation, warrant control by judges who are trained to distinguish trustworthy from less reliable economic evidence. However, compared with the relative underdevelopment of economic analysis in other areas of EU competition law (particularly regarding vertical restrictions and abuse of a dominant position), EU merger control has evolved up to a point where the marriage of competition economics and competition law has become relatively stable.

9.6   Bibliography

Baker J (1999), 'Developments in Antitrust Economics' 13 *Journal of Economic Perspectives* 181

Baker J (1997), 'Contemporary Empirical Merger Analysis' 5 *George Mason Law Review* 347

Baker J, Rubinfeld D (1999), 'Empirical Methods Used in Antitrust Litigation: Review and a Critique' 1 *American Law and Economics Review* 386

Bhattacharya S (2016), *Competition Law and the Bounded Rationality of Firms* (EDLE – Erasmus University Rotterdam) <http://repub.eur.nl/pub/93069>

Bishop S (2013), 'Snake-Oil with Mathematics Is Still Snake-Oil: Why Recent Trends in the Application of So-Called "Sophisticated" Economics Are Hindering Good Competition Policy Enforcement' 9 *European Competition Journal* 67

Bishop S (2001), 'Economic Aspects of Recent Merger Cases' (Speech held at Brussels, April 27)

Bishop S, Walker M (2010), *The Economics of EU Competition Law. Concepts, Application and Measurement* (Sweet & Maxwell, 3rd ed.)

Bishop S, Walker M (2002), *The Economics of EC Competition Law: Concepts, Application and Measurement* (Sweet & Maxwell, 2nd ed.)

Bishop S, Lofaro A, Rosati F, Young J (2005), 'The Efficiency-Enhancing Effects of Non-Horizontal Mergers' (Office for Official Publications of the European Communities)

Blair R, Harrison J (2010), *Monopsony in Law and Economics* (Cambridge University Press)

Camesasca P (2000), *European Merger Control: Getting The Efficiencies Right* (Intersentia)

Coate M (1992), 'Economics, the Guidelines and the Evolution of Merger Policy' 37 *Antitrust Bulletin* 997

Coate M, McChesney F (1992), 'Empirical Evidence on FTC Enforcement of the Merger Guidelines' 30 *Economic Inquiry* 277

Compte O, Jenny F, Rey P (2002), 'Capacity Constraints, Mergers and Collusion' 46 *European Economic Review* 1

Davidson C, Deneckere R (1984), 'Horizontal Mergers and Collusive Behavior' 2 *International Journal of Industrial Organization* 117

Davis P, Reilly A (2010), 'Market Power, Market Outcomes, and Remedies in the UK Groceries Market' 41 *Agricultural Economics* 93

De la Mano M (2002), 'For the Customer's Sake: The Competitive Effects of Efficiencies in European Merger Control' (Final Report Prepared for DG Enterprise) (Office for Official Publications of the European Communities)

Engle R, Granger C (1987), 'Co-integration and Error Correction: Representation, Estimation and Testing' 18 *Antitrust Bulletin* 45

Epstein R, Rubinfeld D (2004), 'Effects of Mergers Involving Differentiated Products' (Final Report Prepared for DG Comp (Office for Official Publications of the European Communities)

Farrell J, Shapiro C (1990), 'Horizontal Mergers: An Equilibrium Analysis' 80 *American Economic Review* 107

Fisher A, Lande R (1983), 'Efficiency Considerations in Merger Enforcement' 71 *California Law Review* 1580

Fisher F (1987), 'Horizontal Mergers: Triage and Treatment' 1 *Journal of Economic Perspectives* 23

Fox E (2002), 'Mergers in Global Markets: *GE/Honeywell* and the Future of Merger Control' 23 *University of Pennsylvania Journal of International Law* 457

Froeb L, Werden G (1998), 'A Robust Test for Consumer Welfare Enhancing Mergers Among Sellers of a Homogeneous Product' 58 *Economics Letters* 367

Gore D, Lewis S, Lofaro A, Dethmers F (2013), *The Economic Assessment of Mergers under European Competition Law* (Cambridge University Press)

Granger C (1969), 'Investigating Causal Relations by Econometric Models and Cross-Spectral Methods' 37 *Econometrica* 424

Grant J, Neven D (2005), 'The Attempted Merger Between General Electric and Honeywell: A Case Study of Transatlantic Conflict' 1 *Journal of Competition Law and Economics* 595

Greenfield J (1984), 'Beyond Herfindahl: Non-Structural Elements of Merger Analysis' 53 *Antitrust Law Journal* 229

Hausman J, Leonard G (1997), 'Economic Analysis of Differentiated Products Mergers Using Real World Data' 5 *George Mason Law Review* 321

Hausman J, Leonard G, Zona J (1992), 'A Proposed Method for Analysing Competition Among Differentiated Products' 60 *Antitrust Law Journal* 889

Hovenkamp H (2017), 'Appraising Merger Efficiencies' (U Iowa Legal Studies Research Paper No. 16-02) <https://ssrn.com/abstract=2664266>

Ivaldi M, Jullien B, Rey P, Seabright P, Tirole J (2003), 'Economics of Unilateral Effects' (Final Report Prepared for DG Comp) (Office for Official Publications of the European Communities)

Ivaldi M, Verboven F (2005), 'Quantifying the Effects from Horizontal Mergers in European Competition Policy' 23 *International Journal of Industrial Organization* 669

Jacquemin A (1990), 'Horizontal Concentration and European Merger Policy' 34 *European Economic Review* 539

Jemison D, Sitkin S (1986), 'Corporate Acquisitions: A Process Perspective' 11 *Academy of Management Review* 145

Kassamali R (1996), 'Competition Law Survey. From Fiction to Fallacy: Reviewing the E.C. Merger Regulation's Community Dimension Thresholds in the Light of Economics and Experience in Merger Control' 21 *European Law Review* 89

Klemperer P (2004), *Auctions: Theory and Practice* (Princeton University Press)

Klemperer P (2002), 'How (Not) to Run Auctions: The European 3G Telecom Auctions' 46 *European Economic Review* 829

Kolasky W (2002), 'Coordinated Effects in Merger Review: From Dead Frenchmen to Beautiful Minds and Mavericks' (Remarks Before ABA Section of Antitrust Law Spring Meeting) <http://www.usdoj.gov/atr/public/speeches/11050.htm>

Kovacic W (1997), 'Administrative Adjudication and the Use of New Economic Approaches in Antitrust Analysis' 5 *George Mason Law Review* 313

Kovacic, W, Marshall R, Marx L, Schulenberg S (2006), 'Coordinated Effects in Merger Review: Quantifying the Payoffs from Collusion', in B Hawk (ed.), *International Antitrust Law & Policy: Fordham Corporate* 271 (Juris Publishing)

Mueller D, Sirower M (2003), 'The Causes of Mergers: Tests Based on the Gains to Acquiring Firms' Shareholders and the Size of Premia' 24 *Managerial and Decision Economics* 373

Neven D, Nuttall R, Seabright P (1993), *Merger in Daylight. The Economics and Politics of European Merger Control* (Centre for Economic Policy Research)

Nevo H (2013), 'Market Definition Under Attack: How Relevant is the Relevant Market?', in M Faure and X Zhang (eds.), *The Chinese Anti-Monopoly Law* 301 (Edward Elgar)

Perry M, Porter R (1985), 'Oligopoly and the Incentive for Horizontal Merger' 75 *American Economic Review* 219 (1985)

Powell T, Lovallo D, Fox C (2011), 'Behavioral Strategy' 32 *Strategic Management Journal* 1369

Rill J (1997), 'Practising What One Preaches: One Lawyer's View of Econometric Models in Differentiated Products Mergers' 5 *George Mason Law Review* 393

Roll R (1986), 'The Hubris Hypothesis of Corporate Takeovers' 59 *Journal of Business* 197

Rubinfeld D, Epstein R (2010), 'Understanding UPP' 10 *B.E. Journal of Theoretical Economics* 21

Salant S, Switzer S, Reynolds R (1983), 'Losses from Horizontal Merger: The Effects of an Exogenous Change in Industry Structure on Cournot-Nash Equilibrium' 98 *Quarterly Journal of Economics* 185

Schmalensee R (1987), 'Horizontal Merger Policy: Problems and Changes' 1 *Journal of Economic Perspectives* 41

Schwalbe U, Zimmer D (2009), *Law and Economics in European Merger Control* (Oxford University Press)

Seabright P (1994), 'Regulatory Capture, Subsidiarity and European Merger Policy' 57 *European Economy* 81

Shapiro C (1996), 'Mergers with Differentiated Products' 10 *Antitrust* 23

Stigler G (1950), 'Monopoly and Oligopoly by Merger' 40 *American Economic Review* 23

Verbeek M (2004), *A Guide to Modern Econometrics* (John Wiley & Sons, 2nd ed.)

Verboven F (1995), 'Corporate Restructuring in a Collusive Oligopoly' 13 *International Journal of Industrial Organization* 335

Weinstock D (1982), 'Using the Herfindahl Index to Measure Concentration' 27 *Antitrust Bulletin* 285

Werden G (1997), 'Simulating the Effects of Differentiated Products Mergers: An Alternative to Structural Merger Policy' 5 *George Mason Law Review* 363

Werden G (1996), 'A Robust Test for Consumer Welfare Enhancing Mergers Among Sellers of Differentiated Products' 44 *Journal of Industrial Economics* 409

Williamson O (1969), 'Economies as an Antitrust Defense: Reply' 59 *American Economic Review* 954

Williamson O (1968), 'Economies as an Antitrust Defense: The Welfare Tradeoffs' 58 *American Economic Review* 18

Willig R (1991), 'Merger Analysis, Industrial Theory, and Merger Guidelines', in M Baily and C Winston (eds.), *Brookings Papers on Economic Activity: Microeconomics* 281 (Brookings Institution)

Index

allocative efficiency *see under* goals of competition law
antidote theory *see under* Harvard School, workable
    competition concept
Arrow, Kenneth 53–4
as-if competition *see under* Ordoliberal School
asset specificity *see under* transaction cost approach
Aubert, C 406
Austrian School *see under* dynamic vision

Bain, Joe
    entry barriers 166, 171–2
    paradigm 34–6, 40, 139–40
barriers to entry *see under* market power/definition/
    entry barriers
Baumol, William 57
Becker, Garry 397–8
behavioural economics 69–76, 79–80
    anchoring 70, 73–4
    antitrust commentators 71, 75–6
    availability heuristic 70, 74
    biases and relevance 72–6
    bounded rationality/willpower/self-interest 70
    confirmation bias 74–5
    decision making errors 73–5
    endowment effect 72
    framing bias 73
    hierarchical structures 75–6
    hyperbolic discounting 73
    loss averse bias 73
    overconfidence bias 74
    paternalism, soft/hard-core 71
    preference formation errors 72–3
    prospect theory 70
    rationality assumption 69–71
    regulatory intervention 71
    representativeness 70
    status quo bias 72–3
    US antitrust law 76
    see also economic approaches
Bertrand, Joseph 462–3, 465, 472, 492
Böhm, Franz 31, 32

Bork, Robert 86, 102, 104
Brazil
    cement cartel 213–14
    enforcement of competition law 429–30
    merger control 522–3
    vertical restrictions 267–8
Buchanan, James 99
bundling *see* tying and bundling

Carlton, Denis 124
Chamberlin, Edward 34–5
Chicago School 44–52, 77–8
    anti-trust guide 45, 50–1
    collusion/efficiency issues 48–9
    entry barriers 49–50
    EU competition law impact 52
    free-riding argument 47
    Harvard School differences 40, 44, 46, 49
    merger control 47–9
    origins 44
    policy conclusions 50–2
    price-theory re-emergence 45–6
    US antitrust law impact 51–2
    vertical restraints 46–7
    see also Harvard School
China
    enforcement of competition law 428–9
    goals 86, 90
    merger control 496–9
    price fixing 212
    vertical restrictions 266–7
Clark, John 37, 39
classical economics 17–21, 76–7
    collusive price fixing 18–19, 20
    dynamic view 17–19
    invisible hand concept 17–18
    laissez faire principle 19–20
    origins of competition theory 17
    perfect competition *see* perfect competition
        model
    policy conclusions 19–20

Printed and bound by CPI Group (UK) Ltd, Croydon, CR0 4YY

04/03/2024

14461326-0001